STRUCTURED PASCAL

STRUCTURED PASCAL

Jean-Paul Tremblay
Richard B. Bunt
Lyle M. Opseth

Department of Computational Science
University of Saskatchewan
Saskatoon, Canada

McGraw-Hill Book Company

New York   St. Louis   San Francisco   Auckland   Bogotá   Hamburg
Johannesburg   London   Madrid   Mexico   Montreal   New Delhi
Panama   Paris   São Paulo   Singapore   Sydney   Tokyo   Toronto

STRUCTURED PASCAL

3 4 5 6 7 8 9 0   SMSM   8 9 8 7 6 5 4 3 2

This book was set in Souvenir by the authors.
The editors were Charles E. Stewart and Annette Hall;
the production supervisor was Dominick Petrellese.
The cover was designed by Robin Hessel.
Semline, Inc., was printer and binder.

Library of Congress Cataloging in Publication Data

Tremblay, Jean-Paul, date
    Structured PASCAL.

    Includes bibliographies and index.
    1.   PASCAL (Computer program language)   2.   Struc-
tured programming.   I.   Bunt, Richard B., date
joint author.   II.   Opseth, Lyle M., joint author.
III.   Title.
QA76.73.P2T73   001.64′24   80-15601
ISBN 0-07-065159-0

CONTENTS

PREFACE

The first course in a computer science curriculum is certainly one of the most important. For most students this constitutes their initial exposure to fundamental notions such as the algorithm, and to the description of solutions in a manner sufficiently precise for computer interpretation. It is important that these notions be properly taught for, as the ancient Roman poet Horace observed, "A new cask will long preserve the tincture of the liquor with which it was first impregnated."

To this end we have prepared a package of instructional materials which reflects our own view of how the first course should be organized and taught. The cornerstone of this package is a book entitled "An Introduction to Computer Science: An Algorithmic Approach" (Tremblay/Bunt, 1979). This book presents computer science concepts in an algorithmic framework, with a strong emphasis on problem solving and solution development. We feel this to be particularly important for the first course.

Clearly the use of a programming language is an important part of the first course too. For that reason we have prepared a series of supplementary integrated programming guides (of which this is one) to provide the needed support. The supplementary guides are not intended to re-teach the ideas of the main book, but rather to supplement them with the programming concepts required to implement them in a particular programming language (here, PASCAL), and thereby provide the student with the practical programming framework that we feel to be important.

It has been our experience that students learn by "doing" and by "viewing." The "viewing" aspect is particularly important in the case of programming where it seems that there are immense barriers of bewilderment for many students at the outset. To try to flatten these barriers we present worked-out sample programs, in many cases complete with actual run output from a PASCAL compiler available to us at the University of Saskatchewan. The particular compiler used was developed at the University of Manitoba for the IBM S/370 series of computers. In addition to examples presented for the sake of illustration, most chapters end with a number of more detailed applications that attempt to draw together the material presented in the chapter. These are the same applications that are discussed in the main book; their choice reflects our emphasis on the nonnumeric aspects of computing. As in the main book, this same bias is carried over into the exercises as well. Exercises are found at the end of most sections and at the end of most chapters.

Much has been said and written in the past few years about the merits of an approach to programming loosely termed "structured programming." Studies of the programming task itself have shown that adherence to certain basic principles can result in the production of better quality programs. Our approach is based on many of these principles, and our presentation and examples are designed accordingly. Chapter 7, on programming style, examines the process of programming itself in more depth.

Finally, since we view this guide both as an instructional vehicle and as a reference document, we have included as an appendix a reference summary of the PASCAL language.

SUMMARY BY CHAPTERS

The book begins with a brief introduction to programming from a PASCAL perspective.

Chapter 2 provides an introduction to basic concepts of computing and programming as well as the first examples of complete PASCAL programs. Some simple applications are described.

The notion of "flow of control" is introduced in Chapter 3, along with two fundamental control structures: selection and repetition. Solutions to several fairly elaborate applications are developed.

The concept of the array is the topic of Chapter 4. Processing of single-dimensional arrays, or vectors, is discussed first. The chapter then moves to a consideration of arrays of higher dimension. Some typical applications of vectors and arrays are discussed. Among these are the important applications of searching and sorting.

String processing is the topic of Chapter 5. The representation of strings in a computer is described, and some basic mechanisms for handling them in PASCAL are developed. A number of simple applications involving string processing are discussed. More advanced topics are deferred to Chapter 9. Chapter 5 also deals for the first time with the concepts of formatted I/0.

Chapter 6 deals with functions and procedures. Topics discussed include the correspondence of arguments and parameters and the way in which functions and procedures are invoked and values are returned. Three applications involving the use of functions and procedures are considered.

Programming style is the topic of Chapter 7. This we feel to be an important chapter of the main book. In this book we try to consider the effects of style on the production of PASCAL programs. Examples of actual programs are included to illustrate the points made.

Chapter 8 deals with the subject of numerical computation. The chapter begins with a discussion of precision and numerical error in PASCAL. Then, PASCAL programs are given for the solution of problems discussed in the main book. These include root finding, numerical integration, the solution of simultaneous linear equations, and curve fitting.

Chapter 9 returns to the topic of string processing, with the presentation dealing with more advanced applications such as KWIC indexing and text editing. The CASE construct is introduced for the first time in this chapter.

Chapter 10 offers an introduction to the support of linear data structures in PASCAL. Simple structures such a linear lists, stacks, and queues are discussed. A number of important applications are described. These include the compilation of expressions, the symbolic manipulation of polynomials, and simulation. Also discussed in this chapter are hash-table techniques.

Chapter 11 considers the PASCAL support for the most important non-linear data structure — the tree. Topics include the representation of trees in PASCAL and the application of trees to problems such as the symbolic manipulation of expressions, searching, and sorting.

As already mentioned, the book concludes with an appendix containing a reference summary of the PASCAL language.

This book is intended for use in conjunction with the book by Tremblay and Bunt entitled "An Introduction to Computer Science: An Algorithmic Approach" (Tremblay/Bunt, 1979). The material covered by these two books encompasses courses CS1 and CS2 in the revised curriculum proposals of the Association for Computing Machinery (Austing et al., 1979).

As was done in the main book, we make assumptions as to the nature of available computing facilities. For convenience of presentation we assume a card reader/line printer environment throughout. Since we recognize that this may not be the case for many students, the dependency on such matters is minor. Should an alternative environment exist, a simple comment from the instructor should suffice to overcome any possible problems of comprehension.

ACKNOWLEDGMENTS

This project would not have been possible without the active involvement of a number of people. Guy Friswell worked on Chapter 8. Brenda Kovalsky assisted in chapters 10 and 11. Dave Hrenewich assisted with the index. We are grateful for the support and comments of our colleagues and students in the Department of Computational Science at the University of Saskatchewan, who have class-tested preliminary versions of our books over the past four years. Finally, we acknowledge the efforts of the Department of Printing Services at the University of Saskatchewan. In particular, thanks go to Bill Snell, Anne Wright, Lilly Mae Millham, Tammina Epp, Joan Tilk, Jo Scappaticci, and Lorraine Voth whose efforts on this book and others have made it possible to meet a difficult production schedule.

Jean-Paul Tremblay

Richard B. Bunt

Lyle M Opseth

REFERENCES

AUSTING, R. H., BARNES, B. H., BONNETTE, D. T., ENGEL, G. L., and STOKES D. G.: "CURRICULUM '78: Recommendation for the Undergraduate Program in Computer Science," *Communications of the ACM*, Vol. 22, No. 3, March 1979, pp. 147-166.

TREMBLAY, J. P. and BUNT, R. B.: *An Introduction to Computer Science: An Algorithmic Approach*, McGraw-Hill Book Co., New York, 1979.

STRUCTURED
PASCAL

CHAPTER

1

INTRODUCTION TO PASCAL PROGRAMMING

Interactions involving humans are most effectively carried out through the medium of language. Language permits the expression of thoughts and ideas, and without it, communication as we know it would be very difficult indeed.

In computer programming, a programming language serves as the means of communication between the person with a problem and the computer used to help solve it. Languages are said to affect the thought and culture of those who use them. Eskimos, for example, have a large vocabulary simply on the subject of snow. An effective programming language enhances both the development and the expression of computer programs. It must bridge the gap between the too often unstructured nature of human thought and the precision required for computer execution. The programming language shapes the thought processes of the programmer, and the quality of the language has a large effect on the quality of the programs produced with it.

1-1 INTRODUCTION

This book is intended to supplement the text, *An Introduction to Computer Science: An Algorithmic Approach*. Its purpose is to provide an introduction to the programming language PASCAL, sufficient to enable you to implement the algorithms of the main text.

As much as possible, we attempt to parallel the presentation of the main text. In our presentation, we assume that the pertinent sections of the main text have been read. The algorithmic language of the main text has been designed for easy translation into several popular programming languages, including PASCAL.

The purpose of this chapter is to define a perspective for the material in this book by providing a brief overview of the development and use of the PASCAL language.

1-2 A SHORT HISTORY OF THE PASCAL LANGUAGE

In the early days of computing, programming was a very formidable task. Many of the early computers were "hard wired" to perform a specific task: to change the "program" required rewiring components. John von Neumann was the first to propose the concept of the stored program, that is, that the instructions of the program be stored in the memory of the computer along with the data. Before long, people began to look for more convenient ways of specifying these instructions, moving from low-level (i.e., machine-oriented) symbolic assembly languages through to higher-level, problem-oriented programming languages.

One of the first general-purpose problem-oriented programming languages was FORTRAN (FORmula TRANslator), introduced in 1954 and designed for the solution of scientific numerical problems. FORTRAN was instrumental in demonstrating the value and cost effectiveness of problem-oriented programming languages, and soon other such languages began to appear with COBOL (Common Business Oriented Language) for business applications, ALGOL (ALGOrithmic Language) for problems in numerical mathematics, LISP for list processing applications primarily in artificial intelligence, SNOBOL for applications involving string manipulation, and PL/I, a large general-purpose language, proving to be the most enduring.

The language PASCAL, named after the seventeenth-century French mathematician, was proposed in 1968 by Niklaus Wirth of the Federal Institute of Technology in Zurich, Switzerland. The first PASCAL compiler was not available until 1970, but by December 1978 there were reported to be more than 110 different PASCAL compilers.

PASCAL is a general-purpose language in the sense that it can be used for a wide range of applications. Despite its programming power, it is relatively compact and easy to learn. A particularly strong feature of the language is its data structuring capabilities that permit a great deal of work, normally required on the part of the programmer, to be shifted instead to the compiler. The popularity of the language has grown rapidly since its introduction and, at the time of writing, a number of standardization efforts are underway. The present *de facto* standard is defined in a document known as *The PASCAL Report [see Jensen and Wirth (1974)]*.

The suitability of any programming language for use in a classroom environment is enhanced by the availability of low-cost, fast-compile, ultra-diagnostic, student-oriented compilers. Such compilers as WATFOR/WATFIV, developed at the University of Waterloo, and PL/C, developed at Cornell University, have played a large part in the acceptance of FORTRAN and PL/I, respectively, by the academic community. Because of its relative simplicity, PASCAL lends itself naturally to such an environment. In fact, many compilers are available for both minicomputers and microcomputers.

1-3   THE USE OF PROGRAMMING LANGUAGE

As described earlier, a programming language serves to aid in the transformation of a problem solution into an executable computer program. In fact, the language that is well-designed enhances not only the *expression* of the solution, but also its *development* as well.

Once a problem solution has been formulated in terms of a computer program in some programming language, it must then be translated into the machine language of the computer on which the program is to be run. Machine language is not programmer-oriented; machine language programs are nothing more than long strings of numbers, which are written in such a way as to be meaningful to the computer. The translation of a program written in a high-level programming language (sometimes called the *source program*) to its machine language equivalent (sometimes called the *object program*) is handled through a special program known as a *compiler*.

For a given programming language, there may be many compilers. For example, there will be a different compiler for every different type of machine that supports the language. Even on the same machine, there may be several compilers for the same language, each emphasizing different features or capabilities.

Often the action of a compiler appears transparent to the programmer, but never completely so. For example, the compiler can often detect errors made in the writing of the program that would prevent it from running correctly. Other errors may escape its detection and not be discovered until the translated machine language program (or the object program) is actually in execution. The distinction between *compile-time* and *run-time* errors is described more completely in Chap. 2.

1-4   THE APPROACH OF THE BOOK

Although we are dealing with the *language* PASCAL, we have run our example programs under a compiler supplied by the University of Manitoba for an IBM S/370 environment. There may be some minor differences between the language as defined by the Manitoba compiler and the language described in the PASCAL report. These differences ought not to affect the beginning programmer, but may be more concern as more programming experience is acquired.

When first learning any programming language, it is very easy to be overpowered by detail. We have tried to ease this problem through a layered presentation that matches the presentation of the main text. When a feature of the language is first introduced, it is described in such a way as to be useful immediately to the beginning programmer. Variations and additional options are deferred until motivated by actual problem requirements.

Much has been said and written in recent years on an approach to programming known as "structured programming". Structured programming is really little more than the application of a particular discipline to the practice of programming. The evidence seems clear that students produce better programs in a shorter time span with this philosophy. The presentation in this book is consistent with the teachings of structured programming.

With this short introduction, you are now ready to begin your study of the PASCAL language.

BIBLIOGRAPHY

Backus, J. W. et al: "The FORTRAN Automatic Coding System," (ed., S. Rosen), in *Programming Systems and Languages,* McGraw-Hill Book Company, New York, 1967.

Foulkes, W. B.: *Manitoba PASCAL User Guide,* Scientific Report No. 83, Department of Computer Science, University of Manitoba, Winnipeg, Manitoba, May 1976, revised June 1977.

Jensen, K., and Wirth, N.: *PASCAL: User Manual and Report* (second edition) Springer-Verlag, New York, 1974.

Sammet, J. E.: *Programming Languages: History and Fundamentals,* Prentice-Hall Inc., Englewood Cliffs, N.J., 1969.

Tremblay, J. P., and Bunt, R. B.: *An Introduction to Computer Science: An Algorithmic Approach,* McGraw-Hill Book Company, New York, 1979.

CHAPTER

2

FUNDAMENTAL PASCAL CONCEPTS

This chapter introduces several of the fundamental concepts of programming in the PASCAL language. The presentation closely follows that of Chap. 2 in the main text. The chapter begins with a simple overview of solving problems in PASCAL, including data, data representation and manipulation, and the use of variables. Simple input and output operations are discussed. This discussion should be sufficient to allow the novice to write very simple PASCAL programs. The process of preparing a program to run under the PASCAL compiler is explained and some instruction on program execution, testing and tracing is given. The chapter concludes with complete PASCAL programs for the applications developed in Chap. 2 of the main text.

2-1   DATA, DATA TYPES, AND PRIMITIVE OPERATIONS

The computer is used to perform tasks involving pieces of information or *data*. By submitting a series of instructions to the computer by means of a program, the programmer specifies exactly how these data are to be processed. The PASCAL language, unlike many other languages, provides the programmer with several primitive data types and allows him or her to define new data types based upon the primitive data type provided. In this section, we discuss some of the primitive data types, their representations in a PASCAL program, and the kinds of operations that can be used to manipulate data.

2-1.1   Data Types

In PASCAL, five primitive data types can be used: numeric, nonnumeric, and logical, and two other special types, pointer and set. All of these, with the exception of set, are described in more detail in the main text. Each of these various data types has a distinct internal representation, and different machine instructions are used for each. Rules for expressing data of each type in a program must be followed by the programmer in order for the computer to interpret the data correctly.

Numeric data in PASCAL can be represented in two different ways: as integer numbers or as real numbers.

Numbers of type integer are written as a string of digits, which might be preceded by a plus or minus sign. The maximum allowed magnitude of an integer depends on the restrictions of the particular computer and compiler used. The following are examples of integer constants:

        1
        +1
        0
    −425678
    999999

Numbers of type real correspond to the real numbers described in the main text. They are specified by any string of digits, signed or unsigned, containing a decimal point. These can be written in conventional decimal form or, for very large or very small numbers, in scientific notation or *floating-point* form. The latter form consists of a real or integer number followed by the letter E (for exponent) and a signed or unsigned integer constant which is the exponent. This is interpreted to mean that the number preceding the letter E is to be multiplied by 10 to the power given by the integer after the E. Examples of real number constants written in both forms are

41341413.35	4.134141335E7
+22.2	+2.22E+01
75.	75E0
−.000000000000000003	−3E−18

The *character string* (a nonnumeric datum) is the second major data type in the PASCAL language. A character string is a sequence of character symbols, where each character must be either an alphabetic letter, one of the digits

(0123456789), or one of the set of special characters +–*/()=.,$'blank. For presentation purposes, character strings are enclosed in single quotes. The quotes themselves are not considered part of the string, but are used as markers for the start and end of the string (or *delimiters*). The following are examples of valid string constants:

'COMPUTER SCIENCE'
'67'
'$.50 GOLD PIECES'
'3+3–4=2'

The string format may present a problem if the string desired contains within itself a quotation mark. The problem is solved by using two single quotes to represent one quote embedded in the string. For example, the correct string representation for the contraction of 'COULD NOT' is not 'COULDN'T', but 'COULDN''T'.

The length of a character string is defined as the number of characters in the string (including the blank characters). An embedded pair of quotes is counted as just one character, since it actually represents only one single quote. Thus, the length of the string 'DON''T' is 5 and not 6. The minimum length that any string may have is 1; the maximum length varies from compiler to compiler, but is typically quite large. For our purposes, we will assume this maximum length to be 256 characters.

The third data type in PASCAL is the logical type, where the data values allowed are the true and false values, represented as TRUE and FALSE, respectively. Applications involving logical data are considered in Chap. 9. The fourth data type, the pointer, is described in Chap. 10.

Unlike many other languages, PASCAL allows the programmer to define a set, which is a data type consisting of specified elements that are associated with names. We shall see examples of this data type in Sec. 2-2.

For the computer to represent data correctly, the data must be specified in a certain format. The programmer, therefore, must determine the particular type of data he or she plans to use, and follow the rules for expressing values of that type. The type of data used will also determine the possible operations that may be used to manipulate its value. This subject is the topic of the next section.

2-1.2 Data Manipulation

The numeric operation is a fundamental component of PASCAL. The symbols and use of the numeric operators are described in this section. With one exception, the symbols used are the same as those of the algorithmic language in the main text. Numeric functions are also available and are discussed in Sec. 2-2.

NUMERIC OPERATORS

The operators used in PASCAL are of two types, *binary* and *unary*. Binary operators are used in operations which contain two operands. The binary numeric operators include:

1. For subtraction –, i.e., 3 – 4

2. For addition +, i.e., 4 + 3
3. For multiplication *, i.e., 3 * 4
4. For division /, i.e., 4 / 3 (real divide)
    and DIV, i.e., 4 DIV 3 (integer divide)

The exponentiation operator which is described in the main text is unavailable in PASCAL. Exponentiation can be computed using multiple multiplications or using logarithms.

TYPES OF NUMERIC OPERATION

All operators (except the division operators) may be used with integer operands, with real operands, or with any combination of these. When two operands of differing types are involved in a binary operation, a copy of one of the values is converted to the other's type. If one operand is of type real and the other is of type integer, a copy of the integer operand is converted into a real operand and the operation is carried out with the two real operands. Some examples of the different types of operations are:

Operation	Type of Result
5.6E02 + 7.8E33	real
4 + 3	integer
4.32 - 8.9	integer
5 * 7.45E-34	real
5.99E 23 * 3.87E 34	real

There are two different operators for division : / and DIV. The DIV operator can have only integer operands and performs integer division. Thus 1 DIV 3 yields 0, 4 DIV 4 yields 1, and 1 DIV 3.0 results in an error since one operand is a real number. The / operator can have either integer or real operands and has a real result. Thus 1 / 3 yields 0.3333333, as does 1. / 3 or 1E+0 / 3.00.

Some of the operators discussed above also perform other operations, for example, operations on sets, and will be discussed in later chapters.

Any numeric operation raises the possibility of certain problems. Two such problems are overflow and underflow.

Overflow is an error condition that occurs when the result of a computation is too large to be represented in the storage space for integer or real values.

Overflow can occur when:

1. Adding two large positive or negative numbers,
2. Subtracting a large negative number from a large positive number,
3. Multiplying two large numbers, negative or positive,
4. Dividing a very large number by a very small one,
    (using the / operator only).

Underflow is an error condition which occurs when the result of a computation is too small to be represented in the storage space for integer or real values.

Underflow can occur when:

1. Mutliplying two very small numbers,
2. Dividing a very small number by a very large number,
    (using the / operator only).

It is the responsibility of the programmer to ensure that the results of the computations fall within the limits of the integer and real number values that can be stored. Since the value of the overflowed or underflowed number retained by the computer would be incomplete and, therefore, usually worthless, the usual response of the computer is to print an overflow or underflow error message and terminate execution of the program. In some computations, however, a warning message may not be given, and the computer may continue to execute using the incomplete value. The programmer must be very careful, therefore, in situations in which the data values are such that overflow or underflow may occur.

In this section, operators, types of operations, and problems that can occur when using operators have been discussed. The variable, its use and representation, is the topic of the next section.

Exercises for Sec. 2-1

1. Give the type of each of the following constants:

(i)	723		(v)	–2456
(ii)	723E0		(vi)	–63E–11
(iii)	'723'		(vii)	45E+26
(iv)	+723E+1		(viii)	786

2. Give the result and its type for each of the following operations:

(i)	6 + 3		(v)	76 / 10 + 2
(ii)	.536E3 – 536		(vi)	35E–1 / 3.5 – 2
(iii)	5 * 30		(vii)	2 * 3
(iv)	.77E2 / .11E+2		(vii)	4 * 2 – 3E0

2-2 IDENTIFIERS AND EXPRESSIONS

We have seen in the previous section that PASCAL allows various types of data values. This section introduces the concept of an identifier and gives rules for the use of identifiers in PASCAL programs. Identifiers are used to represent variables, labels, programmer-defined data types, and constants. Also, the *assignment* and *compound* statements of PASCAL are explored. Finally, we look at combining simple operations into complex expressions.

2-2.1 Identifiers and Their Declaration

An *identifier* in a programming language stands for a location in memory that is capable of holding a value and is referenced by its *identifier name*. As we shall see, identifiers in PASCAL are also used to name programs and represent labels, programmer-defined data types, and constants. In PASCAL, some rules are imposed on the naming of identifiers. These are very similar to the naming rules given in the main text for variables in the algorithmic language. First, an identifier must begin with a letter and can contain no blanks or special characters except for the underscore (_). Some versions of PASCAL do not allow any special characters for identifiers. In other words, only the letters A through Z, the digits 0 through 9, and the underscore may be used. While there is in theory no size limit on an identifier name (i.e., it can be as long as the programmer likes), PASCAL limits the number of characters it uses to recognize the identifier. The language definition for the PASCAL version used in this book considers only the first 31 characters as significant and the remaining characters are not important to the identifier's name. Other versions of PASCAL consider only 8 characters as significant. PASCAL imposes further restrictions on the naming of identifiers by not allowing the use of certain *keywords* of the language. Words like END, BEGIN, and DO, for example, have special meaning in the PASCAL language. Examples of correct and incorrect identifiers follow.

LOG	valid
$MONEY	invalid ($ not allowed in an identifier.)
X3	valid
BANK_ACC	valid (Invalid in some versions of PASCAL.)
#8778	invalid
WHEN?	invalid (? is not allowed in an identifier.)
X+Z	invalid (+ is a special symbol.)
VARIABLE NAME	invalid (Blanks are not allowed within variable names.)
1AB	invalid (Variable name must start with a letter.)

THIS_SEQUENCE_IS_TOO_LONG_FOR_A_VARIABLE_NAME valid
(this identifier is considered to be the same as
THIS_SEQUENCE_IS_TOO_LONG_FOR_A
if 31 characters are significant. Other PASCAL versions allow only 8 characters in which case only THIS_SEQ is used to recognize the identifier name.)

   All identifiers used in a program must be introduced by means of *declaration statements*. These declarations simultaneously associate memory locations, memory addresses, and data types (or values in the case of constants), with identifiers. PASCAL declarations appear at the beginning of the program, and this is discussed later in this section and in Sec. 2-4. The declarations are divided into four sections, one for defining labels, one for defining constants, one for defining data types, and one for defining the variables. If no declarations are to be done in any section, that section can be omitted.
   The first section to appear is the label section, where all label names to be used in a program are defined. These labels must be unique to all other identifiers used in the program, and cannot be reserved words. Labels are used to associate a name with a statement which is done by prefixing the label, followed by a colon, onto the statement. Thus a labelled statement would appear as

ADD: *statement*

The label ADD must be defined in the label section. All labels defined in the label section are separated by commas. The list is begun with the word LABEL and ends with a semicolon. Thus a typical declaration might appear as

LABEL ADD, RESULT, DONE;

The next section, the *constant definition* section, allows the programmer to associate an identifier with a constant of a particular data type (integer, real, or character string). Once associated, the value of the identifier is fixed and cannot be changed during program execution. The form of this section is

CONST $identifier_1$ = $constant_1$;
      $identifier_2$ = $constant_2$;
         .
         .
         .
      $identifier_n$ = $constant_n$;

Each identifier must be unique and cannot be redefined in any other declaration section. For example, in a program we may wish to define the value of π, e, and a character string. The following example illustrates how this would be done.

CONST PI = 3.14159;
      E = 2.718281828;
      STARS = '***************';

The next section is used to define programmer-defined data types. PASCAL allows two types of data definitions in this section: the definition of sets and programmer-defined data types that are built upon existing PASCAL data types or previously defined data types. In this section, identifiers are associated with the new data type. The section begins with the reserved word TYPE and each data declaration is followed by a semicolon.

Sets can be defined as a list of identifiers, where the identifiers are the elements of the set. For example, we can define the names of persons to be a set as shown

NAMES = (JOHN, JACK, JOSEPH, JILL, JANE);

PASCAL provides operations on sets, such as union, intersection, and set membership. Note that all identifiers which represent set elements must be unique and can store no value as they merely represent the elements in a set.

New data types can be defined as subranges of existing data types. Thus, we can define a subrange of a set as follows

MEN = (JOHN..JOSEPH);

which means that all elements defined in NAMES between JOHN and JOSEPH, inclusive, are found in the set MEN. Parentheses surround the subrange, indicating that it is a set. Since set elements consist of unique elements, the PASCAL compiler will identify JOHN and JOSEPH as elements of the NAMES set, provided this subrange definition follows that of the set definition. It is not necessary that it immediately follow the original set definition, however. We can define the subrange 1 to 12 of integers as

    DOZEN = 1..12;

Parentheses do not surround the 1..12 because this is not a set, but a subrange of integers. Note that subranges of the type real cannot be defined. Subranges of character strings can only be defined for single characters. Thus the definition

    LETTER = 'A'..'Z';

is legal, but

    CHARACTERS = 'AA'..'ZZ'

is not.

The next section, beginning with the reserved word VAR, defines the variables to be used in a program. Variables must be defined to be of one of the standard types, such as integer, real, or character, or one of the types defined in the data type declaration section.

All variables used in a program must be introduced in the variable declaration section. These declarations simultaneously serve to associate memory locations with the variables and to tell the compiler the particular data type that the variable will hold (and, therefore, the storage representation to use for its values). An integer variable is declared to be of type integer using the declaration statement

    variable-name: INTEGER;

where the name of the variable is placed before the keyword INTEGER. The declaration for a real variable is

    variable-name: REAL;

where REAL is the keyword used. Similarly, logical variables can be declared to the compiler using the keyword BOOLEAN, as in

    variable-name: BOOLEAN;

The character type declaration in PASCAL has two forms. One form is

    variable-name: STRING(n);

where n is an integer constant which gives the length of the character strings that the character variable named will hold. The compiler will allocate to the variable an area of memory sufficient to accommodate a string n characters long. If a character variable is given a string value which is shorter than the declared length, then the string is padded on its right with blanks to make it the required length. If the string is longer than the declared length, then the string is truncated on its right to reduce it to the required length. The second form is

> *variable-name:* CHAR;

The variable can only hold a single character.

Declarations of variables for programmer-defined data types follow in a similar manner. Also, a programmer may omit a type declaration and use it in place of the type identifier for a variable in the variable declaration section. For example, rather than using the type declaration

> RANGE = 0..100;

and the variable declaration

> SCOPE: RANGE;

SCOPE can be defined as

> SCOPE: 0..100;

or, a subset of names can be defined as

> MENS_NAMES: (JOHN..JOSEPH);

If several variables in a program are to have the same type attribute, then the programmer may, instead of using separate type declarations for each, use only one combined declaration, replacing the *variable-name* field in the declaration format by a list of variable names, separated by commas. Therefore, the previous declaration formats may also have the form

> *variable-list:* INTEGER;
> *variable-list:* REAL;

and so on for all types.

Suppose, for example, we want the variable SUM to have integer values in a program: the variables TEST and ALPHA to hold character strings of length 2 and 18, respectively; the variables BETA and LINE both to hold strings of length 5; and the variables SIDE, TOP, LOWER, and UPPER to hold real values. An appropriate set of declaration statements might be

> VAR SUM: INTEGER;
>   TEXT: STRING(2);
>   ALPHA: STRING(18);
>   BETA, LINE: STRING(5);
>   SIDE, TOP, LOWER, UPPER: REAL;

All variable declarations must be placed at the beginning of a program, just after the TYPE declarations and preceded by VAR which denotes the beginning of the variable declaration section. The programmer must be careful that all values assigned to a variable in a program are of the type declared for that variable, unless type conversion is allowed.

The character type declaration format allows limited variations in length specification for character variables. The maximum length allowed by our PASCAL compiler, for example, is 256.

We have seen in this section the concept of variables, and how they are typed in PASCAL. The important notion concerning a variable is that it represents values, though only one at a time. How does the programmer specify a value in his or her program? We turn now to one method for doing this, which uses an important programming feature—numeric expressions.

2-2.2   Evaluation of Numeric Expressions

The arithmetic expression is a basic element of the PASCAL language. An *expression* can be:

1. A constant,
2. A variable,
3. Two or more constants or variables (or combinations of constants and variables) separated by operators.

The following are all examples of expressions.

```
5
6.387
APPLE
–7
+3.9
A + B
3 / 9
78 * 8.9
INT + 5 / 6
(98 – 78) / (34 * 78)
7 * A + 3 / 2 – 6
```

The order in which the terms of an expression are evaluated is based on the rules of precedence described in the main text. For example, in the statement

$$7.0 + 6.0 * 3.0 - 2.0$$

the multiplication is done first, followed by the addition and subtraction, yielding the following sequence of intermediate results:

```
6.0 * 3.0 = 18.0   intermediate result: 7.0 + 18.0 – 2.0
7.0 + 18.0 = 25.0  intermediate result: 25.0 – 2.0
25.0 – 2.0 = 23.0
```

The rules of precedence in PASCAL are summarized in Table 2-1.

Table 2-1 Order of precedence for PASCAL operators

	Operation	Symbol	Order of Evaluation
1.	Parentheses	( )	inner to outer, (i.e., inner-most first)
2.	Multiplication	*	left to right
	Division	/ and DIV	
3.	Addition	+	left to right
	Subtraction	–	

Notice the absence of the unary operators + and – from this table. PASCAL does not have these two operators *per se*; thus if two operators follow each other where the second indicates the sign of the number, the sign and number must be surrounded with parentheses. For example, the expression

    3 * –5

is invalid, and must be expressed in the form

    3 * (–5)

On the other hand, the expression

    –5 * 3

is allowed since no operator appears before the minus sign; hence, the minus sign is taken to indicate the sign of the number rather than the subtraction operator.

PASCAL allows variables of different subranges, but having the same type, to be used in the same expression. That is, if two variable declarations are

    SMALL_INT: –10..10;

and

    DOZEN: 1..12;

then the expression

    SMALL_INT * DOZEN

is valid.

NUMERIC BUILT-IN FUNCTIONS

PASCAL provides many built-in functions that can be used in expressions. Built-in functions allow the programmer to perform frequently used operations which cannot be easily handled by the conventional operators. The general form of a built-in function is

function-name(expression)

The expression which appears in the parentheses following the function-name is called the *argument*. The argument (or arguments in the case of functions with more than one argument) of the built-in function is evaluated and then the indicated function is performed with that value. For example, the expression

SQRT(5 + 4)

is evaluated in the following manner. First, the expression 5 + 4 is evaluated, leaving an intermediate result of SQRT(9). Then, this function is evaluated and a final value of 3 results.

A built-in function may be the argument of another built-in function. For example, the statement

LN (ABS (25 – 80))

results in the natural log of the absolute value of 25 – 80.

The type of result from the evaluation of a built-in function is determined by the type of function and the argument (or arguments) it possess. In most cases, the argument of the built-in numeric functions is a numeric data type. A list of the commonly used built-in functions appears in Table 2-2. Restrictions on their use with certain numeric data types are described.

2-2.3   The Assignment Operator

The assignment operation allows the programmer to give a variable a value during the execution of a program. In PASCAL, the assignment operator is a colon followed by the equals sign (:=), rather than the left-pointing arrow (←) used in the main text. An assignment operation in PASCAL is indicated by a statement of the form

variable := expression

where the expression can be any valid PASCAL expression.

The rules governing assignment operators in PASCAL closely parallel those of the algorithmic language of the main text. The following are examples of correct and incorrect assignments.

X := 3.0	correct
Y := 8.0E0	correct
A := 2.0 + 3.0	correct
NAME := 'JUDY'	correct
X + Y := A * B	incorrect (The item on the left-hand side of the assignment operator, X + Y, is an expression, not a variable.)

Table 2-2 Some useful built-in functions

Function Name	Argument and Type	Meaning and Type of Result
ABS(n)	n: a real or integer expression	absolute value: result is $|n|$, same type as n
SQRT(n)	n: a real or integer expression	square root: result is $\sqrt{n}$, type real
SQR(n)	n: a real or integer expression	square: result is n^2, same type as n
TRUNC(n)	n: a real expression	truncate: result is the larger integer smaller than or equal to n
ROUND(n)	n: a real expression	round: result is n rounded to the nearest integer
LN(n)	n: a real or integer expression, n must be greater than 0	logarithm base e: result is the natural (Napierian) logarithm of n, type real
EXP(n)	n: a real or integer expression	exponent: result is e^n, type real
SIN(n)	n: a real or integer expression	sine: result is the sine of n radians, type real
COS(n)	n: a real or integer expression	cosine: result is the cosine of n radians, type real

3.0 := R	incorrect (The item on the left-hand side of the assignment operator, 3.0, is a constant, not a variable.)

TYPE CONVERSIONS

As was the case in the algorithmic language, the concept of type is important in the processing of assignment statements in PASCAL. It is expected that the value on the right-hand side of the assignment operator will be the same type as the variable to which it is being assigned. Where this is not the case, PASCAL will generate an error message. The only exception is integer expressions being assigned to real variables. In this case, the integer value is converted before the assignment is performed. In the case of assigning real values to integer variables, the value of the expression must be converted to integer by using either the TRUNC or the ROUND function. For example, if the expression AVERAGE * NUM results in a real value and this value is to be assigned to the integer variable RESULT, the assignment could be performed by

RESULT := TRUNC (AVERAGE * NUM);

if no rounding of the real value is required.

An assignment may be performed on a variable provided the value received is within its range. For example, if the variable declaration

       VAR SMALL_INT: 0..10;
             NUMBER: INTEGER;

appeared in a program, the assignment

       SMALL_INT := NUMBER

is valid provided the value contained in NUMBER has a value between 0 and 10; otherwise an error will result. The assignment

       NUMBER := SMALL_INT;

is always valid.

Notice again that the assignment operator is denoted by :=. This is not to be confused with the equals sign used in some of the declaration sections. The declaration sections use the equals sign to define an identifier as representing a constant value, rather than assigning it to the identifier.

This concludes our discussion of identifiers and expressions. In the first part of this discussion, the concept of a variable or identifier was introduced. The rules for naming and declaring identifiers were given. The evaluation of expressions was the topic of Sec. 2-2.2. Finally, in Sec. 2-2.3 the assignment operator was discussed.

Exercises for Sec. 2-2

1.   Which of the following identifiers are valid?

         (i)   WATER
         (ii) $STAR
         (iii)   76354
         (iv)   NUM@
         (v)   A37_621
         (vi)   TAX
         (vii)   THE_END_OF_THIS_QUESTION?

2.   Evaluate the following expressions, giving the intermediate and final results:

         (i)   –7 + 8 * 3
         (ii)   32 / 4E0 – 9 * 2
         (iii)   11 – 9 + 2 – 3
         (iv)   60 / 3E0 + (5 * 2) * SQR (2)
         (v)   24 * (2 + 3) – 45
         (vi)   6 * 2 – 8 * (3 * 1)
         (vii)   45 / 5E1 + 2
         (viii) 11 – 16 * (+17)

3. Assume that A, B, and C have been declared as REAL variables and that I, J, and K have been declared as INTEGER variables. Given A = 5E0, B = 5E0, and I = 4, what is the final value requested in each of the following if the assignment is valid?

(i) C := A * B – I	C = ——————
(ii) K := I DIV 4 * 6 – B	K = ——————
(iii) C := B / A + 1.53 – 2	C = ——————
(iv) K := TRUNC (B / A + 4.7)	K = ——————
(v) J := ROUND (A / (5 / I))	J = ——————
(vi) K := ABS (A – B) * 2 + I	K = ——————

2-3 STATEMENTS AND COMPOUNDS STATEMENTS

In PASCAL, statements describe actions that are to be performed, such as an assignment. That is

variable := expression

is considered to be an assignment statement. PASCAL statements are separated from each other by semicolons, just as a list of names is separated by commas. For example, consider the list of statements

A := 3 * 5;
SUM := A + B;
DIFF := A – B

The semicolon is used to separate the statements. We have not put a semicolon after the last statement since one may not be necessary as we shall see shortly.

The main text specifies that the statements in an algorithm are executed in the order that they are specified. PASCAL has a *compound statement* which is of the form

BEGIN
.
.
.
END

where an arbitrary number of statements can appear between the BEGIN and END. The compound statement is used to specify that all statements between the BEGIN and END are to be executed in their specified order. We shall see in the next chapter many examples where this statement is very useful. It is necessary to begin the executable part of a PASCAL program, which follows the declarations, with a BEGIN statement and end the program with an END. A period follows the END to denote the physical end of the program. The executable part of the program is placed between the BEGIN and the END. It is our philosophy to indent any statements appearing between a BEGIN and an END to improve program readability.

PASCAL uses the semicolon as a statement delimiter. That is, the semicolon is used to separate statements, not end them. The following example might be the executable portion of a PASCAL program.

```
BEGIN
      X := 3;
      Y := 4;
      Z := 5;
      SUM := X + Y + Z
END.
```

Notice that the semicolon separates each assignment statement from the rest. There is no need to put a semicolon after the BEGIN or after the last assignment statement since the assignment statements are embedded within the compound statement and the BEGIN and END are considered to be in the same statement. Note the following legal PASCAL program body:

```
BEGIN
      BEGIN
            BEGIN
                  X := 3;
                  Y := 4;
                  Z := 5
            END
      END;
      SUM := X + Y + Z
END.
```

This example illustrates that even the END of a compound statement must end with a semicolon if it is to be separated from another statement. This is not the case if the next line is another END (since END itself is an equally valid delimiter). Our indentation scheme helps to clarify this. If the next statement is at the same level (i.e., carries the same amount of indentation as the current one), a semicolon should separate them. This rule of thumb should not be followed too strictly, as we shall see examples in Chap. 3 where it does not always hold.

2-4 SIMPLE INPUT AND OUTPUT

In any computing environment, input and output provide the final interface between the user of a program and the computer executing the program. Input statements in the program allow the computer to read data during the execution of the program. This allows the programmer to write general programs that can be used repeatedly on different sets of data, the exact values of which the programmer need not know at the time the program is written. Without output statements, most programs would be useless, as the users would have no way of knowing what results were obtained.

The PASCAL language provides a number of different methods of input and output. Methods that are easy to use have certain restrictions associated with them. For more advanced applications, where the format of the input data or the printed results, for example, is of particular importance, more sophisticated methods must be used. The discussion of these methods will be deferred until Chap. 5.

The simplest type of input and output is free-style or format-free. This corresponds almost exactly to the form of input/output employed in the main text. The form of a free-style READ statement is

READ (*input list*);

The *input list* consists of one or more variables separated by commas. Each variable in the input list corresponds to an item in the data (which, for the sake of discussion, we will assume to be on punched cards). For example, given the declaration

VAR A, B, C: INTEGER;

execution of the statement

READ (A, B, C);

with the data card:

7 8 9

causes the data card to be scanned. The first value on the card, 7, is assigned to A. The second value, 8, is assigned to B, and the third value, 9, is assigned to C. The data type of the variable and corresponding data item must be the same. If the data types are not the same, a conversion error message is printed and execution of the program terminates.

Adjacent data items should be separated by one or more blanks on the data card. Blanks may, therefore, not appear within a single numeric data item. No commas can appear within a number. Twelve thousand and forty-three is, for example, represented on a data card as 12043, not 12,043. Data may appear in any column of the data card.

Note that data are written on the cards in a form identical to the form for writing constants of the same type. Integers are written as a series of digits, with no decimal point. Real numbers can be written using either of the two forms discussed in Sec. 2-1. Character strings must be enclosed in quote marks. For example,

THIS IS WRONG

is an invalid string data item, but

'THIS IS CORRECT.'

is valid.

Individual data items, except for character strings, may not be broken across card boundaries. For example,

5bbbbbbbb3b...b3.7bbbb'HE
bWALKED,'bbb2.78

(where "b" represents a blank column) is valid, but

> 5bbbbbbbb3b...b3.7bbbbbb2
> .78bbb'HE WALKED'

is invalid, since the data value 2.78 is split across the card boundary.

In all cases but one, reading resumes at the next nonblank character. When reading a value of type character (not type string), reading starts at the current character being scanned which is the one following the last character read. That is, when reading a single character, the character on the data card cannot be surrounded by quotes as a leading quote will be considered as the next character and will be assigned to the corresponding variable. Thus, if SUM is an integer variable and LETTER is a variable defined to be of type CHAR, the statement

> READ (SUM, LETTER);

and the data card

> 15COME

results in SUM receiving the value 15 and LETTER the character C. On the other hand, if LETTER was defined to be of type STRING, quotes would be needed around COME. Blanks can be removed on the data card if no ambiguity results.

If there are more values on the data card than there are variables in the READ statement, the remaining values are ignored. If another input statement occurs in the program, reading resumes from the point where the previous input statement stopped. Each value is read only once. Consider the following program segments and data card.

> VAR LENGTH, WIDTH, HEIGHT: INTEGER;
> 　　　NAME: STRING (20):

and

> READ (NAME);
> READ (LENGTH, WIDTH);

> Data card:
> 'BOX' 7 5 8

This causes the assignment of 'BOX' to NAME, and the assignment of 7, 5, and 8 to LENGTH, WIDTH, and HEIGHT, respectively. If there are insufficient data items on a card to *satisfy* the READ statement (i.e., to give each of the variables in the input list a value), more data cards will be read until all the variables have values. In the example,

> VAR NUMBER, COUNT: INTEGER;
> 　　　AVERAGE, MEAN: REAL;

and

>   READ (NUMBER, AVERAGE, COUNT, MEAN);

Data cards:
>   7
>   8.978E–03
>   9
>   10.345E23

the first card is scanned and 7 is assigned to NUMBER. Since there are no more values on that card, the next card is scanned and 8.978E–03 is assigned to AVERAGE. Finally, the last two cards are scanned and COUNT and MEAN are assigned the values 9, and 10.345E23, respectively.

PASCAL offers output methods similar to those described for input. The free-style output statement has two forms:

>   WRITE (*output-list*)

or

>   WRITELN (*output-list*)

A list of variables, constants, expressions, and literals enclosed in parentheses comprises the *output list* for the WRITE and WRITELN statements. As in the main text, we will assume (unless stated otherwise) that the output device is a line printer.

The WRITE statement is used to add items to the end of the current output line, but does not cause a new line to be started. The WRITELN statement, after adding the items to be printed to the current output line, causes it to be printed so that the next WRITE or WRITELN statement starts a new line on the printer. For example, if the programmer wants three numbers to be printed on the same line, but using different output statements, the following could be specified:

>   WRITE (' ', 1);
>   WRITE (2);
>   WRITELN (3);

The first WRITE statement adds a blank and the number 1 to the current output line. The second statement adds the number 2. The last statement adds 3 to the end of this line and prints the line. If all the output has been added to the output line and the programmer wishes to print it without adding any new data items, the WRITELN statement can be given without any parentheses enclosing items. Thus, the same output for the example given above can be achieved with the statements

>   WRITE (' ', 1, 2);
>   WRITE (3);
>   WRITELN;

As you have probably noticed, the beginning of a new output line has a blank character added. That is, a "character string" is always given first and its first character is usually a blank. Many computer installations use the first character in an output line to determine line spacing and do not print the character. Thus, some characters cause other than single-line spacing to occur. This first character is called the carriage control character and it is used to determine what spacing is to be used before the line is printed. Table 2-3 gives the complete list of carriage control characters and what they do. Any invalid carriage control characters are changed to the blank character. The programmer should always include a carriage control character, otherwise unexpected output results may occur. For example, the line

WRITELN ('1968 WAS THE YEAR.')

causes a page to be skipped before printing the characters 968 WAS THE YEAR. Each line to be printed is divided into a number of *print fields*, each a specified number of print positions wide. In the implementation of PASCAL used in this book, the print field for a real number is 18 print positions wide, while the print field for an integer is 13 positions wide. A characters string is printed in a field whose width is equal to the length of the string. No blanks appear between print fields. The following example shows the spacing of the print fields.

```
VAR A: REAL;
    N: INTEGER;
    A := 6.372;
    N := 7;
    WRITELN (' ', A, N)
END.
```

Output:
bbbbbb6.372000E 00bbbbbbbbbbbbb7

The b's represent blank spaces that occur in the output. Notice that integer and real numbers are *right adjusted*, that is, placed as far right as possible in a *print field*. In this example the first five blanks and the real number (including the blank for the sign) take up 18 print positions. The next 13 positions are made up of 12 leading blanks in the print field of the integer.

The preceding example shows that where variables are involved in the output list, their values (not their names) are printed. In the case of expression, the expression is evaluated and the resulting value printed. Constants, which are just simple expressions, are printed as is.

A string of characters enclosed in quotes appearing in an output list is referred to as a *literal*. When a literal is used in a print statement, whatever is inside the quotes is copied directly into the output. Here is an example of two literals.

WRITELN ('bCOMPUTER SCIENCE', 'MATH')

Output:
COMPUTER SCIENCEMATH

Table 2-3 Carriage Control Characters

Character	Result
'b'	single spacing
'0'	double spacing
'_'	triple spacing
'1'	start a new page
'+'	overprint (suppress line spacing)

The size of the print field for the literal is the length of the literal. Notice that quotes are not printed. If a quote is to be printed as part of a literal, it is necessary to use two quote marks, as in the following WRITELN statement.

```
WRITELN ('bRYAN''S FANCY')
```

Output:
RYAN'S FANCY

Literals are very useful in output statements, because they give the programmer a way of identifying parts of the output. In this way, literals can make the output easier to read. For example, in the following example, the values of two marks are printed.

```
VAR MARK1, MARK2: INTEGER;
BEGIN
        MARK1 := 67;
        MARK2 := 78;
        WRITELN ('bMARK1 =b', MARK1, 'bbMARK2 =b', MARK2)
END.
```

Output:
MARK1 =bbbbbbbbbbbb67bbMARK2 =bbbbbbbbbbbb78

Note the addition of blanks before MARK2 to allow suitable spacing between the integer 67 and the literal output.

Expressions are also allowed in output statements. Examples of output statements containing expressions are shown in the following examples.

```
WRITELN ('b', A + B, A – B)
WRITELN ('bTHE SUM ISb', A + B + C)
WRITE ('1', 6 / 3 – 1, (10 – 2) * 3)
```

The b's represent blanks.

WRITE and WRITELN statements may contain combinations of literals, expressions, and variables. If the length of the output line generated is too long to be put on a single printer line, the output line is continued on the printer's next line.

This brings us to the end of the section on free-style input and output. We now have assembled a body of information sufficient to write simple PASCAL programs. In the next section, the steps involved in preparing a program for execution on a computer and in interpreting the information that is returned are described. A number of complete sample programs are given and discussed.

Exercises for Sec. 2-4

1. Describe the results of the following three print statements:

    WRITE ('–STATEMENT ONE');
    WRITELN ('bbbbbbSTATEMENT TWO');
    WRITELN ('STATEMENT THREE')

2. Give the values of the variables MARK, SUM and AMOUNT following the input statement

    READ (MARK, AVERAGE, NAME, SUM, SOC_INS, ACCOUNT)

    assuming the following input data values:

    65 62 'JOE GREEN' 42 655302111 57321

3. Write a program to read a person's name in the form given name followed by surname and print the name in the form surname followed by given name.

    Example: Input 'URIAH' 'HEEP'
    Output HEEP, URIAH

2-5   PREPARING A PASCAL PROGRAM

The process of preparing and running any program is often needlessly perplexing for the novice programmer. However, after the first few times, the procedure will become more familiar. Again, following the lead of the main text, we will assume that programs are submitted to the computer through punched cards and output is handled by a line printer.

The first step is the coding of the program statements. This process is aided by the use of a special coding form, such as that shown in Fig. 2-1. This form contains printed rows of squares; the 80 squares in a row corresponding to the 80 columns on a punch card. Usually, one statement is printed in each row of the coding sheet. Later, each row will be keypunched onto a separate card. Only one character may be printed in a square.

After the program statements have been printed onto the coding forms, the next step is usually to have the program keypunched onto program punch cards. A keypunch machine (see Fig. 2-2) has a keyboard similar to that of a typewriter, but has automatic facilities for punching holes in cards.

For every character the keypunch operator types, the machine prints the character at the top of the card and punches a certain combination of holes below. Every character is assigned its own unique pattern of holes. The computer is able to interpret the pattern of holes and thereby understand what character the combination represents.

Various compilers have various rules concerning the positioning of program statements on the card. Some PASCAL compilers, such as the one used in this book, allow program statements to be punched anywhere in columns 1 to 72 of the punch cards. Blanks (signified on the card by no holes punched in the column) may appear anywhere within a statement (except, of course, in the middle of an identifier, constant, or keyword). In order to improve the readability of the program, the convention of punching only one statement per card is usually adopted. Several statements, however, may appear on one card. If a PASCAL statement is too long to be punched on one card, it may be continued onto the next card (starting between columns 1 and 72). If this happens, the programmer must ensure that the point in the statement where the next card is begun does not fall in the middle of a constant, keyword, or identifier. Columns 73 through 80 are not normally considered in the processing of the PASCAL program. These columns may be used to number the cards in order or left empty.

Two special statements are used to mark the beginning and end of every PASCAL program. The first statement in a program must always be a PROGRAM statement of the following form:

PROGRAM *program-name* (INPUT, OUTPUT);

where the *program-name* must be a valid PASCAL identifier containing eight characters or less. Characters following the first eight characters are allowed but are not recognized as part of the program name. This name uniquely identifies the program.

The two words INPUT and OUTPUT are required only if input and output is performed in the program. For example, if no data cards are required to be read, INPUT can be omitted. If there is no output (i.e., no WRITE or WRITELN statements appear in the program), OUTPUT can be omitted. If only one of INPUT and OUTPUT is given, the comma is also omitted. For example, a program named SUMMARY that does not read data cards could be given as

PROGRAM SUMMARY (OUTPUT);

or

PROGRAM SUMMARY (INPUT, OUTPUT);

After the PROGRAM statement come the declarations, which are given in the order LABEL, CONST, TYPE, and VAR. While any declaration may be omitted, those that are present must be given in the order listed. After the declarations, the word BEGIN of the compound statement appears first, to indicate the start of the executable program body.

It is good programming practice to include, directly in a program, various narrative explanations or comments. These can be used, for example, to describe the purpose of a particular statement or group of statements or to state conditions in effect at certain points of the program. In this way, other people who may look at the program can read these comments along with the actual statements and thereby understand the program more readily. Comments interspersed with the program statements aid the reader in clarifying the purpose and meaning of the instructions, but play no part in the actual processing of the PASCAL statements. In

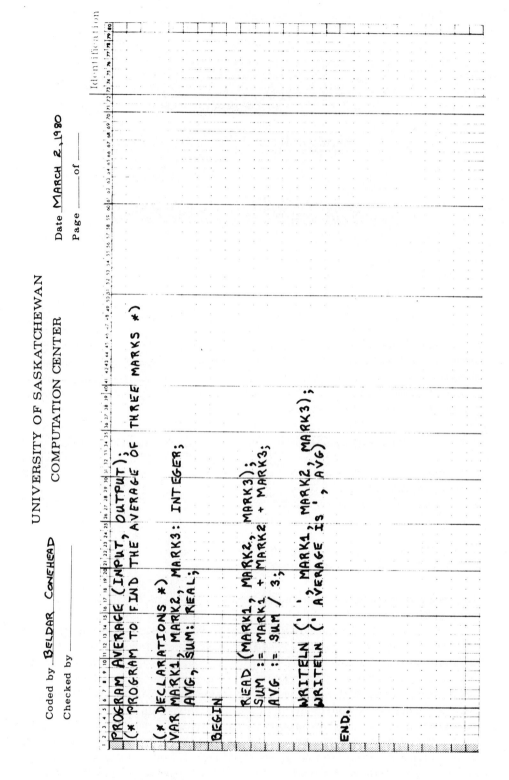

UNIVERSITY OF SASKATCHEWAN
COMPUTATION CENTER

Coded by BELDAR CONEHEAD
Checked by _____

Date MARCH 2, 1980
Page ____ of ____

```
PROGRAM AVERAGE (INPUT, OUTPUT);
(* PROGRAM TO FIND THE AVERAGE OF THREE MARKS *)

(* DECLARATIONS *)
VAR MARK1, MARK2, MARK3: INTEGER;
    AVG, SUM: REAL;

BEGIN

READ (MARK1, MARK2, MARK3);
SUM := MARK1 + MARK2 + MARK3;
AVG := SUM / 3;

WRITELN (' ', MARK1, MARK2, MARK3);
WRITELN (' ', AVERAGE IS ', AVG)

END.
```

Fig. 2-1 A coding form

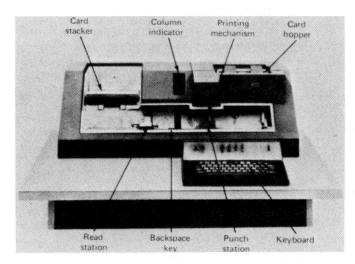

Fig. 2-2 A keypunch machine

order to distinguish between PASCAL program statements and comments, a comment is always preceded by the character pair (* and followed by the pair *) (sometimes referred to as comment brackets or delimiters). Other PASCAL versions use { and } to delimit comments. In this book, we shall use (* and *) to enclose comments. When punching both the beginning and terminating pairs, no blanks may appear between the * and bracket symbols. An example of an acceptable comment is the following:

(* THIS PROGRAM READS 3 NUMBERS AND AVERAGES THEM *)

If the programmer wishes to include a comment which cannot entirely fit on one card, it can be continued on the next card. A comment does not end until a } or a *) is reached, which may be on another card. As an example, consider the following comment placed on two cards

(* IF THE INPUT NUMBERS SUM TO A NUMBER GREATER THAN THIRTY, THEN PRINT OUT AN ERROR MESSAGE *)

As with program statements, no part of a comment should appear in columns 73 through 80 of any card.

Finally, PASCAL programs are entirely free-form, meaning that any number of blanks may appear within or between program statements. This means that the programmer has complete freedom as to where statements can appear on cards. They can be grouped or spread out at will. For example, the programmer may insert blank unpunched cards at various locations among his or her program statement cards. When the computer prints out the program, it prints a blank line for every blank card encountered and thus improves the spacing of the program statements. This approach can reduce the clutter of the program listing, and thereby increase its readability. Also, program statements may be made more readable by indenting and including blanks within and around the program statement. The "white space" can be very effective.

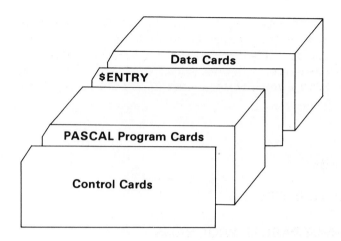

Fig. 2-3   Layout of a program deck

Input data are also usually keypunched on cards, although the rules for keypunching data cards are different from those for program statements. The format for data cards was discussed in Sec. 2-3.

After a program and necessary data have been keypunched on cards, the set of all these cards (the *card deck*) is almost ready to be input to the computer for processing. Prior to this step, however, the programmer must arrange the cards in the following order. At the front of the input card deck must appear certain *control cards*— special cards containing information needed by the computer concerning the program, such as the identification of the programmer and computer account and the programming language used. Control cards, usually one or two in number, will normally be supplied by the class instructor or by the computer installation itself. Following these come the program statement cards in the exact order in which the statements appeared on the coding sheet. For the PASCAL programs read on a card reader, the next card usually indicates the start of the data. Starting in column 1 may appear a card with

$ENTRY

punched on it. A $ENTRY card tells the compiler that the remaining cards in the deck, if any, are data cards. Finally, the data cards should appear at the end of the deck. If no data cards are required by the program, then the $ENTRY card may be omitted from the deck. Figure 2-3 illustrates the complete layout of a program deck.

The deck is now ready to be input to the card reader, which reads the cards and passes the information to the computer for processing. The program output is normally printed on paper by the line printer. This printout consists of a complete listing of the submitted PASCAL program, followed by any output generated by its execution. Any error messages generated by the processing of the program are printed as well.

This guide to preparing a PASCAL program should aid the beginning programmer in successfully running his or her first jobs. After some practice, the novice should become familiar with the use of a keypunch, card reader, and line printer. Also with practice, the coding and card layout rules in PASCAL will become less difficult to remember, along with the required card deck sequence rules. The final step mentioned in running a job was receiving the printed output. The programmer must then try to discover why errors occurred by recreating exactly the steps that the computer performed. This important aspect of programming is the subject of the next section.

Exercises for Sec. 2-5

1. What are control cards?

2. What is the purpose of a $ENTRY card?

2-6 EXECUTING SIMPLE PASCAL PROGRAMS

Once a program has been prepared according to the steps outlined in Sec. 2-5, it is ready to be submitted to the computer. The first stage of its processing involves execution of another program called the *compiler,* whose function is to translate your program into an equivalent program in machine language ready for execution. During compilation of the program, the compiler reports any errors that have been made in the use of the programming language. After the program has been compiled successfully, it is executed. Figure 2-4 contains the printout from the execution of a simple program. Let's examine it.

The statements that appear on the cards submitted to the computer are printed in the listing of the program. The third column of numbers that appears on the lefthand side of the listing contain line numbers generated by the compiler to be used for referencing statements within the listing. Note that all cards, including blank cards, are numbered. The second column of numbers refers to storage addresses. After the listing of the program, the output generated by WRITE and WRITELN statements within the program is printed.

The program begins with a comment describing its purpose and a statement naming the program. Following this, the variables are declared. Next the three marks are read in. The variables, MARK1, MARK2, and MARK3, are assigned the values 65, 72, and 83, respectively, from the data cards (not shown). In the next statement, the sum of MARK1, MARK2, and MARK3 is calculated and assigned to the variable SUM. Next, the sum of the marks is divided by 3 to produce the average, which is assigned to the variable AVG. Finally, the marks and the average are printed. The END. at the end of the program is required to mark the physical end of the program.

The program of Fig. 2-5 is somewhat more difficult. This program reads in the radius of a circle in metres and finds the circumference and area of that circle and of another circle 2 metres larger in radius.

The variables used in this program are declared in the lines 4 through 6. Notice that PI is defined to be a constant in the constant declaration section. Line 9 reads in the radius of the circle. In lines 10, 11, 12, 13, and 14 the values of AREA and CIR are calculated and printed. The radius is increased by 2 meters, and new values for AREA and CIR are calculated and printed.

Both of these sample programs were correct. Often, however, despite the *best* intentions of the programmer, errors are made during the writing of programs. These may result from misuse of some feature of the programming language or, perhaps a misunderstanding of exactly what certain statements do in a program.

```
0  0000   00001   (* PROGRAM TO FIND THE AVERAGE OF THREE MARKS *)
0  0000   00002
0  0000   00003   PROGRAM AVERAGE (INPUT, OUTPUT);
0  0000   00004
0  0000   00005   VAR MARK1, MARK2, MARK3: INTEGER;
0  0038   00006       AVG, SUM: REAL;
0  0038   00007
0  0038   00008   BEGIN
0  0038   00009       READ (MARK1, MARK2, MARK3);
0  006E   00010       SUM := MARK1 + MARK2 + MARK3;
0  008E   00011       AVG := SUM / 3;
0  009A   00012
0  009A   00013       WRITELN (' MARK1 =', MARK1);
0  00BE   00014       WRITELN (' MARK2 =', MARK2);
0  00E2   00015       WRITELN (' MARK3 =', MARK3);
0  0106   00016       WRITELN (' AVERAGE =', AVG)
0  012A   00017   END.
-----------------------------------
| COMPILE TIME:    0.047 SECOND(S) |
|     NO WARNING(S) DETECTED       |
|     NO ERROR(S) DETECTED         |
-----------------------------------
--EXECUTION-->
MARK1 =          65
MARK2 =          72
MARK3 =          83
AVERAGE =     7.333333E 01
```

Fig. 2-4   Program to find the average of three marks

```
0  0000   00001   (* AREA AND CIRCUMFERENCE *)
0  0000   00002   PROGRAM CIRCLE (INPUT, OUTPUT);
0  0000   00003
0  0000   00004   CONST PI = 3.14159;
0  0038   00005   VAR AREA, CIR: REAL;
0  0038   00006       RADIUS: INTEGER;
0  0038   00007
0  0038   00008   BEGIN
0  0038   00009       READ (RADIUS);
0  004A   00010       AREA := PI * RADIUS * RADIUS;
0  007C   00011       CIR := PI * RADIUS * 2;
0  009C   00012       WRITELN (' RADIUS =', RADIUS);
0  00C0   00013       WRITELN (' AREA =', AREA);
0  00E4   00014       WRITELN (' CIRCUMFERENCE =', CIR);
0  0108   00015
0  0108   00016       (* CALCULATE AND PRINT SECOND RADIUS, AREA, AND CIRCUMFERENCE *)
0  0108   00017       WRITELN ('-SECOND RADIUS');
0  011A   00018       RADIUS := RADIUS + 2;
0  0126   00019       AREA := PI * RADIUS * RADIUS;
0  0158   00020       CIR := PI * RADIUS * 2;
0  0178   00021       WRITELN (' RADIUS =', RADIUS);
0  019C   00022       WRITELN (' AREA =', AREA);
0  01C0   00023       WRITELN (' CIRCUMFERENCE =', CIR)
0  01E4   00024   END.
-----------------------------------
| COMPILE TIME:    0.075 SECOND(S) |
|     NO WARNING(S) DETECTED       |
|     NO ERROR(S) DETECTED         |
-----------------------------------
--EXECUTION-->
RADIUS =          7
AREA =       1.539378E 02
CIRCUMFERENCE =    4.398224E 01


SECOND RADIUS
RADIUS =          9
AREA =       2.544686E 02
CIRCUMFERENCE =    5.654858E 01
```

Fig. 2-5   Program to find the area and circumference of two circles

```
0  0000   00001  (* VOLUME OF A SPHERE *)
0  0000   00002  PROGRAM VOLUME (OUTPUT);
0  0000   00003
0  0000   00004  CONST PI = 3.14159;
0  0038   00005  VAR RADIUS, VOLUME: REAL;
0  0038   00006
0  0038   00007  BEGIN
0  0038   00008      RADIUS := 7.8;
0  0040   00009      VOLUME := 4 / 3 * PI * RADIUS * RADIUS * RADIUS;
0  007E   00010      WRITELN ( ' VOLUME =' VOLUME)
                                                   $
... WARNING ...      INSERTED A MISSING  )
                                                   $
>>>> ERROR >>>>      INVALID SYNTAX
0  0090   00011  END.
---------------------------------------
| COMPILE TIME:    0.036 SECOND(S) |
|     1 WARNING(S) DETECTED         |
|     1 ERROR(S) DETECTED           |
---------------------------------------
RETURN CODE 0012
```

Fig. 2-6   Syntax error

The computer often aids in finding these errors by printing error messages, for example, if statements are not properly specified or if an illegal operation is attempted. It is the programmer's task to remove all these errors from the program; this important process is often referred to as *debugging*.

There are three types of errors that are common in programs. The first type of error is the *syntax error (or compile-time error)*. A syntax error is a violation of one of the grammatical rules of the programming language itself— illegally forming one of the statements, for example. As was previously mentioned, syntax errors are detected during the compilation of the program. If a syntax error is discovered by the PASCAL compiler, an error message is printed. The program given in Fig. 2-6 illustrates a syntax error. In this example, the error occurs in line 10. A comma should appear between the literal 'bVOLUMEb=' and the variable VOLUME. The correct statement is

WRITELN ('bVOLUMEb=', VOLUME)

The second type of error occurs during the execution of a program, and is appropriately called an *execution error* (or *run-time error*). An execution error occurs when the program directs the computer to perform an operation that for some reason it cannot perform. When an execution error occurs, the computer stops executing the program and prints an error message. Consider the example program which appears in Fig. 2-7. In this example the computer is unable to calculate a value for VOLUME in line 9 since a division by 0 error occurs. The error is in fact a keypunching error — 0 should have been 3. The statement should read:

VOLUME = 4 / 3 * *PI* * RADIUS * RADIUS * RADIUS

The third type of error is more insidious than the other two, as it is perhaps the most difficult type of error to detect. It is more difficult to detect because it usually does not generate an error message. In the case of this type of error (sometimes referred to as a *logical error*), messages appear only if an execution error is generated later in the program. For example, at one point in a program, a variable may, through an error, be given a value of 0. If this variable is used as a divisor in a subsequent part of the program, the computer would terminate execution at that point and print an error message, since dividing by zero is an illegal operation (although the error actually occurred when the variable *was given* the value 0). If, however, this error does not cause a problem during execution, then the error may remain undetected, invalidating the result of the program. Some of the causes of logic errors are keypunching mistakes in constants, hidden truncation of values, and misuse of operators and their precedence. The program which appears in Fig. 2-8 contains two errors of this type. In this example, a mistake has been made in assigning the value of the constant PI in line 4. PI has been assigned 3.14259 instead of 3.14159. The second error occurs in line 9. The value of RADIUS should be raised to the third power (i.e., multiplied by itself three times) rather than squared, as this statement indicates.

A correct program to find the volume of a sphere with radius 7.8 metres is given in Fig. 2-9.

One of the ways to find logic errors is through *program testing*. The main text offers useful comments on methods of program testing. Program testing involves executing the program with carefully selected data for which the answer is known. When the correct results are known, the results of the program can be easily checked. The data used should be picked with regard to the program specifications rather than the program itself. This is to ensure that the program does what it is supposed to do, rather than what it was written to do; this approach to testing will often detect omissions in the implementation of a problem. Care must be taken to ensure that the data are representative of all possible cases. This does not mean that all possible data must be tested; however, it does mean that all possible situations should be tested. For example, consider the problem of writing a program that reads in an employee's name and hours worked and calculates the amount of pay received per hour, given a fixed weekly salary. The program is then to print the employee's name, hours worked, and weekly and hourly salary. The program which appears in Fig. 2-10 is one possible solution. This program has been tested using the test data,

'JOHN DOE' 40

This program appears to satisfy the specifications of the problem, but not all situations have been tested. Suppose, for some reason (a paid vacation, for example), an employee did not work at all that week and, therefore, the "hours" entry on his card was 0. Running the program with this employee's information would result in an error, as an attempt to divide by zero would be made in line 11. Testing of this program should include this possibility.

Often, extra print statements can be inserted to help locate errors. These extra statements are used to print intermediate values or messages which allow the programmer to follow the execution of the program.

The program of Fig. 2-11 illustrates this method of locating errors. The added statements in this program print the values of all the variables. It is clear from this printout that, for the given values of A, B, and C, the value of SUM is too small. A recheck of the statement in which the SUM is calculated indicates an obvious mistake. Line 11 should be SUM := A + B + C, not SUM := A + B − C. Though the use of this extra print statement was not necessary to find the error in this particular program, it might be important in a situation in which a similar error was embedded in a program containing hundreds of statements.

```
0   0000    00001   (* VOLUME OF A SPHERE *)
0   0000    00002   PROGRAM VOLUME (OUTPUT);
0   0000    00003
0   0000    00004   CONST PI = 3.14159;
0   0038    00005   VAR RADIUS, VOLUME: REAL;
0   0038    00006
0   0038    00007   BEGIN
0   0038    00008       RADIUS := 7.8;
0   0040    00009       VOLUME := 4 / 0 * PI * RADIUS * RADIUS * RADIUS;
0   007E    00010       WRITELN (´ VOLUME =´, VOLUME)
0   00A2    00011   END.
-----------------------------------
¦ COMPILE TIME:    0.037 SECOND(S) ¦
¦     NO WARNING(S) DETECTED       ¦
¦     NO ERROR(S) DETECTED         ¦
-----------------------------------
--EXECUTION-->

*** RUN ERROR: FLOATING-POINT DIVIDE (OCF)              AT OFFSET  006A  IN  VOLUME
RETURN CODE 0016
```

Fig. 2-7   Execution error

```
0   0000    00001   (* VOLUME OF A SPHERE *)
0   0000    00002   PROGRAM VOLUME (OUTPUT);
0   0000    00003
0   0000    00004   CONST PI = 3.14259;
0   0038    00005   VAR RADIUS, VOLUME: REAL;
0   0038    00006
0   0038    00007   BEGIN
0   0038    00008       RADIUS := 7.8;
0   0040    00009       VOLUME := 4 / 3 * PI * RADIUS * RADIUS;
0   007A    00010       WRITELN (´ VOLUME =´, VOLUME)
0   009E    00011   END.
-----------------------------------
¦ COMPILE TIME:    0.035 SECOND(S) ¦
¦     NO WARNING(S) DETECTED       ¦
¦     NO ERROR(S) DETECTED         ¦
-----------------------------------
--EXECUTION-->
VOLUME =    2.549266E 02
```

Fig. 2-8   Logical errors

```
0   0000    00001   (* VOLUME OF A SPHERE *)
0   0000    00002   PROGRAM VOLUME (OUTPUT);
0   0000    00003
0   0000    00004   CONST PI = 3.14159;
0   0038    00005   VAR RADIUS, VOLUME: REAL;
0   0038    00006
0   0038    00007   BEGIN
0   0038    00008       RADIUS := 7.8;
0   0040    00009       VOLUME := 4 / 3 * PI * RADIUS * RADIUS * RADIUS;
0   007E    00010       WRITELN (´ VOLUME =´, VOLUME)
0   00A2    00011   END.
-----------------------------------
¦ COMPILE TIME:    0.036 SECOND(S) ¦
¦     NO WARNING(S) DETECTED       ¦
¦     NO ERROR(S) DETECTED         ¦
-----------------------------------
--EXECUTION-->
VOLUME =    1.987794E 03
```

Fig. 2-9   Correct volume of a sphere program

```
0  0000   00001  (* PROGRAM TO CALCULATE PAY RATES *)
0  0000   00002  PROGRAM PAY (INPUT, OUTPUT);
0  0000   00003
0  0000   00004  VAR WEEKLY_PAY, HOURLY_PAY: REAL;
0  0038   00005      HOURS: INTEGER;
0  0038   00006      EMPLOYEE: STRING (25);
0  0038   00007
0  0038   00008  BEGIN
0  0038   00009      READ (EMPLOYEE, HOURS);
0  005C   00010      WEEKLY_PAY := 150.00;
0  0064   00011      HOURLY_PAY := WEEKLY_PAY / HOURS;
0  0082   00012      WRITELN (' EMPLOYEE: ', EMPLOYEE, ' HOURS =', HOURS);
0  00CA   00013      WRITELN (' WEEKLY PAY =', WEEKLY_PAY);
0  00EE   00014      WRITELN (' HOURLY PAY =', HOURLY_PAY)
0  0112   00015  END.
-----------------------------------
| COMPILE TIME:    0.047 SECOND(S) |
|     NO WARNING(S) DETECTED       |
|     NO ERROR(S) DETECTED         |
-----------------------------------
--EXECUTION-->
EMPLOYEE: JOHN DOE              HOURS =           40
WEEKLY PAY =      1.500000E 02
HOURLY PAY =      3.750000E 00
```

Fig. 2-10   Program to calculate hourly pay

```
0  0000   00001  (* PROGRAM TO FIND THE AVERAGE OF THREE MARKS *)
0  0000   00002  PROGRAM AVERAGE (OUTPUT);
0  0000   00003
0  0000   00004  VAR A, B, C, SUM: INTEGER;
0  0038   00005      AVG: REAL;
0  0038   00006
0  0038   00007  BEGIN
0  0038   00008      A := 68;
0  0040   00009      B := 72;
0  0048   00010      C := 31;
0  0050   00011      SUM := A + B - C;
0  0060   00012      WRITELN (' A =', A, ' B =', B, ' C =', C);
0  00CC   00013      WRITELN (' SUM =', SUM);
0  00F0   00014      AVG := SUM / 3;
0  011E   00015      WRITELN (' AVERAGE =', AVG)
0  0142   00016  END.
-----------------------------------
| COMPILE TIME:    0.051 SECOND(S) |
|     NO WARNING(S) DETECTED       |
|     NO ERROR(S) DETECTED         |
-----------------------------------
--EXECUTION-->
A =          68 B =          72 C =          31
SUM =       109
AVERAGE =     3.633333E 01
```

Fig. 2-11   Example of output statements used to find errors

This ends the discussion on the preparation and execution of simple PASCAL programs. In this section, examples of executed programs were shown. The concepts of program testing and debugging were discussed, and the types of errors found in programs were illustrated.

In the next section, more elaborate sample programs are given.

Exercises for Sec. 2-6

1. Name three types of programming errors.

2. What is program testing?

2-7 APPLICATIONS

In this section, complete PASCAL programs are given for the applications discussed in Sec. 2-6 of the main text. In each case, the reader is expected to have followed through the relevant material in the main text carefully, from problem specification, through the process of algorithm design, to the production of the final algorithm itself. The programs given in this section have resulted from a straightforward implementation of the algorithms given in the main text. The same solution approach has been used and, where possible, the same names have been used for the variables. Sample input and output are given for each program.

The subsection numbering employed in this section parallels that of the main text.

2-7.1 Reporting Student Grades

This section presents the programmed solution to the problem of reporting student grades given in Sec. 2-6.1 of the main text. The problem as given in the main text is to calculate the final grade of a student given his or her mark in three aspects of a year's work. The three marks to be considered are the result of the mid-term examination which is to count 30% toward the final mark, the mark given for the laboratory work which is to count 20%, and finally, the result of the final examination which is to count for the remaining 50%. The input data are to consist of the student's name and mark in each of the three designated areas. The variables used in the PASCAL solution given in Fig. 2-12 are:

Variable	Type	Usage
LAB_WORK	INTEGER	Mark received for lab work
MIDTERM	INTEGER	Mark received on mid-term exam
FINAL	INTEGER	Mark received on final exam
GRADE	REAL	Final grade
NAME	STRING (20)	Student's name

The data card used with this program contained the following values:

'ARTHUR FONZARELLI', 72, 68, 65

In line 12, the student's name and three aspects of his year's work are read into the respective variables. The student's final grade is calculated in line 15. Lines 18 to 22 print the input information and the student's grade. Note that the three items comprising the final grades are declared to be of type integer, while the final grade itself is of type real. This results in different output formats for the numeric values printed. In line 23, execution is terminated.

2-7.2 Gauging Inflation

The program presented in this section is the solution to the gauging inflation problem given in Sec. 2-6.2 of the main text. The problem is to calculate the algebraic and percentage differences in the prices of the same product bought a

```
0  0000  00001  (* COMPUTE THE FINAL GRADE OF A STUDENT WITH WEIGHTINGS OF 20%, 30%,
0  0000  00002     AND 50% *)
0  0000  00003  PROGRAM REPORT (INPUT, OUTPUT);
0  0000  00004
0  0000  00005  VAR LAB_WORK, MIDTERM, FINAL: INTEGER;
0  0038  00006      GRADE: REAL;
0  0038  00007      NAME: STRING (20);
0  0038  00008
0  0038  00009  BEGIN
0  0038  00010
0  0038  00011      (* INPUT DATA *)
0  0038  00012      READ (NAME, LAB_WORK, MIDTERM, FINAL);
0  0080  00013
0  0080  00014      (* COMPUTE FINAL GRADE *)
0  0080  00015      GRADE := 0.20 * LAB_WORK + 0.30 * MIDTERM + 0.50 * FINAL;
0  00D0  00016
0  00D0  00017      (* DISPLAY RESULTS *)
0  00D0  00018      WRITELN (' STUDENT NAME: ', NAME);
0  00F4  00019      WRITELN (' LABORATORY MARK: ', LAB_WORK);
0  0118  00020      WRITELN (' MIDTERM EXAMINATION: ', MIDTERM);
0  013C  00021      WRITELN (' FINAL EXAMINATION: ', FINAL);
0  0160  00022      WRITELN (' FINAL GRADE: ', GRADE)
0  0184  00023  END.
------------------------------------
| COMPILE TIME:    0.058 SECOND(S) |
|      NO WARNING(S) DETECTED      |
|      NO ERROR(S) DETECTED        |
------------------------------------
--EXECUTION-->
STUDENT NAME: ARTHUR FONZARELLI
LABORATORY MARK:          72
MIDTERM EXAMINATION:           68
FINAL EXAMINATION:             65
FINAL GRADE:      6.729999E 01
```

Fig. 2-12   Program for the reporting student grades problem

month apart. The input values are the name of the product followed by its price this month and the price paid last month. The variables used in the PASCAL program which appears in Fig. 2-13 are:

Variable	Type	Usage
ITEM	STRING (20)	Description of item
CURRENT_PRICE	REAL	Price paid this month
OLD_PRICE	REAL	Price paid last month
ALG_DIFF	REAL	Algebraic difference
PC_DIFF	REAL	Percentage difference

The following data card was used with this program:

'COOKING OIL', 4.79, 4.38

In line 11, the three input values are read into ITEM, CURRENT_PRICE, and OLD_PRICE, respectively. Line 14 uses the current price and old price to calculate the algebraic difference (ALG_DIFF). The percentage difference (PC_DIFF) is calculated in line 17. Lines 20 through 24 print the input values and the calculated algebraic and percentage differences for that item. In line 25, execution of the program is terminated.

```
0  0000   00001  (* CALCULATES THE ALGEBRAIC AND PERCENTAGE DIFFERENCE IN THE PRICES OF
0  0000   00002     IDENTICAL ITEMS BOUGHT IN DIFFERENT MONTHS *)
0  0000   00003  PROGRAM GUAGE (INPUT, OUTPUT);
0  0000   00004
0  0000   00005  VAR ITEM: STRING (20);
0  0038   00006     CURRENT_PRICE, OLD_PRICE, ALG_DIF, PC_DIFF: REAL;
0  0038   00007
0  0038   00008  BEGIN
0  0038   00009
0  0038   00010     (* INPUT THE INFORMATION *)
0  0038   00011     READ (ITEM, CURRENT_PRICE, OLD_PRICE);
0  006E   00012
0  006E   00013     (* COMPUTE THE ALGEBRAIC DIFFERENCE IN PRICES *)
0  006E   00014     ALG_DIF := CURRENT_PRICE - OLD_PRICE;
0  007A   00015
0  007A   00016     (* COMPUTE THE PERCENTAGE DIFFERENCE *)
0  007A   00017     PC_DIFF := ALG_DIF / OLD_PRICE * 100;
0  008A   00018
0  008A   00019     (* OUTPUT THE FINDINGS *)
0  008A   00020     WRITELN (' ITEM PURCHASED: ', ITEM);
0  00AE   00021     WRITELN (' PRICE THIS MONTH: $', CURRENT_PRICE);
0  00D2   00022     WRITELN (' PRICE LAST MONTH: $', OLD_PRICE);
0  00F6   00023     WRITELN (' ALGEBRAIC DIFFERENCE: $', ALG_DIF);
0  011A   00024     WRITELN (' PRECENTAGE DIFFERENCE: ', PC_DIFF, '%')
0  0150   00025  END.
-------------------------------------
| COMPILE TIME:    0.057 SECOND(S) |
|     NO WARNING(S) DETECTED       |
|     NO ERROR(S) DETECTED         |
-------------------------------------
--EXECUTION-->
ITEM PURCHASED: COOKING OIL
PRICE THIS MONTH: $       4.790000E 00
PRICE LAST MONTH: $       4.379999E 00
ALGEBRAIC DIFFERENCE: $     4.100008E-01
PRECENTAGE DIFFERENCE:      9.360748E 00%
```

Fig. 2-13   Program for the gauging inflation problem

2-7.3 Parimutuel Payoffs

The program given in Fig. 2-14 is a solution to the parimutuel payoff problem given in Sec. 2-6.3 of the main text. This problem concerns parimutuel betting at a racetrack. Under this system, persons who bet on the winning horse share the total amount which was bet for the race minus a percentage of the total for the racetrack expenses (including purses for the races) and for taxes. The rate of taxation is 10.6% of all money bet. In addition, the racetrack owners take another 12% to cover expenses. The remaining money is divided among those who bet on the winning horse in proportion to the size of their bets.

The problem, then, is to write a PASCAL program which takes as input data, the total amount bet on a race, the name of the winning horse for the race, and the amount bet on that horse, in that order and calculates the payoff on a $2 bet. The variables used in the PASCAL solution are the following:

Variable name	Type	Usage
WIN_POOL	REAL	Total amount bet in the race
WINNER	STRING(20)	Name of winning horse
BET	REAL	Amount bet on winning horse
RATIO	REAL	Payoff ratio for each dollar bet
TRACK_SHARE	REAL	Track owners' share
GOVT_SHARE	REAL	Governments' share (taxes)
PAYOFF	REAL	Amount paid on a $2 bet

```
0  0000   00001   (* COMPUTE THE CALCULATE PAYOFF AND THE MINIMUM REQUIRED PAYOFF FOR
0  0000   00002      A $2 BET. *)
0  0000   00003   PROGRAM PAY_OFF (INPUT, OUTPUT);
0  0000   00004
0  0000   00005   VAR WINNER: STRING (20);
0  0038   00006       BET, WIN_POOL, GOVT_SHARE, TRACK_SHARE, RATIO, PAYOFF: REAL;
0  0038   00007
0  0038   00008   BEGIN
0  0038   00009
0  0038   00010       (* INPUT *)
0  0038   00011       READ (WIN_POOL, WINNER, BET);
0  006E   00012
0  006E   00013       (* DETERMINE GOVERNMENT'S AND TRACK'S SHARES OF POOL *)
0  006E   00014       GOVT_SHARE := 0.106 * WIN_POOL;
0  007A   00015       TRACK_SHARE := 0.12 * WIN_POOL;
0  0086   00016
0  0086   00017       (* REDUCE POOL ACCORDINGLY *)
0  0086   00018       WIN_POOL := WIN_POOL - (GOVT_SHARE + TRACK_SHARE);
0  0098   00019
0  0098   00020       (* COMPUTE PAYOFF RATIO FOR EACH DOLLAR WAGERED *)
0  0098   00021       RATIO := WIN_POOL / BET;
0  00A4   00022
0  00A4   00023       (* COMPUTE POSTED PAYOFF *)
0  00A4   00024       PAYOFF := RATIO * 2.0;
0  00B0   00025       WRITELN (' ', WINNER, ' WINS AND PAYS $', PAYOFF)
0  00F8   00026   END.
------------------------------------------
| COMPILE TIME:    0.056 SECOND(S) |
|     NO WARNING(S) DETECTED       |
|     NO ERROR(S) DETECTED         |
------------------------------------------
--EXECUTION-->
COMPUTER DELIGHT     WINS AND PAYS $     2.814545E 01
```

Fig. 2-14   Program for the parimutual payoffs problem

The sample data card run with the above program in Fig. 2-14 contained the following input values:

10000 'COMPUTER DELIGHT' 550

In line 11, the three input data values are read into the respective variables. Lines 14 and 15 compute the track's and taxes' shares of the amount bet (10000), and line 18 reduces the WIN_POOL amount accordingly. The payoff ratio for each dollar bet on the winning horse COMPUTER DELIGHT is computed in line 21, by dividing the value of WIN_POOL by the amount bet on COMPUTER DELIGHT, which is the value of BET, (550). This value is then doubled to give the payoff on a $2 bet. Line 25 serves to print the results of the computations. In line 26, execution is terminated.

The reader, at this point should be familiar with the basic concepts of PASCAL programming. In this chapter, data and data types were introduced, along with principles of data manipulation. The use of variables in PASCAL programming was discussed. Expressions and their evaluation were the topic of the next section, and the PASCAL concepts of statement and compound statement was also presented. The set of simple fundamental programming tools discussed thus far was completed with the section on input and output. The remainder of the chapter concerned the approach to preparing and executing PASCAL programs, and the reader was provided with sample problems and solutions.

In the next chapter, more complex programming concepts are given to expand the reader's programming capabilities.

EXERCISES FOR CHAPTER 2

1. The Canadian weather office has recently undergone a conversion to the metric system.

   (i) Write a program to find the Fahrenheit equivalent of a Celsius temperature (integer value) input to the program (conversion formula: $F° = 9/5\,C° + 32$). Test your program by finding the Fahrenheit equivalent of 26 degrees Celsius.

   (ii) Write a program that reads a rainfall amount given in inches (real value) and prints its equivalent in millimetres (conversion formula: 25.4 millimetres = 1 inch). Test your program by finding the millimetre equivalent of 1.75 inches.

2. The roots of a quadratic equation of the form

   $$ax^2 + bx + c = 0$$

   are real if and only if the discriminant given by

   $$b^2 - 4ac$$

   is nonnegative. Write a program to read the values of the coefficients a, b, and c and print the coefficients and the value of the discriminant. Use the SQR function to compute b^2

   Example   Input: 2 3 1
             Output: COEFFICIENTS ARE: 2 3 1
                       DISCRIMINANT IS: 1
   Test your program on the values a = 5, b = 6, and c = 8.

3. The cost to the consumer of a new car is the sum of the wholesale cost of the car, the dealer's percentage markup, and the provincial or state sales tax (applied to the "marked up" price). Assuming a dealer's markup of 12% on all units and a sales tax of 6%, write a program to read the wholesale cost of the car and print the consumer's cost. Using your program, find the consumer's cost of a car that has a wholesale cost of $7500.

4. Honest John's Used Car Company pays its sales staff a salary of $250 per month plus a commission of $15 for each car they sell plus 5% of the value of the sale. Each month, Honest John's bookkeeper prepares a single punched card for each salesperson, containing his/her name, the number of cars sold and the value of the cars sold.

   Write a program to compute and display a salesperson's salary for a given month. Include in the output the salesperson's name and salary. Test your program on the data values

   'DON SWIFT', 4, 32000

5. Three masses m_1, m_2, and m_3 are separated by distances r_{12}, r_{13}, and r_{23}, as

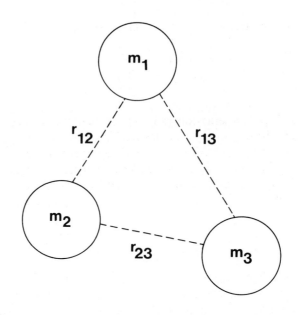

Fig. 2-15   Distances between three masses

shown in Fig. 2-15. If G is the universal gravitational constant, the binding energy holding the mass particles together is given by the following formula:

$$E = G \left(\frac{m_1 \, m_2}{r_{12}} + \frac{m_1 \, m_3}{r_{13}} + \frac{m_2 \, m_3}{r_{23}} \right)$$

Write a program to read values of m_1, m_2, m_3, r_{12}, r_{13}, and r_{23}; then compute and print the binding energy along with the initial data values. For mass in kilograms and distance in metres, $G = 6.67 \times 10^{-11}$ newton- metre^2 / kg^2. The values of m_1, m_2, and m_3 are punched on the first data card, and values of r_{12}, r_{13}, and r_{23} are punched on the second. Assume that all data are punched as real values. Using your program, find the binding energy given the following data:

637E24	3651E36	4531E29
96E65	531E50	75E45

6.   The cost of hail insurance in a typical farming community is 3.5% of the desired amount of coverage per acre, multiplied by the number of acres seeded.

Assuming that the crop possibilities are limited to wheat, oats and barley, write a program that reads the desired coverage and the number of acres planted for each of the three crops and computes the total cost of hail insurance for this customer.

Test your program on the following data:

Desired Coverage Per Acre	Number of Acres
30.00	140
25.00	240
30.0	300

7. Although the speed of light remains constant regardless of the relative speeds of the light source and the observer, the measured frequency and wavelength do change — an effect first predicted by Johann Doppler and thereby dubbed the "Doppler effect." The wavelength λ emitted by a source moving towards an observer with velocity v appears to be compressed by an amount $\triangle\lambda$, which is given by the formula

$$\triangle\lambda = \frac{v\lambda}{c}$$

where c is the speed of light.

Suppose an airplane is travelling towards a radio station at a constant velocity of 360 km/hour (or 10^4 cm. per sec.). If the radio station is broadcasting at a wavelength of 30 metres, the change in wavelength due to the Doppler effect is

$$\triangle\lambda = \frac{v\lambda}{c}$$

$$= \frac{(10^4 \text{ cm per sec}) \times (3 \times 10^3 \text{ cm})}{(3 \times 10^{10} \text{ cm per sec})} = 10^{-3} \text{ cm.}$$

Thus the pilot of this airplane must adjust his receiving set to a wavelength of 3000 cm. *minus* 10^{-3} cm., or 2999.999 cm., until he reaches the station and then to a wavelength of 3000.001 cm. as he moves away from the station.

Write a program to read the broadcast wavelength (in metres) of a radio station and the speed of an approaching plane (in km/hour) and then print out the actual setting (in cm.) at which the pilot will receive the signal. Note that your program will have to make the necessary conversions before calculating the change in wavelength (conversions are: 1000 m. = 1 km., 100 cm. = 1 m.). Use your program to find the proper wavelength setting if a pilot travelling at 440 km/hour wishes to receive a radio station with a broadcast wavelength of 25 metres.

CHAPTER

3

DECISION STRUCTURES

The preceding chapter presented some basic tools of PASCAL which allow the programmer to design and to run simple programs involving input of values, computations, and output of results. More complex problems, however, require the use of additional capabilities. This chapter introduces the PASCAL capabilities of choosing one course of action from several alternatives and of causing the repeated execution of a group of statements. Central to both of these constructs is the concept of a decision: in the former, to determine which alternative to take; in the latter, whether to perform the set of statements one more time. The bases for these decisions are written in a program as expressions called "conditions" which are also developed at this point. Programs using the concepts introduced in this chapter are then presented.

3-1 INTRODUCTION

Chapter 3 of the main text presents key programming constructs to effect the flow of control through an algorithm or program. These constructs, known as *control structures*, represent a major factor in determining the power and usability of a programming language.

The PASCAL language offers a wide range of powerful control structures, that go even beyond those introduced in the algorithmic language. The implementation of two control structures in PASCAL is presented in this chapter, along with some discussion of their application.

3-2 THE SELECTION FROM ALTERNATIVE ACTIONS

3-2.1 The IF...THEN...ELSE Statement

The If-then-else statement represented in the algorithmic language by

If condition
then statement(s)
else statement(s)

has a direct counterpart in PASCAL. The general form of the IF... THEN...ELSE statement in PASCAL is

IF *condition*
THEN single statement
ELSE single statement

As an aid to improved readability, we have adopted the convention that the "IF", "THEN", and "ELSE" all begin in the same column, although this is not a requirement of the PASCAL language.

As in the algorithmic language, the PASCAL IF statement is a double alternative statement; that is, there are two alternatives. If the expressed condition is true, the "true alternative" (or "THEN clause") is executed; otherwise, the "false alternative" (or "ELSE clause") is executed.

The condition is expressed as a PASCAL *logical expression,* that is, an expression which can have only two values, *"true"* or *"false"* (represented in PASCAL by TRUE and FALSE). As is done in the algorithmic language, the condition is normally expressed using *relational operators,* to compare two operands. Table 3-1 shows the relational operators used in the algorithmic language and their representation in PASCAL.

In PASCAL, as in the algorithmic language, logical expressions may also contain the logical connectives, *and, not,* and *or.* The use of these operators in conditional statements is discussed in Sec. 3-4. Here are some examples of logical expressions in PASCAL.

A = B	(This is an expression which is "true" if the value of A equals that of B.)
3 < 7	
TRUE	(logical constant)

Table 3-1   Relational operators and their symbols

Operator	Algorithmic Language Symbol	PASCAL Symbol
Greater than	$>$	$>$
Less than	$<$	$<$
Equal	$=$	$=$
Greater than or equal to	$\geq$	$>=$
Less than or equal to	$\leq$	$<=$
Not equal	$\neq$	$<>$

FALSE	(logical constant)
SWITCH	(A variable that has been declared BOOLEAN.)
'CAT' = 'DOG'	

The last example is a comparison between two strings. Character strings can be compared using any of the relational operators. In this chapter, we compare strings only for equality (i.e., whether or not the strings are equal) for which the interpretation is clear. Complete rules governing the comparison of character strings are left to Chap. 5.

Here is a simple example of a PASCAL IF...THEN...ELSE statement.

```
IF A < B
THEN WRITELN (' A IS SMALLER THAN B')
ELSE WRITELN (' B IS SMALLER THAN OR EQUAL TO A')
```

Notice that there is no semicolon following the WRITELN of the THEN part of the IF statement. Recall that a semicolon is used to separate statements; hence, it would indicate the end of the IF statement and the start of a new statement. A semicolon after the THEN clause in this case would result in an error. A semicolon may appear at the very end of the IF...THEN...ELSE statement if it is needed to separate this statement from following statements. The use of the semicolon for this and all other PASCAL statements follows the rules described in Sec. 2-3 for the compound statement.

In many cases, a group of statements, rather than a single statement, is required in the true or false alternative. For this to be done in PASCAL, the alternative must be contained in a BEGIN ... END construct. The "BEGIN" and "END" which enclose these statements indicate that they are to be considered as one statement (referred to as a *compound statement*). The following is an example of an IF structure which contains compound statements in both the true and false alternatives. Notice the use of the semicolons.

```
IF COUNT >= COUNT1
THEN BEGIN
        COUNT := COUNT + 1;
        WRITELN (' TRUE ALTERNATIVE SELECTED.');
        PLACE := 7 * 34
        END
```

```
ELSE BEGIN
     COUNT1 := COUNT1 + 2;
     WRITELN (' FALSE ALTERNATIVE SELECTED.');
     PLACE := 8 * 34
     END
```

A compound statement may be used in either or both the true and false alternatives. An example in which the true alternative is a single statement and the false alternative is a compound statement is the following:

```
IF NUM < SUM
THEN WRITELN (' TRUE ALTERNATIVE SELECTED.')
ELSE BEGIN
     COUNT := COUNT + 1;
     WRITELN (' FALSE ALTERNATIVE SELECTED.')
     END
```

As in the algorithmic language, the PASCAL IF statement can also be used if there is just one alternative. In the following program segment, for example, one is added to COUNT if the value of NUM is less than zero; otherwise, nothing is done.

```
COUNT := 0;
READ(NUM);
IF NUM < 0
THEN COUNT := COUNT + 1;
WRITELN (' COUNT =', COUNT)
```

In this example there is no ELSE clause. The semicolon after the THEN part of the IF statement indicates the end of the IF statement. The action of the single alternative IF statement is to perform the statement included within the IF statement, if the condition is true. If the condition is false, execution continues with the next executable statement after the true alternative, in this case, the WRITELN statement. The following is another example of a single alternative IF structure in which the alternative is a compound statement.

```
IF MARK < 50
THEN BEGIN
     WRITE (' STUDENT HAS FAILED');
     SUM := SUM + MARK
     END;
WRITELN (' THE SUM IS ', SUM);
```

In this example if MARK is less than 50, the literal 'STUDENT HAS FAILED' is printed and MARK is added to SUM. No matter what the value of MARK is, the value of SUM is always printed after executing the IF statement.

The IF...THEN...ELSE structure also allows the testing of a number of conditions that may occur in sequence. The next section illustrates a way of testing conditions, based on the results of previous tests, through the use of nested IF statements.

3-2.2 Nested IF Statements

In PASCAL, as in the algorithmic language, it is often desirable to include an IF statement in one of the alternatives of another IF...THEN...ELSE. This second IF statement is said to be *nested* within the first IF statement.

For example, consider the following program segment which reads in a student's name and mark, and prints a message if the student has passed (i.e., mark is greater than or equal to 50). If the student has received a passing grade, a further check is made to see if he or she is an "A" student (i.e., the mark is greater than or equal to 80).

```
READ (NAME, MARK);
IF MARK >= 50
THEN BEGIN
        WRITELN (' ', NAME, 'HAS PASSED.');
        IF MARK >= 80
        THEN WRITELN (' ', NAME, 'IS AN "A" STUDENT.')
        ELSE WRITELN (' ', NAME, 'IS NOT AN "A" STUDENT.')
        END
```

In this program, the student's name and mark are read in. If the mark is greater than or equal to 50, the student's name and the literal, HAS PASSED. are printed. In addition, if the mark is greater than or equal to 80, the student's name and the literal IS AN 'A' STUDENT. are printed. If, however, the mark is between 50 and 80 inclusive, the name of the student and the message IS NOT AN 'A' STUDENT. is printed. Again notice the absence of the semicolon at the end of the second IF statement. It can be omitted because the next line is the END of a BEGIN ... END statement.

As was pointed out in the main text, the programmer must be very careful when using nested IF statements. For example, consider the following program segment.

```
READ (NAME, MARK);
IF MARK >= 50
THEN IF MARK >= 80
        THEN WRITELN (' ', NAME, 'IS AN "A" STUDENT.')
ELSE WRITELN (' ', NAME, 'HAS FAILED.')
```

The intent of the programmer was to have the ELSE belong to the first IF statement (i.e., IF MARK >= 50), and the indenting appears to suggest that this is the case, but is it? The answer is no. The ELSE is always associated with the innermost preceding IF that has not been ended; in this case that is IF MARK >= 80.

There are two ways that the desired interpretation can be achieved. One way is to put the nested IF statement in a compound statement, as is done in the following example.

```
READ (NAME, MARK);
IF MARK >= 50
THEN BEGIN
        IF MARK >= 80
```

```
    THEN WRITELN (' ', NAME, 'IS AN "A" STUDENT.')
    END
ELSE WRITELN (' ', NAME, 'HAS FAILED.')
```

Another method is to insert a *dummy* ELSE. A dummy ELSE is simply an ELSE with no statement following. The following example uses this technique.

```
    READ (NAME, MARK);
    IF MARK >= 50
    THEN IF MARK >= 80
            THEN WRITELN (' ', NAME, 'IS AN "A" STUDENT.')
            ELSE
    ELSE WRITELN (' ', NAME, 'HAS FAILED.')
```

In this version, the dummy ELSE inserted after the THEN clause of the nested IF closes the innermost IF, and thereby causes the second ELSE clause to be interpreted as belonging to the outermost IF statement. The erroneous version of this particular program example serves to illustrate another important point; namely that indenting acts as a guide only to the human reader; it has no effect whatsoever on the actions of the computer.

IF statements can, of course, be nested to an arbitrary depth. An example of a multilevel nesting of such statements is contained in the following program.

```
    READ (A, B, C, D, E);
    IF A < B
    THEN BEGIN
            WRITELN (' A IS LESS THAN B');
            IF A < C
            THEN BEGIN
                    WRITELN (' A IS LESS THAN C');
                    IF A < D
                    THEN BEGIN
                            WRITELN (' A IS LESS THAN D');
                            IF A < E
                            THEN BEGIN
                                    WRITELN (' A IS LESS THAN E')
                                    END
                            END
                    END
            END
    END
```

In this program, A is compared to B. If A is less than B, a message is printed and then A is compared to C. If A is less than C, another message is printed and then A is compared to D. If A is less than D, a third message is printed and then A is compared to E. If A is less than E, a final message is printed. Notice that if A is not less than B, nothing is printed.

In this section, the PASCAL IF statement was introduced. This control structure allows decisions to be made during the execution of the program, based on certain conditions that are usually unknown before run time. Nested IF statements were also introduced. The programmer is again cautioned that undisciplined use of this type of structure might impair the clarity of programs, and so proper care must be exercised when using nested IF statements.

The next section deals in more depth with the concept of conditions which are much more complex than the simple relations used in examples thus far. Additional operators to allow the formation of such conditional expressions will be presented.

Exercises for Sec. 3-2

1. Write a program to read in the base and height of a triangle and print out the area of the triangle (area = ½ * base * height). During the preparation of data for this program, it is entirely possible that a mistake be made that may inadvertently result in one of the values base or height being negative. Clearly, this is undesirable since it will result in a negative area being printed. Design into your program the capability to check for negative values on input. If one is encountered, you should print it out along with a message identifying it as the base or height (this may make it easier for someone to correct the error). Test your program on the values base = 34 and height = –64.

2. Write a program to read the lengths of the three sides of a triangle (S1, S2, S3) and determine what type of triangle it is based on the following cases:
   Let A denote the largest of S1, S2 and S3, and B and C the other two.
   Then,

if $A \geqslant B + C$	, no triangle is formed;
if $A^2 = B^2 + C^2$	, a right-angled triangle is formed;
if $A^2 > B^2 + C^2$	, an obtuse triangle is formed;
if $A^2 < B^2 + C^2$	, an acute triangle is formed;
if $A^2 = B^2 = C^2$	, an equilateral triangle is formed.

   Your program should print the lengths of the three sides, followed by the triangle's type

   > (e.g., SIDES ARE: 3 4 5
   >   TYPE OF TRIANGLE: RIGHT_ANGLED)

   Use your program to decide what type of triangle has sides of lengths 6, 7, and 8.

3. (i) Write a program to read an integer value and determine whether the value is even or odd.
   (ii) Generalize the program written in part (i) to decide, given m and n, whether, n divides m. (i.e., there is no remainder for m/n)

3-3 USE OF COMPOUND CONDITIONS

In Sec. 3-4 of the main text, a set of logical connectives "and," "or," and "not" was introduced to allow the formation of compound conditions. Similar connectives are provided in PASCAL, denoted by the symbols AND, OR, and NOT.

Table 3-2 Truth tables of PASCAL logical connectives

1. AND (conjunction)

C1	C2	C1 AND C2
TRUE	TRUE	TRUE
TRUE	FALSE	FALSE
FALSE	TRUE	FALSE
FALSE	FALSE	FALSE

2. OR (disjunction)

C1	C2	C1 OR C2
TRUE	TRUE	TRUE
TRUE	FALSE	TRUE
FALSE	TRUE	TRUE
FALSE	FALSE	FALSE

3. NOT (negation)

C1	NOT C1
TRUE	FALSE
FALSE	TRUE

The truth tables for the connectives, AND, OR, and NOT, are shown in Table 3-2, where C1 and C2 denoted simple conditions.

Here are three examples of compound conditions. The simple conditions, 30 <= 40 (which is true) and 50 <= 30 (which is false), are used.

    (30 <= 40) AND (50 <= 30)
    (30 <= 40) OR (50 <= 30)
    NOT (30 <= 40)

In the first example, the first simple condition is true and the second is false. The compound condition created by the AND operator is, therefore, false. Again in the second example, the first simple condition is true and the second is false. Table 3-2 indicates that when one condition is true and the other false, the OR compound condition is true. Finally, the third compound condition is false. The NOT operator has the effect of reversing the value of the simple condition (which is true); therefore, the compound condition is false.

PRECEDENCE OF LOGICAL AND RELATIONAL OPERATORS

Unlike the expected precedence order, which is used in the main text, in PASCAL the logical connectives are given higher precedence than the relational operators — equal, in fact, to the numeric operators. NOT has the highest precedence. Because of the precedence of the operators, parentheses should

Table 3-3   Precedence of operators and logical connectives

Operation	Operator	Order of Evaluation
1. Built-in functions		left to right
2. Logical "not"	NOT	left to right
3. Multiplication,	*	left to right
Division, and	/ and DIV	
Logical "and"	AND	
4. Addition and	+	left to right
Subtraction, and	–	
Logical "or"	OR	
5. Relational Operators	=	left to right
	>=	
	<=	
	< >	
	<	
	>	

always enclose conditions involving numeric and relational operators to which the logical operators apply. A complete table of the precedence rules appears in Table 3-3.

The following example illustrates the evaluation of a more complex condition.

$$(5 + 6 <= 7 * 9) \text{ AND NOT } (7 - 11 <= 4)$$

In this example, the expressions within parentheses are evaluated first. Within these expressions, the arithmetic operations are evaluated first, leaving an intermediate result of

$$(11 <= 63) \text{ AND NOT } (-4 <= 4)$$

and then the relational operations are performed leaving the result

TRUE AND NOT TRUE

Then the NOT operation is evaluated, leaving an intermediate result of

TRUE AND FALSE

Finally, the last logical operation, AND, is evaluated giving a final result of FALSE. Notice that the operations performed in each step are performed in a left-to-right manner.

COMPOUND CONDITIONS IN DECISION STRUCTURES

As was previously mentioned, compound conditions can be used in IF statements and, as we shall see in the next section, in conditional loops. Compound conditions are often used to clarify programs in which complex nesting might otherwise be required. Unfortunately, complex compound conditions can also cause confusion and, therefore, nesting and compound conditions should be used together judiciously to produce the clearest possible programs.

The choice of using either nesting or compound conditions depends on the circumstances of the program and must be left to the programmer's judgement. The following two programs have been written using nesting (Program 1) and compound conditions (Program 2). Both programs read in three distinct numbers and determine the largest of the three values.

```
(*PROGRAM 1: THE LARGEST OF THREE VALUES (NESTED VERSION) *)
PROGRAM MAXIMUM (INPUT, OUTPUT);
VAR A, B, C, MAX: REAL;
BEGIN
    (*READ THREE VALUES *)
    IF A > B
    THEN IF A > C
            THEN MAX := A
            ELSE  MAX := C
    ELSE IF B > C
            THEN MAX := B
            ELSE  MAX := C
    WRITELN (' THE LARGEST VALUES IS', MAX)
END.
```

```
(* PROGRAM 2: THE LARGEST OF THREE VALUES (COMPOUND CONDITIONS) *)
PROGRAM MAXIMUM (INPUT, OUTPUT);
VAR A, B, C, MAX REAL;
BEGIN
    (* READ VALUES *)
    READ (A, B, C);
    (* FIND LARGEST VALUE *)
    IF (A > B) AND (A > C)
    THEN MAX := A;
    IF (B > A) AND (B > C)
    THEN MAX := B;
    IF (C > A) AND (C > B)
    THEN MAX := C;
    WRITELN (' THE LARGEST VALUE IS', MAX)
END.
```

The next section deals with another control structure which allows the programmer to alter the flow of control during execution. The looping structure allows the programmer to have sections of a program repeated during execution.

Exercise for Sec. 3-3

1. Suppose I and J are INTEGER variables with values 4 and 8, respectively. Which of the following conditions are true?

(i) $2 * I < = J$
(ii) $2 * I - 1 < J$
(iii) $(I > 0)$ AND $(I < = 10)$
(iv) $(I > 25)$ OR $((I < 50)$ AND $(J < 50))$
(v) $(I < 4)$ OR $(J > 5)$
(vi)   NOT $(I > 6)$

3-4 LOOPING

As described in the main text, the programmer may indicate the repetition of a group of statements using a construct called a *loop*. The general format for any loop is usually as follows:

> *loop control statement*
>   *group of statements which are to be repeated*

The group of statements to be repeated is called the *range* of the loop; the number of times that the range is repeated is determined by the loop control statement which must directly precede the range. The loop end statement serves to indicate the end of the statements that make up the range, but is not always required in some kinds of loops.

In the algorithmic language, we introduced two forms of loop: the conditional loop and the counted loop. The conditional loop was given as

> Repeat while condition
>   *statement*$_1$
>   *statement*$_2$
>   .
>   .
>   .
>   *statement*$_n$

where *statement*$_1$ through *statement*$_n$ were statements to be performed while the condition was true. Another form of the conditional loop was

> Repeat thru step *n* while condition

where step *n* referred to the last step of the range. The counted loop was given as

> Repeat for *name* = *start-value, start-value + increment, . . ., end-value*
>   *statement*$_1$
>   *statement*$_2$
>   .
>   .
>   .
>   *statement*$_n$

where *statement*$_1$ through *statement*$_n$ represent the range of the loop or

> Repeat thru step *n* for *name* = *start-value, start-value + increment, . . .,*
>   *end-value*

where *n* denotes the last step in the range.

Both the conditional loop and the counted loop have direct parallels in PASCAL. In this section we look first at the types of loop provided in PASCAL, discussing the rules for their use. We then discuss the concept of writing loops inside loops or loop nesting.

3-4.1 Conditional Loops

There are two forms of the conditional loop in PASCAL. One form is

WHILE *condition* DO
    single statement to do if condition is true

The *condition* is a valid PASCAL logical expression which is evaluated either as "true" or "false." The *statement* can be any valid PASCAL statement. A semicolon may follow this statement if it is to be separated from a following statement. The interpretation given is identical to that of the "Repeat ... while" construct of the algorithmic language. Upon encountering the loop control statement for the first time, the condition is evaluated using the present values of all variables found in the condition. If the truth value resulting from this evaluation is "false," then the loop will not be performed at all and the next statement executed will be the one which follows the single statement after the WHILE ... DO. If, however, the truth value is "true", then the statement following the WHILE ... DO is executed. After this execution, control returns to the loop control statement and the condition is once again evaluated. Note that the values of the variables involved in the condition may have been changed in the loop. If the truth value obtained from this evaluation is "false," then the statement following the WHILE ...DO is not performed any more and control is relinquished to the statement after the loop. If the truth value is "true," the process of loop execution and subsequent condition testing occurs again. This process continues until a condition evaluation produces a "false" value. If more than one statement is required in the range of the WHILE ... DO, a compound statement is used to to enclose these statements. For example, consider the following segment (notice the indentation convention that we adopt for the statements in the range of a loop):

```
COUNT := 0;
SUM := 0;
NUM := 6;
WHILE SUM < NUM DO
BEGIN
     COUNT := COUNT + 1;
     SUM := SUM + 2
END;
WRITELN (' ', SUM, COUNT)
```

Execution of this segment produces the following output:

      6   3

Notice that if this program segment were altered somewhat, by changing the assignment statement

        NUM := 6

to

        NUM := 0

then execution of the segment would produce the output:

            0   0

since the condition would yield a value of "false" upon the initial evaluation, and thus, the loop range is not entered even once.

PASCAL has one other conditional loop, the REPEAT ... UNTIL loop which has the general form:

    REPEAT
            range statement$_1$;
            range statement$_2$;
                    .
                    .
                    .
            range statement$_n$
    UNTIL *condition*

where the last statement is the loop control statement. Notice that unlike the WHILE ... DO statement, this statement allows an arbitrary number of range statements which are placed between the REPEAT and the UNTIL and can be any valid PASCAL statements. The *condition* can be any valid logical expression.

The interpretation given to this loop is not the same as the algorithmic "Repeat ... while" construct. The "Repeat ... while" is top-tested, but the "Repeat ... until" is bottom-tested. In a bottom-tested loop, the range statements are executed before evaluating the condition. Thus the loop is *always* executed at least once. At the end of each loop iteration, the condition is evaluated. If its value is "true," execution of the loop terminates and the statement following the UNTIL condition is executed next. If, however, its value is "false," the loop is executed again. Thus execution of the loop differs from the WHILE ... DO statement in the following ways: the loop is always executed at least once, execution of the loop terminates when the loop condition becomes "true" (unlike "false" in the WHILE ... DO case), and more than one statement may constitute the range of the loop. (That is, the BEGIN...END statement becomes unnecessary when the range of the loop consists of more than one statement.)

To illustrate these differences, the WHILE ... DO example given earlier in this section is rewritten using REPEAT ... UNTIL.

    CONST := 0;
    SUM := 0;
    NUM := 6;
    REPEAT
            COUNT := COUNT + 1;
            SUM := SUM + 2

UNTIL SUM >= NUM;
WRITELN (' ', SUM, COUNT)

Notice that the condition (SUM >= NUM) is the opposite of that used for the WHILE ... DO loop (SUM < NUM). Execution of this segment produces the same output as in the previous example, that is,

    6   3

In this case, if the assignment

    NUM := 6

were changed to

    NUM := 0

then execution of the segment would produce the output

    2   1

since the loop is always executed at least once.

The conditional loops use the truth value of the condition for each loop repetition to determine if the range statements will be repeated once more. Thus, the number of times the repetition actually occurs is not fixed, but instead is dependent upon the logical value of the condition. As shown in the main text, there are certain applications where the loop range must be performed a fixed number of times, controlled by a counter, and independent of any condition. The counted loop is the subject of the next section.

3-4.2 Counted Loops

The PASCAL *counted loop* differs in form from that given in the algorithmic language, although the general principle is very similar.

Both forms of the counted loop involve a loop control statement based on a special *loop variable* that takes on a sequence of values. The essential difference lies in the specification of this sequence. In the algorithmic language, the sequence is expressed in the form

$val_1, val_2, \ldots, val_n$

In PASCAL, it is expressed in the form

start-value TO *end-value* DO

or

start-value DOWNTO *end-value* DO

where *start-value,* and *end-value* are each expressions evaluating to a scalar type other than REAL. This restriction will be discussed in more detail later. TO and DOWNTO are special keywords. The complete construct has the following general form:

> FOR *loop-variable* := start-value TO *end-value* DO
> *single range statement*

The loop control statement is followed by a single statement. If the range is to consist of more than one statement, the BEGIN ... END construct must be used.

The execution of a counted loop in PASCAL proceeds as follows. First, the expressions for the start-value and end-value are evaluated and stored, and the value of the start-value expression is assigned to the loop variable. A comparison is then made between the value of the loop variable and the end-value. If the loop variable value is greater than the end-value (assuming that TO is used rather than DOWNTO), then the statement following is not executed even once. Instead, control passes immediately to the statement following the loop's range statement. If, however, the loop variable's value is less than or equal to the end-value, then loop execution continues as follows. The loop statement is performed once, followed by an increment of the loop variable by choosing the next largest value (e.g., the next integer value in the case of integers). Next, another comparison is made between the incremented loop variable and the end-value. Again, if the value of the former is less than or equal to the value of the latter then the loop is executed once again, followed by another increment of the loop variable and a subsequent comparison. This process continues until the loop variable has a value greater than the end-value, at which point the loop is finally terminated.

Note that the preceding description of the execution applies to a counted loop using TO. If, however, DOWNTO had been used instead, then the loop execution proceeds in basically the same fashion as just described. One change is that, for each comparison made, the loop is terminated if the loop variable is, not greater than, but less than the end-value. Thus, if the value of the loop variable is greater than or equal to the end-value, then the loop execution continues. The other difference concerns the loop-variable, which is decremented on each loop iteration; that is, its next smallest value is chosen.

As an example, consider the following program segment:

```
SUM := 0;
FOR COUNT := 1 TO 3 DO
      SUM := SUM + COUNT;
WRITELN (' SUM = ', SUM)
```

The loop variable is COUNT. The start-value and end-value entries are 1 and 3, respectively. The range of the loop consists of an assignment statement. Execution of the loop begins with the storing of the values of the start-value and end-value, and the assignment of the start-value 1 to COUNT. The initial comparison is then made between the COUNT value 1 and the end-value 3. Since COUNT is to be incremented and the COUNT value 1 is less than the end-value 3, the assignment statement is performed. After this, SUM has the value 1. The increment of the COUNT value to 2 is then done automatically, and the subsequent comparison between the COUNT value 2 and the end-value 3 causes execution of the range statement to take place once again, since 2 is not greater than 3. The assignment statement leaves the value 3 in SUM (since COUNT now has the value 2); the subsequent incrementing of COUNT then results in it getting the value 3. Once again, the comparison is made and COUNT is found to be equal to the end-value 3. Thus, the range statement is repeated once more, leaving the value 6 in SUM. COUNT is next incremented to 4 and the comparison finds that this time the value of COUNT is greater than 3. Therefore, the loop is terminated and the WRITELN statement is the next statement executed.

Note that it is possible for a counted loop to have its range executed zero times. This happens when the start-value given is greater than the end-value (or, if DOWNTO had been used, when the start-value is less than the end-value). For example, the program segment:

```
LIMIT := 4;
WRITE (' ');
FOR J := 5 TO LIMIT DO
        WRITE (J);
next statement
```

causes the assignment of the value 5 to the loop variable J and then performs the initial comparison. Since J is to be incremented and the J value 5 is greater than the end-value 4, the loop is terminated immediately, with control passing to the next statement. Thus, the WRITE statement is never executed.

It is an error for a statement in the range of a loop to attempt to change the value of the loop variable, start-value, or end-value. It is perfectly legal, however, to use these entries in the range in a context where their values will not be changed, as shown in the first program example of this subsection.

Another notable characteristic of counted loops is that, upon completion of the loop execution and normal exit to the statement after the object, the value of the loop variable is indeterminate. This means that it cannot be assumed to contain the last value if possessed within the loop. Therefore, that value should not be used in any computation in the program following the loop.

In all the examples given thus far, the loop variable and the variables in the expressions in the loop control have all been of type INTEGER. Variables of any scalar type other than REAL may be used in these contexts as well. For example, loops which increment (or decrement) set, character, or logical loop variables may be used. In the case of logical variables, FALSE is less than TRUE. For example, we can use characters as follows:

```
FOR C := 'C' DOWNTO 'A' DO
        WRITE (' ', C);
WRITELN
```

The line

    CbBbA

would be printed. Assume that a set of names is defined as

    NAMES = (ALLAN, HOWARD, DAVE, LYLE, PAUL, JOHN)

then in the statement

    FOR LIST := HOWARD TO PAUL DO

LIST would take the values HOWARD, DAVE, LYLE, and PAUL, in that order. Notice that the loop variable takes on the values of a set in the order they were defined (or in the reverse order if DOWNTO is used).

The counted loop is a very useful structure in situations where a group of statements must be repeated a definite number of times, under control of a counter. The programmer should be able to determine, for a given application requiring a loop, whether a counted or conditional loop is more appropriate.

As you may have noticed, we have not referred to increments by values other than 1 or –1. PASCAL does not allow such increments, thus the programmer may find it necessary for such an application to use conditional loops that simulate the counted loop. Furthermore, real variables may be required in counted loops when fractional increments are required. Again, WHILE ... DO loops may be used to simulate the counted loop for these circumstances. The general form of a conditional loop which simulates a counted loop as used in the algorithmic notation which has the form

    For LOOPVAL = STARTVAL, STARTVAL + STEPVAL, ..., ENDVAL

where LOOPVAL, ENDVAL, and STEPVAL are either of type integer or type real, and STEPVAL is positive as follows:

```
LOOPVAL := start-value;
ENDVAL := end-value;
STEPVAL := step-value;
WHILE LOOPVAL <= ENDVAL DO
BEGIN
        range statement₁;
        range statement₂;
            .

            .

            .
        range statementₙ;
        LOOPVAL = LOOPVAL + STEPVAL
END
```

For counted loops with negative step-values, the conditional loop form just given must be changed by replacing the DO WHILE statement by:

    WHILE LOOPVAL >= ENDVAL DO

The programmer must be aware, however, when using REAL variables in the loop control entries, that the actual sequence of values taken by the loop variable may not be exactly as intended because of the way REAL variables are stored internally. For example, the following segment:

```
LOOPVAL := 2.2;
STEPVAL := 1.0;
```

```
ENDVAL := 4.2;
WHILE LOOPVAL <= ENDVAL DO
BEGIN
      .
      .
      .
         LOOPVAL := LOOPVAL + STEPVAL
END
```

causes the correct number of repetitions, but the sequence of values taken by the variable LOOPVAL is 2.199999E0, 3.199999E0, 4.199999E0, rather than the expected sequence 2.2, 3.2, 4.2. These values result because of the way real numbers are stored internally. With this method of internal storage some real values cannot be represented exactly and so are approximated as shown by these results.

From this format we see that, although it is possible, the simulation of counted loops by conditional loops is somewhat awkward. If counted repetition is required, it is much less cumbersome for the programmer to use a counted loop instead of a conditional loop. For counted loops, the compiler looks after many of the execution details, such as assigning the start-value, incrementing the loop variable, and performing the comparisons. In many other looping situations, though, the conditional loop will be found to be more useful, since its repetition is based on conditions, and not on a fixed sequence of values assigned to a loop variable.

3-4.3 Loop-controlled Input

Section 3-3 of the main text deals with the problem of loop-controlled input and presents three ways in which this might be handled. Counter-controlled input and sentinel-controlled input are logical schemes that can be implemented in any programming language.

For example, suppose a program is required for a consumer study which is comparing the prices of goods in two stores. Suppose further that we are told that the data deck is composed of an arbitrary number of cards, each containing three data values: the name of a product sold in both stores, the price of that product in the first store, and the price of the product in the second store. The very first data card in the deck contains only one value, an integer, which is the number of data cards following. The program must, for each set of values, print the product name, the name of the store ('STORE1' or 'STORE2') whose price for the product is higher, and the product's price. A PASCAL solution for this problem is given here, utilizing a counted loop to perform counter-controlled input. The variables PRICE1 and PRICE2 represent the respective prices of STORE1 and STORE2; PROD holds the product name.

```
PROGRAM PRICES (INPUT, OUTPUT);
VAR NUM, COUNT, PRICE1, PRICE2: INTEGER;
      PROD STRING(20);
BEGIN
      READ (NUM);
```

```
          FOR COUNT := 1 TO NUM DO
          BEGIN
                  READ (PROD, PRICE1, PRICE2);
                  IF PRICE1 > PRICE2
                  THEN WRITELN (' ', PROD, 'STORE 1 IS MORE EXPENSIVE', PRICE1)
                  ELSE IF PRICE1 < PRICE2
                          THEN WRITELN ('', PROD, 'STORE 2 IS MORE EXPENSIVE', PRICE2)
                          ELSE WRITELN (' PRICES ARE THE SAME')
          END
      END.
```

In this approach, the programmer has controlled the input loop by ensuring that the number of cards is, first of all, read as a value into a variable (NUM). This variable is subsequently used as the end-value in a counted loop which starts the loop variable COUNT at 1 and successively increments it by 1. Thus, the loop is performed the correct number of times for the number of accompanying sets of data values.

To demonstrate the use of sentinel-controlled input using a conditional loop, suppose the consumer prices problem were altered such that the extra integer at the front of the data is no longer provided. Instead, we are told that an extra set of values

    'END'   0.0   0.0

will be added at the end of the regular data cards. The altered solution is now as follows:

```
      PROGRAM PRICES (INPUT, OUTPUT);
      VAR PRICE1, PRICE2: INTEGER;
          PROD: STRING(20);
      BEGIN
              READ (PROD, PRICE1, PRICE2);
              WHILE PROD < > 'END       ' DO
              BEGIN
                  IF PRICE1 > PRICE2
                  THEN WRITELN (' ', PROD, 'STORE 1 IS MORE EXPENSIVE', PRICE1)
                  ELSE IF PRICE2 > PRICE1
                          THEN WRITELN (' ', PROD, 'STORE 2 IS MORE EXPENSIVE', PRICE2)
                          ELSE WRITELN (' PRICES ARE THE SAME');
                  READ (PROD, PRICE1, PRICE2)
              END
      END.
```

The third approach described in the main text for controlling input loops is the "end-of-file" method which is indicated in the algorithmic language by the phrase, "If there is no more data," or by the condition, "while there is input data". This phrase is very language dependent. PASCAL provides such a feature through the use of a special feature: EOF. No extra data cards are required. Instead, the value of the function EOF is always "false" until an end of file is detected, in which case its value becomes "true." No parentheses follow the function name. When used with an input loop, this function is used as a conditional test within the loop. The interpretation given to this input method is as follows. The computer continues the looping and reading of values until it finds that there are no more data left to read. When this happens, the value of EOF becomes "true" and can be used to terminate execution of the loop.

The most convenient type of input loop using this approach is a conditional loop. The condition in the loop control statement in this context tests whether or not the end of the input data has been reached. As long as there are more data to be read, the condition yields a value of "true" for a WHILE ... DO loop or "false" for a REPEAT ... UNTIL loop. After the last values have been read, however, the next execution of the loop's READ statement causes the value of EOF to become "false." This action must, in some manner, cause the condition in the loop control to change its value. This in turn brings about loop termination.

For example, suppose the consumer prices problem is again changed, so that no special data cards are provided with the regular data cards. In this situation, we must use the end-of-file approach with a conditional input loop. The solution is now as follows:

```
PROGRAM PRICES (INPUT, OUTPUT);
VAR PRICE1, PRICE2: INTEGER;
    PROD STRING(20);
BEGIN
    READ (PROD, PRICE1, PRICE2);
    WHILE NOT EOF DO
    BEGIN
        IF PRICE > PRICE2
        THEN WRITELN (' ', PROD, 'STORE 1 IS MORE EXPENSIVE', PRICE1)
        ELSE IF PRICE2 > PRICE1
            THEN WRITELN (' ', PROD, 'STORE 2 IS MORE EXPENSIVE', PRICE2)
            ELSE WRITELN (' PRICES ARE THE SAME');
        READ (PROD, PRICE1, PRICE2)
    END
END.
```

In this approach, the function EOF serves as an indicator for controlling the input loop. Its initial value is "false" and it continues to hold that value until all the input data have been read and processed, when its value is changed to "true." Therefore, the conditional loop terminates when the value of EOF is no longer "false," but "true." Assuming there is at least one set of data provided, the first READ statement reads in the first of the input sets of data. The loop is then entered, since the first evaluation of the condition NOT EOF gives a "true" value. The prices are compared and the associated results printed. The READ statement at the bottom of the loop then attempts to read in the next set of values. If there are no more data values, then that READ statement fails. Consequently, the value of EOF becomes "true." Control is then passed to the statement after the READ statement, which is the end of the compound statement. The subsequent evaluation of the condition NOT EOF in the loop control, in that case, gives a "false" value and the loop terminates. If, however, the READ statement succeeds in finding another set of values to input, then the value of EOF remains "false." In this case, the evaluation of the condition in the loop control yields a "true" value and the loop is performed once again. This process continues until the loop's READ statement fails in an attempt to input another set of values.

Observe that correct action is taken by the program for the special case of no data cards being present. In such an instance the first READ statement outside the loop fails in its attempt to input a set of data values and the loop cannot be executed. This causes the changing of the value of EOF to "true." Thus, when the condition in the loop control statement is evaluated the first time, a "false" value results. The loop is then bypassed entirely and program execution terminates.

Another form of the end-of-file method uses the REPEAT ... UNTIL loop, and it has the following form:

```
READ (...);
IF NOT EOF
THEN REPEAT
            .
            .
            .
                READ (...)
        UNTIL EOF
```

Notice that since the loop is always executed at least once, we must test inside the loop for the possibility (however remote) that no data cards were present. For this reason an end-of-file test occurs with the first read.

PASCAL contains an additional control structure that we will introduce at this point. A GOTO statement consists of the words

```
GOTO label
```

This statement specifies that execution of the program is to continue with the statement with the label as is given in the GOTO statement. PASCAL allows any program statement to be assigned a unique *label*, where each label must be a valid identifier, which precedes the statement it names. A labelled statement has the following form:

```
label: program statement
```

Since the GOTO allows branching to other parts of the program, the use of many GOTO's may obscure the flow structure of the program. For this reason the use of the GOTO statement is discouraged and this troublesome statement will only be used when necessary in the remainder of this book. Notice that the label must be declared in the label declaration section.

3-4.4 Nested Loops

As described in the main text, a nested loop is one which is embedded within the range of another loop. This means that the nested loop has *all* its repetitions executed entirely for *each* of the repetitions of the "outer" loop. All types of loop in PASCAL may be nested, although certain rules for doing so must be followed. An example of a valid nesting of two loops is the following:

```
READ (VALUE);
WHILE VALUE < 9999 DO
BEGIN
        FOR VAR := 1 TO 9 DO
                WRITELN (' ', VALUE * (VAR + 1));
        READ (VALUE)
END
```

Execution of this segment causes the outer loop to repeat until a value greater than or equal to 9999 is read into VALUE, and for each of its repetitions, the inner loop repeats for values of the loop variable VAR of 1, 2, 3, ..., 8, and 9.

Nested loops of any type must be entirely contained within the range of the loop which envelops them. Therefore, no part of the range of the nested loop may be physically outside the range of the "outer" loop. The compiler matches every END of the BEGIN ... END statement with the nearest preceding unmatched BEGIN. Thus, if part of the intended range of the nested loop is outside the bounds of the outer loop's intended range, then the result of the matching of the END statements with the loop control statements, as performed by the compiler, produces a different interpretation of the nesting than was desired by the programmer. For example, the following shows invalid nesting of two loops. The first loop is

```
FOR COUNT1 := 2 TO 5 DO
BEGIN
        WRITE (COUNT1);
        COUNT2 := COUNT1 * 2
END
```

and the second loop, a conditional loop, is

```
WHILE COUNT2 < (COUNT1 + 2) * 2 DO
BEGIN
        WRITE (COUNT2);
        COUNT2 := COUNT2 + 1
END
```

An incorrect nesting of these two loops follows.

```
FOR COUNT1 := 2 TO 5 DO
BEGIN
        WRITE (COUNT1);
        COUNT2 := COUNT1 * 2;
        WHILE COUNT2 < (COUNT1 + 2) * 2 DO
        BEGIN
END
        WRITE (COUNT2);
        COUNT2 := COUNT2 + 1
        END
```

In this example, the compiler matches the first END statement with the BEGIN on the conditional loop control statement and the last END with the BEGIN of the counted loop, thereby producing entirely different loop ranges than were originally intended. Notice again that the indentation scheme has no effect on the actions of the compiler.

The next section illustrates problems that have been solved using some of the concepts that are described in this section.

Exercises for Sec. 3-4

1. In each of the following segments, give the value printed for the variable VAR. Assume INTEGER variables throughout.

    (i)   VAR := 0;
         FOR INDEX := 1 TO 15 DO
            VAR := VAR + 1;
         WRITELN (' ', VAR)

    (ii) VAR := 0;
         FOR INDEX := 4 DOWNTO –13 DO
            VAR := VAR + 1;
         WRITELN (' ', VAR)

    (iii) VAR := 0;
         REPEAT
            VAR := VAR – 1
         UNTIL VAR <= 0;
         WRITELN (' ', VAR)

    (iv) VAR := 0;
         FOR INDEX1 := 1 TO 15 DO
            FOR INDEX2 := 5 TO 9 DO
               VAR := VAR + 1;
         WRITELN (' ', VAR)

    (v)   VAR := 0;
         WHILE VAR >= 0 DO
         BEGIN
            VAR := VAR + 1
            WHILE VAR >= –2 DO
               VAR := VAR – 1
          END;
         WRITELN (' ', VAR)

    (vi) VAR := 0;
         REPEAT
            VAR := VAR + 1;
            WHILE VAR > –2 DO
               VAR := VAR – 2
          UNTIL VAR >= –2;
         WRITELN (' ', VAR)

2. Penny Programmer is worried about her performance in her computer science class. On her first program, she made one mistake; on her second, she made two; on the third, four, and so on. It appears that she makes twice the number of mistakes on each program as she made on the program before. The class runs for thirteen weeks, with two programming problems per week. Write a program to compute the total number of errors Penny can expect on all her programs, at her current rate of performance.

3. Saskatchewan fishing regulations impose a limit on the total poundage of a day's catch. Suppose that you take your portable computer terminal with you on your next fishing trip, and you require a program to tell you when you have exceeded your limit.

    Write a program that first reads the daily limit (in total pounds) and then reads input values one by one (the weights of the fish recorded as they are caught) and prints a message at the point when the limit is exceeded. A weight of 0 indicates the end of input. After each fish is recorded, your program should print the total poundage caught up to that time.

    Test your program on the following input values:

    50
    6
    7
    3
    8
    6
    10
    3
    7
    6
    8
    5
    0

4. Manny Motorist has just returned from a recent motoring holiday. At each stop for gas, he recorded his odometer reading and the amount of gas purchased. In addition, he purchased gas and took odometer readings prior to leaving for the trip and immediately upon return. Write a program to read first the total number of stops made (including the first and the last) and then the data recorded for gas purchases, and compute

    (i) the gas mileage achieved between every pair of stops on the trip, and
    (ii) the gas mileage achieved through the entire trip.

    The following is a record of Manny's trip:

Gas purchased	Odometer reading
15 gal.	4500
10 gal.	4700
18 gal.	5060
15 gal.	5360

10 gal.	5560
14 gal.	5840
10 gal.	6040
20 gal.	6440
15 gal.	6740
10 gal.	6940

5. The Who-Do-You Trust Company plans to use a computer to prepare customer statements for their deposit accounts. For each customer, a set of data cards is prepared, containing information on his deposits and withdrawals for that month. The data for each customer begins with a special card containing his name, address and balance forwarded from the previous month. This is then followed by transaction cards, which contain the customer's name, a description of the transaction and the amount of the transaction. Account withdrawals will have a negative amount of transaction. Typical input would be as follows:

```
'N. WOLFE', '914 WEST 35TH ST.', 18075.00

    'A. BUNKER', 'CASH WITHDRAWAL', -75.00

        'A. BUNKER', 'MACYS', -50.00

            'A. BUNKER', 'PAY CHEQUE', 500.00

                'A. BUNKER', '704 HOWSER ST.', 1000.00
```

Write a program to produce a statement of account for each customer. These statements appear as follows:

WHO-DO-YOU TRUST COMPANY
416 FIFTH AVE.
NEW YORK, NEW YORK

TO: A. BUNKER
704 HOWSER ST.
QUEENS, NEW YORK

ITEM	DEPOSITS	WITHDRAWALS	TOTAL
OPENING BALANCE	1000.00		1000.00
PAY CHEQUE	500.00		1500.00
MACYS		50.00	1450.00
CASH WITHDRAWAL		75.00	1375.00
SERVICE CHARGE		.50	1374.50
INTEREST PAID	3.75		1378.25

The service charge must be calculated for each customer at a rate of 25¢ for each withdrawal. Interest is to be calculated by your program at 1% on any final balance over $1000.00. A new customer's leading card is detected by a change in name.

Test your program on the following data:

'J. GREEN'	'432 JACKSON AVE.'	1200.00
'J. GREEN'	'PAYLESS DRUGS'	−45.00
'J. GREEN'	'PAY CHEQUE'	850.00
'J. GREEN'	'DOMINION'	−50.00
'G. BROWN'	'648 WALKER DR.'	46.00
'G. BROWN'	'CASH WITHDRAWAL'	−30.00
'G. BROWN'	'PAY CHEQUE'	700.00
'M. BLACK'	'73 ALLEN ST.'	5000.00
'M. BLACK'	'SAAN STORE'	−45.00
'M. BLACK'	'SAM"S JEWELRY'	−75.00
'M. BLACK'	'WONDERLAND FOODS'	−60.00

6. Students are recommended for graduate fellowships according to their overall undergraduate average. The nature of the recommendations is based on the following table:

Average	Recommendation
≥ 90%	highest recommendation
≥ 80% but < 90%	strong recommendation
≥ 70% but < 80%	recommended
< 70%	not recommended

A card is prepared for each student applicant according to the following format:

student's name, overall average

Design a program to read the deck of cards for the applicants and prepare a list giving the name of each student, his or her average and the recommendation. At the end of the list (denoted by a sentinel card with student name 'END OF LIST'), give the overall average of the applicants and a count of the number recommendations of each type.

Use your program to evaluate the following list of applicants:

Student	Overall Average
M. ALLEN	85
K. BELL	65
R. CORMAN	90
L. DICKSON	70
J. ELLIOT	95
S. FORMAN	75
D. GRAY	55
H. HUGHES	81

7. Students were given five examinations (A, B, C, D, E). Statistics are required to determine the number that

   (i)   Passed all exams
   (ii) Passed A, B, and D, but not C or E
   (iii) Passed A and B, C or D, but not E

Write a program to compute these statistics for the following set of marks (each out of 100). Each line represents the marks received by one student.

Student's Marks

45	60	55	70	40
65	70	89	90	77
35	45	75	60	55
50	65	55	40	75
65	72	35	66	42
75	85	90	85	75
100	90	95	92	89
45	70	65	55	42
23	32	46	35	41
65	54	49	55	60

3-5 APPLICATIONS

This section gives PASCAL program solutions to the application problems found in Sec. 3-5 of the main text.

3-5.1 Book Store Orders

The program which appears in Fig. 3-1 is a solution to the book store order problem given in Sec. 3-5.1 of the main text. The problem is to estimate the number of books that the book store should order and the profit the book store will make in the coming academic term. For each book that is to be used, a card has been prepared containing the following information:

1. The book order number (a 6 digit code)
2. The quantity in stock
3. Classification of the book (1 for a prescribed text and 2 for a text recommended for supplementary reading)
4. Estimated student enrollment in course requiring this book
5. Indication whether this book is being used for the first time (1 indicates that the book is being used for the first time and 0 indicates that the book has been used before)
6. Wholesale cost of the book.

It has been found that for required texts that have been previously used, sales are 60% of estimated enrollment and for new books that are required sales are 85% of estimated enrollment. Sales for books required for supplementary reading have been estimated at 25% of estimated enrollment for books that have been previously used and 40% of estimated enrollment for new books. The number of books required in stock is based on these figures. The number to order is determined by subtracting the number currently in stock from the number required. If the result is negative, more books are held in stock than are required and the extra books are to be returned. In this case a message indicating the overstocked condition and the number of books to be returned is required. The profit margin is based on a 25% mark up on books with a wholesale value of ten dollars or less and a 20% mark up on all other books. Given this information, the following report is to be generated:

ORDER NO.	ON HAND	TO ORDER	PROFIT MARGIN
386054	13	67	200
389854	IS OVERSTOCKED 7 COPIES TO RETURN		
.	.	.	.
.	.	.	.
.	.	.	.

TOTAL PROFIT   25653.72

The variables used in this program are:

Variable	Type	Usage
IDENT	STRING(6)	Book identification number
STOCK	INTEGER	Quantity currently in stock
TYPE	INTEGER	Classification of the book as prescribed text or supplementary reading
ENROLMENT	INTEGER	Estimated course enrollment
NEW_TEXT	INTEGER	Indicates text as new or previously used
COST	REAL	Wholesale cost of the book
NUMBER_REQUIRED	INTEGER	Number of copies required
ORDER	INTEGER	Number of copies to be ordered
PROFIT	REAL	Profit margin on this book
TOTAL_PROFIT	REAL	Total profit margin

The following input values were used in this program:

'394072'	20	1	80	1	20.40
'794362'	10	2	10	0	10.20
'767231'	25	1	100	1	11.95
'472315'	12	2	50	0	14.36
'399789'	20	1	135	1	25.30
'699233'	30	2	14	0	23.00
'629111'	15	1	123	1	14.70
'567124'	21	2	179	0	12.30
'791121'	24	1	60	1	26.40
'654315'	6	1	43	1	12.50
'731717'	7	2	110	0	13.75

```
0  0000   00001   (* PROGRAM TO DETERMINE THE PROFIT MARGIN ON BOOK ORDERS *)
0  0000   00002   PROGRAM BOOKSTORE (INPUT, OUTPUT);
0  0000   00003
0  0000   00004   VAR IDENT: STRING (6);          (* BOOK IDENTIFICATION NUMBER *)
0  0038   00005       STOCK,                      (* QUANTITY IN STOCK *)
0  0038   00006       CLASS,                      (* CLASSIFICATION OF THE BOOK *)
0  0038   00007       ENROLMENT,                  (* ESTIMATED COURSE ENROLMENT *)
0  0038   00008       NEW_TEXT,                   (* NEW TEXT OR USED PREVIOUSLY *)
0  0038   00009       NUM_REQUIRED,               (* NUMBER NEEDED *)
0  0038   00010       ORDER: INTEGER;             (* NUMBER TO BE ORDERED *)
0  0038   00011       COST,                       (* WHOLESALE COST *)
0  0038   00012       PROFIT,                     (* PROFIT MARGIN ON BOOK *)
0  0038   00013       TOTAL_PROFIT: REAL;         (* TOTAL PROFIT MARGIN *)
0  0038   00014
0  0038   00015   BEGIN
0  0038   00016
0  0038   00017       (* INITIALIZE *)
0  0038   00018       TOTAL_PROFIT := 0.00;
0  0040   00019
0  0040   00020       (* PRINT REPORT HEADINGS *)
0  0040   00021       WRITELN (' IDENTIFICATION  ON HAND   TO ORDER    ',
0  0052   00022          'PROFIT MARGIN');
0  0064   00023
0  0064   00024       (* PROCESS BOOKS *)
0  0064   00025       READ (IDENT, STOCK, CLASS, ENROLMENT, NEW_TEXT, COST);
0  00D0   00026       WHILE NOT EOF DO
0  00D8   00027       BEGIN
0  00D8   00028
0  00D8   00029           (* DETERMINE NUMBER OF COPIES REQUESTED *)
0  00D8   00030           IF CLASS = 1
0  00D8   00031           THEN IF NEW_TEXT = 1
0  00E4   00032                THEN NUM_REQUIRED := ROUND (0.85 * ENROLMENT)
0  0108   00033                ELSE NUM_REQUIRED := ROUND (0.60 * ENROLMENT)
0  0138   00034           ELSE IF NEW_TEXT = 1
0  0150   00035                THEN NUM_REQUIRED := ROUND (0.40 * ENROLMENT)
0  0174   00036                ELSE NUM_REQUIRED := ROUND (0.25 * ENROLMENT);
0  01B8   00037
0  01B8   00038           (* DETERMINE SIZE OF ORDER AND, IF NECESSARY, ISSUE
0  01B8   00039              OVERSTOCKED NOTICE *)
0  01B8   00040           ORDER := NUM_REQUIRED - STOCK;
0  01C4   00041           IF ORDER < 0
0  01C4   00042           THEN WRITELN (' ', IDENT, ' IS OVERSTOCKED: ', ABS (ORDER),
0  021C   00043                ' COPIES TO RETURN');
0  022E   00044
0  022E   00045           (* DETERMINE PROFIT ON THIS BOOK *)
0  022E   00046           IF COST <= 10.00
0  022E   00047           THEN PROFIT := NUM_REQUIRED * 0.25 * COST
0  0252   00048           ELSE PROFIT := NUM_REQUIRED * 0.20 * COST;
0  027E   00049
0  027E   00050           (* UPDATE TOTAL PROFIT STATISTIC *)
0  027E   00051           TOTAL_PROFIT := TOTAL_PROFIT + PROFIT;
0  028A   00052
0  028A   00053           (* PRINT LINE FOR THIS BOOK *)
0  028A   00054           WRITELN (' ', IDENT, STOCK, ORDER, PROFIT);
0  02E4   00055
0  02E4   00056           (* READ INFORMATION FOR NEXT BOOK *)
0  02E4   00057           READ (IDENT, STOCK, CLASS, ENROLMENT, NEW_TEXT, COST)
0  0350   00058       END;
0  0354   00059
0  0354   00060       (* PRINT TOTAL PROFIT OF ALL BOOKS *)
0  0354   00061       WRITELN (' TOTAL PROFIT', TOTAL_PROFIT)
0  0378   00062   END.
```

```
--EXECUTION-->
IDENTIFICATION  ON HAND   TO ORDER    PROFIT MARGIN
394072            20         48       2.774397E 02
794362 IS OVERSTOCKED:               7 COPIES TO RETURN
794362            10         -7       6.119999E 00
767231            25         60       2.031498E 02
472315            12          1       3.733598E 01
399789            20         95       5.818992E 02
699233 IS OVERSTOCKED:              26 COPIES TO RETURN
699233            30        -26       1.839999E 01
629111            15         90       3.086997E 02
567124            21         24       1.106999E 02
791121            24         27       2.692798E 02
654315             6         31       9.249997E 01
731717             7         21       7.699998E 01
TOTAL PROFIT    1.982523E 03
```

Fig. 3-1   Program for book store orders problem

Line 18 initializes the TOTAL_PROFIT to 0. Next, the information on the first book is read. Then in line 26, the loop that is to handle the processing of the book orders is begun. For each book, the number required is calculated, using information concerning the book's type and whether or not the book has been used before. The size of the order, ORDER, is calculated by subtracting the number in stock, STOCK, from the number required, NUMBER_REQUIRED. If there are more books in stock than are required (i.e., ORDER is negative), a message indicating the number of books to be returned is printed. The profit for this book is calculated and then added to the total profit. Finally, the identification number, the number in stock, the number to order, and the profit to be made on this book are printed. Then information on the next book is read and execution of the loop begins again if not all data cards have been read. The total profit is printed and execution is terminated when all input values have been processed.

3-5.2 Mortgage Payments

The program in Fig. 3-2 is a solution to the mortgage payment problem given in Sec. 3-5.2 of the main text. The calculation of monthly payments on a mortgage depends on three components — the principal involved, the mortgage rate, and the length of the term for the mortgage. The basic formula used in the calculation is

$$\text{Monthly Payment} = \frac{P * IR * (IR + 1) \uparrow N}{(IR + 1) \uparrow N}$$

Where P is the principal, IR is the interest rate per month, and N is the number of months in the term. (Normally, the customer is given the interest rate and term of his mortgage in yearly figures, and therefore, these must be converted to monthly figures for use in the formula.)

Each monthly payment is the sum of the monthly interest required, as dictated by the monthly interest rate applied to the outstanding principal, and a portion of the principal. That is, for any month during the term of N months, the payment is composed of the interest required for the month, given by P * IR, and an amount deducted from the outstanding principal in an attempt to reduce it to zero over the mortgage term.

The problem is then to write a PASCAL program that takes as input the amount of the principal of a mortgage, the yearly interest rate, and the term in years of that mortgage. The output produced must contain the calculated monthly payment and for each of the term years the payments to interest and the principal for each month of the year, and year-ends totals of these monthly amounts. The variables used in the following PASCAL program are:

Variable	Type	Usage
PRINC	REAL	Principal amount
IRATE	REAL	Yearly interest rate
TERM	INTEGER	Term, in years
IR	REAL	Monthly interest rate
N	INTEGER	Term, in months
PAYMENT	REAL	Calculated monthly payment
INTTOT	REAL	Yearly total of interest payments

```
0  0000   00001  (* COMPUTE THE MONTHLY MORTGAGE PAYMENT FOR EACH TERM YEAR, PRINT AND
0  0000   00002     TOTAL UP THE MONTHLY INTEREST PAYMENTS AND MONTHLY PAYMENTS ON THE
0  0000   00003     PRINCIPAL. *)
0  0000   00004  PROGRAM MORTPAY (INPUT, OUTPUT);
0  0000   00005
0  0000   00006  VAR PRINC,                    (* PRINCIPAL AMOUNT *)
0  0038   00007      IRATE,                    (* YEARLY INTEREST RATE *)
0  0038   00008      IR: REAL;                 (* MONTHLY INTEREST RATE *)
0  0038   00009      TERM,                     (* TERM IN YEARS *)
0  0038   00010      N: INTEGER;               (* TERM IN MONTHS *)
0  0038   00011      PAYMENT,                  (* CALCULATED MONTHLY PAYMENT *)
0  0038   00012      INTTOT,                   (* YEARLY TOTAL OF INTEREST PAYMENTS *)
0  0038   00013      PRTOT,                    (* YEARLY TOTAL OF PRINCIPAL PAYMENTS *)
0  0038   00014      MONINT,                   (* MONTHLY INTEREST PAYMENT *)
0  0038   00015      MONPR: REAL;              (* MONTHLY PRINCIPAL PAYMENT *)
0  0038   00016      TEMP: REAL;               (* TEMPORARY VARIABLE *)
0  0038   00017      I, YEAR, MONTH: INTEGER;  (* LOOP VARIABLES *)
0  0038   00018
0  0038   00019  BEGIN
0  0038   00020
0  0038   00021      (* INPUT DATA VALUES AND CHECK THEIR VALIDITY *)
0  0038   00022      READ (PRINC, IRATE, TERM);
0  006E   00023      IF (PRINC <= 0.0) OR (IRATE <= 0.0) OR (TERM <= 0)
0  0092   00024      THEN WRITELN (' INVALID INPUT VALUE')
0  00A4   00025      ELSE BEGIN
0  00A8   00026
0  00A8   00027          (* CONVERT YEARLY FIGURES TO MONTHLY, AND COMPUTE MONTHLY
0  00A8   00028             PAYMENT AFTER COMPUTING IR + 1 TO THE NTH POWER *)
0  00A8   00029          IR := IRATE / 12;
0  00B4   00030          N := TERM * 12;
0  00C4   00031          TEMP := 1;
0  00CC   00032          FOR I := 1 TO N DO
0  00F0   00033              TEMP := TEMP * (IR + 1);
0  0104   00034          PAYMENT := (PRINC * IR * TEMP) / (TEMP - 1);
0  011E   00035          WRITELN (' MONTHLY PAYMENT IS $', PAYMENT);
0  0142   00036          WRITELN ('          YEAR      MONTH  AMOUNT PAID TO ',
0  0154   00037              ' PRINCIPAL  AMOUNT PAID TO INTEREST');
0  0166   00038
0  0166   00039          (* FOR EACH YEAR, PRINT THE MONTHLY AND YEARLY STATISTICS *)
0  0166   00040          FOR YEAR := 1 TO TERM DO
0  018A   00041          BEGIN
0  018A   00042
0  018A   00043              (* INITIALIZE YEARLY TOTALS *)
0  018A   00044              INTTOT := 0; PRTOT := 0;
0  019A   00045
0  019A   00046              (* FOR EACH MONTH, COMPUTE AMOUNTS, PRINT, AND
0  019A   00047                 UPDATE TOTALS *)
0  019A   00048              FOR MONTH := 1 TO 12 DO
0  01BE   00049              BEGIN
0  01BE   00050                  MONINT := IR * PRINC;
0  01CA   00051                  MONPR := PAYMENT - MONINT;
0  01D6   00052                  INTTOT := INTTOT + MONINT;
0  01E2   00053                  PRTOT := PRTOT + MONPR;
0  01EE   00054
0  01EE   00055                  (* PRINT AMOUNTS FOR THE MONTH *)
0  01EE   00056                  WRITELN (YEAR, MONTH, MONPR, '          ', MONINT);
0  0248   00057                  PRINC := PRINC - MONPR
0  0248   00058              END;
0  0258   00059
0  0258   00060              (* PRINT TOTALS FOR THE YEAR *)
0  0258   00061              WRITELN (' YEAR END SUMMARY');
0  026A   00062              WRITELN (' PRINCIPAL PAID: ', PRTOT);
0  028E   00063              WRITELN (' INTEREST PAID: ', INTTOT);
0  02B2   00064              WRITELN (' OUTSTANDING PRINCIPAL: ', PRINC)
0  02D6   00065          END
0  02D6   00066      END
0  02DA   00067  END.
```

```
-----------------------------------
| COMPILE TIME:    0.158 SECOND(S) |
|    NO WARNING(S) DETECTED         |
|    NO ERROR(S) DETECTED           |
-----------------------------------
```

Fig. 3-2 Program for mortgage payments problem

```
--EXECUTION-->
MONTHLY PAYMENT IS $      1.613440E 02
          YEAR      MONTH  AMOUNT PAID TO  PRINCIPAL  AMOUNT PAID TO INTEREST
            1          1    1.196774E 02              4.166664E 01
            1          2    1.206747E 02              4.066931E 01
            1          3    1.216803E 02              3.966368E 01
            1          4    1.226944E 02              3.864964E 01
            1          5    1.237168E 02              3.762718E 01
            1          6    1.247478E 02              3.659619E 01
            1          7    1.257874E 02              3.555661E 01
            1          8    1.268356E 02              3.450838E 01
            1          9    1.278926E 02              3.345142E 01
            1         10    1.289584E 02              3.238564E 01
            1         11    1.300330E 02              3.131099E 01
            1         12    1.311166E 02              3.022737E 01
YEAR END SUMMARY
PRINCIPAL PAID:      1.503814E 03
INTEREST PAID:     4.323125E 02
OUTSTANDING PRINCIPAL:        3.496171E 03
            2          1    1.322093E 02              2.913474E 01
            2          2    1.333110E 02              2.803299E 01
            2          3    1.344219E 02              2.692206E 01
            2          4    1.355421E 02              2.580188E 01
            2          5    1.366716E 02              2.467236E 01
            2          6    1.378106E 02              2.353343E 01
            2          7    1.389590E 02              2.238501E 01
            2          8    1.401170E 02              2.122702E 01
            2          9    1.412846E 02              2.005937E 01
            2         10    1.424620E 02              1.888200E 01
            2         11    1.436492E 02              1.769482E 01
            2         12    1.448463E 02              1.649774E 01
YEAR END SUMMARY
PRINCIPAL PAID:      1.661284E 03
INTEREST PAID:     2.748430E 02
OUTSTANDING PRINCIPAL:        1.834884E 03
            3          1    1.460533E 02              1.529069E 01
            3          2    1.472704E 02              1.407358E 01
            3          3    1.484977E 02              1.284632E 01
            3          4    1.497351E 02              1.160884E 01
            3          5    1.509829E 02              1.036105E 01
            3          6    1.522411E 02              9.102861E 00
            3          7    1.535098E 02              7.834186E 00
            3          8    1.547890E 02              6.554936E 00
            3          9    1.560790E 02              5.265026E 00
            3         10    1.573796E 02              3.964367E 00



            3         11    1.586911E 02              2.652869E 00
            3         12    1.600136E 02              1.330443E 00
YEAR END SUMMARY
PRINCIPAL PAID:      1.835242E 03
INTEREST PAID:     1.008851E 02
OUTSTANDING PRINCIPAL:      -3.602753E-01
```

Fig. 3-2   Program for mortgage payments problem (cont'd.)

PRTOT	REAL	Yearly total of principal payments
MONINT	REAL	Monthly interest payment
MONPR	REAL	Monthly principal payment
YEAR	INTEGER	Loop variable
MONTH	INTEGER	Loop variable
TEMP	REAL	Used to calculate $(IR + 1)^N$
I	INTEGER	Loop variable

The data used in the run consisted of the following values:

5000. .10 3

Lines 6 to 17 contain the declarations for the variables used. Line 22 serves to read the input values. The IF statement beginning in line 23 checks the data values that have been input for the three variables to ensure that they are reasonable and have viable values. It is assumed that if any of the principal amount, the interest rate, or the term length values is less than or equal to 0, then such a data value was most likely mispunched on the data card, and therefore, execution is not continued. Otherwise, the values are accepted as valid, and the processing proceeds within the ELSE clause of the IF...THEN...ELSE statement. Lines 31 to 33 are used to compute $(IR + 1)^N$ by using a loop to multiply $IR + 1$ by itself N times and storing the result in TEMP. In line 40, a counted loop is used to cause the repetitions of the yearly computations, once for each year in the term. Line 48 is the loop control for the inner counted loop, which controls the twelve repetitions of the monthly calculations, one for each month of the year, YEAR.

3-5.3 Cheque Reconciliation

The program presented in Fig. 3-3 is the solution to the cheque reconciliation problem given in Sec. 3-5.3 of the main text. The management of the Red Nose Winery company requires a program to reconcile cheques issued to their employees. For each cheque issued, a card is prepared containing the cheque number and the amount for which the cheque was written. At the end of each month similar cards are prepared for the cashed cheques. The cards containing information on the issued and cashed cheques are merged manually and are used as input for the program. The program is to list the cheques that have been issued but have not yet been cashed and the cheque number and the two amounts of any cheque that has been issued and cashed for differing amounts. After all the cheques have been processed, the total amount of the cheques cashed and the total amount of the cheques outstanding (i.e., cheques that have not been cashed) are to be printed.

The variables used in this program are:

Variable	Type	Usage
CASHED	REAL	Total amount of cheques cashed
OUTSTANDING	REAL	Total amount of cheques outstanding
CARD_REQUIRED	INTEGER	Type of card required
CHEQUE1_NO	INTEGER	Identification number of issued cheque
CHEQUE1_AMT	REAL	Amount of issued cheque
CHEQUE2_NO	INTEGER	Identification number of cashed cheque
CHEQUE2_AMT	REAL	Amount of cashed cheque

The following data values were used for this run:

```
23871       48.50
23871       48.50
```

23872	150.00
23873	36.00
23873	236.00
23874	200.00
23875	230.00
23875	130.00
23876	150.00
23876	150.00
23877	75.00
23877	175.00
23878	75.00
23879	45.00
23880	50.00
23880	50.00

Lines 15 through 17 initialize variables to be used in the program. In line 20, a REPEAT ... UNTIL loop which controls the processing of the cheques is begun. Execution of this loop terminates when all cheques have been processed. If the variable CARD_REQUIRED equals 1, the information concerning the next cheque is read. If there are no more cheques, the amount of total cashed and total outstanding is printed, and execution of the program is terminated. If there is indeed more data, the input values are read into CHEQUE1_NO and CHEQUE1_AMT, respectively. The following data card is read. If the end of the data is reached at this point, the last cheque was uncashed; therefore, the amount outstanding is updated accordingly, and the totals of cashed and outstanding cheques are printed. If, however, the end of the data is not reached, the next input values are read into CHEQUE2_NO and CHEQUE2_AMT, respectively. If the indentification numbers of the two cheques (i.e., CHEQUE1_NO and CHEQUE2_NO) are the same, then the amounts that the cheque was issued for and cashed for are compared. If the two amounts are identical, the value of the cheque is added to the total of cashed cheques; otherwise, a message is printed indicating that the cheque has been issued and cashed for different amounts. In line 52, the flag CARD_REQUIRED is set to 1 to indicate that a complete pair of cards has been read and the next card read contains information concerning an issued cheque.

If it is found in the comparison made in line 44 that the cheque numbers are not identical, then the issued cheque has not been cashed. In line 58, the outstanding total is updated by adding the amount of the uncashed cheque, and lines 61 and 62 transfer the information concerning the second card to the variables representing the issued cheque. The flag, CARD_REQUIRED, is assigned the value 2, indicating that the issued cheque has already been read and information concerning the cashed cheque is required.

This concludes the chapter on decision structures. In Sec. 3-2, the IF statement, which allows selection from alternative actions, was introduced. Next under discussion was the use of complex conditions in IF statements. The next section dealt with the repetition of instructions, using the different forms of the loop structure. Finally, in the last section, the important concepts of this chapter were illustrated, through the use of three programmed examples.

In the next chapter, the programmer is introduced to further programming techniques which involve an important data structure, the array.

```
0   0000   00001   (* PROGRAM TO RECONCILE DATA ON CHEQUES ISSUED AND CHECKS CASHED *)
0   0000   00002   PROGRAM RECON (INPUT, OUTPUT);
0   0000   00003
0   0000   00004   VAR CASHED,                    (* TOTAL AMOUNT OF CHEQUES CASHED *)
0   0038   00005       OUTSTANDING: REAL;         (* TOTAL AMOUNT OUTSTANDING *)
0   0038   00006       CARD_REQUIRED: INTEGER;    (* TYPE OF CARD REQUIRED *)
0   0038   00007       CHEQUE1_NO: INTEGER;       (* NUMBER OF CHEQUE ISSUED *)
0   0038   00008       CHEQUE1_AMT: REAL;         (* AMOUNT OF CHEQUE ISSUED *)
0   0038   00009       CHEQUE2_NO: INTEGER;       (* NUMBER OF CHEQUE CASHED *)
0   0038   00010       CHEQUE2_AMT: REAL;         (* AMOUNT OF CHEQUE CASHED *)
0   0038   00011
0   0038   00012   BEGIN
0   0038   00013
0   0038   00014       (* INITIALIZE *)
0   0038   00015       CASHED := 0.0;
0   0040   00016       OUTSTANDING := 0.0;
0   0048   00017       CARD_REQUIRED := 1;
0   0050   00018
0   0050   00019       (* PROCESS CHEQUES *)
0   0050   00020       REPEAT
0   0050   00021
0   0050   00022           (* READ FIRST CARD OF A PAIR IF NOT PREVIOUSLY READ *)
0   0050   00023           IF CARD_REQUIRED = 1
0   0050   00024           THEN READ (CHEQUE1_NO, CHEQUE1_AMT);
0   0080   00025           IF EOF
0   0080   00026           THEN BEGIN
0   0088   00027               WRITELN (' TOTAL CASHED = $', CASHED);
0   00AC   00028               WRITELN (' TOTAL OUTSTANDING = $', OUTSTANDING)
0   00D0   00029               END
0   00D0   00030           ELSE BEGIN
0   00D4   00031
0   00D4   00032               (* READ SECOND CARD OF PAIR *)
0   00D4   00033               READ (CHEQUE2_NO, CHEQUE2_AMT);
0   00F8   00034               IF EOF
0   00F8   00035               THEN BEGIN (* LAST CHEQUE WAS NOT CASHED *)
0   0100   00036                   WRITELN (CHEQUE1_NO, CHEQUE1_AMT);
0   0124   00037                   WRITELN (' TOTAL CASHED = $', CASHED);
0   0148   00038                   OUTSTANDING := OUTSTANDING + CHEQUE1_AMT;
0   0154   00039                   WRITELN (' TOTAL OUTSTANDING = $', OUTSTANDING)
0   0178   00040                   END
0   0178   00041               ELSE BEGIN
0   017C   00042
0   017C   00043                   (* PROCESS THE PAIR OF CARDS *)
0   017C   00044                   IF CHEQUE1_NO = CHEQUE2_NO
0   017C   00045                   THEN BEGIN
0   0188   00046                       IF CHEQUE1_AMT = CHEQUE2_AMT
0   0188   00047                       (* ISSUED AND CASHED FOR THE SAME AMOUNT *)
0   0188   00048                       THEN CASHED := CASHED + CHEQUE1_AMT
0   0194   00049                       (* ISSUED AND CASHED FOR DIFFERENT AMOUNTS *)
0   0194   00050                       ELSE WRITELN (CHEQUE1_NO, CHEQUE1_AMT,
0   01C8   00051                           CHEQUE2_AMT);
0   01DA   00052                       CARD_REQUIRED := 1  (* PAIR HAS BEEN READ *)
0   01DA   00053                       END
0   01E2   00054                   ELSE BEGIN
0   01E6   00055
0   01E6   00056                       (* CHEQUE NOT CASHED YET *)
0   01E6   00057                       WRITELN (CHEQUE1_NO, CHEQUE1_AMT);
0   020A   00058                       OUTSTANDING := OUTSTANDING + CHEQUE1_AMT;
0   0216   00059
0   0216   00060                       (* SECOND CARD BECOMES FIRST CARD *)
0   0216   00061                       CHEQUE1_NO := CHEQUE2_NO;
0   021E   00062                       CHEQUE1_AMT := CHEQUE2_AMT;
0   0226   00063                       CARD_REQUIRED := 2
0   0226   00064                       END
0   022E   00065                       END
0   022E   00066               END
0   022E   00067       UNTIL EOF
0   022E   00068   END.
--EXECUTION-->
        23872   1.500000E 02
        23873   3.600000E 01   2.360000E 02
        23874   2.000000E 02
        23875   2.300000E 02   1.300000E 02
        23877   7.500000E 01   1.750000E 02
        23878   7.500000E 01
        23879   4.500000E 01
TOTAL CASHED = $       2.485000E 02
TOTAL OUTSTANDING = $       4.700000E 02
```

Fig. 3-3   Program for cheque reconciliation problem

EXERCISES FOR CHAPTER 3

1. Write a program to compute the sum of the squares of the first 100 integers.

2. Commercial fishermen are required to report monthly information on their catch to the Department of Fisheries. The data are analyzed regularly to determine the growth or reduction of the various species of fish and to indicate any possible trouble. From the catch reports and previous data, a card is prepared containing the following information:

    region fished (integer code from 1 to 20), species name (character),
             number caught this year (integer), number caught last year (integer)
    e.g., 16, 'HALIBUT', 20485, 18760

    This sample card indicates that in region 16, a total of 20,485 halibut were caught, as compared to 18,760 in the same month last year.
    Write a program to read the following data:

5,	'SALMON',	25632,	19276
4,	'COD',	35789,	40256
12,	'HERRING',	56792,	20543
19,	'TUNA',	30625,	21872
1,	'HALIBUT',	20892,	23671
7,	'WHITEFISH',	30925,	30900
6,	'SALMON',	39625,	29521
13,	'HERRING',	45631,	40872
-1,	'FISH',	0,	0

    Note that data is terminated by a card with a negative region number. After reading the data, your program should flag any unusual growth or reduction in catches. An unusual growth or reduction is defined as one in which the percentage change exceeds 30%, where percentage change is defined as

    $$\frac{\text{(this year)} - \text{(last year)}}{\text{(last year)}} \times 100\%$$

3. The Saskatchewan Government Insurance Office has compiled data on all traffic accidents in the province over the past year. For each driver involved in an accident, a card has been prepared with the following pieces of information:

    year driver was born (integer), sex ('M' or 'F'),
        registration code (1 for Saskatchewan
            registration, 0 for everything else)

    Design a program to read the deck of data cards and print the following summary statistics on drivers involved in accidents:

    (i) percentage of drivers under 25 years of age

(ii) percentage of drivers who are female

(iii) percentage of drivers who are males between the ages of 18 and 25

(iv) percentage of drivers with out-of-province registration.

Use the end-of-file method to signal the end of input.

Using your program, calculate the four statistics for the following list of data:

1947	'M'	1
1962	'F'	0
1958	'M'	1
1936	'F'	1
1957	'M'	1
1945	'F'	0
1961	'M'	1
1948	'F'	0
1955	'F'	1
1950	'M'	1

4. The city police department has accumulated information on speeding violations over a period of time. The department has divided the city into four quadrants and wishes to have statistics on speeding violations by quadrant. For each violation, a card is prepared containing the following information:

vehicle registration number (eight digit code),
quadrant in which offense occured (1-4),
speed limit in kilometers per hour (integer),
actual speed travelled in kilometers per hour (integer).

This set of cards is terminated by a special card with a vehicle registration number of 0.

Write a program to produce two reports. First, give a listing of speeding fines collected, where the fine is calculated as the sum of court costs ($20) plus $1.25 for every kilometer per hour by which the speed limit was exceeded. Prepare a table with the following headings:

SPEEDING VIOLATIONS

VEHICLE REGISTRATION	SPEED RECORDED (KM/H)	SPEED LIMIT (KM/H)	FINE

This report is to be followed by a second report in which an analysis of violations by quadrant is given. For each of the four quadrants, give the number of violations processed and the average fine.

Test your program on the list of traffic violations given in Table 3-4.

5. (i) Write a program to compute and tabulate the values of the function

$$f(x, y) = \frac{x^2 - y^2}{x^2 + y^2}$$

Table 3-4   Traffic violations

Registration Number	Quadrant	Speed Limit	Actual Speed
45631288	2	25	30
76822131	1	40	55
65331245	3	65	73
55129871	4	70	78
61234891	3	25	35
77891348	1	100	150
67543111	2	25	32
98432918	3	25	29
79144855	4	65	78
23579812	1	30	45

for x = 2, 4, 6, 8
and y = 6, 9, 12, 15, 18, 21.

(ii) Write a program to compute the number of points with integer-valued coordinates that are contained within the ellipse

$$\frac{x^2}{16} + \frac{y^2}{25} = 1$$

(Notes:
1. Points on the ellipse are considered to be within it.
2. Range of coordinate values is limited by the major and minor axes of of the ellipse.
   i.e., $-4 \leqslant x \leqslant 4$
   and $-5 \leqslant y \leqslant 5$.)

6. (i) Design a program to compute the amount of savings you would have at the end of ten years, if you were to deposit $100 each month. Assume a constant annual interest rate of 6%, compounded every six months (that is, interest in the amount of 3% is awarded each six months).
(ii) We want to invest a sum of money that will grow to be X dollars in Y years time. If the interest rate is R percent, then the amount we have to invest (the present value of X) is given by the formula

$$\frac{X}{(1 + .01 * R)^Y}$$

Write a program that will print out a table of the present value of $5000 at 7.5% interest, for periods of one to twenty years, in steps of two years.

7. Assume that a particular store sells all of its merchandise for a price of $1.00 or less. Assume further that all customers pay for each purchase with a $1.00 bill.
   Design a program that reads in the purchase price of an article, and calculates the number of each type of coin to be given in change so that

the smallest number of coins is returned. For example, if the purchase price is 65¢ the change will be 1 quarter, 1 dime, and 2 pennies.

Using your program, find the change to be received from a purchase of 14¢ assuming the customer pays with a $1.00 bill.

CHAPTER

VECTORS
AND
ARRAYS

A subscripted variable in a programming language such as PASCAL is a variable that represents an element in a finite ordered set. In this chapter, we examine the use of subscripted variables in PASCAL to implement the important data structures known as vectors and arrays, as discussed in Chap. 4 of the main text. We begin with a consideration of vectors and operations that can be performed on them. Sorting and searching are very important operations on vectors; these are discussed in Sec. 4-2. We then turn to arrays of higher dimensions. The chapter closes with complete PASCAL programs for the applications discussed in the main text.

4-1 VECTORS AND OPERATIONS ON VECTORS

This section explains the rules for the use of vectors in the PASCAL programming language, introducing the common operations that may be performed on vectors. In the algorithmic language a vector is represented by a variable name and an element of the vector is represented by the variable name followed by the index of the element enclosed in square parentheses. In PASCAL, a vector and its elements have representations similar to those of the algorithmic language. In PASCAL each element is represented as

vector-name (subscript)

The *vector-name* is the name of the set and can be any valid PASCAL variable name. The *subscript* entry must yield an integer value which identifies a particular element in the set. Many versions of PASCAL use the square brackets ("[" and "]") to enclose the subscript, but since keypunches do not always have square brackets, "(" and ")" or "(." and ".)" are often used. In this book we shall use the round parentheses "(" and ")" for subscripts.

Before a vector or any of its elements may be used in a program, the vector must be declared. For example, the statement

VAR PRICE: ARRAY (1..100) OF REAL;

identifies PRICE as the name of a vector. The 1..100, which appears in the parentheses following the vector-name, defines the *lower bound* and the *upper bound* (i.e., the values of the minimum and maximum possible subscripts, respectively) of the vector or the *range* of the vector. Elements of this vector, therefore, may be referenced by subscripts ranging from 1 to 100. Observe that two consecutive periods (..) are used to separate the two bounds. The type attribute specified (i.e., REAL) applies to all the elements of the vector. All vector elements are stored in consecutive storage locations in the computer's memory. The *size* of any vector (i.e., the number of elements in the vector) can thus be determined by the following formula:

Vector size = upper bound – lower bound + 1

In most cases, the specified lower and upper bounds in a declaration statement are positive or negative integer constants. Other types are allowed and will be discussed later in this section.

Often a lower bound of other than 1 is desired for a vector. For example, suppose a vector CARS is to be used to contain the number of cars produced in the years 1957 through 1965. This vector could be referenced by subscripts ranging from 1 to 9, but a more meaningful designation is to use subscripts that range from 1957 to 1965. The statement

VAR CARS: ARRAY(1957..1965) OF REAL;

declares CARS to be a vector of nine elements which are referenced by subscripts that range from 1957 to 1965. In this example, 1957 is the lower bound and 1965 is the upper bound.

In order to refer to a specific element of a vector in a program, it is necessary to use a subscript to identify that element. In PASCAL, a subscript may be any valid PASCAL expression which results in a numeric value less than or equal to the declared upper bound and greater than or equal to the declared lower bound. Note that the resulting type must be of the same type as the range of the array. If the vector NUM is declared in a program with the following statement

    VAR NUM: ARRAY(1..15) OF INTEGER;

a subscript reference to NUM(25) or NUM(−11) in the program is invalid. Nor is the subscripted variable

    NUM(12.867)

allowed, because the range of NUM must be an integer between 1 and 15. Subscripted variables may appear anywhere that simple variables of the same type are used. This means that subscripted variables may be used in expressions which are subscripts. For example, the statement

    MARK(NUM(I) − 2) := 3;

is valid, if the expression NUM(I) − 2 yields a valid subscript for MARK.

To illustrate the use of vectors in a PASCAL program, let us consider the following problem. Suppose we are given a list of stores and their retail prices for bread. We require a program that will print out a list of all the stores that have prices which exceed the average of the retail prices read. Using data from 100 stores, the following program uses vectors to solve this problem.

```
(* RETAIL PRICE OF BREAD *)
PROGRAM PRICE: (INPUT, OUTPUT);
VAR I: INTEGER;
        PRICES: ARRAY(1..100) OF REAL;
        SUM, AVG: REAL;
        STORE: ARRAY(1..100) OF STRING;
BEGIN
        SUM := 0.0;
        FOR I := 1 TO 100 DO
        BEGIN
                READ (STORE(I), PRICES(I));
                SUM := SUM + PRICES(I)
        END;
        AVG := SUM / 100.0;
        FOR I := 1 TO 100 DO
                IF PRICES(I) > AVG
                THEN WRITELN (' ', STORE(I), PRICES(I))
END.
```

Occasionally, during the execution of a program it may be necessary to perform assignments on an entire vector. PASCAL facilitates this by allowing the programmer to specify the entire vector when the elements of one vector are to be assigned to their corresponding elements in another vector. In order to specify the entire vector, the vector name is written without a subscript. For example, with the declaration

    VAR SUM, A, B: ARRAY(1..10) OF REAL;

the statement

    SUM := A

results in each of the ten elements of the vector SUM being assigned the values of the corresponding elements of A. Note that PASCAL does not allow operations on entire vectors such as

    SUM := A + B

or assignments of vectors with different type descriptors. Nor can one assign a constant to a vector; thus

    SUM := 0.0

is not allowed. Note that when single elements are used in an expression or assignment statement (rather than the entire vector), the bounds of the associated vectors need not be the same.

The type descriptors must be exactly alike for assignments to be made. Thus if the following declarations occur

    TYPE VECTOR: ARRAY(1..10) OF REAL;
    VAR A: VECTOR;
        B: ARRAY(1..10) OF REAL;

an assignment such as

    B := A

is not allowed and will result in an error message.

Entire vectors cannot be be specified in input and output statements, as is done on occasion in the main text. All input and output of vectors must be done using loops.

In order to illustrate some of the concepts presented in this section, the example given in Fig. 4-1 is presented. The problem is to find the range (i.e., the difference between the largest and smallest element) of a list of values. For example, the range of the following list

    2 4 6 7 9 3 12 4 2

is 10 (i.e., 12(largest value) − 2(smallest value) = 10).

The variables used in the following program, which calculates the range of a list of ten values, are:

```
0  0000   00001   (* RANGE OF A VECTOR *)
0  0000   00002   PROGRAM RANGE (INPUT, OUTPUT);
0  0000   00003
0  0000   00004   VAR MAX, MIN, RANGE, I: INTEGER;
0  0038   00005       VALUE: ARRAY(1..9) OF INTEGER;
0  0038   00006
0  0038   00007   BEGIN
0  0038   00008       FOR I := 1 TO 9 DO
0  005C   00009           READ (VALUE(I));
0  0092   00010       WRITELN (' VECTOR');
0  00A4   00011       FOR I := 1 TO 9 DO
0  00C8   00012           WRITE (VALUE(I));
0  0100   00013       WRITELN;
0  010E   00014       MAX :=VALUE(1);
0  011A   00015       MIN :=VALUE(1);
0  0144   00016       FOR I := 1 TO 9 DO
0  0168   00017       BEGIN
0  0168   00018           IF VALUE(I) > MAX
0  018E   00019           THEN MAX := VALUE(I);
0  01C0   00020           IF VALUE(I) < MIN
0  01E6   00021           THEN MIN := VALUE(I)
0  0214   00022       END;
0  021C   00023       RANGE := MAX - MIN;
0  0228   00024       WRITELN (' RANGE IS ', RANGE)
0  024C   00025   END.
```

```
---------------------------------------
| COMPILE TIME:    0.084 SECOND(S) |
|    NO WARNING(S) DETECTED        |
|    NO ERROR(S) DETECTED          |
---------------------------------------
--EXECUTION-->
VECTOR
        7         9        11        5        6        9       20       30       52
RANGE IS         47
```

Fig. 4-1 Program to find the range of a list of values

Variable	Type	Usage
VALUE	ARRAY(1..10) OF INTEGER	Vector of values for which the range is to be found
MAX	INTEGER	Value of the largest element
MIN	INTEGER	Value of the smallest element
RANGE	INTEGER	Range of the vector VALUE
I	INTEGER	Loop variable

The data used in this program are

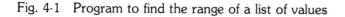

7 9 11 5 6 9 20 30 52

After the appropriate variables have been declared, the list of values is read in and printed. MAX and MIN are both set initially to the value of the first element of the vector VALUE. A loop is then entered in which each element of the vector is compared with the present values of MAX and MIN. If an element is greater than the current value of MAX, MAX is assigned the value of that element. If the element is less than the current value of MIN, the value of that element is assigned to MIN. When all the elements have been processed, the range is computed by subtracting MIN from MAX. This value is then assigned to the variable RANGE. The value of the range is then printed.

Vector subscripts can also be defined as any other scalar type other than reals. This includes the character and logical data types, or programmer-defined data types. For example, a vector could be defined as follows:

```
TYPE RANGE = 1..10;
VAR A: ARRAY(RANGE) OF INTEGER;
```

or

```
TYPE VECTOR = ARRAY(1..10) OF INTEGER;
VAR A: VECTOR;
```

which are both equivalent to the declaration

```
VAR A: ARRAY(1..10) OF INTEGER;
```

The scalar type or range of a vector can be of type character as the following declaration illustrates.

```
VAR A: ARRAY('C'..'F') OF REAL;
```

where A('C') is the first element, A('D') the second, A('E') the third, and A('F') the last.

Vectors can be defined to be of any programmer-defined scalar type. For example, if we define the days of the week as

```
TYPE WEEK = (MONDAY, TUESDAY, WEDNESDAY, THURSDAY, FRIDAY,
             SATURDAY, SUNDAY);
```

a vector could be defined as

```
VAR DAYS: ARRAY(WEEK) OF INTEGER;
```

or a subrange of the week as

```
VAR WORK_DAYS = ARRAY(MONDAY..FRIDAY) OF INTEGER;
```

Notice that the order in which the elements of the sets are defined determines the subscript/array element correspondence. Thus for the DAYS vector, DAYS(MONDAY) is the first element, DAYS(TUESDAY) is the second, ..., and DAYS(SUNDAY) is the last. Changing the order of the elements in the set WEEK will result in new subscript element names for the various array elements. Thus if WEEK is defined as

```
TYPE WEEK = (SUNDAY, MONDAY, FRIDAY, TUESDAY, SATURDAY,
             WEDNESDAY, THURSDAY)
```

then DAYS(MONDAY) is the second element, DAYS(TUESDAY) the fourth, and DAYS(SUNDAY) the first.

This concludes our discussion of simple vector operations. The next section deals with the important applications of sorting and searching with vectors.

Exercises for Sec. 4-1

1. Give the declarations for two arrays whose subscript ranges are the

months of the year and the three summer months, respectively. Use the TYPE declaration to define the set of the months.

2. Write a program that will determine the largest and second largest elements of a list containing no more than 50 real numbers. The data is to consist of an integer specifying the number of elements in the list followed by the elements of the list.

    Using your program, find the largest and second largest elements in the following list.

    75.63
    71.77
    68.31
    82.94
    66.11
    79.81
    67.79
    92.34
    88.11

3. Design a program which reads an unsorted vector A of n integers, and prints the vector in the same sequence after ignoring duplicate values found in the given vector. The number of remaining elements (m) is also required. For example, given the vector

A_1	A_2	A_3	A_4	A_5	A_6	A_7	A_8	A_9	A_{10}
15	31	23	15	75	23	41	15	31	85

    of ten integers, the compressed vector returned would be

A_1	A_2	A_3	A_4	A_5	A_6	A_7	A_8	A_9	A_{10}
15	31	23	75	41	85				

    with m = 6.

    Test your program on the following input values.

    16, 21, 23, 16, 25, 21, 41, 31, 23

4. Formulate a program to convert decimal (base 10) integers to their octal (base 8) representations by successive divisions. Let NUMBER denote the integer to be converted and BASE the base to which the integer is to be converted (8 in our case).

    For example, to compute the octal representation of 150, it is repeatedly divided by eight and the resulting remainders are saved in order.

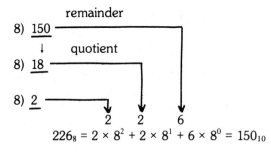

$$226_8 = 2 \times 8^2 + 2 \times 8^1 + 6 \times 8^0 = 150_{10}$$

Using your program find the octal representation of 1022.

5. As the shaft concrete lining was poured at a nearby potash mine, samples of the concrete were taken and tested for maximum strength. The record book of shaft depth versus concrete strength has been keypunched as follows:

> -first card contains the starting shaft depth and the total number of test results for consecutive one foot increments down the shaft
> -the following cards all contain ten test results per card, but the last card may contain less than ten results depending on the total number of results taken.

Example input:

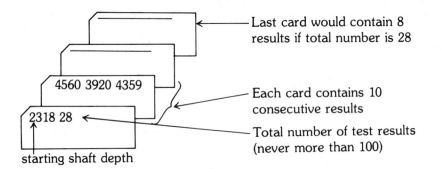

A running average of eight results is used as an indication of the average concrete strength and would indicate any extremely weak section in the shaft. The running average is the average of the readings at that depth and the next seven feet below. The running average for each of the last seven feet is the average of the remaining readings.

Obtain a program to generate a running average table as follows:

Depth	Test Result	Running Average
2318	4560	4341
2319	3920	4265
.	.	.
.	.	.
.	.	.
2339	4820	4515
.	.	.

.   .   .

2345   4500   4500

The "length" of the running average, in this case eight feet, varies with each application. After you have a solution to the preceding problem, generalize your program so only one data card must be changed to change the length of the average.

With your program, print a running average table for the following values.

> 2500 (starting shaft depth)   11 (no. of test results)
> 5500, 6511, 5615, 6000, 5791, 5821, } Test Results
> 5651, 6345, 5796, 6312, 6200   }

6. An important problem in statistics concerns the predictability of the value of one variable from the value of another variable. Two variables that can be used in this way with good chance of success are said to be *strongly correlated*. The strength of correlation is determined by the *correlation coefficient*.

   We wish to conduct an experiment to determine the strength of correlation between a student's final high school average and his or her performance on first year university classes. Following final examinations, a card is prepared for each first year student containing two real values: high school average (H) and first year average (F). Assume there are N students involved in this study. (N is never greater than 100). Write a program to read these data into two vectors H[i] and F[i], i = 1, 2, ..., N. Then compute the correlation coefficient R according to the following formula

$$\frac{N \Sigma H[i]F[i] - \Sigma H[i] \Sigma F[i]}{\sqrt{(N \Sigma H[i]^2 - (\Sigma H[i])^2)(N \Sigma F[i]^2 - (\Sigma F[i])^2)}}$$

If the correlation coefficient exceeds 0.85, a message is to be printed saying that these variables appear to be strongly correlated.

   Test your program on the following input values.

> 12 (no. of students)
>
> | | |
> |---|---|
> | 78 | 65 |
> | 85 | 80 |
> | 65 | 50 |
> | 80 | 75 |
> | 90 | 88 |
> | 67 | 62 |
> | 79 | 75 |
> | 80 | 80 |
> | 69 | 54 |
> | 75 | 70 |
> | 70 | 70 |
> | 82 | 80 |

7. Write a program which generates a yearly sales report. The report is to give a breakdown of sales for each month of the year, and, in addition, a yearly total. Each sales transaction is recorded on a card as follows:

   Sales amount, Month number

   where each month of the year is numbered from 1 to 12. The number of input cards is unknown and these cards are not in any sequence. Use an end-of-file test to detect the end of the data.

   Use your program to generate a report for the following input values.

6032	2
6030	6
7841	1
7963	12
8967	11
3852	3
7789	4
8561	4
9921	12
6754	1
6251	1

4-2 SORTING AND SEARCHING WITH VECTORS

This section deals with two important applications that commonly involve vectors. These are sorting and searching. In Sec. 4-2.1 techniques of sorting, with particular emphasis on the selection sort, are discussed. In the next section, searching is introduced. Finally, in Sec. 4-2.3, merging and merge-sorting are presented. Programs are given for each technique.

4-2.1 Selection Sort

The technique of selection sorting is discussed in Sec. 4-3.1 of the main text. Suppose, for example, we wish to sort a vector into ascending (i.e., increasing) order. Using the selection method, the vector is scanned for the smallest element, and this element is assigned to the first element of a vector that is to contain the sorted elements. In order to distinguish the element that has already been selected, it is replaced in the original vector by some distinguishing value that is known not to exist as one of the elements of the vector. The original vector is then scanned (ignoring the distinguishing value) and the second smallest element is found. This element is then placed in the second position of the new vector. Its value in the original vector is replaced by the distinguishing value. The sort continues in this manner until each element of the original vector has been placed in the sorted vector.

The process of scanning the vector and selecting the next element in the ordering is called a *pass*. In a vector of *n* elements, this method of sorting requires *n* passes, with one element selected on each pass. A program to perform this selection sort appears in Fig. 4-2. The data values used in this program are:

9
5 10 1 7 9 23 46 32 12

The variables used are:

Variable	Type	Usage
K	ARRAY(1..100) OF INTEGER	Vector containing list of values to be sorted
OUTPUT	ARRAY(1..100) OF INTEGER	Sorted vector
NUM	INTEGER	Number of values to be sorted
PASS	INTEGER	Number of current pass
MIN	INTEGER	Subscript which references current smallest element
I	INTEGER	Loop variable

In this program the unsorted vector K is read in and printed. The selection sort is then begun. A counted loop controls the passes made. During each pass, the smallest element is selected (ignoring elements that have been given the distinguishing value 999) and placed in the vector OUTPUT. It is then replaced in the original vector by the value 999. Finally, after all the passes have been made, the sorted vector OUTPUT is printed. This particular selection sort may present problems if the vector to be sorted is large or if one of the elements in the vector happens to be the special value 999. If the vector to be sorted is large, then a large amount of storage space may be required for the two vectors (original and sorted copy). Also, since the number of passes required is equal to the number of elements and each element must be checked on each pass, the time consumed in sorting a very large vector may be impractical. Notice that the vector K is declared to accommodate up to 100 elements. In any particular run (such as the one shown) there may be fewer elements. The actual number is given by N.

Another version of the selection sort, which saves both storage space and computing time, involves using the original vector to hold the selected elements, as described in the main text. The program given in Fig. 4-3 uses this method to sort the numbers

5 10 1 7 9 23 46 32 12

into ascending order. The following variables are used in this program:

Variable	Type	Usage
K	ARRAY(1..100) OF INTEGER	Vector containing list of values to be sorted
NUM	INTEGER	Number of values to be sorted
PASS	INTEGER	Number of current pass
MIN	INTEGER	Subscript which references current smallest element
I	INTEGER	Loop variable

```
0   0000   00001   (* SELECTION SORT (VERSION 1) *)
0   0000   00002   PROGRAM SELECT1 (INPUT, OUTPUT);
0   0000   00003
0   0000   00004   VAR K, OUTPUT: ARRAY(1..100) OF INTEGER;
0   0038   00005       PASS, MIN, NUM, I: INTEGER;
0   0038   00006
0   0038   00007   BEGIN
0   0038   00008
0   0038   00009       (* READ IN VECTOR *)
0   0038   00010       READ (NUM);
0   004A   00011       FOR I := 1 TO NUM DO
0   006E   00012           READ (K(I));
0   00A4   00013
0   00A4   00014       (* PRINT UNSORTED VECTOR *)
0   00A4   00015       WRITELN ('UNSORTED VECTOR');
0   00B6   00016       FOR I := 1 TO NUM DO
0   00DA   00017           WRITE (K(I));
0   0112   00018       WRITELN;
0   0120   00019       WRITELN;
0   012E   00020
0   012E   00021       (* MAKE ONE PASS FOR EACH ELEMENT *)
0   012E   00022       FOR PASS := 1 TO NUM DO
0   0152   00023       BEGIN
0   0152   00024           MIN := 1;
0   015A   00025
0   015A   00026           (* FIND SMALLEST ELEMENT *)
0   015A   00027           FOR I := 2 TO NUM DO
0   017E   00028               IF (K(I) < K(MIN)) AND (K(I) <> 999)
0   01FE   00029               THEN MIN := I;
0   0206   00030           OUTPUT(PASS) := K(MIN);
0   0256   00031           K(MIN) := 999
0   0278   00032       END;
0   0284   00033
0   0284   00034       (* PRINT SORTED VECTOR *)
0   0284   00035       WRITELN ('SORTED VECTOR');
0   0296   00036       WRITELN;
0   02A4   00037       FOR I := 1 TO NUM DO
0   02C8   00038           WRITE (OUTPUT(I));
0   0300   00039       WRITELN
0   0300   00040   END.
-----------------------------------
¦ COMPILE TIME:    0.099 SECOND(S) ¦
¦    NO WARNING(S) DETECTED        ¦
¦    NO ERROR(S) DETECTED          ¦
-----------------------------------
--EXECUTION-->
UNSORTED VECTOR
        5          10          1          7          9          23          46          32          12

SORTED VECTOR

        1          5          7          9          10          12          23          32          46
```

Fig. 4-2　Selection sort (version 1)

| NEXT | INTEGER | Subscript used to reference the first element of the remaining unsorted elements |
| TEMP | INTEGER | Temporarily holds the value of an element during an exchange |

As in the first version of the selection sort, the vector to be sorted is read in. The first counted loop controls the number of passes. The second counted loop controls the search of the remaining elements in the vector. If the smallest element found is not already in the correct position, it is exchanged for the current element in that position. When N – 1 passes have been completed, the now sorted vector is printed.

Sorting may be performed on nonnumerical elements as well as numerical elements. For examples of sorting involving character string elements, see Chap. 5.

```
0  0000   00001   (* SELECTION SORT (VERSION 2) *)
0  0000   00002   PROGRAM SELECT2 (INPUT, OUTPUT);
0  0000   00003
0  0000   00004   VAR PASS, MIN, NUM, I, NEXT, TEMP: INTEGER;
0  0038   00005       K: ARRAY(1..100) OF INTEGER;
0  0038   00006
0  0038   00007   BEGIN
0  0038   00008
0  0038   00009       (* READ IN VECTOR *)
0  0038   00010       READ (NUM);
0  004A   00011       FOR I := 1 TO NUM DO
0  006E   00012           READ (K(I));
0  00A4   00013
0  00A4   00014       (* PRINT UNSORTED VECTOR *)
0  00A4   00015       WRITELN (' UNSORTED VECTOR');
0  00B6   00016       FOR I := 1 TO NUM DO
0  00DA   00017           WRITE (K(I));
0  0112   00018       WRITELN;
0  0120   00019
0  0120   00020       (* REPEAT FOR NUM - 1 PASSES *)
0  0120   00021       FOR PASS := 1 TO NUM - 1 DO
0  0148   00022       BEGIN
0  0148   00023           MIN := PASS;
0  0150   00024           NEXT := PASS + 1;
0  015C   00025           FOR I := NEXT TO NUM DO
0  0180   00026               IF K(I) < K(MIN)
0  01CC   00027               THEN MIN := I;
0  01DA   00028           IF MIN <> PASS
0  01DE   00029           THEN BEGIN
0  01EA   00030               TEMP := K(PASS);
0  0214   00031               K(PASS) := K(MIN);
0  0260   00032               K(MIN) := TEMP
0  0282   00033               END
0  028A   00034       END;
0  028E   00035
0  028E   00036       (* PRINT SORTED VECTOR *)
0  028E   00037       WRITELN (' SORTED VECTOR');
0  02A0   00038       FOR I := 1 TO NUM DO
0  02C4   00039           WRITE (K(I));
0  02FC   00040       WRITELN
0  02FC   00041   END.
```

```
| COMPILE TIME:    0.105 SECOND(S) |
|    NO WARNING(S) DETECTED        |
|    NO ERROR(S) DETECTED          |

--EXECUTION-->
UNSORTED VECTOR
        5        10         1         7         9        23        46        32        12
SORTED VECTOR
        1         5         7         9        10        12        23        32        46
```

Fig. 4-3 Selection sort (version 2)

This concludes the section on selection sorts. In the next section, methods of searching for elements in vectors are introduced.

4-2.2 Basic Searching

Searching refers to the process of scanning a vector for a particular element. Two types of search were discussed in the main text; namely, the *linear* search and the *binary* search.

A linear search involves scanning the elements of a vector in sequential order (i.e., element by element) until the desired element is found. A program to perform this task is given in Fig. 4-4. The data values used in this run were

9
5 10 1 7 9 23 46 32 12
12

```
0  0000  00001  (* LINEAR SEARCH *)
0  0000  00002  PROGRAM LSEARCH (INPUT, OUTPUT);
0  0000  00003
0  0000  00004  VAR N, I, X: INTEGER;
0  0038  00005      K: ARRAY(1..100) OF INTEGER;
0  0038  00006
0  0038  00007  BEGIN
0  0038  00008
0  0038  00009      (* READ VECTOR *)
0  0038  00010      READ (N);
0  004A  00011      FOR I := 1 TO N DO
0  006E  00012          READ (K(I));
0  00A4  00013
0  00A4  00014      (* READ ELEMENT SOUGHT *)
0  00A4  00015      READ (X);
0  00B6  00016
0  00B6  00017      (* PRINT VECTOR TO BE SEARCHED AND VALUE SOUGHT *)
0  00B6  00018      WRITELN (' VECTOR');
0  00C8  00019      WRITELN;
0  00D6  00020      FOR I := 1 TO N DO
0  00FA  00021          WRITE (K(I));
0  0132  00022      WRITELN;
0  0140  00023      WRITELN (' VALUE SOUGHT EQUALS', X);
0  0164  00024
0  0164  00025      (* CHECK EACH ELEMENT UNTIL X IS FOUND *)
0  0164  00026      I := 1;
0  016C  00027      WHILE (K(I) <> X) AND (I <> N) DO
0  01A6  00028          I := I + 1;
0  01B6  00029      IF K(I) = X
0  01DC  00030      THEN WRITELN (' SUCCESSFUL SEARCH. VALUE IN POSITION', I)
0  0208  00031      ELSE WRITELN (' UNSUCCESSFUL SEARCH')
0  021E  00032  END.
-------------------------------------
| COMPILE TIME:    0.080 SECOND(S) |
|     NO WARNING(S) DETECTED        |
|     NO ERROR(S) DETECTED          |
-------------------------------------
--EXECUTION-->
VECTOR

      5          10          1          7          9          23          46          32          12
VALUE SOUGHT EQUALS          12
SUCCESSFUL SEARCH. VALUE IN POSITION          9
```

Fig. 4-4   Linear search

The following variables appear in this program:

Variable	Type	Usage
K	ARRAY(1..100) OF INTEGER	Vector to be searched
N	INTEGER	Number of elements in vector
I	INTEGER	Loop variable
X	INTEGER	Value sought

After the appropriate variables are declared, the vector and particular element sought are read in and printed. The search then proceeds in a sequential manner until the desired element is found or the end of the vector is reached. If the element is found, the message SUCCESSFUL SEARCH and the position of the element in the vector is printed; otherwise, the message UNSUCCESSFUL SEARCH is printed.

A more efficient method of searching, which can be performed only on sorted vectors, is the *binary search*. Suppose the elements of a vector are stored in ascending order. A binary search performed on this vector proceeds in the following manner. The middle (or approximately the middle) element of the vector is chosen. If the value sought is greater than the middle element, the search continues with the second half of the vector. If, on the other hand, the value sought is less than the value of the middle element, the search continues with the first half of the vector. A new middle element, which is the middle of the new search interval, is found. The process is repeated with this new search interval and again the appropriate half (now one quarter of the whole vector) is chosen. This process is repeated until the element sought is found or until the search interval is empty, the latter indicating that the desired element is not present in the vector. A PASCAL program to perform a binary search appears in Fig. 4-5. This program performs a binary search for the element 45 in the ordered vector:

10 11 25 30 39 45 56 72 88

The variables that appear in this program are:

Variable	Type	Usage
K	ARRAY(1..100) OF INTEGER	Vector of values to be searched
LOW	INTEGER	Subscript of smallest element in current search interval
HIGH	INTEGER	Subscript of largest element in current search interval
MIDDLE	INTEGER	Subscript of middle element in current search interval
N	INTEGER	Number of values in K
X	INTEGER	Value sought
I	INTEGER	Loop variable

Notice in lines 27 and 34 that the built-in function TRUNC is used to obtain an integer value that is less than or equal to the calculated middle value. This is done to ensure that the subscript used to locate the middle element of the vector is always an integer. X is then compared with the middle element. If X is less than the middle element, then the variable HIGH is set to MIDDLE − 1, and the search interval becomes the lower half of the present search interval. If X is greater than the value of the middle element, then LOW is assigned the value of MIDDLE + 1, and the search interval is reduced to the upper half of the current search interval. The position of the middle element in this new search interval is then calculated. This process continues until X equals the value of the middle element (i.e., the search is successful), or until the search interval is empty (this is indicated by a value of LOW which is larger than the value of HIGH).

We close this section with a more elaborate problem. The city of Lowly Heights is experiencing a housing shortage. As a consequence, the price of rental accommodations has become unreasonable. In order to keep down the inflationary price of new apartments in the city, the city fathers have decided to implement a basic maximum allowable rent for apartments. This maximum is based on the amount of floor space contained in the apartment. The schedule of areas and corresponding rents is as follows.

```
0   0000    00001   (* BINARY SEARCH *)
0   0000    00002   PROGRAM BSEARCH (INPUT, OUTPUT);
0   0000    00003
0   0000    00004   VAR LOW, HIGH, N, I, MIDDLE, X: INTEGER;
0   0038    00005       K: ARRAY(1..100) OF INTEGER;
0   0038    00006
0   0038    00007   BEGIN
0   0038    00008
0   0038    00009       (* READ VECTOR *)
0   0038    00010       READ (N);
0   004A    00011       FOR I := 1 TO N DO
0   006E    00012           READ (K(I));
0   00A4    00013
0   00A4    00014       (* READ ELEMENT SEARCHED FOR *)
0   00A4    00015       READ (X);
0   00B6    00016
0   00B6    00017       (* PRINT VECTOR AND VALUE SOUGHT *)
0   00B6    00018       WRITELN (' VECTOR');
0   00C8    00019       FOR I := 1 TO N DO
0   00EC    00020           WRITE (K(I));
0   0124    00021       WRITELN;
0   0132    00022       WRITELN (' VALUE SOUGHT EQUALS', X);
0   0156    00023
0   0156    00024       (* PERFORM SEARCH *)
0   0156    00025       LOW := 1;
0   015E    00026       HIGH := N;
0   0166    00027       MIDDLE := TRUNC ((LOW + HIGH) / 2.0);
0   0196    00028       WHILE (LOW <= HIGH) AND (X <> K(MIDDLE)) DO
0   01D0    00029       BEGIN
0   01D0    00030           IF X < K(MIDDLE)
0   01F6    00031           THEN HIGH := MIDDLE - 1
0   01FE    00032           ELSE IF X > K(MIDDLE)
0   0234    00033               THEN LOW := MIDDLE + 1;
0   0248    00034           MIDDLE := TRUNC ((LOW + HIGH) / 2.0)
0   0264    00035       END;
0   027C    00036       IF X = K(MIDDLE)
0   02A2    00037       THEN WRITELN (' SUCCESSFUL SEARCH.  VALUE IN POSITION ', MIDDLE)
0   02CE    00038       ELSE WRITELN (' UNSUCCESSFUL SEARCH')
0   02E4    00039   END.
------------------------------------
| COMPILE TIME:    0.109 SECOND(S) |
|    NO WARNING(S) DETECTED        |
|    NO ERROR(S) DETECTED          |
------------------------------------
--EXECUTION-->
VECTOR
        10        11        25        30        39        45        56        72        88
VALUE SOUGHT EQUALS         45
SUCCESSFUL SEARCH.  VALUE IN POSITION        6
```

Fig. 4-5   Binary search

Floor space	145	165	180	190	220	235	245	270	280	300	340	350
Rent	90	100	125	140	150	165	175	190	200	210	225	250

If the floor space is below 145 square feet, the apartment is exempt from rent control. If the floor space is above 350 square feet, the apartment is to be placed in a special category. The problem is to write a program that reads in the location of an apartment and the amount of floor space it contains and finds the maximum allowable rent that, according to the previous table, may be charged. If the floor space is below 145 square feet or above 350 square feet, the messages, "IS NOT COVERED UNDER RENT CONTROL", and "REFER TO SPECIAL CATEGORY", respectively are to be printed. In addition, a record must be kept of the number of apartments that fall into each of the 12 space and rent categories just given. The floor space read in is rounded to the nearest rent category. The program must generate the following reports:

APARTMENT REPORT

LOCATION	MAXIMUM ALLOWABLE RENT
APT. 5 SPRUCE CRES.	150
APT. 7 WRANGLER ROAD	90
APT. 9 CHARLY HTS.	125
APT. 4 WILLOW AVE.	190

and

REPORT ON RENTAL ACCOMMODATIONS

APPROXIMATE AREA	MAXIMUM ALLOWABLE RENT	NUMBER OF UNITS
145	90	1
165	100	0
.	.	.
.	.	.
.	.	.
350	250	0

A general outline of the steps involved in solving this problem follows.

1) Read in the data on the first apartment.
2) Repeat through step 5 until there is no more data
3) Check if the floor space is below or above the specified minimum and maximum,
   then print the appropriate message
   else use a binary search to find the position of the designated floor space in the vector of areas and use that position to determine the rent for the apartment.
5) Print the location of the apartment and the maximum rent. Increment a counter which keeps track of the number of units of that area.
6) Read in data concerning the next apartment.
7) Print a report consisting of the various apartment floor spaces, the maximum rent that can be charged for each, and the number of apartments in that category.

The variables used in the program of Fig. 4-6 are:

Variable	Type	Usage
AREA	ARRAY(1..12) OF INTEGER	Vector of floor spaces
RENT	ARRAY(1..12) OF INTEGER	Vector of rents
NUM	ARRAY(1..12) OF INTEGER	Number of available units in each category
LOW	INTEGER	Subscript which points to the beginning of the search interval

```
0  0000   00001   (* APARTMENT RENTAL REPORT *)
0  0000   00002   PROGRAM REPORT (INPUT, OUTPUT);
0  0000   00003
0  0000   00004   VAR AREA, RENT, NUM: ARRAY(1..12) OF INTEGER;
0  0038   00005       SPACE, LOW, HIGH, MIDDLE, I: INTEGER;
0  0038   00006       LOCATION: STRING(24);
0  0038   00007
0  0038   00008   BEGIN
0  0038   00009
0  0038   00010       (* INITIALIZE VARIABLES *)
0  0038   00011       FOR I := 1 TO 12 DO
0  005C   00012       BEGIN
0  005C   00013           READ (AREA(I), RENT(I));
0  00C0   00014           NUM(I) := 0
0  00E2   00015       END;
0  00EC   00016
0  00EC   00017       (* PRINT HEADER *)
0  00EC   00018       WRITELN (' APARTMENT REPORT');
0  00FE   00019       WRITELN (' LOCATION              MAXIMUM ALLOWABLE RENT');
0  0110   00020
0  0110   00021       (* PROCESS CARDS UNTIL TRAILER IS REACHED *)
0  0110   00022       READ (LOCATION, SPACE);
0  0134   00023       WHILE LOCATION <> 'END                 ' DO
0  013E   00024       BEGIN
0  013E   00025
0  013E   00026           (* CHECK IS AREA BELOW 145 OR OVER 350 *)
0  013E   00027           IF SPACE < 145
0  013E   00028           THEN WRITELN (' ', LOCATION, 'IS NOT COVERED UNDER RENT ',
0  0180   00029               'CONTROL')
0  0192   00030           ELSE IF SPACE > 350
0  0196   00031               THEN WRITELN (' ', LOCATION, 'REFER TO SPECIAL CATEGORY')
0  01D8   00032               ELSE BEGIN
0  01DC   00033
0  01DC   00034                   (* SEARCH FOR LOCATION *)
0  01DC   00035                   LOW := 1;
0  01E4   00036                   HIGH := 12;
0  01EC   00037                   WHILE (LOW <= HIGH) DO
0  01F8   00038                   BEGIN
0  01F8   00039                       MIDDLE := TRUNC ((LOW + HIGH) / 2.0);
0  0228   00040                       IF SPACE < AREA(MIDDLE)
0  024E   00041                       THEN HIGH := MIDDLE - 1
0  0256   00042                       ELSE IF SPACE > AREA(MIDDLE)
0  028C   00043                           THEN LOW := MIDDLE + 1
0  0294   00044                           ELSE BEGIN
0  02A4   00045                               WRITELN (' ', LOCATION,
0  02C8   00046                                   RENT(MIDDLE));
0  02FC   00047                               NUM(MIDDLE) := NUM(MIDDLE) + 1;
0  034C   00048                               LOW := HIGH + 1
0  034C   00049                           END
0  0358   00050                   END
0  0358   00051               END;
0  035C   00052           READ (LOCATION, SPACE)
0  0380   00053       END;
0  0384   00054
0  0384   00055       (* PRINT SECOND REPORT *)
0  0384   00056       WRITELN;
0  0392   00057       WRITELN (' REPORT ON TOTAL RENTAL ACCOMODATIONS');
0  03A4   00058       WRITELN ('    FLOOR SPACE  MAXIMUM RENT  NUMBER OF UNITS');
0  03B6   00059       FOR I := 1 TO 12 DO
0  03DA   00060           WRITELN (' ', AREA(I), RENT(I), NUM(I))
0  0488   00061   END.
```

Fig. 4-6 Apartment Report Program

HIGH	INTEGER	Subscript which points to end of the search interval
MIDDLE	INTEGER	Subscript which points to the middle of the search interval
I	INTEGER	Loop variable
LOCATION	STRING(24)	Address of the rental unit
SPACE	INTEGER	Amount of floor space in the rental unit

```
------------------------------------
| COMPILE TIME:    0.173 SECOND(S) |
|      NO WARNING(S) DETECTED      |
|      NO ERROR(S) DETECTED        |
------------------------------------
--EXECUTION-->
APARTMENT REPORT
LOCATION                    MAXIMUM ALLOWABLE RENT
APT. 5 234 ELM ST.                    100
APT. 12 452 SCYRA DRIVE               190
APT. 5 452 JASMIN ST.                 150
APT. 4 125 YEOMAN AVE.                165
APT. 23 756 ROVER LANE                190
APT. 3 52 TARA COURT                  250
APT. 6 25 SORRO PLACE                  90
APT. 6 10 JOY ST.       IS NOT COVERED UNDER RENT CONTROL
APT. 2 335 GOPHER LANE                100
APT. 15 234 APPLE CRES.               140
APT. 1 24 RODE ST.                    100
APT. 4 124 GRAY ST.                   200
APT. 8 45 RYERS CRES.                 125
APT. 25 435 TALLY DRIVE               210
APT. 42 534 RIVER ST.                 140

REPORT ON TOTAL RENTAL ACCOMODATIONS
   FLOOR SPACE  MAXIMUM RENT  NUMBER OF UNITS
          145         90           1
          165        100           3
          180        125           1
          190        140           2
          220        150           1
          235        165           1
          245        175           0
          270        190           2
          280        200           1
          300        210           1
          340        225           0
          350        250           1
```

Fig. 4-6   Apartment Report Program (cont'd.)

The data for the program given in Fig. 4-6 include information given in the rent schedule and a list of apartments and their rents. The input list of apartments and areas used in this program follows.

'APT. 5 234 ELM ST.'	165
'APT. 12 452 SCYRA DRIVE'	270
'APT. 5 452 JASMIN ST.'	220
'APT. 4 125 YEOMAN AVE.'	235
'APT. 23 756 ROVER LANE'	270
'APT. 3 52 TARA COURT'	350
'APT. 6 25 SORRO PLACE'	145
'APT. 6 10 JOY ST.'	125
'APT. 2 335 GOPHER LANE'	165
'APT. 15 234 APPLE CRES.'	190
'APT. 1 24 RODE ST.'	165
'APT. 4 124 GRAY ST.'	280
'APT. 8 45 RYERS CRES.'	180
'APT. 25 435 TALLY DRIVE'	300
'APT. 42 534 RIVER ST.'	190
'END'	0

At the start of the program, the schedule of rental rates and floor spaces is read. A loop processes each of the apartments, using a binary search to locate the

```
0  0000   00001  (* PROGRAM TO MERGE TWO VECTORS *)
0  0000   00002  PROGRAM MERGE (INPUT, OUTPUT);
0  0000   00003
0  0000   00004  VAR A, B, C: ARRAY(1..100) OF INTEGER;
0  0038   00005      N, M, I, J, K, R: INTEGER;
0  0038   00006
0  0038   00007  BEGIN
0  0038   00008
0  0038   00009      (* READ AND PRINT THE TWO VECTORS *)
0  0038   00010      READ (N, M);
0  005C   00011      WRITELN (' VECTOR A');
0  006E   00012      FOR I := 1 TO N DO
0  0092   00013      BEGIN
0  0092   00014         READ (A(I));
0  00C4   00015         WRITE (A(I))
0  00F8   00016      END;
0  00FC   00017      WRITELN;
0  010A   00018      WRITELN (' VECTOR B');
0  011C   00019      FOR I := 1 TO M DO
0  0140   00020      BEGIN
0  0140   00021         READ (B(I));
0  0172   00022         WRITE (B(I))
0  01A6   00023      END;
0  01AA   00024      WRITELN;
0  01B8   00025      I := 1; J := 1; K := 1;
0  01D0   00026
0  01D0   00027      (* PROCESS VECTORS UNTIL THE END OF ONE IS REACHED *)
0  01D0   00028      WHILE (I <= N) AND (J <= M) DO
0  01E8   00029          IF A(I) <= B(J)
0  0234   00030          THEN BEGIN
0  023A   00031              C(K) := A(I);
0  0286   00032              I := I + 1;
0  0292   00033              K := K + 1
0  0292   00034              END
0  029E   00035          ELSE BEGIN
0  02A2   00036              C(K) := B(J);
0  02EE   00037              J := J + 1;
0  02FA   00038              K := K + 1
0  02FA   00039              END;
0  030A   00040
0  030A   00041      (* ADD REMAINING ELEMENTS TO SORTED VECTOR *)
0  030A   00042      IF I > N
0  030A   00043      THEN FOR R := J TO M DO
0  033A   00044          BEGIN
0  033A   00045              C(K) := B(R);
0  0386   00046              K := K + 1
0  0386   00047          END
0  0392   00048      ELSE FOR R := 1 TO N DO
0  03BE   00049          BEGIN
0  03BE   00050              C(K) := A(R);
0  040A   00051              K := K + 1
0  040A   00052          END;
0  041A   00053
0  041A   00054      (* PRINT MERGED VECTOR *)
0  041A   00055      WRITELN (' MERGED VECTOR');
0  042C   00056      FOR I := 1 TO N + M DO
0  0454   00057          WRITE (C(I));
0  048C   00058      WRITELN
0  048C   00059  END.
------------------------------------
| COMPILE TIME:    0.162 SECOND(S) |
|     NO WARNING(S) DETECTED       |
|     NO ERROR(S) DETECTED         |
------------------------------------
--EXECUTION-->
VECTOR A
      1       3       5       7       9      12      14
VECTOR B
      2       4       6       8       9      11      14      25      26
MERGED VECTOR
      1       2       3       4       5       6       7       8       9       9
     11      12      14      14      25      26
```

Fig. 4-7   Program to merge two vectors

appropriate rent. The location and allowable rent are printed for each apartment. In addition, a counter which contains the number of apartments in this category is incremented. When all apartments have been processed, a counted loop is used to print the number of apartments that fall into each category.

4-2.3 Merging and Merge Sorting

As described in the main text, merging vectors is the process of taking two sorted vectors and combining them into a single sorted vector. In this section, we present first a program that performs a merge, then a program that uses the technique of merging to effect a sort.

The program given in Fig. 4-7 merges two integer vectors that have been sorted in ascending order. The variables used in this program are

Variable	Type	Usage
A	ARRAY(1..100) OF INTEGER	Vector to be merged
B	ARRAY(1..100) OF INTEGER	Vector to be merged
C	ARRAY(1..200) OF INTEGER	Merged vector
N	INTEGER	Number of elements in vector A
M	INTEGER	Number of elements in vector B
I	INTEGER	Subscript
J	INTEGER	Subscript
K	INTEGER	Subscript
R	INTEGER	Loop variable

In this program, a card which contains two integers, N, the number of elements in the first vector, and M, the number of elements in the second, is read in. The first element of each vector is checked and the smallest is selected and placed in vector C. This process continues until all the elements of vector A or vector B have been used. The remaining unprocessed elements are then added to the vector containing the merged elements. Finally, the merged vector is printed.

Multiple merging or *K-way merging* is the merging of a number of sorted vectors into one sorted vector. The following program uses this method to sort a vector that contains 2^m elements where 2^m is less than 128. The program can be modified to handle vectors with a number of elements that are not an exact power of two, although this is not done here. The variables used in this program are:

Variable	Type	Usage
K	ARRAY(1..128) OF INTEGER	Vector to be sorted
C	ARRAY(1..128) OF INTEGER	Output sorted vector

```
0   0000   00001   (* MERGE SORT *)
0   0000   00002   PROGRAM MSORT (INPUT, OUTPUT);
0   0000   00003
0   0000   00004   VAR K, C: ARRAY(1..128) OF INTEGER;
0   0038   00005       PASS, P, Q, I, J, R, S, T, N, LAST,
0   0038   00006       SIZE, SUBPASS, S1: INTEGER;
0   0038   00007
0   0038   00008   BEGIN
0   0038   00009
0   0038   00010       (* READ IN VECTOR *)
0   0038   00011       READ (N);
0   004A   00012       WRITELN (' UNSORTED VECTOR');
0   005C   00013       FOR I := 1 TO N DO
0   0080   00014       BEGIN
0   0080   00015           READ (K(I));
0   00B2   00016           WRITE (K(I))
0   00E6   00017       END;
0   00EA   00018       WRITELN;
0   00F8   00019
0   00F8   00020       (* CALCULATE NUMBER OF PASSES *)
0   00F8   00021       LAST := ROUND (LN (N) / LN (2.0));
0   013E   00022       FOR PASS := 1 TO LAST DO
0   0162   00023       BEGIN
0   0162   00024
0   0162   00025           (* COMPUTE 2 TO THE PASS - 1TH POWER *)
0   0162   00026           SIZE := 1;
0   016A   00027           FOR J := 1 TO PASS - 1 DO
0   0192   00028               SIZE := SIZE * 2;
0   01A6   00029           P := 1;
0   01AE   00030           Q := P + SIZE;
0   01BA   00031           SUBPASS := TRUNC (N / (2 * SIZE));
0   0200   00032
0   0200   00033           (* PERFORM THE SUBPASSES *)
0   0200   00034           FOR S1 := 1 TO SUBPASS DO
0   0224   00035           BEGIN
0   0224   00036               I := P;
0   022C   00037               J := Q;
0   0234   00038               T := P;
0   023C   00039               WHILE (I + 1 - P <= SIZE) AND (1 + J - Q <= SIZE) DO
0   0264   00040               BEGIN
0   0264   00041
0   0264   00042                   (* IF THE PASS IS ODD *)
0   0264   00043                   IF ODD (PASS)
0   0264   00044                   THEN IF K(I) <= K(J)
0   02BE   00045                       THEN BEGIN
0   02C4   00046                           C(T) := K(I);
0   0310   00047                           I := I + 1;
0   031C   00048                           T := T + 1
0   031C   00049                           END
0   0328   00050                       ELSE BEGIN
0   032C   00051                           C(T) := K(J);
0   0378   00052                           J := J + 1;
0   0384   00053                           T := T + 1
0   0384   00054                           END
0   0390   00055                   ELSE IF C(I) <= C(J)
0   03E0   00056                       THEN BEGIN
0   03E6   00057                           K(T) := C(I);
0   0432   00058                           I := I + 1:
0   043E   00059                           T := T + 1
0   043E   00060                           END
0   044A   00061                       ELSE BEGIN
0   044E   00062                           K(T) := C(J);
0   049A   00063                           J := J + 1;
0   04A6   00064                           T := T + 1
0   04A6   00065                           END
0   04B2   00066               END;
0   04B6   00067
0   04B6   00068                   (* COPY REMAINING ELEMENTS INTO OUTPUT AREA *)
0   04B6   00069               IF I + 1 - P > SIZE
0   04C2   00070               THEN BEGIN
0   04CA   00071                   S := Q + SIZE - 1;
0   04DA   00072
0   04DA   00073                   (* IF PASS IS ODD *)
0   04DA   00074                   IF ODD (PASS)
0   04DA   00075                   THEN FOR R := J TO S DO
0   050C   00076                       BEGIN
0   050C   00077                           C(T) := K(R);
0   0558   00078                           T := T + 1
0   0558   00079                           END
```

Fig. 4-8   Merge sort

```
0   0564   00080                          ELSE FOR R := J TO S DO
0   0590   00081                                   BEGIN
0   0590   00082                                       K(T) := C(R);
0   05DC   00083                                       T := T + 1
0   05DC   00084                                   END
0   05E8   00085                          END
0   05EC   00086                      ELSE BEGIN
0   05F0   00087                          S := P + SIZE - 1;
0   0600   00088
0   0600   00089                          (* IF PASS IS ODD *)
0   0600   00090                          IF ODD (PASS)
0   0600   00091                          THEN FOR R := I TO S DO
0   0632   00092                                   BEGIN
0   0632   00093                                       C(T) := K(R);
0   067E   00094                                       T := T + 1
0   067E   00095                                   END
0   068A   00096                          ELSE FOR R := I TO S DO
0   06B6   00097                                   BEGIN
0   06B6   00098                                       K(T) := C(R);
0   0702   00099                                       T := T + 1
0   0702   00100                                   END
0   070E   00101                               END;
0   0712   00102                          P := Q + SIZE;
0   071E   00103                          Q := P + SIZE
0   071E   00104                      END
0   072A   00105                  END;
0   0732   00106
0   0732   00107          (* RECOPY VECTOR IF NEEDED *)
0   0732   00108          IF ODD (LAST)
0   0732   00109          THEN FOR I := 1 TO N DO
0   0764   00110                  K(I) := C(I);
0   07B4   00111
0   07B4   00112          (* PRINT THE SORTED VECTOR *)
0   07B4   00113          WRITELN (' SORTED VECTOR');
0   07C6   00114          FOR I := 1 TO N DO
0   07EA   00115                  WRITE (K(I));
0   0822   00116          WRITELN
0   0822   00117  END.
----------------------------------------
| COMPILE TIME:     0.294 SECOND(S) |
|     NO WARNING(S) DETECTED        |
|     NO ERROR(S) DETECTED          |
----------------------------------------
--EXECUTION-->
UNSORTED VECTOR
        5          10         1          7          9          23         46         32
SORTED VECTOR
        1           5         7          9         10          23         32         46
```

Fig. 4-8 Merge sort (cont'd.)

N	INTEGER	Number of elements in vector K
I	INTEGER	Used as a subscript
J	INTEGER	Used as a subscript
T	INTEGER	Used as a subscript
R	INTEGER	Loop variable
PASS	INTEGER	Number of current pass
P	INTEGER	Subscript of the first element of first subvector
Q	INTEGER	Subscript of the first element of second subvector
S	INTEGER	Subscript of last element in subvector
LAST	INTEGER	Number of passes to be made
SIZE	INTEGER	Size of the current subvector
SUBPASS	INTEGER	Number of subpasses
S1	INTEGER	Loop variable

The vector to be sorted is read in, and the number of passes needed to sort the vector is calculated. The number of passes needed for a vector of 2^m elements is m. In order to calculate m, it is necessary to find the $\log_2$ of the number of elements. Since PASCAL does not have a built-in $\log_2$ function, $\log_2$ is calculated using the natural (or base e) logarithm as follows:

$$\log_2 n = \log_e n \ / \ \log_e 2$$

The function ROUND is then called to round the log value obtained to the nearest integer. The variable SIZE refers to the number of elements contained in a subvector during a particular pass. The variables P and Q contain the first elements of the subvectors to be merged on a particular subpass. The variable SUBPASS contains the number of subpasses to be performed during that pass. Each subpass consists of merging two subvectors and placing the result in vector C if PASS is odd, or in vector K if pass is even. Whether the pass is even or odd is determined by calling the function ODD which returns the value "true" if the value of its integer argument is odd. After each subpass is completed, the values of P and Q are updated, and the next subpass with the next two subvectors is performed until all subvectors within the vector have been processed. The next pass is then initiated, and this process continues until the entire vector has been sorted. If the number of passes required is odd, then the sorted vector C is recopied into vector K. Finally, the sorted vector K is printed.

This ends our discussion of vectors in PASCAL. In this section, some vector applications were introduced. In Sec. 4-2.1, two versions of the selection sort were presented. Searching was the topic of Sec. 4-2.2. Programs which illustrated linear and binary searches were given. Finally in Sec. 4-2.3, the process of merging and its use as a sorting technique were introduced.

Note that in PASCAL, as in most programming languages, a vector is simply a special case of a one-dimensional array. In the next section, arrays with more than one dimension are presented. The multidimensional array and its use with certain operations are discussed.

Exercises for Sec. 4-2

1. Given a vector X of n integer elements where n is odd, write a program to calculate the median of this vector. The median is the value such that half the numbers are greater than that value and half are less. For example, given the vector X

X_1	X_2	X_3	X_4	X_5	X_6	X_7	X_8	X_9
17	–3	21	2	9	–4	6	8	11

    containing nine elements, the execution of your program should give a value of 8.

2. Program MSORT given in this text only works if $n = 2^m$. Extend this program so it can handle any value of n.

3. A large firm has plants in five different cities. The firm employs a total of n employees. Each employee record contains (in part) the following fields:

1. Employee name
2. City
3. Employee number

These records are not kept in any order. Assume that the City field is coded with an integer value of 1 to 5. The information on the employees can be represented by three vectors: NAME, CITY, and NUMBER. Write a program which sorts all the employees records such that they are printed by increasing employee number within each city. That is, the format is as follows:

1st City

        name number
        name number
         .
         .
         .
        name number

2nd City

        name number
        name number
         .
         .
         .
        name number

     .
     .
     .

5th City

        name number
        name number
         .
         .
         .
        name number

4. Management information systems are becoming more common. They allow an administrator to type a request into a computer and obtain the answer to the request. In this problem, we will consider one such request; given the name of an employee, find the department in which the employee works. These requests come in the form of the keyword 'DEPARTMENT' followed by the name of the employee. The last of these requests has a keyword of 'FINISHED'.

    In order to respond to such requests, the following information is available. First there is a file of employee information. This file contains the employee's name and the name of his supervisor. This information is in alphabetical order by employee name, and the last record in the file has a sentinel employee name of 'ZZZZZ'.

The company has a large number of employees, the current number (which changes from time to time) is 134. Since the number of employees is large and the file is in alphabetical order by employee name, when seeking the record for a specific employee, a binary search should be used.

It is known that every supervisor is also the manager of some department. Thus in order to determine the department in which an employee works, we must determine the name of the department that the employee's supervisor manages. This information can be determined from a second file, the department file. This file contains the name of each department and the name of the manager of the department. This file is ordered by department name. Note there is always fewer than 50 departments.

Write a program to respond to this type of request. For your data, assume the department file comes first, preceded by a number specifying the number of records (departments) in the department file. The employee file comes next. Last come the requests for information.

4-3   ARRAYS

An array in PASCAL, like a vector, is an ordered set consisting of a fixed number of data elements. For a general array, however, more than one subscript must be used after the variable name to single out a particular element. To represent a two-dimensional table, for example, we require a subscripted variable having two subscripts, where, by convention, the first specifies the row number and the second the column number. Thus, if the array that represents the table is TOTALS, the TOTALS(2, 1) indicates the value in the second row and first column of the array. Note that the two subscripts are separated by a comma. If the table contained 5 rows and 3 columns, the array named TOTALS would require enough memory space to accommodate the 5 rows of values, with each row having 3 columns (that is, 15 memory locations must be reserved by the computer for that array).

Arrays such as the TOTALS array are examples of "two-dimensional" arrays —the rows constituting one dimension and the columns the second. For any two-dimensional array, two subscripts are always used with the array name to reference a particular element; thus the array reference has the form:

array-name (subscript$_1$, subscript$_2$)

where subscript$_1$ refers to the number of the row desired and subscript$_2$ to the number of the column. As mentioned, the vector structure is actually just an array with only a single dimension, and thus requires only 1 subscript. Generally, if an array structure contains "n" dimensions, then "n" subscripts must be used following the array name in order to select a particular element in the array. Arrays having more than two dimensions are mentioned later in this section.

PASCAL also allows an array element to be specified by having each subscript enclosed in brackets. Thus, array elements can also be referenced by:

array-name (subscript$_1$) (subscript$_2$)

As in one-dimensional arrays, (and for all arrays, for that matter), elements in a two-dimensional array must all be of the same type and the range of *each* subscript must be from some lower bound to some upper bound for that subscript. In fact, the rules for specifying both subscripts are identical to those given in Sec. 4-1 for a vector subscript. When arrays of two dimensions are used, the bounds on both subscripts must be declared, just as is required for vectors. For example, the TOTALS array described previously may be declared by the following:

```
VAR TOTALS: ARRAY(1..5, 1..3) OF INTEGERS;
```

or by

```
VAR TOTALS: ARRAY(1..5) OF ARRAY(1..3) OF INTEGER;
```

The declaration just given informs the compiler that the storage allocated for the array TOTALS must accommodate a table with 5 rows and 3 columns, with the successive rows numbered 1, 2, 3, 4, and 5 and the columns numbered 1, 2, and 3. Notice that the second form allows the array declarations to be broken up. This also allows the TOTALS array to be declared as

```
TYPE VECTOR: ARRAY(1..3) OF INTEGER;
VAR TOTALS: ARRAY(1..5) OF VECTOR;
```

If the programmer wishes the values in an array to be read in or printed out, subscripts must always be used with the array name with some form of looping construct to control when printing or reading. For example, in the program segment:

```
VAR NAMES: ARRAY(1..3, 1..4) OF STRING(20);
    VARB INTEGER;
BEGIN
        .
        .
        .
    WRITE(' ');
    FOR VARB := 1 TO 4 DO
        WRITE (NAMES(1, VARB));
    WRITELN
END.
```

only the array elements NAMES(1, 1), NAMES(1, 2), NAMES(1, 3), and NAMES(1, 4), that is, the four elements of the first row of the array NAMES, are printed, in that order.

To print out the entire NAMES array, for example, by columns, that is, such that the entries of the first column are printed, then the second column entries, and so on for all the columns, nested looping must be used, as follows:

```
VAR ROW, COL: INTEGER;
    NAMES: ARRAY(1..3, 1..4) OF STRING(20);
BEGIN
        .
        .
        .
```

```
FOR COL := 1 TO 4 DO
    FOR ROW := 1 TO 3 DO
        WRITELN (' ', NAMES(ROW, COL))
END.
```

Array elements may be assigned values through assignment statements, just as was discussed for vector elements. The assignment of a value to a single array element requires that both subscripts be used in the array reference to specify that element. For example, the following program segment

```
VAR TOTALS, ACCOUNT: ARRAY (1..5, 1..2) OF REAL;
BEGIN
        .
        .
        .
    TOTALS := ACCOUNT
```

assigns the values in ACCOUNT to the array TOTALS. In this form of assignment, it is important to note that the arrays on the left-hand and right-hand sides must have the same number of dimensions and identical bounds for each dimension. For example, if the declaration in the previous segment is changed to

```
VAR TOTALS: ARRAY(1..6, 1..2) OF REAL;
    ACCOUNT: ARRAY(1..5, 1..2) OF REAL;
```

then the subsequent assignment statement in the segment results in an error message. Note that the following declaration, when used in place of the preceding in the segment is also not acceptable:

```
VAR TOTALS: ARRAY(0..4, 1..2) OF REAL;
    ACCOUNT: ARRAY(1..5, 1..2) OF REAL;
```

Although both arrays contain two dimensions and both contain the same number of rows and columns, the bounds on the ranges of the row numbers differ, and therefore, the assignment statement cannot be performed. Note that assignments are not allowed unless the type descriptors match exactly. For example, given the declarations

```
MATRIX1: ARRAY(1..7, 1..3) OF INTEGER;
MATRIX2: ARRAY(1..7) OF ARRAY(1..3) OF INTEGER;
```

the assignment

```
MATRIX1 := MATRIX2;
```

is not allowed although the arrays are both of type integer and have the same bounds.

Assignment of array segments (or cross sections) is allowed to a limited extent. For example, if the two statements

VAR FIRST, LAST: ARRAY(1..3, 1..8) OF INTEGER;

and

FIRST(2) := LAST(3);

occur in a program, the second row of FIRST is assigned the values of the elements in the third row of LAST. Notice that this only applies to rows and not to columns since arrays are stored in row-major order. That is, PASCAL always stores array values row by row, not column by column. Thus the entries of the first row are followed by the entries of the second row, then the third, and so on, for all the rows in the array.

   Array references in PASCAL expressions can occur only for single elements in the arrays unless one array is being assigned to another. Thus while assignment of arrays is allowed, manipulating entire arrays in expressions is not. For example, if the arrays X, Y, and SUM have the same type descriptors, the statement

SUM := X;

is allowed, but

SUM := X + Y;

is not.

MULTI-DIMENSIONAL ARRAYS

   Until now, we have dealt mainly with one-dimensional arrays (or vectors) and two-dimensional arrays (often called matrices). PASCAL allows arrays to be defined with many dimensions. Basically the same rules apply to arrays with three or more dimensions as those discussed thus far for arrays of lower dimension. The storage order given for two-dimensional arrays may be generalized to apply to arrays of any dimension. That is, array entries are stored in consecutive storage locations in an order such that every subscript is taken through its entire range of values for *each* of the values of the range of the subscript on its immediate left. Arrays of dimension greater than, say, three, are usually avoided by programmers, since they are more difficult to visualize, and thus to manipulate.

   The program given in Fig. 4-9 illustrates one application of a three-dimensional array. This program is based on the algorithm given in Sec. 4-4 of the main text. In this problem a program is required to find the average condition of all known antique cars from a particular year. Information concerning all reported cars is to be stored in a three-dimensional array named CARS where the first subscript represents the manufacturer's code (an integer from 0 to 30), the second represents the year the car was built (from 1900 to 1950), and the third represents the car's condition (an integer from 1 to 4). Each element of the array contains the number of cars found that were built by the manufacturer in the year and in the condition given by the three subscripts. The variables used in this program are:

```
0  0000  00001  (* REPORT ON ANTIQUE CARS *)
0  0000  00002  PROGRAM CARREPORT (INPUT, OUTPUT);
0  0000  00003
0  0000  00004  VAR CARS: ARRAY(0..30, 1900..1950, 1..4) OF INTEGER;
0  0038  00005                                      (* ARRAY OF ANTIQUE CARS *)
0  0038  00006       YEAR,                           (* YEAR CAR WAS MADE *)
0  0038  00007       COUNT,                          (* NO OF CARS FOUND IN A CERTAIN YEAR *)
0  0038  00008       AVG_COND,                       (* AVERAGE CONDITION OF CARS *)
0  0038  00009       MAKE,                           (* MAKE OF CAR *)
0  0038  00010       COND,                           (* CONDITION OF CAR *)
0  0038  00011       NUM,                            (* NUMBER OF CARS OF A CERTAIN MAKE,
0  0038  00012                                          CONDITION, AND YEAR *)
0  0038  00013       I, J, K: INTEGER;               (* LOOP VARIABLES *)
0  0038  00014
0  0038  00015  BEGIN
0  0038  00016
0  0038  00017       (* INITIALIZE ARRAY *)
0  0038  00018       FOR I := 0 TO 30 DO
0  005C  00019           FOR J := 1900 TO 1950 DO
0  0080  00020               FOR K := 1 TO 4 DO
0  00A4  00021                   CARS(I, J, K) := 0;
0  0114  00022
0  0114  00023       (* READ DATA ON CARS *)
0  0114  00024       FOR I := 1 TO 10 DO
0  0138  00025       BEGIN
0  0138  00026           READ (MAKE, YEAR, COND);
0  016E  00027           CARS(MAKE, YEAR, COND) := CARS(MAKE, YEAR, COND) + 1
0  022E  00028       END;
0  023A  00029
0  023A  00030       (* READ REQUESTED YEAR *)
0  023A  00031       READ (YEAR);
0  024C  00032
0  024C  00033       (* INITIALIZE COUNTERS *)
0  024C  00034       COUNT := 0;
0  0252  00035       AVG_COND := 0;
0  0258  00036
0  0258  00037       (* PROCESS ALL MAKES OF CARS FOR THAT YEAR *)
0  0258  00038       FOR MAKE := 0 TO 30 DO
0  027C  00039           FOR COND := 1 TO 4 DO
0  02A0  00040               BEGIN
0  02A0  00041                   NUM := CARS(MAKE, YEAR, COND);
0  0306  00042                   IF NUM <> 0
0  0306  00043                   THEN BEGIN
0  0312  00044                       AVG_COND := AVG_COND + COND * NUM;
0  0326  00045                       COUNT := COUNT + NUM
0  0326  00046                       END
0  0332  00047               END;
0  033A  00048
0  033A  00049       (* OUTPUT COMPUTED STATISTICS *)
0  033A  00050       WRITELN (´ YEAR: ´, YEAR, ´      CARS RECORDED: ´, COUNT,
0  0382  00051                ´      AVERAGE CONDITION: ´, AVG_COND / COUNT)
0  03CE  00052  END.
----------------------------------
| COMPILE TIME:    0.125 SECOND(S) |
|     NO WARNING(S) DETECTED       |
|     NO ERROR(S) DETECTED         |
----------------------------------
--EXECUTION-->
YEAR:      1949    CARS RECORDED:         3    AVERAGE CONDITION:    2.000000E 00
```

Fig. 4-9 Car Report Program

Variable	Type	Usage
CARS	ARRAY(0..30, 1900..1950, 1..4) OF INTEGER	Number of cars of each make, year, and condition found
YEAR	INTEGER	Year car was made
COUNT	INTEGER	Number of cars found in a certain year
AVG_COND	FLOAT	Average condition of cars
MAKE	INTEGER	Make of car

COND	INTEGER	Condition of car
NUM	INTEGER	Number of cars of a certain year with a certain make and condition
I, J, K	INTEGER	Loop variables

The input values used in this run were:

3	1946	3
5	1949	1
20	1936	4
25	1948	2
16	1949	2
11	1905	1
30	1922	3
24	1901	2
26	1907	4
15	1949	3
1949		

Information concerning ten cars is read in and the appropriate elements of the array CARS are incremented. Once this is done, the year for which information is requested is read. The variables COUNT and AVG_COND are initialized to zero. Two counted loops are then used to calculate the weighted average of the cars' conditions. Finally, the requested year, the number of cars recorded for that year, and the average condition of the cars are printed.

This section has presented the concept of dimension, focusing on the array data structure of dimension two. Operations with two-dimensional arrays were discussed by expanding on those given for vectors. The capability of defining several dimensions in arrays greatly increases the scope of problems that may be solved with the subscripted variable. Section 4-4 illustrates some particular applications which require the use of arrays in order to program efficient solutions.

Exercises for Sec. 4-3

1. A matrix A of the form

$$\begin{pmatrix} a_{11} & a_{12} & \dots & a_{1m} \\ a_{21} & a_{22} & \dots & a_{2m} \\ \cdot & \cdot & & \cdot \\ \cdot & \cdot & & \cdot \\ \cdot & \cdot & & \cdot \\ a_{n1} & a_{n2} & \dots & a_{nm} \end{pmatrix}$$

is symmetric if

$$a_{ij} = a_{ji} \text{ for } 1 \leqslant i \leqslant n \text{ and } 1 \leqslant j \leqslant m.$$

Write a program which reads a matrix (never greater than 10 x 10) and determines whether or not it is symmetric. Assume that the elements of the matrix are integers. Test your program on the symmetric matrix

$$\begin{pmatrix} 1 & 4 & 7 \\ 4 & 2 & 9 \\ 7 & 9 & 3 \end{pmatrix}$$

2. Given the two matrices A and B where

$$A = \begin{pmatrix} a_{11} & a_{12} & \dots & a_{1m} \\ a_{21} & a_{22} & \dots & a_{2m} \\ . & . & & . \\ . & . & & . \\ . & . & & . \\ a_{n1} & a_{n2} & \dots & a_{nm} \end{pmatrix} \qquad B = \begin{pmatrix} b_{11} & b_{12} & \dots & b_{1r} \\ b_{21} & b_{22} & \dots & b_{2r} \\ . & . & & . \\ . & . & & . \\ . & . & & . \\ b_{m1} & b_{m2} & \dots & b_{mr} \end{pmatrix}$$

the *product* of A and B is given by

$$C = \begin{pmatrix} c_{11} & c_{12} & \dots & c_{1r} \\ c_{21} & c_{22} & \dots & c_{2r} \\ . & . & & . \\ . & . & & . \\ . & . & & . \\ c_{n1} & c_{n2} & \dots & c_{nr} \end{pmatrix}$$

where

$$c_{ij} = \sum_{k=1}^{m} a_{ik} * b_{kj}$$

For example, given

$$A = \begin{pmatrix} 1 & 2 & 3 \\ 4 & 5 & 6 \end{pmatrix} \quad \text{and } B = \begin{pmatrix} 1 & 4 \\ 2 & 5 \\ 3 & 6 \end{pmatrix}$$

the product is

$$C = \begin{pmatrix} 14 & 32 \\ 32 & 77 \end{pmatrix}$$

Using your program find the product of A and B where

$$A = \begin{pmatrix} 1 & 4 & 6 \\ 3 & 2 & 9 \\ 1 & 6 & 7 \end{pmatrix} \quad \text{and } B = \begin{pmatrix} 6 & 5 \\ 7 & 2 \\ 8 & 1 \end{pmatrix}$$

3. A study concerning the occurrence of traffic accidents is being conducted in Saskatoon. For convenience the city is divided into a grid as follows:

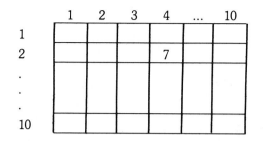

where the rows and column headings denote the streets and avenues, respectively, in the city. For example, 7 traffic accidents have occured at the intersection of 2nd Street and 4th Avenue. An unknown number of accident data are to be read in. Each accident gives the grid location of a traffic accident and takes the form of a pair of numbers. For example, the pair 2,4 describes the location of an accident at the intersection of 2nd Street and 4th Avenue. Formulate a program which reads in this information and counts the number of accidents at each intersection. Furthermore, produce a list of the 10 most dangerous intersections. Use an end-of-file test to determine the end of the data.

4. Using the three-dimensional array CARS described in this section, write a program to compute the following statistics:

    (i) The number of cars made before 1910 with condition rated good or excellent
    (ii) The most popular make of car, as judged by the number recorded
    (iii) The manufacturer whose cars appear to be in the best average condition.

    Test your program on the data used with the program CARREPORT.

4-4 APPLICATIONS OF VECTORS AND ARRAYS

This section presents PASCAL programs for the applications introduced in Sec. 4-5 of the main text.

4-4.1 Family Allowance Payments

The program which appears in Fig. 4-10 is a solution to the family allowance payments problem given in Sec. 4-5.1 of the main text. The problem is to calculate the monthly family allowance payment for the families in the kingdom of Fraziland. These monthly payments are based on the family's yearly income and on the number of children according to Table 4-1.

For each family, a card containing the yearly income of the family and the number of children in the family is prepared. Given this information, the program is to calculate and print the amount of payment. The following variables are used in this program:

Table 4-1   Schedule of Family Allowance Payments

Yearly Income	Number of Children						
	0	1	2	3	4	5	6 and up
less than $3000	0	17	19	20	22	24	25
$3000 - 3999	0	16	18	19	21	23	24
$4000 - 4999	0	15	17	18	20	22	23
$5000 - 5999	0	14	16	17	19	21	22
$6000 - 6999	0	13	15	16	18	20	21
$7000 - 7999	0	12	14	15	17	19	20
$8000 - 8999	0	11	13	14	16	18	19
$9000 - 9999	0	10	12	13	15	17	18
$10,000 and over	0	9	11	12	14	16	17

Variable	Type	Usage
SCHED	ARRAY(1..9, 1..6) OF INTEGER	Schedule of payments
INCOME	INTEGER	Family's income
CHILDREN	INTEGER	Number of children
R	INTEGER	Row subscript
C	INTEGER	Column subscript
I	INTEGER	Loop variable
J	INTEGER	Loop variable

The input values for this run were:

```
0     17    19    20    22    24    25
0     16    18    19    21    23    24
0     15    17    18    20    22    23
0     14    16    17    19    21    22
0     13    15    16    18    20    21
0     12    14    15    17    19    20
0     11    13    14    16    18    19
0     10    12    13    15    17    18
0      9    11    12    14    16    17
7600   3
3950   4
2500   0
12700  8
5634   7
9820   5
4000   6
13872  1
42561  1
2500   2
```

```
0   0000    00001  (* PROGRAM TO COMPUTE THE MONTHLY FAMILY ALLOWANCE PAYMENTS *)
0   0000    00002  PROGRAM BENEFIT (INPUT, OUTPUT);
0   0000    00003
0   0000    00004  VAR SCHED: ARRAY(1..9, 0..6) OF INTEGER;
0   0038    00005                               (* SCHEDULE OF PAYMENTS *)
0   0038    00006      INCOME,                  (* FAMILY'S INCOME *)
0   0038    00007      CHILDREN,                (* NUMBER OF CHILDREN *)
0   0038    00008      R,                       (* ROW SUBSCRIPT *)
0   0038    00009      C,                       (* COLUMN SUBSCRIPT *)
0   0038    00010      I, J: INTEGER;           (* LOOP VARIABLES *)
0   0038    00011
0   0038    00012  BEGIN
0   0038    00013
0   0038    00014      (* READ SCHEDULE OF FAMILY ALLOWANCE PAYMENTS *)
0   0038    00015      FOR I := 1 TO 9 DO
0   005C    00016          FOR J := 0 TO 6 DO
0   0080    00017              READ (SCHED(I, J));
0   00D8    00018
0   00D8    00019      (* PROCESS FAMILIES *)
0   00D8    00020      READ (INCOME, CHILDREN);
0   00FC    00021      WHILE NOT EOF DO
0   0104    00022      BEGIN
0   0104    00023          (* DETERMINE APPROPRIATE ROW SUBSCRIPT *)
0   0104    00024          IF INCOME < 3000
0   0104    00025          THEN R := 1
0   0110    00026          ELSE IF INCOME >= 10000
0   011C    00027              THEN R := 9
0   0128    00028              ELSE R := (INCOME - 1000) DIV 1000;
0   014A    00029
0   014A    00030          (* DETERMINE APPROPRIATE COLUMN SUBSCRIPT *)
0   014A    00031          IF CHILDREN >= 6
0   014A    00032          THEN C := 6
0   0156    00033          ELSE C := CHILDREN;
0   016A    00034
0   016A    00035          (* SELECT CORRECT PAYMENT *)
0   016A    00036          WRITELN (' PAYMENT IS ', SCHED(R, C));
0   01CE    00037
0   01CE    00038          (* READ DATA FOR NEXT FAMILY *)
0   01CE    00039          READ (INCOME, CHILDREN)
0   01F2    00040      END
0   01F2    00041  END.
-----------------------------------
| COMPILE TIME:    0.090 SECOND(S) |
|    NO WARNING(S) DETECTED        |
|    NO ERROR(S) DETECTED          |
-----------------------------------
--EXECUTION-->
PAYMENT IS        15
PAYMENT IS        21
PAYMENT IS         0
PAYMENT IS        17
PAYMENT IS        22
PAYMENT IS        17
PAYMENT IS        23
PAYMENT IS         9
PAYMENT IS         9
PAYMENT IS        19
```

Fig. 4-10   Program for family allowance payments problem

Lines 15 to 17 read in the schedule of family allowance payments. Line 21 begins a loop which handles the calculation and printing of payments for each of the families after reading the first family's income and number of children. Using this information, the appropriate row and column subscripts are obtained. In line 36, the payment for this particular family is printed. In line 39, information concerning the next family's income and number of children is read. Finally, when all the data have been read, the value of the function EOF becomes true, the loop is exited, and execution of the program is terminated.

4-4.2   Overweights Anonymous

The program given in Fig. 4-11 is based on the Overweights Anonymous problem given is Sec. 4-5.2 of the main text. In this problem fifteen members (rather than 50 as stated in the main text) of the Saskatoon branch of the Overweights Anonymous have been selected for a study of the effectiveness of the group's program. For each selected member a card has been prepared containing the subject's recorded weight (rounded to the nearest pound) for the last twelve months. Using this information the group wishes to determine the following:

1. The average weight change for all subjects over the entire 12 month period.
2. The number of subjects whose total weight exceeded the average.
3. The average monthly weight change per subject.
4. The number of instances during the year in which a subject lost more than the average monthly weight change during a single month.

The variables used in the program are:

Variable	Type	Usage
POUNDS	ARRAY(1..15, 1..12) OF INTEGER	Array for input data
Y_COUNT	INTEGER	Number exceeding yearly average loss
M_COUNT	INTEGER	Number of times monthly average loss is exceeded
TEMP	INTEGER	Temporary sum
SUBJECT	INTEGER	Loop variable
MONTH	INTEGER	Loop variable
PY_AVG	REAL	Average weight loss for the year
PM_AVG	REAL	Average weight loss for a month for one subject

In the program, lines 23 to 34 read the data values into the array POUNDS and simultaneously compute the running total of the subjects' weight losses for the year. Next, the average of the year's weight losses is computed. Another pass through the array elements is then performed in order to arrive at two figures; namely, the total number of subjects whose weight loss for the year exceeds the average (line 44) and the sum of the subjects' averages of their monthly weight losses (lines 47 to 49). The subjects' average for the latter is computed in line 50. The third pass through the array entries then occurs to count the number of times this average is surpassed.

4-4.3   The Global Hockey League

The program in Fig. 4-12 is a solution to the Global Hockey League problem given in Sec. 4-5.3 of the main text. In this problem a newly-formed hockey organization, the Global Hockey League, is developing a system for processing all league game results, using a computer. This involves recording wins and losses for all teams and the current point totals. Upon completion of each league game, the result is sent to the league headquarters, in the following format.

home-team's name   home-team's score   visiting-team's name   visiting-team's score

For example, the following is a sample result:

'BURMA'   5   'CHILE'   4

A team is given 2 points for every win, 1 point for every tie, and no points for a game lost. These point totals, along with separate totals for each team's number of wins, losses, ties, and games played are kept as running totals and are updated regularly, after an appropriate number of new game results are received at the headquarters. After each update the latest league standings are produced as a report in the following form:

TEAM   GAMES PLAYED   WINS   LOSSES   TIES   POINTS
$team_1$
$team_2$
.
.
.
$team_{12}$

The report lists the teams (there are currently 12), with their respective statistics, in decreasing order of points.

The headquarters desires a program to be written which first inputs the current league standings (the team's totals), and stores them appropriately. Next, it must input as data a batch of the latest game results received (punched one set of results to a card, in the same format as received). For each result card, it must update the current team totals for the teams involved. After having processed all the results input, the program must then print out a new standings report in the form just given. The variables used in this program are:

Variable	Type	Usage
STATS	ARRAY(1..12, 1..5) OF INTEGER	Array for teams' statistics
TEAMS	ARRAY(1..12) OF STRING(15)	Vector for teams' names
ROW	INTEGER	Loop variable
COLUMN	INTEGER	Loop variable
SCORE1	INTEGER	Team's score
SCORE2	INTEGER	Team's score
ROW1	INTEGER	Save position in array
ROW2	INTEGER	Save position in array
PASS	INTEGER	Loop variable in sort
TOP	INTEGER	Save subscript in sort
TEAM	INTEGER	Loop counter

```
0  0000   00001  (* FOR 15 SUBJECTS, COMPUTE THE REQUESTED TOTALS AND AVERAGES *)
0  0000   00002  PROGRAM WEIGHT (INPUT, OUTPUT);
0  0000   00003
0  0000   00004  VAR POUNDS: ARRAY(1..15, 1..12) OF INTEGER;
0  0038   00005                                  (* ARRAY FOR SUBJECTS' WEIGHTS *)
0  0038   00006      Y_COUNT,                     (* NUMBER EXCEEDING YEARLY AVERAGE LOSS *)
0  0038   00007      M_COUNT,                     (* NUMBER OF TIMES MONTHLY AVERAGE LOSS
0  0038   00008                                      COUNT EXCEEDED *)
0  0038   00009      SUBJECT, MONTH,              (* LOOP VARIABLES *)
0  0038   00010      TEMP: INTEGER;               (* TEMPORARY SUM *)
0  0038   00011      PY_AVG,                      (* AVERAGE LOSS FOR THE YEAR *)
0  0038   00012      PM_AVG: REAL;                (* AVERAGE LOSS FOR A MONTH FOR 1 SUBJECT*)
0  0038   00013
0  0038   00014  BEGIN
0  0038   00015
0  0038   00016      (* INITIALIZE *)
0  0038   00017      Y_COUNT := 0;  M_COUNT := 0;
0  0044   00018      PY_AVG := 0.0;  PM_AVG := 0.0;
0  0054   00019
0  0054   00020      (* INPUT THE DATA TABLE AND SUM THE WEIGHT LOSSES FOR THE YEAR FOR
0  0054   00021         ALL SUBJECTS *)
0  0054   00022      WRITELN (' SUBJECT WEIGHTS');
0  0066   00023      FOR SUBJECT := 1 TO 15 DO
0  008A   00024      BEGIN
0  008A   00025          WRITELN;
0  0098   00026          WRITELN;
0  00A6   00027          FOR MONTH := 1 TO 12 DO
0  00CA   00028          BEGIN
0  00CA   00029              READ (POUNDS(SUBJECT, MONTH));
0  011A   00030              WRITE (POUNDS(SUBJECT, MONTH))
0  016C   00031          END;
0  0170   00032          WRITELN;
0  017E   00033          PY_AVG := PY_AVG + POUNDS(SUBJECT, 1) - POUNDS(SUBJECT, 12)
0  01E2   00034      END;
0  01FC   00035
0  01FC   00036      (* COMPUTE PER SUBJECT YEARLY AVERAGE WEIGHT LOSS *)
0  01FC   00037      PY_AVG := PY_AVG / 15;
0  0208   00038      WRITELN (' PER SUBJECT, PER YEAR WEIGHT CHANGE IS ', PY_AVG);
0  022C   00039
0  022C   00040      (* COUNT NUMBER EXCEEDING THIS AVERAGE AND SUM THE AVERAGE MONTHLY
0  022C   00041         WEIGHT LOSSES OF ALL SUBJECTS *)
0  022C   00042      FOR SUBJECT := 1 TO 15 DO
0  0250   00043      BEGIN
0  0250   00044          IF POUNDS(SUBJECT, 1) - POUNDS(SUBJECT, 12) > PY_AVG
0  02A2   00045          THEN Y_COUNT := Y_COUNT + 1;
0  02C6   00046          TEMP := 0;
0  02CC   00047          FOR MONTH := 2 TO 12 DO
0  02F0   00048              TEMP := TEMP + POUNDS(SUBJECT, MONTH - 1) -
0  033E   00049                      POUNDS(SUBJECT, MONTH);
0  038C   00050          PM_AVG := PM_AVG + TEMP / 11.0
0  038C   00051      END;
0  03B0   00052      WRITELN ('   NUMBER OF SUBJECTS EXCEEDING THIS FIGURE IS ',
0  03C2   00053          Y_COUNT);
0  03D4   00054
0  03D4   00055      (* COMPUTE THE AVERAGE OF THE MONTHLY AVERAGES OF THE SUBJECTS *)
0  03D4   00056      PM_AVG := PM_AVG / 15;
0  03E0   00057      WRITELN (' PER SUBJECT, PER MONTH WEIGHT CHANGE IS ', PM_AVG);
0  0404   00058
0  0404   00059      (* COUNT THE NUMBER EXCEEDING THIS AVERAGE *)
0  0404   00060      FOR MONTH := 2 TO 12 DO
0  0428   00061          FOR SUBJECT := 1 TO 15 DO
0  044C   00062              IF POUNDS(SUBJECT, MONTH - 1) - POUNDS(SUBJECT, MONTH)
0  04DA   00063                  > PM_AVG
0  04DC   00064              THEN M_COUNT := M_COUNT + 1;
0  0500   00065      WRITELN ('   NUMBER OF TIMES THIS FIGURE EXCEEDED IS ', M_COUNT)
0  052C   00066  END.
```

Fig. 4-11 Program for Overweights Anonymous problem

TEMP	INTEGER	Save value when switching elements
TEAM1	STRING(15)	Team's name
TEAM2	STRING(15)	Team's name

```
--EXECUTION-->
SUBJECT WEIGHTS

    165     164     164     162     163     162     162     161     160     160
    155     155

    175     175     173     173     171     170     169     170     168     168
    164     165

    210     212     209     207     207     207     204     203     201     201
    201     200

    222     220     223     220     216     214     214     212     210     210
    208     205

    140     138     136     135     134     130     128     127     126     125
    126     125

    179     175     175     175     172     170     168     169     165     164
    163     162

    191     190     190     188     186     185     184     184     182     181
    180     172

    189     190     189     188     188     187     187     187     186     186
    183     182

    211     210     209     207     206     205     205     203     201     200
    199     194

    256     254     253     250     248     246     245     243     242     239
    236     230

    301     295     292     290     288     288     289     291     286     285
    284     280
    176     174     170     168     168     165     166     164     163     162
    160     158

    151     150     149     147     145     146     142     140     138     135
    133     132

    199     198     196     194     194     194     192     189     185     182
    182     180

    239     238     235     237     232     231     228     227     226     223
    221     221
PER SUBJECT, PER YEAR WEIGHT CHANGE IS       1.620000E 01
   NUMBER OF SUBJECTS EXCEEDING THIS FIGURE IS            10
PER SUBJECT, PER MONTH WEIGHT CHANGE IS       1.472724E 00
   NUMBER OF TIMES THIS FIGURE EXCEEDED IS            76
```

Fig. 4-11 Program for Overweights Anonymous problem (cont'd.)

The data used in this run consisted of the following values:

'BURMA'	14	8	2	4	20
'CHILE'	14	8	3	3	19
'HAMMOND'	14	7	3	4	18

```
0   0000   00001   (* UPDATE CURRENT TEAM STANDINGS USING NEW GAME RESULTS AND PRINT A
0   0000   00002          REPORT ON THE UPDATED LEAGUE STANDINGS. *)
0   0000   00003   PROGRAM HOCKEY (INPUT, OUTPUT);
0   0000   00004
0   0000   00005   VAR STATS: ARRAY(1..12, 1..5) OF INTEGER;
0   0038   00006                                  (* TEAM'S STATISTICS *)
0   0038   00007       ROW, COLUMN,               (* LOOP VARIABLES *)
0   0038   00008       SCORE1, SCORE2,            (* TEAMS' SCORES *)
0   0038   00009       ROW1, ROW2,                (* TO SAVE LOCATIONS IN ARRAY *)
0   0038   00010       PASS,                      (* LOOP VARIABLE IN SORT *)
0   0038   00011       TOP,                       (* TO SAVE SUBSCRIPT IN SORT *)
0   0038   00012       TEAM,                      (* LOOP COUNTER *)
0   0038   00013       TEMP: INTEGER;             (* SAVES VALUE WHEN SWITCHING ELEMENTS *)
0   0038   00014       TEAMS: ARRAY(1..12) OF STRING(15);
0   0038   00015                                  (* TEAMS' NAMES VECTOR *)
0   0038   00016       TEAM1, TEAM2: STRING(15);(* TEAM NAMES *)
0   0038   00017
0   0038   00018   BEGIN
0   0038   00019
0   0038   00020       (* INPUT THE CURRENT TOTALS *)
0   0038   00021       FOR ROW := 1 TO 12 DO
0   005C   00022       BEGIN
0   005C   00023           READ (TEAMS(ROW));
0   008E   00024           FOR COLUMN := 1 TO 5 DO
0   00B2   00025               READ (STATS(ROW, COLUMN))
0   0102   00026       END;
0   010A   00027
0   010A   00028       (* INPUT THE FIRST OF THE NEW GAME RESULT CARDS *)
0   010A   00029       READ (TEAM1, SCORE1, TEAM2, SCORE2);
0   0152   00030
0   0152   00031       (* BEGIN LOOP TO INPUT AND PROCESS NEW GAME RESULTS *)
0   0152   00032       WHILE NOT EOF DO
0   015A   00033       BEGIN
0   015A   00034
0   015A   00035           (* FIND POSITIONS OF THE 2 TEAMS NAMES IN THE VECTORS *)
0   015A   00036           FOR ROW := 1 TO 12 DO
0   017E   00037               IF TEAMS(ROW) = TEAM1
0   01A0   00038               THEN ROW1 := ROW
0   01AA   00039               ELSE IF TEAMS(ROW) = TEAM2
0   01D8   00040                   THEN ROW2 := ROW;
0   01EA   00041
0   01EA   00042           (* UPDATE THE GAMES PLAYED TOTALS FOR BOTH TEAMS *)
0   01EA   00043           STATS(ROW1, 1) := STATS(ROW1, 1) + 1;
0   023E   00044           STATS(ROW2, 1) := STATS(ROW2, 1) + 1;
0   028E   00045
0   028E   00046           (* DETERMINE GAME OUTCOME AND UPDATE TOTALS ACCORDINGLY *)
0   028E   00047           IF SCORE1 > SCORE2
0   028E   00048           THEN BEGIN
0   029A   00049               STATS(ROW1, 2) := STATS(ROW1, 2) + 1;
0   02F2   00050               STATS(ROW2, 3) := STATS(ROW2, 3) + 1
0   0342   00051           END
0   034A   00052           ELSE IF SCORE2 > SCORE1
0   034E   00053               THEN BEGIN
0   035A   00054                   STATS(ROW1, 3) := STATS(ROW1, 3) + 1;
0   03B2   00055                   STATS(ROW2, 2) := STATS(ROW2, 2) + 1
0   0402   00056               END
0   040A   00057               ELSE BEGIN
0   040E   00058                   STATS(ROW1, 4) := STATS(ROW1, 4) + 1;
0   0466   00059                   STATS(ROW2, 4) := STATS(ROW2, 4) + 1
0   04B6   00060               END;
0   04BE   00061
0   04BE   00062           (* READ NEXT GAME RESULT CARD *)
0   04BE   00063           READ (TEAM1, SCORE1, TEAM2, SCORE2)
0   0506   00064       END;
```

Fig. 4-12 Program for the Global Hockey League problem

'KENTUCKY'	14	8	4	2	18
'LABRADOR'	14	6	3	5	17
'LOUISIANA'	14	6	5	3	15
'MOBILE'	14	5	7	2	12
'PEKING'	14	4	8	2	10
'SCOTLAND'	14	2	11	1	5

```
0  050A  00065
0  050A  00066        (* COMPUTE UPDATED TOTALS *)
0  050A  00067        FOR ROW := 1 TO 12 DO
0  052E  00068            STATS (ROW, 5) := 2 * STATS(ROW, 2) + STATS(ROW, 4);
0  05BC  00069
0  05BC  00070        (* SORT BY DECREASING ORDER OF POINTS *)
0  05BC  00071        FOR PASS := 1 TO 11 DO
0  05E0  00072        BEGIN
0  05E0  00073            TOP := PASS;
0  05E8  00074
0  05E8  00075            (* FIND THE LARGEST OF THE UNSORTED ELEMENTS *)
0  05E8  00076            FOR ROW := TOP + 1 TO 12 DO
0  0612  00077                IF STATS(ROW, 5) > STATS(TOP, 5)
0  0666  00078                THEN TOP := ROW;
0  0674  00079
0  0674  00080            (* INTERCHANGE ROWS *)
0  0674  00081            IF PASS <> TOP
0  0678  00082            THEN BEGIN
0  0684  00083                FOR COLUMN := 1 TO 5 DO
0  06A8  00084                  BEGIN
0  06A8  00085                    TEMP := STATS(PASS, COLUMN);
0  06F0  00086                    STATS(PASS, COLUMN) := STATS(TOP, COLUMN);
0  0778  00087                    STATS(TOP, COLUMN) := TEMP
0  07B8  00088                  END;
0  07C4  00089                TEAM1 := TEAMS(PASS);
0  07EC  00090                TEAMS(PASS) := TEAMS(TOP);
0  0836  00091                TEAMS(TOP) := TEAM1
0  0858  00092                END
0  085E  00093        END;
0  0862  00094
0  0862  00095        (* PRINT HEADINGS FOR THE REPORT *)
0  0862  00096        WRITELN (' TEAM             GAMES PLAYED      WINS          ',
0  0874  00097          'LOSSES          TIES          POINTS');
0  0886  00098
0  0886  00099        (* PRINT NEW TOTALS *)
0  0886  00100        WRITELN;
0  0894  00101        FOR TEAM := 1 TO 12 DO
0  08B8  00102        BEGIN
0  08B8  00103            WRITE (' ', TEAMS(TEAM));
0  08FC  00104            FOR COLUMN := 1 TO 5 DO
0  0920  00105                WRITE (STATS(TEAM, COLUMN));
0  0976  00106        WRITELN
0  0976  00107        END
0  0984  00108  END.
```

```
-----------------------------------
| COMPILE TIME:    0.299 SECOND(S) |
|    NO WARNING(S) DETECTED        |
|    NO ERROR(S) DETECTED          |
-----------------------------------
--EXECUTION-->
```

TEAM	GAMES PLAYED	WINS	LOSSES	TIES	POINTS
TORONTO	16	13	3	0	26
BURMA	16	9	3	4	22
CHILE	16	8	3	5	21
VICHY	15	9	3	3	21
HAMMOND	15	8	3	4	20
KENTUCKY	14	8	4	2	18
LABRADOR	15	6	4	5	17
LOUISIANA	15	6	5	4	16
MOBILE	15	6	7	2	14
PEKING	16	5	8	3	13
TRAFALGAR	14	5	7	2	12
SCOTLAND	15	2	12	1	5

Fig. 4-12   Program for the Global Hockey League problem (cont'd.)

'TORONTO'	14	12	2	0	24
'TRAFALGAR'	14	5	7	2	12
'VICHY'	14	9	2	3	21
'BURMA'	5	'SCOTLAND'	3
'LOUISIANA'	2	'CHILE'	2
'VICHY'	1	'MOBILE'	6
'CHILE'	5	'PEKING'	5

'HAMMOND'	7	'TORONTO'	5
'TORONTO'	9	'LABRADOR'	0
'BURMA'	0	'PEKING'	1

Lines 21 to 26 serve to read in the current standings in the appropriate order. Next, a conditional loop is constructed to input the game result cards one at a time. For each game result, a search is made of the TEAMS vector to locate in it the respective input names (lines 36 through 40). The appropriate statistical totals are then updated by using nested IF...THEN... ELSE statements. When the input game results have all been processed, execution is passed to line 67, where the computation of the new point totals begins. Lines 71 to 93 perform the (selection) sort of the arrays. Finally, the report on the latest standings is output.

4-4.4   Computer Dating Service

The program which appears in Fig. 4-13 is a solution to the dating service problem given in Sec. 4-5.4 of the main text. In this problem, Universal Dating Inc., a nationwide dating service, requires a program that will choose the most compatable candidates for an applicant based on the ratings of some factors. Each factor is rated with a number between 1 and 7 according to the following code:

> 1 - intense dislike
> 2 - moderate dislike
> 3 - mild dislike
> 4 - neutral
> 5 - mild like
> 6 - moderate like
> 7 - intense like

The input data begins with a card containing the date, the number of candidates, and the number of factors surveyed. Then for each candidate a card containing the candidate's name, sex (1 for male, 2 for female), and the ratings of the factors by increasing factor number (i.e., the first rating is for factor 1, the second for factor 2, etc.) follows. These cards are followed by cards containing the name, sex, and factor ratings for applicants. The most compatible dates are chosen from the candidates for each of the applicants using the least squares method. That is, each of the factor ratings are compared and the squares of the differences between the factor ratings of an applicant and candidate are summed. The candidate (or candidates) with the least sum of squares are considered the most compatable. The program, therefore, is to select and print the most suited candidates for each applicant based on the previously stated criteria.

The variables used in this program are:

Variable	Type	Usage
N	INTEGER	Number of candidates
M	INTEGER	Number of factors
RATINGS	ARRAY(1..10, 1..10) OF INTEGER	Candidate's rating of factors
SEX	ARRAY(1..10) OF INTEGER	Candidate's sex

FACTOR	ARRAY(1..10) OF INTEGER	Applicant's rating of factors
A_SEX	INTEGER	Applicant's sex
STAT	ARRAY(1..10) OF INTEGER	Sum of squares statistics for the candidates
BEST	ARRAY(1..10) OF INTEGER	Candidates with smallest sum of squares statistics
ACCEPT	INTEGER	Number of candidates with least sum of squares
MIN	INTEGER	Least sum of squares
DATE	STRING(20)	Current date
APPLICANT_ID	STRING(20)	Applicant's name
NAME	ARRAY(1..10) OF STRING(20)	Candidates' names
I	INTEGER	Index variable
J	INTEGER	Index variable

The following input values were used in this run.

'MARCH 1, 1979'	5	3		
'MARY MATCH'	2	1	6	5
'TIM TALL'	1	2	4	5
'FRED FUN'	1	2	5	7
'GARY GALLANT'	1	1	6	7
'LINDA LOVE'	2	2	4	6
'BARBARA BEAUTY'	2	2	5	6
'JIM BLACK'	1	2	5	6

In line 28, the date, number of candidates, and number of factors are read into DATE, N, and M, respectively. Lines 31 through 36 serve to read the candidate profiles. In line 40, a loop to process each of the applicants is begun, after reading the first applicant's identification number, sex, and factor ratings. Lines 48 to 52 designate a loop which calculates the least squares statistic for each candidate of opposite sex to the applicant. The candidates (or candidate) of opposite sex to the applicant with the smallest least square statistic are then selected. Finally the date, applicant's name, and the names of the candidate who are best suited to the applicant are printed, and the next applicant is read.

This concludes the discussion of arrays. In Sec. 4-1 operations on vectors in PASCAL were introduced. Section 4-2 presented methods of sorting and searching vectors. In Sec. 4-3 arrays of more than one dimension were disscussed. Finally, in Sec. 4-4 programmed solutions to the applications discussed in Sec. 4-5 of the main text were given. In the next chapter operations and applications involving strings are considered.

EXERCISES FOR CHAPTER 4

1. It has been discovered by the leaders of two international espionage organizations (called CONTROL and KAOS) that a number of employees are on the payrolls of both groups! A secret meeting is to be held for loyal employees of CONTROL and KOAS (i.e., excluding those on both payrolls) to determine a suitable course of action to be taken against the "double agents".

```
0   0000   00001   (* GENERATE FROM THE CANDIDATES GIVEN THE ONE THAT IS MOST SUITED TO
0   0000   00002       AN APPLICANT´S PROFILE *)
0   0000   00003   PROGRAM DATING (INPUT, OUTPUT);
0   0000   00004
0   0000   00005   VAR N, M,                      (* NUMBER OF CANDIDATES AND FACTORS *)
0   0038   00006       I, J,                      (* INDEX VARIABLES *)
0   0038   00007       A_SEX,                     (* APPLICANT´S SEX *)
0   0038   00008       ACCEPT,                    (* NUMBER OF CANDIDATES WITH LEAST SUM OF
0   0038   00009                                      SQUARES *)
0   0038   00010       MIN: INTEGER;              (* LEAST SUM OF SQUARES *)
0   0038   00011       SEX,                       (* CANDIDATE´S SEX *)
0   0038   00012       FACTOR,                    (* APPLICANT´S RATINGS *)
0   0038   00013       STAT,                      (* SUM OF SQUARES STATISTICS FOR THE
0   0038   00014                                      CANDIDATES *)
.0  0038   00015       BEST: ARRAY(1..10) OF INTEGER;
0   0038   00016                                  (* CANDIDATES WITH SMALLEST SUM OF SQUARES
0   0038   00017                                      STATISTICS *)
0   0038   00018       RATINGS: ARRAY(1..10, 1..10) OF INTEGER;
0   0038   00019                                  (* CANDIDATES´ RATINGS *)
0   0038   00020       DATE,                      (* TODAY´S DATE *)
0   0038   00021       APPLICANT_ID: STRING(20);  (* APPLICANT´S NAME *)
0   0038   00022       NAME: ARRAY(1..10) OF STRING(20);
0   0038   00023                                  (* CANDIDATES´ NAMES *)
0   0038   00024
0   0038   00025   BEGIN
0   0038   00026
0   0038   00027       (* INPUT DATE, NUMBER OF CANDIDATES, AND NUMBER OF FACTORS *)
0   0038   00028       READ (DATE, N, M);
0   006E   00029
0   006E   00030       (* INPUT THE CANDIDATES´ PROFILES *)
0   006E   00031       FOR I := 1 TO N DO
0   0092   00032       BEGIN
0   0092   00033           READ (NAME(I), SEX(I));
0   00F6   00034           FOR J := 1 TO M DO
0   011A   00035               READ (RATINGS(I, J))
0   016A   00036       END;
0   0172   00037
0   0172   00038       (* PROCESS ALL APPLICANTS *)
0   0172   00039       READ (APPLICANT_ID, A_SEX);
0   0196   00040       WHILE NOT EOF DO
0   019E   00041       BEGIN
0   019E   00042           FOR J := 1 TO M DO
0   01C2   00043               READ (FACTOR(J));
0   01F8   00044
0   01F8   00045           (* COMPUTE THE CANDIDATE´S SUM OF SQUARES STATISTICS *)
0   01F8   00046           FOR I := 1 TO N DO
0   021C   00047               STAT(I) := 0;
0   0248   00048           FOR I := 1 TO N DO
0   026C   00049               IF A_SEX <> SEX(I)
0   0292   00050               THEN FOR J := 1 TO M DO
0   02BE   00051                           STAT(I) := STAT(I) + (RATINGS(I, J) -
0   034A   00052                               FACTOR(J)) * (RATINGS(I, J) - FACTOR(J));
0   03F0   00053
0   03F0   00054           (* DETERMINE THE MINIMUM SUM OF SQUARES STATISTIC *)
0   03F0   00055           I := 1;
0   03FC   00056           WHILE A_SEX = SEX(I) DO
0   042A   00057               I := I + 1;
0   043A   00058           MIN := STAT(I);
0   0464   00059           FOR J := 1 TO N DO
0   0488   00060               IF A_SEX <> SEX(J)
0   04AE   00061               THEN IF STAT(J) < MIN
0   04DC   00062                   THEN MIN := STAT(J);
0   050E   00063
0   050E   00064           (* SELECT THOSE CANDIDATES WITH SMALLEST STATISTIC *)
0   050E   00065           ACCEPT := 0;
0   0518   00066           FOR I := 1 TO N DO
0   053C   00067               IF A_SEX <> SEX(I)
0   0562   00068               THEN IF STAT(I) = MIN
0   0590   00069                   THEN BEGIN
0   0598   00070                       ACCEPT := ACCEPT + 1;
0   05A4   00071                       BEST(ACCEPT) := I
0   05C6   00072                       END;
0   05CE   00073
0   05CE   00074           (* OUTPUT THE DESIRED REPORT FOR THIS APPLICANT *)
0   05CE   00075           WRITELN;
0   05E0   00076           WRITELN (´ DATE IS ´, DATE);
0   0604   00077           WRITELN (´ APPLICANT´´S NAME IS: ´, APPLICANT_ID);
0   0628   00078           WRITELN (´ THE BEST MATCHED CANDIDATES ARE:´);
0   063A   00079           FOR I := 1 TO ACCEPT DO
0   065E   00080               WRITELN (´ ´, NAME(BEST(I)));
```

Fig. 4-13   Program for the Computer Dating Service problem

```
0  06CA   00081
0  06CA   00082                (* READ NEXT APPLICANT'S PROFILE *)
0  06CA   00083                READ (APPLICANT_ID, A_SEX)
0  06EE   00084       END
0  06EE   00085  END.
```
```
-----------------------------------
¦ COMPILE TIME:    0.216 SECOND(S) ¦
¦      NO WARNING(S) DETECTED      ¦
¦       NO ERROR(S) DETECTED       ¦
-----------------------------------
```
```
--EXECUTION-->

DATE IS MARCH 1, 1979
APPLICANT'S NAME IS: BARBARA BEAUTY
THE BEST MATCHED CANDIDATES ARE:
FRED FUN

DATE IS MARCH 1, 1979
APPLICANT'S NAME IS: JIM BLACK
THE BEST MATCHED CANDIDATES ARE:
LINDA LOVE
```

Fig. 4-13 Program for the Computer Dating Service problem (cont'd.)

Design a program which will accomplish the following task:
Read as input two alphabetically ordered list of names, one name per data card, the first list containing the names of agents on the CONTROL payroll and the second containing names of agents on the KAOS payroll. (Each of the two lists is followed by a card with the name 'ZZZZ'.) Then scan the two lists together and print in alphabetical order the names of those agents who should be invited to the proposed meeting (i.e., all those whose name appears on one list but not on both).

Example input:

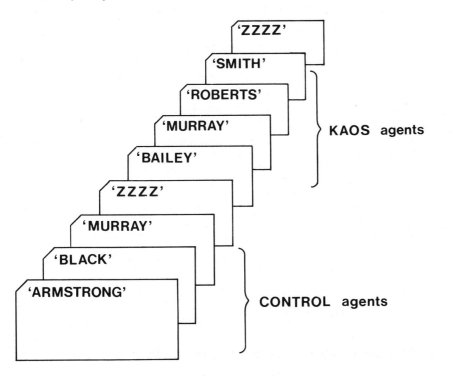

Corresponding Example Output:

ARMSTRONG
BAILEY
BLACK
ROBERTS
SMITH

2. At any school or university the task of drafting an exam timetable is both difficult and time consuming. An aid to the development of an exam timetable is a program which would "check out" all students against a tentative exam timetable and determine if any exam conflicts exist (an exam conflict means the student writes more than one exam at any one time). Input to the program consists of the tentative exam timetable and student records indicating the classes taken by each student. This input is punched on cards as follows:

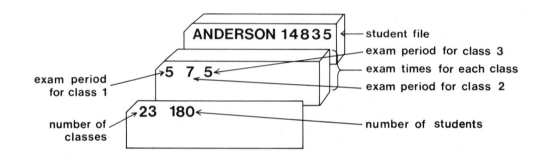

The first card contains two numbers — the number of classes and the number of students. The next set of cards indicates the exam period for each class with the first card indicating the exam periods for classes 1 to 10, the second card indicating the exam periods for classes 11 to 20, etc.

The final set of cards consists of the student's name and the number of classes the student takes. Each student always takes five classes. In the example illustrated, Anderson takes classes numbered 1, 4, 8, 3, and 5. Both classes 1 and 3 have been scheduled for exam period 5, therefore Anderson has an exam conflict. Your program must print the names of all students who have exam timetable conflicts.

3. Assume that the Saskatchewan Real Estate Board has conducted a survey of each of its licensees. Each licensee fills in a questionnaire of the following form:

Item	Answer Code
License type	1 = broker
	2 = salesperson
Residence town	840 towns coded from 1 to 840
Age	Age in years
Sex	1 = male
	2 = female

Education

                 1 = less than high school diploma
                 2 = high school diploma
                 3 = technical institute or community
                     college
                 4 = college degree

Write a program which analyzes these questionnaires. In particular, calculate the following for the group of respondents:

(a) Total number of respondents.
(b) Percentage brokers and percentage salespeople.

Calculate the following separately for brokers and salespersons:

(a) Number of respondents from each town.
(b) Average age
(c) Percentage male and percentage female
(d) Number of respondents in each educational classification.

The input data for each questionnaire consists of five questionnaire answer codes representing license type, residence town, age, sex, and education. Use an end-of-file test to determine the end of the data.

4. A profile of student attitudes towards a certain course is being determined by a method that requires each student in the course to assess the degree of his or her feelings of like or dislike towards certain factors. Each student is requested to rate each factor by associating a number with every factor, according to the following scale of values:

         1 - intense dislike   4 - neutral
         2 - moderate dislike   5 - mild like
         3 - mild dislike   6 - moderate like
                                7 - intense like

It is required to formulate a program which will perform a simple analysis of these data and produce a report giving:

(a) the average rating of each factor
(b) information on the students whose ratings are "closest" to the average ratings. More will be said about what is meant by "closest" shortly.

The input data is punched on cards and consists of one header card followed by a number of survey cards, one for each student surveyed. The header card contains 3 data items:

     - name of the course
     - the number of students surveyed
     - the number of factors surveyed

Each survey card contains a student's identification number and this student's ratings of the factors by increasing factor number. That is, the first rating is for factor 1, the second rating is for factor 2, and so on.

The sample input data

Course name	Number of students	Student number	Number of factors	Ratings for factors 1, 2, and 3, respectively		
'CMPT 180A'	5		3			
		10175		1	6	5
		12791		2	4	5
		99818		2	5	7
		38005		1	6	7
		27091		2	4	6

describes the ratings obtained on three factors from five students in course CMPT 180A.

As mentioned earlier, the program must produce the average rating for each factor in the course and output the student or students whose ratings are "closest" to the average ratings. The "closeness" is measured by the statistic S_j which is computed for the jth student from his or her ratings for the various factors and the average for each of these factors. The lower the S_j value for a student, the "closer" the student's ratings are to the averages. S_i is defined as follows:

$$S_i = \sqrt{\sum_{j=1}^{n}(r_{ij} - \bar{r}_j)^2}$$

where S_i is the "closeness" statistic for person i
   n is the number of factors surveyed
   r_{ij} is the ith student's rating of the jth factor
   $\bar{r}_j$ is the average rating of the jth factor

The output report is to consist of

(a) name of the course
(b) the "smallest" (i.e., the smallest S_j) statistic for the course
(c) the average rating for each factor
(d) for each of these "closest" students, the difference between each of their ratings and the corresponding averages
(e) the identification numbers of those students "closest" to the averages

A sample report of the previous data follows:

ATTITUDE REPORT FOR CMPT 180A
SMALLEST S: 1.077

FACTOR	AVERAGE VALUE
1	1.60

2	5.00
3	6.00

CLOSEST STUDENTS
STUDENT NUMBER 99818

FACTOR	DIFF. FROM AVG.
1	0.40
2	0.00
3	1.00

CLOSEST STUDENTS
STUDENT NUMBER 27091

FACTOR	DIFF. FROM AVG.
1	0.40
2	−1.00
3	0.00

5. The College of Arts and Science wishes to determine the age distribution of the faculty members in its various departments. In particular, they want to know for each department, how many faculty members are in each of the following categories:

```
< 20
20 - 29
30 - 39
40 - 49
50 - 59
> 59
```

The following data have been prepared for the program. The first card gives the number of departments in the College. This is followed by the names of the departments in alphabetical order. These names are in quotes. After all the department names comes the information on the individual faculty members. This information consists of the faculty member's name (in quotes), the name of the department in which the faculty member is located, and the faculty member's age. This information is in alphabetical order by the name of the faculty member. The following is a set of sample data:

```
33
'ANATOMY'
'ANTHROPOLOGY'
        .
        .
        .

'SOCIOLOGY'
'ABBOT'         'HISTORY'          37
'ACKERMAN'      'PSYCHOLOGY'       53
   .                .               .
   .                .               .
   .                .               .
'ZOOK'          'ART'              42
'END'           'DATA'             0
```

Give a program that will use this data to output the age distribution for each department.

Output from the program should have the following format:

DEPARTMENT	AGE CATEGORIES					
	< 20	20 - 29	30 - 39	40 - 49	50 - 59	> 59
ANATOMY	0	2	5	4	2	2
ANTHROPOLOGY	0	1	2	4	2	1
.			.			
.			.			
.			.			
SOCIOLOGY	0	4	5	6	4	1

CHAPTER

5

STRINGS AND THINGS

Although the concept of a string was introduced in Chap. 2, this chapter formally introduces the basic notions of string processing as they apply to the PASCAL language. The first section introduces an alternative to free-style input and output — formatted input and output. Section 5-2 deals with the concatenation of strings and rules that govern their comparison. Section 5-3 discusses several primitive string-handling functions. Finally, the chapter terminates with complete PASCAL programs for the applications developed in Chap. 5 of the main text.

5-1 FORMATTED INPUT AND OUTPUT

In Sec. 2-3 the READ, WRITE, and WRITELN statements were introduced. Though useful, these statements as presented have several disadvantages in that the programmer has little control over the format with which information may be read or printed. For example, suppose we wish to print a table of integers such that the first integer appears in column one, the second in column three, the third in column five, and so on. Without formatting the output, this desired output is not possible. Formatted input and output statements, however, provide us with this capability. These statements associate one or two format numbers with each item in the input or output list. For example, to print data items an output item can have one of the two forms.

    output-item

or

    output-item: w

The output item can be an expression including variables, literals, or constants. For input, the format is the same except that only variables can be used. Input and output data items were discussed in Chap. 2. w is an optional control that specifies the number of characters that the next input or output item takes in the input or output field. It must be an expression that evaluates to an integer.

When printing numeric values, w specifies the minimum field width, that is, the minimum number of characters to be used for printing the number. The number is always right-adjusted in this field and blanks are padded onto the left of the number to fill out the unused portion of the print field. For example, execution of the statement

    WRITELN (' ', 14: 7, 7.326: 5 * 2 + 3)

causes the output

    bbbbb14b7.326000E 00

Notice that if the field size is too small for the item being printed, the size of the field will be increased to a size that will allow the number to be printed. The following example illustrates this.

    WRITELN (' ', –7.9: 5, 14: 6, 123: 2)

Output

    b–7.9Eb00bbbb14123

The minimum field width for a real number is 9 and it has the form

    bsd.dEsyy

where b represents a blank,
      s represents the sign (– for negative, blank for positive)
      d represents the digits, and
      y represents the exponent digits.

Notice that a minimum of 2 digits must be printed plus a leading blank, two positions for signs and four positions for the exponent digits, decimal point and "E". All increases in the size of the field result in more digits after the decimal.
      Strings are right-justified in the field if the field is larger than the size of the string, and are truncated on the right if the field width is too small. For example,

      WRITELN (' HARMONY': 11, ' AND BLISS': 4)

will result in the output

      bbbbHARMONY AND

      Finally, logical values are always printed as T or F, right-adjusted in their field.
      For input, w specifies that the next w characters on the data card contain the input value. In the case of numbers (real or integer), they should be right-justified, as any blanks to the right of the number are considered to be zeros. Blanks may precede the number, but cannot appear within it. No characters other than digits, blanks, an optional sign, and an optional E for numbers written in exponential form may appear within this field. Any invalid characters will result in an error. Given the data card

      bb17bb14.3bb17.625E1

the statement

      READ(NUMBER: 4, CODE: 5, CODE2: 10)

assigns 17 to NUMBER, 14.3 to CODE1, and 17.625E1 to CODE2. On the other hand, the statement

      READ (NUMBER: 6. CODE1: 4, CODE2: 8, RESULT: 2)

would assign 1700 to NUMBER, 14.3 to CODE1, and 17.625 to CODE2. Since E1 alone is not a valid real number, an error would result when attempting to read a value into RESULT.
      When reading strings and single characters, no quotes are given around the string, as the field width indicates what characters on the data card contain the string. For example, if a data card contained

      bb'RYAN''S FANCY'bb14

where the variable NAME is declared to be of type STRING(20) and NUM is an integer variable, after executing the READ statement

READ (NAME: 17, NUM: 3)

NAME would contain bb′RYAN″SbFANCY′bbb, and not RYAN′SbFANCYbbbbbbbb. NUM would have the value 1 and not 14.

When reading logical values, the field is scanned from left to right until the first T or F is found, in which case the associated variable is assigned TRUE or FALSE, respectively. If no T or F is found within the field, an error results. It should be noted that standard PASCAL does not allow logical values to be read.

One other form is allowed in input or output statements and it can only be associated with real variables, constants, or expressions. It has the form

output-item: w: d

where w behaves as described and d indicates the number of digits to the right of the decimal point using a fixed decimal format. That is, for an input statement, only d digits to the right of the decimal point are printed, the last one being rounded if necessary. All digits to the left of the decimal point are printed and the number is always preceded by a blank and one character position which is a blank if the number is positive or is a minus sign if the number is negative. Thus, the minimum field width is 4 and it appears as

bsd.

As an example, the statement

WRITELN (′ ′, –7.623E01: 11: 5, 14.23678: 7: 2)

causes the output

bb–76.23000bb14.24

On input, the number should be right-adjusted in its field but it can either be in fixed-point format or in exponent format. The decimal point is assumed to be d digits from the right of the field for fixed-point format: for numbers with an exponent the decimal point is assumed to be d digits to the left of E. Note that the d specification is ignored if a decimal point already appears in the number. As an example, assume that a data card contains the following:

123.456b1234567654321E01bb765.4321E01

The statement

READ (A1: 7: 4, A2: 7: 4, B1: 10: 3, B2: 13: 2)

would result in A1, A2, B1, and B2 receiving the values 123.456, 12.3456, 7654.321E01, and 765.4321E01, respectively. Since decimal points are present in the numbers for A1 and B2, the d specification is ignored in these cases.

Formatted items can be mixed with nonformatted items within the same input and output statement. For example, the statement

WRITELN (′ ′, 17: 3, 17 * 16: 8, 13.0, ′ALOHA′: 6, ′bHAWAII′)

can be used. The first item, 17, is formatted, as is the second, 17 * 16; these are printed in field widths of 3 and 8, respectively. The next number, 13.0, is printed unformatted, that is, with a field width of 18. The literal 'ALOHA' is printed formatted in a field width of 6. The last literal, 'bHAWAII', is unformatted and is printed in a field of 8 characters. This results in the output

b17bbbbb172bbbbbb1.300000Eb01bALOHAbHAWAII

Note that no blanks are inserted before or after an output item. The same output can be achieved with the statement

READ (' ', 17: 3, 17 * 16: 8, 13.0: 14, 'ALOHA': 6, 'bHAWAII': 7)

Often it may be necessary to skip over columns in input or output. For output, this can be achieved with the formatted output literal

' ': x

where x contains the number of blanks to be skipped. For example, the statement

WRITELN (' ': 10, 'START')

prints START starting in printer column 10. Notice that while 10 blanks precede START, one of them is used as a carriage control so that only 9 blanks are printed before START. On input, it is necessary to use a "dummy" variable which is assigned the value of the characters to be skipped on the data card, that is, a variable for which we are not concerned about the value it has. For example, if we wish to start reading a data card in column 12, the READ statement would appear as

READ (DUMMY: 11, ...)

where DUMMY is a string or character variable. Its length is not important, nor is the value it receives.

PASCAL also includes another input statement, which is used in the same manner as the READ statement. READLN after reading a data card causes the next READ or READLN statement to begin reading the *next* data card. Thus, any remaining data on the current data card are omitted. This statement is sometimes useful, for example, when reading formatted strings.

This section has introduced several concepts concerning formatted input and output. The WRITE, WRITELN, READ, and READLN statements can be used to format output and in the reading of formatted data. In the next section string-handling operations are presented. The input and output of these strings use some of the concepts presented in this section.

Exercises for Sec. 5-1

1. Give the results of the following output statements:

    (i)   WRITELN (' ABBOTT AND COSTELLO': 9)
    (ii) WRITELN (' ', 56.78: 5: 1)

   (iii)   WRITELN ('−', 65.33: 11)
   (iv)   WRITELN (' THE': 4, 'LAST': 5)
   (v)   WRITELN (' COME': 3, 'HERE': 6)
   (vi)   WRITELN (' ', 7777.: 12)
   (vii)   WRITELN ('+', 7777.: 5: 1)
   (viii)   WRITELN ('−', 7777: 6)
   (ix)   WRITELN (' ', 14: 2, 24.: 1: 1, 36.6: 5:1)

2. Write a formatted READ statement that will read the following information:

   (i) A five-digit integer in columns 5 through 10
   (ii) A string in columns 13 through 19
   (iii) A real number in columns 20 through 30

3. Given a card containing the following information

Card column	1	2	3	4	5	6	7	8
Values	1	1	7	8	5	6	7	9

what would the values of MARK, SUM and AVERAGE be after each of the following input statements:

   (i)   READ (MARK: 2, SUM: 2, AVERAGE: 2)
   (ii)   READ (MARK: 3: 1, SUM: 2: 1, AVERAGE: 4: 0)
   (iii)   READ (MARK: 4: 2, SUM: 3: 1, AVERAGE)

4. Write a program which reads in a 4 x 4 array column by column and prints the array row by row.
    For example,

Input	1	2	3	4
	5	6	7	8
	9	10	11	12
	13	14	15	16
Output	1	5	9	13
	2	6	10	14
	3	7	11	15
	4	8	12	16

5-2 STRING CONCEPTS AND TERMINOLOGY

The definition of a string constant was given in Sec. 2-1.1. Unfortunately, PASCAL does not support the processing of character strings of variable length. In this section, we will introduce a method that will allow us to process such character strings. This will involve using a vector of single character elements.

Because PASCAL does not allow variable-length strings, they must be simulated. Whenever such strings are required, as is the case in many of the string-processing applications discussed in the main text, we will use a delimiter to signal the end of the string. The delimiter we have chosen is the pair of characters '*/'. Should the programmer expect this sequence to appear within a string, it is possible to use a different delimiter to mark the end of the string. No delimiter is required if the strings are to be used strictly for comparison, reading, or writing. When string processing does occur, the delimiter is often included on the data card, or in a literal or constant.

Because the strings in PASCAL are of a fixed length, there may in fact be characters after the first '*/' of the value of a string variable which are considered to be undefined. Those characters preceding the '*/' are considered to constitute the string. As mentioned in Chap. 2, the maximum length of a string variable is 256 characters. To allow variable strings to be as long as possible, it will be necessary for the programmer to define all string variables to be STRING(256) if they are to be used by the string-handling subprograms introduced in this section. For example, a declaration might be

EXAMPLE: STRING(256);

and the assignment

STRING := 'THIS IS A STRING OF 33 CHARACTERS*/'

Since the character sequence '*/' requires two characters, the maximum length of the actual string (not including the delimiter) is 254 characters.

Another solution to the problem of handling variable-length strings is to store the lengths of the strings in separate variables and to use these variables in conjunction with the strings. Using a delimiter to mark the end of a string may be less efficient, but the methods of handling the strings are then similar to those of the main text. With more sophisticated storage management techniques, the efficiency of string handling can be improved, but this requires a better understanding of data and storage structures. These structures are introduced in Chaps. 10 and 11.

Although PASCAL does not allow the processing of character strings, a vector of single character elements can be processed, because it is possible to access the individual characters within the string. PASCAL allows vectors of characters to be used in most cases where string variables would be used. For example, input and output of entire vectors of strings can be done by specifying the vector name in the output or input statement, as is done for string variables, and omitting the subscripts. In the case of a character vector, quotes are used to delimit the string, unlike single character variables. Furthermore, character vectors and string variables can be compared, or one type assigned to the other. That is, if we have declarations

STRING1: STRING(10);
STRING2: ARRAY (1..15) OF CHAR;

then a statement such as

STRING1 := STRING2

is allowed, although the lengths of the variables are not the same.

Our discussion on the compatibility of STRING variables with a vector of CHARACTER elements implies that the declaration STRING(n) is equivalent to ARRAY(1..n) OF CHAR, but this is not always the case, as we shall see.

STRING-HANDLING FUNCTIONS FOR PASCAL

As we have stated earlier, there are no primitive string-handling functions such as concatenation in PASCAL. By using vectors of CHAR elements, however, we can write program segments that will perform these operations. A problem occurs at this point. Every time we wish to perform an operation on a string in a program, we will have to write a program segment to perform this operation. Recall that a built-in function performs an operation, such as the TRUNC function, which gives the truncated value of the number that it is given. Such functions may be several statements long, and it would become tedious for the programmer to include these statements wherever the function is required. The string-handling operations require program segments that are much longer, and in a program requiring several operations, the program could become extremely large if this operation were not included in a subprogram. Therefore, we will imitate the built-in functions by developing our own *subprograms*. These subprograms will be used in a similar fashion to the built-in functions we have seen. By doing this, a program to perform an operation will need to be given only once in a program.

While it should be obvious to you that this can greatly reduce the length of a program and improve its readability, we will defer the explanation of how these programs actually work until Chap. 6. At this point, it will suffice to know that they work somewhat like the built-in functions, although some will be invoked in a slightly different manner.

Concatenation

In the main text, concatenation is denoted by the symbol "o." Since there is no concatenation operator in PASCAL, the procedure CONCAT will be used instead. This procedure, which is shown in Fig. 5-1, requires three arguments. Its method of use is quite similar to that of built-in functions.

In the procedure CONCAT, the second string (STR2) is concatenated to the end of the first string (STR1) and then the resulting string is returned through the third parameter (ANSWER). Algorithmically, this effect can be denoted as

ANSWER ← STR1 o STR2

The arguments STR1 and STR2 must each end with the delimiter '*/'. The three arguments must be defined as STRING(256).

When calling this procedure, only the statement

CONCAT (*string*$_1$, *string*$_2$, *result-string*)

should be used. It is not necessary to have *result-string* initialized before calling the procedure; after execution of the procedure it will have the value of *string*$_1$ o *string*$_2$. Therefore, the concatenation of two strings A and B is specified by the statement

CONCAT (A, B, C)

```
0  0000   00001  PROCEDURE CONCAT (VAR S1, S2, RESULT: STRING(256));
1  0000   00002  (* THIS SUBROUTINE PERFORMS THE OPERATION
1  0000   00003            ANSWER := STR1 O STR2        *)
1  0000   00004  VAR I, J: INTEGER;        (* INDEX VARIABLES *)
1  0060   00005      STR1, STR2, ANSWER: ARRAY(1..256) OF CHAR;
1  0070   00006                          (* VECTORS FOR ACCESSING SINGLE CHARACTERS *)
1  0070   00007
1  0070   00008  BEGIN
1  0070   00009
1  0070   00010      (* SET FIRST STRING EXCEPT DELIMITER TO RESULT STRING *)
1  0070   00011      ANSWER := ' ';
1  009A   00012      STR1 := S1;
1  00A4   00013      STR2 := S2;
1  00AE   00014      I := 1;
1  00B6   00015      WHILE ((STR1(I) <> '*') OR (STR1(I + 1) <> '/')) AND (I < 255) DO
1  0118   00016      BEGIN
1  0118   00017          ANSWER(I) := STR1(I);
1  015A   00018          I := I + 1
1  015A   00019      END;
1  016A   00020
1  016A   00021      (* CHECK IF NO DELIMITERS ON STRING *)
1  016A   00022      IF (I = 255) AND (STR1(255) <> '*') AND (STR1(256) <> '/')
1  019A   00023      THEN BEGIN
1  019A   00024          WRITELN;
1  01A8   00025          WRITELN (' ERROR - MISSING DELIMITER ON FIRST ARGUMENT.');
1  01BA   00026          WRITELN (' DELIMITER ADDED; LENGTH OF FIRST STRING IS 254.');
1  01CC   00027          STR1(255) := '*';
1  01DA   00028          STR1(256) := '/';
1  01E8   00029          I := 255
1  01E8   00030          END;
1  01F0   00031
1  01F0   00032      (* ADD SECOND STRING UNLESS RESULT STRING BECOMES TOO LARGE *)
1  01F0   00033      J := 1;
1  01F8   00034      WHILE ((STR2(J) <> '*') OR (STR2(J + 1) <> '/')) AND (I < 256) DO
1  025A   00035      BEGIN
1  025A   00036          ANSWER(I) := STR2(J);
1  029C   00037          I := I + 1;
1  02A8   00038          J := J + 1
1  02A8   00039      END;
1  02B8   00040
1  02B8   00041      (* ADD DELIMITER TO END OF STRING AND CHECK FOR OVERFLOW *)
1  02B8   00042      IF I >= 256
1  02B8   00043      THEN BEGIN
1  02C4   00044          ANSWER(255) := '*';
1  02D2   00045          ANSWER(256) := '/';
1  02E0   00046          WRITELN;
1  02EE   00047          WRITELN (' ERROR - CONCATENATION RESULTS IN TOO LONG CHARA',
1  0300   00048              'CTER STRING.  STRING TRUNCATED TO LENGTH 254.')
1  0312   00049          END
1  0312   00050      ELSE BEGIN
1  0316   00051          ANSWER(I) := '*';
1  033A   00052          ANSWER(I + 1) := '/'
1  035E   00053          END;
1  0364   00054
1  0364   00055      (* FINISHED, RETURN RESULT *)
1  0364   00056      RESULT := ANSWER;
1  036E   00057      S1 := STR1;
1  0378   00058      S2 := STR2
1  0378   00059  END;
```

Fig. 5-1   Procedure to concatenate two strings

The result of evaluating this statement is the string A o B, which is stored in the variable C. Because of the limitations of the PASCAL language, this is not as general a facility as one would like. For instance, the arguments of the procedure CONCAT cannot be string constants. For example, the program segment

    A = 'COMPUTERb*/';
    CONCAT (A, 'SCIENCE*/', B)

is invalid because the second argument of CONCAT is a string constant.

String Comparisons

In earlier chapters, the notion of testing strings for equality (or inequality) was introduced. The relational operators in PASCAL were given in Table 3-1. The comparison feature for "=" and "≠" can be expanded to include the other four relational operators. The basis of this comparison is the collating sequence of a character set. The collating sequence of the PASCAL character set on the IBM 360/370 is defined to be

b.(<+|&!$*);–/,%_>?:#@'=ABCDEFGHIJKLMNOPQRSTUVWXYZ0123456789

for the English alphabet, digits, and special characters. Note that b represents the blank character, which is valued less than any other character.

When two strings having an unequal number of characters are compared, only the characters up to the length of the shorter string are compared. This holds for string variables and arrays of characters. Some compilers issue warning messages if strings of unequal length are compared. For example, in comparing the strings 'JOE' and 'JOHN', JOE, the shorter string, has three characters. Thus, only the first three characters (i.e., JOH) are compared with JOE on a character-by-character basis in a left-to-right scan. In the current example the condition

'JOE' = 'JOHN'

is false, However, the condition

'JOE' < 'JOHN'

is true since 'E' lexically precedes 'H'. Also notice that the following condition is true.

'JOE' = 'JOEY'

Other examples of conditions involving strings are given in the following:

'BILL' = 'BILLY'	true
'BILLb' < 'BILLY'	true
'BOB' <= 'ALAN'	false
'TREMBLAY' > 'BUNT'	true
'AND' = 'ANDb'	true

The comparison of characters strings is very important in the sorting of string data. Such a sorting operation is required in many data processing and string manipulation applications. As an example, the following program performs a selection sort on a set of names. In the program, variable-length strings are not used since no processing of the strings is required.

```
PROGRAM SORT (INPUT, OUTPUT);
( * PROGRAM TO SORT A SET OF NAMES * )
VAR NAME(100), TEMP: STRING(20);
     PASS, MIN_INDEX, I, N: INTEGER;
```

```
BEGIN
      ( * READ NAMES * )
      READ (N);
      FOR I:= 1 TO N DO
            READ (NAME(I));
      ( * PERFORM SELECTION SORT * )
      MIN_INDEX := PASS;
      FOR PASS := 1 TO N – 1 DO
      BEGIN
            FOR I := PASS + 1 TO N DO
                  IF NAME(I) < NAME(MIN_INDEX))
                  THEN MIN_INDEX := I;
            IF MIN_INDEX <> PASS
            THEN BEGIN
                  TEMP := NAME(PASS);
                  NAME(PASS) := NAME(MIN_INDEX);
                  NAME(MIN_INDEX) := TEMP
                  END
      END;
      ( * PRINT SORTED LIST * )
      FOR I := 1 TO N DO
            WRITELN (' ', NAME(I))
END.
```

So far, the only string operation we have introduced is concatenation. Clearly, if we are going to write string manipulation programs, a greater variety of operators is required. Some of these operators are introduced in the next section.

5-3 BASIC STRING OPERATIONS

The notions of string manipulation discussed in the previous section involved the concatenation and the comparison of two strings. Other operations required by a string manipulation system include the following:

1) Obtain the length of a string.
2) Extract a portion (i.e., a substring) of a string.
3) Search and replace (if necessary) a given substring within a string.

As we mentioned in Sec. 5-2, there are no primitive string-handling functions in PASCAL. Therefore, to handle the operations just mentioned, we will again give subprograms to perform these operations. As with procedure CONCAT, these subprograms will be user-defined functions and procedures that will be invoked in a similar manner to procedure CONCAT. The programming aspects of these operations in PASCAL are discussed in this section.

Length of a String

For computing the length of a string in PASCAL, we will use the user-defined function LENGTH which is shown in Fig. 5-2. This function is invoked in exactly the

```
0   0000   00001   FUNCTION LENGTH (VAR STR: STRING(256)): INTEGER;
1   0000   00002   (* THIS FUNCTION COMPUTES THE LENGTH OF THE GIVEN STRING *)
1   0000   00003
1   0000   00004   VAR I: INTEGER;              (* INDEX VARIABLE *)
1   004C   00005       VECTOR: ARRAY(1..256) OF CHAR;
1   005C   00006
1   005C   00007   BEGIN
1   005C   00008
1   005C   00009       (* COMPUTE THE LENGTH OF THE STRING *)
1   005C   00010       VECTOR := STR;
1   0076   00011       I := 1;
1   007E   00012       WHILE ((VECTOR(I) <> '*') OR (VECTOR(I + 1) <> '/')) AND
1   00D4   00013           (I < 255) DO
1   00E0   00014               I := I + 1;
1   00F0   00015
1   00F0   00016       (* CHECK FOR NO DELIMITERS ON STRING *)
1   00F0   00017       IF (I = 255) AND (VECTOR(255) <> '*') AND (VECTOR(256) <> '/')
1   0120   00018       THEN BEGIN
1   0120   00019               WRITELN;
1   012E   00020               WRITELN (' ERROR - DELIMITER MISSING ON ARGUMENT STRING.');
1   0140   00021               WRITELN (' DELIMITER ADDED; LENGTH OF STRING IS 254.');
1   0152   00022               VECTOR(255) := '*';
1   0160   00023               VECTOR(256) := '/';
1   016E   00024               LENGTH := 254
1   016E   00025               END
1   0176   00026       ELSE (* RETURN LENGTH OF STRING *)
1   0176   00027               LENGTH := I - 1;
1   0186   00028       STR := VECTOR
1   0186   00029   END;
```

Fig. 5-2　Function to compute the length of a string

same way as any built-in function, that is, to call this function, the programmer uses

LENGTH *(string-variable)*

Given any string-variable, this function will return the length of the string (excluding delimiting characters) as an integer. The length of the empty or null string (i.e., '*/') is defined to be zero.

To demonstrate the use of this function, the program segment

A = 'COMPUTER SCIENCE*/';
B = LENGTH(A)

gives B a value of 16. Since the result of invoking this function is numeric, it can be used in arithmetic computations. For example, the expression

LENGTH(NAME1) + LENGTH(NAME2)

where NAME1 and NAME2 have the values 'OPSETH*/' and 'HAMILTON*/', respectively, yields a value of 14. Once again, string constants are not allowed as arguments to this function. Therefore,

LENGTH('OOPS*/')

will result in an error.

Substring Extraction

The task of extracting a particular substring from a given string is accomplished in PASCAL by using a programmer-defined procedure such as procedure SUB which is shown in Fig. 5-3. This procedure is very similar to the function SUB of the main text, except that the resulting substring is returned through a fourth parameter. In this manner, its use is the same as procedure CONCAT which was introduced in the previous section. Invoking procedure SUB is done by the following statement

SUB(*string-variable, initial-position, length, result-string*)

where

string-variable is a variable name that gives a string
from which a substring is desired
initial-position is the character position in the original string
at which the substring begins

```
0 0000  00001  PROCEDURE SUB (VAR S: STRING(256); POS, NUM: INTEGER; VAR RESULT:
1 0000  00002      STRING(256));
1 0000  00003  (* THIS PROCEDURE TAKES THE SUBSTRING OF STRING S, STARTING AT POSITION
1 0000  00004     POS FOR NUM CHARACTERS AND RETURNS IT THROUGH THE PARAMETER RESULT.*)
1 0000  00005
1 0000  00006  VAR STR, RSLT: ARRAY(1..256) OF CHAR;
1 007E  00007                              (* STRING AND RESULTING SUBSTRING *)
1 007E  00008     LNTH: INTEGER;           (* LENGTH OF STRING *)
1 007E  00009     J, K, L, M: INTEGER;     (* INDEX VARIABLES *)
1 007E  00010  FUNCTION LENGTH (VAR STR: STRING(256)): INTEGER; EXTERNAL;
1 0096  00011
1 0096  00012  BEGIN
1 0096  00013
1 0096  00014      (* CHECK IF VALUE OF POS OR NUM IS OUT OF BOUNDS *)
1 0096  00015      STR := S;
1 00A0  00016      RSLT := ' ';
1 00AA  00017      LNTH := LENGTH (S);
1 00CC  00018      IF (POS <= 0) OR (NUM <= 0) OR (POS > LNTH)
1 00F0  00019      THEN RESULT := '*/'
1 00F0  00020      ELSE BEGIN
1 00FA  00021
1 00FA  00022          (* IF NUM GOES BEYOND END OF SUBSTRING, RESET *)
1 00FA  00023          IF POS + NUM > LNTH + 1
1 0102  00024          THEN M := LNTH - POS + 1
1 0118  00025          ELSE M := NUM;
1 012C  00026
1 012C  00027          (* OBTAIN THE SUBSTRING *)
1 012C  00028          J := POS;
1 0134  00029          FOR L := 1 TO M DO
1 0158  00030          BEGIN
1 0158  00031              RSLT(L) := STR(J);
1 019A  00032              J := J + 1
1 019A  00033          END;
1 01AA  00034
1 01AA  00035          (* ADD DELIMITER AND RETURN STRING *)
1 01AA  00036          RSLT(M + 1) := '*';
1 01D4  00037          RSLT(M + 2) := '/';
1 01FE  00038          RESULT := RSLT
1 01FE  00039      END
1 0208  00040  END;
```

Fig. 5-3 Procedure to compute the required substring of a given string

length denotes the length of the desired substring
result-string is the variable that is to contain the resulting
substring after execution of the procedure.
(The result string does not need to be initialized when calling
procedure SUB.)

This procedure returns through its fourth argument the substring starting at the given position POS for NUM characters except in the following cases:

1) If NUM $\leq$ 0, then the empty string is returned.
2) If POS $\leq$ 0, then the empty string is returned.
3) If POS $>$ length of STRING, then the empty string is returned.
4) If POS + NUM $>$ k + 1, where k is the length of STRING, then NUM is assumed to be k – POS + 1.

An example of invoking this procedure is

SUB(A, 1, 8, B)

If A has the value 'MONTREAL, QUEBEC*/', then after the execution of SUB, B will have the value 'MONTREAL*/'. The substring that is returned will also end with the delimiter '*/'. The expression

SUB(A, 11, 6, B)

on the other hand, assigns the value 'QUEBEC*/' to B. It should be emphasized that if the substring being referenced doesn't exist, a null string is returned. For example, the program segment

A := 'OTTAWA*/';
SUB(A, 7, 1, B)

results in B receiving the value '*/' as the string 'OTTAWA' contains fewer than seven characters. Notice also that the expression

SUB(A, 5, 4, B)

assigns a value of 'WA*/' to B since the total length of the string 'OTTAWA*/' is less than the sum of the initial position (5) and the length of the substring (4). Unlike function SUB in the main text, the programmer cannot omit the third argument when calling procedure SUB if he or she desires a substring starting at the given position and containing all characters to the end of the string. To get around this problem, either enough characters in NUM to include the end of the string (which is its length) or a value large enough to exceed this value must be given. Therefore, the value 254 could be used as it is the maximum possible length of the string. For example, the following statement will delete the first seven characters from a string of unknown length.

SUB(LIST, 8, 254, LIST)

Notice that the two string variables specified may be the same. Thus LIST gets changed to the substring that was extracted from the string in LIST.

As another example, the PASCAL program shown in Fig. 5-4 transforms a name which has the form

first-name middle-name last-name

to the output form

last-name, first-initial middle-initial

where the names are separated by one blank. For example, a person's name is given as

'JOHN ALBERT MACDONALD*/'.

The delimiter */ is used to mark the end of the string as the string is read into a string variable which has a fixed length of 256 characters. Blanks are padded onto the end of the string being read to bring its length up to 256 characters.

```
0  0000   00001  PROGRAM NAME_ED (INPUT, OUTPUT);
0  0000   00002  (* GIVEN A NAME IN THE FORM
0  0000   00003       FIRST-NAME MIDDLE-NAME LAST-NAME
0  0000   00004     THIS PROGRAM GENERATES AN EQUIVALENT NAME IN THE FORM
0  0000   00005       LAST-NAME, FIRST-INITIAL MIDDLE-INITIAL     *)
0  0000   00006
0  0000   00007  VAR NAME, LAST, DESIRED_NAME, FI, MI,
0  0038   00008      TEMP, BLANK, BLANKS, COMMA: STRING(256);
0  0038   00009      I: INTEGER;
0  0038   00010  PROCEDURE SUB (VAR S: STRING(256); POS, NUM: INTEGER; VAR RESULT:
1  0000   00011      STRING(256)); EXTERNAL;
0  0038   00012  PROCEDURE CONCAT (VAR STR1, STR2, RESULT: STRING(256)); EXTERNAL;
0  0038   00013
0  0038   00014  BEGIN
0  0038   00015
0  0038   00016     (* INITIALIZE *)
0  0038   00017     BLANK := ' */';
0  003E   00018     BLANKS := '                     */';
0  0044   00019     COMMA := ', */';
0  004A   00020
0  004A   00021     (* READ NAME AND OBTAIN FIRST INITITAL *)
0  004A   00022     READ (NAME);
0  005C   00023     SUB (NAME, 1, 1, FI);
0  0092   00024
0  0092   00025     (* SCAN THE NAME FOR THE FIRST BLANK *)
0  0092   00026     I := 1;
0  009A   00027     SUB (NAME, I, 1, TEMP);
0  00D0   00028     WHILE TEMP <> BLANK DO
0  00DA   00029     BEGIN
0  00DA   00030         I := I + 1;
0  00E6   00031         SUB (NAME, I, 1, TEMP)
0  0106   00032     END;
0  0120   00033
0  0120   00034     (* OBTAIN THE SECOND INITIAL *)
0  0120   00035     SUB (NAME, I + 1, 1, MI);
0  0162   00036
0  0162   00037     (* GET RID OF FIRST NAME AND BLANK *)
0  0162   00038     SUB (NAME, I + 1, 254, NAME);
0  01A4   00039
```

Fig. 5-4 Program to transform names

```
0  01A4   00040        (* SCAN THE NAME FOR THE SECOND BLANK *)
0  01A4   00041        I := 1;
0  01AC   00042        SUB (NAME, I, 1, TEMP);
0  01E2   00043        WHILE TEMP <> BLANK DO
0  01EC   00044        BEGIN
0  01EC   00045            I := I + 1;
0  01F8   00046            SUB (NAME, I, 1, TEMP)
0  0218   00047        END;
0  0232   00048
0  0232   00049        (* OBTAIN THE LAST NAME *)
0  0232   00050        SUB (NAME, I + 1, 254, LAST);
0  0274   00051
0  0274   00052        (* OUTPUT THE DESIRED NAME *)
0  0274   00053        CONCAT (LAST, COMMA, TEMP);
0  02A2   00054        CONCAT (TEMP, FI, TEMP);
0  02D0   00055        CONCAT (TEMP, BLANK, TEMP);
0  02FE   00056        CONCAT (TEMP, MI, TEMP);
0  032C   00057
0  032C   00058        (* MOVE THE DELIMITER SO IT ISN'T PRINTED *)
0  032C   00059        CONCAT (TEMP, BLANKS, DESIRED_NAME);
0  035A   00060        WRITELN (' ', DESIRED_NAME: 20)
0  037E   00061  END.
-----------------------------------
| COMPILE TIME:     0.163 SECOND(S) |
|       NO WARNING(S) DETECTED      |
|       NO ERROR(S) DETECTED        |
-----------------------------------
--EXECUTION-->
TREMBLAY, J P
```

Fig. 5-4   Program to transform names (cont'd.)

In the main text, the function SUB was also used as a pseudo-variable on the left-hand side of an assignment statement. Unfortunately, there is no such pseudo-variable in PASCAL, nor can procedure SUB be used to perform this operation. Therefore, in PASCAL we will use procedure PSDSUB for this purpose. This procedure is given in Fig. 5-5.

This procedure is similar in behaviour to function SUB. It replaces the indicated characters starting at position POS for NUM characters for those characters given by ADD. If POS or NUM is less than or equal to zero, then the assignment is not executed. If POS is greater than the length of STRING, then the characters are assigned to positions beyond the right-hand side of STRING, starting at the given position. Intermediate blanks are added between the end of STRING and the position of the first character of the substring that is added onto STRING.

To illustrate the simulation of a pseudo-variable, consider the following statements:

S = 'JOHNbPAULbGETTY*/';
A = 'JONES*/';
PSDSUB(S, 11, 5, A)

In this example, the substring 'GETTY' in S has been replaced by the string 'JONES' thus yielding an updated value of 'JOHNbPAULbJONES*/'. In the statements

S = 'CHARLESbF.bKANE*/';
B = 'FOSTER*/';
PSDSUB(S, 9, 2, B)

the substring 'F.' has been replaced by the string 'FOSTER'. The updated value of S has become 'CHARLESbFOSTERbKANE*/'. Once again, the character string

```
0   0000   00001   PROCEDURE PSDSUB (VAR S: STRING(256); POS, NUM: INTEGER; VAR ADD:
1   0000   00002       STRING(256));
1   0000   00003   (* GIVEN STRING, AND A POSITION POS FOR NUM CHARACTERS, THIS PROCEDURE
1   0000   00004      CHANGES THOSE CHARACTERS TO THE CHARACTERS CONTAINED IN THE STRING
1   0000   00005      ADD. *)
1   0000   00006
1   0000   00007   VAR STR, CHANGE,              (* STRING AND NEW SUBSTRING TO ADD *)
1   006E   00008       SAVE: ARRAY(1..256) OF CHAR;
1   007E   00009                                 (* TEMPORARY SUBSTRING *)
1   007E   00010      J, K, L,                   (* INDEX VARIABLES *)
1   007E   00011      LNTH, SVLNTH,              (* INDICATES LENGTH OF STRING *)
1   007E   00012      LAST: INTEGER;             (* LAST CHARACTER IN NEW STRING *)
1   007E   00013   FUNCTION LENGTH (VAR STR: STRING(256)): INTEGER; EXTERNAL;
1   009E   00014
1   009E   00015   BEGIN
1   009E   00016
1   009E   00017      (* INITIALIZE AND PROCESS IF POS AND NUM GREATER THAN ZERO *)
1   009E   00018      IF (POS > 0) AND (NUM > 0)
1   00B6   00019      THEN BEGIN
1   00B6   00020          STR := S;
1   00C0   00021          CHANGE := ADD;
1   00CA   00022
1   00CA   00023          (* ADD INTERMEDIATE BLANKS AND RESET LENGTH OF POS > LENGTH
1   00CA   00024             OF STRING *)
1   00CA   00025          LNTH := LENGTH (S);
1   00EC   00026          LAST := LNTH;
1   00F4   00027          IF POS > LNTH
1   00F4   00028          THEN BEGIN
1   0100   00029              FOR K := LNTH + 1 TO POS DO
1   012A   00030                  STR(K) := ' ';
1   0152   00031              LNTH := POS + LENGTH (ADD) - 1
1   0174   00032              END;
1   017C   00033
1   017C   00034          (* SAVE THE END OF THE STRING AFTER THE CHARACTERS TO BE
1   017C   00035             SUBSTITUTED, INCLUDING THE DELIMITER. *)
1   017C   00036          SVLNTH := 0;
1   0182   00037          FOR K := POS + NUM TO LAST DO
1   01AC   00038          BEGIN
1   01AC   00039              SVLNTH := SVLNTH + 1;
1   01B8   00040              SAVE(SVLNTH) := STR(K)
1   01F4   00041          END;
1   01FE   00042          SAVE(SVLNTH + 1) := '*';
1   0228   00043          SAVE(SVLNTH + 2) := '/';
1   0252   00044          SVLNTH := SVLNTH + 2;
1   025E   00045
1   025E   00046          (* REPLACE THE CHARACTERS IN STRING BY THOSE IN CHANGE IF
1   025E   00047             CHANGE IS NOT THE NULL STRING *)
1   025E   00048          J := 1;
1   0266   00049          LAST := POS + LENGTH (ADD) - 1;
1   0290   00050          FOR K := POS TO LAST DO
1   02B4   00051          BEGIN
1   02B4   00052              STR(K) := CHANGE(J);
1   02F6   00053              J := J + 1
1   02F6   00054          END;
1   0306   00055
1   0306   00056          (* ADD END OF STRING, SVLNTH IS LENGTH OF SAVED CHARACTERS *)
1   0306   00057          FOR K := 1 TO SVLNTH DO
1   032A   00058          BEGIN
1   032A   00059              LAST := LAST + 1;
1   0336   00060              STR(LAST) := SAVE(K)
1   0372   00061          END;
1   037C   00062
1   037C   00063          (* SET CHARACTERS FOLLOWING THE END OF THE STRING TO BLANKS *)
1   037C   00064          FOR K := LAST + 1 TO 256 DO
1   03A6   00065              STR(K) := ' ';
1   03CE   00066
1   03CE   00067          (* RETURN RESULTING STRING *)
1   03CE   00068          S := STR
1   03CE   00069          END
1   03D8   00070   END;
```

Fig. 5-5 Procedure to simulate the substring function as a pseudo-variable

arguments for both the SUB and PSDSUB procedures cannot be string constants. Thus,

SUB('HELLO LYLE*/', 7, 4, B)

is an invalid call to procedure SUB.

Searching for a Given Substring

In the program given earlier for the transformation of a name, the positions of each blank in the name had to be determined. Although it was possible to determine these positions by using the SUB procedure, this approach was somewhat tedious.

An alternate way of accomplishing the same task involves the introduction of the function INDEX. This function behaves identically in every respect to its counterpart in the main text. The function, as shown in Fig. 5-6, in its general form, is

INDEX(S, P)

where S denotes the subject string which is to be examined for the leftmost occurrence of the given pattern string P. If the search is successful, then the result of invoking this function is an integer which gives the leftmost position in the subject where the pattern string begins; otherwise, a value of zero is returned. As before, the arguments of INDEX cannot be string constants.

As an example, the program segment

A = 'SANDOR*/';
B = 'MURRAY SANDOR MAZER*/';
POS = INDEX(B, A)

gives POS a value of 8. If A had had the value 'SANDY*/' instead, POS would have received the value zero.

The programmer may include the string-processing functions and procedures introduced in this chapter immediately after the declarations, but before the executable portion of the program or they may also be called from a library. In the latter case, the functions and procedures need only be declared after the variable declaration section. The declaration required for any function or procedure used is the top line given for the subprogram that is desired. This line tells the compiler whether the subprogram is a function or a procedure and what to expect in the way of parameters. Immediately following this, FORWARD; or EXTERNAL; must be given. For example, if the function INDEX is used in the program, the declaration

FUNCTION INDEX (VAR S, PATTERN: STRING(256)): INTEGER; EXTERNAL;

is used. The CONCAT procedure requires the following declaration:

PROCEDURE CONCAT (VAR S1, S2, RESULT: STRING(256)); FORWARD;

EXTERNAL; and FORWARD; may be used interchangeably.

```
0  0000    00001  FUNCTION INDEX (VAR S, PATTERN: STRING(256)): INTEGER;
1  0000    00002  (* THIS FUNCTION RETURNS THE LEFTMOST OCCURENCE OF THE PATTERN STRING
1  0000    00003         IN THE STRING S. *)
1  0000    00004
1  0000    00005  VAR STR, PATTN: ARRAY(1..256) OF CHAR;
1  0066    00006                          (* SUBJECT STRING AND PATTERN STRING *)
1  0066    00007      LNTH,               (* LENGTH OF PATTERN STRING *)
1  0066    00008      L,                  (* NUMBER OF POSITIONS TO SEARCH IN SUBJECT *)
1  0066    00009      I,J, K,             (* INDEX VARIABLES *)
1  0066    00010      FLAG: INTEGER;      (* DENOTES IF PATTERN FOUND *)
1  0066    00011  FUNCTION LENGTH (VAR STR: STRING(256)): INTEGER; EXTERNAL;
1  007E    00012
1  007E    00013  BEGIN
1  007E    00014
1  007E    00015      (* INITIALIZE *)
1  007E    00016      PATTN := PATTERN;
1  0088    00017      STR := S;
1  0092    00018
1  0092    00019      (* SEARCH FOR PATTERN STRING IN STR *)
1  0092    00020      LNTH := LENGTH (PATTERN);
1  00B4    00021      L := LENGTH (S) - LNTH + 1;
1  00DE    00022
1  00DE    00023      (* NOT FOUND IF EITHER STRING IS THE NULL STRING *)
1  00DE    00024      INDEX := 0;
1  00E4    00025      IF (LNTH > 0) AND (L > 0)
1  00FC    00026      THEN BEGIN
1  00FC    00027
1  00FC    00028          (* SEARCH FOR FIRST CHARACTER OF PATTERN STRING *)
1  00FC    00029          I := 1;
1  0104    00030          WHILE I <= L DO
1  0110    00031          BEGIN
1  0110    00032
1  0110    00033              (* USE FLAG TO CHECK IF PATTERN FOUND IN POSITION
1  0110    00034                  STARTING AT I FOR NUMBER OF CHARACTERS IN PATTERN. *)
1  0110    00035              J := I;
1  0118    00036              K := 1;
1  0120    00037              FLAG := 0;
1  0126    00038              WHILE (K <= LNTH) AND (FLAG = 0) DO
1  013E    00039              BEGIN
1  013E    00040                  IF STR(J) <> PATTN(K)
1  017A    00041                  THEN FLAG := 1;
1  018C    00042                  K := K + 1;
1  0198    00043                  J := J + 1
1  0198    00044              END;
1  01A8    00045
1  01A8    00046              (* CHECK IF PATTERN HAS BEEN FOUND *)
1  01A8    00047              IF FLAG = 0
1  01A8    00048              THEN BEGIN
1  01B4    00049                  INDEX := I;
1  01BC    00050                  I := L + 1
1  01BC    00051                  END
1  01C8    00052              ELSE I := I + 1
1  01CC    00053          END
1  01D8    00054          END;
1  01DC    00055      PATTERN := PATTN;
1  01E6    00056      S := STR
1  01E6    00057  END;
```

Fig. 5-6 Function to return the position of a substring in a given string

The program given in Fig. 5-7 is a reformulation of the earlier program to transform a name.

The second version of this program is very similar to the first version with the WHILE DO statements having been replaced by the statements containing the INDEX function.

Applications of the functions and procedures discussed in this section will be exhibited in the next section.

```
0  0000   00001  PROGRAM NAME_ED (INPUT, OUTPUT);
0  0000   00002  (* GIVEN A NAME IN THE FORM
0  0000   00003      FIRST-NAME MIDDLE-NAME LAST-NAME
0  0000   00004      THIS PROGRAM USES THE INDEX AND SUB FUNCTIONS TO PRINT AN EQUIVALENT
0  0000   00005      NAME IN THE FORM
0  0000   00006          LAST-NAME, FIRST-INITIAL MIDDLE-INITIAL     *)
0  0000   00007
0  0000   00008  VAR NAME, LAST, DESIRED_NAME, MI, FI,
0  0038   00009      TEMP, BLANK, BLANKS, COMMA: STRING(256);
0  0038   00010      I: INTEGER;
0  0038   00011  PROCEDURE CONCAT (VAR STR1, STR2, RESULT: STRING(256)); EXTERNAL;
0  0038   00012  FUNCTION INDEX (VAR S, PATTERN: STRING(256)): INTEGER; EXTERNAL;
0  0038   00013  PROCEDURE SUB (VAR S: STRING(256); POS, NUM: INTEGER; VAR RESULT:
1  0000   00014      STRING(256)); EXTERNAL;
0  0038   00015
0  0038   00016  BEGIN
0  0038   00017
0  0038   00018      (* INITIALIZE *)
0  0038   00019      BLANK := ' */';
0  003E   00020      BLANKS := '                      */';
0  0044   00021      COMMA := ', */';
0  004A   00022
0  004A   00023      (* READ NAME AND OBTAIN FIRST INITIAL *)
0  004A   00024      READ (NAME);
0  005C   00025      SUB (NAME, 1, 1, FI);
0  0092   00026
0  0092   00027      (* SCAN THE NAME FOR THE FIRST BLNAK *)
0  0092   00028      I := INDEX (NAME, BLANK);
0  00BE   00029
0  00BE   00030      (* OBTAIN SECOND INITIAL *)
0  00BE   00031      SUB (NAME, I + 1, 1, MI);
0  0100   00032
0  0100   00033      (* GET RID OF FIRST NAME AND BLANK *)
0  0100   00034      SUB (NAME, I + 1, 254, NAME);
0  0142   00035
0  0142   00036      (* SCAN THE NAME FOR THE SECOND BLANK *)
0  0142   00037      I := INDEX (NAME, BLANK);
0  016E   00038
0  016E   00039      (* OBTAIN THE LAST NAME *)
0  016E   00040      SUB (NAME, I + 1, 254, LAST);
0  01B0   00041
0  01B0   00042      (* OUTPUT THE DESIRED NAME *)
0  01B0   00043      CONCAT (LAST, COMMA, TEMP);
0  01DE   00044      CONCAT (TEMP, FI, TEMP);
0  020C   00045      CONCAT (TEMP, BLANK, TEMP);
0  023A   00046      CONCAT (TEMP, MI, TEMP);
0  0268   00047
0  0268   00048      (* MOVE DELIMITER SO IT ISN'T PRINTED *)
0  0268   00049      CONCAT (TEMP, BLANKS, DESIRED_NAME);
0  0296   00050      WRITELN (' ', DESIRED_NAME: 20)
0  02BA   00051  END.
-----------------------------------
| COMPILE TIME:    0.133 SECOND(S) |
|     NO WARNING(S) DETECTED        |
|     NO ERROR(S) DETECTED          |
-----------------------------------
--EXECUTION-->
TREMBLAY, J P
```

Fig. 5-7 Revised program to transform names

Exercises for Sec. 5-3

1. Assume that STR1, STR2, and STR3 have the values 'ALPHA*/', 'BET*/', and 'ѢSOUP*/', respectively. Give the values of STR4 after executing the following program segments:

    (i) CONCAT (STR1, STR2, STR4);
         CONCAT (STR4, STR3, STR4)

    (ii) SUB (STR3, LENGTH (STR3) – 4, 255, STR4)

    (iii) STR4 = STR3;
          PSDSUB (STR4, 2, 4, STR2)

2. (i) You are given two cards with names written on them. Each name is separated by a comma, e.g., JOHN, SUE, ..., JIM. Assume that a name appears only once on any one card. Write a program that will read these two cards and print out the union of the names on both cards. The union is the set of all the names that appear on one list or the other list or both lists (if on both, only print once). Typical input and output are as follows:

   JOHN, MARY, JIM, JERRY, SUE, BOB, BARB*/
   BILL, BARB, JILL, BOB, SUE, JOHN*/

   UNION IS JOHN, MARY, JIM, JERRY, SUE, BOB, BARB, BILL, JILL

   (ii) Repeat part (i) and print the intersection of the names on both cards. The intersection is the set of all names that appear on both lists. For the input data just given, the output is

   INTERSECTION IS JOHN, SUE, BOB, BARB

   Note that the output suggested in this problem is one possible form of the result.

3. Write a program that inputs the name of a person which is punched on one card in the form

   'EMILEbJEANbPAULbTREMBLAY*/'

   and outputs

   TREMBLAY, E.J.P.

   (Note that the character 'b' represents a blank.) Your program should handle an arbitrary number of names before the surname (up to a maximum of ten).

4. Write a program which inputs a string and replaces all occurrences of 'MRS.b' or 'MISSb' by 'MS.b' and all occurrences of 'CHAIRMAN' by 'CHAIRPERSON'. (Note that the character 'b' represents a blank.)

5. Devise a program that deletes all occurrences of trailing blanks in a given string. For example, the string 'R.B.bBUNTbbbb*/' should be transformed to the string 'R.B.bBUNT*/'. (Note that the character 'b' represents a blank.)

6. Write a program which inputs a string S and a replication factor N, and replicates the given string N times. For example, the results for the input

   'HO!*/', 3

   would be

   'HO!HO!HO!*/'

5-4 BASIC STRING APPLICATIONS

This section presents PASCAL programs for the applications introduced in Sec. 5-4 of the main text.

5-4.1 Analysis of Textual Material

The problem as stated in the main text concerns the analysis of natural language text. In this problem English text is to be analyzed in order to produce a frequency table which gives the words used in the text (listed in alphabetical order) and the frequency with which they appear. For example, the line

'THE LAST MILE WAS THE HARDEST'

results in the following frequency table:

WORD	FREQUENCY
HARDEST	1
LAST	1
MILE	1
THE	2
WAS	1

In solving this problem we assume that the words are separated by one blank, and that all punctuation symbols have been removed. Furthermore, we assume that the words of the text are not hyphenated or broken across card boundaries. The number of cards containing the text is unknown, although it is known that the number of distinct words is less than 100 and no word contains more than 20 characters. For convenience we assume that the text contains no more than 256 characters (including separating blanks). A solution to this problem is given in Fig. 5-8. The following variables are used in this program:

Variable	Type	Usage
WORD	ARRAY(1..20) OF STRING(256)	Vector containing words used in text
FREQ	ARRAY(1..20) OF STRING(256)	Vector containing count of number of times word used
TEXT	STRING(256)	Text to be analyzed
NEXT	INTEGER	Next free vector element
CARD	STRING(256)	Input line of text
P	INTEGER	Position of the leftmost blank
I	INTEGER	Index variable
PASS	INTEGER	Current pass in selection sort
MIN_INDEX	INTEGER	Index of smallest element in a pass
WORD_COUNT	INTEGER	Number of distinct words
NEW_WORD	STRING(256)	Current word
TEMP_WORD	STRING(256)	Temporary variable used in exchange

| BLANK | STRING(256) | Blank character |
| TEMP_FREQ | INTEGER | Temporary variable used in exchange |

The data analyzed by this program was the passage

'YOU CAN FOOL SOME OF THE PEOPLE ALL OF THE TIME AND ALL
OF THE PEOPLE SOME OF THE TIME BUT NOT ALL OF THE PEOPLE
ALL OF THE TIME'

```
0   0000   00001   PROGRAM WORD_FREQ (INPUT, OUTPUT);
0   0000   00002   (* ANALYSIS OF THE FREQUENCY OF WORDS IN ENGLISH TEXT *)
0   0000   00003
0   0000   00004   VAR WORD: ARRAY(1..20) OF STRING(256);
0   0038   00005                               (* WORD TABLE *)
0   0038   00006      FREQ: ARRAY(1..20) OF INTEGER;
0   0038   00007                               (* FREQUENCY TABLE *)
0   0038   00008      TEXT,                     (* TEXT TO BE ALALYZED *)
0   0038   00009      CARD,                     (* INPUT LINE OF TEXT *)
0   0038   00010      NEW_WORD,                 (* CURRENT WORD *)
0   0038   00011      BLANK,                    (* BLANK CHARACTER *)
0   0038   00012      TEMP_WORD: STRING(256);   (* USED TO SORT WORD VECTOR *)
0   0038   00013      NEXT,                     (* NEXT FREE VECTOR ELEMENT *)
0   0038   00014      P,                        (* POSITION OF LEFTMOST BLANK *)
0   0038   00015      I,                        (* INDEX VARIABLE *)
0   0038   00016      PASS,                     (* CURRENT PASS IN SELECTION SORT *)
0   0038   00017      MIN_INDEX,                (* INDEX OF SMALLEST ELEMENT IN PASS *)
0   0038   00018      WORD_COUNT,               (* NUMBER OF DISTINCT WORDS *)
0   0038   00019      TEMP_FREQ: INTEGER;       (* TEMPORARY VARIABLE *)
0   0038   00020   PROCEDURE CONCAT (VAR STR1, STR2, RESULT: STRING(256)); EXTERNAL;
0   0038   00021   PROCEDURE SUB (VAR S: STRING(256); POS, NUM: INTEGER; VAR RESULT:
1   0000   00022        STRING(256)); EXTERNAL;
0   0038   00023   FUNCTION INDEX (VAR S, PATTERN: STRING(256)): INTEGER; EXTERNAL;
0   0038   00024
0   0038   00025   BEGIN
0   0038   00026
0   0038   00027      (* INITIALIZE *)
0   0038   00028      NEXT := 1;
0   0040   00029      WORD_COUNT := 0;
0   0046   00030      FOR I := 1 TO 20 DO
0   006A   00031          FREQ(I) := 0;
0   0096   00032      BLANK := ' */';
0   009C   00033
0   009C   00034      (* READ IN PASSAGE OF NARRATIVE TEXT *)
0   009C   00035      TEXT := '*/';
0   00A2   00036      READ (CARD: 80);
0   00B4   00037      WHILE NOT EOF DO
0   00BC   00038      BEGIN
0   00BC   00039          CONCAT (TEXT, CARD, TEXT);
0   00EA   00040          READ (CARD: 80)
0   00FC   00041      END;
0   0100   00042
0   0100   00043      (* PROCESS TEXT *)
0   0100   00044      P := INDEX (TEXT, BLANK);
0   012C   00045      WHILE P <> 0 DO
0   0138   00046      BEGIN
0   0138   00047
0   0138   00048          (* SCAN THE NEXT WORD OF TEXT *)
0   0138   00049          SUB (TEXT, 1, P - 1, NEW_WORD);
0   017A   00050          SUB (TEXT, P + 1, 254, TEXT);
0   01BC   00051
0   01BC   00052          (* SEARCH AND UPDATE WORD TABLE FOR THE WORD JUST SCANNED *)
0   01BC   00053          I := 1;
0   01C4   00054          WORD(NEXT) := NEW_WORD;
0   01EC   00055          WHILE WORD(I) <> NEW_WORD DO
0   0218   00056              I := I + 1;
0   0228   00057          IF I = NEXT
0   0228   00058          THEN NEXT := NEXT + 1;
```

Fig. 5-8   Program to analyze the frequency of words in English text

```
0   0240   00059
0   0240   00060                    (* UPDATE THE FREQUENCY COUNT OF WORD JUST SCANNED *)
0   0240   00061                    FREQ(I) := FREQ(I) + 1;
0   0290   00062
0   0290   00063                    (* OBTAIN POSITION OF NEXT BLANK IN THE REMAINING
0   0290   00064                       NARRATIVE TEXT *)
0   0290   00065                    P := INDEX (TEXT, BLANK)
0   02A0   00066              END;
0   02C0   00067
0   02C0   00068         (* USING A SELECTION SORT, SORT THE WORD TABLE AND ASSOCIATED
0   02C0   00069            FREQUENCY COUNT *)
0   02C0   00070         WORD_COUNT := NEXT - 1;
0   02CC   00071         FOR PASS := 1 TO WORD_COUNT DO
0   02F0   00072         BEGIN
0   02F0   00073              MIN_INDEX := PASS;
0   02F8   00074              FOR I := PASS + 1 TO WORD_COUNT DO
0   0322   00075                   IF WORD(I) < WORD(MIN_INDEX)
0   0366   00076                   THEN MIN_INDEX := I;
0   0378   00077              IF MIN_INDEX <> PASS
0   037C   00078              THEN BEGIN
0   0388   00079                   TEMP_WORD := WORD(PASS);
0   03B0   00080                   WORD(PASS) := WORD(MIN_INDEX);
0   03FA   00081                   WORD(MIN_INDEX) := TEMP_WORD;
0   0422   00082                   TEMP_FREQ := FREQ(PASS);
0   044C   00083                   FREQ(PASS) := FREQ(MIN_INDEX);
0   0498   00084                   FREQ(MIN_INDEX) := TEMP_FREQ
0   04BA   00085                   END
0   04C2   00086         END;
0   04C6   00087
0   04C6   00088         (* PRINT THE DESIRED REPORT *)
0   04C6   00089         WRITELN (' WORD               FREQUENCY');
0   04D8   00090         BLANK := '            */';
0   04DE   00091         FOR I := 1 TO WORD_COUNT DO
0   0502   00092         BEGIN
0   0502   00093              CONCAT (WORD(I), BLANK, WORD(I));
0   056C   00094              WRITELN (' ', WORD(I): 10, FREQ(I))
0   05E4   00095         END
0   05E4   00096   END.
```

```
-------------------------------------
| COMPILE TIME:    0.239 SECOND(S) |
|     NO WARNING(S) DETECTED        |
|     NO ERROR(S) DETECTED          |
-------------------------------------

--EXECUTION-->
WORD            FREQUENCY
ALL                 4
AND                 1
BUT                 1
CAN                 1
FOOL                1
NOT                 1
OF                  6
PEOPLE              3
SOME                2
THE                 6
TIME                3
YOU                 1
```

Fig. 5-8   Program to analyze the frequency of words in English text (cont'd.)

The program begins by reading the text to be analyzed. In line 45 a loop is begun to scan each word of the text. New words are added to the WORD vector and the frequency count for the words is updated accordingly. Lines 70 through 86 comprise a selection sort which sorts the WORD vector into alphabetic order. Finally, the frequency table is printed and execution of the program is terminated.

The second problem involving text analysis concerns the calculation of statistics for a passage of natural language (i.e., English) text. Three statistics which are of interest are:

1) The number of sentences in the passage of text,

2) The average number of words in a sentence, and
3) The average number of symbols per word

In solving this problem we assume words in the passage are separated by one blank. Secondly, we assume that commas, colons, semicolons, question marks, exclamation marks, hyphens, and periods are valid punctuation symbols which are not to be considered as textual characters in the calculation of the previously mentioned statistics. Sentences are denoted by a period, and for convenience we assume that periods are not allowed for any other purpose. The last sentence of the text is followed by a blank, the symbol "@," and another blank. Finally, the text to be analyzed contains at least one sentence and contains no more than 256 characters. The solution to this problem is given in Fig. 5-9. The following variables were used in this solution:

Variable	Type	Usage
SENTENCE_CTR	REAL	Number of sentences in narrative text
AVG_WORDS	REAL	Average number of words per sentence
AVG_SYMBOLS	REAL	Average number of symbols per word
CARD	STRING(256)	Input line of text
WORD	STRING(256)	Word in text
TEXT	STRING(256)	Text to be analyzed
P	INTEGER	Position of the leftmost blank in text
SYMBOL_CTR	REAL	Number of symbols in text
WORD_CTR	REAL	Number of words in text
STR	STRING(256)	Temporary string variable
BLANK, AT	STRING(256)	Blank and @ character
CHAR	STRING(256)	Next character of word being scanned
I	INTEGER	Index variable
TEMP	INTEGER	Temporary variable

This program was used to analyze the following text taken from Chap. 1.

'INTERACTIONS INVOLVING HUMANS ARE MOST EFFECTIVELY CARRIED OUT THROUGH THE MEDIUM OF LANGUAGE. LANGUAGE PERMITS THE EXPRESSION OF THOUGHTS AND IDEAS, AND WITHOUT IT, COMMUNICATION, AS WE KNOW IT, WOULD BE VERY DIFFICULT INDEED. @ '

The text to be analyzed is read into the string variable TEXT. In line 40 a REPEAT ...UNTIL loop is begun which scans through the text counting the number of sentences, words, and symbols that appear. If the special symbol "@" is found, the average number of words (AVG_WORDS) and average number of symbols (AVG_SYMBOLS) is computed and printed along with the number of sentences (SENTENCE_CTR) found in the text. If a period is encountered, the sentence

```
0   0000   00001   PROGRAM TEXT_AN (INPUT, OUTPUT);
0   0000   00002   (* CALCULATION OF STATISTICS FOR NARRATIVE TEXT *)
0   0000   00003
0   0000   00004   VAR SENTENCE_CTR,           (* NUMBER OF SENTENCES *)
0   0038   00005       AVG_WORDS,              (* AVERAGE NUMBER OF WORDS PER SENTENCE *)
0   0038   00006       AVG_SYMBOLS,            (* AVERAGE NUMBER OF SYMBOLS PER WORD *)
0   0038   00007       SYMBOL_CTR,             (* NUMBER OF SYMBOLS IN TEXT *)
0   0038   00008       WORD_CTR: REAL;         (* NUMBER OF WORDS IN TEXT *)
0   0038   00009       P,                      (* POSITION OF LEFTMOST BLANK *)
0   0038   00010       TEMP,                   (* TEMPORARY VARIABLE *)
0   0038   00011       I: INTEGER;             (* COUNTED LOOP VARIABLE *)
0   0038   00012       CARD,                   (* INPUT LINE OF TEXT *)
0   0038   00013       WORD,                   (* WORD IN TEXT *)
0   0038   00014       TEXT,                   (* TEXT TO BE ANALYZED *)
0   0038   00015       BLANK, AT,              (* BLANK AND @ CHARACTERS *)
0   0038   00016       STR,                    (* TEMPORARY STRING VARIABLE *)
0   0038   00017       CHAR: STRING(256);      (* NEXT CHARACTER OF WORD *)
0   0038   00018   FUNCTION INDEX (VAR S, PATTERN: STRING(256)): INTEGER; EXTERNAL;
0   0038   00019   FUNCTION LENGTH (VAR STR: STRING(256)): INTEGER; EXTERNAL;
0   0038   00020   PROCEDURE SUB (VAR S: STRING(256); POS, NUM: INTEGER; VAR RESULT:
1   0000   00021       STRING(256)); EXTERNAL;
0   0038   00022   PROCEDURE CONCAT (VAR S1, S2, RESULT: STRING(256)); EXTERNAL;
0   0038   00023
0   0038   00024   BEGIN
0   0038   00025
0   0038   00026       (* INITIALIZE *)
0   0038   00027       WORD_CTR := 0; SYMBOL_CTR := 0; SENTENCE_CTR := 0;
0   0050   00028       BLANK := ' */';
0   0056   00029       AT := '@*/';
0   005C   00030
0   005C   00031       (* READ TEXTUAL MATERIAL *)
0   005C   00032       TEXT := '*/';
0   0062   00033       READ (CARD: 80);
0   0074   00034       REPEAT
0   0074   00035           CONCAT (TEXT, CARD, TEXT);
0   00A2   00036           READ (CARD: 80)
0   00B4   00037       UNTIL EOF;
0   00BC   00038
```

Fig. 5-9   Program to calculate statistics for narrative text

counter is incremented. Finally the symbol counter is incremented by the length of the word found. If the word ends in a punctuation mark, the symbol counter is decremented by one to reflect the true number of nonpunctuation symbols.

5-4.2   Justification of Text

The program given in Fig. 5-10 is a solution to the problem given in Sec. 5-4.2 of the main text. This problem concerns the justification of text. To reduce the complexity of this problem we assume that words are not to be split between lines and that each line (except for the last line of text) is to be both left-and right-justified. Extra blanks used in the justification of text are to be distributed evenly between the words of a line. As in the previous application each word is separated from each other word by a blank and each punctuation symbol is followed by a blank. The text to be justified is read as data and is preceded by an integer representing the number (a maximum of 100) of characters per line of justified text. The following variables were used in the solution to this program:

Variable	Type	Usage
TEXT	STRING(256)	Text to be justified
CARD	STRING(256)	Input text
RMARGIN	INTEGER	Number of characters in a justified line of text

```
0  00BC  00039        (* PROCESS TEXTUAL MATERIAL *)
0  00BC  00040        REPEAT
0  00BC  00041            P := INDEX (TEXT, BLANK);
0  00E8  00042            SUB (TEXT, 1, P - 1, WORD);
0  012A  00043            IF LENGTH (TEXT) = P
0  014A  00044            THEN TEXT := '*/'
0  0152  00045            ELSE SUB (TEXT, P + 1, 254, TEXT);
0  019E  00046
0  019E  00047            (* END OF TEXT *)
0  019E  00048            IF WORD = AT
0  019E  00049            THEN BEGIN
0  01A8  00050                AVG_WORDS := WORD_CTR / SENTENCE_CTR;
0  01B4  00051                AVG_SYMBOLS := SYMBOL_CTR / WORD_CTR;
0  01C0  00052                WRITELN (' THE NUMBER OF SENTENCES IS', SENTENCE_CTR:
0  01D6  00053                    4: 0);
0  01E4  00054                WRITELN (' THE AVERAGE NUMBER OF WORDS IN A SENTENCE IS',
0  01F6  00055                    AVG_WORDS: 6: 3);
0  0208  00056                WRITELN (' THE AVERAGE NUMBER OF SYMBOLS IN A WORD IS',
0  021A  00057                    AVG_SYMBOLS: 6: 3)
0  022C  00058                END
0  022C  00059            ELSE BEGIN
0  0230  00060
0  0230  00061                (* END OF SENTENCE *)
0  0230  00062                STR := '.*/';
0  0236  00063                IF INDEX (WORD, STR) <> 0
0  025E  00064                THEN SENTENCE_CTR := SENTENCE_CTR + 1;
0  0272  00065
0  0272  00066                (* UPDATE THE WORD COUNTER *)
0  0272  00067                WORD_CTR := WORD_CTR + 1;
0  027E  00068
0  027E  00069                (* UPDATE THE SYMBOL COUNTER *)
0  027E  00070                SYMBOL_CTR := SYMBOL_CTR + P - 1;
0  029E  00071                STR := '.,:;!?-*/';
0  02A4  00072                TEMP := 0;
0  02AA  00073                FOR I := 1 TO LENGTH (WORD) DO
0  02EA  00074                BEGIN
0  02EA  00075                    SUB (WORD, I, 1, CHAR);
0  0320  00076                    TEMP := TEMP + INDEX (STR, CHAR)
0  0330  00077                END;
0  0354  00078                IF TEMP <> 0
0  0354  00079                THEN SYMBOL_CTR := SYMBOL_CTR - 1
0  0360  00080                END
0  036C  00081        UNTIL WORD = AT
0  036C  00082  END.
```

```
-------------------------------------
| COMPILE TIME:    0.204 SECOND(S)  |
|     NO WARNING(S) DETECTED        |
|     NO ERROR(S) DETECTED          |
-------------------------------------
--EXECUTION-->
THE NUMBER OF SENTENCES IS  2.
THE AVERAGE NUMBER OF WORDS IN A SENTENCE IS 17.000
THE AVERAGE NUMBER OF SYMBOLS IN A WORD IS 5.529
```

Fig. 5-9 Program to calculate statistics for narrative text (cont'd.)

BLANKS	INTEGER	Number of blanks to be inserted to justify line
BFIELD	STRING(256)	String of blanks
I	INTEGER	Index variable used in scanning line of text
J	INTEGER	Loop variable
LINE	STRING(256)	Justified line of text
STR1, STR2	STRING(256)	Temporary string variables
BLANK	STRING(256)	Blank character
TEMP	INTEGER	Temporary variable

The text justified during this run contained of the following passage.

'INTERACTIONS INVOLVING HUMANS ARE MOST EFFECTIVELY CARRIED OUT THROUGH THE MEDIUM OF LANGUAGE. LANGUAGE PERMITS THE EXPRESSION OF THOUGHTS AND IDEAS, AND WITHOUT IT, COMMUNICATION, AS WE KNOW IT WOULD BE VERY DIFFICULT INDEED.'

```
0  0000   00001   PROGRAM JUSTIFY (INPUT, OUTPUT);
0  0000   00002   (* PROGRAM TO JUSTIFY NARRATIVE TEXT *)
0  0000   00003
0  0000   00004   VAR TEXT,                (* TEXT TO BE JUSTIFIED *)
0  0038   00005       CARD,                (* INPUT TEXT *)
0  0038   00006       BFIELD,              (* BLANK STRING *)
0  0038   00007       LINE,                (* EDITED LINE OF TEXT *)
0  0038   00008       STR1, STR2,          (* TEMPORARY STRING VARIABLE *)
0  0038   00009       BLANK: STRING(256);  (* BLANK CHARACTER *)
0  0038   00010       RMARGIN,             (* SPECIFIED RIGHT MARGIN *)
0  0038   00011       BLANKS,              (* NUMBER OF BLANKS TO BE INSERTED *)
0  0038   00012       TEMP,                (* TEMPORARY VARIABLE *)
0  0038   00013       I,                   (* INDEX VARIABLE *)
0  0038   00014       J: INTEGER;          (* LOOP VARIABLE *)
0  0038   00015   FUNCTION INDEX (VAR S, PATTERN: STRING(256)): INTEGER; EXTERNAL;
0  0038   00016   FUNCTION LENGTH (VAR STR: STRING(256)): INTEGER; EXTERNAL;
0  0038   00017   PROCEDURE SUB (VAR S: STRING(256); POS, NUM: INTEGER; VAR RESULT:
1  0000   00018       STRING(256)); EXTERNAL;
0  0038   00019   PROCEDURE CONCAT (VAR S1, S2, RESULT: STRING(256)); EXTERNAL;
0  0038   00020
0  0038   00021   BEGIN
0  0038   00022
0  0038   00023       (* INITIALIZE *)
0  0038   00024       TEXT := '*/';
0  003E   00025       BLANK := ' */';
0  0044   00026
0  0044   00027       (* READ ENGLISH TEXT AND CHARACTERS PER LINE *)
0  0044   00028       READ (RMARGIN);
0  0056   00029       READ (CARD);
0  0068   00030       WHILE NOT EOF DO
0  0070   00031       BEGIN
0  0070   00032           CONCAT (TEXT, CARD, TEXT);
0  009E   00033           READ (CARD)
0  00B0   00034       END;
0  00B4   00035
0  00B4   00036       (* JUSTIFY TEXT *)
0  00B4   00037       WHILE LENGTH (TEXT) > RMARGIN DO
0  00DC   00038       BEGIN
0  00DC   00039
0  00DC   00040           (* NO JUSTIFICATION REQUIRED *)
0  00DC   00041           SUB (TEXT, RMARGIN, 1, STR1);
0  0112   00042           SUB (TEXT, RMARGIN + 1, 1, STR2);
0  0154   00043           IF (STR1 <> BLANK) AND (STR2 = BLANK)
0  0168   00044           THEN SUB (TEXT, 1, RMARGIN, LINE)
0  0188   00045
0  0188   00046           (* BLANKS MUST BE INSERTED IN THE OUTPUT LINE *)
0  0188   00047           ELSE BEGIN
0  01A2   00048
0  01A2   00049               (* CHECK TO SEE IF POSITION RMARGIN CONTAINS A NONBLANK
0  01A2   00050                  CHARACTER *)
0  01A2   00051               I := RMARGIN - 1;
0  01AE   00052               SUB (TEXT, RMARGIN, 1, STR1);
0  01E4   00053               IF STR1 <> BLANK
0  01E4   00054               THEN BEGIN
0  01EE   00055                   SUB (TEXT, I, 1, STR2);
0  0224   00056                   WHILE STR2 <> BLANK DO
0  022E   00057                   BEGIN
0  022E   00058                       I := I - 1;
0  023A   00059                       SUB (TEXT, I, 1, STR2)
0  025A   00060                   END
0  0270   00061                   END;
0  0274   00062               I := I - 1;
0  0280   00063
```

Fig. 5-10   Program to justify text

```
0  0280   00064                    (* ESTABLISH A LOOP FOR INSERTING BLANKS *)
0  0280   00065                    BLANKS := RMARGIN - I;
0  028C   00066                    BFIELD := ' */';
0  0292   00067                    FOR J := 1 TO BLANKS DO
0  02B6   00068                    BEGIN
0  02B6   00069
0  02B6   00070                        (* SUCCESSFULLY ADD BLANKS TO THE BLANK FIELDS SEP-
0  02B6   00071                            ARATING WORD *)
0  02B6   00072                        TEMP := LENGTH (BFIELD);
0  02DA   00073                        SUB (TEXT, I, TEMP, STR1);
0  0310   00074                        WHILE INDEX (STR1, BFIELD) = 0 DO
0  0340   00075                        BEGIN
0  0340   00076                            I := I - 1;
0  034C   00077                            IF I = 0
0  034C   00078                            THEN BEGIN
0  0358   00079                                I := RMARGIN - BLANKS + J - 1;
0  036C   00080                                CONCAT (BFIELD, BLANK, BFIELD);
0  039A   00081                                TEMP := TEMP + 1
0  039A   00082                                END;
0  03A6   00083                            SUB (TEXT, I, TEMP, STR1)
0  03C6   00084                        END;
0  03E0   00085                        SUB (TEXT, 1, I, STR1);
0  0416   00086                        SUB (TEXT, I + 1, 254, STR2);
0  0458   00087                        CONCAT (STR1, BLANK, TEXT);
0  0486   00088                        CONCAT (TEXT, STR2, TEXT);
0  04B4   00089                        I := I - 1
0  04B4   00090                    END;
0  04C4   00091                    SUB (TEXT, 1, RMARGIN, LINE)
0  04E4   00092                END;
0  04FA   00093
0  04FA   00094                (* OUTPUT JUSTIFED LINE, REMOVING DELIMITER *)
0  04FA   00095                BFIELD := '                                        */';
0  0500   00096                CONCAT (LINE, BFIELD, LINE);
0  052E   00097                WRITELN (' ': 6, LINE: 50);
0  0552   00098                SUB (TEXT, RMARGIN + 1, 254, TEXT);
0  0594   00099                SUB (TEXT, 1, 1, STR1);
0  05CA   00100                IF STR1 = BLANK
0  05CA   00101                THEN SUB (TEXT, 2, 254, TEXT)
0  05F4   00102            END;
0  060E   00103
0  060E   00104            (* OUTPUT LAST LINE *)
0  060E   00105            BFIELD := '                                        */';
0  0614   00106            CONCAT (TEXT, BFIELD, TEXT);
0  0642   00107            WRITELN (' ': 6, TEXT: 50)
0  0666   00108 END.
```

```
----------------------------------
¦ COMPILE TIME:    0.306 SECOND(S) ¦
¦     NO WARNING(S) DETECTED       ¦
¦     NO ERROR(S) DETECTED         ¦
----------------------------------
--EXECUTION-->
    INTERACTIONS INVOLVING HUMANS ARE MOST EFFECTIVELY
    CARRIED  OUT  THROUGH  THE  MEDIUM  OF  LANGUAGE.
    LANGUAGE PERMITS THE EXPRESSION OF  THOUGHTS  AND
    IDEAS, AND WITHOUT IT, COMMUNICATION, AS  WE  KNOW
    IT, WOULD BE VERY ·DIFFICULT INDEED.
```

Fig. 5-10 Program to justify text (cont'd.)

In line 28 the number of characters per justified line of text (i.e., RMARGIN) is read. The next statements accomplish the reading in of the text to be justified. In line 37 a loop is begun to justify the input text. A check is made to see if a word ends at the right margin. If this is the case, then no justification is required and LINE is assigned a substring of TEXT up to the end of that word; otherwise, blanks must be inserted to justify the text. The number of blanks needed is calculated, then in line 67 a loop is begun to insert the blanks into the text. Finally, in line 97 the justified text is printed, and in the next statement the line of justified text is removed from TEXT. When the length of TEXT is less than the length of justified text, the loop to justify text is terminated and the final line of text is printed unjustified.

5-4.3   Form Letter Generation

The program presented in this section is a solution to the form letter generation problem given in Sec. 5-4.3 of the main text. The problem as given in the main text is to write a program for generating personalized form letters. The input data consist of a number of cards, each card containing a line of the letter. The lines of the form letter contain certain keywords which are to be replaced by information concerning the recipient of the letter in order to make the letter more personal. The keywords to be used in this form are

Keyword	Replacement information
DATE	Date given in the customer's information
ADDRESS	Customer's address
CITY	Customer's city
PROVINCE	Customer's province
N	Number of weeks until salesperson's visit
X	Customer's full name (e.g., MR. R.B. BROWN)
Z	Customer's last name (e.g., MR. BROWN)

In addition to these keywords an indentation code represented by "+number" is used to specify the indentation to be used for the following line. The number (containing no more than two digits) represents the number of characters the line is to be indented. The end of the form letter is denoted by a card containing the string '***/'. Following this card, information concerning an unknown number of recipients is supplied. For each recipient (or customer) the following information is supplied:

'Date*/'
'MR. (or MRS., etc.) bInitialsbSurname*/'
'Street Address*/'
'City,bProvince*/'
'Number of weeks before salesperson's visit*/'

where b represents a blank within the string. The program is to read in the form letter and, for each customer, produce a personalized form letter using the information given for that customer. A program which solves this problem is given in Fig. 5-11. The variables used in this program are

Variable	Type	Usage
LETTER	ARRAY(1..50) OF STRING(256)	Form letter
NUM_LINES	INTEGER	Number of lines in the form letter
DATE	STRING(256)	Date to be placed on the letter
NAME	STRING(256)	Customer's name
ADDRES	STRING(256)	Customer's address
CITY_PROV	STRING(256)	Customer's city and province

WEEKS	STRING(256)	Weeks until salesperson's visit
LAST_NAME	STRING(256)	Customer's last name
PROVINCE	STRING(256)	Customer's province
CITY	STRING(256)	Customer's city
RESULT	STRING(256)	String to replace keyword
VALUE	INTEGER	Number of spaces line is to be indented
BLANKS	STRING(256)	String of 80 blanks
LINE	STRING(256)	Input line of letter
KEY	STRING(256)	Keyword in form letter
KEYWORD	STRING(12)	Used in comparisons
STR1	STRING(256)	Temporary string variable
STR2	STRING(256)	Temporary string variable
I, J, K, CC	INTEGER	Loop variables

The following data were used in this run.

```
'+40 187 MAIN STREET*/'
'+40 WINNIPEG 1, MANITOBA*/'
'+40 *DATE**/'
'*X**/'
'*ADDRESS**/'
'*CITY*, *PROVINCE**/'

'DEAR *Z**/'
'          THE BUSINESS WORLD IS RAPIDLY CHANGING AND OUR CORPORATION*/'
'HAS BEEN KEEPING PACE WITH THE NEW REQUIREMENTS FORCED UPON OFFICE*/'
'MACHINERY, WE ARE GIVING, YOU, *Z*, AS A KEY FIGURE IN THE *CITY**/'
'BUSINESS COMMUNITY, AN OPPORTUNITY TO BECOME FAMILIAR WITH THE */'
'LATEST ADVANCEMENTS IN OUR EQUIPMENT. A REPRESENTATIVE OF OUR*/'
'CORPORATION IN *PROVINCE* WILL BE SEEING YOU IN *N* WEEKS. HE WILL*/'
'TAKE SEVERAL MACHINES TO *CITY* WHICH ARE INDICATIVE OF A WHOLE NEW*/'
'LINE OF OFFICE MACHINES WE HAVE RECENTLY DEVELOPED.*/'
'          OUR SALES REPRESENTATIVE IS LOOKING FORWARD TO HIS VISIT IN *CITY**/'
'HE KNOWS THAT THE MACHINES HE SELLS COULD BECOME AN INTEGRAL PART*/'
'OF YOUR OFFICE ONLY A FEW DAYS AFTER IMPLEMENTATION.*/'

'+40 SINCERELY,*/'
'+40 ROGER SMITH, MANAGER*/'
'+40 OFFICE DEVICES CORPORATION*/'
'***/'
'JANUARY 1, 1978*/'
'MR. R.B. BROWN*/'
'1712 ELK DRIVE*/'
'JASPER, ALBERTA*/'
'FOUR*/'
'JANUARY 10, 1978*/'
'MRS. C.T. ALLAN*/'
'336 RIVER ST.*/'
'REGINA, SASKATCHEWAN*/'
'SEVEN*/'
```

```
0   0000   00001   PROGRAM FORM (INPUT, OUTPUT);
0   0000   00002   (* PROGRAM TO GENERATE PERSONALIZED FORM LETTERS *)
0   0000   00003
0   0000   00004   VAR DATE,                      (* LETTER'S DATE *)
0   0038   00005       ADDRESS:                   (* CUSTOMER'S ADDRESS *)
0   0038   00006         ARRAY(1..256) OF CHAR;
0   0038   00007       NAME,                      (* CUSTOMER'S NAME *)
0   0038   00008       CITY_PROV,                 (* CUSTOMER'S CITY AND PROVINCE *)
0   0038   00009       WEEKS,                     (* WEEKS UNTIL VISIT *)
0   0038   00010       LAST_NAME,                 (* CUSTOMER'S LAST NAME *)
0   0038   00011       PROVINCE,                  (* CUSTOMER'S PROVINCE *)
0   0038   00012       CITY,                      (* CUSTOMER'S CITY *)
0   0038   00013       LINE,                      (* INPUT LINE OF LETTER *)
0   0038   00014       RESULT,                    (* KEYWORD REPLACEMENT *)
0   0038   00015       BLANKS,                    (* A STRING OF 80 BLANKS *)
0   0038   00016       KEY,                       (* KEYWORD IN FORM LETTER *)
0   0038   00017       STR1, STR2: STRING(256);   (* TEMPORARY STRING VARIABLES *)
0   0038   00018       KEYWORD: STRING(12);       (* KEYWORD TO REPLACE *)
0   0038   00019       NUM_LINES,                 (* NUMBER OF LINES IN FORM LETTER *)
0   0038   00020       I, J, K, CC,               (* LOOP VARIABLES *)
0   0038   00021       VALUE: INTEGER;            (* VALUE OF NUMBER AS AN INTEGER *)
0   0038   00022       LETTER: ARRAY(1..50) OF STRING(256);   (* FORM LETTER *)
0   0038   00023   FUNCTION INDEX (VAR S, PATTERN: STRING(256)): INTEGER; EXTERNAL;
0   0038   00024   FUNCTION LENGTH (VAR STR: STRING(256)): INTEGER; EXTERNAL;
0   0038   00025   PROCEDURE SUB (VAR S: STRING(256); POS, NUM: INTEGER; VAR RESULT:
1   0000   00026       STRING(256)); EXTERNAL;
0   0038   00027   PROCEDURE CONCAT (VAR S1, S2, RESULT: STRING(256)); EXTERNAL;
0   0038   00028
0   0038   00029   BEGIN
0   0038   00030
0   0038   00031       (* INPUT FORM LETTER *)
0   0038   00032       READ (LINE: 80);
0   004A   00033       NUM_LINES := 0;
0   0050   00034       STR1 := '***/';
0   0056   00035       WHILE STR1 <> LINE DO
0   0060   00036       BEGIN
0   0060   00037           NUM_LINES := NUM_LINES + 1;
0   006C   00038           LETTER (NUM_LINES) := LINE;
0   0094   00039           READ (LINE: 80);
0   00A6   00040       END;
0   00AA   00041
0   00AA   00042       (* ENGAGE THE LOOP TO WRITE PERSONALIZED LETTERS *)
0   00AA   00043       BLANKS := '                                    */';
0   00B0   00044
0   00B0   00045       (* A STRING OF 80 BLANKS *)
0   00B0   00046       CONCAT (BLANKS, BLANKS, BLANKS);
0   00DE   00047       READ (DATE, NAME, ADDRESS, CITY_PROV, WEEKS);
0   0138   00048       WHILE NOT EOF DO
0   0140   00049       BEGIN
0   0140   00050
0   0140   00051           (* SPLIT UP THE PERSONALIZED DATA FOR ONE CUSTOMER *)
0   0140   00052           STR2 := ' */';
0   0146   00053           I := INDEX (NAME, STR2);
0   0172   00054           SUB (NAME, I + 1, 254, STR1);
0   01B4   00055           J := INDEX (STR1, STR2);
0   01E0   00056           SUB (NAME, 1, I - 1, STR1);
0   0222   00057           CONCAT (STR1, STR2, LAST_NAME);
0   0250   00058           SUB (NAME, I + J + 1, 254, STR1);
0   0296   00059           CONCAT (LAST_NAME, STR1, LAST_NAME);
0   02C4   00060           STR1 := ',*/';
0   02CA   00061           I := INDEX (CITY_PROV, STR1);
0   02F6   00062           SUB (CITY_PROV, I + 2, 254, PROVINCE);
0   0338   00063           SUB (CITY_PROV, 1, I - 1, CITY);
0   037A   00064
0   037A   00065           (* GENERATE A PERSONALIZED LETTER FOR CURRENT CUSTOMER *)
0   037A   00066           FOR CC := 1 TO NUM_LINES DO
0   037A   00067           BEGIN
0   039E   00068
0   039E   00069               (* GET THE NEXT LINE OF THE FORM LETTER *)
0   039E   00070               LINE := LETTER(CC);
0   03C6   00071
0   03C6   00072               (* PERFORM ALL KEYWORD SUBSTITUTIONS *)
0   03C6   00073               I := 0;
0   03CC   00074               J := 0;
0   03D2   00075               STR2 := '**/';
0   03D8   00076               K := INDEX (LINE, STR2);
```

Fig. 5-11 Program to generate a personalized form letter

```
0  0404  00077                    WHILE K <> 0 DO
0  0410  00078                    BEGIN
0  0410  00079                        I := K + J + I;
0  0420  00080                        SUB (LINE, I + 1, 254, STR1);
0  0462  00081                        STR2 := '**/';
0  0468  00082                        J := INDEX (STR1, STR2);
0  0494  00083                        SUB (LINE, I, J + 1, KEY);
0  04D6  00084                        (* SHORTEN KEY DOWN TO SHORTER LENGTH STRING *)
0  04D6  00085                        KEYWORD := KEY;
0  04DC  00086                        IF KEYWORD = '*DATE**/'
0  04DC  00087                        THEN RESULT := DATE
0  04E6  00088                        ELSE IF KEYWORD = '*ADDRESS**/'
0  04F4  00089                             THEN RESULT := ADDRESS
0  04FE  00090                             ELSE IF KEYWORD = '*CITY**/'
0  050C  00091                                  THEN RESULT := CITY
0  0516  00092                                  ELSE IF KEYWORD = '*PROVINCE**/'
0  0520  00093                                       THEN RESULT := PROVINCE
0  052A  00094                                       ELSE IF KEYWORD = '*N**/'
0  0534  00095                                            THEN RESULT := WEEKS
0  053E  00096                                            ELSE IF KEYWORD = '*X**/'
0  0548  00097                                                 THEN RESULT := NAME
0  0552  00098                                                 ELSE IF KEYWORD = '*Z**/'
0  0552  00099                                                      THEN RESULT := LAST_NAME;
0  056C  00100                        SUB (LINE, 1, I - 1, STR1);
0  05AE  00101                        SUB (LINE, I + J + 1, 254, STR2);
0  05F4  00102                        CONCAT (STR1, RESULT, LINE);
0  0622  00103                        CONCAT (LINE, STR2, LINE);
0  0650  00104                        J := LENGTH (RESULT);
0  0674  00105                        IF LENGTH (LINE) < I + J + 1
0  069C  00106                        THEN K := 0
0  06A6  00107                        ELSE BEGIN
0  06B0  00108                             SUB (LINE, I + J + 1, 254, STR1);
0  06F6  00109                             STR2 := '**/';
0  06FC  00110                             K := INDEX (STR1, STR2)
0  070C  00111                             END
0  0728  00112                    END;
0  072C  00113
0  072C  00114                    (*PERFORM INDENTATION IF REQUIRED *)
0  072C  00115                    SUB (LINE, 1, 1, STR1);
0  0762  00116                    STR2 := '+*/';
0  0768  00117                    IF STR1 = STR2
0  0768  00118                    THEN BEGIN
0  0772  00119                         STR2 := ' */';
0  0778  00120                         I := INDEX (LINE, STR2);
0  07A4  00121                         VALUE := 0;
0  07AA  00122                         STR1 := '0123456789*/';
0  07B0  00123                         SUB (LINE, 2, I - 2, STR2);
0  07F2  00124                         IF LENGTH (STR2) = 2
0  0812  00125                         THEN BEGIN
0  081A  00126                              SUB (STR2, 1, 1, RESULT);
0  0850  00127                              VALUE := (INDEX (STR1, RESULT) - 1) * 10;
0  088C  00128                              SUB (STR2, 2, 254, STR2)
0  08AC  00129                              END;
0  08C2  00130                         VALUE := VALUE + INDEX (STR1, STR2) - 1;
0  08F6  00131                         SUB (BLANKS, 1, VALUE, STR1);
0  092C  00132                         SUB (LINE, I + 1, 254, LINE);
0  096E  00133                         CONCAT (STR1, LINE, LINE)
0  0986  00134                         END;
0  099C  00135
0  099C  00136                    (* OUTPUT NEXT LINE OF PERSONALIZED LETTER *)
0  099C  00137                    CONCAT (LINE, BLANKS, LINE);
0  09CA  00138                    WRITELN (' ': 6, LINE: 80)
0  09EE  00139                    END;
0  09F2  00140                    WRITELN ('-');
0  0A04  00141
0  0A04  00142                    (* READ NEXT PERSON *)
0  0A04  00143                    READ (DATE, NAME, ADDRESS, CITY_PROV, WEEKS)
0  0A5E  00144              END
0  0A5E  00145  END.
---------------------------------------
| COMPILE TIME:    0.437 SECOND(S) |
|    NO WARNING(S) DETECTED        |
|    NO ERROR(S) DETECTED          |
---------------------------------------
```

Fig. 5-11   Program to generate a personalized form letter (cont'd.)

```
--EXECUTION-->
                                        187 MAIN STREET
                                        WINNIPEG 1, MANITOBA
                                        JANUARY 1, 1978

        MR. R.B. BROWN
        1712 ELK DRIVE
        JASPER, ALBERTA

        DEAR MR. BROWN
             THE BUSINESS WORLD IS RAPIDLY CHANGING AND OUR CORPORATION
        HAS BEEN KEEPING PACE WITH NEW NEW REQUIREMENTS FORCED UPON OFFICE
        MACHINERY.  WE ARE GIVING, YOU, MR. BROWN, AS A KEY FIGURE IN THE JASPER
        BUSINESS COMMUNITY, AN OPPORTUNITY TO BECOME FAMILIAR WITH THE
        LATEST ADVANCEMENTS IN OUR EQUIPMENT.  A REPRESENTATIVE OF OUR
        CORPORATION IN ALBERTA WILL BE SEEING YOU IN FOUR WEEKS.  HE WILL
        TAKE SEVERAL MACHINES TO JASPER WHICH ARE INDICATIVE OF A WHOLE NEW
        LINE OF OFFICE MACHINES WE HAVE RECENTLY DEVELOPED.
             OUR SALES REPRESENTATIVE IS LOOKING FORWARD TO HIS VISIT IN JASPER.
        HE KNOWS THAT THE MACHINES HE SELLS COULD BECOME AN INTEGRAL PART
        OF YOUR OFFICE ONLY A FEW DAYS AFTER IMPLEMENTATION.




                                        SINCERELY,

                                        ROGER SMITH, MANAGER
                                        OFFICE DEVICES CORPORATION


                                        187 MAIN STREET
                                        WINNIPEG 1, MANITOBA
                                        JANUARY 10, 1978

        MRS. C.T. ALLAN
        336 RIVER ST.
        REGINA, SASKATCHEWAN

        DEAR MRS. ALLAN
             THE BUSINESS WORLD IS RAPIDLY CHANGING AND OUR CORPORATION
        HAS BEEN KEEPING PACE WITH NEW NEW REQUIREMENTS FORCED UPON OFFICE
        MACHINERY.  WE ARE GIVING, YOU, MRS. ALLAN, AS A KEY FIGURE IN THE REGINA
        BUSINESS COMMUNITY, AN OPPORTUNITY TO BECOME FAMILIAR WITH THE
        LATEST ADVANCEMENTS IN OUR EQUIPMENT.  A REPRESENTATIVE OF OUR
        CORPORATION IN SASKATCHEWAN WILL BE SEEING YOU IN SEVEN WEEKS.  HE WILL
        TAKE SEVERAL MACHINES TO REGINA WHICH ARE INDICATIVE OF A WHOLE NEW
        LINE OF OFFICE MACHINES WE HAVE RECENTLY DEVELOPED.
             OUR SALES REPRESENTATIVE IS LOOKING FORWARD TO HIS VISIT IN REGINA.
        HE KNOWS THAT THE MACHINES HE SELLS COULD BECOME AN INTEGRAL PART
        OF YOUR OFFICE ONLY A FEW DAYS AFTER IMPLEMENTATION.

                                        SINCERELY,

                                        ROGER SMITH, MANAGER
                                        OFFICE DEVICES CORPORATION
```

Fig. 5-11   Program to generate a personalized form letter (cont'd.)

Line 35 of the program begins a loop to read the lines of the form letter. In line 48 a loop to produce the personalized form letters for each of the customers is begun. The information concerning the recipient is read in and then split into the components that are to be used in the personalized letter. Each line of the form letter is then scanned and the keywords are replaced by the appropriate customer information. After this is done, the line is indented (if necessary). The line of the form letter is then printed.

This concludes our discussion of string applications in PASCAL. In this chapter, the concepts of string manipulation and operations on strings have been discussed. Several concepts in formatted input and output were introduced. The next section presented some basic string functions. Finally the ideas presented in the chapter were illustrated in the solution of the application problems given in Chap. 5 of the main text.

In the next chapter the use of procedures and functions is introduced.

EXERCISES FOR CHAPTER 5

1. Many programming languages, such as PASCAL, permit the programmer to use blanks anywhere within certain parts of each statement of a program. The compiler of such a program would probably remove all the unnecessary blanks. Usually in these languages, there is a label field associated with each statement that is processed in a different manner. In the case of PASCAL, the label is ended with a colon. Furthermore, the remaining part of the statement must lie within a fixed field, such as columns 7 through 72 in PASCAL.

    Write a program that will

    (i) Read in a text of 80 characters.
    (ii) Delete the last eight of them.
    (iii) Delete any leading or following blanks from the label (if one exists).
    (iv) Remove all blanks from the statement.
    (v) Print the modified text.

2. Write a program for converting Roman numerals to Arabic numerals. The input consists of a sequence of Roman numerals. For each of these Roman numerals, the corresponding Arabic numeral is to be generated. Table 5-1 gives the correspondence between the two number systems.

3. The usual way of writing a cheque requires five fields to be filled in, namely, the date, the person being paid, the amount as a number, the amount in words, and the signature of the issuer. The amount is written twice for consistency and protection. Computer-generated cheques sometimes do not generate the amount in words, since it is believed by some that a machine-printed amount is

Table 5-1

Roman symbol	Arabic equivalent
I	1
V	5
X	10
L	50
C	100
D	500
M	1000

Table 5-2

Input (in pennies)	Amount (in figures)	Amount in words
17573	$175.73	ONE HUNDRED SEVENTY-FIVE AND 73/100
2900	$ 29.00	TWENTY-NINE AND 00/100
48050	$480.50	FOUR HUNDRED EIGHTY AND 50/100
1362	$ 13.62	THIRTEEN AND 62/100

more difficult to change than its hand-written counterpart. Many companies have learned, however, that such is not the case and, consequently, these companies do print on each check the amount in words. Formulate a program which, given an integer amount, will print the amount in words. The integer amount lies in the range 100 through 99999 in pennies. Table 5-2 contains examples of numbers and their corresponding outputs.

4. A coded message is received on punched cards in groups of five letters separated by a blank. The last group of letters is followed by five 9's. The initial step in the decoding process is to replace each letter by another, according to a table which changes each day. This table precedes the coded message information and occupies one card. For example, the string

ABCDEFGHIJKLMNOPQRSTUVWXYZ
'DEFGHIJKLMNOPQRSTUVWXYZABC*/'

represents a coding table in which D replaces A, E replaces B, F replaces C, . . . , B replaces Y, and C replaces Z. Using this code, the encoded message

WKHZRbUOGLYbFRPLQbJWRDKbHKGCCb99999

with 'b' interpreted as a blank, will be decoded as

THEWORLDISCOMINGTOANENDZZ

Formulate a program which inputs the given data and decodes the message.

CHAPTER

SUBPROGRAMS: FUNCTIONS AND PROCEDURES

Chapter 6 of the main text deals with the notion of the subalgorithm. Any large problem is more easily solved if first it is broken into a number of smaller subproblems. The notion of "subprograms" is important in the programming process.

PASCAL supports the two forms of subprogram described in the main text — the function and the procedure. The use of functions and procedures in PASCAL is the topic of this chapter.

6-1 FUNCTIONS IN PASCAL

A PASCAL function is a group of statements within a program which form a somewhat independent and separate block or component. This block of statements constitutes a subprogram which performs a particular set of operations on a supplied set of arguments and returns a single value. Each time the function is invoked, control transfers to the block of statements defined for that function. After these statements have been performed, execution returns to the statement from which the function was called or *invoked*. A similar type of subprogram block, the *procedure*, is discussed in the next section.

The block of statements belonging to a function is written as a *function definition* in PASCAL and is almost always included with the main program. A transfer of execution from outside the program statements to the function is caused by a function *invocation*, written in the form:

entry-name (argument1, argument2, ...)

where *entry-name* is the name of the function being called. The arguments to be used by the function are listed in parentheses following the name of the function. Each argument may be any valid variable, constant, or expression.

In addition to the code comprising the statements to be executed, the definition of a function also includes the definition of its parameters. The general form of a function definition is as follows:

FUNCTION *entry-name (parameter declarations): attribute;*
 local identifier declarations
BEGIN
        executable statements
END;

The first statement is called the definition "head." The *entry-name* portion of the head is the name by which the particular function is known. This name must be a valid PASCAL identifier. The

(parameter declarations)

portion of the head statement constitutes the *parameter list* for the function. It lists the parameters, each which must be valid PASCAL identifiers, and their associated data types. The order of the list defines the order of correspondence with the arguments in the argument list of the invocation. That is, the first parameter in the parameter list will always correspond to the first argument in the argument list, the second parameter to the second argument, and so on. Therefore, the number of arguments in the invocation and parameters in the definition head must always be equal. If a particular function requires no parameters to be passed, then the list of arguments and the corresponding list of parameters are omitted, giving an invocation of the form:

entry-name

and a definition head of the form:

FUNCTION *entry-name: attribute;*

The *attribute* part of the definition head serves to indicate the type attribute of the value which the function returns. Only numeric, character, logical, set, or subrange values are allowed to be returned by functions; that is, only scalars can be returned.

As stated earlier, the definition head includes the *parameter declarations*. These consist of valid type declarations for the function parameters, and should, for each parameter, define attributes which agree with those of the corresponding argument. In PASCAL, the arguments and parameters must be of the same type. Parameter declarations appear in a similar format to that of the variable declarations, but with a few differences. The declarations of the parameters have the following form

VAR *variable$_1$, variable$_2$, . . ., variable$_n$: type identifier*

where VAR is optional. VAR's use is discussed in Sec. 6-3 as it determines the type of parameter passing that is to be used. The sequence may be repeated any number of times, allowing all variables to be defined according to their various types. For example, if the first parameter of a function is a 10-element vector of integers, the second and third are strings of equal length, and the last is a character variable, we could have the parameter declaration:

(VAR RECORDS: VECTOR; VAR NAME, ADDRESS: STRING(20); INITIAL INTEGER)

where VECTOR is defined to be of type ARRAY(1..10) OF INTEGER. In all cases VAR is optional, except if the corresponding argument is an expression or a constant, in which case it must be omitted. The reason for this is explained in Sec. 6-3.

An important restriction in PASCAL is that only type identifiers are allowed. Thus, the type declarations can be an identifier name such as INTEGER, STRING(*n*), or BOOLEAN, or the identifier for a programmer-defined data type , such as VECTOR in the example above. The type declarations cannot be arrays, set definitions, and so on. Thus declarations such as

NAMES: (AL, JOE, DAVE);
NUMBER, SIZE: 1..20;
DATES: ARRAY(1..10) OF INTEGER;

are not allowed. In order to pass arguments of these types, type identifiers must be associated with these types and are declared in the main (or calling) program.

The declaration head must be followed by the declarations of the *local* identifiers; that is, the variables which are not parameters and the labels, constants, and data types used by the function. All these declarations follow the same form as that for any identifier declaration, as discussed in Chap. 2.

The actual statements of the function (i.e., the function body) appear next in the definition, and are composed of any valid PASCAL statements. This body is enclosed in the BEGIN ... END construct as is done in the main program. The programmer must, for one of these statements, specify the value to be returned by the function through an assignment statement which assigns a value to the function name. This value must have the same type attribute as indicated in the declaration head, or at least attributes which can be converted to those of the function. Note that an array may not be returned, since it contains more than one value. Return to the calling program occurs when execution of the function "falls through" to the end of the function. This occurs when the END of the outermost compound statement is encountered. Control is then passed back to the point outside the program from which the function was invoked. The value obtained by the function name is returned to the invocation point as the value of the function. Notice that unlike the algorithmic notation, returning from a function always occurs at the end of the function. There is no RETURN statement in PASCAL. Also, the value to be returned is assigned to the function name instead.

The final line of the function definition, the "END" of the BEGIN ... END construct, indicates the *physical* termination of the executable part of the function.

As an example, the following is the complete definition of a function named MAXIMUM:

```
FUNCTION MAXIMUM (NUM1, NUM2, NUM3: REAL): REAL;
/* FIND THE MAXIMUM OF 3 NUMBERS */
VAR MAX: REAL;
BEGIN
    IF NUM1 > NUM2
    THEN MAX := NUM1
    ELSE MAX := NUM2;
    IF NUM3 > MAX
    THEN MAX := NUM3;
    MAXIMUM := MAX
END;
```

An invocation of this function must supply three values as arguments; these are represented in the function by parameters NUM1, NUM2, and NUM3. The function compares these values, which are integers, and returns the largest of the three as the value of MAXIMUM. A local variable MAX is used, and, after the comparisons are completed, it holds the value of the largest number. The function name MAXIMUM can only be used on the left-hand side of an assignment statement (without any parameters given). An ambiguity results if it appears on the right-hand side as to whether it means using a value previously assigned to the function, or another invocation of the function. Suppose that the following invocation appears in a program which contains this definition:

```
VALUE := MAXIMUM(A, B, C);
```

where variables VALUE, A, B, and C have previously been declared as having type INTEGER, and A, B, and C currently possess the values 37, 25, and 89, respectively. Execution of this statement causes control to transfer to the function definition statements, where the argument values are passed to the parameters. The statements of the function are performed, leaving the value 89 in the local variable MAX. When the MAXIMUM := MAX statement is executed, the value of the function effectively becomes 89. Then the end of the function is reached, and control returns to the invocation point in the calling program. The value 89 is returned as the resulting value of MAXIMUM, and thus the variable VALUE receives, through the assignment, the value 89.

Consider the result if the function's attributes of the definition head were changed from REAL to INTEGER, and also the variable VALUE was declared to be INTEGER. Execution of the function statements would produce the value 89 for MAX, as before. Before the value 89 may be returned to the point of invocation, however, the compiler converts 89 to a real value in the assignment of MAX to MAXIMUM. Notice that the conversion rules and restrictions follow those of assignment statements as discussed in Chap. 2.

Function definitions, as discussed thus far, are embedded inside a main program, and called from an invocation in the program. Function definitions always occur after the variable declaration section, but before the program body. More than one function may appear. In PASCAL this type of function is termed an *internal* function, since its definition is written within bounds of the main program. For example, in the following program skeleton:

```
PROGRAM HELLO (INPUT, OUTPUT);
declaration statements
        FUNCTION AVERAGE (VAR FIRST, SECOND: REAL): REAL;

                .

                .

                .

        END;
        program body
    END.
```

the function named AVERAGE is internal to the main program, and may be invoked by a function call anywhere in the section marked *program body*. This includes the executable part of the program and any other subprograms which may be defined. If a function definition is not included in the main program, then it is said to be an *external* function. Further discussion of internal and external functions is found in Sec. 6-4.

PASCAL requires that the declaration head of the function be declared before it is used. This serves to provide the compiler with information concerning the function. This is normally of no concern since the function is invoked in the program body. Problems occur when several functions occur in a program and one function may call another. This can be solved by ordering the functions in such a way so that if function A calls function B, function B's definition precedes that of function A. Unfortunately, this cannot always be done, as we shall see in Chap. 10. In such cases PASCAL allows the declaration head of the function to be placed before the function, in effect, separating the function head from the rest of the function. The function head is given as previously defined but it is immediately followed by FORWARD; which indicates it is a *forward reference* to a function. The function head then becomes

```
FUNCTION entry-name;
```

without any parameters or attributes. They are not necessary since they have been previously defined. As an example, suppose a function named ST_DEV calls a function SUM. We may have the following form for the function declarations:

```
TYPE VECTOR = ARRAY(1..10) OF REAL;
      .
      .
      .

FUNCTION SUM (VAR X: VECTOR): REAL; FORWARD;
FUNCTION ST_DEV (VAR X: VECTOR): REAL;
      .
      .
      .

      VALUE := SUM (A);
      .
      .
      .

FUNCTION SUM;
      .
      .
      .
```

Notice that if the function SUM had been placed before the function ST_DEV, the forward reference would not be required.

The use of functions is illustrated further in the following program example:

```
PROGRAM LIST (INPUT, OUTPUT);
TYPE STRINGS: ARRAY(1..50) OF STRING(256);
VAR NAMES: STRINGS;
      CTR, A_B_NUM: INTEGER;
      FUNCTION COUNT (VAR ARR: STRINGS): INTEGER;
      VAR TALLY, J: INTEGER;
          STR: STRING(256);
          A, B: STRING(256);
      PROCEDURE SUB (VAR S: STRING(256); POS, NUM: INTEGER;
          VAR ADD: STRING(256)); EXTERNAL;
      BEGIN
          TALLY := 0;
          A := 'A*/';
          B := 'B*/';
          FOR J := 1 TO 50 DO
          BEGIN
              SUB (ARR(J), 1, 1, STR);
              IF (STR = A) OR (STR = B)
              THEN TALLY := TALLY + 1
          END;
          COUNT := TALLY
      END;
```

```
BEGIN
      FOR CTR := 1 TO 10 DO
            READ (NAMES(CTR));
            .
            .
            .
      A_B_NUM := COUNT (NAMES);
      WRITELN ('', A_B_NUM, ' OF THE FOLLOWING NAMES BEGIN WITH',
            'THE LETTER A OR B');
      FOR CTR := 1 TO 50 DO
            WRITELN ('', NAMES(CTR): 100);
            .
            .
            .
      END.
```

The main program begins execution by reading a list of 50 names into the array NAMES. The function was not executed because it does not appear in the executable part of the program. After some intervening statements, an invocation of the function COUNT is encountered, in the assignment A_B_NUM := COUNT (NAMES);. At this point, execution is transferred to the function COUNT. The entire array NAMES is the only argument passed, and is represented in the function statements by the parameter ARR. Notice that the data identifier STRINGS was used to declare its data type in the declaration head. This head also indicates that the value to be returned is an integer. After the parameter ARR is declared, the local identifiers are declared. Execution of the counted loop then occurs. This serves to count the number of names in the array which begin with the letter A or the letter B. This number is held in the variable TALLY. After termination of the loop, an assignment of TALLY to COUNT is performed, giving the function a value which can be returned, and the transfer of control back to the invocation point occurs. The assignment to the variable A_B_NUM can now be completed, giving it the returned value. Execution of the main program statements now continues, in normal sequence, until the end of the program.

Arrays cannot be dimensioned in subprograms at runtime in PASCAL. That is, we cannot pass an argument to a subprogram which is used within the subprogram to define the size of an array. A constant, given as either an identifier or a value, must be used, but in the case of an identifier, it can be defined in the main program.

The ability to define functions and to call them from any point in a program is a powerful programming tool. First of all, it allows the programmer to defer writing certain program portions until later, while still being able to write the main part of the program. For example, in the previous outline example, the main program statements could have been written without also having to worry, at that time, about writing the statements for counting the names beginning with the letter A or the letter B. The programmer need only remember that, later he or she will have to compose a function named COUNT to do this operation and then to include it inside the main program before it is run. This permits the programmer to concentrate on one task at a time, and thus one cause of error is eliminated. Second, if a particular operation or set of operations is required at several different points in a program, the programmer is spared having to write out the statements to perform the task each time. Instead, the operation statements may be written once, in the form of a single function to be included with the program, and an invocation to the function written at each point where the operation is required.

We turn now to a second type of subprogram available in PASCAL, which provides the same programming enhancements in a slightly different way.

Exercises for Sec. 6-1

1. Design a function that takes a parameter X and returns the following value:

$$\frac{1}{X^5(\dfrac{e^{1.432}}{X} - 1)}$$

2. (i) In Chap. 2, built-in functions TRUNC and ROUND were introduced. Although convenient for programming, ROUND is acutally redundant. Design a function to perform the action of ROUND using TRUNC.

   (ii) The function FLOOR(X) is defined as the largest integer value not exceeding X. This is not quite the same as the TRUNC function. For example, FLOOR (4.72) is 4, but FLOOR(–16.8) is –17. Use the built-in functions listed in Chap. 2 to design a function to compute FLOOR(X).

   (iii) The function MOD(X, Y) is defined as the remainder that results from the division of X by Y (X and Y are both integers, as is the remainder). For example, MOD(8, 3) is 2. Formulate a function to compute MOD(X, Y).

3. Design functions MEAN and STD to compute the mean and standard deviation, respectively, of the N elements of a vector X, according to the following formulas:

$$MEAN\ (X) = \frac{1}{N}\sum_{i=1}^{N} X_i$$

$$STD\ (X) = \frac{1}{N}\sum_{i=1}^{N}(X_i - MEAN(X))^2$$

N is never greater than 25.

4. An expression involving a variable X such as

$$A(1)*X^1 + A(2)*X^2 + A(3)*X^3 + CONSTANT$$

can be evaluated for many values of X. For example, if

A(1) = 3, A(2) = 1, A(3) = 0.5 and CONSTANT = 5.2,

then the value of the expression for X = 2 is

$$(3)*(2) + 1*(2)^2 + 0.5*(2)^3 + 5.2 = 19.2$$

Desired is a function that would calculate

$$A(1)*X^1 + A(2)*X^2 + A(3)*X^3 + ... + A(N)*X^N + CONSTANT$$

given the value of N, a particular set of coefficients (a vector A, never containing more than 20 elements), a CONSTANT and the value of X. Design a function EVAL that will accept the value of N, the CONSTANT, the coefficients (vector A) and a value for X. It will then evaluate the given expression for the value of X and return the resulting value to the point of call.

6-2 PROCEDURES IN PASCAL

As we saw in the previous section, a function is a block of statements, which, when invoked, performs the specified operations, and returns a single value.

A procedure in PASCAL is a block of statements similar to a function, but with two important differences. First, it is invoked in a different manner; that is, the PASCAL statement consists of the entry-name and the arguments to the procedure, as follows

entry-name (argument1, argument2, ...)

where *entry-name* is the name given to the procedure block. The list of arguments following it is identical in format to the argument list in a function invocation, serving to pass values to the corresponding procedure parameters. The execution of this statement causes immediate transfer of control to the statements of the procedure's definition (to be discussed later), and establishes the correspondence between arguments and parameters. After execution of the procedure statements, control is returned to the statement which immediately follows the statement which invoked the procedure.

The second important difference is that no single value is returned by a procedure to the point of invocation. Instead, any number of values can be passed back to the main program through the parameters. Thus, the particular method used to set up the correspondence between arguments and parameters must allow "reverse" passing of values (that is, from parameters to arguments) as well as the usual passing of values from arguments to parameters (see Sec. 6-3).

To illustrate the use of "two-way" value passing between an argument and parameter in a procedure, suppose a procedure named SORT has been defined, which sorts a given array. We wish to invoke it in the main program, to sort an array named NAMES. A valid invocation would be

SORT (NAMES)

where the argument is the array itself. The invocation transfers execution to the SORT definition statements, and passes the argument value to the parameter of the procedure. After the sort operations have been performed on the parameter array, the NAMES array in the main program should also contain the sorted array entries (not the original, unsorted entries). In the next section we will examine methods of argument-parameter correspondence which result in this and other effects.

A procedure definition in PASCAL is very similar to a function definition, but with a few important differences. First, the keyword FUNCTION is replaced by the PROCEDURE in the declaration head indicating that the subprogram is a procedure. The definition head for a procedure does not contain an attribute after the parameter declarations since no single value is returned as is the case for a function. The parameters, listed in the definition head, are given the values of the corresponding arguments upon invocation of the procedure. Procedures which do not have any parameters may also be defined, with a definition head of the form:

PROCEDURE *entry-name;*

and invocations of the form:

entry-name

Notice the absence of the CALL which was used to invoke a procedure in the main text; this does not imply that procedures can be used in expressions, because they do not return a value. The procedure parameters, listed in the parameter declarations, and local variable declarations are the same as for a function. The statements in the procedure perform the desired operations on the parameters, and usually pass values back to the main program through the parameters. Unlike functions, no assignment of a value to the procedure name occurs. Execution of a procedure is terminated by reaching the end of the procedure. Note that as in the case of a function, no "RETURN" statement is available to specify returning to the calling program. The following example is a procedure which when given two integer values returns the quotient and remainder produced by the division of the first integer by the second.

```
PROCEDURE DIVIDE (VAR DIVIDEND, DIVISOR, QUOTIENT, REMAINDER: INTEGER);
BEGIN
    (* PERFORM INTEGER DIVISION *)
    QUOTIENT := DIVIDEND DIV DIVISOR;
    (* DETERMINE REMAINDER *)
    REMAINDER := DIVIDEND - QUOTIENT * DIVISOR
END;
```

As with functions in PASCAL, a forward declaration for a procedure may be required if an invocation of the procedure appears before it is defined. The format of a forward declaration is the same as for functions.

It should be noticed that if a parameter is to return a value to its corresponding argument, it must be preceded by VAR. If VAR is absent, any change made to the value of the parameter will not be transferred to its argument (see Sec. 6-3).

Procedures may be defined inside or outside the main program body, yielding *internal* and *external* procedures, respectively. We will study added features of the use of internal procedures in Sec. 6-4.

Let us turn now to a more complete example of the use of a procedure. A program is required to input and sort a set of data cards concerning a store's employees. Each card contains two character strings — the name of an employee, and the employee's five-character identification code. The last card contains dummy data values of

'LAST_NAME' 'AOOOO'

The program must print two lists: first a sorted list of the employees names, and then a sorted list of the identification codes. A procedure SORT is used in the solution given in Fig. 6-1. The main program begins by reading in the employee names and codes into separate vectors NAMES and CODES, counting them as they are read using the variable NUM. The first invocation of the procedure SORT is then encountered, with the NAMES array and the variable NUM as arguments. Control transfers immediately to the SORT procedure. The two parameters are LIST and COUNT, which receive the values of the NAMES array and NUM, respectively. Local variables TEMP, MIN, POS, and PASS are declared and created at the start of the procedure execution. A selection sort is then performed on the array

```
0  0000   00001   PROGRAM EMP_EES (INPUT, OUTPUT);
0  0000   00002   (* THIS PROGRAM INPUTS AND SORTS A LIST OF EMPLOYEES BY BOTH THEIR
0  0000   00003      NAMES AND THEIR IDENTIFICATION CODES. *)
0  0000   00004
0  0000   00005   TYPE VECTOR = ARRAY(1..50) OF STRING(20);
0  0038   00006   VAR NAMES,                     (* EMPLOYEE NAMES LIST *)
0  0038   00007      CODES: VECTOR;             (* IDENTIFICATION CODES LIST *)
0  0038   00008      NUM,                       (* NUMBER OF EMPLOYEES *)
0  0038   00009      K : INTEGER;               (* COUNTED LOOP VARIABLE *)
0  0038   00010
0  0038   00011      PROCEDURE SORT (VAR LIST: VECTOR; VAR COUNT: INTEGER);
1  0000   00012      (* THIS PROCEDURE SORTS THE ARRAY LIST OF COUNT ELEMENTS *)
1  0000   00013
1  0000   00014      VAR MIN,                    (* MINIMUM VALUE IN A PASS *)
1  0056   00015         POS, PASS: INTEGER;      (* COUNTED LOOP VARIABLES *)
1  0056   00016         TEMP: STRING(20);        (* USED TO EXCHANGE ELEMENTS *)
1  0056   00017
1  0056   00018      BEGIN
1  0056   00019
1  0056   00020         (* PERFORM THE PASSES *)
1  0056   00021         FOR PASS := 1 TO COUNT - 1 DO
1  007E   00022         BEGIN
1  007E   00023
1  007E   00024            (* FIND MINIMUM ELEMENT *)
1  007E   00025            MIN := PASS;
1  0086   00026            FOR POS := PASS + 1 TO COUNT DO
1  00B0   00027               IF LIST(POS) < LIST(MIN)
1  00F4   00028               THEN MIN := POS;
1  0106   00029
1  0106   00030            (* EXCHANGE ELEMENT IF NECESSARY *)
1  0106   00031            IF MIN <> PASS
1  010A   00032            THEN BEGIN
1  0116   00033               TEMP := LIST(MIN);
1  013E   00034               LIST(MIN) := LIST(PASS);
1  0188   00035               LIST(PASS) := TEMP
1  01AA   00036               END
1  01B0   00037         END
1  01B0   00038   END;
```

Fig. 6-1 Program EMP_EES

```
0   0038   00039   BEGIN
0   0038   00040
0   0038   00041       (* READ EMPLOYEES *)
0   0038   00042       NUM := 1;
0   0040   00043       READ (NAMES(1), CODES(1));
0   0064   00044       WHILE NAMES(NUM) <> 'LAST_NAME          ' DO
0   0090   00045       BEGIN
0   0090   00046           NUM := NUM + 1;
0   009C   00047           READ (NAMES(NUM), CODES(NUM))
0   0100   00048       END;
0   0104   00049       NUM := NUM - 1;
0   0110   00050
0   0110   00051       (* SORT THE LIST OF EMPLOYEE NAMES INTO ASCENDING ORDER *)
0   0110   00052       SORT (NAMES, NUM);
0   0136   00053
0   0136   00054       (* SORT THE LIST OF EMPLOYEE CODES INTO ASCENDING ORDER *)
0   0136   00055       SORT (CODES, NUM);
0   015C   00056
0   015C   00057       (* PRINT THE SORTED LISTS *)
0   015C   00058       WRITELN (' EMPLOYEE NAMES LIST:');
0   016E   00059       FOR K := 1 TO NUM DO
0   0192   00060           WRITELN (' ', NAMES(K));
0   01DA   00061       WRITELN ('-EMPLOYEE CODES LIST:');
0   01EC   00062       FOR K := 1 TO NUM DO
0   0210   00063           WRITELN (' ', CODES(K))
0   0254   00064   END.
```

```
-----------------------------------
¦ COMPILE TIME:     0.150 SECOND(S) ¦
¦     NO WARNING(S) DETECTED        ¦
¦     NO ERROR(S) DETECTED          ¦
-----------------------------------
--EXECUTION-->
EMPLOYEE NAMES LIST:
BUNT, RICK
MAZER, MURRAY
OPSETH, LYLE
SMITH, JANE
TREMBLAY, JEAN PAUL


EMPLOYEE CODES LIST:
B5672
M1298
O8736
S7311
T1234
```

Fig. 6-1   Program EMP_EES (cont'd.)

parameter LIST. The COUNT parameter contains the value of NUM, and thus indicates the actual number of elements in the array being sorted. When the end of the procedures is reached, the array is in sorted order. Execution of the procedure then terminates and control reverts to the main program statement following the first invocation, which turns out to be a second invocation, with the argument NAMES now containing the array in sorted order. On this second invocation, the first argument is the CODES array, and the second is again NUM (CODES also has NUM elements in it). Once again, control transfers to the SORT procedure, with the parameter LIST now corresponding to the CODES array. As a result, the execution of the SORT procedure causes the CODES array to be sorted. Termination of the second execution of SORT returns control to the statement following the second invocation, namely the first of the output statements. The two ordered lists are then printed. The next statements performed are the final output statements, after which the program terminates. Notice that local variables TEMP, MIN, POS, and PASS are created and destroyed on two separate occasions, once for each execution of SORT. Note also the relationship between the parameter COUNT and the argument NUM to which it corresponds during both calls to the procedure. During procedure execution, if any change to its current value had occurred, the value of NUM would also be so altered, causing unexpected results on the second call of the procedure. Fortunately, however, the SORT operations never cause a change in the value given to COUNT.

We have seen, in this section, that a PASCAL procedure is similar in many respects to a function. The major differences between the two forms of subprogram are the manner in which they are invoked, and the manner in which results are returned to the point of call. The programmer, in deciding what type to use in a particular program, must determine which is most suitable for the given application.

Exercises for Sec. 6-2

1. One of the earliest applications of computers was the calculation of shell trajectories. If a shell is fired with an initial velocity V (feet per second) at an angle of inclination B (radians), its position in the vertical x,y plane at time t (seconds) is calculated from the following:

   $$x = (V \cos\Theta) t$$
   $$y = (V \sin\Theta) t - \tfrac{1}{2}g t^2$$

   where $0 < \Theta < \pi/2$ and g = 32 feet per second^2.

   Design a procedure with parameters Θ and V that will list the x,y co-ordinates at intervals of 0.01 seconds for a particular firing, terminating the list when the shell hits the ground.

2. Design a procedure to center a title. The procedure it to take as an input parameter a card image string, somewhere in which appears a title. The procedure is to produce a print line image string (of length 120) in which the input text (excluding the leading and trailing blanks) is to be centered as nearly as possible within the string; that is, to within one blank, the number of blanks before the title is the same as the number after. This print line image is then to be returned to the point of call.

3. Design a procedure to accept as a parameter a vector which may contain duplicate entries. The procedure is to replace each repeated value by −1 and return to the point of call the altered vector and the number of altered entries.

4. Design a procedure TRIM to accept as a parameter an arbitrary character string and return a string in which all the trailing blanks are removed.
   For example,

   > Input   'JOHNbSTEEDbbb*/'
   > Output   JOHNbSTEED

   where 'b' represents a blank.

5. Design a procedure REVERSE to accept as a parameter an arbitrary character string and return a string of the same length in which the order of the characters is reversed. That is, the first character of the output string is the last character of the input string, and so on.

6-3 ARGUMENT-PARAMETER CORRESPONDENCE

An association or correspondence is formed between each argument and its parameter *every time a* procedure or function is invoked. Section 6-4 of the main text discusses two methods by which this correspondence can be achieved. These are known as call by value (or, pass by value) and call by reference (or pass as variable). Both of these methods are available in PASCAL.

Call by value simply involves assigning the value of the argument concerned, upon invocation of the procedure or function, to its parameter in the subprogram definition. The parameter is, in effect, a newly-created independent variable, with its own memory location, that receives the value of the argument upon the start of the subprogram execution. Since the parameter and argument are independent variables, any change to the parameter that occurs during subprogram execution has no effect whatsoever on the value of the original argument. This means that when call by value is employed, the passing of values back to the point of invocation through the parameter is impossible. Call by value is, therefore, most useful for parameters where initial transmission of the argument value to the parameter is required upon invocation, to be followed by a severance of any further communication between argument and parameter. Upon termination of subprogram execution, the parameter variable is destroyed and the value(s) which it held, are lost. *Call by reference*, unlike call by value, does not involve creating a separate memory location for the parameter. Instead, invocation causes the passing of the *address* of the actual storage location where the value of the argument is held. The parameter, in effect, becomes merely another name for the same location already created for the argument value. This method of association implies, then, that each time the parameter name is encountered in the subprogram, the actual location which it references is precisely that of the argument. The effect of this is the passing of values in both directions between argument and parameter. That is, the parameter "receives" the current argument value at the time of invocation, and any subsequent assignment of new values to the parameter during subprogram execution causes that assignment to occur on the argument. Call by reference, then, is most useful for parameters where communication of value in both directions is required (for example, Fig. 6-1, the array parameter LIST).

Both forms of correspondence apply to function calls, as well as to procedure calls. A function, therefore, has the ability now to return values back to the main program in two ways — as the value of the function (as discussed in Sec. 6-1), and through arguments governed by call by reference parameter-argument correspondence. For procedures, as mentioned in Sec. 6-2, only the latter method is available for return of results.

PASCAL allows the programmer to specify the type of parameter passing. If a list of parameters is declared to be one type (i.e., they are all separated by commas and are followed by an attribute), and is preceded by VAR, then call by reference (variable) is used. If VAR is absent, call by value is assumed. Note that expressions and constants must be passed by value because the subprogram cannot be allowed to change the value of the parameters. Upon returning to the calling program, an error would result if we try to change a previously computed value of an expression or the value of a constant. In other words, if call by reference is used, the argument must be a variable. Furthermore, arrays should be passed by reference. Call by value requires that new storage be created for the array, and the values of the original array must be copied into the new array. This wastes space and slows down the execution time of the program. Arrays should be passed by value only where necessary.

The following example illustrates theses rules, and the effects of call by value and call by reference. Suppose a program is written which inputs a list of product codes, each being a string between one and six characters long. After some intermediate processing, the program must sequence through the list of codes, counting the number of codes beginning with the character "0." As the search proceeds, each character "0" beginning any code must be changed to the character "1." A function BEGINS is used in the solution given in Fig. 6-2. Notice in this example that the conditions required for call by reference are met for the argument CODES and parameter VALS in the function invocation, and thus, as desired, the VALS parameter is merely another name for the array stored in CODES. The function execution causes the required replacement to occur directly on the codes in the CODES array. The second argument in the invocation is an expression NBR – 1, meaning call by value must be used. This implies the value obtained from evaluation of this simple expression is assigned to the location newly created in storage for parameter NUM. Upon completion of the function, the variable NUM, and its value, are destroyed.

Consider the effect if the declaration for the parameter VALS had been written without the VAR prefix. The result is a call by value correspondence

```
0  0000   00001   PROGRAM PRODUCT (INPUT, OUTPUT);
0  0000   00002   (* THIS PROGRAM INPUTS A LIST OF PRODUCT CODES AND COUNTS THE NUMBER OF
0  0000  '00003      CODES BEGINNING WITH ZERO, CHANGING EACH' ONE TO A ONE. *)
0  0000   00004
0  0000   00005   TYPE VECTOR = ARRAY(1..30) OF STRING(256);
0  0038   00006   VAR CODES: VECTOR;                    (* PRODUCT CODES LIST *)
0  0038   00007       REPLACE,                          (* NUMBER OF REPLACEMENTS *)
0  0038   00008       NBR,                              (* NUMBER OF CODES READ *)
0  0038   00009       I: INTEGER;                       (* COUNTED LOOP VARIABLE *)
0  0038   00010
0  0038   00011       PROCEDURE SUB (VAR S: STRING(256); POS, NUM: INTEGER;
1  0000   00012            VAR RESULT: STRING(256)); EXTERNAL;
0  0038   00013       PROCEDURE PSDSUB (VAR S: STRING(256); POS, NUM: INTEGER;
1  0000   00014            VAR ADD: STRING(256)); EXTERNAL;
0  0038   00015
0  0038   00016       FUNCTION BEGINS (VAR VALS: VECTOR; NUM: INTEGER): INTEGER;
1  0000   00017       (* SUBSTITUTE ALL INITIAL '0' BY '1' AND COUNT THE NUMBER OF
1  0000   00018          REPLACEMENTS REQUIRED. *)
1  0000   00019
1  0000   00020       VAR COUNT,                        (* NUMBER OF REPLACEMENTS *)
1  0056   00021           K: INTEGER;                   (* COUNTED LOOP VARIABLE *)
1  0056   00022           ONE, ZERO,                    (* VALUES '1' AND '0' *)
1  0056   00023           STR: STRING(256);             (* TEMPORARY STRING VARIABLE *)
1  0056   00024
1  0056   00025       BEGIN
1  0056   00026           ONE := '1*/';
1  005C   00027           ZERO := '0*/';
1  0062   00028           COUNT := 0;
1  0068   00029           FOR K := 1 TO NUM DO
1  008C   00030           BEGIN
1  008C   00031               SUB (VALS(K), 1, 1, STR);
1  00DE   00032               IF STR = ZERO
1  00DE   00033               THEN BEGIN
1  00E8   00034                   COUNT := COUNT + 1;
1  00F4   00035                   PSDSUB (VALS(K), 1, 1, ONE)
1  0132   00036                   END
1  0146   00037           END;
1  014A   00038           BEGINS := COUNT
1  014A   00039       END;
```

Fig. 6-2 Program PRODUCT

```
0   0038   00040
0   0038   00041   BEGIN
0   0038   00042
0   0038   00043        (* INPUT LIST OF PRODUCT CODES *)
0   0038   00044        WRITELN (' THE CODES READ ARE:');
0   004A   00045        NBR := 1;
0   0052   00046        READ (CODES(NBR));
0   0084   00047        WHILE NOT EOF DO
0   008C   00048        BEGIN
0   008C   00049             WRITELN ('  ', CODES(NBR): 6);
0   00D0   00050             NBR := NBR + 1;
0   00DC   00051             READ (CODES(NBR))
0   010E   00052        END;
0   0112   00053
0   0112   00054        (* REPLACE BEGINNING '0' BY '1' AND COUNT *)
0   0112   00055        REPLACE := BEGINS (CODES, NBR - 1);
0   014A   00056        WRITELN ('-', REPLACE: 2, ' REPLACEMENTS WERE MADE');
0   0180   00057        WRITELN (' THE NEW CODE LIST IS');
0   0192   00058        FOR I := 1 TO NBR - 1 DO
0   01BA   00059             WRITELN ('  ', CODES(I): 6)
0   01FE   00060   END.
-------------------------------------
| COMPILE TIME:     0.152 SECOND(S) |
|     NO WARNING(S) DETECTED        |
|     NO ERROR(S) DETECTED          |
-------------------------------------
--EXECUTION-->
THE CODES READ ARE:
025387
124316
521333
001238
098287
123456


 3 REPLACEMENTS WERE MADE
THE NEW CODE LIST IS
125387
124316
521333
101238
198287
123456
```

Fig. 6-2   Program PRODUCT (cont'd.)

between the two, not the previous call by reference association. Thus, no replacements made in the VALS array by the function operations would be affected in the CODES array, and the contents of the latter following the execution of the function would remain unchanged from its contents prior to the invocation.

The programmer must always be cautious, when implementing subprograms, that the conditions required by PASCAL for establishment of the type of correspondence he or she desires for certain arguments are met. Errors may result if expressions, for example, are passed by reference.

In Sec. 6-1 and Sec. 6-2 a classification of functions and procedures into internal and external types was mentioned. These types are further examined in the section to follow, along with special features of each.

Exercises for Sec. 6-3

1.   A procedure is desired to accept as a parameter an arbitrary vector of numeric elements. The procedure is to calculate certain statistics concerning the

vector. The vector is to be returned unchanged, though the procedure in calculating the required statistics may change elements in the vector. What type of parameter passing is required? Why?

2. Consider the following procedure ADD, with parameters A and B, which calculates the sum of A and B rounded to the nearest integer and returns the value in B.

```
 PROCEDURE ADD (VAR A, B: REAL);
BEGIN
      B := ROUND (A + B)
END;
```

This procedure is invoked in the following program:

```
PROGRAM TEST (INPUT, OUTPUT);
VAR A, B: REAL;
BEGIN
      READ (A, B);
      ADD (A, B);
      WRITELN (' ROUNDED SUM IS ', B)
END.
```

Give the results of the WRITELN statement, explaining in detail what happens. Suppose the declaration in the ADD procedure call were changed to

```
PROCEDURE ADD (A, B: REAL);
```

How would this affect the execution of the program and procedure? What would be the result of the WRITELN statement now?

6-4 INTERNAL AND EXTERNAL SUBPROGRAMS IN PASCAL

We have already stated that both functions and procedures may be placed either inside or outside the statements of the main program, yielding, respectively, internal and external subprograms. The use of external subprograms was mentioned in Chap. 5. The notions of internality and externality are examined in this section, illustrating important differences between the two.

An internal subprogram is one which is defined within the main program statements, and thus one which is called by invocations in the main program. Internal subprograms may themselves contain definitions of other subprograms, which are called from within the outer subprogram. Thus, several levels of internal nesting are possible. The levels of nesting define where invocations can and cannot be made. In fact, the levels of nesting define what is known as the *scope* of a name. For example, consider the following program outline:

```
PROGRAM PGM (INPUT, OUTPUT);
program declarations
        PROCEDURE B1
        procedure declarations
                PROCEDURE B2
                procedure declarations
                BEGIN
                    .
                    .
                    .
                END;
        BEGIN
            .
            .
            .
        END;
BEGIN
    .
    .
    .
END.
```

Two subprograms (procedures are used, but any of these may be functions) are present, named B1 and B2, and both are internal to the main program. Note, however, that B2 is itself internal to the B1 subprogram. The subprogram B1 may be invoked by an invocation in the main program statements, but, because of its nesting level, the subprogram B2 may only be invoked from within the B1 statements. That is, the main program cannot call the subprogram B2. The general rule is that reference is permitted to something within the current scope (or nesting level), or a scope *enclosing* the current scope, but not to something in an *enclosed* scope. This rule will be elaborated on shortly.

The use of internal subprograms permits another means through which communication between a subprogram and a main program (or, more generally, between two compatible scopes) can occur. This involves the use of *global variables*. To demonstrate global variables, consider the following outline:

```
PROGRAM PGM (INPUT, OUTPUT);
VAR VAR1: INTEGER;
        PROCEDURE SORT ...;
        VAR VAR2: INTEGER;
        BEGIN
            .
            .
            .
        END;
BEGIN
    .
    .
    .
END.
```

The subprogram SORT is internal to the main program PGM, and may be called by an invocation in PGM. The variable VAR2 is *local* to the subprogram SORT, since it is declared within it. Thus it is known only to the subprogram SORT. It is created only when SORT is invoked and destroyed upon termination of an execution of SORT. Consider now the variable VAR1, which is declared in the main program. Because it is declared where it is (in an enclosing scope), VAR1 is said to be *global* to the internal subprogram SORT, meaning that it may be used not only in the main program, but also within the SORT statements. Generally, any variable name which is declared in a particular scope is global to all scopes which are internal to it. A global variable need not be redeclared inside a subprogram definition, unless the name is intended for reuse, that is, intended to represent a separate, local variable, not related to the variable of the same name in the invoking block. Note that if execution of an internal subprogram uses and alters the current value of one of the variables that are global to it, then the value of the variable, upon termination of the subprogram, is then the latest, and not the original, value which it received. In this way, global variables can provide a simple method for communication of values in both directions between an internal subprogram and the main program (or block from which invocation occurred), but at the same time can lead to dangerous side effects for the unwitting programmer.

As an illustration of nested internal subprograms, and the use of global variables in subprograms, consider the modified version appearing in Fig. 6-3 of the program EMP_EES, first given in Sec. 6-2. The procedure SORT is internal to the main program EMP_EES, as before. The differences in this version are within the SORT procedure, where the switching of two elements in the array is now performed by invoking procedure references the local variables declared in the SORT procedure, since they are global to EXCHNGE. Thus, EXCHNGE uses the variables TEMP, LIST, MIN, and PASS just as if they were declared within that procedure. After an execution of EXCHNGE, the two elements LIST(MIN) and LIST(PASS) have exchanged values, which in turn implies that those two elements in the main program have also switched values (by call by reference between NAMES and LIST).

The program EMP_EES could further be rewritten to make more extensive use of the communication provided by global variables in internal subprograms. This is done in the third version of the same program given in Fig. 6-4. In this version, an invocation of the SORT procedure does not require the passing of a second argument, which previously was necessary to inform that procedure of the number of elements in the array to be sorted. This item of information, held in the variable, NUM, is now communicated to SORT using the fact that NUM is global to the procedure. Thus, the variable name NUM is used directly in the SORT statements. When using internal subprograms, as in this case, the programmer is often faced with the decision of whether to establish communication between a variable in the invoking block and a variable in the subprogram by argument-parameter correspondence in the parameter list or by global variables. Although the latter method (use of global variable reference) may appear to be less troublesome to implement than the former, we advocate that you consider its use very carefully since it decreases the modularity of the subprogram and can lead to errors that are very hard to detect.

Let us now look briefly at the second type of subprogram to be discussed in this section — external subprograms. These are subprograms which are not contained within the main program, nor within any other subprogram. Instead, the

```
0  0000  00001  PROGRAM EMP_EES (INPUT, OUTPUT);
0  0000  00002  (* THIS PROGRAM INPUTS AND SORTS A LIST OF EMPLOYEES BY BOTH THEIR
0  0000  00003     NAMES AND THEIR IDENTIFICATION CODES. *)
0  0000  00004
0  0000  00005  TYPE VECTOR = ARRAY(1..50) OF STRING(20);
0  0038  00006  VAR NAMES,                          (* EMPLOYEE NAMES LIST *)
0  0038  00007     CODES: VECTOR;                   (* IDENTIFICATION CODES LIST *)
0  0038  00008     NUM,                             (* NUMBER OF EMPLOYEES *)
0  0038  00009     K: INTEGER;                      (* COUNTED LOOP VARIABLE *)
0  0038  00010
0  0038  00011     PROCEDURE SORT (VAR LIST: VECTOR; VAR COUNT: INTEGER);
1  0000  00012     (* THIS PROCEDURE SORTS THE ARRAY LIST OF COUNT ELEMENTS *)
1  0000  00013
1  0000  00014     VAR MIN,                         (* MINIMUM VALUE IN A PASS *)
1  0056  00015         POS, PASS: INTEGER;          (* COUNTED LOOP VARIABLES *)
1  0056  00016         TEMP: STRING(20);            (* USED TO EXCHANGE ELEMENTS *)
1  0056  00017
1  0056  00018        PROCEDURE EXCHNGE;
2  0000  00019        (* EXCHANGE TWO ELEMENTS IN THE LIST ARRAY *)
2  0000  00020
2  0000  00021        BEGIN
2  003C  00022            TEMP := LIST(MIN);
2  0064  00023            LIST(MIN) := LIST(PASS);
2  00AE  00024            LIST(PASS) := TEMP
2  00D0  00025        END;
1  0056  00026
1  0056  00027     BEGIN
1  0056  00028
1  0056  00029        (* PERFORM THE PASSES *)
1  0056  00030        FOR PASS := 1 TO COUNT - 1 DO
1  007E  00031        BEGIN
1  007E  00032
1  007E  00033            (* FIND THE MINIMUM ELEMENT *)
1  007E  00034            MIN := PASS;
1  0086  00035            FOR POS := PASS + 1 TO COUNT DO
1  00B0  00036                IF LIST(POS) < LIST(MIN)
1  00F4  00037                THEN MIN := POS;
1  0106  00038
1  0106  00039            (* EXCHANGE ELEMENT IF NECESSARY *)
1  0106  00040            IF MIN <> PASS
1  010A  00041            THEN EXCHNGE
1  0116  00042        END
1  0122  00043     END;
0  0038  00044
0  0038  00045  BEGIN
0  0038  00046
0  0038  00047     (* READ EMPLOYEES *)
0  0038  00048     NUM := 1;
0  0040  00049     READ (NAMES(1), CODES(1));
0  0064  00050     WHILE NAMES(NUM) <> 'LAST_NAME          ' DO
0  0090  00051     BEGIN
0  0090  00052         NUM := NUM + 1;
0  009C  00053         READ (NAMES(NUM), CODES(NUM))
0  0100  00054     END;
0  0104  00055     NUM := NUM - 1;
0  0110  00056
0  0110  00057     (* SORT THE LIST OF EMPLOYEE NAMES INTO ASCENDING ORDER *)
0  0110  00058     SORT (NAMES, NUM);
0  0136  00059
0  0136  00060     (* SORT THE LIST OF EMPLOYEE CODES INTO ASCENDING ORDER *)
0  0136  00061     SORT (CODES, NUM);
0  015C  00062
0  015C  00063     (* PRINT THE SORTED LISTS *)
0  015C  00064     WRITELN (' EMPLOYEE NAMES LIST:');
0  016E  00065     FOR K := 1 TO NUM DO
0  0192  00066         WRITELN ('  ', NAMES(K));
0  01DA  00067     WRITELN ('-EMPLOYEE CODES LIST:');
0  01EC  00068     FOR K := 1 TO NUM DO
0  0210  00069         WRITELN ('  ', CODES(K))
0  0254  00070  END.
```

```
----------------------------------
| COMPILE TIME:   0.154 SECOND(S) |
|    NO WARNING(S) DETECTED        |
|    NO ERROR(S) DETECTED          |
----------------------------------
```

Fig. 6-3 Modified EMP_EES using nested internal subprograms

```
0  0000   00001  PROGRAM EMP_EES (INPUT, OUTPUT);
0  0000   00002  (* THIS PROGRAM INPUTS AND SORTS A LIST OF EMPLOYEES BY BOTH THEIR
0  0000   00003     NAMES AND THEIR IDENTIFICATION CODES. *)
0  0000   00004
0  0000   00005  TYPE VECTOR = ARRAY(1..50) OF STRING(20);
0  0038   00006  VAR NAMES,                       (* EMPLOYEE NAMES LIST *)
0  0038   00007     CODES: VECTOR;                (* IDENTIFICATION CODES LIST *)
0  0038   00008     NUM,                          (* NUMBER OF EMPLOYEES *)
0  0038   00009     K: INTEGER;                   (* COUNTED LOOP VARIABLE *)
0  0038   00010
0  0038   00011     PROCEDURE SORT (VAR LIST: VECTOR);
1  0000   00012     (* THIS PROCEDURE SORTS THE ARRAY LIST OF COUNT ELEMENTS *)
1  0000   00013
1  0000   00014     VAR MIN,                      (* MINIMUM VALUE IN A PASS *)
1  004A   00015        POS, PASS: INTEGER;        (* COUNTED LOOP VARIABLES *)
1  004A   00016        TEMP: STRING(20);          (* USED TO EXCHANGE ELEMENTS *)
1  004A   00017
1  004A   00018        PROCEDURE EXCHNGE;
2  0000   00019        (* EXCHANGE TWO ELEMENTS IN THE LIST ARRAY *)
2  0000   00020
2  0000   00021        BEGIN
2  003C   00022            TEMP := LIST(MIN);
2  0064   00023            LIST(MIN) := LIST(PASS);
2  00AE   00024            LIST(PASS) := TEMP
2  00D0   00025        END;
1  004A   00026
1  004A   00027     BEGIN
1  004A   00028
1  004A   00029        (* PERFORM THE PASSES *)
1  004A   00030        FOR PASS := 1 TO NUM - 1 DO
1  0072   00031        BEGIN
1  0072   00032
1  0072   00033            (* FIND THE MINIMUM ELEMENT *)
1  0072   00034            MIN := PASS;
1  007A   00035            FOR POS := PASS + 1 TO NUM DO
1  00A4   00036                IF LIST(POS) < LIST(MIN)
1  00E8   00037                THEN MIN := POS;
1  00FA   00038
1  00FA   00039            (* EXCHANGE ELEMENT IF NECESSARY *)
1  00FA   00040            IF MIN <> PASS
1  00FE   00041            THEN EXCHNGE
1  010A   00042        END
1  0116   00043     END;
0  0038   00044
0  0038   00045  BEGIN
0  0038   00046
0  0038   00047     (* READ EMPLOYEES *)
0  0038   00048     NUM := 1;
0  0040   00049     READ (NAMES(1), CODES(1));
0  0064   00050     WHILE NAMES(NUM) <> 'LAST_NAME           ' DO
0  0090   00051     BEGIN
0  0090   00052        NUM := NUM + 1;
0  009C   00053        READ (NAMES(NUM), CODES(NUM))
0  0100   00054     END;
0  0104   00055     NUM := NUM - 1;
0  0110   00056
0  0110   00057     (* SORT THE LIST OF EMPLOYEE NAMES INTO ASCENDING ORDER *)
0  0110   00058     SORT (NAMES);
0  012E   00059
0  012E   00060     (* SORT THE LIST OF EMPLOYEE CODES INTO ASCENDING ORDER *)
0  012E   00061     SORT (CODES);
0  014C   00062
0  014C   00063     (* PRINT THE SORTED LISTS *)
0  014C   00064     WRITELN (' EMPLOYEE NAMES LIST:');
0  015E   00065     FOR K := 1 TO NUM DO
0  0182   00066        WRITELN (' ', NAMES(K));
0  01CA   00067     WRITELN ('-EMPLOYEE CODES LIST:');
0  01DC   00068     FOR K := 1 TO NUM DO
0  0200   00069        WRITELN (' ', CODES(K))
0  0244   00070  END.
```

```
----------------------------------
| COMPILE TIME:    0.153 SECOND(S) |
|     NO WARNING(S) DETECTED        |
|     NO ERROR(S) DETECTED          |
----------------------------------
```

Fig. 6-4 Modified version of EMP_EES using global variables

subprograms may be stored in a program library. An external subprogram may be invoked from the main program or from any internal or external subprogram, but its head must be declared within the program; that is, the original definition head followed by EXTERNAL; or FORWARD;. Some compilers do not have EXTERNAL;, and thus FORWARD; must be used. EXTERNAL;, where available, is preferred since it makes the meaning of the declaration head more obvious. Global variables are not possible with external subprograms. That is, variables declared in the invoking program may not be referenced in the external subprogram. Thus, communication between the external subprogram, and the invoking program may only occur through argument-parameter correspondence and, if the subprogram is a function, by returning a value on the function name. We shall not go into any more detail concerning external subprograms.

The concept of scope is important in any programming language that has what is known as a *block structure*. PASCAL, ALGOL, and PL/I are all examples of block structured languages. To rephrase the basic rule, scopes are inherited inward; that is, any name (variable name or subprogram name) is known to any enclosed block where a block is a subprogram. Figure 6-5 uses boxes to represent blocks. X, Y, Z are identifiers; S_1, S_2, and S_3 represent statements. Table 6-1 shows which variables can be referenced by which statements according to the rules of scope. Notice that Y and Z cannot be referenced from outside the blocks in which they are defined; scopes are inherited *inward*. Notice also that there is no place where both Y and Z can be referenced. Their scopes are incompatible.

It should be noted that if the block defining the identifier Y also redefines X, then any reference in S_2 to X would refer to the new definition of X, that is, the innermost one. Any reference to X in S_3 would refer only to the original definition of X.

In this section we have discussed several of the important issues involving the use of subprograms in PASCAL, and the notion of subprograms being internal to others. In the next section, PASCAL programs for the applications of Chap. 6 in the main text are developed and discussed.

Exercises for Sec. 6-4

1. Give the value of MAX following the execution of this program and subprogram, assuming

   (i)   The subprogram is internal, as shown
   (ii) The subprogram is external, and the procedure declaration is replaced by

   PROCEDURE LARGE; EXTERNAL;

   ```
   PROGRAM MAXI (INPUT, OUTPUT);
   VAR MAX, A, B: INTEGER;
        PROCEDURE LARGE;
        BEGIN
            IF A > B
            THEN MAX := A
            ELSE MAX := B
        END;
   ```

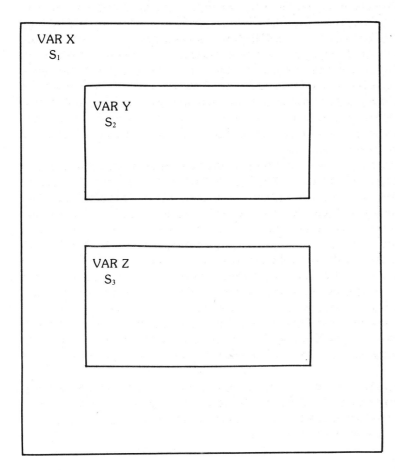

Fig. 6-5   Block structure

```
BEGIN
      A := 4;
      B := 3;
      LARGE;
      WRITELN ( ' ', MAX)
END.
```

Table 6-1   Allowed reference in Fig. 6-5

Statements	Names to which reference is permitted
S_1	X
S_2	X, Y
S_3	X, Z

What if the call is written

      LARGE(A, B);

and the subprogram begins

      PROCEDURE LARGE (A, B: INTEGER);

2.   What are the advantages and disadvantages of using global variables?

3.   Consider the following program outline:

```
PROGRAM PGM1 (INPUT, OUTPUT);
VAR X, Y: ...
        PROCEDURE PGM2;
        VAR A, B, C: ...
        BEGIN
              .
              .
              .
        END;
        PROCEDURE PGM3;
        VAR M, N: ...
                PROCEDURE PGM4;
                VAR S, T: ...
                BEGIN
                      .
                      .
                      .
                END;
        BEGIN
              .
              .
              .
        END;
        PROCEDURE PGM5; EXTERNAL;
BEGIN
      .
      .
      .
END.
```

PGM5 is a programmer-defined procedure stored in a program library. Based on the preceding outline, answer the following questions:

  (i)   What variables are global to PGM2?
  (ii) Is it possible for PGM3 to access the value of variable A?
  (iii) List all the variables global to PGM4.
  (iv) Draw a block diagram like the one given in Fig. 6-5 for the above program outline.

6-5 APPLICATIONS

This section presents PASCAL program solutions to the application problems found in Sec. 6-5 of the main text.

6-5.1 Processing Symbol Tables

The program given in Fig. 6-6 is a solution to the symbol table problem presented in Sec. 6-5.1 of the main text. In order to illustrate programs that perform the functions of the subalgorithms described in the main text, a main program called TEST_R is used to call the routines. TEST_R uses the INSERT procedure to create a symbol table containing 10 elements. Once the elements have been inserted, the contents of the symbol table are printed. Elements are then retrieved from the symbol table in a random order using the RETRIEVE procedure. The SEARCH function is used in both the INSERT and RETRIEVE procedures. The following is a general outline of the TEST_R program.

1. Enter 10 elements into the symbol table using the procedure INSERT.
2. Print the created symbol table.
3. Repeat through step 6 for all remaining input.
4. Read name of variable sought.
5. Find the variable's type and position using the RETRIEVE procedure.
6. Print the variable's name, type, and address.

The following identifiers appear in the TEST_R program:

Identifier	Type	Usage
MAXNUM	CONST	Maximum number of table positions
NAMES	ARRAY(1..MAXNUM) OF STRING(31)	Type of variable names vector
TYPES	ARRAY(1..MAXNUM) OF STRING(7)	Type of variable type vector
ADDRESSES	ARRAY(1..MAXNUM) OF INTEGER	Type of variable addresses vector
NAME	NAMES	Vector of variable names
V_TYPE	TYPES	Vector of variable types
ADDRESS	ADDRESSES	Vector of variable addresses
VARIABLE	STRING(31)	Name of variable to be inserted or retrieved
VARIABLE_TYPE	STRING(7)	Type of variable
VARIABLE_ADDRESS	INTEGER	Address of variable
NUMBER	INTEGER	Number of elements inserted
I	INTEGER	Loop variable

Variables used in the INSERT procedure:

VAR_NAME	STRING(31)	Name of variable to be inserted

VAR_TYPE	STRING(7)	Type of variable to be inserted
VAR_ADDRESS	INTEGER	Address of variable to be inserted
SIZE	INTEGER	Number of entries in the symbol table

Variables used in the RETRIEVE procedure:

VAR_NAME	STRING(31)	Name of variable sought
VAR_TYPE	STRING(7)	Type of variable sought
VAR_ADDRESS	INTEGER	Address of variable sought
SIZE	INTEGER	Number of variables in the symbol table
POS	INTEGER	Position of variable in the symbol table

Variables used in the SEARCH function:

LIST	NAMES	List containing element sought
N	INTEGER	Number of elements in the list
ELEMENT	STRING(31)	Element sought
I	INTEGER	Loop variable
FOUND	BOOLEAN	Flag indicating if element found

The following input values were used during this run.

'ALPHA'	'INTEGER'	6030
'BETA'	'REAL'	6034
'GAMMA'	'INTEGER'	6038
'LETTERS'	'STRING'	7010
'TOTAL'	'INTEGER'	7124
'AVERAGE'	'REAL'	7388
'SUM'	'INTEGER'	7764
'WORD'	'STRING'	7777
'NAME'	'STRING'	7900
'COUNT'	'INTEGER'	7944
'LETTERS'		
'WORD'		
'BETA'		
'TOTAL'		
'SUM'		

Line 96 initializes NUMBER to 0. In line 99, a loop to read and insert 10 elements is begun. Once this loop has been completed, lines 106 through 109 print the elements of the symbol table. A WHILE ... DO loop is then used to control the input of variable names and the retrieval of the corresponding type and address. Execution is terminated when the end of the input values has been reached.

```
0  0000   00001   PROGRAM TEST_R (INPUT, OUTPUT);
0  0000   00002   (* PROGRAM TO TEST SYMBOL TABLE ROUTINES, SEARCH, INSERT, AND
0  0000   00003      RETRIEVE. *)
0  0000   00004
0  0000   00005   CONST MAXNUM = 10;            (* MAXIMUM NUMBER OF TABLE POSITIONS *)
0  0038   00006   TYPE NAMES = ARRAY(1..MAXNUM) OF STRING(31);
0  0038   00007        TYPES = ARRAY(1..MAXNUM) OF STRING(7);
0  0038   00008        ADDRESSES = ARRAY(1..MAXNUM) OF INTEGER;
0  0038   00009   VAR NAME: NAMES;              (* VECTOR OF VARIABLE NAMES *)
0  0038   00010       ADDRESS: ADDRESSES;       (* VECTOR OF VARIABLE ADDRESSES *)
0  0038   00011       V_TYPE: TYPES;            (* VECTOR OF VARIABLE TYPES *)
0  0038   00012       VARIABLE: STRING(31);     (* VARIABLE TO BE INSERTED OR RETRIEVED *)
0  0038   00013       VARIABLE_TYPE: STRING(7);(* VARIABLE'S TYPE *)
0  0038   00014       VARIABLE_ADDRESS,         (* VARIABLE'S ADDRESS *)
0  0038   00015       NUMBER,                   (* NUMBER OF ELEMENTS INSERTED *)
0  0038   00016       I: INTEGER;               (* LOOP VARIABLE *)
0  0038   00017
0  0038   00018       FUNCTION SEARCH (LIST: NAMES; N: INTEGER; ELEMENT: STRING(31)):
1  0000   00019            INTEGER;
1  0000   00020       (* FUNCTION TO FIND AN ELEMENT IN A VECTOR *)
1  0000   00021
1  0000   00022       VAR I: INTEGER;           (* LOOP VARIABLE *)
1  0078   00023           FOUND: BOOLEAN;       (* DETERMINES IF ELEMENT FOUND *)
1  0078   00024
1  0078   00025       BEGIN
1  0078   00026
1  0078   00027           (* SEARCH THE VECTOR *)
1  0078   00028           FOUND := FALSE;
1  0080   00029           FOR I := 1 TO N DO
1  00A4   00030               IF LIST(I) = ELEMENT
1  00C6   00031               THEN BEGIN
1  00D0   00032                   FOUND := TRUE;
1  00D8   00033                   SEARCH := I
1  00D8   00034                   END;
1  00E0   00035
1  00E0   00036           (* ELEMENT NOT FOUND *)
1  00E0   00037           IF FOUND = FALSE
1  00E4   00038           THEN SEARCH := 0;
1  00F6   00039       END;
0  0038   00040
0  0038   00041       PROCEDURE INSERT (VAR_NAME: STRING(31); VAR_TYPE: STRING(7);
1  0000   00042            VAR_ADDRESS: INTEGER; VAR SIZE: INTEGER);
1  0000   00043       (* PROCEDURE TO INSERT A VARIABLE INTO A SYMBOL TABLE.  NAME,
1  0000   00044         TYPE, AND ADDRESS ARE GLOBAL VECTORS COMPRISING THE
1  0000   00045         SYMBOL TABLE. *)
1  0000   00046
1  0000   00047       VAR NUM: INTEGER;         (* NUMBER OF ELEMENTS *)
1  006E   00048
1  006E   00049       BEGIN
1  006E   00050
1  006E   00051           (* CHECK IF VARIABLE HAS ALREADY BEEN DEFINED *)
1  006E   00052           IF SEARCH (NAME, SIZE, VAR_NAME) <> 0
1  009C   00053           THEN WRITELN (' ***ERROR - VARIABLE ', VAR_NAME, ' HAS BEEN ',
1  00DA   00054               'PREVIOUSLY DEFINED.')
1  00EC   00055           ELSE BEGIN
1  00F0   00056
1  00F0   00057               (* COMPUTE THE NEXT AVAILABLE POSITION *)
1  00FC   00058               SIZE := SIZE + 1;
1  00FC   00059               IF SIZE > MAXNUM
1  00FC   00060               THEN WRITELN (' ***ERROR - TOO MANY VARIABLES DEFINED')
1  011A   00061               ELSE BEGIN
1  011E   00062
1  011E   00063                   (* MAKE INSERTION INTO THE POSITION FOUND *)
1  011E   00064                   NAME(SIZE) := VAR_NAME;
1  0146   00065                   V_TYPE(SIZE) := VAR_TYPE;
1  016E   00066                   ADDRESS(SIZE) := VAR_ADDRESS
1  0190   00067                   END
1  0198   00068               END
1  0198   00069       END;
0  0038   00070
```

Fig. 6-6 Program for symbol table application

```
0  0038  00071        PROCEDURE RETRIEVE (VAR_NAME: STRING(31); VAR VAR_TYPE: STRING(7);
1  0000  00072              VAR VAR_ADDRESS: INTEGER; SIZE: INTEGER);
1  0000  00073        (* PROCEDURE TO RETRIEVE THE TYPE AND ADDRESS OF A VARIABLE FROM
1  0000  00074           A SYMBOL TABLE. *)
1  0000  00075
1  0000  00076        VAR POS: INTEGER;        (* POSITION OF VARIABLE IN SYMBOL TABLE *)
1  006E  00077
1  006E  00078        BEGIN
1  006E  00079
1  006E  00080            (* CHECK IF VARIABLE IS IN TABLE *)
1  006E  00081            POS := SEARCH (NAME, SIZE, VAR_NAME);
1  00A0  00082            IF POS = 0
1  00A0  00083            THEN WRITELN (' ***ERROR - VARIABLE ', VAR_NAME, ' HAS NOT ',
1  00E2  00084                 'BEEN DEFINED.')
1  00F4  00085            ELSE BEGIN
1  00F8  00086
1  00F8  00087                (* SUPPLY THE REQUIRED INFORMATION *)
1  00F8  00088                VAR_TYPE := V_TYPE(POS);
1  0120  00089                VAR_ADDRESS := ADDRESS(POS)
1  0146  00090                END
1  014A  00091        END;
0  0038  00092
0  0038  00093  BEGIN    (* MAIN PROGRAM *)
0  0038  00094
0  0038  00095        (* INITIALIZE *)
0  0038  00096        NUMBER := 0;
0  003E  00097
0  003E  00098        (* READ AND INSERT TEN ELEMENTS INTO THE SYMBOL TABLE VECTORS *)
0  003E  00099        FOR I := 1 TO MAXNUM DO
0  0062  00100        BEGIN
0  0062  00101            READ (VARIABLE, VARIABLE_TYPE, VARIABLE_ADDRESS);
0  0098  00102            INSERT (VARIABLE, VARIABLE_TYPE, VARIABLE_ADDRESS, NUMBER)
0  00B8  00103        END;
0  00D2  00104
0  00D2  00105        (* PRINT OUT SYMBOL TABLE ENTRIES *)
0  00D2  00106        WRITELN (' ': 20, 'SYMBOL TABLE');
0  00F6  00107        WRITELN (' VARIABLE', 'TYPE': 29, 'ADDRESS': 21);
0  012C  00108        FOR I := 1 TO NUMBER DO
0  0150  00109            WRITELN (' ', NAME(I), ' ', V_TYPE(I), ' ', ADDRESS(I));
0  0222  00110
0  0222  00111        (* TEST RETRIEVE PROCEDURE AND PRINT HEADINGS *)
0  0222  00112        WRITELN ('-VARIABLE SOUGHT', 'TYPE': 22, 'ADDRESS': 21);
0  0258  00113        READ (VARIABLE);
0  026A  00114        WHILE NOT EOF DO
0  0272  00115        BEGIN
0  0272  00116            RETRIEVE (VARIABLE, VARIABLE_TYPE, VARIABLE_ADDRESS, NUMBER);
0  02A8  00117            WRITELN (' ', VARIABLE, ' ', VARIABLE_TYPE, ' ',
0  0302  00118                VARIABLE_ADDRESS);
0  0314  00119            READ (VARIABLE)
0  0326  00120        END
0  0326  00121  END.
------------------------------------
| COMPILE TIME:    0.268 SECOND(S) |
|    NO WARNING(S) DETECTED         |
|    NO ERROR(S) DETECTED           |
------------------------------------
--EXECUTION-->
                SYMBOL TABLE
VARIABLE                   TYPE           ADDRESS
ALPHA                      INTEGER        6030
BETA                       REAL           6034
GAMMA                      INTEGER        6038
LETTERS                    STRING         7010
TOTAL                      INTEGER        7124
AVERAGE                    REAL           7388
SUM                        INTEGER        7764
WORD                       STRING         7777
NAME                       STRING         7900
COUNT                      INTEGER        7944


VARIABLE SOUGHT            TYPE           ADDRESS
LETTERS                    STRING         7010
WORD                       STRING         7777
BETA                       REAL           6034
TOTAL                      INTEGER        7124
SUM                        INTEGER        7764
```

Fig. 6-6   Program for symbol table application (cont'd.)

6-5.2 The Transposition of Musical Scores

The program appearing in Fig. 6-7 is a solution to the problem of transposing musical scores given in Sec. 6-5.2 of the main text. The problem concerns shifting a score written in one key to a different key. Both the original key and the new key are to be read in along with the musical score. The amount of shift between these two keys defines the amount of shift needed. The possible keys are represented by the following character string:

'AbbBbCbbDbbEbFbbGbbAbbBbCbbDbbEbFbbGb'

The blanks between the notes, represented here by b's, denote the tones separating notes: a single blank represents a semitone and two blanks represent a full tone. Besides the shift between keys, sharps and flats must be taken into consideration as they imply a semitone shift. This means that to convert a chord that is a sharp or flat, 1 must be added (for a sharp) or subtracted (for a flat) to the amount of the shift to produce a correct shift. For example, suppose the following score was to be transposed from the key of E to C.

'E'
'A'
'G#'

According to the string of notes given previously, the shift from E to C is eleven. The transposed score would then be

'C'
'E'
'D#'

Note that in transposing the last chord, one was added to the basic shift of eleven. Variations of the basic chords such as minors or sevenths are simply concatenated to the transposed key. For example, Gm7 in the key of G transposed to the key of D would be Dm7. Using this information the program given in Fig. 6-7 can be used to transpose simple musical scores. The variables used in this program are

Variable	Type	Usage
NOTES	STRING(256)	Basic scale
ORIGINAL_KEY	STRING(256)	Original key of the score
KEY_DESIRED	STRING(256)	Desired key of the score
POSITION	INTEGER	Position of note in the scale
SHIFT	INTEGER	Number of notes chords must be shifted
CHORD	STRING(256)	Chord of score to be transposed
RESULT	STRING(256)	Transposed chord
FLAT	STRING(256)	Flat symbol (!)
SHARP	STRING(256)	Sharp symbol (#)
TEMP1, TEMP2	STRING(256)	Temporary string variables
BLANKS	STRING(256)	String of blank characters

The variables used in the TRANSPOSE procedure are

IN_CHORD	STRING(256)	Chord to be transposed
DIST	INTEGER	Distance chord is to be transposed
OUT_CHORD	STRING(256)	Transposed chord
P1, P2	STRING(256)	Indices into the string of notes
TEMP	STRING(256)	Temporary string variable
BLANK	STRING(256)	Single blank character

The following input values were used in this run.

```
'C'      'F'
'C'
'AM'
'F'
'G7'
'E!'
'D#M7'
```

In line 74, the variable NOTES is assigned the basic scale. The original key (C) and the desired key (F) are read. In lines 84 through 88, the position in the scale of the original key and the shift required to transpose the score to the desired key are calculated. Lines 91 through 100 perform any adjustment that may be required for a sharp or flat. Lines 104 to 112 read each chord and, using the TRANSPOSE function, print the original chord and its transposed counterpart.

6-5.3 Finding Paths in a Graph

The program given in Fig. 6-8 is a programmed solution to the problem of finding paths in a graph presented in Sec. 6-5.3 of the main text. The program is to determine if a path exists between two points (read in) and to print the length of the path. The graph is represented in the program by an *adjacency matrix* which is a n x n matrix where n equals the number of nodes in the corresponding graph. The element in row i, column j is TRUE if there is an edge of the graph between nodes i and j; otherwise the element is FALSE. One method of determining whether a path exists between two nodes i and j is the following. We first check if i and j are adjacent (i.e., there is an edge of the graph between i and j). If this is not true, a check is made to see if there is a vertex k such that there is a path from i to k to j. Again, if this is not true, we test whether there are two vertices, k and h, such that there is a path from i to k to h to j. This process continues until all possible paths have been checked or until a path between i and j has been found. This search can be done by a program that performs logical operations on the adjacency matrix of the graph. The logical operation "and" performed on the adjacency matrix and itself produces a new matrix A^2 in which the i, j entry is

$$a_{ij}^2 = (a_{i1} \text{ AND } a_{1j}) \text{ OR } (a_{i2} \text{ AND } a_{2j}) \text{ OR } \ldots \text{ OR } (a_{in} \text{ AND } a_{nj})$$

In other words a_{ij}^2 = TRUE if there is a path from i to 1 to j, or i to 2 to j, or i to 3 to j, . . ., or i to n to j; that is, if a path of length two exists. Similarly, A^3 represents all

```
0  0000   00001  PROGRAM KEYS (INPUT, OUTPUT);
0  0000   00002  (* THIS PROGRAM TRANSPOSES CHORDS OF A MUSICAL SCORE *)
0  0000   00003
0  0000   00004  VAR NOTES,                    (* BASIC SCALE *)
0  0038   00005      ORIGINAL_KEY,             (* ORIGINAL KEY OF MUSIC *)
0  0038   00006      KEY_DESIRED,              (* DESIRED KEY OF THE MUSIC *)
0  0038   00007      CHORD,                    (* CHORD TO BE TRANSPOSED *)
0  0038   00008      RESULT,                   (* RESULTING CHORD *)
0  0038   00009      FLAT, SHARP,              (* FLAT (!) AND SHARP (#) SYMBOLS *)
0  0038   00010      TEMP1, TEMP2,             (* TEMPORARY STRING VARIABLES *)
0  0038   00011      BLANKS: STRING(256);      (* STRING OF BLANKS *)
0  0038   00012      POSITION,                 (* POSITION OF NOTE IN SCALE *)
0  0038   00013      SHIFT: INTEGER;           (* NUMBER OF NOTES MUSIC MUST BE SHIFTED *)
0  0038   00014
0  0038   00015      PROCEDURE SUB (VAR S: STRING(256); POS, NUM: INTEGER;
1  0000   00016           VAR RESULT: STRING(256)); EXTERNAL;
0  0038   00017      FUNCTION INDEX (VAR S, PATTERN: STRING(256)): INTEGER; EXTERNAL;
0  0038   00018      PROCEDURE CONCAT (VAR S1, S2, RESULT: STRING(256)); EXTERNAL;
0  0038   00019
0  0038   00020      PROCEDURE TRANSPOSE (IN_CHORD: STRING(256); DIST: INTEGER;
1  0000   00021           VAR OUT_CHORD: STRING(256));
1  0000   00022      (* THIS FUNCTION TRANSPOSES THE GIVEN CHORD *)
1  0000   00023
1  0000   00024      VAR P1, P2: INTEGER;      (* INDICES TO THE STRING OF NOTES *)
1  0062   00025          BLANK,                (* BLANK CHARACTER *)
1  0062   00026          TEMP: STRING(256);    (* TEMPORARY STRING VARIABLE *)
1  0062   00027
1  0062   00028      BEGIN
1  0062   00029
1  0062   00030          (* FIND POSITION OF BASIC CHORD, SHIFTING IF NECESSARY FOR
1  0062   00031             FLAT OR SHARP *)
1  0062   00032          SUB (IN_CHORD, 1, 1, TEMP);
1  0096   00033          P1 := INDEX (NOTES, TEMP);
1  00C0   00034
1  00C0   00035          (* REMOVE CHARACTERS JUST CONSIDERED *)
1  00C0   00036          SUB (IN_CHORD, 2, 256, IN_CHORD);
1  00F4   00037          SUB (IN_CHORD, 1, 1, TEMP);
1  0128   00038          IF TEMP = SHARP
1  0128   00039          THEN BEGIN
1  0132   00040              P1 := P1 + 1;
1  013E   00041              SUB (IN_CHORD, 2, 256, IN_CHORD)
1  015E   00042          END;
1  0172   00043          SUB (IN_CHORD, 1, 1, TEMP);
1  01A6   00044          IF TEMP = FLAT
1  01A6   00045          THEN BEGIN
1  01B0   00046              P1 := P1 - 1;
1  01BC   00047              SUB (IN_CHORD, 2, 256, IN_CHORD)
1  01DC   00048              END;
1  01F0   00049
1  01F0   00050          (* DETERMINE TRANSPOSED CHORD *)
1  01F0   00051          P2 := P1 + DIST;
1  01FC   00052          SUB (NOTES, P2, 1, OUT_CHORD);
1  0230   00053          BLANK := ' */';
1  0236   00054          IF OUT_CHORD = BLANK
1  0236   00055          THEN BEGIN
1  0240   00056              SUB (NOTES, P2 + 1, 1, TEMP);
1  0280   00057              IF TEMP <> BLANK
1  0280   00058              THEN CONCAT (TEMP, FLAT, OUT_CHORD)
1  02A2   00059              ELSE BEGIN
1  02BA   00060                  SUB (NOTES, P2 - 1, 1, TEMP);
1  02FA   00061                  IF TEMP <> BLANK
1  02FA   00062                  THEN CONCAT (TEMP, SHARP, OUT_CHORD)
1  031C   00063                  ELSE WRITELN (' ***ERROR***')
1  0346   00064                  END
1  0346   00065              END;
1  0346   00066
1  0346   00067          (* RETURN TRANSPOSED CHORD *)
1  0346   00068          CONCAT (OUT_CHORD, IN_CHORD, OUT_CHORD)
1  035E   00069          END;
0  0038   00070
0  0038   00071  BEGIN
0  0038   00072
0  0038   00073      (* INITIALIZE *)
0  0038   00074      NOTES := 'A  B C  D E F  G  A  B C  D  E F  G */';
0  003E   00075      SHARP := '#*/';
0  0044   00076      FLAT := '!*/';
0  004A   00077      BLANKS := '                        */';
0  0050   00078
0  0050   00079
```

Fig. 6-7   Program for music transposition problem

```
0   0050   00080           (* READ KEYS *)
0   0050   00081           READ (ORIGINAL_KEY, KEY_DESIRED);
0   0074   00082
0   0074   00083           (* COMPUTE SHIFT *)
0   0074   00084           SUB (ORIGINAL_KEY, 1, 1, TEMP1);
0   00AA   00085           POSITION := INDEX (NOTES, TEMP1);
0   00D6   00086           SUB (NOTES, POSITION + 1, 256, TEMP1);
0   0118   00087           SUB (KEY_DESIRED, 1, 1, TEMP2);
0   014E   00088           SHIFT := INDEX (TEMP1, TEMP2);
0   017A   00089
0   017A   00090           (* CHECK IF ADJUSTMENT REQUIRED *)
0   017A   00091           SUB (ORIGINAL_KEY, 2, 1, TEMP1);
0   01B0   00092           IF TEMP1 = SHARP
0   01B0   00093           THEN SHIFT := SHIFT - 1;
0   01C6   00094           IF TEMP1 = FLAT
0   01C6   00095           THEN SHIFT := SHIFT + 1;
0   01DC   00096           SUB (KEY_DESIRED, 2, 1, TEMP1);
0   0212   00097           IF TEMP1 = SHARP
0   0212   00098           THEN SHIFT := SHIFT + 1;
0   0228   00099           IF TEMP1 = FLAT
0   0228   00100           THEN SHIFT := SHIFT - 1;
0   023E   00101
0   023E   00102           (* TRANSPOSE CHORDS OF COMPLETE SCORE *)
0   023E   00103           WRITELN ('  ORIGINAL CHORD', '  ': 8, 'TRANSPOSED CHORD');
0   0274   00104           READ (CHORD);
0   0286   00105           WHILE NOT EOF DO
0   028E   00106           BEGIN
0   028E   00107               TRANSPOSE (CHORD, SHIFT, RESULT);
0   02BC   00108               CONCAT (CHORD, BLANKS, CHORD);
0   02EA   00109               CONCAT (RESULT, BLANKS, RESULT);
0   0318   00110               WRITELN ('  ', CHORD: 20, '  ', RESULT: 20);
0   0360   00111               READ (CHORD)
0   0372   00112           END;
0   0376   00113   END.
-----------------------------------------
| COMPILE TIME:    0.322 SECOND(S) |
|     NO WARNING(S) DETECTED        |
|     NO ERROR(S) DETECTED          |
-----------------------------------------
--EXECUTION-->
ORIGINAL CHORD      TRANSPOSED CHORD
C                   F
AM                  DM
F                   B!
G7                  C7
E!                  A!
D#M7                G#M7
```

Fig. 6-7   Program for music transposition problem (cont'd.)

paths of length three, A^4 represents all paths of length 4, etc. The program given in Fig. 6-8 uses this method to find a path between two nodes. The function POWER is used by this program to calculate the different powers of the adjacency matrix. The following variables appear in this solution, where GRAPH is a type identifier for ARRAY(1..25, 1..25) OF BOOLEAN.

Variable	Type	Usage
N	INTEGER	Number of nodes in the graph
A	GRAPH	Adjacency matrix of the graph
I	INTEGER	End point of path sought
J	INTEGER	End point of path sought
AL, T	GRAPH	Arrays used for temporary results
L	INTEGER	Current power of the adjacency matrix
G, H	INTEGER	Loop variables
FOUND	BOOLEAN	Flag which indicates if a path is found

The variables used in the POWER procedure are:

A, B	GRAPH	Graphs to compute next power
C	GRAPH	Result of A AND B
N	INTEGER	Number of nodes in the graph
I, J, K	INTEGER	Loop variables

The following data values were used in this program:

```
5
F   T   F   F   F
T   F   F   T   F
F   F   F   T   T
F   T   T   F   T
F   F   T   T   F
2   5
```

In line 37, the number of nodes in the graph is read. Using this information, lines 38 through 43 accomplish the input of the adjacency matrix of the graph into arrays A and AL. The values of the nodes between which a path is sought is read. A counted loop is then used to find the paths in the graph. The element in row i and column j of the adjacency matrix is inspected, and if it has a value of TRUE, FOUND is set to TRUE indicating a path has been found. If, however, this condition is not true, the POWER procedure is called to calculate the next power of the adjacency matrix. Lines 54 through 56 then copy the result into the temporary array AL. If all possible paths have been found (i.e., the counted loop has been completely executed) without a path between the two specified nodes being found, FOUND has the value FALSE and a message indicating that no path between the nodes exists is printed; otherwise, the length of the path is printed.

EXERCISES FOR CHAPTER 6

1. The scalar product (also called the inner or dot product) of two vectors A and B of length n is defined as

$$A \cdot B = \sum_{i=1}^{n} a_i b_i = a_1 b_1 + a_2 b_2 + \cdots + a_n b_n$$

(i) Design a function with three parameters A, B, and N that computes the scalar product according to this formula.

(ii) If the scalar product of two vectors is zero, the vectors are said to be orthogonal. Design a program that calls the function from part (i). If the value returned is less than .00001, the message 'ORTHOGONAL VECTORS' is to be printed.

2. Design a function FACTORIAL(N) that computes the factorial of the argument

```
0  0000   00001  PROGRAM PATHS (INPUT, OUTPUT);
0  0000   00002  (* PROGRAM TO DETERMINE WHETHER OR NOT A PATH EXISTS BETWEEN TWO
0  0000   00003     SPECIFIED NODES, I AND J, FOR A 5 X 5 GRAPH, A. *)
0  0000   00004
0  0000   00005  TYPE GRAPH = ARRAY (1..25, 1..25) OF BOOLEAN;
0  0038   00006  VAR N,                           (* NUMBER OF NODES IN THE GRAPH *)
0  0038   00007      I, J,                        (* NODES BETWEEN WHICH A PATH IS SOUGHT *)
0  0038   00008      L,                           (* POWER OF THE ADJACENCY MATRIX BEING
0  0038   00009                                      COMPUTED *)
0  0038   00010      G, H: INTEGER;               (* LOOP VARIABLES *)
0  0038   00011      A,                           (* ADJACENCY MATRIX OF THE GRAPH *)
0  0038   00012      AL, T: GRAPH;                (* TEMPORARY ARRAYS *)
0  0038   00013      FOUND: BOOLEAN;              (* DETERMINES IF PATH FOUND *)
0  0038   00014
0  0038   00015      PROCEDURE POWER (VAR A, B, C: GRAPH; N: INTEGER);
1  0000   00016      (* PROCEDURE TO CALCULATE A AND B FOR N X N ARRAYS A AND B. *)
1  0000   00017
1  0000   00018      VAR I, J, K: INTEGER;   (* LOOP VARIABLES *)
1  0066   00019
1  0066   00020      BEGIN
1  0066   00021
1  0066   00022          (* INITIALIZE RESULT ARRAY *)
1  0066   00023          FOR I := 1 TO N DO
1  008A   00024              FOR J := 1 TO N DO
1  00AE   00025                  C(I, J) := FALSE;
1  00FE   00026
1  00FE   00027          (* COMPUTE A AND B *)
1  00FE   00028          FOR I := 1 TO N DO            (* COMPUTE ROW ELEMENTS *)
1  0122   00029              FOR J := 1 TO N DO        (* COMPUTE COLUMN ELEMENTS *)
1  0146   00030                  FOR K := 1 TO N DO (* COMPUTE I, J ELEMENT *)
1  016A   00031                      C(I, J) := C(I, J) OR (A(I, K) AND B(K, J))
1  0288   00032      END;
0  0038   00033
0  0038   00034  BEGIN
0  0038   00035
0  0038   00036      (* INPUT DATA VALUES AND INITIALIZE TEMPORARY ARRAY *)
0  0038   00037      READ (N);
0  004A   00038      FOR G := 1 TO N DO
0  006E   00039          FOR H := 1 TO N DO
0  0092   00040          BEGIN
0  0092   00041              READ (A(G, H));
0  00E2   00042              AL(G, H) := A(G, H)
0  0166   00043          END;
0  0172   00044      READ (I, J);
0  0196   00045
0  0196   00046      (* DETERMINE ALL POSSIBLE PATHS IN THE GRAPH *)
0  0196   00047      FOUND := FALSE;
0  019E   00048      L := 1;
0  01A6   00049      WHILE (FOUND = FALSE) AND (L <= N) DO
0  01BE   00050          IF AL(I, J) = TRUE
0  0202   00051          THEN FOUND := TRUE
0  020A   00052          ELSE BEGIN
0  0216   00053              POWER (AL, A, T, N);
0  024C   00054              FOR G := 1 TO N DO
0  0270   00055                  FOR H := 1 TO N DO
0  0294   00056                      AL(G, H) := T(G, H);
0  0324   00057              L := L + 1
0  0324   00058          END;
0  0334   00059
0  0334   00060      (* CHECK IF PATH FOUND *)
0  0334   00061      IF FOUND = TRUE
0  0334   00062      THEN WRITELN (´ A PATH OF LENGTH ´, L: 2, ´ EXISTS´)
0  0376   00063      ELSE WRITELN (´ NO PATH EXISTS´)
0  038C   00064  END.
```

```
------------------------------------
¦ COMPILE TIME:    0.195 SECOND(S) ¦
¦    NO WARNING(S) DETECTED        ¦
¦    NO ERROR(S) DETECTED          ¦
------------------------------------
--EXECUTION-->
A PATH OF LENGTH  2 EXISTS
```

Fig. 6-8   Program to find paths in graphs

N (sometimes written as N!). For an integer N, N! is by definition

$$N! = N * (N - 1) * (N - 2) * \cdots * 1$$

Incorporate in your function the special case

$$0! = 1.$$

3. Design a procedure to accept as a parameter an arbitrary string containing a series of words separated by one or more blanks and return to the point of call the average number of letters in each word.

4. Design a procedure to accept as a parameter an adjacency matrix for a graph (containing no more than 10 nodes) and a length k, and return to the point of call the number of paths of *exactly* length k in the graph. Test your procedure on the adjacency matrix given in Sec. 6-4.3.

5. The Saskatoon Police Department requires a program to assist them in determining the identities of criminals from filed descriptions supplied by their victims. The police have cards describing known criminals. These cards have the following format:

      name   height (in inches)   weight (in pounds)   address

Example:

      'BUGSY MALONE'   53   119   '68 TOWN ST.'

Design a program that first reads in the deck of cards giving the descriptions of known criminals and prepares a table of information on "known criminals". This set of cards is terminated by a special card of the form

'***' 0 0 '***'

A second set of cards follows, containing descriptions of criminals participating in unsolved crimes. These cards have the format:

     description of crime   estimated height of criminal   estimated weight

Example:

     '21 JULY: MUGGING'   68   155

This second set of cards is terminated by a special card of the form

     '***' 0 0

For each of the unsolved crimes, call a procedure (which you must also write) to determine possible suspects for the crime. This determination is based on the estimated height and weight of the criminals as given by the victims of the crimes. If the height is within two inches *and* the weight is within ten pounds, the person is to be listed as a possible suspect for the crime involved. The parameters are to include the table of "known criminals" and the card image on which the current crime is described.

CHAPTER

7

PROGRAMMING STYLE IN PASCAL PROGRAMS

The issue of programming style has been addressed informally throughout the first six chapters of this book. This chapter deals with the subject in more depth, and considers the effect of style on the production of programs. The first section provides an introduction and motivation. Section 2 looks at issues of program implementation and introduces the notion of "structured programming" as it relates to the use of control structures. Section 3 deals with the proper use of variables in a program. Section 4 considers questions of the presentation of a program. The chapter concludes with some final reflections and an annotated bibliography of suggested readings.

7-1 INTRODUCTION

Chapter 7 of the main text deals with the issue of programming style. The programming profession is presently undergoing a critical review of its own practices, motivated largely by the disappointingly poor quality of many programs. It is widely believed that this is due less to the talents of the individual programmers than to the methods by which programs have been produced. The past decade has seen an influx of techniques reputed to improve the production of programs. These run the gamut from systematic methodologies to graphical aids to informal guidelines. If there is an underlying theme in these suggestions, it could well be the importance of programming style to the quality of programs.

In the main text, Chap. 7 looks at the issue of programming style from several vantage points. First, some thoughts are offered on what constitutes a good program. We then review the individual phases of the programming process: problem analysis, solution development, solution implementation, testing, and maintenance. Section 7-4 deals with a methodology for solution development that we refer to as *top-down* design. In Sec. 7-5, we consider the actual implementation or coding of programs and show that considerations of style at this stage can be very important. The chapter concludes with some thoughts on human elements and their effect on the programming process.

In this chapter, we look more closely at implementation issues, with specific emphasis on their relation to the PASCAL programming language. The language used to implement programs has an undeniably profound effect on their quality. Some languages offer a rich set of features, carefully designed to support successful programming styles. Other languages are much less generous. Whatever the language used, it is important to remember that the appropriate design work must precede any implementation effort. One is hard-pressed to produce a good program, in any language, from an inadequate, ill-conceived, or imcomplete design. As the saying goes, you can't make a silk purse out of a sow's ear. Although we will not dwell on issues of solution design in this book, we will assume that you are completely comfortable with the notions of solution design as presented in Sec. 7-4 (and, to some extent, Sec. 7-5) of the main text.

A single chapter cannot hope to do justice to the topic of programming style. As in the main text, we draw your attention to the books "The Elements of Programming Style", by Kernighan and Plauger, and "Programming Proverbs", by Ledgard, both of which deal with the subject in considerable depth. Although we can only scratch the surface of the topic, we hope that our examples serve to start you thinking in the right direction, and whet your appetite for more. The style that you ultimately choose to adopt will be largely personal; to convince you of the importance of style is our objective in this chapter.

7-2 IMPLEMENTING A PROGRAM

There are a number of considerations that go into the writing of a good computer program. Much of this falls under the heading of solution design. First and foremost, one must ensure that the requirements of the program are completely understood. This includes full details of the input that is to be presented to the program, and the output that it is to produce. Then one must take pains to choose the appropriate data structures, for example, the use of vectors and/or arrays where warranted, or even more sophisticated structures (see Chaps. 10 and 11) if required. Next one ensures that the best algorithm is employed, focusing here on questions of elegance and efficiency. Only after all of this has been done, does one turn to the implementation of this solution in the programming language at hand. Programming encompasses all of this, although the term is often applied to the coding of programming language statements. Even at this stage, however, there are useful guidelines on how best to proceed.

As stated in the main text, the "structure" of a program is a function of the constructs used to direct the flow of control through its statements. One of the first principles of "structured programming" is a restriction on the type of control structure that are to be used. In the main text we advocate restricting yourself to the IF-THEN-ELSE and REPEAT algorithmic constructs, and combinations of these. PASCAL offers the full range of these constructs, along with additional constructs to be introduced later in the book. Programs written using only these "structured" constructs can be composed as a series of nested *action modules,* each of which has a single point of entry and a single point of exit. This greatly enhances the understanding and verifiability of the code. For example, Fig. 7-1 illustrates the concept of action modules in a segment taken from the program PATHS produced in Chap. 6 to determine the paths of a graph. The *structure* of the program (as distinct from its *logic*) is clearly shown by the orderly nesting of the boxes. The program code reads in a straightforward fashion from top-to-bottom and executes similarly, without unnecessarily jumping about in the code. The code controlling these actions (that is, the FOR's and the IF's) is clearly seen as well.

There has been a great deal written on the merits of "structured programming." The technique is not a panacea, guaranteed to produce perfect programs. It is no more than a useful guideline that, with practice, can lead to high-quality programs in shorter periods of time. By reducing the degrees of freedom for a programmer, the technique reduces the chances of errors being made. The overall emphasis on structure as opposed to logic has proven to have a significant effect on quality, as well. As was pointed out in Sec. 7-5.2 of the main text, however, it is not sufficient to adhere to the *letter* of the law in producing structured programs; more important is a recognition of the *spirit* of the law in attempting to arrive at a clear, logical structure. This section is worth re-reading. Because of the similarity in control structures between the algorithmic language and those provided by PASCAL, the comments in that section are highly pertinent.

Considerations of structure should be borne in mind throughout the development of a program, not only in the coding phase, but also in the solution development phase. Good structure cannot be an afterthought. It must be seen as an important component of a good program that can aid as much in its creation as in its understanding and subsequent enhancements.

7-3 THE USE OF VARIABLES

Variables constitute an essential part of programming in any language like PASCAL. It is important that they be used to best advantage. PASCAL offers the programmer considerable flexibility in the choice of variable names. This flexibility can be, and should be, exploited to make programs as self-documenting as possible. This point is made again and again in the main text that variable names should be chosen to reflect the purpose of the variable in a program. This has a

```
0   0038   00036        (* INPUT DATA VALUES AND INITIALIZE TEMPORARY ARRAY *)
0   0038   00037        READ (N);
0   004A   00038        FOR  G := 1 TO N DO
0   006E   00039            FOR H := 1 TO N DO
0   0092   00040            BEGIN
0   0092   00041                READ (A(G, H));
0   00E2   00042                AL(G, H) := A(G, H)
0   0166   00043            END;
0   0172   00044        READ (I, J);
0   0196   00045
0   0196   00046        (* DETERMINE ALL POSSIBLE PATHS IN THE GRAPH *)
0   0196   00047        FOUND := FALSE;
0   019E   00048        L := 1;
0   01A6   00049        WHILE (FOUND = FALSE) AND (L <= N) DO
0   01BE   00050            IF AL(I, J) = TRUE
0   0202   00051            THEN FOUND := TRUE
0   020A   00052            ELSE BEGIN
0   0216   00053                POWER (AL, A, .T, N);
0   024C   00054                FOR G := 1 TO N DO
0   0270   00055                    FOR H := 1 TO N DO
0   0294   00056                        AL(G, H) := T(G, H);
0   0324   00057                L := L + 1
0   0324   00058            END;
0   0334   00059
0   0334   00060        (* CHECK IF PATH FOUND *)
0   0334   00061        IF FOUND = TRUE
0   0334   00062        THEN WRITELN (' A PATH OF LENGTH ', L: 2, ' EXISTS')
0   0376   00063        ELSE WRITELN (' NO PATH EXISTS')
```

Fig. 7-1 Action modules in a PASCAL program

major impact on the readability of the code, and also on its ability to be modified. Not only is it easier to understand the function of an individual statement when the variables in the statement are named so that their role in the program is clear, but if a functional change should be required in the program, it is easier to target on the variables involved. Figure 7-2 is a case in point. The first version of this program (Fig. 7-2a) is identical to that given in Sec. 3-5 for processing orders in a university book store. The second version (Fig. 7-2b) is the same program, but written using single letter variable names. Which is easier to understand? Which would you rather modify? Although partly a matter of style and partly a matter of good programming practice, the thoughtful use of variables can make a significant contribution toward the production of high quality computer programs.

```
0  0000   00001  (* PROGRAM TO DETERMINE THE PROFIT MARGIN ON BOOK ORDERS *)
0  0000   00002  PROGRAM BOOKSTORE (INPUT, OUTPUT);
0  0000   00003
0  0000   00004  VAR IDENT: STRING (6);        (* BOOK IDENTIFICATION NUMBER *)
0  0038   00005      STOCK,                    (* QUANTITY IN STOCK *)
0  0038   00006      CLASS,                    (* CLASSIFICATION OF THE BOOK *)
0  0038   00007      ENROLMENT,                (* ESTIMATED COURSE ENROLMENT *)
0  0038   00008      NEW_TEXT,                 (* NEW TEXT OR USED PREVIOUSLY *)
0  0038   00009      NUM_REQUIRED,             (* NUMBER NEEDED *)
0  0038   00010      ORDER: INTEGER;           (* NUMBER TO BE ORDERED *)
0  0038   00011      COST,                     (* WHOLESALE COST *)
0  0038   00012      PROFIT,                   (* PROFIT MARGIN ON BOOK *)
0  0038   00013      TOTAL_PROFIT: REAL;       (* TOTAL PROFIT MARGIN *)
0  0038   00014
0  0038   00015  BEGIN
0  0038   00016
0  0038   00017      (* INITIALIZE *)
0  0038   00018      TOTAL_PROFIT := 0.00;
0  0040   00019
0  0040   00020      (* PRINT REPORT HEADINGS *)
0  0040   00021      WRITELN (' IDENTIFICATION  ON HAND   TO ORDER      ',
0  0052   00022          'PROFIT MARGIN');
0  0064   00023
0  0064   00024      (* PROCESS BOOKS *)
0  0064   00025      READ (IDENT, STOCK, CLASS, ENROLMENT, NEW_TEXT, COST);
0  00D0   00026      WHILE NOT EOF DO
0  00D8   00027      BEGIN
0  00D8   00028
0  00D8   00029          (* DETERMINE NUMBER OF COPIES REQUESTED *)
0  00D8   00030          IF CLASS = 1
0  00D8   00031          THEN IF NEW_TEXT = 1
0  00E4   00032              THEN NUM_REQUIRED := ROUND (0.85 * ENROLMENT)
0  0108   00033              ELSE NUM_REQUIRED := ROUND (0.60 * ENROLMENT)
0  0138   00034          ELSE IF NEW_TEXT = 1
0  0150   00035              THEN NUM_REQUIRED := ROUND (0.40 * ENROLMENT)
0  0174   00036              ELSE NUM_REQUIRED := ROUND (0.25 * ENROLMENT);
0  01B8   00037
0  01B8   00038          (* DETERMINE SIZE OF ORDER AND, IF NECESSARY, ISSUE
0  01B8   00039              OVERSTOCKED NOTICE *)
0  01B8   00040          ORDER := NUM_REQUIRED - STOCK;
0  01C4   00041          IF ORDER < 0
0  01C4   00042          THEN WRITELN (' ', IDENT, ' IS OVERSTOCKED: ', ABS (ORDER),
0  021C   00043              ' COPIES TO RETURN');
0  022E   00044
0  022E   00045          (* DETERMINE PROFIT ON THIS BOOK *)
0  022E   00046          IF COST <= 10.00
0  022E   00047          THEN PROFIT := NUM_REQUIRED * 0.25 * COST
0  0252   00048          ELSE PROFIT := NUM_REQUIRED * 0.20 * COST;
0  027E   00049
0  027E   00050          (* UPDATE TOTAL PROFIT STATISTIC *)
0  027E   00051          TOTAL_PROFIT := TOTAL_PROFIT + PROFIT;
0  028A   00052
0  028A   00053          (* PRINT LINE FOR THIS BOOK *)
0  028A   00054          WRITELN (' ', IDENT, STOCK, ORDER, PROFIT);
0  02E4   00055
0  02E4   00056          (* READ INFORMATION FOR NEXT BOOK *)
0  02E4   00057          READ (IDENT, STOCK, CLASS, ENROLMENT, NEW_TEXT, COST)
0  0350   00058      END;
0  0354   00059
0  0354   00060      (* PRINT TOTAL PROFIT OF ALL BOOKS *)
0  0354   00061      WRITELN (' TOTAL PROFIT', TOTAL_PROFIT)
0  0378   00062  END.
```

Fig. 7-2 (a)   The importance of choice of variable names

```
0  0000   00001   (* PROGRAM TO DETERMINE THE PROFIT MARGIN ON BOOK ORDERS *)
0  0000   00002   PROGRAM B (INPUT, OUTPUT);
0  0000   00003
0  0000   00004   VAR I: STRING(6);                 (* BOOK IDENTIFICATION NUMBER *)
0  0038   00005       S,                            (* QUANTITY IN STOCK *)
0  0038   00006       T,                            (* CLASSIFICATION OF BOOK *)
0  0038   00007       E,                            (* ESTIMATED COURSE ENROLMENT *)
0  0038   00008       N,                            (* NEW TEXT OR USED PREVIOUSLY *)
0  0038   00009       R,                            (* NUMBER NEEDED *)
0  0038   00010       O: INTEGER;                   (* NUMBER TO BE ORDERED *)
0  0038   00011       C,                            (* WHOLESALE COST *)
0  0038   00012       P,                            (* PROFIT MARGIN ON BOOK *)
0  0038   00013       Q: REAL;                      (* TOTAL PROFIT MARGIN *)
0  0038   00014
0  0038   00015   BEGIN
0  0038   00016
0  0038   00017       (* INITIALIZE *)
0  0038   00018       Q := 0.00;
0  0040   00019
0  0040   00020       (* PRINT REPORT HEADINGS *)
0  0040   00021       WRITELN (' IDENTIFICATION  ON HAND   TO ORDER
0  0052   00022           'PROFIT MARGIN');
0  0064   00023
0  0064   00024       (* PROCESS BOOKDS *)
0  0064   00025       READ (I, S, T, E, N, C);
0  00D0   00026       WHILE NOT EOF DO
0  00D8   00027       BEGIN
0  00D8   00028
0  00D8   00029           (* DETERMINE NUMBER OF COPIES REQUESTED *)
0  00D8   00030           IF T = 1
0  00D8   00031           THEN IF N = 1
0  00E4   00032               THEN R := ROUND (0.85 * E)
0  0108   00033               ELSE R := ROUND (0.60 * E)
0  0138   00034           ELSE IF N = 1
0  0150   00035               THEN R := ROUND (0.40 * E)
0  0174   00036               ELSE R := ROUND (0.25 * E);
0  01B8   00037
0  01B8   00038           (* DETERMINE SIZE OF ORDER AND, IF NECESSARY, ISSUE
0  01B8   00039               OVERSTOCKED NOTICE *)
0  01B8   00040           O := R - S;
0  01C4   00041           IF O < 0
0  01C4   00042           THEN WRITELN (' ', I, ' IS OVERSTOCKED: ', ABS (O),
0  021C   00043               ' COPIES TO RETURN');
0  022E   00044
0  022E   00045           (* DETERMINE PROFIT ON THIS BOOK *)
0  022E   00046           IF C <= 10.00
0  022E   00047           THEN P := R * 0.25 * C
0  0252   00048           ELSE P := R * 0.20 * C;
0  027E   00049
0  027E   00050           (* UPDATE TOTAL PROFIT STATISTIC *)
0  027E   00051           Q := Q + P;
0  028A   00052
0  028A   00053           (* PRINT LINE FOR THIS BOOK *)
0  028A   00054           WRITELN (' ', I, S, O, P);
0  02E4   00055
0  02E4   00056           (* READ INFORMATION FOR NEXT BOOK *)
0  02E4   00057           READ (I, S, T, E, N, C)
0  0350   00058       END;
0  0354   00059
0  0354   00060       (* PRINT TOTAL PROFIT ON ALL BOOKS *)
0  0354   00061       WRITELN (' TOTAL PROFIT', Q)
0  0378   00062   END.
```

Fig. 7-2 (b)   The importance of choice of variable names

7-4 PROGRAM PRESENTATION

Section 7-5.3 of the main text deals with two facets of the program presentation question: comments and paragraphing. As stated, the program code itself serves as the front line of documentation for a program. It is essential that it be easy to read. Comments and paragraphing play important roles to this end.

The comment facility in any programming language can be and should be used to great advantage. Lengthy comments, extending perhaps over several lines, can be used to explain the purpose and assumptions of a section of code (for example, a procedure). Figure 7-3 shows the use of such a comment to describe the purpose and key variables of the procedure INSERT from Sec. 6-5.1. Notice also the presence of three additional comments on lines 51, 57, and 63 to describe the purpose of each of these sections of code. Additionally, one might incorporate *elaborative* comments; that is, comments that elaborate on the piece of code, providing some information or insight not discernible from the code itself. Both types of comment are useful and important.

Section 7-5.3 contains some good material on the use of comments, much of it taken from the aforementioned books by Kernighan and Plauger, and Ledgard, as well as an article by Sachs entitled "Some Comments on Comments." In general, comments exist to explain and support program code. They should not be expected to improve bad code. Be wary of overcommenting, which serves only to add clutter to an already cluttered visual display. Do not just "parrot" the code by repeating it in comment form, but try to add something that will be of value to a reader trying to understand what is going on. Lastly, ensure that comments and code agree at all times. Too often changes are made to code without the corresponding changes to the related comments. This increases confusion immeasurably.

```
0  0038   00041      PROCEDURE INSERT (VAR_NAME: STRING(31); VAR_TYPE: STRING(7);
1  0000   00042          VAR_ADDRESS: INTEGER; VAR SIZE: INTEGER);
1  0000   00043      (* PROCEDURE TO INSERT A VARIABLE INTO A SYMBOL TABLE.  NAME,
1  0000   00044         TYPE, AND ADDRESS ARE GLOBAL VECTORS COMPRISING THE
1  0000   00045         SYMBOL TABLE. *)
1  0000   00046
1  0000   00047      VAR NUM: INTEGER;        (* NUMBER OF ELEMENTS *)
1  006E   00048
1  006E   00049      BEGIN
1  006E   00050
1  006E   00051          (* CHECK IF VARIABLE HAS ALREADY BEEN DEFINED *)
1  006E   00052          IF SEARCH (NAME, SIZE, VAR_NAME) <> 0
1  009C   00053          THEN WRITELN (' ***ERROR - VARIABLE ', VAR_NAME, ' HAS BEEN ',
1  00DA   00054              'PREVIOUSLY DEFINED.')
1  00EC   00055          ELSE BEGIN
1  00F0   00056
1  00F0   00057              (* COMPUTE THE NEXT AVAILABLE POSITION *)
1  00F0   00058              SIZE := SIZE + 1;
1  00FC   00059              IF SIZE > MAXNUM
1  00FC   00060              THEN WRITELN (' ***ERROR - TOO MANY VARIABLES DEFINED')
1  011A   00061              ELSE BEGIN
1  011E   00062
1  011E   00063                  (* MAKE INSERTION INTO THE POSITION FOUND *)
1  011E   00064                  NAME(SIZE) := VAR_NAME;
1  0146   00065                  V_TYPE(SIZE) := VAR_TYPE;
1  016E   00066                  ADDRESS(SIZE) := VAR_ADDRESS
1  0190   00067                  END
1  0198   00068              END
1  0198   00069      END;
```

Fig. 7-3   The use of descriptive comments

The writing of good comments can be as difficult as the writing of good code; yet, at the same time, it can also be as important. It is a skill that you will develop through practice, provided that you recognize it as important. It is.

Paragraphing, that is, the judicious use of blank space, is another important element of program presentation. A programmer has considerable freedom in the positioning of statements on cards and, through this, in the appearance of the source listing. If used properly, paragraphing can provide valuable assistance in identifying structural and logical program units, as is done in the spacing of the algorithms in the main text. To illustrate, Fig. 7-4 shows the same program presented in two ways: linear alignment (that is, all statements begin in the same column (Fig. 7-4a)), and our preferred indentation scheme with blank cards judiciously placed to increase separation (Fig. 7-4b). The readability advantages of form (b) should be evident.

Paragraphing is particularly valuable when nesting is employed. The program in Fig. 7-4b contains various types of nesting. In each case the paragraphing scheme removes confusion by indicating clearly what corresponds to what. For example, in the program beginning with the comment

(*READ IN SCHEDULE OF FAMILY ALLOWANCE PAYMENTS*)

it is readily apparent that the loop

FOR J := 0 TO 6 DO

is completely under control of the loop

FOR I := 1 TO 9 DO

In the section of code beginning with the comment

(*DETERMINE APPROPRIATE ROW SUBSCRIPT*)

the statement

R := (INCOME – 1000) DIV 1000

is clearly seen to be executed only when the value of INCOME is between 3000 and 10000 (including 3000).

As you have undoubtedly observed, the "END" statement is used to close BEGIN ... END constructs which are often nested. The correct use of paragraphing can alleviate any confusion that this might induce by indicating what BEGIN a particular END is meant to close. This is shown to advantage in the example given in Fig. 7-4b.

As stated in the main text, issues of program presentation seldom *cause* errors, but they can play a large role in avoiding them. In addition to the pride felt by a programmer when a program listing has a pleasing, professional appearance, he or she should also recognize that the presentation of a program is a key determinant of its readability, and through this, of its quality.

```
0  0000    00001   (* PROGRAM TO COMPUTE THE MONTHLY FAMILY ALLOWANCE PAYMENTS *)
0  0000    00002   PROGRAM BENEFIT (INPUT, OUTPUT);
0  0000    00003   VAR SCHED: ARRAY(1..9, 0..6) OF INTEGER; (* SCHEDULE OF PAYMENTS *)
0  0038    00004   INCOME, (* FAMILY'S INCOME *)
0  0038    00005   CHILDREN, (* NUMBER OF CHILDREN *)
0  0038    00006   R, (* ROW SUBSCRIPT *)
0  0038    00007   C, (* COLUMN SUBSCRIPT *)
0  0038    00008   I, J: INTEGER; (* LOOP VARIABLES *)
0  0038    00009   BEGIN
0  0038    00010   (* READ SCHEDULE OF FAMILY ALLOWANCE PAYMENTS *)
0  0038    00011   FOR I := 1 TO 9 DO
0  005C    00012   FOR J := 0 TO 6 DO
0  0080    00013   READ (SCHED(I, J));
0  00D8    00014   (* PROCESS FAMILIES *)
0  00D8    00015   READ (INCOME, CHILDREN);
0  00FC    00016   WHILE NOT EOF DO
0  0104    00017   BEGIN
0  0104    00018   (* DETERMINE APPROPRIATE ROW SUBSCRIPT *)
0  0104    00019   IF INCOME < 3000
0  0104    00020   THEN R := 1
0  0110    00021   ELSE IF INCOME >= 10000
0  011C    00022   THEN R := 9
0  0128    00023   ELSE R := (INCOME - 1000) DIV 1000;
0  014A    00024   (* DETERMINE APPROPRIATE COLUMN SUBSCRIPT *)
0  014A    00025   IF CHILDREN >= 6
0  014A    00026   THEN C := 6
0  0156    00027   ELSE C := CHILDREN;
0  016A    00028   (* SELECT CORRECT PAYMENT *)
0  016A    00029   WRITELN (' PAYMENT IS ', SCHED(R, C));
0  01CE    00030   (* READ DATA FOR NEXT FAMILY *)
0  01CE    00031   READ (INCOME, CHILDREN)
0  01F2    00032   END
0  01F2    00033   END.
```

Fig. 7-4 (a)   Two program presentations

7-5   REFLECTIONS

The theme in this chapter has been the role of programming style in the production of good programs. This is an important aspect, to be sure, but one must be careful not to interpret "style" in too restrictive a manner. There are many elements involved in the production of a program. Is the problem completely understood? Is the program adequately specified? Has the best algorithm been employed? Have the most appropriate data structures been used? And the list continues.

The purpose of this chapter has not been to suggest that good programs follow directly from attention to matters of style. This is an overly naive view, and is certainly not the case. However, an awareness of programming style can provide a suitable starting point. We are encouraging the proper mental attitude toward the production of programs. If you care enough to do your best always, then you stand a good chance of succeeding as a programmer.

BIBLIOGRAPHY

The items in this list deal with various issues related to the practice of programming, some of which have been dealt with in this chapter, many of which have not. Comments are offered on the content and relative difficulty of the items.

```
0  0000   00001   (* PROGRAM TO COMPUTE THE MONTHLY FAMILY ALLOWANCE PAYMENTS *)
0  0000   00002   PROGRAM BENEFIT (INPUT, OUTPUT);
0  0000   00003
0  0000   00004   VAR SCHED: ARRAY(1..9, 0..6) OF INTEGER;
0  0038   00005                              (* SCHEDULE OF PAYMENTS *)
0  0038   00006       INCOME,                (* FAMILY'S INCOME *)
0  0038   00007       CHILDREN,              (* NUMBER OF CHILDREN *)
0  0038   00008       R,                     (* ROW SUBSCRIPT *)
0  0038   00009       C,                     (* COLUMN SUBSCRIPT *)
0  0038   00010       I, J: INTEGER;         (* LOOP VARIABLES *)
0  0038   00011
0  0038   00012   BEGIN
0  0038   00013
0  0038   00014       (* READ SCHEDULE OF FAMILY ALLOWANCE PAYMENTS *)
0  0038   00015       FOR I := 1 TO 9 DO
0  005C   00016           FOR J := 0 TO 6 DO
0  0080   00017               READ (SCHED(I, J));
0  00D8   00018
0  00D8   00019       (* PROCESS FAMILIES *)
0  00D8   00020       READ (INCOME, CHILDREN);
0  00FC   00021       WHILE NOT EOF DO
0  0104   00022       BEGIN
0  0104   00023
0  0104   00024           (* DETERMINE APPROPRIATE ROW SUBSCRIPT *)
0  0104   00025           IF INCOME < 3000
0  0104   00026           THEN R := 1
0  0110   00027           ELSE IF INCOME >= 10000
0  011C   00028               THEN R := 9
0  0128   00029               ELSE R := (INCOME - 1000) DIV 1000;
0  014A   00030
0  014A   00031           (* DETERMINE APPROPRIATE COLUMN SUBSCRIPT *)
0  014A   00032           IF CHILDREN >= 6
0  014A   00033           THEN C := 6
0  0156   00034           ELSE C := CHILDREN;
0  016A   00035
0  016A   00036           (* SELECT CORRECT PAYMENT *)
0  016A   00037           WRITELN (' PAYMENT IS ', SCHED(R, C));
0  01CE   00038
0  01CE   00039           (* READ DATA FOR NEXT FAMILY *)
0  01CE   00040           READ (INCOME, CHILDREN)
0  01F2   00041       END
0  01F2   00042   END.
```

Fig. 7-4 (b)   Two program presentations

ACM: *Computing Surveys*, special issue on programming (edited by
      Peter J. Denning), 6, December, 1974.

This special issue contains a number of articles of varying degrees of
difficulty. These range from articles of a general survey flavor to articles on
specific technical topics, which are the most difficult.

Brooks, Frederick P., JR.: "The Mythical Man-Month," Addison-Wesley,
      Reading, Mass., 1975.

This is an entertaining and informative collection of essays on programming
and the management of programming projects, specifically slanted to very large
projects. The style is light and casual.

Dijkstra, Edsger W.: "The Humble Programmer," *Comm. ACM*,
      15, October, 1972, p. 859.

This article was the text of the author's Turing lecture to the Association for
Computing Machinery. It offers some interesting insights on programming and the
computing profession in an easy-to-read style.

Dijkstra, Edsger W.: "A Discipline of Programming," Prentice-Hall Inc.,
Englewood Cliffs, N.J., 1976.
A major work, this book is difficult, and is intended for the particularly
serious student of programming.

Jackson, Michael A.: "Principles of Program Design," Academic Press Inc.,
London, 1975.
The author offers a constructive and repeatable method for the design of
"correct" programs that does not rely heavily on inspiration and insight on the
designer's part. The approach differs from that which we have presented, and a
comparison of the two methods would certainly be of value.

Kernighan, Brian W., and Plauger, P.J.: "The Elements of Programming
Style," McGraw-Hill Book Co., New York, 1974. 2/e, 1979.
This is a concise, well-written, and entertaining book that operates in a
critical mode. Working from existing published programs, the authors show how
they can be improved through considerations of style.

Ledgard, Henry F.: "Programming Proverbs," Hayden Book Company,
Rochelle Park, New Jersey, 1975.
Written in a light, amusing style, this book contains many good
programming tips with ample illustration.

Mills, Harlan D.: "Software Development," *IEEE Transactions on
Software Engineering*, SE-2, 1976, p. 265.
This is a good overview of the present state of software development. The
article is well-written and very readable.

Sachs, Jon: "Some Comments on Comments," * (Systems Documentation
Newsletter), 3, December, 1976.
This easy-to-read article offers some good suggestions on the use of
comments in programs.

Weinberg, Gerald M.: *The Psychology of Computer Programming*,
Van Nostrand Reinhold, New York, 1971.
This is good reading for anyone interested in more than just the technical
issues of programming. Highly anecdotal in style, it offers entertaining and
informative reading.

Wirth, Niklaus: "Program Development by Stepwise Refinement,"
Comm. ACM, 14, April 1971, p. 221.
This article is a good discussion, complete with examples, of the top-down
design approach. It may be somewhat heavy going for the novice.

CHAPTER

**NUMERICAL
COMPUTATIONS**

This chapter explains the programming aspects of numerical computations in PASCAL. We begin with a discussion of the specification of precision in PASCAL arithmetic computations. The rest of the chapter presents methods and programs for dealing with various numerical applications such as: finding roots of equations, numerical integration, solving simultaneous equations, and least-squares curve fitting.

8-1 THE SPECIFICATION OF PRECISION IN PASCAL

Chapter 2 of the main text presented an introduction to the representation of numeric information in a computer. This section contains a more detailed discussion of number representation than that given previously.

The *precision* of a variable specifies the range of values that it can hold. From our discussion in the main text, it is clear that a computer can represent numbers only within some finite precision. When we declare a variable of type INTEGER, a specific amount of storage is set aside for the representation of that variable. If we know the amount of storage set aside, we will be able to determine the precision of a given INTEGER variable. For example, IBM 360/370 versions of PASCAL programs store INTEGER variables in 32 bits. One of these bits is used to indicate the sign of the number, leaving 31 bits to represent the magnitude of the number. The range of values representable in this manner is -2147483648 to $+2147483647$. As a rule of thumb, numbers under ten decimal digits in length can be stored in an INTEGER variable.

For IBM 360/370 versions of PASCAL programs, the declaration of a variable as type REAL also sets aside 32 bits for the representation of the value of the variable. Section 2-3 of the main text introduced the notion of floating-point numbers and their representation. Within a computer, they are in the form $\pm f * 16^e$, where f represents a binary fraction different from zero, and e represents the exponent of the base 16. Seven bits are used for the exponent, 24 bits for the fraction, and 1 bit for the sign. This results in a precision of approximately seven decimal digits for the fraction and allows a range in magnitude of approximately $.5397605 * 10^{-78}$ to $.7237005 * 10^{76}$.

So far we have been dealing with the precision of variables. The use of a constant within a program necessitates the use of a certain amount of storage. The precision of a constant is determined by its implicit type. Constants written in the same form as an integer have the same precision as an INTEGER variable. Similarly, constants written in the same form as a floating-point number have the same precision as a REAL variable.

This section has presented an insight into the range of numbers representable in PASCAL using conventional methods. The next section deals with numerical methods for determining the roots of functions.

8-2 FINDING THE ROOTS OF NONLINEAR FUNCTIONS

Recall that the *root* of a function of a single variable is defined to be that value of the variable that results in a value of zero for the function. For nonlinear polynomials of degree two, three, and four, there exist solution formulas for obtaining these roots. However, for polynomials of higher degree and other nonlinear equations, such as those involving the transcendental functions, there are no general formulas for the roots. Thus we require some other methods for finding the roots of functions.

One such method is that of *successive bisection*. To find the root of a given function f, we choose two values of x, say, x_1 and x_2, such that $f(x_1) * f(x_2) < 0$; in other words, we choose two values of x for which f has the opposite sign. If a function never changes sign, the requirement cannot be met and so the method cannot be applied. If we assume that $f(x)$ is continuous on the interval (x_1, x_2), there must exist a root between x_1 and x_2. The idea of this method is to reduce the size of the interval by half iteratively, while keeping the root within the interval.

The program given in Fig. 8-1 uses the method of successive bisection to find the solution of the function

$$f(x) = x^3 - x^2 - 2x + 1$$

given the initial boundaries $x_1 = 0.0$ and $x_2 = 1.0$ and a desired precision in the root of .00001.

The variables used in the main program are:

Variable	Type	Usage
A	REAL	Initial lower bound of the interval
B	REAL	Initial upper bound of the interval
PRECIS	REAL	Accuracy of the solution

The variables used in procedure SUCCESSIVE_BISECTION are:

X1	REAL	Lower bound of the interval
X2	REAL	Upper bound of the interval
PRECIS	REAL	Accuracy of the solution
ROOT	REAL	Estimated root of F
FROOT	REAL	Value of F(ROOT)
FX1	REAL	Value of F(X1)
I	INTEGER	Counted loop variable
FOUND	BOOLEAN	Indicates the root has been found

```
0   0000   00001   PROGRAM TEST_SB (INPUT, OUTPUT);
0   0000   00002   (*   THE MAIN PROGRAM DEMONSTATES A TYPICAL CALL TO THE SUCCESSIVE
0   0000   00003        BISECTION PROCEDURE.  INPUT DATA CONSISTS OF TWO VALUES (A AND B)
0   0000   00004        WHICH HAVE FUNCTIONAL VALUES OF OPPOSITE SIGN, AND THE DESIRED
0   0000   00005        ACCURACY OF THE ROOT (PRECIS). *)
0   0000   00006
0   0000   00007   VAR A, B, PRECIS: REAL;
0   0038   00008
0   0038   00009   PROCEDURE SUCCESSIVE_BISECTION(X1, X2, PRECIS: REAL);
1   0000   00010   (*  GIVEN X1 AND X2, TWO VALUES SUCH THAT F(X1) * F(X2) < 0,
1   0000   00011       AND PRECIS, THE DESIRED ACCURACY, THIS PROCEDURE FINDS ROOT,
1   0000   00012       A VALUE OF X FOR WHICH F(X) = 0.  I IS THE ITERATIONS COUNTER.
1   0000   00013       FOUND IS A FLAG INDICATING THAT THE ROOT HAS BEEN FOUND.
1   0000   00014       FROOT AND FX1 ARE TEMPORARY FUNCTION VALUES.
1   0000   00015       THE FUNCTION F IS INVOKED AS A FUNCTION CALL.  *)
1   0000   00016
1   0000   00017   VAR  ROOT, FROOT, FX1: REAL;
1   0066   00018        I: INTEGER;
1   0066   00019        FOUND: BOOLEAN;
1   0066   00020
1   0066   00021        FUNCTION F (X: REAL): REAL;
2   0000   00022        (*  THIS FUNCTION CORRESPONDS TO THE FUNCTION F FOR WHICH
2   0000   00023            WE ARE DETERMINING THE ROOT.  IT RETURNS THE VALUE OF
2   0000   00024            F EVALUATED AT THE POINT X.  *)
2   0000   00025        BEGIN
2   004E   00026            F := (((X - 1) * X - 2) * X + 1)
2   0066   00027        END;
1   0066   00028
```

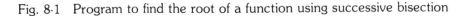

Fig. 8-1   Program to find the root of a function using successive bisection

```
1  0066   00029  BEGIN     (*  SUCCESSIVE BISECTION  *)
1  0066   00030
1  0066   00031          (*  PRINT A HEADING FOR THE ITERATIONS TABLE.  *)
1  0066   00032          WRITELN('0', ' ': 4, 'INTERVAL: (X1,X2)', ' ': 9, 'MIDPOINT',
1  00C0   00033                  ' ': 10, 'F(ROOT)');
1  00E4   00034          WRITELN(' ');
1  00F6   00035
1  00F6   00036          FOUND := FALSE;
1  00FE   00037          I := 1;
1  0106   00038
1  0106   00039          (*  PERFORM THE ITERATIONS TO A MAXIMUM OF 30.  *)
1  0106   00040          WHILE NOT FOUND AND (I <= 30) DO
1  0120   00041          BEGIN
1  0120   00042
1  0120   00043              (*  FIND THE MIDPOINT OF THE INTERVAL.  *)
1  0120   00044              ROOT := (X1 + X2) / 2;
1  0130   00045              FROOT := F(ROOT);
1  0150   00046
1  0150   00047              (*  OUTPUT THE RESULT OF THIS ITERATION.  *)
1  0150   00048              WRITELN(' ', '(', X1:10:6, ',', X2:10:6, ')', ' ': 5,
1  01CE   00049                      ROOT:10:6, ' ': 7, FROOT:10:6);
1  0204   00050
1  0204   00051              (*  ROOT FOUND?  *)
1  0204   00052              IF (FROOT = 0) OR (ABS(X2 - X1) < PRECIS)
1  0222   00053              THEN FOUND := TRUE;
1  022A   00054
1  022A   00055              (*  BISECT THE INTERVAL  *)
1  022A   00056              FX1 := F(X1);
1  024A   00057              IF (FROOT * FX1 < 0.0)
1  025A   00058              THEN X2 := ROOT
1  025A   00059              ELSE X1 := ROOT;
1  026E   00060              I := I + 1
1  026E   00061          END;
1  027E   00062
1  027E   00063          (*  ROOT FOUND?  *)
1  027E   00064          IF FOUND
1  027E   00065          THEN WRITELN('0', ' ': 2, 'SOLUTION: ROOT = ', ROOT:10:6,
1  02D0   00066                      ' ; F(ROOT) = ', F(ROOT):10:6)
1  030C   00067          ELSE WRITELN('0', ' ': 2, 'ROOT NOT FOUND IN 30 ITERATIONS; ',
1  0346   00068                      'ROOT SO FAR IS: ', ROOT:10:6)
1  036A   00069  END;
0  0038   00070
0  0038   00071  BEGIN     (*  TEST SUCCESSIVE BISECTION PROCEDURE  *)
0  0038   00072
0  0038   00073          READ (A, B, PRECIS);
0  006E   00074          SUCCESSIVE_BISECTION(A, B, PRECIS)
0  0086   00075  END.
```

```
-----------------------------------
| COMPILE TIME:    0.174 SECOND(S) |
|     NO WARNING(S) DETECTED        |
|     NO ERROR(S) DETECTED          |
-----------------------------------

--EXECUTION-->

   INTERVAL: (X1,X2)           MIDPOINT          F(ROOT)

(  0.000000,  1.000000)        0.500000        -0.125000
(  0.000000,  0.500000)        0.250000         0.453125
(  0.250000,  0.500000)        0.375000         0.162109
(  0.375000,  0.500000)        0.437500         0.017334
(  0.437500,  0.500000)        0.468750        -0.054230
(  0.437500,  0.468750)        0.453125        -0.018536
(  0.437500,  0.453125)        0.445313        -0.000621
(  0.437500,  0.445313)        0.441406         0.008351
(  0.441406,  0.445313)        0.443359         0.003864
(  0.443359,  0.445313)        0.444336         0.001621
(  0.444336,  0.445313)        0.444824         0.000500
(  0.444824,  0.445313)        0.445068        -0.000060
(  0.444824,  0.445068)        0.444946         0.000220
(  0.444946,  0.445068)        0.445007         0.000080
(  0.445007,  0.445068)        0.445038         0.000009

   SOLUTION: ROOT =    0.445038 ; F(ROOT) =    0.000009
```

Fig. 8-1   Program to find the root of a function using successive bisection (cont'd.)

The main program initializes the boundary of the interval and the desired accuracy of the root. Procedure SUCCESSIVE_BISECTION is then called to find the root of the function. In line 40 of the procedure, a loop is entered which causes the program to terminate if the root does not converge within 30 iterations. Inside the loop, the midpoint of the interval is first computed and printed. If the accuracy of the root is within the specified tolerance, the loop terminates and the procedure returns to the calling program. Otherwise, lines 56 to 59 reduce the size of the interval where the midpoint becomes one of the boundaries. If the values of F(ROOT) and F(X1) are of the same sign, the lower bound (X1) is assigned the value of the midpoint, otherwise the upper bound (X2) receives the value of the midpoint.

Another numerical procedure, called *Newton's method*, approximates the curve of the function by the tangent to the curve at a certain value of x. Given an initial guess, x_1, each successive approximation of the root is the x-axis intersection of the tangent to the curve at the previous guess. This method yields the following iterative formula for determining the successive approximations:

$$x_{n+1} = x_n - f(x_n)/f'(x_n)$$

The iterations continue until $f(x_n)$ is within the specified tolerance of zero.

Figure 8-2 gives a program that finds the root of a function using Newton's method. The function used is

$$f(x) = x^3 - x^2 - 2x + 1$$

where the derivative of $f(x)$ is

$$f'(x) = 3x^2 - 2x - 2$$

The variables used in the main program are:

Variable	Type	Usage
GUESS	REAL	Initial estimate of the root
PRECIS	REAL	Desired accuracy of the root

The variables used in procedure NEWTON are:

X	REAL	Value of x_n
PRECIS	REAL	Desired accuracy of the root
ROOT	REAL	Calculated root of F
I	INTEGER	Counted loop variable
FOUND	BOOLEAN	Indicates root found

The main program calls procedure NEWTON, with an initial guess at the root of the function of 1.0 and the desired accuracy of the root of .00001. In procedure NEWTON, the loop beginning in line 42 stops execution of the procedure if no convergence to the root is found after 30 iterations. Line 46 calculates the value of $x_n - f(x_n)/f'(x_n)$. If the newly computed root is such that F(ROOT) is within the stated tolerance of zero, then the procedure returns to the main program, otherwise the new value of the root is assigned to X. The function F returns the value of the function $f(x)$, while DERIVF returns the value of the derivative of $f(x)$.

```
0  0000   00001  PROGRAM TEST_NEWTON (INPUT, OUTPUT);
0  0000   00002  (*    THE MAIN PROGRAM DEMONSTATES A TYPICAL CALL TO THE NEWTON'S
0  0000   00003        METHOD PROCEDURE.  INPUT DATA CONSISTS OF AN INITIAL GUESS AT THE
0  0000   00004        ROOT OF THE FUNCTION (GUESS), AND THE DESIRED ACCURACY OF THE
0  0000   00005        ROOT (PRECIS).  *)
0  0000   00006
0  0000   00007  VAR  GUESS, PRECIS: REAL;
0  0038   00008
0  0038   00009  PROCEDURE NEWTON(X, PRECIS: REAL);
1  0000   00010  (*    NEWTON'S METHOD: GIVEN X, AN INITIAL GUESS AT THE ROOT OF F(X),
1  0000   00011        AND THE DESIRED ACCURACY, PRECIS, THIS PROCEDURE FINDS ROOT,
1  0000   00012        THE ROOT OF F(X).  I IS THE ITERATIONS COUNTER.  FOUND IS A FLAG
1  0000   00013        INDICATING THAT THE ROOT HAS BEEN FOUND.  THE FUNCTIONS
1  0000   00014        F AND DERIVF ARE INVOKED AS FUNCTION CALLS.  *)
1  0000   00015
1  0000   00016  VAR  ROOT: REAL;
1  005A   00017       I: INTEGER;
1  005A   00018       FOUND: BOOLEAN;
1  005A   00019
1  005A   00020       FUNCTION F (X: REAL): REAL;
2  0000   00021       (*  THIS FUNCTION CORRESPONDS TO THE FUNCTION F FOR WHICH WE ARE
2  0000   00022           DETERMINING THE ROOT.  IT RETURNS THE VALUE OF F EVALUATED
2  0000   00023           AT THE POINT X.  *)
2  0000   00024       BEGIN
2  004E   00025           F := (((X - 1) * X - 2) * X + 1)
2  0066   00026       END;
1  005A   00027
1  005A   00028       FUNCTION DERIVF (X: REAL): REAL;
2  0000   00029       (*  THIS FUNCTION CORRESPONDS TO THE DERIVATIVE OF THE FUNCTION
2  0000   00030           FOR WHICH WE ARE DETERMINING THE ROOT.  IT RETURNS THE VALUE
2  0000   00031           OF THE DERIVATIVE EVALUATED AT THE POINT X.  *)
2  0000   00032       BEGIN
2  004E   00033           DERIVF := ((3 * X - 2) * X - 2)
2  0062   00034       END;
1  005A   00035
1  005A   00036  BEGIN    (*  NEWTON'S METHOD  *)
1  005A   00037
1  005A   00038       FOUND := FALSE;
1  0062   00039       I := 1;
1  006A   00040
1  006A   00041       (*  PERFORM THE ITERATIONS TO A MAXIMUM OF 30.  *)
1  006A   00042       WHILE NOT FOUND AND (I <= 30) DO
1  0084   00043       BEGIN
1  0084   00044
1  0084   00045           (*  CALCULATE IMPROVED ESTIMATE  *)
1  0084   00046           ROOT := X - (F(X) / DERIVF(X));
1  00D0   00047
1  00D0   00048           (*  ROOT FOUND?  *)
1  00D0   00049           IF ABS(F(ROOT)) < PRECIS
1  00EE   00050           THEN FOUND := TRUE;
1  00FE   00051           X := ROOT;
1  0106   00052           I := I + 1
1  0106   00053       END;
1  0116   00054
1  0116   00055       (*  CONVERGENCE?  *)
1  0116   00056       IF FOUND
1  0116   00057       THEN WRITELN('0', ' ': 6, 'ROOT = ', ROOT:10:6, ' ; F(ROOT) = ',
1  017A   00058                    F(ROOT):10:6)
1  01A4   00059       ELSE WRITELN('0', ' ': 6, 'ROOT NOT FOUND IN 30 ITERATIONS; ',
1  01DE   00060                    'ROOT SO FAR = ', ROOT:10:6, ' ; F(ROOT) = ',
1  0214   00061                    F(ROOT):10:6)
1  023E   00062  END;
0  0038   00063
0  0038   00064  BEGIN    (*  TEST NEWTON'S METHOD PROCEDURE  *)
0  0038   00065
0  0038   00066       READ (GUESS, PRECIS);
0  005C   00067       NEWTON(GUESS, PRECIS)
0  006C   00068  END.
```

```
------------------------------------
| COMPILE TIME:    0.155 SECOND(S) |
|    NO WARNING(S) DETECTED         |
|    NO ERROR(S) DETECTED           |
------------------------------------
--EXECUTION-->

     ROOT =   0.445042 ; F(ROOT) =   0.000000
```

Fig. 8-2 Program to find the root of a function using Newton's method

Exercises for Sec. 8-2

1. Use the successive bisection program to compute a root of each of the following functions to an accuracy of 0.0001 on the interval [0, 1].

    (a) $f(x) = 10x^3 - 33x^2 + 29x - 6$
    (b) $f(x) = xe^x - 1$
    (c) $f(x) = x - 2^{-x}$

2. Use Newton's method to devise a program which will compute a root of each of the following functions to an accuracy of 0.0005 using an initial approximation of $x = 1$.

    (a) $f(x) = x^3 - x - 1$
    (b) $f(x) = 3x^2 - e^x$
    (c) $f(x) = 4\cos x - e^x$

3. Construct a program which uses the method of successive bisection to compute the square root of a number N to an accuracy of five decimal places. Use $x_0 = N$ as an initial approximation to the root.

4. Let $f_1 (x)$ and $f_2 (x)$ denote two functions in x. One method of obtaining their solution is by writing a third function $g(x)$ as

    $$g(x) = f_1 (x) - f_2 (x)$$

    and solving for a root of $g(x)$. Given $f_1 (x) = x^2 - 2x$ and $f_2 (x) = \sqrt{3x}$, write a program which uses the above method and the method of successive bisection to determine a point of intersection of the two functions. Use an accuracy of 0.0001 and run the program twice, once on the interval $-.5 \leqslant x \leqslant 1.5$ and once on the interval $1.0 \leqslant x \leqslant 3.5$.

5. The objective of this problem is to find the positive root of the following equation

    $$x^4 - 2x^3 - x^2 - 7x - 4 = 0$$

    You should try (i) the successive bisection method, (ii) the secant method (see main text), and (iii) Newton's method on the equation. Each of the methods should be implemented by means of a function.

    The evaluation of the function and its derivative should also be implemented by means of a function (so that it would be trivial to find the root of another equation by simply replacing these two functions). Thus you should have five separate functions; one for the successive bisection method, one for the secant method, one for Newton's method, one for the evaluation of the function, and one for the evaluation of the derivative of the function (i.e., the evaluation of $4x^3 - 6x^2 - 2x - 7$).

    For the successive bisection and secant methods try initial end points of both 0.0 and 5.0, and 2.5 and 4.0. For Newton's method try the initial guesses of 2.0 and 2.5. In all cases, continue the iterations until the functional value is less than 1.0×10^{-5} (this tolerance should be a parameter to the functions) or 25 iterations have been tried.

8-3 NUMERICAL INTEGRATION

Integration is a standard mathematical technique for computing the area of a closed figure. When we approximate a definite integral of the form $\int_a^b f(x)dx$ using numerical rather than analytical techniques, we are using *numerical integration*. One such method, *Simpson's rule*, calculates the integral of a function by fitting second-degree polynomials to the curve $f(x)$. To approximate the integral of $f(x)$, the interval, (a, b) is divided into n equal subintervals where n must be an even number. Then the integral of $f(x)$ is approximated by:

$$\frac{h}{3} [f(x_0) + 4f(x_1) + 2f(x_2) + \cdots + 2f(x_{n-2}) + 4f(x_{n-1}) + f(x_n)]$$

where h is the length of each subinterval. This formula is exact for all polynomials having a degree of three or lower. In most other cases, its error tends to be small.

A program to compute the integral of a function using Simpson's rule is given in Fig. 8-3. The program computes the integral of $f(x) = 6x^5 - 3x^2$ over the interval $(1, 2)$ to an accuracy of .0001.

The variables used in the main program are:

Variable	Type	Usage
A	REAL	Lower bound of the interval
B	REAL	Upper bound of the interval
PRECIS	REAL	Desired accuracy of the result

The variables used in the procedure SIMPSON are:

A	REAL	Lower bound of the interval
B	REAL	Upper bound of the interval
PRECIS	REAL	Desired accuracy of the result
N	INTEGER	Number of subintervals
H	REAL	Length of the subintervals
SIMP	REAL	Calculated value of the integral of F
SUM	REAL	Sum of the areas under the curve
LAST	REAL	Previous approximation of the integral
I	INTEGER	Counted loop variable
J	INTEGER	Counted loop variable
DONE	BOOLEAN	A flag indicating accuracy reached

The main program initializes the interval and accuracy required before calling the procedure. Within procedure SIMPSON, H is first set to half the size of the given interval. Then in line 39 a loop which performs at most 30 iterations is entered. Thus, if the value of the integral does not converge within 30 iterations, execution of the procedure terminates. Within the loop, the number of subintervals to be used is first calculated. Lines 49 to 55 compute the sum of the areas of the subintervals. The accuracy of this result is then determined; if its value is within the given tolerance, execution of the loop is terminated, the result is printed and the procedure returns to the calling program. If this is not the case, line 65 is used to

```
0  0000  00001  PROGRAM TEST_SIMPSON (INPUT, OUTPUT);
0  0000  00002  (*   THE MAIN PROGRAM DEMONSTRATES A TYPICAL CALL TO THE SIMPSON'S
0  0000  00003         RULE PROCEDURE.  INPUT DATA CONSISTS OF THE UPPER AND LOWER
0  0000  00004         BOUNDS OF INTEGRAL TO BE APPROXIMATED (A AND B), AND THE DESIRED
0  0000  00005         ACCURACY OF THE APPROXIMATION (PRECIS).  *)
0  0000  00006
0  0000  00007  VAR  A, B, PRECIS: REAL;
0  0038  00008
0  0038  00009  PROCEDURE SIMPSON (A, B, PRECIS: REAL);
1  0000  00010  (*   GIVEN A, B, AND PRECIS, THIS PROCEDURE CALCULATES SIMP, THE
1  0000  00011         SIMPSON'S RULE APPROXIMATION OF THE INTEGRAL FROM A TO B OF
1  0000  00012         F(X)DX, TO THE SPECIFIED ACCURACY OF PRECIS.  THE FUNCTION F
1  0000  00013         IS INVOKED AS A FUNCTION CALL.  *)
1  0000  00014
1  0000  00015       VAR  SIMP,           (*   THE APPROXIMATION TO THE INTEGRAL    *)
1  0066  00016            H,              (*   THE LENGTH OF THE SUBINTERVALS       *)
1  0066  00017            LAST,           (*   THE PREVIOUS VALUE OF SIMP           *)
1  0066  00018            SUM: REAL;      (*   THE SUM OF AREAS UNDER THE CURVE     *)
1  0066  00019            N,              (*   THE NUMBER OF SUBINTERVALS           *)
1  0066  00020            I, J: INTEGER;  (*   ITERATION COUNTERS                   *)
1  0066  00021            DONE: BOOLEAN;  (*   A FLAG INDICATING ACCURACY REACHED *)
1  0066  00022
1  0066  00023       FUNCTION F (X: REAL): REAL;
2  0000  00024       (*   THIS FUNCTION CORRESPONDS TO THE FUNCTION F IN THE INTEGRAL
2  0000  00025             WE ARE APPROXIMATING.  IT RETURNS THE VALUE OF F EVALUATED
2  0000  00026             AT THE POINT X.  *)
2  0000  00027       BEGIN
2  004E  00028            F := ((6 * (X * X * X * X * X)) - (3 * (X * X)))
2  0074  00029       END;
1  0066  00030
1  0066  00031  BEGIN     (*  SIMPSON'S RULE  *)
1  0066  00032
1  0066  00033       SIMP := 0;
1  006E  00034       H := (B - A) / 2;
1  007E  00035       DONE := FALSE;
1  0086  00036       I := 1;
1  008E  00037
1  008E  00038       (*  PERFORM THE ITERATIONS TO A MAXIMUM OF 20  *)
1  008E  00039       WHILE NOT DONE AND (I <= 30) DO
1  00A8  00040       BEGIN
1  00A8  00041
1  00A8  00042            (*  SAVE PREVIOUS APPROXIMATION  *)
1  00A8  00043            LAST := SIMP;
1  00B0  00044
1  00B0  00045            (*  CALCULATE NUMBER OF SUBINTERVALS  *)
1  00B0  00046            N := ROUND((B - A) / H);
1  00D0  00047
1  00D0  00048            (*  ACCUMULATE SUM  *)
1  00D0  00049            SUM := F(A) + 4 * F(A + H) + F(B);
1  0148  00050            FOR J := 2 TO N - 2 DO
1  0170  00051            BEGIN
1  0170  00052                 IF NOT ODD(J)
1  0170  00053                 THEN SUM := SUM + 2 * F(A + J * H) +
1  01C2  00054                              4 * F(A + (J + 1) * H)
1  01EE  00055            END;
1  0216  00056
1  0216  00057            (*  CALCULATE SIMPSON'S RULE APPROXIMATION  *)
1  0216  00058            SIMP := H / 3 * SUM;
1  0226  00059
1  0226  00060            (*  TEST ACCURACY  *)
1  0226  00061            IF (ABS(SIMP - LAST) / SIMP) < PRECIS
1  0234  00062            THEN DONE := TRUE
1  023C  00063            ELSE BEGIN
1  0248  00064                 (*  PREPARE FOR NEXT ITERATION  *)
1  0248  00065                 H := H / 2;
1  0254  00066                 I := I + 1
1  0254  00067                 END
1  0260  00068       END;
1  0264  00069
1  0264  00070       (*  ACCURACY ACHIEVED?  *)
1  0264  00071       IF DONE
1  0264  00072       THEN WRITELN('0', ' ': 6, 'ANSWER IS ', SIMP:10:6,
1  02B6  00073                    ' ; TOLERANCE MET IN ', I:2, ' ITERATIONS')
1  02EC  00074       ELSE WRITELN('0', ' ': 6, 'TOLERANCE NOT MET IN 20 ITERATIONS; ',
1  0326  00075                    'CURRENT ANSWER IS ', SIMP:10:6)
1  034A  00076  END;
0  0038  00077
0  0038  00078  BEGIN     (*  TEST SIMPSON'S RULE PROCEDURE  *)
0  0038  00079
```

Fig. 8-3 Program to compute the integral of f(x) using Simpson's method

```
0  0038   00080        READ(A, B, PRECIS);
0  006E   00081        SIMPSON(A, B, PRECIS)
0  0086   00082  END.
-----------------------------------
| COMPILE TIME:    0.183 SECOND(S) |
|     NO WARNING(S) DETECTED       |
|     NO ERROR(S) DETECTED         |
-----------------------------------
--EXECUTION-->

    ANSWER IS  56.000050 ; TOLERANCE MET IN  4 ITERATIONS
```

Fig. 8-3   Program to compute the integral of f(x) using Simpson's method (cont'd.)

halve the size of the subintervals for the next iteration. The function F returns the value of the function $f(x)$.

To illustrate the use of Simpson's Rule we have deliberately chosen a function whose integral is easy to obtain analytically. The exact solution of $\int_1^2(6x^5 - 3x^2)dx$ is

$$\int_1^2(6x^5 - 3x^2)dx = (x^6 - x^3)]_1^2$$
$$= (2^6 - 2^3) - (1^6 - 1^3)$$
$$= 2^6 - 2^3 - 0$$
$$= 56$$

One of the major advantages of numerical integration is that the techniques, once developed, apply equally well to functions whose integrals are difficult, or even impossible, to obtain analytically. Examples of such functions are given in the exercises.

Exercises for Sec. 8-3

1. The answer in Fig. 8-3 is obtained in 4 iterations. Hand trace these 4 iterations, showing the value of H, SUM, SIMP and LAST at each stage.

2. Use the Simpson's rule program to approximate the following integrals to an accuracy of 0.0001.

    (a) $\int_0^2 x^2 e^x dx$
    (b) $\int_0^{\pi/2} \sin^2 x dx$
    (c) $\int_1^\pi \frac{1 - \cos x}{x} dx$

3. Using Simpson's rule, construct a program to compute the area in the first quadrant under the curve $y = x^2$ and inside the circle with unit radius. Use an accuracy of 0.0001.

4. Formulate a program to compute the area of a circle with a radius of 2 units, whose center has coordinates (4, 4). Use Simpson's rule with an accuracy of 0.0001.

5. Use Simpson's Rule to compute the value of π to an accuracy of 6 decimal

places. The value is obtained by observing that the area of a circle with radius r is given by πr^2. Thus the area of a circle with unit radius equals the value of π. Your approximation, therefore, is obtained by calculating the area of a circle, centered at the origin, with a radius of 1 unit.

6. In the main text an optimization technique was discussed for the rectangle and trapezoidal rules for numerical integration. Bascially this revolved around the observation that certain function points were involved in each iteration, and a saving could therefore be realized by not recalculating these points each time. Such a saving is possible as well for Simpson's rule, although the revised calculations are somewhat more difficult to obtain. Develop a modified technique in which only **new** points are considered in each iteration.

8-4   SIMULTANEOUS LINEAR EQUATIONS

In this section, we examine two methods for solving sets of simultaneous linear equations. The first method, known as *Gaussian elimination*, solves equations of the form

$$a_{11}x_1 + a_{12}x_2 + \cdots + a_{1n}x_n = b_1$$
$$a_{21}x_1 + a_{22}x_2 + \cdots + a_{2n}x_n = b_2$$
$$\vdots \qquad\qquad\qquad\qquad \vdots$$
$$a_{n1}x_1 + a_{n2}x_2 + \cdots + a_{nn}x_n = b_n$$

by representing them as a matrix as described in the main text.

The process of Gaussian elimination consists of the two steps:

1. *Forward elimination:* for each row starting from the top row, successively divide the row by its diagonal element, called the *pivot*, leaving a 1 on the diagonal, and then subtract a multiple of the row from each row below it, leaving zeros in the column below the diagonal 1.
2. *Back substitution:* subtract multiples of lower rows from the higher rows, leaving zeros in all positions but those on the diagonal, which contains 1's and the rightmost column.

The program given in Fig. 8-4 solves a system of linear equations using this approach. The variables used in the main program are:

Variable	Type	Usage
SIZE	INTEGER	Number of variables in the system
SYSTEM	REAL	The augmented matrix of size SIZE by SIZE + 1

I	INTEGER	A subscript
J	INTEGER	A subscript

The variables used in the procedure GAUSS are:

SYSTEM	REAL	The system of equations
N	INTEGER	Number of rows in SYSTEM
M	INTEGER	Number of columns in SYSTEM
PIVOT	REAL	Pivot for each row
I	INTEGER	Subscript and counted loop variable
J	INTEGER	Subscript and counted loop variable
K	INTEGER	Subscript and counted loop variable

This program is used to solve the set of equations

$$1.0x_1 + 3.0x_2 - 2.0x_3 = 7.0$$
$$4.0x_1 - 1.0x_2 + 3.0x_3 = 10.0$$
$$-5.0x_1 + 2.0x_2 + 3.0x_3 = 7.0$$

```
0  0000  00001  PROGRAM TEST_GAUSS (INPUT, OUTPUT);
0  0000  00002  (*    THIS PROGRAM SETS UP THE PARAMETERS FOR PROCEDURE GAUSS AND
0  0000  00003        PRINTS THE INITIAL AND FINAL SYSTEMS.  INPUT IS ASSUMED TO BE
0  0000  00004        THE SIZE OF THE SYSTEM FOLLOWED BY THE AUGMENTED MATRIX OF
0  0000  00005        COEFFICIENTS WRITTEN IN ROW-BY-ROW FORM.  THE VARIABLES SIZE
0  0000  00006        AND MATRIX ARE USED FOR THIS PURPOSE.  *)
0  0000  00007
0  0000  00008  CONST MAXROW = 25;    (* MAXIMUM NUMBER OF EQUATIONS IN SYSTEM  *)
0  0038  00009        MAXCOL = 26;    (*  MAXROW + 1 *)
0  0038  00010
0  0038  00011  TYPE MATRIX = ARRAY(1..MAXROW, 1..MAXCOL) OF REAL;
0  0038  00012
0  0038  00013  VAR  SYSTEM: MATRIX;  (*  THE SYSTEM OF EQUATIONS  *)
0  0038  00014       SIZE,            (*  NUMBER OF EQUATIONS  *)
0  0038  00015       I, J: INTEGER;   (*   SUBSCRIPTS  *)
0  0038  00016
0  0038  00017  PROCEDURE GAUSS(N: INTEGER; VAR SYSTEM: MATRIX);
1  0000  00018  (*    GIVEN N, THE NUMBER OF EQUATIONS IN THE SYSTEM, AND SYSTEM,
1  0000  00019        AN AUGMENTED MATRIX OF THE FORM:
1  0000  00020              | A11 A12 . . . A1N | B1 |
1  0000  00021              | A21 A22 . . . A2N | B2 |
1  0000  00022              |  .   .           . |  . |
1  0000  00023              |  .   .          .  |  . |
1  0000  00024              |  .   .         .   |  . |
1  0000  00025              | AN1 AN2 . . . ANN | BN |
1  0000  00026        THIS PROCEDURE FINDS THE CORRESPONDING SOLUTION MATRIX:
1  0000  00027              |  1   0  . . .  0 | X1 |
1  0000  00028              |  0   1  . . .  0 | X2 |
1  0000  00029              |  .   .          . |  . |
1  0000  00030              |  .   .         .  |  . |
1  0000  00031              |  .   .        .   |  . |
1  0000  00032              |  0   0  . . .  1 | XN |
1  0000  00033        WHERE AX = B.  *)
1  0000  00034
1  0000  00035  VAR  PIVOT: REAL;      (*  THE PIVOT ELEMENT OF A ROW  *)
1  0056  00036       M,                (*  NUMBER OF COLUMNS = N + 1  *)
1  0056  00037       I, J, K: INTEGER; (*  SUBSCRIPTS AND ITERATION COUNTERS  *)
```

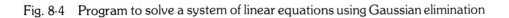

Fig. 8-4 Program to solve a system of linear equations using Gaussian elimination

```
1  0056   00038  BEGIN    (*  GAUSSIAN ELIMINATION  *)
1  0056   00039
1  0056   00040       (*  FORWARD ELIMINATION  *)
1  0056   00041       M := N + 1;
1  0062   00042       FOR I := 1 TO N DO
1  0086   00043       BEGIN
1  0086   00044
1  0086   00045            (*  DIVIDE EACH ELEMENT IN THE ROW BY THE PIVOT  *)
1  0086   00046            PIVOT := SYSTEM(I, I);
1  00CE   00047            FOR J := 1 TO M DO
1  00F2   00048                SYSTEM(I, J) := SYSTEM(I, J) / PIVOT;
1  0182   00049
1  0182   00050            (*  SUBTRACT A MULTIPLE OF THE ROW FROM EACH LOWER ROW  *)
1  0182   00051            FOR J := I + 1 TO N DO
1  01AC   00052            BEGIN
1  01AC   00053                PIVOT := SYSTEM(J, I);
1  01F4   00054                FOR K := I TO M DO
1  0218   00055                    SYSTEM(J, K) := SYSTEM(J, K) - PIVOT * SYSTEM(I, K);
1  02EE   00055                SYSTEM(J, I) := 0
1  032E   00057            END
1  0336   00058       END;
1  033E   00059
1  033E   00060       (*  BACK SUBSTITUTION  *)
1  033E   00061       FOR I := N DOWNTO 2 DO
1  0360   00062       BEGIN
1  0360   00063            FOR J := 1 TO I - 1 DO
1  0388   00064            BEGIN
1  0388   00065                SYSTEM(J, M) := SYSTEM(J, M) - (SYSTEM(J, I)
1  0450   00066                                   * SYSTEM(I, M));
1  049C   00067                SYSTEM(J, I) := 0
1  04DC   00068            END
1  04E4   00069       END
1  04E8   00070  END;
0  0038   00071
0  0038   00072  BEGIN    (*  TEST GAUSSIAN ELIMINATION PROCEDURE  *)
0  0038   00073
0  0038   00074       (*  INPUT THE SYSTEM  *)
0  0038   00075       READ(SIZE);
0  004A   00076       FOR I := 1 TO SIZE DO
0  006E   00077       BEGIN
0  006E   00078            FOR J := 1 TO SIZE + 1 DO
0  0096   00079                READ(SYSTEM(I, J))
0  00E6   00080       END;
0  00EE   00081
0  00EE   00082       (*  OUTPUT THE ORIGINAL SYSTEM  *)
0  00EE   00083       WRITELN('0', ' ': 34, 'ORIGINAL SYSTEM');
0  0124   00084       WRITELN('0', ' ':13, 'X1', ' ': 16, 'X2', ' ': 16, 'X3',
0  01A2   00085                ' ': 9, 'RIGHT HAND SIDE');
0  01C6   00086       FOR I := 1 TO SIZE DO
0  01EA   00087       BEGIN
0  01EA   00088            FOR J := 1 TO SIZE + 1 DO
0  0212   00089                WRITE(' ': 9, SYSTEM(I, J):9:5);
0  027A   00090            WRITELN(' ')
0  028C   00091       END;
0  0290   00092
0  0290   00093       (*  PERFORM GAUSSIAN ELIMINATION ON THE SYSTEM  *)
0  0290   00094       GAUSS(SIZE, SYSTEM);
0  02B6   00095
0  02B6   00096       (*  OUTPUT THE SOLUTION SYSTEM  *)
0  02B6   00097       WRITELN('-', ' ': 34, 'SOLUTION SYSTEM');
0  02EC   00098       WRITELN('0', ' ': 13, 'X1', ' ': 16, 'X2', ' ': 16, 'X3',
0  036A   00099                ' ': 10, 'FINAL SOLUTION');
0  038E   00100       FOR I := 1 TO SIZE DO
0  03B2   00101       BEGIN
0  03B2   00102            FOR J := 1 TO SIZE + 1 DO
0  03DA   00103                WRITE(' ': 9, SYSTEM(I, J):9:5);
0  0442   00104            WRITELN(' ')
0  0454   00105       END
0  0454   00106  END.
```

```
------------------------------------
| COMPILE TIME:   0.281 SECOND(S)  |
|     NO WARNING(S) DETECTED        |
|     NO ERROR(S) DETECTED          |
------------------------------------
--EXECUTION-->
```

```
                   ORIGINAL SYSTEM

        X1              X2              X3          RIGHT HAND SIDE
      1.00000         3.00000        -2.00000          7.00000
```

Fig. 8-4   Program to solve a system of linear equations using Gaussian elimination
            (cont'd.)

```
   4.00000          -1.00000           3.00000          10.00000
  -5.00000           2.00000           3.00000           7.00000


                          SOLUTION SYSTEM

        X1                X2                X3        FINAL SOLUTION
     1.00000           0.00000           0.00000           1.50000
     0.00000           1.00000           0.00000           3.50000
     0.00000           0.00000           1.00000           2.50000
```

Fig. 8-4   Program to solve a system of linear equations using Gaussian elimination
         (cont'd.)

The main program first inputs the system of equations. Procedure GAUSS is then called in line 94 to solve this system of equations. Finally, the solution to this system of equations is printed.

Within the procedure GAUSS, lines 41 to 58 first perform forward elimination. For each row, the elements in that row are divided by the pivot element and a multiple of the row is subtracted from each lower row so that all values below the pivot are zero. Then back substitution is performed in lines 61 to 69, which makes all values above the diagonal zero.

A second method to solve a system of linear equations is called *Gauss-Seidel iteration*. The equations are each solved for one of the variables. For example, the set of equations

$$
\begin{array}{rcrcrcll}
5x_1 & + & x_2 & + & 3x_3 & = & 10 & \quad (1)\\
x_1 & + & x_2 & + & 5x_3 & = & 8 & \quad (2)\\
2x_1 & + & 4x_2 & + & x_3 & = & 11 & \quad (3)
\end{array}
$$

might be written as

$$
\begin{array}{rclclcll}
x_1 & = & 2.00 & - & 0.20x_2 & - & 0.60x_3 & \quad (1)\\
x_2 & = & 2.75 & - & 0.50x_1 & - & 0.25x_3 & \quad (3)\\
x_3 & = & 1.60 & - & 0.20x_1 & - & 0.20x_2 & \quad (2)
\end{array}
$$

and stored in an array as

$$
\begin{array}{rrr}
2.00 & -0.20 & -0.60\\
2.75 & -0.50 & -0.25\\
1.60 & -0.20 & -0.20
\end{array}
$$

An initial estimate for the variables $x_1, x_2, ..., x_n$ is assigned. Zero is used in many cases. When calculating a new value for x_i, the new values for $x_1, x_2, ..., x_{i-1}$ are used as well as the old values for $x_{i+1}, x_{i+2}, ..., x_n$, rather than the entire set of old values, as is done in the *Jacobi method* (see main text). For each iteration, we solve these equations for better estimates of the variables. We stop when the errors are within a prescribed tolerance defined by

$$
\sum_{j=1}^{N} (x_j^i - x_j^{i-1})^2 < \epsilon
$$

where x_j^i is the ith estimation of the jth variable. The program for this method of solving linear equations is given in Fig. 8-5. The variables used in the main program are:

Variable	Type	Usage
N	INTEGER	Number of equations
EQNS	ARRAY(1..3, 1..3) OF REAL	Matrix of coefficients of the equations
PRECIS	REAL	Desired accuracy of the solutions
SOLNS	ARRAY(1..3) OF REAL	Solution vector for the system
I	INTEGER	Counted loop variable
J	INTEGER	Counted loop variable

The variables used in procedure GAUSS_SEIDEL are:

N	INTEGER	Number of equations
EQNS	ARRAY(1..3) OF REAL	Matrix of coefficients of the equations
SOLNS	ARRAY(1..3) OF REAL	Solution vector for the system
PRECIS	REAL	Desired accuracy of the solutions
SUM	REAL	Sum of the squares of differences
OLD	REAL	Previous value in the solution vector
I	INTEGER	Counted loop variable
J	INTEGER	Counted loop variable
K	INTEGER	Counted loop variable
DONE	BOOLEAN	Indicates convergence of the iterations

The program in Fig. 8-5 solves the system of equations

$$
\begin{aligned}
x_1 &= -1.4 + 0.4x_2 + 0.6x_3 \\
x_2 &= 2.3333 - 0.33335x_1 + 0.6666x_3 \\
x_3 &= 3.3333 - 1.3333x_1 + 0.3333x_2
\end{aligned}
$$

The main program first reads the system of equations. Then the solution vector elements are initialized to 0.0. Procedure GAUSS_SEIDEL is then called to solve this system of equations. Within the procedure, a maximum of 30 iterations are performed to find the solution vector. Within this loop, a new set of approximations is computed in lines 60 to 66. A sum of the squared differences between the new value of SOLNS(J) and its previous value is updated in line 67. Next the accuracy of the solution is tested and the procedure returns to the main program if the error is small enough.

```
0  0000   00001  PROGRAM TEST_GS (INOUT, OUTPUT);
0  0000   00002  (*    THE MAIN PROGRAM DEMONSTRATES A TYPICAL CALL TO THE GAUSS-SEIDEL
0  0000   00003        PROCEDURE.  INPUT DATA CONSISTS OF:
0  0000   00004              N - THE NUMBER OF EQUATIONS
0  0000   00005              EQNS - THE MATRIX OF EQUATIONS OF SIZE N BY N
0  0000   00006              PRECIS - THE DESIRED ACCURACY OF THE RESULT.
0  0000   00007        OTHER VARIABLES USED ARE:
0  0000   00008              SOLNS - THE SOLUTION VECTOR OF SIZE N
0  0000   00009              I, J - INDICES.
0  0000   00010        NOTICE THAT THE MAXIMUM NUMBER OF EQUATIONS HAS BEEN LIMITED
0  0000   00011        TO 3, BUT THAT THIS LIMIT CAN BE READILY CHANGED.  *)
0  0000   00012
0  0000   00013  CONST MAXEQNS = 3;
0  0038   00014
0  0038   00015  TYPE EQUATIONS= ARRAY(1..MAXEQNS, 1..MAXEQNS) OF REAL;
0  0038   00016       SOLUTIONS= ARRAY(1..MAXEQNS) OF REAL;
0  0038   00017
0  0038   00018  VAR  PRECIS: REAL;
0  0038   00019       EQNS: EQUATIONS;
0  0038   00020       SOLNS: SOLUTIONS;
0  0038   00021       I, J, N: INTEGER;
0  0038   00022
0  0038   00023  PROCEDURE GAUSS_SEIDEL (N: INTEGER; EQNS: EQUATIONS; SOLNS: SOLUTIONS;
1  0000   00024                          PRECIS: REAL);
1  0000   00025  (*    GIVEN THE PARAMETERS N, EQNS, SOLNS, AND PRECIS AS DESCRIBED IN
1  0000   00026        THE MAIN PROGRAM, THIS PROCEDURE SOLVES THE GIVEN SET OF
1  0000   00027        SIMULTANEOUS LINEAR EQUATIONS USING GAUSS-SEIDEL ITERATION.
1  0000   00028        OTHER VARIABLES USED ARE:
1  0000   00029              SUM - THE SUM OF SQUARES OF DIFFERENCES
1  0000   00030              OLD - A PREVIOUS APPROXIMATION
1  0000   00031              DONE - A FLAG INDICATING THE ITERATIONS CONVERGE
1  0000   00032              I, J, K - INDICES AND ITERATION COUNTERS.  *)
1  0000   00033
1  0000   00034  VAR  SUM, OLD: REAL;
1  009A   00035       I, J, K: INTEGER;
1  009A   00036       DONE: BOOLEAN;
1  009A   00037
1  009A   00038  BEGIN     (*  GAUSS-SEIDEL ITERATION  *)
1  009A   00039
1  009A   00040        (*  PRINT A HEADING FOR THE ITERATIONS TABLE  *)
1  009A   00041        WRITELN('0', ' ': 2, 'ITERATIONS TABLE FOR GAUSS-SEIDEL METHOD');
1  00D0   00042        WRITELN('0', ' ': 8, 'X1', ' ': 10, 'X2', ' ': 10, 'X3');
1  014E   00043
1  014E   00044        DONE := FALSE;
1  0156   00045        I := 1;
1  015E   00046
1  015E   00047        (*  PERFORM THE ITERATIONS TO A MAXIMUM OF 30  *)
1  015E   00048        WHILE NOT DONE AND (I <= 30) DO
1  0178   00049        BEGIN
1  0178   00050
1  0178   00051              (*  PRINT THE CURRENT RESULT  *)
1  0178   00052              WRITELN(' ': 4, SOLNS(1):9:5, ' ': 3, SOLNS(2):9:5, ' ': 3,
1  01DE   00053                    SOLNS(3):9:5);
1  01F8   00054
1  01F8   00055              (*  CALCULATE A NEW SET OF APPROXIMATIONS  *)
1  01F8   00056              SUM := 0.0;
1  0200   00057              FOR J := 1 TO N DO
1  0224   00058              BEGIN
1  0224   00059                    OLD := SOLNS(J);
1  024E   00060                    SOLNS(J) := EQNS(J, 1);
1  029A   00061                    FOR K := 2 TO N DO
1  02BE   00062                    BEGIN
1  02BE   00063                          IF (K <= J)
1  02CA   00064                          THEN SOLNS(J) := SOLNS(J) + EQNS(J, K) * SOLNS(K-1)
1  0382   00065                          ELSE SOLNS(J) := SOLNS(J) + EQNS(J, K) * SOLNS(K)
1  0440   00066                    END;
1  044C   00067                    SUM := SUM + (SOLNS(J) - OLD) * (SOLNS(J) - OLD)
1  04A0   00068              END;
1  04AE   00069
1  04AE   00070              (*  TEST ACCURACY  *)
1  04AE   00071              IF (SUM < PRECIS)
1  04BA   00072              THEN DONE := TRUE
1  04BA   00073              ELSE I := I + 1
1  04C6   00074        END;
1  04D6   00075
```

Fig. 8-5   Program to solve a system of equations using Gauss-Seidel iteration

```
1   04D6   00076        (*  CONVERGENCE?  *)
1   04D6   00077        IF DONE
1   04D6   00078        THEN BEGIN
1   04E0   00079            WRITELN('0', ' ': 2, 'THE VECTOR OF SOLUTIONS FOR ',
1   0516   00080                '3 EQUATIONS IS');
1   0528   00081            FOR I := 1 TO 3 DO
1   054C   00082                WRITELN(' ': 10, 'X', I:1, ' ': 3, SOLNS(I):9:5);
1   05CC   00083            WRITELN(' ': 3, 'WITH AN ACCURACY OF  ', PRECIS:9:6)
1   0602   00084            END
1   0602   00085        ELSE BEGIN
1   0606   00086            WRITELN('0', ' ': 2, 'TOLERANCE NOT MET IN 30 ITERATIONS; ',
1   063C   00087                'ANSWER SO FAR IS: ');
1   064E   00088            FOR I := 1 TO 3 DO
1   0672   00089                WRITELN(' ': 10, 'X', I:1, ' ': 3, SOLNS(I):9:5)
1   06EE   00090            END
1   06F2   00091    END;
0   0038   00092
0   0038   00093    BEGIN     (*  TEST GAUSS-SEIDEL PROCEDURE  *)
0   0038   00094
0   0038   00095        (*  INPUT THE SYSTEM OF EQUATIONS  *)
0   0038   00096        READ (N);
0   004A   00097        FOR I := 1 TO N DO
0   006E   00098            FOR J := 1 TO N DO
0   0092   00099                READ (EQNS(I, J));
0   00EA   00100        READ (PRECIS);
0   00FC   00101
0   00FC   00102        (*  INITIALIZE THE SOLUTIONS VECTOR  *)
0   00FC   00103        FOR I := 1 TO N DO
0   0120   00104            SOLNS(I) := 0.0;
0   014E   00105
0   014E   00106        (*  PERFORM GAUSS-SEIDEL ITERATION ON THE SYSTEM  *)
0   014E   00107        GAUSS_SEIDEL(N, EQNS, SOLNS, PRECIS)
0   016E   00108    END.
```

```
------------------------------------
| COMPILE TIME:   0.288 SECOND(S) |
|    NO WARNING(S) DETECTED        |
|    NO ERROR(S) DETECTED          |
------------------------------------
--EXECUTION-->

ITERATIONS TABLE FOR GAUSS-SEIDEL METHOD

       X1          X2          X3

    0.00000     0.00000     0.00000
   -1.40000     2.79992     6.13313
    3.39985     5.28848     0.56294
    1.05315     2.35754     2.71490
    1.17195     3.75244     3.02142
    1.91383     3.70950     2.01797
    1.29458     3.24699     2.68946
    1.51247     3.62198     2.52393
    1.56315     3.49475     2.41395
    1.44627     3.46040     2.55834
    1.51916     3.53235     2.48514
    1.50402     3.48860     2.49074
    1.48988     3.49705     2.51240
    1.50626     3.50603     2.49356
    1.49855     3.49604     2.50052
    1.49873     3.50062     2.50181
    1.50133     3.50061     2.49833
    1.49924     3.49899     2.50058
    1.49994     3.50025     2.50007

THE VECTOR OF SOLUTIONS FOR 3 EQUATIONS IS
        X1    1.50014
        X2    3.49985
        X3    2.49966
WITH AN ACCURACY OF   0.000001
```

Fig. 8-5 Program to solve a system of equations using Gauss-Seidel iteration (cont'd.)

Exercises for Sec. 8-4

1. Use the Gaussian elimination program to solve the following systems of equations:

   (a)
   $$\begin{aligned}
   x_1 &+ 2x_2 + 3x_3 = 5 \\
   2x_1 &- x_2 + x_3 = 6 \\
   x_1 &+ 3x_2 - 5x_3 = 2
   \end{aligned}$$

   (b)
   $$\begin{aligned}
   x_1 &+ 2x_2 + 3x_3 + 4x_4 = 5 \\
   2x_1 &+ 3x_2 + 4x_3 + 5x_4 = 6 \\
   3x_1 &+ 4x_2 + 5x_3 + 6x_4 = 7 \\
   4x_1 &+ 5x_2 + 6x_3 + 7x_4 = 8
   \end{aligned}$$

2. Repeat exercise 1(a) using the iterative function Gauss-Seidel program. Use $x_1 = x_2 = x_3 = 0$ as the initial guesses and .005 as the accuracy. Compare your results with those obtained in exercise 1(a).

3. Repeat exercise 1(b) using the iterative function Gauss-Seidel program. Use $x_1 = x_2 = x_3 = x_4 = 0$ as the initial guesses and .0001 as the accuracy. Compare your results with those obtained in exercise 1(b).

4. Recall that elimination with partial pivoting is a method in which roundoff errors are reduced by interchanging rows so that the largest number in magnitude is the next pivot. Formulate a program for Gaussian elimination with partial pivoting. Use the equations in exercise 1(a) to test your program.

8-5 CURVE FITTING BY LEAST-SQUARES APPROXIMATION

A curve which gives the best fit for a set of N points is often required. Approximating the curve by a polynomial of degree n which minimizes the squares of the errors is called the *least-squares technique*. For the special case of linear approximations, which we will examine in this section, the method is known as *linear regression*. For example, to find an equation of the form

$$f(x) = a_0 + a_1 x$$

we must solve the set of equations

$$a_0 N + a_1 \sum_{i=1}^{N} x_i = \sum_{i=1}^{N} y_i$$

and

$$a_0 \sum_{i=1}^{N} x_i + a_1 \sum_{i=1}^{N} x_i^2 = \sum_{i=1}^{N} x_i y_i$$

for a_0 and a_1. The program for solving such a system of equations is given in Fig. 8-6. The variables used in the main program are:

Variable	Type	Usage
N	INTEGER	Number of ordered pairs
X	ARRAY(1..50) OF REAL	Vector of X values of size N
Y	ARRAY(1..50) OF REAL	Vector of Y values of size N
SOLUTION	ARRAY(1..2) OF REAL	Vector of solutions of size 2
I	INTEGER	Counted loop variable

The variables used in the procedure LINEAR are:

N	INTEGER	Number of ordered pairs
X	ARRAY(1..50) OF REAL	Vector of X values of size N
Y	ARRAY(1..50) OF REAL	Vector of Y values of size N
COEF	ARRAY(1..2) OF REAL	Solution vector of size 2
SUMX	REAL	Sum of elements in X (x_i)
SUMY	REAL	Sum of elements in Y (y_i)
SUMXX	REAL	Sum of squares of elements in X (x_i^2)
SUMXY	REAL	Sum of products of corresponding elements in X and Y (x_iy_i)
DENOM	REAL	Value of denominator of the determinant
I	INTEGER	Counted loop variable

The data used by the program given in Fig. 8-6 are:

X	Y
0.4501	3.0509
0.9802	1.5078
1.3376	1.0999
2.3999	0.9212
2.7936	1.0012
3.5805	2.2333
3.7201	3.2500

The main program calls procedure LINEAR after reading the set of data points. Lines 63 to 65 print the resulting equation. Procedure LINEAR first computes the sums of x_i, y_i, x_i^2, and x_iy_i and stores them in the variables SUMX, SUMY, SUMXX, and SUMXY, respectively. Then the resulting equations

N * COEFF(1) + SUMX * COEFF(2) = SUMY
SUMX * COEFF(1) + SUMXX * COEFF(2) = SUMXY

are solved in lines 47 to 49 for COEFF(1) and COEFF(2) by using determinants.

```
0  0000   00001   PROGRAM TEST_LINEAR (INPUT, OUTPUT);
0  0000   00002   (*    THIS PROGRAM TESTS PROCEDURE LINEAR WHICH DETERINES A LINEAR
0  0000   00003         EQUATION TO FIT A GIVEN SET OF ORDERED X-Y PAIRS.  *)
0  0000   00004
0  0000   00005   CONST MAXPAIRS = 50;
0  0038   00006
0  0038   00007   TYPE VALUES= ARRAY(1..MAXPAIRS) OF REAL;
0  0038   00008        SOLN= ARRAY(1..2) OF REAL;
0  0038   00009
0  0038   00010   VAR  X, Y: VALUES;  (*  X-Y CORRDINATES OF THE ORDERED PAIRS  *)
0  0038   00011        SOLUTION: SOLN;  (*  LINEAR EQUATION COEFFICIENTS *)
0  0038   00012        N,             (*  THE NUMBER OF ORDERED PAIRS  *)
0  0038   00013        I: INTEGER;    (*  AN INDEX  *)
0  0038   00014
0  0038   00015   PROCEDURE LINEAR(N: INTEGER; X, Y: VALUES; VAR COEF: SOLN);
1  0000   00016   (*    THIS PROCEDURE DETERMINES THE LINEAR REGRESSION LINE FOR THE GIVEN
1  0000   00017         SET OF X AND Y VALUES.  THE DETERMINED COEFFICIENTS ARE RETURNED
1  0000   00018         TO THE CALLING PROCEDURE THROUGH THE ARRAY COEF, WITH THE CONSTANT
1  0000   00019         COEFFICIENT IN THE FIRST POSITION AND THE X-COEFFICIENT IN THE
1  0000   00020         SECOND POSITION.  N IS THE NUMBER OF X-Y PAIRS.  *)
1  0000   00021
1  0000   00022   VAR  SUMX,          (*  SUM OF THE X VALUES                      *)
1  0096   00023        SUMY,          (*  SUM OF THE Y VALUES                      *)
1  0096   00024        SUMXX,         (*  SUM OF SQUARES OF X VALUES               *)
1  0096   00025        SUMXY,         (*  SUM OF PRODUCT OF CORRESPONDING X-Y VALUES  *)
1  0096   00026        DENOM: REAL;   (*  DENOMINATOR OF THE DETERMINANT           *)
1  0096   00027        I: INTEGER;    (*  INDEX AND COUNTER                        *)
1  0096   00028
1  0096   00029   BEGIN     (*  LINEAR REGRESSION  *)
1  0096   00030
1  0096   00031        (*  INITIALIZE  *)
1  0096   00032        SUMX := 0;
1  009E   00033        SUMY := 0;
1  00A6   00034        SUMXX := 0;
1  00AE   00035        SUMXY := 0;
1  00B6   00036
1  00B6   00037        (*  DETERMINE REQUIRED SUMS  *)
1  00B6   00038        FOR I := 1 TO N DO
1  00DA   00039        BEGIN
1  00DA   00040            SUMX := SUMX + X(I);
1  0108   00041            SUMY := SUMY + Y(I);
1  0136   00042            SUMXX := SUMXX + (X(I) * X(I));
1  018C   00043            SUMXY := SUMXY + (X(I) * Y(I))
1  01DA   00044        END;
1  01E6   00045
1  01E6   00046        (*  SOLVE USING DETERMINANTS (CRAMER'S RULE)  *)
1  01E6   00047        DENOM := (N * SUMXX) - (SUMX * SUMX);
1  020C   00048        COEF(1) := ((SUMY * SUMXX) - (SUMXY * SUMX)) / DENOM;
1  022A   00049        COEF(2) := ((N * SUMXY) - (SUMX * SUMY)) / DENOM
1  0254   00050   END;
0  0038   00051
0  0038   00052   BEGIN     (*  TEST LINEAR REGRESSION PROCEDURE  *)
0  0038   00053
0  0038   00054        (*  INPUT THE SYSTEM  *)
0  0038   00055        READ(N);
0  004A   00056        FOR I := 1 TO N DO
0  006E   00057            READ(X(I), Y(I));
0  00D6   00058
0  00D6   00059        (*  DETERMINE THE LEAST-SQUARES APPROXIMATION TO THE CURVE  *)
0  00D6   00060        LINEAR(N, X, Y, SOLUTION);
0  010C   00061
0  010C   00062        (*  PRINT THE SOLUTION  *)
0  010C   00063        WRITELN('0', '  THE RESULTING REGRESSION LINE IS');
0  0130   00064        WRITELN('0', ' ': 5, 'Y = ', SOLUTION(1):9:5, ' + ',
0  018E   00065                SOLUTION(2):9:5, 'X')
0  01BA   00066   END.
--------------------------------------
| COMPILE TIME:    0.157 SECOND(S) |
|    NO WARNING(S) DETECTED        |
|    NO ERROR(S) DETECTED          |
--------------------------------------
--EXECUTION-->

THE RESULTING REGRESSION LINE IS

    Y =    1.66088 +   0.09423X
```

Fig. 8-6 Program to perform linear regression on a set of points

Exercises for Sec. 8-5

1. Write a program to compute the regression line for the data in Table 8-1. Plot the data and the computed regression line. Does your line appear to be a good approximation to the actual curve? Why or why not?

    Table 8-1

X	Y
1.5603	3.6189
2.0157	2.4113
2.3399	1.1346
2.7568	0.5673
3.1346	1.2015
3.4799	2.5682
3.7521	3.3999

2. The midterm averages for a selected sample of freshman computer science students were recorded and tabulated along with their final high school averages. The results are given in Table 8-2.

    Table 8-2

Student	Midterm Average	High School Average
ADAMS	73.5	78.2
BARNES	66.9	71.5
CAMPBELL	83.8	81.7
DOLBY	58.1	77.3
FRIESEN	77.1	85.6
HOOPER	44.3	65.8
JONES	35.8	70.3
MARSHALL	66.2	60.5
REMPEL	72.5	75.3
SCOTT	60.6	66.6
TURNER	85.8	85.2
WALSH	87.9	86.3

    Write a program to compute the regression line for the data. Plot the regression line. Can you predict, with a reasonable degree of accuracy, the midterm average of a specific student given that student's high school average? Why or why not?

3. The purpose of this problem is to write a program to obtain the best-fit polynomial regression line of arbitrary degree for a given set of data. If we let n represent the order of the curve we are approximating and M, the number of data points, then we wish to approximate the curve by a function of the form

    $$f(x) = a_0 + a_1x + a_2x^2 + \cdots + a_nx^n$$

We can find these $n + 1$ unknowns $(a_0, a_1, ..., a_n)$ using Gaussian elimination on the $n + 1$ simultaneous equations given on pages 390 and 391 of the main text. Formulate a program for this purpose.

4. Use the program devised in exercise 3 to determine the best-fit polynomial regression line of degree 2 for the data in Table 8-2. Compare your results with those obtained in exercise 1 by plotting this regression line on your previous graph. Which line fits the data most accurately and why?

CHAPTER

9

ADVANCED STRING PROCESSING

The basic notions of string manipulation in PASCAL were introduced in Chap. 5. These notions are extended to include three additional nonprimitive functions in this chapter. Also a new PASCAL control structure, the CASE statement, is introduced. Finally, four string manipulation applications are presented. In particular these applications deal with lexical analysis, text editing, KWIC indexing, and the use of bit strings in information organization and retrieval.

9-1 BASIC FUNCTIONS

Chapter 5 discussed in some detail the PASCAL programming aspects of string manipulation. The simulation of the concatenation operation and the two primitive functions LENGTH and SUB were discussed in detail. Most other string-manipulation functions can be obtained from these primitives.

In this chapter we provide programs for the three additional functions – MATCH, SPAN, and BREAK – which are discussed in the main text. As was done in that discussion, we associate a *cursor* with the scanning process. The three programs presented in this section concern themselves with the maintenance and updating of the cursor mechanism.

The three PASCAL functions which we present here all have the same six parameters. These parameters are the following:

SUBJECT	Subject string to be examined.
PATTERN	String sought within the subject string.
CURSOR	Character position in SUBJECT at which the pattern matching process is to begin.
MATCH_STR	Desired substring found in SUBJECT in the case of a successful pattern match.
REPLACE_FLAG	Flag indicating whether or not a replacement is required. A value of *true* specifies a replacement and a value of *false* indicates no replacement.
REPLACE_STR	Replacement string for the matched substring.

Figure 9-1 presents a PASCAL function for the MATCH function. This function first determines if the pattern fits within the subject string starting at the position given by CURSOR. If not, MATCH returns a value of *false*. Then lines 28 and 29 attempt to match PATTERN with the substring of equal length starting at the indicated position. If the match is unsuccessful, a value of *false* is returned; otherwise the pattern matched in SUBJECT is replaced by REPLACE_STR if this is so indicated. Finally, the value of CURSOR is updated and MATCH returns the value TRUE.

Figure 9-2 is a PASCAL implementation of the function SPAN. In line 28 a check is made to see if the cursor is greater than the length of SUBJECT and a value of *false* results if this occurs. Next a search is made through the subject string starting at the position indicated by CURSOR until any character in the pattern string is not found in the subject string. If the characters at the position indicated by CURSOR is not found in PATTERN, SPAN returns FALSE; otherwise, it returns TRUE and if REPLACE_FLAG has the value TRUE, the substring matched is replaced by REPLACE_STR. Finally, CURSOR is updated and the value TRUE is returned. SPAN then returns a value of *true*.

Finally, Fig. 9-3 contains a PASCAL program for the function BREAK. This function is very similar to the function SPAN except that we are searching for the first character in SUBJECT which is also in PATTERN. If no character is found, BREAK returns the value FALSE in line 31; otherwise, the value TRUE is returned. Lines 62 to 65 replace the matched substring with REPLACE_STR if this is indicated.

Now that programs for the functions MATCH, SPAN, and BREAK have been presented, we are ready to use them in a variety of string-manipulation applications. Some of these applications allow us to use the CASE statement which is introduced in the next section.

```
0 0000  00001    FUNCTION MATCH (VAR SUBJECT, PATTERN: STRING(256);
1 0000  00002         VAR CURSOR: INTEGER; VAR MATCH_STR: STRING(256);
1 0000  00003         REPLACE_FLAG: BOOLEAN; VAR REPLACE_STR: STRING(256)): BOOLEAN;
1 0000  00004
1 0000  00005    (* THIS FUNCTION RETURNS A VALUE OF TRUE IF THE PATTERN STRING
1 0000  00006        (PATTERN) IS FOUND STARTING AT THE CHARACTER POSITION SPECIFIED  BY
1 0000  00007        CURSOR IN THE STRING SUBJECT; OTHERWISE, IT RETURNS A VALUE OF
1 0000  00008        FALSE.  IF THE PATTERN MATCH SUCCEEDS, MATCH_STR IS SET TO THE
1 0000  00009        VALUE OF PATTERN AND IF REPLACE_FLAG IS TRUE, THE SUBSTRING
1 0000  00010        MATCHED IN SUBJECT IS REPLACED BY THE VALUE IN REPLACE_STR. *)
1 0000  00011
1 0000  00012    VAR TEMP: STRING(256);       (* TEMPORARY STRING VARIABLE *)
1 0082  00013    FUNCTION LENGTH (VAR STR: STRING(256)): INTEGER; EXTERNAL;
1 0082  00014    PROCEDURE SUB (VAR S: STRING(256); POS, NUM: INTEGER; VAR RESULT:
2 0000  00015        STRING(256)); EXTERNAL;
1 0082  00016    PROCEDURE PSDSUB (VAR S: STRING(256); POS, NUM: INTEGER; VAR ADD:
2 0000  00017        STRING(256)); EXTERNAL;
1 0082  00018
1 0082  00019    BEGIN
1 0082  00020
1 0082  00021        (* DOES THE PATTERN FIT WITHIN THE SEARCH BOUNDS OF THE
1 0082  00022           SUBJECT STRING? *)
1 0082  00023        IF CURSOR + LENGTH (PATTERN) > LENGTH (SUBJECT) + 1
1 00C6  00024        THEN MATCH := FALSE
1 00D2  00025
1 00D2  00026        (* PERFORM PATTERN MATCH *)
1 00D2  00027        ELSE BEGIN
1 00DE  00028            SUB (SUBJECT, CURSOR, LENGTH (PATTERN), TEMP);
1 0134  00029            IF (TEMP <> PATTERN)
1 013E  00030            THEN MATCH := FALSE
1 013E  00031
1 013E  00032            (* SET MATCH_STR AND PERFORM INDICATED REPLACEMENT *)
1 013E  00033            ELSE BEGIN
1 014A  00034                MATCH_STR := PATTERN;
1 0150  00035                IF REPLACE_FLAG
1 0150  00036                THEN BEGIN
1 015A  00037                    PSDSUB (SUBJECT, CURSOR, LENGTH (PATTERN),
1 0194  00038                        REPLACE_STR);
1 01B0  00039                    CURSOR := CURSOR + LENGTH (REPLACE_STR)
1 01B8  00040                    END
1 01D6  00041                ELSE CURSOR := CURSOR + LENGTH (PATTERN);
1 0200  00042
1 0200  00043                (* SUCCESSFUL RETURN *)
1 0200  00044                MATCH := TRUE
1 0200  00045                END
1 0208  00046            END
1 0208  00047    END;
```

Fig. 9-1 PASCAL program for the function MATCH

Exercises for Sec. 9-1

1. Write a PASCAL procedure TRIM which will delete all trailing blanks of a given character string. Test your program on the following strings:

    'HELLObbbbb*/'

    and

    'GOODBYEbbbbbbbbb*/'

    where "b" represents blank spaces in the string.

2. Design a PASCAL procedure which acts in the same manner as the REPEAT function illustrated in the main text; that is, produce a string containing *n* replications of *pattern* for the procedure call REPEAT (*pattern, n, result*) and returns the value through *result*.

```
0  0000  00001       FUNCTION SPAN (VAR SUBJECT, PATTERN: STRING(256); VAR CURSOR:
1  0000  00002           INTEGER; VAR MATCH_STR: STRING(256); REPLACE_FLAG: BOOLEAN;
1  0000  00003           VAR REPLACE_STR: STRING(256)): BOOLEAN;
1  0000  00004
1  0000  00005       (* THIS FUNCTION RETURNS TRUE IF THE CHARACTER DENOTED BY CURSOR
1  0000  00006          MATCHES ANY OF THE CHARACTERS IN PATTERN.  IF THE PATTERN MATCH
1  0000  00007          SUCCEEDS, MATCH_STR BECOMES A SEQUENCE OF CHARACTERS CONTAINING
1  0000  00008          THE CHARACTER AT THE POSITION SPECIFIED BY CURSOR AND ALL OTHER
1  0000  00009          CHARACTERS WHICH ARE CONTAINED IN PATTERN.  THE PATTERN MATCH
1  0000  00010          PROCESS TERMINATES ON ENCOUNTERING A CHARACTER NOT IN PATTERN OR
1  0000  00011          THE END OF THE SUBJECT STRING.  IF A REPLACEMENT OPERATION IS
1  0000  00012          SPECIFIED, THE SEQUENCE OF CHARACTERS IS REPLACED BY THE VALUE
1  0000  00013          OF REPLACE_STR. *)
1  0000  00014
1  0000  00015       VAR I: INTEGER;               (* INDEX VARIABLE *)
1  0082  00016           TEMP: STRING(256);        (* TEMPORARY STRING VARIABLE *)
1  0082  00017       FUNCTION LENGTH (VAR STR: STRING(256)): INTEGER; EXTERNAL;
1  0082  00018       FUNCTION INDEX (VAR S, PATTERN: STRING(256)): INTEGER; EXTERNAL;
1  0082  00019       PROCEDURE SUB (VAR S: STRING(256); POS, NUM: INTEGER;
2  0000  00020           VAR RESULT: STRING(256)); EXTERNAL;
1  0082  00021       PROCEDURE PSDSUB (VAR S: STRING(256); POS, NUM: INTEGER; VAR ADD:
2  0000  00022           STRING(256)); EXTERNAL;
1  0082  00023
1  0082  00024       BEGIN
1  0082  00025
1  0082  00026           (* DOES THE PATTERN FIT WITHIN THE BOUNDS OF THE SUBJECT
1  0082  00027              STRING? *)
1  0082  00028           IF CURSOR > LENGTH (SUBJECT)
1  008A  00029           THEN SPAN := FALSE
1  00A8  00030           ELSE BEGIN
1  00B4  00031
1  00B4  00032               (* INITIALIZE PATTERN MATCH *)
1  00B4  00033               I := CURSOR;
1  00BC  00034
1  00BC  00035               (* IS CHARACTER I IN THE PATTERN STRING? *)
1  00BC  00036               SUB (SUBJECT, I, 1, TEMP);
1  00F0  00037               WHILE (I <= LENGTH (SUBJECT)) AND (INDEX (PATTERN, TEMP)
1  0126  00038                   <> 0) DO
1  0144  00039               BEGIN
1  0144  00040                   I := I + 1;
1  0150  00041                   SUB (SUBJECT, I, 1, TEMP)
1  0170  00042               END;
1  0188  00043
1  0188  00044               (* UNSUCCESSFUL PATTERN MATCH? *)
1  0188  00045               IF I = CURSOR
1  0188  00046               THEN SPAN := FALSE
1  0194  00047               ELSE BEGIN
1  01A0  00048
1  01A0  00049                   (* SET UP MATCH_STR AND PERFORM INDICATED REPLACE-
1  01A0  00050                      MENT *)
1  01A0  00051                   SUB (SUBJECT, CURSOR, I - CURSOR, MATCH_STR);
1  01E0  00052                   IF REPLACE_FLAG
1  01E0  00053                   THEN BEGIN
1  01EA  00054                       PSDSUB (SUBJECT, CURSOR, I - CURSOR,
1  020E  00055                           REPLACE_STR);
1  022A  00056                       CURSOR := CURSOR + LENGTH (REPLACE_STR)
1  0232  00057                       END
1  0250  00058                   ELSE CURSOR := I;
1  025C  00059
1  025C  00060                   (* SUCCESSFUL RETURN *)
1  025C  00061                   SPAN := TRUE
1  025C  00062                   END
1  0264  00063               END
1  0264  00064       END;
```

Fig. 9-2 PASCAL program for the function SPAN

9-2 THE CASE STATEMENT

In Sec. 3-2 a method of selecting alternative actions by using the IF ... THEN ... ELSE statement was introduced. PASCAL has another statement, the CASE statement, which can be used for selecting among different actions. The

```
0   0000   00001      FUNCTION BREAK (VAR SUBJECT, PATTERN: STRING(256); VAR CURSOR:
1   0000   00002          INTEGER; VAR MATCH_STR: STRING(256); REPLACE_FLAG: BOOLEAN;
1   0000   00003          VAR REPLACE_STR: STRING(256)): BOOLEAN;
1   0000   00004
1   0000   00005      (* THIS FUNCTION RETURNS A VALUE OF FALSE IF IT ENCOUNTERS A
1   0000   00006          CHARACTER WHICH IS ALSO IN PATTERN FROM THE CHARACTER POSITION
1   0000   00007          ONWARDS; OTHERWISE, IT RETURNS A VALUE OF FALSE. WHEN A SUCCESS-
1   0000   00008          FUL PATTERN MATCH OCCURS, MATCH_STR IS SET TO THE SUBSTRING OF
1   0000   00009          THE SUBJECT STRING FROM THE INITIAL CURSOR POSITION UP TO, BUT
1   0000   00010          NOT INCLUDING THE CHARACTER ALSO FOUND TO BE IN PATTERN.  IF
1   0000   00011          REPLACE_FLAG IS TRUE, THE MATCHED SUBSTRING IN SUBJECT IS
1   0000   00012          REPLACED BY THE VALUE OF REPLACE_STR. FINALLY, CURSOR IS
1   0000   00013          UPDATED. *)
1   0000   00014
1   0000   00015      VAR I: INTEGER;                (* INDEX VARIABLE *)
1   0082   00016          TEMP, SAVE:         (* TEMPORARY STRING VARIABLES *)
1   0082   00017              STRING(256);
1   0082   00018      FUNCTION LENGTH (VAR STR: STRING(256)): INTEGER; EXTERNAL;
1   0082   00019      FUNCTION INDEX (VAR S, PATTERN: STRING(256)): INTEGER; EXTERNAL;
1   0082   00020      PROCEDURE SUB (VAR S: STRING(256); POS, NUM: INTEGER; VAR RESULT:
2   0000   00021          STRING(256)); EXTERNAL;
1   0082   00022      PROCEDURE PSDSUB (VAR S: STRING(256); POS, NUM: INTEGER; VAR ADD:
2   0000   00023          STRING(256)); EXTERNAL;
1   0082   00024      PROCEDURE CONCAT (VAR S1, S2, RESULT: STRING(256)); EXTERNAL;
1   0082   00025
1   0082   00026      BEGIN
1   0082   00027
1   0082   00028          (* DOES THE PATTERN FIT WITHIN THE SEARCH BOUNDS OF THE
1   0082   00029             SUBJECT STRING? *)
1   0082   00030          IF CURSOR > LENGTH (SUBJECT)
1   008A   00031          THEN BREAK := FALSE
1   00A8   00032          ELSE BEGIN
1   00B4   00033
1   00B4   00034              (* INITIALIZE PATTERN MATCH *)
1   00B4   00035              I := CURSOR;
1   00BC   00036
1   00BC   00037              (* IS CHARACTER I IN THE PATTERN STRING? *)
1   00BC   00038              SUB (SUBJECT, I, 1, TEMP);
1   00F0   00039              WHILE (I <= LENGTH (SUBJECT)) AND (INDEX (PATTERN, TEMP)
1   0126   00040                  = 0) DO
1   0144   00041              BEGIN
1   0144   00042                  I := I + 1;
1   0150   00043                  SUB (SUBJECT, I, 1, TEMP)
1   0170   00044              END;
1   0188   00045
1   0188   00046              (* SUCCESSFUL PATTERN MATCH *)
1   0188   00047              IF I = LENGTH (SUBJECT) + 1
1   01A6   00048              THEN BREAK := FALSE
1   01B2   00049              ELSE BEGIN
1   01BE   00050
1   01BE   00051                  (* SET MATCH_STR AND PERFORM INDICATED REPLACE-
1   01BE   00052                     MENT *)
1   01BE   00053                  SUB (SUBJECT, CURSOR, I - CURSOR, MATCH_STR);
1   01FE   00054                  IF REPLACE_FLAG
1   01FE   00055                  THEN BEGIN
1   0208   00056                      IF I <> CURSOR
1   0208   00057                      THEN PSDSUB (SUBJECT, CURSOR, I - CURSOR,
1   0238   00058                              REPLACE_STR)
1   0240   00059                      ELSE BEGIN
1   0258   00060
1   0258   00061                          (* REPLACEMENT OF EMPTY STRING *)
1   0258   00062                          SUB (SUBJECT, 1, CURSOR - 1, TEMP);
1   0298·  00063                          CONCAT (TEMP, REPLACE_STR, TEMP);
1   02C4   00064                          SUB (SUBJECT, CURSOR, 256, SAVE);
1   02F8   00065                          CONCAT (TEMP, SAVE, SUBJECT)
1   0310   00066                          END;
1   0324   00067                      CURSOR := CURSOR + LENGTH (REPLACE_STR)
1   032C   00068                      END
1   034A   00069                  ELSE CURSOR := I;
1   0356   00070
1   0356   00071                  (* SUCCESSFUL RETURN *)
1   0356   00072                  BREAK := TRUE
1   0356   00073                  END
1   035E   00074          END
1   035E   00075      END;
```

Fig. 9-3 PASCAL program for the function BREAK

CASE statement allows an arbitrary number of different actions to be defined and it has the form:

```
CASE expression OF
        label₁: statement;
        label₂: statement;
            .
            .
            .
        labelₙ: statement
END
```

Expression is any PASCAL expression which can evaluate to one of the scalar types: integer, logical, character, or a user-defined scalar type (user-defined scalars were introduced in Sec. 4-1). Each CASE label consists of a list of possible values to which the expression may evaluate. Examples of CASE statement labels are:

```
0:
1, 2, 7, 6:
'A', 'B', 'Z':
TRUE, FALSE:
MONDAY, TUESDAY, WEDNESDAY, THURSDAY, FRIDAY:
```

The final example is a list of user-defined scalar values representing the days of the week. Identifiers in the CONST section of the declarations may also be used as labels, but type identifiers, variables, or function or procedure identifiers cannot be used. Furthermore, all labels must be of the same type as the CASE expression and their ordering is arbitrary.

The labels must be mutually exclusive. Since no scalar value may be used more than once, the CASE statement

```
CASE A + B OF
        0, 1, 2, 3: statement;
        1, 5, 9: statement
END
```

is invalid as "1" appears more than once.

The statement following a label may be any valid PASCAL statement including a null statement. A null statement is defined to have no action and is merely inserted whenever a PASCAL statement should appear but none is given. For example, two consecutive semicolons (;;) have a null statement between them. A CASE statement may have any number of label-statement pairs.

The behavior of the CASE statement is as follows. The *expression* (which also may be a variable name) is first evaluated to yield a value. Then a scan of the CASE statement labels is made until a value within the list is found that equals the value of the expression. The statement associated with this label is then executed. An error results for some PASCAL compilers if no such label is found. After executing the statement, control passes to the end of the CASE statement.

For example, consider the following PASCAL program segment:

```
ACTION := OLD_ACTION - NEW_ACTION;
CASE ACTION OF
        2: A := A + 2;
        3: B := B + 3;
        4: BEGIN
                CALL CHECK (A, B);
                WRITELN (' INVALID ACTION')
            END
END;
WRITELN (' ', A, B)
```

Assume that ACTION is assigned the value 3. The label 3, found in the second label-statement pair, has the same value as ACTION. This results in the statement of the second label-statement pair to be executed; that is, B is incremented by 3. After incrementing B, control passes to the end of the CASE statement, where the values of A and B are printed. As another example of the CASE statement, consider the following program segment:

```
CASE DAY OF
        MON, TUES, WED, THURS, FRI:
                REGULAR_HRS := REGULAR_HRS + HOURS;
        SAT, SUN: OVERTIME := OVERTIME + HOURS
END
```

This CASE statement adds the number of hours an employee has worked either to his regular pay or overtime pay, depending upon whether he worked a weekday or the weekend. The variable DAY must be of the same type as the week-name identifiers.

As a final example, it is interesting to note that the statement

```
IF condition
THEN statement₁
ELSE statement₂
```

can also be written using a CASE statement as follows:

```
CASE condition OF
        TRUE: statement₁;
        FALSE: statement₂
END
```

If the ELSE part of the IF statement had been omitted, a null statement could be substituted for $statement_2$ after the FALSE label of the CASE statement. In other words,

```
CASE condition OF
        TRUE: statement₁;
        FALSE:
END
```

would have been given. This implies that no action is performed if *condition* evaluates to FALSE.

This section has introduced the CASE statement. This statement is a useful control structure and will be used in some string-manipulation application programs which are given in the next section.

Exercises for Sec. 9-2

1. Write a PASCAL program which reads an arbitrary number of days of the week and prints an abbreviation for these days. If the first letter of the name is not unique (i.e., Saturday and Sunday, Tuesday and Thursday), the first two letters of the name are printed; otherwise, only the first letter is printed. Use a CASE statement to print the required abbreviations.

2. Design a PASCAL program which reads a series of strings which can either be PASCAL identifiers (including keywords), integer constants, operators (i.e., +, *, etc.), or other special symbols (i.e., ;, ,, :, etc.). For each string, print its type, such as identifier, integer, operator, or special symbol.

3. Give a PASCAL function which reads the name of a month and returns the number of days in the month.

9-3 APPLICATIONS

This section presents PASCAL solutions to the application problems found in Sec. 9-2 of the main text.

9-3.1 Lexical Analysis

The program given in Fig. 9-4 is a solution to the lexical analysis problem discussed in Sec. 9-2.1 of the main text. The problem consists of designing a scanner that is able to isolate words or tokens of an assignment statement and separate them into classes to be used by a syntactic analyzer. For this example, we assume that the allowable tokens in the assignment statement are identifiers; integers; the addition, subtraction, multiplication, division, exponentiation, and assignment operators; and left and right parentheses. The exponentiation operator in this example is assumed to be the exclamation punctuation mark (i.e., !). In addition to these tokens, the scanner must also be able to handle blanks within the assignment statement. Table 9-1 lists the name of the classes, the tokens in the classes, and the number assigned to each class.

The following variables appear in this program:

Variable	Type	Usage
SOURCE	STRING (256)	Statement to be scanned
CHAR	STRING (256)	Current character being examined
TOKEN	STRING (256)	Current token being isolated

Table 9-1 Tokens of an assignment statement

Name	Tokens	Number
Identifier	Valid identifier	1
Integer	String of digits	2
Addition and subtraction operators	+ and –	3
Multiplication and division operators	* and /	4
Exponentiation operator	!	5
Assignment operator	=	6
Left parenthesis	(	7
Right parenthesis	)	8

LETTERS	STRING (256)	Letters of the alphabet
DIGITS	STRING (256)	String containing digits 0 through 9
REP_NO	INTEGER	Representation number of a token
CURSOR	INTEGER	Position of character in SOURCE currently being examined
F	INTEGER	Temporary variable
DUMMY	BOOLEAN	Temporary variable
ALPHA	STRING (256)	All characters and digits
BLANK	STRING (256)	Blank character
BLANKS	STRING (256)	String of blank characters
NULL	STRING (256)	Null string ('*/')
SPECIAL	STRING (256)	String containing characters +, *, !, =, (, and)
MIN_DIV	STRING (256)	String containing characters – and /
TEMP	STRING (256)	Temporary string variable

The program uses the following input data:

'A1 = A + 5*/'

In the first part of the program, the variables representing the letters and digits are initialized. The variable CURSOR is also initialized to one. The statement to be analyzed is then read and assigned to the variable SOURCE. After the statement to be analyzed is printed, a loop is begun which separates the tokens of the statement and prints a copy of the tokens preceded by their classifications. The function SPAN is used to move the CURSOR to the next nonblank character of SOURCE. A number of nested IF statements are then used to determine the classification of the token consisting of (or begun by, in the case of an identifier or digit) the character(s) found and to print the appropriate message. When the end of the statement has been reached, the program terminates.

```
0   0000   00001   PROGRAM SCAN (INPUT, OUTPUT);
0   0000   00002   (* GIVEN A SOURCE STATEMENT (SOURCE), THIS PROGRAM SEPARATES THIS
0   0000   00003      STATEMENT'S TOKENS WITH THEIR CORRESPONDING REPRESENTATION
0   0000   00004      NUMBERS. *)
0   0000   00005
0   0000   00006   VAR SOURCE,                    (* SOURCE STATEMENT *)
0   0038   00007       CHAR,                      (* CURRENT CHARACTER BEING EXAMINED *)
0   0038   00008       TOKEN,                     (* CURRENT TOKEN BEING EXAMINED *)
0   0038   00009       TEMP,                      (* TEMPORARY VARIABLE *)
0   0038   00010       LETTERS,                   (* LETTERS OF ALPHABET *)
0   0038   00011       DIGITS,                    (* DIGITS 0 THROUGH 9 *)
0   0038   00012       ALPHA,                     (* ALPHANUMERIC CHARACTERS *)
0   0038   00013       BLANK, BLANKS,             (* BLANK CHARACTERS *)
0   0038   00014       NULL,                      (* EMPTY STRING *)
0   0038   00015       SPECIAL,                   (* CHARACTERS +, *, !, =, (, ) *)
0   0038   00016       MIN_DIV: STRING(256);      (* SUBTRACTION AND DIVISION CHARACTERS *)
0   0038   00017       REP_NO,                    (* REPRESENTATION NUMBER OF TOKEN *)
0   0038   00018       CURSOR,                    (* POSITION OF CHARACTER BEING EXAMINED *)
0   0038   00019       F: INTEGER;                (* TEMPORARY VARIABLE *)
0   0038   00020       DUMMY: BOOLEAN;            (* DUMMY VARIABLE *)
0   0038   00021   FUNCTION INDEX (VAR S, PATTERN: STRING(256)): INTEGER; EXTERNAL;
0   0038   00022   FUNCTION LENGTH (VAR STR: STRING(256)): INTEGER; EXTERNAL;
0   0038   00023   PROCEDURE SUB (VAR S: STRING(256); POS, NUM: INTEGER; VAR RESULT:
1   0000   00024       STRING(256)); EXTERNAL;
0   0038   00025   PROCEDURE CONCAT (VAR S1, S2, RESULT: STRING(256)); EXTERNAL;
0   0038   00026
0   0038   00027       FUNCTION SPAN (VAR SUBJECT, PATTERN: STRING(256); VAR CURSOR:
1   0000   00028           INTEGER; VAR MATCH_STR: STRING(256); REPLACE_FLAG: BOOLEAN;
1   0000   00029           VAR REPLACE_STR: STRING(256)): BOOLEAN;
1   0000   00030
1   0000   00031       (* THIS FUNCTION RETURNS TRUE IF THE CHARACTER DENOTED BY CURSOR
1   0000   00032          MATCHES ANY OF THE CHARACTERS IN PATTERN.  IF THE PATTERN MATCH
1   0000   00033          SUCCEEDS, MATCH_STR BECOMES A SEQUENCE OF CHARACTERS CONTAINING
1   0000   00034          THE CHARACTER AT THE POSITION SPECIFIED BY CURSOR AND ALL OTHER
1   0000   00035          CHARACTERS WHICH ARE CONTAINED IN PATTERN.  THE PATTERN MATCH
1   0000   00036          PROCESS TERMINATES ON ENCOUNTERING A CHARACTER NOT IN PATTERN OR
1   0000   00037          THE END OF THE SUBJECT STRING.  IF A REPLACEMENT OPERATION IS
1   0000   00038          SPECIFIED, THE SEQUENCE OF CHARACTERS IS REPLACED BY THE VALUE
1   0000   00039          OF REPLACE_STR. *)
1   0000   00040
1   0000   00041       VAR I: INTEGER;            (* INDEX VARIABLE *)
1   0082   00042           TEMP: STRING(256);     (* TEMPORARY STRING VARIABLE *)
1   0082   00043       FUNCTION LENGTH (VAR STR: STRING(256)): INTEGER; EXTERNAL;
1   0082   00044       FUNCTION INDEX (VAR S, PATTERN: STRING(256)): INTEGER; EXTERNAL;
1   0082   00045       PROCEDURE SUB (VAR S: STRING(256); POS, NUM: INTEGER;
2   0000   00046           VAR RESULT: STRING(256)); EXTERNAL;
1   0082   00047       PROCEDURE PSDSUB (VAR S: STRING(256); POS, NUM: INTEGER; VAR ADD:
2   0000   00048           STRING(256)); EXTERNAL;
1   0082   00049
1   0082   00050       BEGIN
1   0082   00051
1   0082   00052           (* DOES THE PATTERN FIT WITHIN THE BOUNDS OF THE SUBJECT
1   0082   00053              STRING? *)
1   0082   00054           IF CURSOR > LENGTH (SUBJECT)
1   008A   00055           THEN SPAN := FALSE
1   00A8   00056           ELSE BEGIN
1   00B4   00057
1   00B4   00058               (* INITIALIZE PATTERN MATCH *)
1   00B4   00059               I := CURSOR;
1   00BC   00060
1   00BC   00061               (* IS CHARACTER I IN THE PATTERN STRING? *)
1   00BC   00062               SUB (SUBJECT, I, 1, TEMP);
1   00F0   00063               WHILE (I <= LENGTH (SUBJECT)) AND (INDEX (PATTERN, TEMP)
1   0126   00064                   <> 0) DO
1   0144   00065               BEGIN
1   0144   00066                   I := I + 1;
1   0150   00067                   SUB (SUBJECT, I, 1, TEMP)
1   0170   00068               END;
1   0188   00069
1   0188   00070               (* UNSUCCESSFUL PATTERN MATCH? *)
1   0188   00071               IF I = CURSOR
1   0188   00072               THEN SPAN := FALSE
1   0194   00073               ELSE BEGIN
1   01A0   00074
1   01A0   00075                   (* SET UP MATCH_STR AND PERFORM INDICATED REPLACE-
1   01A0   00076                      MENT *)
1   01A0   00077                   SUB (SUBJECT, CURSOR, I - CURSOR, MATCH_STR);
1   01E0   00078                   IF REPLACE_FLAG
1   01E0   00079                   THEN BEGIN
1   01EA   00080                       PSDSUB (SUBJECT, CURSOR, I - CURSOR,
```

Fig. 9-4 Program to perform a lexical scan of an assignment statement

```
1  020E   00081                                              REPLACE_STR);
1  022A   00082                            CURSOR := CURSOR + LENGTH (REPLACE_STR)
1  0232   00083                            END
1  0250   00084                   ELSE CURSOR := I;
1  025C   00085
1  025C   00086                      (* SUCCESSFUL RETURN *)
1  025C   00087                      SPAN := TRUE
1  025C   00088                      END
1  0264   00089               END
1  0264   00090        END;
0  0038   00091
0  0038   00092   BEGIN
0  0038   00093
0  0038   00094        (* INITIALIZE *)
0  0038   00095        LETTERS := 'ABCDEFGHIJKLMNOPQRSTUVWXYZ*/';
0  003E   00096        DIGITS := '0123456789*/';
0  0044   00097        ALPHA := 'ABCDEFGHIJKLMNOPQRSTUVWXYZ0123456789*/';
0  004A   00098        SPECIAL := '+*!=()*/';
0  0050   00099        MIN_DIV := '-/*/';
0  0056   00100        BLANK := ' */';
0  005C   00101        BLANKS := '                         */';
0  0062   00102        NULL := '*/';
0  0068   00103        CURSOR := 1;
0  0070   00104
0  0070   00105        (* INPUT AND PRINT SOURCE STATEMENT *)
0  0070   00106        READ (SOURCE);
0  0082   00107        CONCAT (SOURCE, BLANKS, TEMP);
0  00B0   00108        WRITELN (' ', TEMP: 20);
0  00D4   00109
0  00D4   00110        (* SCAN SOURCE STATEMENT *)
0  00D4   00111        WHILE CURSOR <= LENGTH (SOURCE) DO
0  00FC   00112        BEGIN
0  00FC   00113
0  00FC   00114             (* OBTAIN NEXT TOKEN AFTER CHECKING FOR NON-BLANK CHARACTER *)
0  00FC   00115             IF NOT SPAN (SOURCE, BLANK, CURSOR, TEMP, FALSE, NULL)
0  012C   00116             THEN BEGIN
0  014A   00117
0  014A   00118                  (* ISOLATE NEXT CHARACTER *)
0  014A   00119                  SUB (SOURCE, CURSOR, 1, CHAR);
0  0180   00120
0  0180   00121                  (* CHECK FOR IDENTIFIER *)
0  0180   00122                  IF INDEX (LETTERS, CHAR) <> 0
0  01A8   00123                  THEN BEGIN
0  01B0   00124                       DUMMY := SPAN (SOURCE, ALPHA, CURSOR, TOKEN, FALSE,
0  01D8   00125                            NULL);
0  01FC   00126                       CONCAT (TOKEN, BLANKS, TEMP);
0  022A   00127                       WRITELN (' ', 1: 2, ' ': 5, TEMP: 20)
0  0272   00128                       END
0  0272   00129
0  0272   00130                  (* CHECK FOR IDENTIFIER *)
0  0272   00131                  ELSE IF INDEX (DIGITS, CHAR) <> 0
0  029E   00132                       THEN BEGIN
0  02A6   00133                            DUMMY := SPAN (SOURCE, DIGITS, CURSOR, TOKEN,
0  02C6   00134                                 FALSE, NULL);
0  02F2   00135                            CONCAT (TOKEN, BLANKS, TEMP);
0  0320   00136                            WRITELN (' ', 2: 2, ' ': 5, TEMP: 20)
0  0368   00137                            END
0  0368   00138                       ELSE BEGIN
0  036C   00139
0  036C   00140                            (* CHECK FOR +, *, !, =, (, OR ) *)
0  036C   00141                            IF INDEX (SPECIAL, CHAR) <> 0
0  0394   00142                            THEN BEGIN
0  039C   00143                                 REP_NO := INDEX (SPECIAL, CHAR) + 2;
0  03CC   00144                                 CONCAT (CHAR, BLANKS, TEMP);
0  03FA   00145                                 WRITELN (' ', REP_NO: 2, ' ': 5, TEMP: 20)
0  0442   00146                                 END
0  0442   00147                            ELSE BEGIN
0  0446   00148
0  0446   00149                                 (* CHECK FOR - OR / *)
0  0446   00150                                 IF INDEX (MIN_DIV, CHAR) <> 0
0  046E   00151                                 THEN BEGIN
0  0476   00152                                      REP_NO := INDEX (MIN_DIV, CHAR) + 2;
0  04A6   00153                                      CONCAT (CHAR, BLANKS, TEMP);
0  04D4   00154                                      WRITELN (' ', REP_NO: 2, ' ': 5,
0  050A   00155                                           TEMP: 20)
0  051C   00156                                      END
0  051C   00157                                 END;
0  051C   00158                            CURSOR := CURSOR + 1
0  051C   00159                            END
```

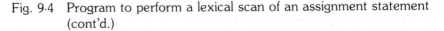

Fig. 9-4   Program to perform a lexical scan of an assignment statement
            (cont'd.)

```
  0  0528   00160                        END
 '0  0528   00161          END
  0  0528   00162  END.
-------------------------------------
| COMPILE TIME:    0.410 SECOND(S) |
|     NO WARNING(S) DETECTED       |
|     NO ERROR(S) DETECTED         |
-------------------------------------
--EXECUTION-->
A1 = A + 5
  1      A1
  6      =
  1      A
  3      +
  2      5
```

Fig. 9-4   Program to perform a lexical scan of an assignment statement
          (cont'd.)

9-3.2   Keyword-In-Context (KWIC) Indexing

KWIC indexing is a popular method of indexing which produces a listing of
all the lines in a document that contain any of a particular list of keywords. In the
program presented in Fig. 9-5 of this section, KWIC indexing is applied to a list of
titles. The program consists of two procedures. The first procedure, called
KWIC_C, creates the KWIC index by scanning each title for keywords which specify
the meaning of the document. (The words "a", "an", "and", "its", "the", "to" and
"with" are considered to be ordinary words and are ignored in the creation of KWIC
index.) For each keyword found in the title of a document, an entry is made in the
vector T_INDEX which indicates the title's position in the vector TITLE.

The second procedure uses the T_INDEX entries of each of the keywords in
order to produce a listing of the KWIC index. In listing the KWIC index, each line is
permuted so that the keyword appears first. The following variables are used in the
main program:

Variable	Type	Usage
LAST_KEY	INTEGER	Index of last keyword
ORD_WORD	ARRAY (1..7) OF STRING (256)	Vector of ordinary words
TITLE	ARRAY (1..50) OF STRING (256)	Document titles
KEYWORD	ARRAY (1..100) OF STRING (256)	Document keywords
T_INDEX	ARRAY (1..100) OF STRING (256)	Title indices for a particular keyword

The variables used in the procedure KWIC_C are:

LAST_TITLE	INTEGER	Index of last title
KEY_IND	INTEGER	Index of keyword
NUM, TEMP	INTEGER	Temporary variables
DUMMY	BOOLEAN	Temporary variable
WORD	STRING(256)	Current word being processed
LBLANK, TCHAR	STRING(256)	Temporary strings

CHARNO	STRING(256)	Character string of title index number
PHRASE	STRING(256)	Input title
BLANK	STRING(256)	String of one blank
BLANKS	STRING(256)	String of many blanks used for printing
SLASHS	STRING(256)	String of two slashes, i.e.,//
DIGITS	STRING(256)	String of digits 0 to 9

The variables used in the procedure KWIC_G are:

KEYSTRING	STRING (256)	String of title indices
KWIC_LINE	STRING (256)	Line of output
DUMMY	STRING (256)	Dummy variable
TCHAR	STRING (256)	Temporary string variable
NULL	STRING (256)	Empty string
BLANK	STRING (256)	Blank character
BLANKS, DIGITS	STRING (256)	String of blanks and digits
INDEX_NO	INTEGER	Particular title index
I, J	INTEGER	Counted loop variables
POS, TEMP	INTEGER	Temporary variables

The variables used in the function KEY_SEARCH are:

WORD	STRING (256)	Word to be searched for
NULL	STRING (256)	Empty string
I, J	INTEGER	Index variables

The variables used in the function ORD_SEARCH are:

| WORD | STRING(256) | Word to be searched for |
| I | INTEGER | Index variable |

The sample input data used in the program consist of the following titles:

'AN INTRODUCTION TO COMPUTER SCIENCE AN ALGORITHMIC APPROACH */'
'STRUCTURED PL/I PROGRAMMING */'
'STRUCTURED WATFIV-S PROGRAMMING */'
'PL/I PROGRAMMING WITH APPLICATIONS */'
'AN INTRODUCTION TO PASCAL PROGRAMMING */'

The main program initializes the ORD_WORDS vector to seven ordinary words and then calls the two procedure KWIC_C and KWIC_G to create and generate the KWIC index. In the first part of the procedure KWIC_C, the counters LAST_TITLE and LAST_KEY are initialized to zero. A loop is then begun to read in all the titles. Once a title is read, any initial blanks are removed using the SPAN function, and the end marker // is appended to the end of the title. The title is then added to the TITLE vector. Lines 195 through 228 define a loop which is used to process all the words in the current title. First a check is made to see if the word is

```
0  0000   00001   PROGRAM KWIC (INPUT, OUTPUT);
0  0000   00002
0  0000   00003   (* THIS PROGRAM CALLS KWIC_C CREATES THE VECTORS NECESSARY FOR THE KWIC
0  0000   00004      INDEXING SYSTEM.  THEN IT CALLS KWIC_G TO ACTUALLY GENERATE A KWIC
0  0000   00005      INDEX ORDERED LEXICALLY BY KEYWORDS. *)
0  0000   00006
0  0000   00007   VAR LAST_KEY: INTEGER;              (* INDEX OF LAST KEYWORD *)
0  0038   00008       ORD_WORD: ARRAY(1..7) OF STRING(256);
0  0038   00009                                      (* ORDINARY WORDS *)
0  0038   00010     TITLE: ARRAY(1..50) OF STRING(256);
0  0038   00011                                      (* DOCUMENT TITLES *)
0  0038   00012     KEYWORD,                         (* DOCUMENT KEYWORDS *)
0  0038   00013     T_INDEX: ARRAY(1..100) OF STRING(256);
0  0038   00014                                      (* INDICES OF TITLES *)
0  0038   00015
0  0038   00016   FUNCTION INDEX (VAR S, PATTERN: STRING(256)): INTEGER; EXTERNAL;
0  0038   00017   FUNCTION LENGTH (VAR STR: STRING(256)): INTEGER; EXTERNAL;
0  0038   00018   PROCEDURE SUB (VAR S: STRING(256); POS, NUM: INTEGER; VAR RESULT:
1  0000   00019       STRING(256)); EXTERNAL;
0  0038   00020   PROCEDURE CONCAT (VAR S1, S2, RESULT: STRING(256)); EXTERNAL;
0  0038   00021   PROCEDURE PSDSUB (VAR S: STRING(256); POS, NUM: INTEGER; VAR ADD:
1  0000   00022       STRING(256)); EXTERNAL;
0  0038   00023
0  0038   00024       FUNCTION SPAN (VAR SUBJECT, PATTERN: STRING(256); VAR CURSOR:
1  0000   00025           INTEGER; VAR MATCH_STR: STRING(256); REPLACE_FLAG: BOOLEAN;
1  0000   00026           VAR REPLACE_STR: STRING(256)): BOOLEAN;
1  0000   00027
1  0000   00028       (* THIS FUNCTION RETURNS TRUE IF THE CHARACTER DENOTED BY CURSOR
1  0000   00029          MATCHES ANY OF THE CHARACTERS IN PATTERN.  IF THE PATTERN MATCH
1  0000   00030          SUCCEEDS, MATCH_STR BECOMES A SEQUENCE OF CHARACTERS CONTAINING
1  0000   00031          THE CHARACTER AT THE POSITION SPECIFIED BY CURSOR AND ALL OTHER
1  0000   00032          CHARACTERS WHICH ARE CONTAINED IN PATTERN.  THE PATTERN MATCH
1  0000   00033          PROCESS TERMINATES ON ENCOUNTERING A CHARACTER NOT IN PATTERN OR
1  0000   00034          THE END OF THE SUBJECT STRING.  IF A REPLACEMENT OPERATION IS
1  0000   00035          SPECIFIED, THE SEQUENCE OF CHARACTERS IS REPLACED BY THE VALUE
1  0000   00036          OF REPLACE_STR. *)
1  0000   00037
1  0000   00038       VAR I: INTEGER;                (* INDEX VARIABLE *)
1  0082   00039           TEMP: STRING(256);         (* TEMPORARY STRING VARIABLE *)
1  0082   00040       FUNCTION LENGTH (VAR STR: STRING(256)): INTEGER; EXTERNAL;
1  0082   00041       FUNCTION INDEX (VAR S, PATTERN: STRING(256)): INTEGER; EXTERNAL;
1  0082   00042       PROCEDURE SUB (VAR S: STRING(256); POS, NUM: INTEGER;
2  0000   00043           VAR RESULT: STRING(256)); EXTERNAL;
1  0082   00044       PROCEDURE PSDSUB (VAR S: STRING(256); POS, NUM: INTEGER; VAR ADD:
2  0000   00045           STRING(256)); EXTERNAL;
1  0082   00046
1  0082   00047       BEGIN
1  0082   00048
1  0082   00049           (* DOES THE PATTERN FIT WITHIN THE BOUNDS OF THE SUBJECT
1  0082   00050              STRING? *)
1  0082   00051           IF CURSOR > LENGTH (SUBJECT)
1  008A   00052           THEN SPAN := FALSE
1  00A8   00053           ELSE BEGIN
1  00B4   00054
1  00B4   00055               (* INITIALIZE PATTERN MATCH *)
1  00B4   00056               I := CURSOR;
1  00BC   00057
1  00BC   00058               (* IS CHARACTER I IN THE PATTERN STRING? *)
1  00BC   00059               SUB (SUBJECT, I, 1, TEMP);
1  00F0   00060               WHILE (I <= LENGTH (SUBJECT)) AND (INDEX (PATTERN, TEMP)
1  0126   00061                   <> 0) DO
1  0144   00062               BEGIN
1  0144   00063                   I := I + 1;
1  0150   00064                   SUB (SUBJECT, I, 1, TEMP)
1  0170   00065               END;
1  0188   00066
1  0188   00067               (* UNSUCCESSFUL PATTERN MATCH? *)
1  0188   00068               IF I = CURSOR
1  0188   00069               THEN SPAN := FALSE
1  0194   00070               ELSE BEGIN
1  01A0   00071
1  01A0   00072                   (* SET UP MATCH_STR AND PERFORM INDICATED REPLACE-
1  01A0   00073                      MENT *)
1  01A0   00074                   SUB (SUBJECT, CURSOR, I - CURSOR, MATCH_STR);
1  01E0   00075                   IF REPLACE_FLAG
1  01E0   00076                   THEN BEGIN
1  01EA   00077                       PSDSUB (SUBJECT, CURSOR, I - CURSOR,
1  020E   00078                           REPLACE_STR);
1  022A   00079                       CURSOR := CURSOR + LENGTH (REPLACE_STR)
1  0232   00080                   END
```

Fig. 9-5   Program to generate a KWIC indexing system

```
1   0250   00081                              ELSE CURSOR := I;
1   025C   00082
1   025C   00083                                 (* SUCCESSFUL RETURN *)
1   025C   00084                                 SPAN := TRUE
1   025C   00085                              END
1   0264   00086                           END
1   0264   00087   END;
0   0038   00088
0   0038   00089   FUNCTION ORD_SEARCH (VAR WORD: STRING (256)): INTEGER;
1   0000   00090   (* THIS FUNCTION SEARCHES THE VECTOR ORD_WORD TO DETERMINE WHETHER
1   0000   00091      OR NOT A WORD IN A PARTICULAR TITLE IS AN ORDINARY WORD. *)
1   0000   00092
1   0000   00093   VAR I: INTEGER;           (* INDEX VARIABLE *)
1   004C   00094
1   004C   00095   BEGIN
1   004C   00096
1   004C   00097       ORD_SEARCH := 0;
1   0052   00098       FOR I := 1 TO 7 DO
1   0076   00099          IF ORD_WORD(I) = WORD
1   0098   00100             THEN ORD_SEARCH := I  (* SUCCESSFUL MATCH *)
1   00A2   00101   END;
0   0038   00102
0   0038   00103   FUNCTION KEY_SEARCH (VAR WORD: STRING(256)): INTEGER;
1   0000   00104   (* FUNCTION TO SEARCH THE VECTOR KEY_WORD TO DETERMINE WHETHER OR
1   0000   00105      NOT A KEYWORD HAS BEEN ENCOUNTERED IN THE TITLES.  LAST_KEY IS A
1   0000   00106      COMMON VARIABLE THAT CONTAINS THE INDEX OF THE LAST KEY
1   0000   00107      IN KEY_WORD. *)
1   0000   00108
1   0000   00109   VAR NULL: STRING(256);  (* EMPTY STRING *)
1   004C   00110       I, J: INTEGER;       (* INDEX VARIABLES *)
1   004C   00111
1   004C   00112   BEGIN
1   004C   00113
1   004C   00114       (* SEARCH KEYWORD VECTOR FOR WORD *)
1   004C   00115       I := 1;
1   0054   00116       NULL := '*/';
1   005A   00117       WHILE (I < LAST_KEY) AND (KEYWORD(I) < WORD) DO
1   0092   00118          I := I + 1;
1   00A2   00119
1   00A2   00120       (* FOUND KEYWORD *)
1   00A2   00121       IF KEYWORD(I) = WORD
1   00C4   00122       THEN KEY_SEARCH := I
1   00CE   00123       ELSE BEGIN
1   00DA   00124          IF KEYWORD(I) > WORD
1   00FC   00125          THEN BEGIN
1   0106   00126
1   0106   00127             (* WORD IS NOT IN KEYWORD VECTOR.  MOVE REMAINING
1   0106   00128                KEYWORDS ONE POSITION UP IN THE KEYWORD VECTOR.*)
1   0106   00129             J := LAST_KEY;
1   010E   00130             WHILE (J >= I) DO
1   011A   00131             BEGIN
1   011A   00132                KEYWORD(J + 1) := KEYWORD(J);
1   016A   00133                T_INDEX(J + 1) := T_INDEX(J);
1   01BA   00134                J := J - 1
1   01BA   00135             END
1   01C6   00136          END
1   01CA   00137          ELSE BEGIN
1   01CE   00138
1   01CE   00139             (* PLACE NEW KEYWORD AT END OF KEYWORD VECTOR *)
1   01CE   00140             I := LAST_KEY + 1
1   01CE   00141             END;
1   01DA   00142          KEYWORD(I) := WORD;
1   0202   00143          T_INDEX(I) := NULL;
1   022A   00144          LAST_KEY := LAST_KEY + 1;
1   0236   00145          KEY_SEARCH := I;
1   023E   00146          END
1   023E   00147   END;
0   0038   00148
0   0038   00149   PROCEDURE KWIC_C;
1   0000   00150   (* GIVEN AN INPUT SEQUENCE OF PHRASES (THAT IS, TITLES) IN THE FORM
1   0000   00151      OF CHARACTER STRINGS AND THE ORDERED LIST OF ORDINARY WORDS,
1   0000   00152      ORD_WORDS, AS DESCRIBED IN THE MAIN TEXT, THIS PROCEDURE
1   0000   00153      CONSTRUCTS THE VECTORS TITLE, KEYWORDS, AND T_INDEX. *)
1   0000   00154
1   0000   00155   VAR LAST_TITLE,                 (* INDEX OF THE LAST TITLE TO BE ADDED
1   0000   00156                                      TO TITLE *)
1   003C   00157       KEY_IND,                   (* INDEX FOR VECTOR KEYWORD *)
1   003C   00158       ONE,                       (* NUMERIC VALUE 1 *)
1   003C   00159       NUM, TEMP: INTEGER;        (* TEMPORARY VARIABLES *)
```

Fig. 9-5 Program to generate a KWIC indexing system (cont'd.)

```
1  003C  00160          WORD,                        (* CURRENT WORD BEING PROCESSED *)
1  003C  00161          CHAR_NO,                     (* STRING CONTAINING TITLE INDEX
1  003C  00162                                          NUMBER *)
1  003C  00163          PHRASE,                      (* INPUT TITLE *)
1  003C  00164          TCHAR, LBLANK,               (* TEMPORARY VARIABLES *)
1  003C  00165          BLANK, BLANKS, SLASHS, DIGITS, NULL: STRING(256);
1  003C  00166                                       (* STRINGS OF CHARACTERS *)
1  003C  00167          DUMMY: BOOLEAN;              (* TEMPORARY VARIABLE *)
1  003C  00168
1  003C  00169      BEGIN
1  003C  00170
1  003C  00171          (* INITIALIZE *)
1  003C  00172          NULL := '*/';
1  0042  00173          BLANK := ' */';
1  0048  00174          BLANKS := '                                   */';
1  004E  00175          SLASHS := '//*/';
1  0054  00176          DIGITS := '0123456789*/';
1  005A  00177          ONE := 1;
1  0062  00178          LAST_TITLE := 0;
1  0068  00179          LAST_KEY := 0;
1  006E  00180
1  006E  00181          (* PROCESS ALL TITLES *)
1  006E  00182          READ (PHRASE);
1  0080  00183          WHILE NOT EOF DO
1  0088  00184          BEGIN
1  0088  00185
1  0088  00186              (* REMOVE ANY LEADING BLANKS AND APPEND END MARKERS // TO
1  0088  00187                 STORE CURRENT DOCUMENT TITLE *)
1  0088  00188              DUMMY := SPAN (PHRASE, BLANK, ONE, LBLANK, TRUE, NULL);
1  00D2  00189              CONCAT (PHRASE, SLASHS, PHRASE);
1  00FE  00190              LAST_TITLE := LAST_TITLE + 1;
1  010A  00191              TITLE (LAST_TITLE) := PHRASE;
1  0132  00192
1  0132  00193              (* PROCESS ALL WORDS IN CURRENT TITLE *)
1  0132  00194              SUB (PHRASE, 1, 2, TCHAR);
1  0166  00195              WHILE TCHAR <> SLASHS DO
1  0170  00196              BEGIN
1  0170  00197
1  0170  00198                  (* SCAN AND REMOVE NEXT WORD FROM CURRENT TITLE *)
1  0170  00199                  SUB (PHRASE, 1, INDEX (PHRASE, BLANK) - 1, WORD);
1  01D2  00200                  SUB (PHRASE, INDEX(PHRASE, BLANK) + 1, 256, PHRASE);
1  0234  00201
1  0234  00202                  (* IS WORD A KEYWORD? *)
1  0234  00203                  IF ORD_SEARCH (WORD) = 0
1  0252  00204                  THEN BEGIN
1  025A  00205                      KEY_IND := KEY_SEARCH (WORD);
1  027C  00206
1  027C  00207                      (* CONVERT INDEX NUMBER INTO CHARACTER STRING*)
1  027C  00208                      NUM := LAST_TITLE;
1  0284  00209                      CHAR_NO := NULL;
1  028A  00210                      WHILE NUM > 0 DO
1  0296  00211                      BEGIN
1  0296  00212                          SUB (DIGITS, NUM - (NUM DIV 10) * 10 + 1,
1  02C8  00213                              1, TCHAR);
1  02EC  00214                          CONCAT (TCHAR, CHAR_NO, CHAR_NO);
1  0318  00215                          NUM := NUM DIV 10
1  0318  00216                      END;
1  032C  00217                      CONCAT (T_INDEX(KEY_IND), BLANK,
1  035A  00218                          T_INDEX(KEY_IND));
1  0394  00219                      CONCAT (T_INDEX(KEY_IND), CHAR_NO,
1  03C2  00220                          T_INDEX(KEY_IND));
1  03FC  00221
1  03FC  00222                      (* REMOVE INITIAL BLANK FROM PHRASE *)
1  03FC  00223                      SUB (T_INDEX(KEY_IND), 1, 1, TCHAR);
1  044E  00224                      IF TCHAR = BLANK
1  044E  00225                      THEN PSDSUB (T_INDEX(KEY_IND), 1, 1, NULL)
1  0496  00226                  END;
1  04AA  00227                  SUB (PHRASE, 1, 2, TCHAR)
1  04CA  00228              END;
1  04E2  00229              READ (PHRASE)
1  04F4  00230          END
1  04F4  00231      END;
0  0038  00232
0  0038  00233      PROCEDURE KWIC_G;
1  0000  00234      (* THIS PROCEDURE GENERATES A KWIC INDEX WHICH IS ORDERED LEXICALLY
1  0000  00235         BY KEYWORDS. *)
1  0000  00236
1  0000  00237      VAR KEYSTRING,               (* STRING OF TITLE INDICES *)
1  003C  00238          KWIC_LINE,               (* LINE OF OUTPUT *)
```

Fig. 9-5 Program to generate a KWIC indexing system (cont'd.)

```
1   003C   00239              DUMMY, TCHAR,              (* TEMPORARY VARIABLES *)
1   003C   00240              NULL, BLANK, BLANKS, DIGITS: STRING(256);
1   003C   00241                                        (* STRINGS OF CHARACTERS *)
1   003C   00242              INDEX_NO,                  (* PARTICULAR TITLE NUMBER INDEX *)
1   003C   00243              I, J,                      (* COUNTED LOOP VARIABLE *)
1   003C   00244              POS, TEMP: INTEGER;        (* TEMPORARY VARIABLES *)
1   003C   00245
1   003C   00246      BEGIN
1   003C   00247
1   003C   00248          (* INITIALIZE *)
1   003C   00249          NULL := '*/';
1   0042   00250          BLANK := ' */';
1   0048   00251          BLANKS := '                                        */';
1   004E   00252          DIGITS := '0123456789*/';
1   0054   00253
1   0054   00254          (* PROCESS EACH KEYWORD IN KEYWORD VECTOR *)
1   0054   00255          FOR I := 1 TO LAST_KEY DO
1   0078   00256          BEGIN
1   0078   00257
1   0078   00258              (* OBTAIN INDEX LIST FOR CURRENT KEYWORD *)
1   0078   00259              CONCAT (T_INDEX(I), BLANK, KEYSTRING);
1   00C2   00260
1   00C2   00261              (* PROCESS ALL TITLE INDICES IN KEYSTRING *)
1   00C2   00262              WHILE LENGTH (KEYSTRING) > 1 DO
1   00E8   00263              BEGIN
1   00E8   00264
1   00E8   00265                  (* OBTAIN AND DELETE NEXT TITLE INDEX *)
1   00E8   00266                  SUB (KEYSTRING, 1, INDEX (KEYSTRING, BLANK) - 1,
1   012E   00267                      DUMMY);
1   014A   00268                  SUB (KEYSTRING, INDEX (KEYSTRING, BLANK) + 1, 256,
1   0190   00269                      KEYSTRING);
1   01AC   00270
1   01AC   00271                  (* CONVERT CHARACTER STRING TO INTEGER *)
1   01AC   00272                  INDEX_NO := 0;
1   01B2   00273                  FOR J := 1 TO LENGTH (DUMMY) DO
1   01F0   00274                  BEGIN
1   01F0   00275                      SUB (DUMMY, J, 1, TCHAR);
1   0224   00276                      INDEX_NO := INDEX_NO * 10 + (INDEX (DIGITS,
1   0238   00277                          TCHAR) - 1)
1   025E   00278                  END;
1   026A   00279
1   026A   00280                  (* OBTAIN AND OUTPUT KWIC LINE *)
1   026A   00281                  KWIC_LINE := TITLE (INDEX_NO);
1   0292   00282                  POS := INDEX (KWIC_LINE, KEYWORD(I));
1   02DA   00283                  IF POS <> 0
1   02DA   00284                  THEN BEGIN
1   02E6   00285
1   02E6   00286                      (* RECREATE KWIC LINE WITH KEYWORD IN FIRST
1   02E6   00287                          POSITION *)
1   02E6   00288                      SUB (KWIC_LINE, POS + LENGTH (KEYWORD(I)), 256,
1   0342   00289                          TCHAR);
1   035E   00290                      CONCAT (KEYWORD(I), TCHAR, TCHAR);
1   03A8   00291                      CONCAT (TCHAR, BLANK, TCHAR);
1   03D4   00292                      SUB (KWIC_LINE, 1, POS - 1, KWIC_LINE);
1   0414   00293                      CONCAT (TCHAR, KWIC_LINE, KWIC_LINE);
1   0440   00294
1   0440   00295                      (* PRINT CURRENT KWIC LINE WITHOUT DELIMITER *)
1   0440   00296                      TCHAR := KWIC_LINE;
1   0446   00297                      CONCAT (TCHAR, BLANKS, TCHAR);
1   0472   00298                      WRITELN (' ', TCHAR: 70)
1   0496   00299                  END
1   0496   00300                  ELSE WRITELN (' ERROR - KEYWORD NOT FOUND IN TITLE')
1   04AC   00301              END
1   04AC   00302          END
1   04B0   00303      END;
0   0038   00304
0   0038   00305  BEGIN
0   0038   00306
0   0038   00307      (* INITIALIZE THE ORDINARY WORD VECTOR *)
0   0038   00308      ORD_WORD(1) := 'A*/';
0   0042   00309      ORD_WORD(2) := 'AN*/';
0   0050   00310      ORD_WORD(3) := 'AND*/';
0   005E   00311      ORD_WORD(4) := 'ITS*/';
0   006C   00312      ORD_WORD(5) := 'THE*/';
0   007A   00313      ORD_WORD(6) := 'TO*/';
0   0088   00314      ORD_WORD(7) := 'WITH*/';
0   0096   00315
0   0096   00316      (* CALL KWIC_C TO CREATE THE NECESSARY VECTORS *)
0   0096   00317      KWIC_C;
0   00A4   00318
```

Fig. 9-5 Program to generate a KWIC indexing system (cont'd.)

```
0  00A4   00319      (* CALL KWIC_G TO GENERATE KWIC INDEX *)
0  00A4   00320      KWIC_G
0  00A4   00321 END.
------------------------------------
¦ COMPILE TIME:    0.769 SECOND(S) ¦
¦     NO WARNING(S) DETECTED       ¦
¦     NO ERROR(S) DETECTED         ¦
------------------------------------
--EXECUTION-->
ALGORITHMIC APPROACH // AN INTRODUCTION TO COMPUTER SCIENCE AN
APPLICATIONS // PL/I PROGRAMMING WITH
APPROACH // AN INTRODUCTION TO COMPUTER SCIENCE AN ALGORITHMIC
COMPUTER SCIENCE AN ALGORITHMIC APPROACH // AN INTRODUCTION TO
INTRODUCTION TO COMPUTER SCIENCE AN ALGORITHMIC APPROACH // AN
INTRODUCTION TO PASCAL PROGRAMMING // AN
PASCAL PROGRAMMING // AN INTRODUCTION TO
PL/I PROGRAMMING // STRUCTURED
PL/I PROGRAMMING WITH APPLICATIONS //
PROGRAMMING // STRUCTURED PL/I
PROGRAMMING // STRUCTURED WATFIV-S
PROGRAMMING WITH APPLICATIONS // PL/I
PROGRAMMING // AN INTRODUCTION TO PASCAL
SCIENCE AN ALGORITHMIC APPROACH // AN INTRODUCTION TO COMPUTER
STRUCTURED PL/I PROGRAMMING //
STRUCTURED WATFIV-S PROGRAMMING //
WATFIV-S PROGRAMMING // STRUCTURED
```

Fig. 9-5   Program to generate a KWIC indexing system (cont'd.)

one of the ordinary words. The function ORD_SEARCH returns a value of zero if the word is not one of the words in ORD_WORDS; otherwise, it returns the position of the word in the ORD_WORDS vector. If the word is not ordinary, the function KEY_SEARCH is used to find the position of the word in the keyword vector. If the word is not present in KEY_WORD, the function KEY_SEARCH adds the word to the vector preserving the lexical ordering of KEY_WORD. The index of the title from which the keyword comes is then concatenated to the element of T_INDEX which corresponds to the keyword. If this is the first time the keyword appears, then the initial blank is removed from T_INDEX. Once all the titles have been processed, the procedure KWIC_G is called to print the KWIC index. The T_INDEX entry corresponding to each keyword is used to find the titles containing that keyword. The corresponding titles are permuted so that the keyword is at the beginning of the title. The titles are then printed.

9-3.3   The Application of Bit Strings to Information Retrieval

The program presented in Fig. 9-6 uses bit strings to represent information gathered about a number of students. Each bit of the bit string represents a student, with the first bit representing the first student, the second bit the second student, and so on. Since PASCAL does not have bit strings *per se*, they can be represented as vectors declared to be of type BOOLEAN. Thus a bit string of 100 bits can be represented as a vector BIT_STRING and declared as

BIT_STRING: ARRAY (1..100) OF BOOLEAN;

The information concerning the students is contained in three logical arrays representing the sex, college, and marital status of the students. Thus a particular array element is TRUE for a given student and category if the student fits into this category where the rows represent the students and the columns represent the categories. The program consists of two procedures: the first builds the bit strings from information read concerning the students and the second prints information concerning the students based on queries made in the main program. The variables used in this program are:

Variable	Type	Usage
ARRAY_SIZE	CONST	Size of arrays
SEXES	CONST	Number of sexes
COLLEGES	CONST	Number of colleges
STATUS	CONST	Number of different marital statuses
NUMBER	ARRAY (1..ARRAY_SIZE) OF STRING(6)	Student's number
NAME	ARRAY (1..ARRAY_SIZE) OF STRING(20)	Student's name
SEX	ARRAY (1..ARRAY_SIZE) OF INTEGER	Student's sex
COLLEGE	ARRAY (1..ARRAY_SIZE) OF INTEGER	Student's college
MARITAL_STATUS	ARRAY (1..ARRAY_SIZE) OF INTEGER	Student's marital status
SEX_WORD	ARRAY(1..SEXES) OF STRING(6)	Name of sexes
COLLEGE_WORD	ARRAY(1..COLLEGES) OF STRING(16)	Name of colleges
STATUS_WORD	ARRAY(1..STATUS) OF STRING(7)	Names of marital statuses
SEX_FILE	ARRAY(1..ARRAY_SIZE, 1..SEXES) OF BOOLEAN	Logical vector of students' sexes
COLLEGE_FILE	ARRAY(1..ARRAY_SIZE, 1..COLLEGES) OF BOOLEAN	Logical vector of students' colleges
STATUS_FILE	ARRAY(1..ARRAY_SIZE, 1..STATUS) OF BOOLEAN	Logical vector of students' marital statuses
I	INTEGER	Counted loop variable
VECTOR	ARRAY(1..ARRAY_SIZE) OF BOOLEAN	Temporary logical vector
N	INTEGER	Number of students

The variables used in the procedure BUILD are:
(Note that the global variables are not included.)

I, J, K	INTEGER	Index variables

The variables used in the procedure OUTPUT are:

TITLE	STRING(29)	Title of report

VECTOR	ARRAY(1..ARRAY_SIZE) OF BOOLEAN	Vector of students who satisfy the query
I	INTEGER	Counted loop variable

The data used in this program are:

Number	Name	Sex	College	Marital Status
'596426'	'LARRY R BROWN'	1	2	2
'600868'	'ROY B ANDERSON'	1	4	2
'621655'	'DAVID N PARKER'	1	3	2
'640621'	'JOHN M BROWN'	1	1	2
'652079'	'PATRICIA L FOX'	2	1	2
'672915'	'JOE E WALL'	1	3	3
'672919'	'LINDA R GARDNER'	2	2	2
'683369'	'SUSAN C FROST'	2	1	3
'690528'	'SUSAN L WONG'	2	5	2
'703062'	'JAKE L FARMER'	1	6	1

```
0  0000  00001  PROGRAM STUDENT (INPUT, OUTPUT);
0  0000  00002  (* THIS PROGRAM BUILDS A MASTER FILE OF BIT STRINGS AND PRODUCES THE
0  0000  00003      REPORTS CONSISTING OF ALL STUDENTS, ALL FEMALE STUDENTS, ALL SCIENCE
0  0000  00004      STUDENTS, AND ALL UNMARRIED STUDENTS. *)
0  0000  00005
0  0000  00006  CONST ARRAY_SIZE = 100;
0  0038  00007        COLLEGES = 6;
0  0038  00008        STATUS = 3;
0  0038  00009        SEXES = 2;
0  0038  00010        STUD_NO_LEN = 6;
0  0038  00011  TYPE BOOLEAN_ARRAY = ARRAY(1..ARRAY_SIZE) OF BOOLEAN;
0  0038  00012  VAR I,                        (* COUNTED LOOP VARIABLE *)
0  0038  00013      N: INTEGER;               (* NUMBER OF STUDENTS *)
0  0038- 00014      SEX,                      (* STUDENT'S SEX *)
0  0038  00015      COLLEGE,                  (* STUDENT'S COLLEGE *)
0  0038  00016      MARITAL_STATUS:           (* STUDENT'S MARITAL STATUS *)
0  0038  00017          ARRAY(1..ARRAY_SIZE) OF INTEGER;
0  0038  00018      NUMBER:                   (* STUDENTS' NUMBERS *)
0  0038  00019          ARRAY(1..ARRAY_SIZE) OF STRING(6);
0  0038  00020      NAME:                     (* STUDENTS' NAMES *)
0  0038  00021          ARRAY(1..ARRAY_SIZE) OF STRING(20);
0  0038  00022      SEX_WORD:                 (* MALE OR FEMALE *)
0  0038  00023          ARRAY(1..SEXES) OF STRING(6);
0  0038  00024      COLLEGE_WORD:             (* NAMES OF COLLEGES *)
0  0038  00025          ARRAY(1..COLLEGES) OF STRING(16);
0  0038  00026      STATUS_WORD:              (* NAMES OF MARITAL STATUSES *)
0  0038  00027          ARRAY(1..STATUS) OF STRING(7);
0  0038  00028      SEX_FILE:                 (* BIT STRING OF STUDENTS' SEXES *)
0  0038  00029          ARRAY(1..SEXES, 1..ARRAY_SIZE) OF BOOLEAN;
0  0038  00030      COLLEGE_FILE:             (* BIT STRING OF STUDENTS' COLLEGES *)
0  0038  00031          ARRAY(1..COLLEGES, 1..ARRAY_SIZE) OF BOOLEAN;
0  0038  00032      STATUS_FILE:              (* BIT STRING OF STUDENTS' MARITAL *)
0  0038  00033          ARRAY(1..STATUS, 1..ARRAY_SIZE) OF BOOLEAN;
0  0038  00034      VECTOR: BOOLEAN_ARRAY;    (* VECTOR USED TO PROCESS QUERIES *)
0  0038  00035
0  0038  00036      PROCEDURE BUILD;
1  0000  00037      (* THIS PROCEDURE CONSTRUCTS A MASTER FILE CONTAINING THE NUMBERS,
1  0000  00038          NAMES, SEXES, COLLEGES, AND MARITAL STATUSES OF THE STUDENTS. *)
1  0000  00039
1  0000  00040      VAR I, J, K: INTEGER;     (* COUNTED LOOP VARIABLES *)
1  003C  00041
1  003C  00042      BEGIN
1  003C  00043
```

Fig. 9-6 Program to retrieve student information using bit strings

```
1   003C   00044              (* INITIALIZE *)
1   003C   00045              FOR I := 1 TO SEXES DO
1   0060   00046                  FOR J := 1 TO ARRAY_SIZE DO
1   0084   00047                      SEX_FILE(I, J) := FALSE;
1   00D4   00048              FOR I := 1 TO COLLEGES DO
1   00F8   00049                  FOR J := 1 TO ARRAY_SIZE DO
1   011C   00050                      COLLEGE_FILE (I, J) := FALSE;
1   016C   00051              FOR I := 1 TO STATUS DO
1   0190   00052                  FOR J := 1 TO ARRAY_SIZE DO
1   01B4   00053                      STATUS_FILE(I, J) := FALSE;
1   0204   00054
1   0204   00055              (* READ AND PROCESS THE STUDENT RECORDS *)
1   0204   00056              READ (N);
1   0216   00057              FOR I := 1 TO N DO
1   023A   00058              BEGIN
1   023A   00059
1   023A   00060                  (* INPUT A STUDENT RECORD *)
1   023A   00061                  READ (NUMBER(I), NAME(I), SEX(I), COLLEGE(I),
1   0302   00062                      MARITAL_STATUS(I));
1   0334   00063
1   0334   00064                  (* UPDATE BIT STRING VECTORS *)
1   0334   00065                  SEX_FILE(SEX(I), I) := TRUE;
1   03A0   00066                  COLLEGE_FILE(COLLEGE(I), I) := TRUE;
1   040C   00067                  STATUS_FILE(MARITAL_STATUS(I), I) := TRUE
1   0470   00068              END
1   0478   00069          END;
0   0038   00070
0   0038   00071      PROCEDURE OUTPUT (TITLE: STRING(29); VECTOR: BOOLEAN_ARRAY);
1   0000   00072      (* THIS PROCEDURE PRODUCES A REPORT LISTING ALL STUDENT INFORMATION
1   0000   00073          PERTAINING TO A QUERY. *)
1   0000   00074
1   0000   00075      VAR I: INTEGER;          (* INDEX VARIABLE *)
1   006C   00076
1   006C   00077      BEGIN
1   006C   00078
1   006C   00079          (* OUTPUT TITLE OF REPORT *)
1   006C   00080          WRITELN ('-', TITLE);
1   0090   00081
1   0090   00082          (* GENERATE THE DETAILS OF THE REPORT *)
1   0090   00083          FOR I := 1 TO ARRAY_SIZE DO
1   00B4   00084              IF VECTOR(I)
1   00DA   00085              THEN WRITELN (' ', NUMBER(I), ' ', NAME(I), ' ',
1   017A   00086                  SEX_WORD(SEX(I)), ' ', COLLEGE_WORD(COLLEGE(I)),
1   0238   00087                  ' ', STATUS_WORD(MARITAL_STATUS(I)))
1   02A0   00088      END;
0   0038   00089
0   0038   00090  BEGIN
0   0038   00091
0   0038   00092      (* INITIALIZE *)
0   0038   00093      SEX_WORD(1) := 'MALE';
0   0042   00094      SEX_WORD(2) := 'FEMALE';
0   0050   00095      STATUS_WORD(1) := 'SINGLE';
0   005A   00096      STATUS_WORD(2) := 'MARRIED';
0   0068   00097      STATUS_WORD(3) := 'OTHER';
0   0076   00098      COLLEGE_WORD(1) := 'SCIENCE';
0   0080   00099      COLLEGE_WORD(2) := 'COMMERCE';
0   008E   00100      COLLEGE_WORD(3) := 'ENGINEERING';
0   009C   00101      COLLEGE_WORD(4) := 'GRADUATE STUDIES';
0   00AA   00102      COLLEGE_WORD(5) := 'HOME ECONOMICS';
0   00B8   00103      COLLEGE_WORD(6) := 'AGRICULTURE';
0   00C6   00104
0   00C6   00105      (* BUILD THE BIT STRINGS *)
0   00C6   00106      BUILD;
0   00D4   00107
0   00D4   00108      (* PROCESS THE QUERIES *)
0   00D4   00109      FOR I := 1 TO ARRAY_SIZE DO
0   00F8   00110          VECTOR(I) := SEX_FILE(1, I) OR SEX_FILE(2, I);
0   0188   00111      OUTPUT ('ALL STUDENTS              ', VECTOR);
0   01AE   00112      FOR I := 1 TO ARRAY_SIZE DO
0   01D2   00113          VECTOR(I) := SEX_FILE(2, I);
0   0226   00114      OUTPUT ('FEMALE STUDENTS           ', VECTOR);
0   024C   00115      FOR I := 1 TO ARRAY_SIZE DO
0   0270   00116          VECTOR(I) := COLLEGE_FILE(1, I);
0   02C0   00117      OUTPUT ('SCIENCE STUDENTS          ', VECTOR);
0   02E6   00118      FOR I := 1 TO ARRAY_SIZE DO
0   030A   00119          VECTOR(I) := COLLEGE_FILE(1, I) AND NOT STATUS_FILE(2, I);
0   039A   00120      OUTPUT ('UNMARRIED STUDENTS IN SCIENCE', VECTOR)
0   03AA   00121  END.
```

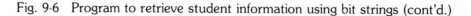

Fig. 9-6 Program to retrieve student information using bit strings (cont'd.)

```
--EXECUTION-->


ALL STUDENTS
596426 LARRY R BROWN        MALE    COMMERCE          MARRIED
600868 ROY B ANDERSON       MALE    GRADUATE STUDIES  MARRIED
621655 DAVID N PARKER       MALE    ENGINEERING       MARRIED
640621 JOHN M BROWN         MALE    SCIENCE           MARRIED
652079 PATRICIA L FOX       FEMALE  SCIENCE           MARRIED
672915 JOE E WALL           MALE    ENGINEERING       OTHER
672919 LINDA R GARDNER      FEMALE  COMMERCE          MARRIED
683369 SUSAN C FROST        FEMALE  SCIENCE           OTHER
690528 SUSAN L WONG         FEMALE  HOME ECONOMICS    MARRIED
703062 JAKE L FARMER        MALE    AGRICULTURE       SINGLE


FEMALE STUDENTS
652079 PATRICIA L FOX       FEMALE  SCIENCE           MARRIED
672919 LINDA R GARDNER      FEMALE  COMMERCE          MARRIED
683369 SUSAN C FROST        FEMALE  SCIENCE           OTHER
690528 SUSAN L WONG         FEMALE  HOME ECONOMICS    MARRIED


SCIENCE STUDENTS
640621 JOHN M BROWN         MALE    SCIENCE           MARRIED
652079 PATRICIA L FOX       FEMALE  SCIENCE           MARRIED
683369 SUSAN C FROST        FEMALE  SCIENCE           OTHER


UNMARRIED STUDENTS IN SCIENCE
683369 SUSAN C FROST        FEMALE  SCIENCE           OTHER
```

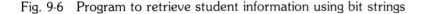

Fig. 9-6 Program to retrieve student information using bit strings

The main program first initializes the vectors SEX_WORD, STATUS_WORD, and COLLEGE_WORD. The procedure BUILD is then called to create the logical vectors for the eleven categories. Information concerning each of the students is read in, and using this information the element corresponding to this student is set to TRUE in the appropriate column of the array. After the completion of the procedure BUILD, the OUTPUT procedure is then called four times to produce reports for the following four queries: all students, female students, science students, and unmarried students in science.

Note that the logical vector VECTOR is required to pass those students who satisfy a given query. A position in VECTOR is TRUE if the particular student satisfies all the conditions.

9-3.4 Text Editing

The program presented in this section is a solution to the text editing problem discussed in Sec. 9-2.4 of the main text. The text editor interprets a number of commands to format textual material. Each command is preceded by "##" and is associated with a code which is used by the text editor and must begin in column one of the data card. A summary of the commands is given in Table 9-2.

The program given in Fig. 9-7 consists of a main program and four procedures; namely, FORMAT, SCANNER, PRINTU, and PRINTJ. The main program reads in the line width and calls the procedure FORMAT, which produces the edited version of the text with the line width just read. To produce the edited line of text, the procedure FORMAT uses the procedures SCANNER, PRINTU, and PRINTJ. The procedure SCANNER finds the next item in the text and determines its type. If the end of an input line has been reached, SCANNER inputs another line of

Table 9-2   Summary of commands for the text editor

Command	Code	Description
##JS	2	Right justify text
##NJ	3	Do not right justify text
##NP	4	Begin a new paragraph
##CN/.../	5	Center the text between the two slashes
##BL n	6	Add n blank lines
##ED	7	End of text

text. In determining the next line of text, SCANNER uses the two functions SPAN and BREAK. PRINTU and PRINTJ are used to print an unadjusted line and an adjusted line of text, respectively. The variables used in the main program are:

Variable	Type	Usage
WIDTH	INTEGER	Length of edited line

The variables used in the procedure FORMAT are:

INPUT_LINE	STRING(256)	Line currently being processed
CURSOR	INTEGER	Current character position
WORDS	ARRAY(1..100) OF STRING(256)	Vector of words to be printed
NO_WORDS	INTEGER	Number of words in WORDS vector
LINE_LENGTH	INTEGER	Length of unedited line
ITEM	STRING(256)	Current item
TYPE	INTEGER	Type of command
BLANK_LINE	STRING(256)	Sequence of blanks
NO_LINE	INTEGER	Number of blank lines
JUSTIFY	BOOLEAN	Flag for justification
PADDING	STRING(256)	Padding for edited line
WIDTH	INTEGER	Length of edited line
DIGITS	STRING(256)	String of digits 0 to 9
NO_BLANK	INTEGER	Number of blank characters
TEMP	STRING (256)	Temporary string variable
I, J	INTEGER	Loop variables

The variables used in the procedure SCANNER are:

DUMMY	BOOLEAN	Temporary variable
BLANKS	STRING(256)	Variable to hold any leading blanks
BLANK	STRING(256)	Blank character
NULL	STRING(256)	Null string ('*/')
SLASH	STRING(256)	Stores / character

TEMP	STRING(256)	Temporary string variable
INPUT	STRING(256)	Line of input text
ITEM	STRING(256)	Next item of input line
CURSOR	INTEGER	Current character being examined
C_TYPE	INTEGER	Type of item to be returned
STEMP	STRING(6)	Text command

The variables used in the procedure PRINTU are:

NO_WORDS	INTEGER	Number of words in WORDS vector
LINE	STRING(256)	Line to be output
I	INTEGER	Index variable
BLANK	STRING(256)	Blank character
BLANKS	STRING(256)	String of blank characters

The variables used in the procedure PRINTJ are:

NO_WORDS	INTEGER	Number of words in WORDS vector
LINE_LENGTH	INTEGER	Total length of words to be printed
WIDTH	INTEGER	Length of edited line
TOTAL_PAD	INTEGER	Number of additional blanks needed
AV_PAD	INTEGER	Number of blanks to be inserted between each pair of words
EXTRA_BLANKS	INTEGER	Number of extra blanks that must be distributed
PADDING	STRING(256)	Padding between words
LINE	STRING(256)	Output line of text
J	INTEGER	Loop variable
I	INTEGER	Index variable
BLANK	STRING(256)	Blank character
BLANKS	STRING(256)	String of blank characters

The data used in this program are:

```
##JS*/
THIS LINE ILLUSTRATES THE USE OF THE JUSTIFY TEXT COMMAND.*/
##NP*/
THIS IS THE START OF A NEW PARAGRAPH.*/
##CN/THIS IS CENTERED./*/
##BL 5*/
THE ##BL COMMAND HAS BEEN USED TO LEAVE FIVE BLANK LINES.*/
THE FOLLOWING LINE HAS NOT BEEN JUSTIFIED.*/
##NJ*/
##NP*/
ALL THE WORLD LOVES A TEXT EDITING COMPUTER.*/
##ED*/
```

```
0  0000   00001   PROGRAM TEXT_ED (INPUT, OUTPUT);
0  0000   00002   (* THIS PROGRAM PRODUCES AN EDITED VERSION OF INPUT TEXT USING A SERIES
0  0000   00003      OF TEXT EDITING COMMANDS. *)
0  0000   00004
0  0000   00005   VAR WIDTH: INTEGER;              (* INPUT LINE WIDTH *)
0  0038   00006   FUNCTION INDEX (VAR S, PATTERN: STRING(256)): INTEGER; EXTERNAL;
0  0038   00007   FUNCTION LENGTH (VAR STR: STRING(256)): INTEGER; EXTERNAL;
0  0038   00008   PROCEDURE SUB (VAR S: STRING(256); POS, NUM: INTEGER; VAR RESULT:
1  0000   00009         STRING(256)); EXTERNAL;
0  0038   00010   PROCEDURE CONCAT (VAR S1, S2, RESULT: STRING(256)); EXTERNAL;
0  0038   00011
0  0038   00012      FUNCTION SPAN (VAR SUBJECT, PATTERN: STRING(256); VAR CURSOR:
1  0000   00013         INTEGER; VAR MATCH_STR: STRING(256); REPLACE_FLAG: BOOLEAN;
1  0000   00014         VAR REPLACE_STR: STRING(256)): BOOLEAN;
1  0000   00015
1  0000   00016      (* THIS FUNCTION RETURNS TRUE IF THE CHARACTER DENOTED BY CURSOR
1  0000   00017         MATCHES ANY OF THE CHARACTERS IN PATTERN.  IF THE PATTERN MATCH
1  0000   00018         SUCCEEDS, MATCH_STR BECOMES A SEQUENCE OF CHARACTERS CONTAINING
1  0000   00019         THE CHARACTER AT THE POSITION SPECIFIED BY CURSOR AND ALL OTHER
1  0000   00020         CHARACTERS WHICH ARE CONTAINED IN PATTERN.  THE PATTERN MATCH
1  0000   00021         PROCESS TERMINATES ON ENCOUNTERING A CHARACTER NOT IN PATTERN OR
1  0000   00022         THE END OF THE SUBJECT STRING.  IF A REPLACEMENT OPERATION IS
1  0000   00023         SPECIFIED, THE SEQUENCE OF CHARACTERS IS REPLACED BY THE VALUE
1  0000   00024         OF REPLACE_STR. *)
1  0000   00025
1  0000   00026      VAR I: INTEGER;                (* INDEX VARIABLE *)
1  0082   00027         TEMP: STRING(256);          (* TEMPORARY STRING VARIABLE *)
1  0082   00028      FUNCTION LENGTH (VAR STR: STRING(256)): INTEGER; EXTERNAL;
1  0082   00029      FUNCTION INDEX (VAR S, PATTERN: STRING(256)): INTEGER; EXTERNAL;
1  0082   00030      PROCEDURE SUB (VAR S: STRING(256); POS, NUM: INTEGER;
2  0000   00031         VAR RESULT: STRING(256)); EXTERNAL;
1  0082   00032      PROCEDURE PSDSUB (VAR S: STRING(256); POS, NUM: INTEGER; VAR ADD:
2  0000   00033         STRING(256)); EXTERNAL;
1  0082   00034
1  0082   00035      BEGIN
1  0082   00036
1  0082   00037         (* DOES THE PATTERN FIT WITHIN THE BOUNDS OF THE SUBJECT
1  0082   00038            STRING? *)
1  0082   00039         IF CURSOR > LENGTH (SUBJECT)
1  008A   00040         THEN SPAN := FALSE
1  00A8   00041         ELSE BEGIN
1  00B4   00042
1  00B4   00043            (* INITIALIZE PATTERN MATCH *)
1  00B4   00044            I := CURSOR;
1  00BC   00045
1  00BC   00046            (* IS CHARACTER I IN THE PATTERN STRING? *)
1  00BC   00047            SUB (SUBJECT, I, 1, TEMP);
1  00F0   00048            WHILE (I <= LENGTH (SUBJECT)) AND (INDEX (PATTERN, TEMP)
1  0126   00049               <> 0) DO
1  0144   00050            BEGIN
1  0144   00051               I := I + 1;
1  0150   00052               SUB (SUBJECT, I, 1, TEMP)
1  0170   00053            END;
1  0188   00054
1  0188   00055            (* UNSUCCESSFUL PATTERN MATCH? *)
1  0188   00056            IF I = CURSOR
1  0188   00057            THEN SPAN := FALSE
1  0194   00058            ELSE BEGIN
1  01A0   00059
1  01A0   00060               (* SET UP MATCH_STR AND PERFORM INDICATED REPLACE-
1  01A0   00061                  MENT *)
1  01A0   00062               SUB (SUBJECT, CURSOR, I - CURSOR, MATCH_STR);
1  01E0   00063               IF REPLACE_FLAG
1  01E0   00064               THEN BEGIN
1  01EA   00065                  PSDSUB (SUBJECT, CURSOR, I - CURSOR,
1  020E   00066                     REPLACE_STR);
1  022A   00067                  CURSOR := CURSOR + LENGTH (REPLACE_STR)
1  0232   00068                  END
1  0250   00069               ELSE CURSOR := I;
1  025C   00070
1  025C   00071               (* SUCCESSFUL RETURN *)
1  025C   00072               SPAN := TRUE
1  025C   00073               END
1  0264   00074            END
1  0264   00075      END;
0  0038   00076
0  0038   00077      FUNCTION BREAK (VAR SUBJECT, PATTERN: STRING(256); VAR CURSOR:
1  0000   00078         INTEGER; VAR MATCH_STR: STRING(256); REPLACE_FLAG: BOOLEAN;
1  0000   00079         VAR REPLACE_STR: STRING(256)): BOOLEAN;
```

Fig. 9-7   Program for a text editing system

```
1  0000  00080
1  0000  00081      (* THIS FUNCTION RETURNS A VALUE OF FALSE IF IT ENCOUNTERS A
1  0000  00082         CHARACTER WHICH IS ALSO IN PATTERN FROM THE CHARACTER POSITION
1  0000  00083         ONWARDS; OTHERWISE, IT RETURNS A VALUE OF FALSE. WHEN A SUCCESS-
1  0000  00084         FUL PATTERN MATCH OCCURS, MATCH_STR IS SET TO THE SUBSTRING OF
1  0000  00085         THE SUBJECT STRING FROM THE INITIAL CURSOR POSITION UP TO, BUT
1  0000  00086         NOT INCLUDING THE CHARACTER ALSO FOUND TO BE IN PATTERN.  IF
1  0000  00087         REPLACE_FLAG IS TRUE, THE MATCHED SUBSTRING IN SUBJECT IS
1  0000  00088         REPLACED BY THE VALUE OF REPLACE_STR.  FINALLY, CURSOR IS
1  0000  00089         UPDATED. *)
1  0000  00090
1  0000  00091      VAR I: INTEGER;                   (* INDEX VARIABLE *)
1  0082  00092          TEMP, SAVE:          (* TEMPORARY STRING VARIABLES *)
1  0082  00093              STRING(256);
1  0082  00094      FUNCTION LENGTH (VAR STR: STRING(256)): INTEGER; EXTERNAL;
1  0082  00095      FUNCTION INDEX (VAR S, PATTERN: STRING(256)): INTEGER; EXTERNAL;
1  0082  00096      PROCEDURE SUB (VAR S: STRING(256); POS, NUM: INTEGER; VAR RESULT:
2  0000  00097          STRING(256)); EXTERNAL;
1  0082  00098      PROCEDURE PSDSUB (VAR S: STRING(256); POS, NUM: INTEGER; VAR ADD:
2  0000  00099          STRING(256)); EXTERNAL;
1  0082  00100      PROCEDURE CONCAT (VAR S1, S2, RESULT: STRING(256)); EXTERNAL;
1  0082  00101
1  0082  00102      BEGIN
1  0082  00103
1  0082  00104          (* DOES THE PATTERN FIT WITHIN THE SEARCH BOUNDS OF THE
1  0082  00105             SUBJECT STRING? *)
1  0082  00106          IF CURSOR > LENGTH (SUBJECT)
1  008A  00107          THEN BREAK := FALSE
1  00A8  00108          ELSE BEGIN
1  00B4  00109
1  00B4  00110              (* INITIALIZE PATTERN MATCH *)
1  00B4  00111              I := CURSOR;
1  00BC  00112
1  00BC  00113              (* IS CHARACTER I IN THE PATTERN STRING? *)
1  00BC  00114              SUB (SUBJECT, I, 1, TEMP);
1  00F0  00115              WHILE (I <= LENGTH (SUBJECT)) AND (INDEX (PATTERN, TEMP)
1  0126  00116                  = 0) DO
1  0144  00117              BEGIN
1  0144  00118                  I := I + 1;
1  0150  00119                  SUB (SUBJECT, I, 1, TEMP)
1  0170  00120              END;
1  0188  00121
1  0188  00122              (* SUCCESSFUL PATTERN MATCH *)
1  0188  00123              IF I = LENGTH (SUBJECT) + 1
1  01A6  00124              THEN BREAK := FALSE
1  01B2  00125              ELSE BEGIN
1  01BE  00126
1  01BE  00127                  (* SET MATCH_STR AND PERFORM INDICATED REPLACE-
1  01BE  00128                     MENT *)
1  01BE  00129                  SUB (SUBJECT, CURSOR, I - CURSOR, MATCH_STR);
1  01FE  00130                  IF REPLACE_FLAG
1  01FE  00131                  THEN BEGIN
1  0208  00132                      IF I <> CURSOR
1  0208  00133                      THEN PSDSUB (SUBJECT, CURSOR, I - CURSOR,
1  0238  00134                                      REPLACE_STR)
1  0240  00135                      ELSE BEGIN
1  0258  00136
1  0258  00137                          (* REPLACEMENT OF EMPTY STRING *)
1  0258  00138                          SUB (SUBJECT, 1, CURSOR - 1, TEMP);
1  0298  00139                          CONCAT (TEMP, REPLACE_STR, TEMP);
1  02C4  00140                          SUB (SUBJECT, CURSOR, 256, SAVE);
1  02F8  00141                          CONCAT (TEMP, SAVE, SUBJECT)
1  0310  00142                      END;
1  0324  00143                      CURSOR := CURSOR + LENGTH (REPLACE_STR)
1  032C  00144                  END
1  034A  00145                  ELSE CURSOR := I;
1  0356  00146
1  0356  00147                  (* SUCCESSFUL RETURN *)
1  0356  00148                  BREAK := TRUE
1  0356  00149              END
1  035E  00150          END
1  035E  00151      END;
0  0038  00152
0  0038  00153      PROCEDURE SCANNER (VAR INPUT: STRING(256); VAR CURSOR, C_TYPE:
1  0000  00154          INTEGER; VAR ITEM: STRING(256));
1  0000  00155      (* GIVEN A CHARACTER STRING (INPUT), WHICH REPRESENTS A LINE OF
1  0000  00156         INPUT TEXT AND A CURSOR WHICH DENOTES THE CURRENT CHARACTER
1  0000  00157         BEING EXAMINED, THIS PROCEDURE ISOLATES THE NEXT WORD OR COMMAND
1  0000  00158         AND DETERMINES ITS TYPE. *)
1  0000  00159
```

Fig. 9-7   Program for a text editing system (cont'd.)

```
1 0000   00160      VAR BLANK, NULL, SLASH, (* HOLDS CHARACTER STRINGS *)
1 006E   00161          BLANKS,            (* HOLDS ANY LEADING BLANKS *)
1 006E   00162          TEMP: STRING(256); (* TEXT COMMAND *)
1 006E   00163          DUMMY: BOOLEAN;    (* TEMPORARY VARIABLE *)
1 006E   00164          STEMP: STRING(6);  (* TEXT COMMAND *)
1 006E   00165
1 006E   00166      BEGIN
1 006E   00167
1 006E   00168          (* INITIALIZE *)
1 006E   00169          BLANK := ' */';
1 0074   00170          NULL := '*/';
1 007A   00171          SLASH := '/*/';
1 0080   00172
1 0080   00173          (* SCAN ANY LEADING BLANK CHARACTERS *)
1 0080   00174          DUMMY := SPAN (INPUT, BLANK, CURSOR, BLANKS, FALSE, NULL);
1 00CA   00175
1 00CA   00176          (* HAS THE CURRENT INPUT LINE BEEN ENTIRELY SCANNED? *)
1 00CA   00177          IF CURSOR > LENGTH (INPUT)
1 00D2   00178          THEN BEGIN
1 00F0   00179              READ (INPUT: 80);
1 0102   00180              CONCAT (INPUT, BLANK, INPUT);
1 012E   00181              CURSOR := 1;
1 0136   00182              DUMMY := SPAN (INPUT, BLANK, CURSOR, BLANKS, FALSE,
1 015E   00183                  NULL);
1 0180   00184              DUMMY := BREAK (INPUT, BLANK, CURSOR, ITEM, FALSE,
1 01A8   00185                  NULL);
1 01CA   00186              SUB (INPUT, 1, 4, TEMP);
1 01FE   00187              STEMP := TEMP; (* SHORTEN LENGTH OF STRING TO 5 CHARS. *)
1 0204   00188              IF STEMP = '##JS*/'
1 0204   00189              THEN C_TYPE := 2
1 020E   00190              ELSE IF STEMP = '##NJ*/'
1 021A   00191                  THEN C_TYPE := 3
1 0224   00192                  ELSE IF STEMP = '##NP*/'
1 0230   00193                      THEN C_TYPE := 4
1 023A   00194                      ELSE IF STEMP = '##CN*/'
1 0246   00195                          THEN BEGIN
1 0250   00196                              C_TYPE := 5;
1 0258   00197                              SUB (INPUT, 6, 256, TEMP);
1 028C   00198                              SUB (INPUT, 6, INDEX (TEMP, SLASH)
1 02AC   00199                                  - 1, ITEM);
1 02EE   00200                              CURSOR := LENGTH (INPUT) + 1
1 030C   00201                          END
1 0314   00202                          ELSE IF STEMP = '##BL*/'
1 0318   00203                              THEN BEGIN
1 0322   00204                                  C_TYPE := 6;
1 032A   00205                                  SUB (INPUT, 6, 256, TEMP);
1 035E   00206                                  SUB (INPUT, 6, INDEX (TEMP,
1 0376   00207                                      BLANK) - 1, ITEM);
1 03C0   00208                                  CURSOR := LENGTH (INPUT) + 1
1 03DE   00209                              END
1 03E6   00210                              ELSE IF STEMP = '##ED*/'
1 03EA   00211                                  THEN C_TYPE := 7
1 03F4   00212                                  ELSE C_TYPE := 1
1 0400   00213              END
1 0408   00214
1 0408   00215          (* OBTAIN ORDINARY WORD OF TEXT *)
1 0408   00216          ELSE BEGIN
1 040C   00217              DUMMY := BREAK (INPUT, BLANK, CURSOR, ITEM, FALSE, NULL);
1 0456   00218              C_TYPE := 1
1 0456   00219          END
1 045E   00220      END;
0 0038   00221
0 0038   00222  PROCEDURE FORMAT (WIDTH: INTEGER);
1 0000   00223  (* GIVEN THE LINE WIDTH OF AN EDITED LINE, THIS PROCEDURE CONTROLS
1 0000   00224      THE INPUT OF A PASSAGE OF TEXT AND PRODUCES THE DESIRED EDITED
1 0000   00225      VERSION OF THIS INPUT TEXT. *)
1 0000   00226
1 0000   00227  VAR INPUT_LINE,          (* CURRENT LINE BEING PROCESSED *)
1 004E   00228      ITEM,                (* CURRENT ITEM *)
1 004E   00229      BLANK_LINE,          (* SEQUENCE OF BLANKS *)
1 004E   00230      PADDING,             (* USED TO PAD BLANKS *)
1 004E   00231      DIGITS,              (* DIGITS 0 THROUGH 9 *)
1 004E   00232      TEMP: STRING(256);   (* TEMPORARY STRING VARIABLE *)
1 004E   00233      WORDS: ARRAY(1..100) OF STRING(256);
1 005E   00234                           (* WORDS TO BE OUTPUT *)
1 005E   00235      JUSTIFY: BOOLEAN;    (* FLAG FOR JUSTIFICATION *)
1 005E   00236      CURSOR,              (* CURRENT CHARACTER POSITION *)
1 005E   00237      NO_WORDS,            (* NUMBER OF WORDS IN WORDS VECTOR *)
1 005E   00238      LINE_LENGTH,         (* LENGTH OF UNEDITED LINE *)
1 005E   00239      C_TYPE,              (* COMMAND TYPE *)
```

Fig. 9-7   Program for a text editing system

```
1  005E  00240        NO_LINES,             (* NUMBER OF BLANK LINES *)
1  005E  00241        NO_BLANKS,            (* NUMBER OF BLANKS TO PAD *)
1  005E  00242        I, J: INTEGER;        (* COUNTED LOOP VARIABLE *)
1  005E  00243
1  005E  00244        PROCEDURE PRINTU (NO_WORDS: INTEGER);
2  0000  00245        (* GIVEN A STRING VECTOR, WORDS, WHICH CONTAINS THE WORDS OF A N
2  0000  00246        OUTPUT LINE AND NO_WORDS, THE NUMBER OF WORDS IN THIS LINE,
2  0000  00247        THIS PROCEDURE OUTPUTS THE NEXT LINE WITHOUT ANY RIGHT
2  0000  00248        JUSTIFICATION. *)
2  0000  00249        VAR LINE,             (* LINE TO PRINT *)
2  004E  00250            BLANK, BLANKS: (* STRINGS CONTAINING BLANK AND BLANKS *)
2  004E  00251                  STRING(256);
2  004E  00252            I: INTEGER;       (* COUNTED LOOP VARIABLE *)
2  004E  00253
2  004E  00254        BEGIN
2  004E  00255
2  004E  00256            (* OBTAIN THE CURRENT LINE IN UNJUSTIFIED FORM *)
2  004E  00257            BLANKS := '                                    */';
2  0054  00258            CONCAT (BLANKS, BLANKS, BLANKS);
2  0080  00259            BLANK := ' */';
2  0086  00260            LINE := WORDS(1);
2  0090  00261            FOR I := 2 TO NO_WORDS DO
2  00B4  00262            BEGIN
2  00B4  00263                CONCAT (LINE, BLANK, LINE);
2  00E0  00264                CONCAT (LINE, WORDS(I), LINE)
2  0116  00265            END;
2  012E  00266
2  012E  00267            (* OUTPUT CURRENT LINE *)
2  012E  00268            CONCAT (LINE, BLANKS, LINE);
2  015A  00269            WRITELN (' ', LINE: 80);
2  017E  00270        END;
1  006E  00271
1  006E  00272        PROCEDURE PRINTJ (VAR NO_WORDS, LINE_LENGTH, WIDTH: INTEGER);
2  0000  00273        (* GIVEN A STRING VECTOR, WORDS, WHICH CONTAINS THE WORDS TO
2  0000  00274           BE OUTPUT, THIS PROCEDURE PRODUCES AN OUTPUT LINE OF THE
2  0000  00275           SPECIFIED WIDTH BY INSERTING EXTRA BLANKS BETWEEN WORDS. *)
2  0000  00276
2  0000  00277        VAR TOTAL_PAD,        (* NO. OF ADDITIONAL BLANKS NEEDED *)
2  0066  00278            AV_PAD,           (* NO. OF BLANKS TO BE INSERTED BETWEEN
2  0066  00279                                 EACH PAIR OF WORDS *)
2  0066  00280            EXTRA_BLANKS,     (* NO. OF EXTRA BLANKS THAT MUST BE
2  0066  00281                                 DISTRIBUTED *)
2  0066  00282            I, J: INTEGER;    (* COUNTED LOOP VARIABLES *)
2  0066  00283            PADDING,          (* BLANKS TO PAD ONTO OUTPUT LINE *)
2  0066  00284            LINE,             (* OUTPUT LINE *)
2  0066  00285            BLANK, BLANKS: (* STRINGS OF BLANK AND BLANKS *)
2  0066  00286                  STRING(256);
2  0066  00287
2  0066  00288        BEGIN
2  0066  00289
2  0066  00290            BLANK := ' */';
2  006C  00291            BLANKS := '                                    */';
2  0072  00292            CONCAT (BLANKS, BLANKS, BLANKS);
2  009E  00293
2  009E  00294            (* COMPUTE TOTAL NUMBER OF BLANKS TO BE INSERTED *)
2  009E  00295            TOTAL_PAD := WIDTH - LINE_LENGTH;
2  00AA  00296
2  00AA  00297            (* COMPUTE AVERAGE NUMBER OF BLANKS TO BE PADDED BETWEEN
2  00AA  00298               EACH WORD *)
2  00AA  00299            AV_PAD := TOTAL_PAD DIV (NO_WORDS - 1);
2  00C0  00300
2  00C0  00301            (* COMPUTE EXTRA BLANKS TO BE DISTRBUTED BETWEEN
2  00C0  00302               CERTAIN WORDS *)
2  00C0  00303            EXTRA_BLANKS := TOTAL_PAD MOD (NO_WORDS - 1);
2  00D6  00304
2  00D6  00305            (* OBTAIN OUTPUT LINE *)
2  00D6  00306            LINE := WORDS(1);
2  00E0  00307            PADDING := '*/';
2  00E6  00308            FOR J := 1 TO AV_PAD + 1 DO
2  010E  00309                CONCAT (PADDING, BLANK, PADDING);
2  013E  00310            FOR J := 2 TO NO_WORDS - EXTRA_BLANKS DO
2  0166  00311            BEGIN
2  0166  00312                CONCAT (LINE, PADDING, LINE);
2  0192  00313                CONCAT (LINE, WORDS(J), LINE)
2  01C8  00314            END;
2  01E0  00315            PADDING := '*/';
2  01E6  00316            FOR J := 1 TO AV_PAD + 2 DO
2  020E  00317                CONCAT (PADDING, BLANK, PADDING);
```

Fig. 9-7 Program for a text editing system (cont'd.)

```
2  023E  00318                        FOR J := NO_WORDS - EXTRA_BLANKS + 1 TO NO_WORDS DO
2  026C  00319                        BEGIN
2  026C  00320                             CONCAT (LINE, PADDING, LINE);
2  0298  00321                             CONCAT (LINE, WORDS(J), LINE)
2  02CE  00322                        END;
2  02E6  00323
2  02E6  00324                        (* OUTPUT LINE *)
2  02E6  00325                        CONCAT (LINE, BLANKS, LINE);
2  0312  00326                        WRITELN (' ', LINE: 80)
2  0336  00327                   END;
1  006E  00328
1  006E  00329       BEGIN
1  006E  00330
1  006E  00331           (* INITIALIZE *)
1  006E  00332           DIGITS := '0123456789*/';
1  0074  00333           INPUT_LINE := '*/';
1  007A  00334           CURSOR := 1;
1  0082  00335           JUSTIFY := TRUE;
1  008A  00336           LINE_LENGTH := 0;
1  0090  00337           NO_WORDS := 0;
1  0096  00338           BLANK_LINE := '                                          */';
1  009C  00339           CONCAT (BLANK_LINE, BLANK_LINE, BLANK_LINE);
1  00C8  00340
1  00C8  00341           (* EDIT THE GIVEN TEXT *)
1  00C8  00342           WHILE C_TYPE <> 7 DO
1  00D4  00343           BEGIN
1  00D4  00344               SCANNER (INPUT_LINE, CURSOR, C_TYPE, ITEM);
1  0108  00345
1  0108  00346               (* PROCESS CURRENT WORD OR COMMAND *)
1  0108  00347               CASE C_TYPE OF
1  0108  00348               1: (* ORDINARY LINE OF TEXT *)
1  0126  00349                   BEGIN
1  0126  00350                       IF LINE_LENGTH + LENGTH (ITEM) + 1 <= WIDTH
1  014C  00351                       THEN BEGIN
1  0154  00352
1  0154  00353                           (* ADD THE WORD TO THE CURRENT LINE *)
1  0154  00354                           NO_WORDS := NO_WORDS + 1;
1  0160  00355                           WORDS (NO_WORDS) := ITEM;
1  0188  00356                           IF NO_WORDS = 1
1  0188  00357                           THEN LINE_LENGTH := LENGTH (ITEM)
1  019C  00358                           ELSE LINE_LENGTH := LINE_LENGTH + LENGTH (ITEM)
1  01C2  00359                                     + 1
1  01DC  00360                           END
1  01E4  00361                       ELSE BEGIN
1  01E8  00362
1  01E8  00363                           (* PRINT THE PREVIOUS LINE AND USE NEW ITEM TO
1  01E8  00364                              START NEW LINE *)
1  01E8  00365                           IF JUSTIFY
1  01E8  00366                           THEN PRINTJ (NO_WORDS, LINE_LENGTH, WIDTH)
1  020A  00367                           ELSE PRINTU (NO_WORDS);
1  023E  00368                           WORDS(1) := ITEM;
1  0248  00369                           NO_WORDS := 1;
1  0250  00370                           LINE_LENGTH := LENGTH (ITEM)
1  0258  00371                           END
1  0272  00372                   END;
1  0276  00373
1  0276  00374               2: (* RIGHT JUSTIFY TEXT *)
1  0276  00375                   JUSTIFY := TRUE;
1  0282  00376
1  0282  00377               3: (* DO NOT RIGHT-JUSTIFY TEXT *)
1  0282  00378                   JUSTIFY := FALSE;
1  028E  00379
1  028E  00380               4: (* NEW PARAGRAPH *)
1  028E  00381                   BEGIN
1  028E  00382                       IF LINE_LENGTH <> 0
1  028E  00383                       THEN (* PRINT THE PREVIOUS LINE AND A BLANK LINE,
1  028E  00384                               AND INDENT THE FIRST WORD ON THE NEXT
1  028E  00385                               LINE. *)
1  029A  00386                           PRINTU (NO_WORDS);
1  02B6  00387                       WRITELN (' ');
1  02C8  00388                       SCANNER (INPUT_LINE, CURSOR, C_TYPE, ITEM);
1  02FC  00389                       IF C_TYPE <> 1
1  02FC  00390                       THEN WRITELN (' ERROR IN INPUT')
1  031A  00391                       ELSE BEGIN
1  031E  00392                           NO_WORDS := 1;
1  0326  00393                           TEMP := '    */';
1  032C  00394                           CONCAT (TEMP, ITEM, WORDS(1));
1  0358  00395                           LINE_LENGTH := LENGTH (WORDS(1))
1  0360  00396                           END
1  037A  00397                   END;
```

Fig. 9-7   Program for a text editing system (cont'd.)

```
1  037E  00398
1  037E  00399                          5: (* CENTER ITEM *)
1  037E  00400                             BEGIN
1  037E  00401                                IF LINE_LENGTH <> 0
1  037E  00402                                THEN PRINTU (NO_WORDS);
1  03A6  00403                                NO_BLANKS := (WIDTH - LENGTH (ITEM)) DIV 2;
1  03D8  00404                                PADDING := '*/';
1  03DE  00405                                TEMP := ' */';
1  03E4  00406                                FOR I := 1 TO NO_BLANKS DO
1  0408  00407                                     CONCAT (PADDING, TEMP, PADDING);
1  0438  00408                                CONCAT (PADDING, ITEM, TEMP);
1  0464  00409                                CONCAT (TEMP, BLANK_LINE, TEMP);
1  0490  00410                                WRITELN (' ', TEMP: 80);
1  04B4  00411                                LINE_LENGTH := 0;
1  04BA  00412                                NO_WORDS := 0
1  04BA  00413                             END;
1  04C4  00414
1  04C4  00415                          6: (* BLANK LINE *)
1  04C4  00416                             BEGIN
1  04C4  00417
1  04C4  00418                                (* ADD NUMBER OF BLANK LINES SPECIFIED BY ITEM *)
1  04C4  00419                                IF LINE_LENGTH <> 0
1  04C4  00420                                THEN PRINTU (NO_WORDS);
1  04EC  00421                                NO_LINES := 0;
1  04F2  00422                                FOR I := 1 TO LENGTH (ITEM) DO
1  0530  00423                                BEGIN
1  0530  00424                                     SUB (ITEM, I, 1, TEMP);
1  0564  00425                                     NO_LINES := NO_LINES * 10 +
1  0570  00426                                          INDEX (DIGITS, TEMP) - 1
1  059E  00427                                     END;
1  05AA  00428                                FOR I := 1 TO NO_LINES DO
1  05CE  00429                                     WRITELN (' ');
1  05E4  00430                                LINE_LENGTH := 0;
1  05EA  00431                                NO_WORDS := 0
1  05EA  00432                             END;
1  05F4  00433
1  05F4  00434                          7: (* END OF TEXT *)
1  05F4  00435                             IF LINE_LENGTH <> 0
1  05F4  00436                             THEN PRINTU (NO_WORDS)
1  0608  00437                          END
1  0620  00438                     END
1  0632  00439               END;
0  0038  00440  BEGIN
0  0038  00441
0  0038  00442        (* INPUT LINE WIDTH *)
0  0038  00443        READLN (WIDTH);
0  004A  00444
0  004A  00445        (* INVOKE FORMATER ROUTINE *)
0  004A  00446        FORMAT (WIDTH);
0  0068  00447  END.
```

```
---------------------------------
| COMPILE TIME:    1.124 SECOND(S) |
|    NO WARNING(S) DETECTED         |
|    NO ERROR(S) DETECTED           |
---------------------------------
```

```
--EXECUTION-->
THIS LINE ILLUSTRATES  THE  USE  OF  THE
JUSTIFY TEXT COMMAND.

     THIS   IS  THE  START   OF   A   NEW
PARAGRAPH.
               THIS IS CENTERED.




THE ##BL COMMAND HAS BEEN USED TO  LEAVE
FIVE BLANK LINES. THE FOLLOWING LINE HAS
NOT BEEN JUSTIFIED.

     ALL THE WORLD LOVES A TEXT EDITING
COMPUTER.
```

Fig. 9-7 Program for a text editing system (cont'd.)

The main program reads the width of the line to be used in formatting the text. Procedure FORMAT is then called to process the text. In the procedure FORMAT, INPUT is initially set to the empty string. A loop is then begun to process the input text. At the beginning of the loop, SCANNER is called to isolate the next item in the input text. In SCANNER, if the CURSOR is greater than the length of INPUT (as is the case when the loop in FORMAT is first executed), then a new line of text is read. A blank is then concatenated to the end of the input line, and CURSOR is reset to one. The functions SPAN and BREAK are then called to remove the initial blanks from the input line and place the next item of INPUT into ITEM, respectively. Then a number of IF statements are used to determine if the input line begins with a command. If this is true, then C_TYPE is set to the command's corresponding code number. If the first item on the input line is not a command, however, C_TYPE is assigned the value one. Procedure SCANNER then returns to the FORMAT procedure.

On the other hand, if the CURSOR is less than or equal to the length of INPUT, then the function BREAK is used to place the next item of the line into ITEM. C_TYPE is set to one, and SCANNER returns to the procedure FORMAT.

After the SCANNER has isolated the next item and determined its type, a CASE statement is used to handle the different types of items. If C_TYPE has the value one (i.e., a word of text), then a check is made to see if the word fits on the current line. If this test is true, the word is added to the WORDS vector and NO_WORDS and LINE_LENGTH are updated appropriately; otherwise, either the procedure PRINTJ or PRINTU is used to print the line, depending upon the value of JUSTIFY. If C_TYPE has the value two (i.e., the justify command) or three (i.e., the unjustify command), then the logical variable JUSTIFY is set to TRUE or FALSE, respectively. A C_TYPE value of four (i.e., begin a new paragraph) causes the current line to be printed without justification, and a call to SCANNER to input the next line of text. If the next input item is not a word, then the message "ERROR IN INPUT" is printed; otherwise, NO_WORDS is set to one, five blanks are concatenated to the beginning of the item which is assigned to WORDS(1), and the LINE_LENGTH is set to the length of WORDS(1). If C_TYPE is equal to five (i.e., center the following item), then the previous line is printed using the PRINTU procedure. The item is then centered on the following line. A C_TYPE value of six indicating blank lines, causes the current line to be printed unjustified. The number of lines given by the variable ITEM are then skipped. Finally, a C_TYPE value of seven indicates the end of the text, and the FORMAT procedure ends. Execution of the program then terminates.

EXERCISES FOR CHAPTER 9

1. Modify the program SCAN given in Sec. 9-3.1 so that it can handle a sample language which contains real numbers. A real number is defined to be a sequence of digits (possibly empty) followed by a period (.) followed by a (nonempty) sequence of digits. Test your program on the values:

         3.456
         45.9
         .99999
         1.2

2. Alter the program KWIC given in Sec. 9-3.2 so that it prints only the titles containing keywords which appear as data following the document titles. You may assume that the keywords given as data are in alphabetic order.

3. A company is computerizing its payroll and accounting procedures. The employee file for the company is to contain the following information:

    1. Employee's social insurance number (SIN) — a nine-digit field.
    2. Employee's name (NAME) — a 25-character field.
    3. Employee's sex (SEX) — a one-character field coded as 'M' for male and 'F' for female.
    4. Employee's type of work (TYPE) — a one-character field with 'A' denoting agent, 'D' denoting driver, 'H' denoting driver's helper, and 'P' denoting payroll.
    5. Employee's wage (WAGE) — a one-digit field where 1 denotes $4.00/hour, 2 denotes $4.80/hour, 3 denotes $6.00/hour, and 4 denotes $7.00/hour.
    6. Employee's location (LOCATION) — a one-character field where 'B' denotes Banff, 'J' denotes Jasper, and 'L' denotes Lake Louise.

    The following list of employee records is to be used.

Soc. In. No.	Name	Sex	Type	Wage	Location
693121053	LEW ARCHER	M	D	2	J
686725001	NANCY DREW	F	D	2	B
591146235	ARCHIE GOODWIN	M	H	1	B
661301964	PHILIP MARLOWE	M	A	3	J
529270792	JANE MARPLE	F	P	2	B
637263675	TRAVIS MCGEE	M	P	3	J

    Write a PASCAL procedure (similar to the procedure BUILD) to build a master file containing 13 bit strings, representing the sex, type of work, wage category, and location of the employees.

4. Write a PASCAL program that will use the logical arrays built by the program in exercise 3 to print a list of employees for the following categories: all employees earning $6.00 per hour, all drivers in Lake Louise, and all female employees in Jasper.

CHAPTER

10

LINEAR
DATA
STRUCTURES

Our programming discussion of data structures thus far has been concerned with the programming aspects of simple structures such as numbers, strings, vectors, and arrays. In this chapter we discuss the programming aspects of linear lists. These programming details fall into two categories which deal with the sequential-allocation and linked-allocation methods of storage for linear lists.

The chapter contains a basic discussion of an address. Also present is a description of the PASCAL notation of a structure and an array of structures. A structure is important because it can be used to represent the structural relationship of the constituent parts of an element in a linear list. Programming details of stacks and queues are given. These programming details are exemplified in several applications such as recursion, the translation of expressions to Polish, simulation, and hash-table methods.

10-1 POINTERS IN PASCAL

A *pointer* is an address or reference to a data structure or one of its elements. A pointer is sometimes called a *link*. In PASCAL, a pointer is a programmer-defined data type. The following TYPE declaration statement declares POINTER to be a new data type which allows variables of type POINTER to point to the data type t. P is a variable which is defined to be of type POINTER.

```
TYPE POINTER = @t;
VAR P: POINTER;
```

In this example, t may be either a PASCAL data type or another user-defined data type. P may contain the address to a memory location of type t. Some compilers require that the data type which is to be pointed to be preceded by an upward arrow (↑) rather than @.

Since the PASCAL programmer does not know the precise location in memory where data structures are stored, he or she cannot assign a constant value to a pointer variable as can be done, for example, for a numeric or string variable. Although the programmer can control *when* a pointer variable receives a value (i.e., an address), it is the compiler that controls *what* specific value is assigned to that variable. Such programmer control is discussed throughout this chapter and, in particular, in Sec. 10-8.

Finally, since the actual value received by a pointer variable is under compiler control, PASCAL does not allow the reading and writing of addresses for pointer variables.

10-2 STRUCTURES

Thus far we have encountered PASCAL data types such as strings, integers, real numbers, and arrays. We now introduce nonhomogeneous data aggregates called *structures* or *records*. We first introduce the notion of a structure through the use of a simple example — a complex number.

Structures are programmer-defined data types. For example, the declaration statement

```
TYPE COMPLEX = RECORD
        R,
        I: REAL
        END;
VAR Z: COMPLEX;
```

creates a new data type COMPLEX, consisting of two fields R and I, each of which can store REAL values. The variable Z is defined to be a structure of type COMPLEX and is made up of two fields. Thus, Z can be interpreted as a complex number with the variables R and I representing the real and imaginary parts of a complex number, respectively.

Suppose that we declare two additional complex number structures called X and Y using the statement

```
X, Y: COMPLEX
```

Now assume that we want to refer to the real number part in X. How can this be accomplished? If we simply refer to R, there is an ambiguity since R is a variable name associated with the three variables X, Y, and Z. In order to make the desired reference unambiguous or unique, the *qualified* name X.R specifies that the field associated with X is being selected. The period separates the qualifier (X) from the variable being qualified (R). This name-qualification approach avoids the necessity of having to create variable names for essentially the same class of items, each item of which may be associated with a different but similar hierarchical structure. Note that even if no ambiguity may occur, the qualifier must still be given. For example, for the complex number $-1.5 + 2.3i$, where $i = \sqrt{-1}$, the following sequence of assignment statements.

```
Z.R := -1.5;
Z.I := 2.3
```

assigns the complex number $-1.5 + 2.3i$ to the structure Z.

It is an interesting exercise to formulate a procedure for simulating the subtraction of two complex numbers. Let us assume that this procedure is to have three structure variables, as previously described, called A, B, and C. The following procedure simulates the desired subtraction:

```
PROCEDURE CSUB (VAR A, B, C: COMPLEX);
      (*THIS PROCEDURE SUBTRACTS THE COMPLEX NUMBERS
      A AND B, WHICH ARE STORED IN STRUCTURES
      AND RETURNS THE DIFFERENCE THROUGH THE PARAMETER C.*)
      BEGIN
      C.R := A.R - B.R;
      C.I := A.I - B.I
END;
```

The mainline statement

```
      CSUB (X, Y, Z)
```

invokes the procedure and the desired result is placed in the real and imaginary parts of the structure Z. Similar procedures can be written to simulate other complex arithmetic operations.

The structures just described each have two component variables which are of the same type. This is not always the case. As an example, the following statements create a simplified structure for an employee.

```
TYPE ADDRESS_TYPE = RECORD
      STREET,
      CITY: STRING(20);
      PROVINCE: STRING(15)
      END;
DEDUC_TYPE = RECORD
      NO_OF_DED: INTEGER;
      DEDUCTION_NAME: ARRAY(1..5) OF STRING(10);
      AMOUNT: ARRAY(1..5) OF INTEGER
      END;
```

```
EMPLOYEE_TYPE = RECORD
      NAME: RECORD
            FIRST: STRING(10);
            M_I: CHAR;
            LAST: STRING(19)
            END;
      ADDRESS: ADDRESS_TYPE;
      DEDUCTIONS: DEDUC_TYPE
      END;
VAR EMPLOYEE: EMPLOYEE_TYPE;
```

The names of the structures or record data types are EMPLOYEE_TYPE, ADDRESS_TYPE, and DEDUC_TYPE. Within EMPLOYEE_TYPE, the fields ADDRESS and DEDUCTIONS are defined to be of types ADDRESS_TYPE and DEDUC_TYPE, respectively, which are both structures. The NAME field is also defined to be a structure but the declaration for this structure is given immediately following the identifier name. This example illustrates two different methods of nesting structures or records within other records.

The variable EMPLOYEE references the fields given by the major structure EMPLOYEE_TYPE. EMPLOYEE.NAME refers to the part of the structure dealing with the employee's name and is called a *minor structure*. EMPLOYEE.NAME.LAST. EMPLOYEE.NAME.M_I, and EMPLOYEE.NAME.LAST refer to first name, middle initial, and last name of an employee, respectively, and are called *elementary items*. Elementary items cannot be further subdivided. Similarly, EMPLOYEE.ADDRESS is a minor structure which refers to the employee's address. Finally, EMPLOYEE.DEDUCTIONS refers to a minor structure consisting of three elementary items (NO_OF_DED, DEDUCTION_NAME, and AMOUNT) which describes an employee's deductions. Note that two parts of the DEDUCTIONS structure are arrays. The first array (DEDUCTION_NAME) is a character array; while the second (AMOUNT) is a numeric array. Observe that unlike an array, a structure does not require all of its constituent parts to be of the same type. The qualified name of the deduction array is

EMPLOYEE.DEDUCTIONS.DEDUCTION_NAME

To refer to the Ith deduction of this array, we use

EMPLOYEE.DEDUCTIONS.DEDUCTION_NAME(I).

Note that the hierarchy of the items shown in the previous example can be viewed as having different levels. At the highest level is the major structure name. At an intermediate level are *substructures* or minor structures. Each substructure name at a deeper level is nested within another substructure.

The notion of a structure is easily extended to arrays of structures. This is done in the next section.

Exercises for Sec. 10-2

1. A western farm currently produces several feed grains. In particular, wheat, barley, oats, rape seed, and flax are produced. The production level (in

bushels) and the price per bushel (in dollars and cents) received during the year are recorded. Use a structure to describe the data.

2. A university book store maintains a list of up to twenty requests for any book which is currently out of stock. The information kept for such a book consists of the book title (80 characters), book price (in dollars and cents), and the requests for the book. Each request consists of a person's name (40 characters) and address (100 characters). Use a structure to describe a book with its associated information.

3. Use a PASCAL structure to represent each of the following documents:

   a)   Airline ticket
   b)   Blue Cross or Medicare card
   c)   Gasoline credit card
   d)   Driver's license
   e)   Student identification card

   Make realistic assumptions about the contents of each document.

4. Given the following program segment

```
TYPE STRUC = RECORD
        B: RECORD
            C,
            D: INTEGER
        END;
        E: RECORD
            F: RECORD
                G, C: REAL
            END
        END
        H: RECORD
            I, J: REAL
        END
    END;
VAR A: STRUC;
BEGIN
    READ (A.B.C, A.B.D, A.E.F.G, A.E.F.C, A.H.I, A.H.J)
```

and the data

105   63   20.25   1800.5   −76   38

Obtain:

   a)   The value of B.C.
   b)   The sum of E and H.
   c)   The element that contains 1800.5.
   d)   The sum of B.C and F.C.

5.   A liquor store has the following kinds of alcoholic beverages on hand:

> 60 brands of wine of which:
> > 10 brands are champagne
> > 5 brands are sherry
> > 20 brands are red
> > 10 brands are white
> > 5 brands are sparkling
>
> 15 brands of whiskey of which:
> > 6 brands are rye
> > 6 brands are scotch
> > 3 brands are bourbon
>
> 10 brands of rum
> 5 brands of cognac
> 7 brands of gin
> 5 brands of vodka

Design a structure to store this information.

10-3 ARRAYS OF STRUCTURES

The notion of an array was introduced in Chap. 4. Its use has been illustrated widely throughout the book. In PASCAL, arrays are stored in row-major order. For example, a two-dimensional array is stored row by row. A sometimes undesirable property of an array is that all of its elements must be of the same data type attribute. As mentioned in the previous section, the parts of a structure can be non-homogeneous, i.e., they can be of different data types. In this section we extend the notion of a structure to include arrays of structures.

An *array of structures* is simply an array whose elements are structures. These elements have identical names, levels, and subparts. For example, if a structure MONTH_SALES were used to represent the sales performance of a salesperson for each month of the year, it might be declared as follows:

```
VAR MONTH_SALES: ARRAY(1..12) OF RECORD
        SALESPERSON: RECORD
             NAME: STRING(30);
             REGION: STRING(5)
             END;
        SALES_DETAIL: RECORD
             QUOTA,
             SALES,
             COMMISSION: INTEGER
             END
        END
```

Thus, we can refer to the sales data for the month of May by specifying MONTH_SALES(5). Parts of the May sales are referred to by MONTH_SALES(5).SALESPERSON and MONTH_SALES(5).SALES_DETAIL. MONTH_SALES(2).SALES_DETAIL.SALES, which refers to the sales for the month of February, is called a *subscripted qualified name*.

As an application of an array of structures, let us consider a simplified system for gathering and reporting student grades. Let us assume that the data comprise two parts. The first part contains the number of all students enrolled in courses followed by the details (such as student name, student number, and address) for each student in student number order. The second part of the data specifies the number of courses whose examination results are being reported, followed by the examination results for each course. The results of each course contain the course name and the course enrollment. A list of student descriptions (with grades) follows its course description. For example, the data which follow describe a total of 100 students enrolled in three courses:

100 (number of students)
'LYLE OPSETH' 1 '120 2ND AVE' 'MELFORT' 'SASK' 'S0E1A0'

                        .

                        .   student details in student number order

                        .

'HOWARD HAMILTON' 100 '17 MAZE AVE' 'SASKATOON' 'SASK' 'S5J1B2'
3 (number of courses)
'CMPT 180A' 60   (first course)
1 'LYLE OPSETH' 91

                        .

                        .

                        .

72 'JACK COOPER' 73
'CMPT 181B' 40   (second course)
3 'MARY SMITH' 62

                        .

                        .

90 'JOE BLACK' 55
'CMPT 212A' 25   (third course)
17 'JIM BROWN' 25

                        .

                        .

75 'JANE FORD' 76

The following declaration statement defines an array of structures for representing students and course data:

```
VAR STUDENT: ARRAY(1..100) OF RECORD
        NAME: STRING(20);
        NUMBER: INTEGER;
        ADDRESS: RECORD
            STREET: STRING(20);
            CITY: STRING(15);
            PROVINCE: STRING(15);
            POSTAL_CODE: STRING(16)
            END;
        TRANSCRIPT: RECORD
```

```
            NO_OF_COURSES: INTEGER;
            COURSE_NAME: ARRAY(1..5) OF STRING(10);
            GRADE: ARRAY(1..5) OF INTEGER
            END
      END;
```

Observe that the number of elements in the array of structures is specified by the number of students taking courses. Also, the transcript associated with each student consists of the number of courses he or she has taken (NO_OF_COURSES) and the course descriptions. Each course description contains a course name and a grade for that course. We assume that each student cannot take more than five courses. The vectors COURSE_NAME and GRADE represent the course names and the associated grades, respectively.

A general algorithm for constructing the array of structures from the input data given in the form described earlier follows:

1. Input number of students
2. Repeat for each student
        input student's name, number, and address
        initialize transcript portion of the student's record
3. Input number of courses
4. Repeat thru step 6 for each course
5. Input course title and class size
6. Repeat for each student in this class
        input student in this class
        update transcript portion of student's record
7. Output student file

For convenience, we assume that the student numbers are sequentially ordered from 1 to NO_OF_STUDENTS. In this way a particular student number can be used to access directly that student's record in the array of structures.

Figure 10-1 is a PASCAL program which performs the required task. The list of variables used is as follows:

NO_OF_STUDENTS	Number of students
STUDENT	Array of structures
COURSES	Number of courses being reported
COURSE_TITLE	Title or name of course
CLASS_SIZE	Number of students in a class
STUDENT_NO	Student number of student in a particular course
STUDENT_NAME	Student name of student in a particular course
TEMP	Stores number of courses a student is taking
I	Index to access a particular student
J	Index to access a particular course

The data on enrolled students are read and placed into the array of structures in lines 42 to 45. Then the grades of the students are initialized to zero and the course titles to blanks. Lines 55 and 56 control reading the courses offered.

```
0   0000   00001   PROGRAM GRADE (INPUT, OUTPUT);
0   0000   00002   (* THIS PROGRAM INPUTS A SERIES OF STUDENTS AND
0   0000   00003      THE COURSE LISTS FOR THE STUDENTS, STORING THE STUDENTS
0   0000   00004      STATISTICS IN AN ARRAY OF STRUCTURES. *)
0   0000   00005
0   0000   00006   CONST ARRAY_SIZE = 10;
0   0038   00007
0   0038   00008   TYPE STUDENT_DATA = RECORD   (* STRUCTURE FOR STUDENTS *)
0   0038   00009           NAME: STRING(20);
0   0038   00010           NUMBER: INTEGER;
0   0038   00011           ADDRESS: RECORD
0   0038   00012              STREET: STRING(20);
0   0038   00013              CITY: STRING(15);
0   0038   00014              PROVINCE: STRING(15);
0   0038   00015              POSTAL_CODE: STRING(6);
0   0038   00016              END;
0   0038   00017           TRANSCRIPT: RECORD
0   0038   00018              NO_OF_COURSES: INTEGER;
0   0038   00019              COURSE_NAME: ARRAY (1..5) OF STRING(10);
0   0038   00020              GRADE: ARRAY (1..5) OF INTEGER
0   0038   00021              END
0   0038   00022           END;
0   0038   00023
0   0038   00024   VAR NO_OF_STUDENTS,           (* NUMBER OF STUDENTS *)
0   0038   00025       CLASS_SIZE,               (* SIZE OF CLASS *)
0   0038   00026       STUDENT_NO,               (* STUDENT NUMBER *)
0   0038   00027       MARK,                     (* STUDENT GRADE *)
0   0038   00028       COURSES,                  (* NUMBER OF COURSES *)
0   0038   00029       TEMP,                     (* NUMBER OF COURSES STUDENT IS TAKING *)
0   0038   00030       I, J: INTEGER;            (* COUNTED LOOP VARIABLES *)
0   0038   00031       COURSE_TITLE: STRING(10); (* TITLE OF COURSE *)
0   0038   00032       STUDENT_NAME: STRING(20); (* STUDENT NAME *)
0   0038   00033       STUDENT: ARRAY (1..ARRAY_SIZE) OF STUDENT_DATA;
0   0038   00034                             (* ARRAY OF STRUCTURES FOR THE STUDENTS *)
0   0038   00035
0   0038   00036   BEGIN
0   0038   00037
0   0038   00038       (* INPUT ENROLLED STUDENTS *)
0   0038   00039       READ (NO_OF_STUDENTS);
0   004A   00040       FOR I := 1 TO NO_OF_STUDENTS DO
0   006E   00041       BEGIN
0   006E   00042           READ (STUDENT(I).NAME, STUDENT(I).NUMBER,
0   00D4   00043              STUDENT(I).ADDRESS.STREET, STUDENT(I).ADDRESS.CITY,
0   013C   00044              STUDENT(I).ADDRESS.PROVINCE, STUDENT(I).ADDRESS.
0   0196   00045              POSTAL_CODE);
0   01A4   00046           STUDENT(I).TRANSCRIPT.NO_OF_COURSES := 0;
0   01D0   00047           FOR J := 1 TO 5 DO
0   01F4   00048           BEGIN
0   01F4   00049              STUDENT(I).TRANSCRIPT.COURSE_NAME(J) := ' ';
0   023E   00050              STUDENT(I).TRANSCIPT.GRADE(J) := 0
0   0282   00051           END
0   0288   00052       END;
0   0290   00053
0   0290   00054       (* PROCESS COURSES OFFERED *)
0   0290   00055       READ (COURSES);
0   02A2   00056       FOR I := 1 TO COURSES DO
0   02C6   00057       BEGIN
0   02C6   00058           READ (COURSE_TITLE, CLASS_SIZE);
0   02EA   00059           FOR J := 1 TO CLASS_SIZE DO
0   030E   00060           BEGIN
0   030E   00061              READ (STUDENT_NO, STUDENT_NAME, MARK);
0   0344   00062              STUDENT(STUDENT_NO).TRANSCRIPT.NO_OF_COURSES :=
0   036A   00063                 STUDENT(STUDENT_NO).TRANSCRIPT.NO_OF_COURSES + 1;
0   039C   00064              TEMP := STUDENT(STUDENT_NO).TRANSCRIPT.NO_OF_COURSES;
0   03CA   00065              STUDENT(STUDENT_NO).TRANSCRIPT.COURSE_NAME(TEMP) :=
0   040E   00066                 COURSE_TITLE;
0   0414   00067              STUDENT(STUDENT_NO).TRANSCRIPT.GRADE(TEMP) := MARK
0   0458   00068           END
0   0460   00069       END;
0   0468   00070
0   0468   00071       (* OUTPUT ARRAY OF STRUCTURES *)
0   0468   00072       FOR I := 1 TO NO_OF_STUDENTS DO
0   048C   00073       BEGIN
0   048C   00074           WRITELN ('-', 'NAME: ', STUDENT(I).NAME, 'STUDENT NUMBER: '
0   04F4   00075              STUDENT(I).NUMBER : 5);
0   0528   00076           WRITELN (' ', 'ADDRESS: ', STUDENT(I).ADDRESS.STREET);
```

Fig. 10-1   A program to store the courses students are taking

```
0  0580  00077        WRITELN (' ' : 10, STUDENT(I).ADDRESS.CITY, ', ',
0  05D8  00078              STUDENT(I).ADDRESS.PROVINCE, ' ',
0  061E  00079              STUDENT(I).ADDRESS.POSTAL_CODE);
0  0652  00080        WRITELN ('0', ' ' : 9, 'COURSE NAME', ' ' : 4, 'GRADE');
0  06AC  00081        FOR J := 1 TO STUDENT(I).TRANSCRIPT.NO_OF_COURSES DO
0  06F6  00082              WRITELN (' ' : 10, STUDENT(I).TRANSCRIPT. COURSE_NAME(J),
0  075C  00083                  ' ' : 6, STUDENT(I).TRANSCRIPT.GRADE(J) : 3)
0  07C4  00084        END
0  07C8  00085  END.
```

```
-------------------------------------
| COMPILE TIME:   0.249 SECOND(S) |
|     NO WARNING(S) DETECTED      |
|       NO ERROR(S) DETECTED      |
-------------------------------------
--EXECUTION-->
```

```
NAME: LYLE OPSETH        STUDENT NUMBER:     1
ADDRESS: 120 2ND AVE
         MELFORT         , SASK         S0E1A0

         COURSE NAME   GRADE
         CMPT 180A       91
         CMPT 212A       79
         CMPT 228B       87
         CMPT 313B       69


NAME: HOWARD HAMILTON    STUDENT NUMBER:     2
ADDRESS: 17 MAZE AVE
         SASKATOON       , SASK         M5J1B2

         COURSE NAME   GRADE
         CMPT 180A       85
         CMPT 181B       79
         CMPT 212A       93
         CMPT 220B       77
         CMPT 313B       98


NAME: MARY SMITH         STUDENT NUMBER:     3
ADDRESS: 2 MADISON CRES
         PRINCE ALBERT   , SASK         M3K4P7

         COURSE NAME   GRADE
         CMPT 181B       54
         CMPT 220B       66
         CMPT 377A       68


NAME: JOE BLACK          STUDENT NUMBER:     4
ADDRESS: 43 ARCADIA DRIVE
         SASKATOON       , SASK         S7K2P3

         COURSE NAME   GRADE
         CMPT 181B       49


NAME: JANE FORD          STUDENT NUMBER:     5
ADDRESS: 1137 117TH STREET
         TORONTO         , ONTARIO      P3J7F6

         COURSE NAME   GRADE
         CMPT 180A       73
         CMPT 181B       77
         CMPT 220B       83
```

Fig. 10-1 A program to store the courses students are taking (cont'd.)

Exercises for Sec. 10-3

1. The following declaration statement defines an array of structures:

```
TYPE    SALES_HISTORY = RECORD
            QUOTA,
            SALES,
            COMMISSION: INTEGER
            END;
        SALES = ARRAY(1..200) OF RECORD
          SALESPERSON: RECORD
              NAME,
              ADDRESS: STRING(30);
              CITY: STRING(10);
              DISTRICT: INTEGER
              END;
          SALES_RECORD: RECORD
              YEAR_TO_DATE: SALES_HISTORY;
              CURRENT_MONTH: SALES_HISTORY
              END
          END;
```

a) How many elementary items does this structure have?

b) Give a WRITE statement to output the information associated with the 50th salesperson.

c) Assuming a commission rate of 10%, give a statement to compute and store each salesperson's commission for the current month.

2. The Honest John Motor Corporation has six dealerships of motor vehicle sales. Each dealership markets cars and trucks. The cars are classified into three categories as follows:

Small	Mid-size	Full
Futura	Fairmont	Lincoln
Zephyr	Mustang	Thunderbird
Bobcat	Granada	LTD1
Fiesta		LTD2

The trucks are broken down into the two following classes:

Pick-up	Freight
Courier	F600
F100	F700
F150	F800
F250	
F350	

Each time a vehicle is sold, a card containing the following information is filed:

type
model name

month purchased (1 to 12)
dealership (1 to 6)
purchase price (to the nearest dollar)

Construct a PASCAL program that outputs the following:

a)   The total number of cars sold and total sales in each month.
b)   The total number of cars sold and total sales in each dealership in
      each month.
c)   The most popular pick-up sold overall.
d)   The region with the most cars and trucks sold in a given month.
e)   The most popular small car sold overall.

10-4 STACKS

The notion of a stack is introduced in Sec. 10-4 of the main text. In
particular, a vector is used to simulate a stack structure. Using this representation,
algorithms for pushing an element onto a stack and popping an element from a
stack are developed. Note that these algorithms require a special variable to keep
track of the topmost element in the stack. As mentioned in the main text, the
update of the top element index of a stack is a burden to the programmer. This
burden can be avoided if the programming language being used allows a "pure"
representation of a stack. Unfortunately, PASCAL does not have controlled
storage and the stack operations must be explicity handled by the programmer.
Arrays of structures may be used to simulate stacks if more than one field is
required to represent the stack. We now give a few PASCAL program segments for
handling some stack operations. In many cases, the approach used is often
application-dependent.

To push an element onto a stack, say, S, involves the following PASCAL
statements

```
(* OVERFLOW? *)
IF TOP >= STACK_SIZE
THEN OVERFLOW;
(* INCREMENT TOP *)
TOP := TOP + 1;
(* INSERT NEW ELEMENT *)
S(TOP) := X
```

Note that STACK_SIZE is the size of the vector which represents the stack, and X is
the element to be pushed onto the stack. To pop an element from the stack S
involves the program segment

```
(* UNDERFLOW? *)
IF TOP <= 0
THEN UNDERFLOW;
(* UNSTACK ELEMENT *)
VALUE := S(TOP);
(* DECREMENT TOP *)
TOP := TOP - 1
```

After execution of this program segment, VALUE contains the value of the element which was deleted from the stack.

Note that the variable TOP denotes the top element of a stack and it has the value zero if the stack is empty. Also, the procedures OVERFLOW and UNDERFLOW are called if there is an overflow or underflow in the stack. Their precise function depends upon the particular application.

In the next section we will examine some applications of stacks.

10-5   APPLICATIONS OF STACKS

This section describes the programming aspects associated with the three application areas discussed in Sec. 10-5 of the main text. The first application deals with recursion. Several programming examples of recursion are given. The second application of stacks involves the compilation of arithmetic expressions to machine code. The last application pertains to the use of a stack in performing a sort.

10-5.1   Recursion

Thus far in this book we have encountered instances of a procedure calling another procedure. We now consider the case of a recursive procedure; that is, a procedure which calls itself.

Consider the following recursive formulation of the factorial function:

$$n! = \begin{cases} 1 & \text{if } n = 0 \\ n\,(n-1) & \text{if } n > 0 \end{cases}$$

A recursive PASCAL function for this function and an associated main test procedure are given in Fig. 10-2.

The following recursive definition specifies the nth Fibonacci number:

$$FIB(n) = \begin{cases} 0 & \text{if } n = 1 \\ 1 & \text{if } n = 2 \\ FIB(n-1) + FIB(n-2) & \text{if } n > 2 \end{cases}$$

Figure 10-3 contains the PASCAL recursive function which performs the required evaluation.

As a final example, Fig. 10-4 contains a PASCAL recursive function which performs a binary search for the element X in the vector K. The remaining parameters, TOP and BOTTOM, define the current search interval.

As was mentioned in Chap. 6, forward declarations are required if a procedure is called before it is declared. Indirect recursion requires forward declarations because one procedure must be called before it is declared as is illustrated in the following example.

```
PROGRAM A (INPUT, OUTPUT);
        PROCEDURE C; FORWARD;
        PROCEDURE B;
                .
                .
                .
```

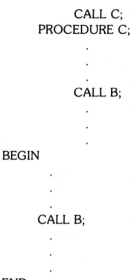

              CALL C;
        PROCEDURE C;
              .
              .
              .
          CALL B;
              .
              .
              .

    BEGIN
            .
            .
            .
        CALL B;
            .
            .
            .

    END.

      Notice that procedure B calls procedure C before the procedure is given. For this reason, a forward reference to procedure C is given before procedure B is declared.

Exercises for Sec. 10-5.1

1. A well-known algorithm for finding the greatest common divisor of two integers is *Euclid's algorithm*. The greatest common divisor function is defined by the following:

$$GCD(M, N) = \begin{cases} GCD(N, M), & \text{if } N > M \\ M, & \text{if } N = 0 \\ GCD(N, M \text{ MOD } N), & \text{if } N > 0 \end{cases}$$

    where M MOD N is M modulo N – the remainder on dividing M by N. Construct a recursive function for this problem and obtain GCD(20, 6).

2. The usual method used in evaluating a polynomial of the form

    $$p_n(x) = a_0 x^n + a_1 x^{n-1} + a_2 x^{n-2} + \cdots + a_{n-1} x + a_n$$

    is by using the technique known as *nesting* or *Horner's rule*. This is an iterative method which is described as follows:

    $$b_0 = a_0, \quad b_{i+1} = x \cdot b_i + a_{i+1} \; ; \; i = 0, 1, \ldots, n-1$$

    from which one can obtain

    $$b_n = p_n(x)$$

```
0  0000   00001  PROGRAM RUNFACT (INPUT, OUTPUT);
0  0000   00002  (* THIS PROGRAM TESTS THE RECURSIVE FACTORIAL FUCTION.*)
0  0000   00003
0  0000   00004  VAR I: INTEGER;
0  0038   00005      FUNCTION FACT (N: INTEGER): INTEGER;
1  0000   00006      (* THIS FUNCTION RETURNS THE FACTORIAL OF N *)
1  0000   00007
1  0000   00008      VAR M: INTEGER;
1  004E   00009
1  004E   00010      BEGIN
1  004E   00011          IF N = 0
1  004E   00012          THEN FACT := 1
1  005A   00013          ELSE FACT := N * FACT (N - 1);
1  0098   00014      END;
0  0038   00015
0  0038   00016  BEGIN
0  0038   00017      FOR I := 1 TO 3 DO
0  005C   00018          WRITELN ('0', 'FACTORIAL (', I * 3 - 1 : 1,
0  009E   00019              ') IS ', FACT (I * 3 - 1) : 5)
0  00F2   00020  END.
-------------------------------------
| COMPILE TIME:    0.058 SECOND(S) |
|     NO WARNING(S) DETECTED        |
|     NO ERROR(S) DETECTED          |
-------------------------------------
--EXECUTION-->

FACTORIAL (2) IS      2

FACTORIAL (5) IS    120

FACTORIAL (8) IS 40320
```

Fig. 10-2   Recursive formulation of the factorial function

```
0  0000   00001  PROGRAM RUNFIB (INPUT, OUTPUT);
0  0000   00002  (* TEST THE RECURSIVE FIBONACCI NUMBER FUNTION *)
0  0000   00003
0  0000   00004  VAR I: INTEGER;
0  0038   00005
0  0038   00006      FUNCTION FIB (N: INTEGER): INTEGER;
1  0000   00007      (* RETURN THE FIBONACCI NUMBER OF N *)
1  0000   00008
1  0000   00009      BEGIN
1  004E   00010          IF N = 1
1  004E   00011          THEN FIB := 0
1  005A   00012          ELSE IF N = 2
1  0064   00013              THEN FIB := 1
1  0070   00014              ELSE FIB := FIB (N - 1) + FIB (N - 2)
1  00B2   00015      END;
0  0038   00016
0  0038   00017  BEGIN
0  0038   00018      FOR I := 0 TO 2 DO
0  005C   00019          WRITELN ('0', 'FIBONACCI (', I * 5 + 2 : 2,
0  009E   00020              ') IS', FIB (I * 5 + 2) : 4)
0  00F2   00021  END.
-------------------------------------
| COMPILE TIME:    0.064 SECOND(S) |
|     NO WARNING(S) DETECTED        |
|     NO ERROR(S) DETECTED          |
-------------------------------------
--EXECUTION-->

FIBONACCI ( 2) IS    1

FIBONACCI ( 7) IS    8

FIBONACCI (12) IS   89
```

Fig. 10-3   Recursive function for computing Fibonacci numbers

```
0  0000   00001   PROGRAM RUN_BSR (INPUT, OUTPUT);
0  0000   00002   (* THIS PROGRAM TESTS THE RECURSIVE BINARY SEARCH PROCEDURE *)
0  0000   00003
0  0000   00004   CONST VECTOR_SIZE = 10;
0  0038   00005   TYPE VECTOR = ARRAY (1..VECTOR_SIZE) OF REAL;
0  0038   00006   VAR LIST: VECTOR;              (* VECTOR TO BE SEARCHED *)
0  0038   00007       VALUE: REAL;               (* VALUE TO SEARCH FOR *)
0  0038   00008       NUM,                       (* POSITION OF ELEMENT SEARCHED FOR *)
0  0038   00009       I: INTEGER;                (* COUNTED LOOP VARIABLE *)
0  0038   00010       FUNCTION B_S_R (K: VECTOR; X: REAL; TOP, BOTTOM: INTEGER): INTEGER;
1  0000   00011       (* THIS RECURSIVE FUNCTION RETURNS THE POSTION OF THE
1  0000   00012          ELEMENT X IN THE SORTED VECTOR X. *)
1  0000   00013
1  0000   00014       VAR MIDDLE: INTEGER; (* MIDDLE OF SEARCH INTERVAL *)
1  0086   00015
1  0086   00016       BEGIN
1  0086   00017
1  0086   00018           (* CHECK IF UNSUCCESSFUL SEARCH *)
1  0086   00019           IF (TOP = BOTTOM) AND (K(TOP) <> X)
1  00C0   00020           THEN BEGIN
1  00C0   00021               WRITELN ('0', 'SEARCH IS UNSUCCESSFUL');
1  00E4   00022               B_S_R := 0
1  00E4   00023               END
1  00EA   00024           ELSE BEGIN
1  00EE   00025
1  00EE   00026               (* DETERMINE MIDDLE ELEMENT AND NEW TOP OR
1  00EE   00027                  BOTTOM OF SEARCH VECTOR *)
1  00EE   00028               MIDDLE := (TOP + BOTTOM) DIV 2;
1  0104   00029               IF K(MIDDLE) = X
1  012A   00030               THEN BEGIN
1  0132   00031                   WRITELN ('0', 'SEARCH IS SUCCESSFUL');
1  0156   00032                   B_S_R := MIDDLE
1  0156   00033                   END
1  015E   00034               ELSE IF K(MIDDLE) < X
1  0188   00035                   THEN B_S_R := B_S_R (K, X, MIDDLE + 1, BOTTOM)
1  01BC   00036                   ELSE B_S_R := B_S_R (K, X, TOP, MIDDLE - 1)
1  01FE   00037               END
1  0210   00038       END;
0  0038   00039
0  0038   00040   BEGIN
0  0038   00041
0  0038   00042       (* INPUT VECTOR *)
0  0038   00043       WRITE (' ', 'VECTOR READ IN IS ');
0  005C   00044       FOR I := 1 TO 10 DO
0  0080   00045       BEGIN
0  0080   00046           READ (LIST(I));
0  00B2   00047           WRITE (' ' : 5, LIST(I) : 2 : 1)
0  00F8   00048       END;
0  00FC   00049
0  00FC   00050       (* TEST B_S_R ON SEVERAL INPUT ITEMS *)
0  00FC   00051       WRITELN;
0  010A   00052       WRITELN ('0');
0  011C   00053       FOR I := 1 TO 5 DO
0  0140   00054       BEGIN
0  0140   00055           READ (VALUE);
0  0152   00056           NUM := B_S_R (LIST, VALUE, 1, 10);
0  018E   00057           WRITELN (' ', 'POSITION OF ', VALUE : 2 : 1, ' IS ', NUM : 2)
0  01E8   00058       END
0  01E8   00059   END.
```

```
-----------------------------------
| COMPILE TIME:    0.181 SECOND(S) |
|    NO WARNING(S) DETECTED         |
|    NO ERROR(S) DETECTED           |
-----------------------------------
--EXECUTION-->
VECTOR READ IN IS    7.0    12.0    15.0    42.0    56.0    59.0    67.0    88.0    89.0    93.0

SEARCH IS SUCCESSFUL
POSITION OF 67.0 IS  7

SEARCH IS SUCCESSFUL
POSITION OF 59.0 IS  6

SEARCH IS SUCCESSFUL
POSITION OF 12.0 IS  2

SEARCH IS SUCCESSFUL
POSITION OF 7.0 IS  1

SEARCH IS UNSUCCESSFUL
POSITION OF 9.0 IS  0
```

Fig. 10-4   Recursive function for performing a binary search

An alternate solution to the problem is to write

$$p_n(x) = x \cdot p_{n-1}(x) + a_0$$

where

$$p_{n-1}(x) = a_0 x^{n-1} + a_1 x^{n-2} + \cdots + a_{n-2} x + a_{n-1}$$

which is the recursive formulation of the problem. Formulate a recursive function for this problem. Test this function with the data

$$n = 3, \ a_0 = 1, \ a_1 = 3, \ a_2 = 3, \ a_3 = 1, \text{ and } x = 3.$$

3. Consider the set of all valid, completely parenthesized, infix arithmetic expressions consisting of single-letter variable names, a digit, and the four operators +, −, *, and /. The following recursive definition specifies the set of valid expressions:

   1. Any single-letter variable (A – Z) or a digit is a valid infix expression.
   2. If α and β are valid infix expressions, then $(\alpha + \beta)$, $(\alpha - \beta)$, $(\alpha * \beta)$, and (α / β) are all valid infix expressions.
   3. The only valid infix expressions are those defined by steps 1 and 2.

   Formulate a recursive function that will input a string of symbols and output either VALID EXPRESSION for a valid infix expression, or INVALID EXPRESSION otherwise. Use the following strings as test data:

   '(((A*B)−C)+D)*/'
   '((A+B*C)*D)*/'
   '(((A*X)+B)*X)+C)*/'
   '(A−B)*C*/'

4. Write a recursive function to compute the square root of a number. Read in triples of numbers N, A, and E, where N is the number for which the square root is to be found, A is an approximation of the square root, and E is the allowable error in the result. Use as your function

$$ROOT(N,A,E) = \begin{cases} A, & \text{if } |A^2 - N| < E \\ ROOT\left(N, \dfrac{A^2 + N}{2A}, E\right), & \text{otherwise} \end{cases}$$

Use the following triples as test data:

2	1.0	.001
3	1.5	.001
8	2.5	.001
225	14.2	.001

5. An important theoretical function, known as *Ackerman's function*, is defined as

$$A(M, N) = \begin{cases} N + 1, & \text{if } M = 0 \\ A(M - 1, 1), & \text{if } N = 0 \\ A(M - 1, A(M, N - 1)), & \text{otherwise} \end{cases}$$

Obtain a recursive function for this problem. As test data, use the values $M = 2$ and $N = 2$.

6. Recursion can be used to generate all possible permutations of a set of symbols. For example, there are six permutations of the set of symbols A, B, and C; namely, ABC, ACB, BAC, BCA, CBA, and CAB. The set of permutations of N symbols is generated by taking each symbol in turn and prefixing it with all the permutations which result from the remaining $N - 1$ symbols. Formulate a recursive procedure for this problem.

7. Certain applications require a knowledge of the number of different partitions of a given integer N; that is, how many different ways N can be expressed as a sum of integer summands. For example, $N = 5$ yields the partitions

$$1 + 1 + 1 + 1 + 1, \ 5, \ 1 + 2 + 2, \ 3 + 1 + 1, \ 2 + 3, \ 1 + 4, \ \text{and } 1 + 1 + 1 + 2$$

If we denote by Q_{MN} the number of ways in which an integer M can be expressed as a sum, each summand of which no larger than N, then the number of partitions of N is given by Q_{NN}. The function Q_{MN} is defined recursively as

$$Q_{MN} = \begin{cases} 1, & \text{if } M = 1 \text{ and for all } N \\ 1, & \text{if } N = 1 \text{ and for all } M \\ Q_{MM}, & \text{if } M < N \\ 1 + Q_{M,M-1}, & \text{if } M = N \\ Q_{M,N-1} + Q_{M-N,N}, & \text{if } M > N \end{cases}$$

Formulate a recursive function for this problem and generate Q_{33} and Q_{55}.

10-5.2 Polish Expressions and Their Compilation

The problem of converting a partially-parenthesized infix expression to suffix Polish form and then converting this intermediate form to object code is discussed in Sec. 10-5.2 of the main text. Table 10-1 summarizes the input and stack precedence values associated with arithmetic expressions. The table also contains the rank value of each symbol. Note that, for convenience, the exponentiation operator (↑) is represented by the symbol @.

A general algorithm for the conversion of partially-parenthesized infix expressions to suffix Polish follows:

1. Place a left parenthesis onto the stack and initialize the rank count of the expression to zero.

2. Obtain the leftmost symbol in the given infix expression and denote this symbol the current input symbol.
3. Repeat thru step 6 while the current symbol is not empty.
4. Repeat while the input precedence of the current input symbol is less than the stack precedence of the stack symbol
    pop and output the stack top symbol
    add the rank of this symbol to the rank count of the expression
    if the rank count is less than one
    then the infix expression is invalid and exit
5. If the current input symbol is a left parenthesis and the stack top symbol is a right parenthesis
    then pop the stack
    else push the current input symbol onto the stack
6. Set the new current input symbol to the next input symbol
7. If the stack is not empty or the rank count is not equal to one
    then the infix expression is invalid
    else the infix expression is valid
    exit

A program to perform this conversion process appears in Fig. 10-5. In addition to a main program segment, the program contains the procedure SUFFIX and the functions F, G, and R. The sample infix expressions used in this program are:

```
'(A+B*C)*(D+E@F@A))*/'
'A+B)*C*(D+E))*/'
'(A+B@C@D)*(E+FD))*/'
```

Note that each expression is padded on the right with a right parenthesis. The variables used in the main program are:

Variable	Type	Usage
INFIX	STRING(256)	Infix expression
POLISH	STRING(256)	Suffix Polish output string
NUM	INTEGER	Number of infix expressions to be converted
I	INTEGER	Counted loop variable

Variables used in the procedure SUFFIX are:

INFIX	STRING(256)	Infix expression
STACK	ARRAY(1..50) OF STRING(256)	Stack
TEMP	STRING(256)	Contains stack top symbol
POLISH	STRING(256)	Suffix Polish output string
CURRENT	STRING(256)	Current input symbol
RANK	INTEGER	Rank of infix expression

Variable used in the functions F, G, and R is:

TOKEN	STRING(256)	An expression symbol

Table 10-1   Input- and stack-precedence values for arithmetic expressions

| Symbol | Precedence | | Rank |
	Input Function(F)	Stack Function(G)	Function(R)
+ –	1	2	–1
* /	3	4	–1
@	6	5	–1
single-letter variables	7	8	1
(	9	0	–
)	0	–	–

The main program inputs the infix expressions, and in line 183 calls procedure SUFFIX to convert the expression to its suffix Polish form. In SUFFIX, a left parenthesis is placed on the stack in line 97. Then the output string Polish and the rank count are initialized. Lines 109 to 154 perform the desired translation of the given expression. Lines 119 to 131 add all stack symbols with a precedence value greater than the input symbol's value to POLISH. A rank of less than one implies an invalid expression. The current symbol is then pushed onto the stack if it is not a right parenthesis; otherwise, the left parenthesis is popped from the stack. Finally, lines 126 to 130 check the validity of the expression. The function F determines the input precedence value of the current symbol contained in TOKEN as given in Table 10-1. The function G returns the stack precedence value of TOKEN, while R determines the rank value of TOKEN.

We now turn to translating a suffix Polish expression to object code. For our purposes we assume that the object code desired is in the form of hypothetical assembly-language instructions. As a matter of convenience, we also assume that the object computer which will execute the object code produced by the translation process is a single-address single-accumulator machine whose memory is sequentially organized into words. Such a computer was described in Sec. 2-1 of the main text. In this subsection we assume a simple assembly-language representation for the machine language instructions introduced there. A summary of these assembly instructions is given in Table 10-2. Note that we have added two new instructions — multiplication (MUL) and division (DIV).

An informal algorithm for the evaluation of a suffix string is given in Sec. 10-5.2.1 of the main text. Let us consider a program for converting suffix expressions consisting of the four basic arithmetic operators and single-letter variables to assembly language. Finally, assume that the basic arithmetic operators generate the following code:

$$
\begin{array}{lll}
a + b \ (ab+) & \text{LOD} & a \\
& \text{ADD} & b \\
& \text{STO} & T_i \\
a - b \ (ab-) & \text{LOD} & a \\
& \text{SUB} & b \\
& \text{STO} & T_i \\
a * b \ (ab*) & \text{LOD} & a \\
& \text{MUL} & b \\
& \text{STO} & T_i \\
\end{array}
$$

```
0  0000   00001   PROGRAM CONVERT (INPUT, OUTPUT);
0  0000   00002
0  0000   00003   (* THIS PROGRAM INPUTS SEVERAL INFIX ECPRESSIONS AND CONVERTS
0  0000   00004      THESE EXPRESSIONS TO THEIR SUFFIX EQUIVALENT. *)
0  0000   00005
0  0000   00006   VAR INFIX,                      (* INFIX EXPRESSION TO BE CONVERTED    *)
0  0038   00007       POLISH,                     (* RESULTING POLISH EXPRESSION         *)
0  0038   00008       BLANKS,                     (* STRING OF BLANK CHARACTERS          *)
0  0038   00009       TEMP: STRING(256);          (* TEMPORARY CHARACTER STRING          *)
0  0038   00010       ALPHAB: STRING(256);        (* STRING OF ALPHABETIC CHARACTERS     *)
0  0038   00011       NUM,                        (* NUMBER OF INFIX EXPRESSIONS TO READ *)
0  0038   00012       I: INTEGER;                 (* COUNTED LOOP VARIABLE               *)
0  0038   00013       INVALID: BOOLEAN;           (* INVALID EXPRESSION FLAG             *)
0  0038   00014       FUNCTION LENGTH (VAR STR: STRING(256)): INTEGER; EXTERNAL;
0  0038   00015       PROCEDURE CONCAT (VAR S1, S2, RESULT: STRING(256)); EXTERNAL;
0  0038   00016       PROCEDURE SUB (VAR S: STRING(256); POS, NUM: INTEGER;
1  0000   00017           VAR RESULT: STRING(256)); EXTERNAL;
0  0038   00018
0  0038   00019       FUNCTION F (TOKEN: STRING(256)): INTEGER;
1  0000   00020       (* THIS FUNCTION RETURNS THE INPUT PROCEDURE VALUE FOR THE
1  0000   00021          CHARACTER GIVEN IN TOKEN. *)
1  0000   00022
1  0000   00023       VAR TOKEN_CHAR: CHAR;   (* TOKEN CHARACTER *)
1  004C   00024       FUNCTION INDEX (VAR S, PATTERN: STRING(256)): INTEGER; EXTERNAL;
1  004C   00025
1  004C   00026       BEGIN
1  004C   00027
1  004C   00028           WRITELN('TOKEN=', TOKEN);
1  0070   00029           WRITELN('ALPHAB=', ALPHAB);
1  0094   00030           (* RETURN PRECEDENCE VALUE *)
1  0094   00031           IF INDEX (ALPHAB, TOKEN) <> 0
1  00BA   00032           THEN F := 7
1  00C2   00033           ELSE BEGIN
1  00CE   00034               TOKEN_CHAR := TOKEN;
1  00D4   00035               CASE TOKEN_CHAR OF
1  00D4   00036                   '+', '-' : F := 1;
1  0100   00037                   '*', '/' : F := 3;
1  010C   00038                       '@' : F := 6;
1  0118   00039                       '(' : F := 9;
1  0124   00040                       ')' : F := 0
1  0124   00041           END
1  012E   00042           END
1  0192   00043       END;
0  0038   00044
0  0038   00045       FUNCTION G (TOKEN: STRING(256)): INTEGER;
1  0000   00046       (* THIS FUNCTION RETURNS THE STACK PRECEDENCE VALUE FOR THE
1  0000   00047          SYMBOL CONTAINED IN TOKEN. *)
1  0000   00048
1  0000   00049       VAR TOKEN_CHAR: CHAR;   (* TOKEN CHARACTER *)
1  004C   00050       FUNCTION INDEX (VAR S, PATTERN: STRING(256)): INTEGER; EXTERNAL;
1  004C   00051
1  004C   00052       BEGIN
1  004C   00053
1  004C   00054           (* RETURN STACK PRECEDENCE VALUE *)
1  004C   00055           IF INDEX (ALPHAB, TOKEN) <> 0
1  0072   00056           THEN G := 8
1  007A   00057           ELSE BEGIN
1  0086   00058               TOKEN_CHAR := TOKEN;
1  008C   00059               CASE TOKEN_CHAR OF
1  008C   00060                   '+', '-' : G := 2;
1  00B8   00061                   '*', '/' : G := 4;
1  00C4   00062                       '@' : G := 5;
1  00D0   00063                       '(' : G := 0
1  00D0   00064           END
1  00DA   00065           END
1  013E   00066       END;
0  0038   00067
0  0038   00068       FUNCTION R (TOKEN: STRING(256)): INTEGER;
1  0000   00069       (* THIS FUNCTION RETURNS THE RANK VALUE FOR THE SYMBOL
1  0000   00070          CONTAINED IN TOKEN. *)
1  0000   00071
1  0000   00072       FUNCTION INDEX (VAR S, PATTERN: STRING(256)): INTEGER; EXTERNAL;
1  004C   00073
1  004C   00074       BEGIN
1  004C   00075
1  004C   00076           (* RETURN RANK VALUE *)
1  004C   00077           IF INDEX (ALPHAB, TOKEN) <> 0
1  0072   00078           THEN R := 1
1  007A   00079           ELSE R := -1
1  0086   00080       END;
0  0038   00081
```

Fig. 10-5 PASCAL program to convert from infix to suffix Polish notation

```
0  0038  00082   PROCEDURE SUFFIX (INFIX: STRING(256); VAR POLISH: STRING(256));
1  0000  00083   (* GIVEN AN INPUT STRING (INFIX) CONTAINING AN INFIX
1  0000  00084       EXPRESSION WHICH HAS BEEN PADDED ON THE RIGHT WITH A RIGHT
1  0000  00085       PARENTHESIS, THIS PROCEDURE CONVERTS INFIX INTO SUFFIX
1  0000  00086       NOTATION AND PLACES THE RESULT IN THE STRING POLISH. *)
1  0000  00087
1  0000  00088   VAR STACK: ARRAY(1..20) OF STRING(256);  (* STACK *)
1  0066  00089       CURRENT: STRING(256); (* SYMBOL BEING EXAMINED *)
1  0066  00090       TOP,                  (* TOP OF STACK *)
1  0066  00091       RANK: INTEGER;        (* EXPRESSION RANK COUNT *)
1  0066  00092
1  0066  00093   BEGIN
1  0066  00094
1  0066  00095       (* INITIALIZE THE STACK *)
1  0066  00096       TOP := 1;
1  007E  00097       STACK(TOP) := '(*/';
1  00A6  00098
1  00A6  00099       (* INITIALIZE OUTPUT STRING AND RANK COUNT *)
1  00A6  00100       POLISH := '*/';
1  00AC  00101       RANK := 0;
1  00B2  00102
1  00B2  00103       (* GET FIRST INPUT SYMBOL *)
1  00B2  00104       CURRENT := '*/';
1  00B8  00105       SUB (INFIX, 1, 1, CURRENT);
1  00EC  00106       SUB (INFIX, 2, 256, INFIX);
1  0120  00107
1  0120  00108       (* TRANSLATE THE INFIX EXPRESSION *)
1  0120  00109       WHILE (CURRENT <> '*/') AND NOT INVALID DO
1  0138  00110       BEGIN
1  0138  00111           WRITELN('CURRENT=', CURRENT);
1  015C  00112
1  015C  00113           (* REMOVE SYMBOLS WITH GREATER PRECEDENCE FROM STACK *)
1  015C  00114           IF TOP = 0
1  015C  00115           THEN BEGIN
1  0168  00116               INVALID := TRUE;
1  0170  00117               WRITELN(' ', 'INVALID')
1  0194  00118               END
1  0194  00119           ELSE WHILE (F (CURRENT) < G (STACK(TOP)))
1  01FE  00120               AND NOT INVALID DO
1  020C  00121               BEGIN
1  020C  00122                   TEMP := STACK(TOP);
1  0234  00123                   TOP := TOP + 1;
1  0240  00124                   CONCAT (POLISH, TEMP, POLISH);
1  026C  00125                   RANK := RANK + R (TEMP);
1  0292  00126                   IF RANK < 1
1  0292  00127                   THEN BEGIN
1  029E  00128                       INVALID := TRUE;
1  02A6  00129                       WRITELN(' ', 'INVALID')
1  02CA  00130                       END
1  02CA  00131               END;
1  02CE  00132
1  02CE  00133           (* IS THE EXPRESSION VALID? *)
1  02CE  00134           IF NOT INVALID
1  02CE  00135           THEN BEGIN
1  02DC  00136
1  02DC  00137               (* ARE THERE MATCHING PARENTHESIS? *)
1  02DC  00138               IF F (CURRENT) <> G (STACK(TOP))
1  0320  00139               THEN BEGIN
1  0342  00140                   TOP := TOP + 1;
1  034E  00141                   STACK(TOP) := CURRENT
1  0370  00142                   END
1  0376  00143               ELSE TOP := TOP - 1;
1  0386  00144
1  0386  00145               (* GET NEXT INPUT SYMBOL *)
1  0386  00146               IF LENGTH (INFIX) > 0
1  03A4  00147               THEN BEGIN
1  03AC  00148                   CURRENT := '*/';
1  03B2  00149                   SUB (INFIX, 1, 1, CURRENT);
1  03E6  00150                   SUB (INFIX, 2, 256, INFIX)
1  0406  00151                   END
1  041A  00152               ELSE CURRENT := '*/'
1  041E  00153               END
1  0424  00154       END;
1  0428  00155
1  0428  00156       (* IS THE EXPRESSION VALID? *)
1  0428  00157       IF NOT INVALID
1  0428  00158       THEN IF (TOP > 0) OR (RANK <> 1)
1  044E  00159           THEN BEGIN
1  044E  00160               INVALID := TRUE;
1  0456  00161               WRITELN(' ', 'INVALID')
1  047A  00162               END
```

Fig. 10-5 PASCAL program to convert from infix to suffix Polish notation
(cont'd.)

```
1  047A   00163                          ELSE WRITELN(' ', 'VALID')
1  04A2   00164          END;
0  0038   00165
0  0038   00166  BEGIN  (* MAIN PROGRAM *)
0  0038   00167
0  0038   00168          (* INITIALIZE STRING OF BLANKS, INVALID EXPRESSION FLAG
0  0038   00169             AND STRING OF ALPHABETIC CHARACTERS *)
0  0038   00170          BLANKS := '                                */';
0  003E   00171          INVALID := FALSE;
0  0046   00172          ALPHAB := 'ABCDEFGHIJKLMNOPQRSTUVWXYZ*/';
0  004C   00173
0  004C   00174          (* READ NUMBER OF EXPRESSIONS *)
0  004C   00175          READ(NUM);
0  005E   00176
0  005E   00177          (* INPUT AND CONVERT EACH EXPRESSION *)
0  005E   00178          FOR I := 1 TO NUM DO
0  0082   00179          BEGIN
0  0082   00180              READ(INFIX);
0  0094   00181              CONCAT (INFIX, BLANKS, TEMP);
0  00C2   00182              WRITELN('-', 'INFIX STRING IS ', TEMP : 20);
0  00F8   00183              SUFFIX (INFIX, POLISH);
0  011E   00184              IF NOT INVALID
0  011E   00185              THEN BEGIN
0  012C   00186                  CONCAT (POLISH, BLANKS, TEMP);
0  015A   00187                  WRITELN(' ', 'POLISH FORM IS ', TEMP : 20)
0  0190   00188                  END
0  0190   00189          END
0  0190   00190  END.
--------------------------------
| COMPILE TIME:    0.492 SECOND(S) |
|     NO WARNING(S) DETECTED       |
|     NO ERROR(S) DETECTED         |
--------------------------------

--EXECUTION-->


INFIX STRING IS (A+B*C)*(D+E@F@A))
VALID
POLISH FORM IS ABC*+DEFA@@+*


INFIX STRING IS A+B)*C*(D+E))
INVALID


INFIX STRING IS (A+B@C@D)*(E+F/D))
VALID
POLISH FORM IS ABCD@@+EFD/+*
```

Fig. 10-5 PASCAL program to convert from infix to suffix Polish notation (cont'd.)

a / b (ab/)	LOD	a
	DIV	b
	STO	T_i

Note that each operator generates three assembly-language instructions. The third instruction in each group is of the form STO T_i, where T_i denotes the address of a location (word) in the computer's memory that is to contain the value of the intermediate result. These addresses are to be created by the desired suffix-to-assembly-language program.

A straightforward algorithm involves the use of a stack. This entails the scanning of the suffix expression in a left-to-right manner. Each variable name in the input must be placed on the stack. On encountering an operator, the topmost two operands are unstacked and used (along with the operator) to generate the desired sequence of assembly instructions. The intermediate result corresponding to the operator in question is also placed on the stack. A general algorithm based on this approach follows:

Table 10-2 Sample assembly-language instruction set

Operation	Meaning
LOD A	load: copy the value of the word addressed by A into the accumulator.
STO A	store: copy the value of the accumulator into the word addressed by A.
ADD A	add: replace the present value of the accumulator with the sum of its present value and the value of the word addressed by A.
SUB A	subtract: replace the present value of the accumulator with the result obtained by subtracting from its present value the value of the word addressed by A.
MUL A	multiply: replace the present value of the accumulator with the result obtained by multiplying its present value by the value of the word addressed by A.
DIV A	divide: replace the present value of the accumulator with the result obtained by dividing its present value by the value of the word addressed by A.

1. Repeat thru step 3 while there still remains an input symbol
2. Obtain the current input symbol
3. If the current input symbol is a variable
   then push this variable on the stack
   else remove the two topmost operands from the stack
      generate the sequence of assembly-language instructions which corresponds to the current arithmetic operator
      stack the intermediate result

A program to perform the required translation appears in Fig. 10-6. In addition to a main-program segment the program contains the procedure CODE. The sample suffix expressions used in this program are:

    'AB*C+DEF/+***/'
    'AB+CEF/-* */'
    'AB/CD+/*/'

The variables used in the main program are:

Variable	Type	Usage
EXPRESSION	STRING(256)	Suffix expression
NUM	INTEGER	Number of suffix expressions to process
I	INTEGER	Counted loop variable

Variables used in the procedure CODE are:

SUFFIX	STRING(256)	Input suffix expression
CURRENT	STRING(256)	Current input symbol

```
0  0000  00001  PROGRAM ASEMBLY (INPUT, OUTPUT);
0  0000  00002  (* THIS PROGRAM TESTS PROCEDURE CODE ON SEVERAL SUFFIX EXPRESSIONS
0  0000  00003     IN ORDER TO GENERATE THEIR ASSEMBLY LANGUAGE INSTRUCTIONS *)
0  0000  00004
0  0000  00005  VAR EXPRESSION,              (* SUFFIX EXPRESSION *)
0  0038  00006      BLANKS,                  (* STRING OF BLANK CHARACTERS *)
0  0038  00007      TEMP,                    (* TEMPORARY CHARACTER STRING *)
0  0038  00008      ALPHAB: STRING(256);     (* STRING OF ALPHABETIC CHARACTERS *)
0  0038  00009      NUM,                     (* NUMBER OF SUFFIX EXPRESSIONS TO READ *)
0  0038  00010      I: INTEGER;              (* COUNTED LOOP VARIABLE *)
0  0038  00011
0  0038  00012      FUNCTION INDEX (VAR S, PATTERN: STRING(256)): INTEGER; EXTERNAL;
0  0038  00013      FUNCTION LENGTH (VAR STR: STRING(256)): INTEGER; EXTERNAL;
0  0038  00014      PROCEDURE CONCAT (VAR S1, S2, RESULT: STRING(256)); EXTERNAL;
0  0038  00015      PROCEDURE SUB (VAR S: STRING(256); POS, NUM: INTEGER;
1  0000  00016           VAR RESULT: STRING(256)); EXTERNAL;
0  0038  00017
0  0038  00018      PROCEDURE CODE (SUFFIX: STRING(256));
1  0000  00019      (* GIVEN A STRING (SUFFIX) REPRESENTING A SUFFIX EXPRESSION
1  0000  00020         EQUIVALENT TO A VALID INFIX EXPRESSION, THIS PROCEDURE
1  0000  00021         TRANSLATES THE STRING SUFFIX TO ASSEMBLY LANGUAGE
1  0000  00022         INSTRUCTIONS. *)
1  0000  00023
1  0000  00024      VAR S: ARRAY(1..20) OF STRING(256);  (* STACK *)
1  005C  00025          CURRENT,                (* SYMBOL BEING EXAMINED *)
1  005C  00026          LEFT, RIGHT,            (* CURRENT OPERANDS *)
1  005C  00027          OPCODE,                 (* OPERATION CODE *)
1  005C  00028          TEMP2, TEMP3: STRING(256);  (* TEMPORARY STORAGE *)
1  005C  00029          CURRENT_CHAR: CHAR; (* CURRENT CHARACTER *)
1  005C  00030          TOP,                    (* TOP OF STACK *)
1  005C  00031          I,                      (* TEMPORARY STORAGE INDEX *)
1  005C  00032          J: INTEGER;             (* COUNTED LOOP INDEX *)
1  005C  00033
1  005C  00034      BEGIN
1  005C  00035
1  005C  00036          (* INITIALIZE *)
1  005C  00037          I := 0;
1  0072  00038          TOP := 0;
1  0078  00039          TEMP3 := '*/';
1  007E  00040
1  007E  00041          (* PROCESS THE SUFFIX EXPRESSION *)
1  007E  00042          FOR J := 1 TO LENGTH (SUFFIX) DO
1  00BC  00043          BEGIN
1  00BC  00044
1  00BC  00045              (* INITIALIZE *)
1  00BC  00046              CURRENT := '*/';
1  00C2  00047
1  00C2  00048              (* OBTAIN AND PROCESS CURRENT INPUT SYMBOL *)
1  00C2  00049              SUB (SUFFIX, J, 1, CURRENT);
1  00F6  00050              IF INDEX (ALPHAB, CURRENT) <> 0
1  011C  00051              THEN BEGIN
1  0124  00052
1  0124  00053                  (* PUSH CURRENT VARIABLE ONTO THE STACK *)
1  0124  00054                  TOP := TOP + 1;
1  0130  00055                  S(TOP) := CURRENT
1  0152  00056              END
1  0158  00057              ELSE BEGIN
1  015C  00058
1  015C  00059                  (* PROCESS CURRENT OPERATOR *)
1  015C  00060                  CURRENT_CHAR := CURRENT;
1  0162  00061                  CASE CURRENT_CHAR OF
1  0162  00062                  '+' : OPCODE := 'ADD */';
1  018C  00063                  '-' : OPCODE := 'SUB */';
1  0196  00064                  '*' : OPCODE := 'MUL */';
1  01A0  00065                  '/' : OPCODE := 'DIV */'
1  01A0  00066                  END;
1  01D6  00067
1  01D6  00068                  (* UNSTACK TWO OPERANDS *)
1  01D6  00069                  RIGHT := SFE   00070                      LEFT := S(TOP - 1);
1  022C  00071                  TOP := TOP - 2;
1  0238  00072
1  0238  00073                  (* OUTPUT LOAD INSTRUCTION *)
1  0238  00074                  TEMP := 'LOD */';
1  023E  00075                  CONCAT (TEMP, LEFT, TEMP);
1  026A  00076                  CONCAT (TEMP, BLANKS, TEMP);
1  0296  00077                  WRITELN(' ', TEMP : 6);
1  02BA  00078
1  02BA  00079                  (* OUTPUT ARITHMETIC INSTRUCTION *)
1  02BA  00080                  CONCAT (OPCODE, RIGHT, TEMP);
1  02E6  00081                  CONCAT (TEMP, BLANKS, TEMP);
1  0312  00082                  WRITELN(' ', TEMP : 6);
```

Fig. 10-6   PASCAL program to convert from suffix to object code

```
1  0336   00083
1  0336   00084                               (* TEMPORARY STORAGE INSTRUCTION *)
1  0336   00085                               I := I + 1;
1  0342   00086                               WRITELN(' ', 'STO T', I : 1);
1  0378   00087
1  0378   00088                               (* STACK INTERMEDIATE RESULT *)
1  0378   00089                               TOP := TOP + 1;
1  0384   00090                               TEMP := '123456789*/';
1  038A   00091                               SUB (TEMP, I, 1, TEMP);
1  03BE   00092                               TEMP2 := 'T*/';
1  03C4   00093                               CONCAT (TEMP2, TEMP, TEMP3);
1  03F0   00094                               S(TOP) := TEMP3
1  0412   00095                             END
1  0418   00096                    END
1  0418   00097           END;
0  0038   00098
0  0038   00099  BEGIN  (* MAIN PROGRAM *)
0  0038   00100
0  0038   00101       (* INITIALIZE *)
0  0038   00102       BLANKS := '                            */';
0  003E   00103       ALPHAB := 'ABCDEFGHIJKLMNOPQRSTUVWXYZ*/';
0  0044   00104
0  0044   00105       (* READ NUMBER OF EXPRESSIONS *)
0  0044   00106       READ(NUM);
0  0056   00107
0  0056   00108       (* INPUT AND CONVERT EACH EXPRESSION *)
0  0056   00109       FOR I := 1 TO NUM DO
0  007A   00110       BEGIN
0  007A   00111            READ(EXPRESSION);
0  008C   00112            CONCAT (EXPRESSION, BLANKS, TEMP);
0  00BA   00113            WRITELN('0', 'THE ASSEMBLY CODE FOR ', TEMP : 20, ' IS');
0  0102   00114            CODE (EXPRESSION)
0  010A   00115       END
0  0120   00116  END.
-------------------------------------
¦ COMPILE TIME:    0.298 SECOND(S) ¦
¦     NO WARNING(S) DETECTED       ¦
¦     NO ERROR(S) DETECTED         ¦
-------------------------------------
--EXECUTION-->

THE ASSEMBLY CODE FOR AB*C+DEF/+*        IS
LOD A
MUL B
STO T1
LOD T1
ADD C
STO T2
LOD E
DIV F
STO T3
LOD D
ADD T3
STO T4
LOD T2
MUL T4
STO T5

THE ASSEMBLY CODE FOR AB+CEF/-*          IS
LOD A
ADD B
STO T1
LOD E
DIV F
STO T2
LOD C
SUB T2
STO T3
LOD T1
MUL T3
STO T4

THE ASSEMBLY CODE FOR AB/CD+/            IS
LOD A
DIV B
STO T1
LOD C
ADD D
STO T2
LOD T1
DIV T2
STO T3
```

Fig. 10-6   PASCAL program to convert from suffix to object code (cont'd.)

S	ARRAY(1..50) OF STRING(256)	Stack which contains operands
OPCODE	STRING(256)	Contains assembly op-code for current instruction
TEMP	STRING(256)	Intermediate result
LEFT	STRING(256)	Left operand of current operator
RIGHT	STRING(256)	Right operand of current operator
I	INTEGER	Counter that keeps track of temporary storage
J	INTEGER	Index associated with suffix string

The main program inputs the suffix expressions and calls the procedure CODE to generate the assembly-language instructions for each expression. In the procedure CODE, line 37 initializes the temporary storage index. Line 42 controls the loop to perform the translation process for each symbol in SUFFIX. If the current symbol is a variable name, then the name is pushed onto the stack; otherwise, in lines 60 to 66, the symbol is an operator so the correct operator is determined. Next, two operands are unstacked. The left operand is used with a load instruction while the right instruction is used with the operator generated in lines 60 to 66. The resulting instructions are printed. Finally, a temporary storage instruction is generated after the storage index is generated in line 85. This storage location is then pushed onto the stack.

Exercises for Sec. 10-5.2

1. Modify the procedure SUFFIX presented in this section so that it will handle the PASCAL relational operators:

    $$<, <=, =, <>, >, \text{ and } >=$$

    Recall that the relational operators should have a lower priority than the arithmetic operators. Note that the functions F, G, and R must also change.

2. Alter procedure CODE given in this section such that it will generate more efficient code when the commutativity of the operators + and * is taken into consideration.

3. Modify the procedure obtained in exercise 2 so that the required number of temporary positions is reduced.

4. Modify the procedure obtained in exercise 3 so that it will handle the unary minus operator.

5. Using the general algorithm given in the main text, formulate a PASCAL function (PREFIX) for converting an infix expression (INFIX) to its equivalent prefix form. Use the following data in checking your function:

```
'(A+B)*(C–D+E)*/'
'A*B*C(C+D)*/'
'(A+B)(C+D)*/'
'A+BD*/'
```

6. Formulate a procedure similar to procedure CODE for generating code for prefix expressions.

7. Modify the procedure obtained in exercise 6 so that the advantage of the commutative operators + and * is taken into consideration.

10-5.3 Partition-Exchange Sorting

For the third and final application of a stack structure, we now consider a sorting technique which performs well on large tables. The approach is to place initially a particular record in its final position within the sorted table. Once this is done, all records which precede this record have smaller keys, while all records that follow it have larger keys. This technique partitions the original table into two subtables. The same process is then applied to each of these subtables and repeated until all records are placed in their final positions.

As an example of this approach to sorting, let us consider the placement of 73 in its final position in the following key set:

| 73 | 65 | 52 | 24 | 83 | 17 | 35 | 96 | 41 | 9 |

We now use two index variables I and J with initial values of 2 and 10, respectively. The two keys 73 and K[I] are compared and, if an exchange is required (i.e., K[I] < 73), then I is incremented by 1 and the process is repeated. When K[I] $\geq$ 73, we proceed to compare keys K[J] and 73. If an exchange is required, then J is decremented by 1 and the process is repeated until K[J] $\leq$ 73. At this point, the keys K[I] and K[J] (i.e., 83 and 9) are interchanged. The entire process is then repeated with J fixed and I being incremented once again. When I $\geq$ J, the desired key is placed in its final position by interchanging the keys 73 and K[J].

Figure 10-7 contains a main program and a recursive procedure QUICK which performs the required sort. The sample input data used in this program are the key set

| 73 | 65 | 52 | 24 | 83 | 17 | 35 | 96 | 41 | 9 |

The variables used in the main program are:

Variable	Type	Usage
VECTOR	ARRAY(1..20) OF REAL	Type definition of vector
LIST	VECTOR	Vector to be sorted
N	INTEGER	Number of elements in table
NUM	INTEGER	Number of tables to be sorted
I	INTEGER	Counted loop variable
J	INTEGER	Counted loop variable

```
0  0000   00001   PROGRAM SORT (INPUT, OUTPUT);
0  0000   00002   (* THIS PROGRAM INPUTS SEVERAL UNSORTED TABLES AND SORTS THEM BY
0  0000   00003      CALLING THE RECURSIVE PROCEDURE QUICK. *)
0  0000   00004
0  0000   00005   TYPE TABLE = ARRAY(1..20) OF INTEGER;
0  0038   00006   VAR NUM,                     (* NUMBER OF TABLES TO BE SORTED *)
0  0038   00007       I, J,                    (* COUNTED LOOP VARIABLES *)
0  0038   00008       N: INTEGER;              (* NUMBER OF ELEMENTS IN TABLE *)
0  0038   00009       VECTOR: TABLE;           (* UNSORTED TABLE *)
0  0038   00010
0  0038   00011       PROCEDURE QUICK (VAR K: TABLE; LB, UB: INTEGER);
1  0000   00012       (* GIVEN A TABLE K OF N RECORDS, THIS RECURSIVE PROCEDURE
1  0000   00013          SORTS THE TABLE INTO ASCENDING ORDER BE THE PARTITION-
1  0000   00014          EXCHANGE SORT. *)
1  0000   00015
1  0000   00016       VAR FLAG: BOOLEAN;       (* INDICATES PLACING RECORD IN
1  0000   00017                                   ITS FINAL POSITION *)
1  0062   00018           I, J,                (* INDEX VARIABLES *)
1  0062   00019           M,                   (* TEMPORARY VARIABLE *)
1  0062   00020           KEY,                 (* KEY VALUE BEING PLACED IN
1  0062   00021                                   FINAL POSITION *)
1  0062   00022           TEMP: INTEGER;       (* USED TO EXCHANGE RECORDS *)
1  0062   00023
1  0062   00024       BEGIN
1  0062   00025
1  0062   00026           (* INITIALIZE *)
1  0062   00027           FLAG := TRUE;
1  006A   00028
1  006A   00029           (* PERFORM SORT *)
1  006A   00030           IF LB < UB
1  006A   00031           THEN BEGIN
1  0076   00032               I := LB;
1  007E   00033               J := UB + 1;
1  008A   00034               KEY := K(LB);
1  00B4   00035               WHILE FLAG DO
1  00BE   00036               BEGIN
1  00BE   00037                   I := I + 1;
1  00CA   00038
1  00CA   00039                   (* SCAN THE KEYS FROM LEFT TO RIGHT *)
1  00CA   00040                   WHILE K(I) < KEY DO
1  00F8   00041                       I := I + 1;
1  0108   00042                   J := J -1;
1  0114   00043
1  0114   00044                   (* SCAN THE KEYS FROM RIGHT TO LEFT *)
1  0114   00045                   WHILE K(J) > KEY DO
1  0142   00046                       J := J - 1;
1  0152   00047                   IF I < J
1  0152   00048                   THEN BEGIN
1  015E   00049
1  015E   00050                       (* INTERCHANGE RECORDS *)
1  015E   00051                       TEMP := K(J);
1  0188   00052                       K(J) := K(I);
1  01D4   00053                       K(I) := TEMP
1  01F6   00054                   END
1  01FE   00055                   ELSE FLAG := FALSE
1  0202   00056               END;
1  020E   00057
1  020E   00058               (* INTERCHANGE RECORDS *)
1  020E   00059               TEMP := K(LB);
1  0238   00060               K(LB) := K(J);
1  0284   00061               K(J) := TEMP;
1  02AE   00062               M := J - 1;
1  02BA   00063               QUICK (K, LB, M);  (* SORT 1ST SUBTABLE *)
1  02DE   00064               M := J + 1;
1  02EA   00065               QUICK (K, M, UB)   (* SORT 2ND SUBTABLE *)
1  0302   00066           END
1  030E   00067       END;
0  0038   00068
0  0038   00069   BEGIN  (* MAIN PROGRAM *)
0  0038   00070
0  0038   00071       (* READ NUMBER OF TABLES TO BE SORTED *)
0  0038   00072       READ(NUM);
0  004A   00073
0  004A   00074       (* PROCESS THE TABLES *)
0  004A   00075       FOR I := 1 TO NUM DO
0  006E   00076       BEGIN
0  006E   00077
0  006E   00078           (* INPUT UNSORTED TABLE *)
0  006E   00079           READ(N);
0  0080   00080           WRITELN('-', 'UNSORTED TABLE IS');
```

Fig. 10-7 Program for a partition-exchange sort

```
0  00A4  00081          WRITELN('0');
0  00B6  00082          FOR J := 1 TO N DO
0  00DA  00083          BEGIN
0  00DA  00084              READ(VECTOR(J));
0  010C  00085              WRITE(VECTOR(J) : 7)
0  0140  00086          END;
0  0144  00087          WRITELN;
0  0152  00088
0  0152  00089          (* SORT VECTOR *)
0  0152  00090          J := 1;
0  015A  00091          VECTOR(N + 1) := 9999;
0  018A  00092          QUICK (VECTOR, J, N);
0  01B8  00093
0  01B8  00094          (* OUTPUT SORTED VECTOR *)
0  01B8  00095          WRITELN('-', 'SORTED TABLE IS');
0  01DC  00096          WRITELN('0');
0  01EE  00097          FOR J := 1 TO N DO
0  0212  00098              WRITE(VECTOR(J) : 7);
0  024A  00099          WRITELN
0  024A  00100      END
0  0258  00101  END.
-----------------------------------
| COMPILE TIME:    0.255 SECOND(S) |
|     NO WARNING(S) DETECTED       |
|     NO ERROR(S) DETECTED         |
-----------------------------------
--EXECUTION-->


UNSORTED TABLE IS


   73     65     52     24     83     17     35     96     41      9


SORTED TABLE IS


    9     17     24     35     41     52     65     73     83     96
```

Fig. 10-7 Program for a partition-exchange sort (cont'd.)

Variables used in the procedure QUICK are:

K(*)	VECTOR	Vector to be sorted
LB	INTEGER	Lower bound of subtable
UB	INTEGER	Upper bound of subtable
FLAG	BOOLEAN	Variable to specify the end of splitting table into two subtables
KEY	REAL	Key to be placed in its final position
TEMP	REAL	Temporary variable in exchange process
I	INTEGER	Index to subtable
J	INTEGER	Index to subtable

The main program reads the number of tables to be sorted in line 72. Then, for each table, the number of elements in the table and the individual elements are read. Line 91 gives a value for the $(n + 1)$th element that is greater than all values in the table. The next statement calls the procedure QUICK to sort the table. Finally, the sorted table is printed.

The procedure QUICK first initializes FLAG to *true*. Then if there is more than one element in the subtable (i.e., LB < UB), the sort is performed. KEY is given the value of the first element in the subtable. Then, the keys are scanned from left to right until KEY has a value less than or equal to the Ith element, and from right to left until the Jth key is greater than KEY. If I is less than J, then the two records for these two indices can be interchanged; otherwise, the position where the table can be broken up into two subtables has been found and FLAG is set to false in order to exit the loop. Finally the Jth record is interchanged with the record at the lower bound of the table, and the procedure QUICK is called twice to sort the two smaller subtables.

Exercise for Sec. 10-5.3

1. Obtain an iterative PASCAL procedure for the partition-exchange method of sorting. Use as data the key set

   42 23 74 11 65 58 94 36 99 87

10-6 QUEUES

As mentioned in the main text a queue structure is a linear list in which insertions are performed at the rear and elements are deleted from the front of the structure. Recall that elements in such a structure are processed on a first-come, first-served basis. A convenient and popular way of representing a FCFS queue is to use a vector. If we assume that the elements in such a vector are arranged in a circular fashion, that is, that its first and last elements are logically adjacent to each other, then a circular queue structure results.

The following PASCAL procedure, CQINS, performs an insertion into a FCFS circular queue which is represented as a vector.

```
PROCEDURE CQINS (VAR Q: VECTOR; N: INTEGER; VAR F, R: INTEGER;
    X: INTEGER);
(*THIS PROCEDURE INSERTS ELEMENT X INTO THE REAR OF THE
    CIRCULAR QUEUE Q WHICH IS REPRESENTED AS A VECTOR OF
    SIZE N. F AND R POINT TO THE FRONT AND REAR OF THE
    QUEUE, RESPECTIVELY.*)
BEGIN
    (* RESET REAR POINTER, IF NECESSARY *)
    IF R = N
    THEN R := 1
    ELSE R := R + 1;
    (* OVERFLOW CONDITION *)
    IF F = R THEN CALL Q_OVER;
    Q(R) := X;
    (* IS F PROPERLY SET? *)
    IF F = 0 THEN F := 1
END;
```

The second conditional statement of the procedure checks for an overflow situation. If an overflow occurs, then the procedure Q_OVER is invoked. Although this procedure is application-dependent, usually its invocation signifies that more storage for the queue is required and that the program must be re-run. Observe that the last conditional statement in the program checks for an insertion into an empty queue. In such an instance F is set to 1.

The following PASCAL procedure, CQDEL, performs a deletion from a circular queue structure which is represented by a vector.

```
PROCEDURE CQDEL (VAR Q: VECTOR; N: INTEGER; VAR F, R, X:
      INTEGER);
(* THIS PROCEDURE DELETES THE FRONT ELEMENT OF THE QUEUE AND
      PLACES IT INTO THE ELEMENT X. F AND R DENOTE THE FRONT
      AND REAR OF THE QUEUE, RESPECTIVELY. *)
BEGIN
      (* UNDERFLOW? *)
      IF F = 0 THEN CALL Q_UNDER;
      (* DELETE FRONT ELEMENT *)
      X := Q(F);
      (* IS QUEUE NOW EMPTY? *)
      IF F = R
      THEN BEGIN
            F := 0;
            R := 0
            END
      ELSE  BEGIN
            (* INCREMENT F *)
            F := F + 1;
            IF F > N THEN F := 1
            END
END;
```

The first conditional statement in the program checks for an underflow situation. If an underflow occurs, then procedure Q_UNDER is invoked. Although this procedure is also application-dependent, an attempt to delete from an empty queue may be valid. The second conditional statement checks for an empty queue after deletion. In such a case the front and rear pointers are set to zero. An alternate representation of a queue, which reflects its variable-size property, is given in Sec. 10-9. The next section examines the application of queues to the area of simulation.

10-7 SIMULATION

In this section, we consider the design of a simulation model of the loading of jobs into main memory by a hypothetical operating system. This application of queues, as well as the nature of simulation, is discussed in Sec. 10-7 of the main text. Prior reading of that discussion is assumed in this section. Recall that a very straightforward scheme for memory allocation is used in this application. Three queues are required, the descriptions of which are provided below. Notice the new organization of these queues, which in turn necessitates new procedures for handling queues of this new type.

The first queue contains information about available memory space and is a *priority queue*; that is, the elements are arranged in decreasing order of memory hole size. The elements stored in the queue are the address and size of the memory holes.

Another priority queue is required to simulate execution of the jobs so that they leave the system in the proper order. This queue, however, is arranged in increasing order of execution time remaining. This is because the execution times of the jobs may vary, so they will not necessarily depart the system at the same relative time. Elements of the execution queue have four components; namely, a job identification number, the load address of this job in memory, the amount of execution time remaining, and the amount of memory occupied by this job. All execution times are assumed to be multiples of one minute to simplify job processing.

The final queue required is a straightforward first-in, first-out (FIFO) queue to represent the arrival of jobs to the system. Elements of this queue consist of three fields; a job identification number, a memory size request, and an execution time request. Again for simplicity, we assume a new job arrives every minute for 30 minutes. Figure 10-8 gives a summary of these queues.

Any computer simulation is the study of the behavior of some system over some time period. Our time simplifications ensure that no accuracy is lost in the state of the memory allocation system. This is because the passage of time is handled by updating the state of the system at regular one minute intervals, while changes occur only at time units which are multiples of one minute. If events in the system occurred irregularly, more elaborate mechanisms would be required to model the passage of time.

In specifying the current model, we use a simple naming convention to illustrate the multiple-component queue entries. Each component will actually be a separate vector, which enables us to use some of the procedures developed in Sec. 10-6 of the main text. The procedures used will be QINSERT and QDELETE, for rear insertion and front deletion, respectively, from a linear queue. These procedures operate on the same principles as CQINS and CQDEL in Sec. 10-6 of this text, except that CQINS and CQDEL are for circular queues.

Table 10-3 describes the vectors involved in each queue and their respective queue pointers. Note that the similarities in names indicate each respective queue. Assume that all queue values are integer.

The model clearly requires mechanisms for insertion and deletion analogous to those given in Sec. 10-6 of the main text, but for priority queues. The deletion is accomplished simply by procedure QDELETE, since we will delete from the front of the queue in all cases. Insertion is more complicated, however. Because of the priority considerations, a new element may be inserted somewhere in the middle of the queue instead of strictly at the rear, as in procedure QINSERT. Also, different orderings may be imposed on a priority queue; the queue elements may be in either descending or ascending order. Procedure QFILE accomplishes the insertion task on a single vector for both orderings by shifting the other elements, if necessary, and inserting the new element in its appropriate position.

Procedure QFILE accommodates only those queues that are represented by a single vector. However, because the position of the inserted element is returned through parameter P, the procedure can easily be used for queues with multiple components, where one of these components is the ordering key. This multiple-component insertion is accomplished as follows. First, procedure QFILE is used to insert into the ordering criterion vector; then the returned value of P is used to place the remaining components in parallel positions in their respective vectors by calling procedure QPLACE for each remaining component vector. This latter procedure simply shifts elements in the vector as required and then inserts the new element in the newly freed position P.

We are now ready to give the complete simulation model. Assume a memory of 10,000 words, which is initially one big hole. Therefore, the memory

Memory queue

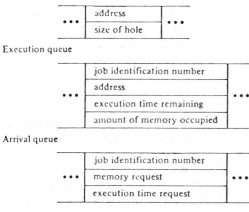

Execution queue

Arrival queue

Fig. 10-8   The queues of the simulation model

queue has one initial entry with address 0000 (assuming four-digit addresses) and size 10,000. As previously stated, we assume the simulation is to run for 30 minutes, with a new job arriving each minute, and that the characteristics of each job (memory and time requests) are read from the input stream at the time of its arrival. In the simulation, the time of arrival is used as the job identification number, and we will count the number of jobs completed.

A general algorithm to perform the simulation follows:

1. Initialize the completions counter, all queue pointers, and all queues to zero, error flag to false, and the timing controller to 1.
2. Insert the full memory size available (10,000) and the initial load address (0000) into the memory queue.
3. Repeat thru step 7 for 30 minutes by steps of one minute.
4. Input and print a memory size request and a corresponding execution time request.
5. Insert the new request at the rear of the arrivals queue.
6. If the largest available memory size is sufficient to handle
   the next memory request of the FIFO arrivals queue,
   then remove the first job from the arrivals queue, adjust the
       memory hole accordingly, file the new hole in the memory
       queue and put the job in the execution queue.
7. Take one minute off the remaining time for each job in the execution queue (parallel processing), and if a job is finished, increment the completions counter, delete the job from the execution queue and return the newly completed job's memory to the memory queue.
8. Print out the number of completions and exit.

The program MEM_SIM given in Fig. 10-9 performs this simulation. The variables used in this program are:

Table 10-3   Queue naming conventions

Queue	Name of Vector	Queue Pointers	Component
Memory queue	MEM_Q_ADDR	MF1, MR1	Address of hole
	MEM_Q_SIZE	MF2, MR2	Size of hole
Execution queue	EXEC_Q_ID	EF1, ER1	Job identification number
	EXEC_Q_ADDR	EF2, ER2	Address of job (after loading)
	EXEC_Q_TIME	EF3, ER3	Remaining execution time
	EXEC_Q_SIZE	EF4, ER4	Memory occupied by job
Arrival queue	ARR_Q_ID	AF1, AR1	Job identification number
	ARR_Q_MEM	AF2, AR2	Memory request
	ARR_Q_TIME	AF3, AR3	Execution time request

Main program MEM_SIM (excluding queues and pointers):

Variable	Type	Usage
VECTOR	ARRAY(1..100) OF INTEGER	Type definition of queues
MEM_REQUEST	INTEGER	Requested size of the memory hole
TIME_REQUEST	INTEGER	Execution time requested corresponding to the memory requested in MEM_REQUEST
COMPLETIONS	INTEGER	Number of jobs completely executed
MINUTE	INTEGER	Present time in the simulation
HOLE_SIZE	INTEGER	Largest available memory size
ADDR	INTEGER	Address of memory hole examined
ID	INTEGER	Identification number of job examined
MEM	INTEGER	Memory size request of job examined
TIME	INTEGER	Execution time request of job examined
P, J	INTEGER	Temporary counter variables
ERROR	BOOLEAN	Error flag

All the queues are declared as integer vectors, each containing 100 elements. All queue pointers are also INTEGER.

Q	VECTOR	Vector for queue for rear insertion
F	INTEGER	Front pointer of Q
R	INTEGER	Rear pointer of Q
X	INTEGER	Element to insert at the rear of Q

The variables used in the procedure QDELETE are:

Q	VECTOR	Vector for queue for front deletion
F	INTEGER	Front pointer of Q
R	INTEGER	Rear pointer of Q
X	INTEGER	Contains deleted element

The variables used in the procedure QFILE are:

Q	VECTOR	Vector for the priority queue for insertion
F	INTEGER	Front pointer of Q
R	INTEGER	Rear pointer of Q
X	INTEGER	Element to insert
P	INTEGER	Position of insertion of X
D	INTEGER	Direction indicator of Q ordering (ascending or descending)
L	INTEGER	Temporary counter variable

The variables used in the procedure QPLACE are:

Q	VECTOR	Vector for the priority queue for insertion
F	INTEGER	Front pointer of Q
R	INTEGER	Rear pointer of Q
X	INTEGER	Element to insert
P	INTEGER	Position of insertion of X
L	INTEGER	Temporary counter variable

A statement of purpose for each of the procedures is as follows:

QINSERT	inserts an element at the rear of a queue (vector).
QDELETE	deletes an element from the front of a queue (vector).
QFILE	inserts an element into a priority queue (vector). The queue is maintained in either descending or ascending order, depending on a parameter value.
QPLACE	inserts into a priority queue (vector) an element corresponding to that used in QFILE above. The same ordering is used for corresponding calls of QFILE and QPLACE.
Q_OVERF	prints an error message and halts the program if a queue (vector) overflow occurs.
Q_UNDER	prints an error message and halts the program if a queue (vector) underflow occurs.

The 30 data values used are:

Memory Request	Time request
500	1
300	4
9200	2
600	4
400	10
500	4
300	5
350	6
400	1
1000	4
200	6
600	2
800	5
300	2
100	5
300	2
400	2
800	5
400	6
253	2
632	2
250	5
321	1
342	2
325	2
123	3
325	8
522	3
3422	10
322	3

The program works as follows. First, the count of completed jobs and all 18 queue pointers are initialized. Then the execution and arrivals queues are initialized, followed by the initialization of the memory queue to contain the entire memory as one hole with address 0000. Note the use of the two procedures QFILE and QPLACE, communicating through a common value of P, to insert the two components of the memory queue entry.

The timing loop for the simulation is engaged in line 227; the loop is to run for 30 minutes in steps of one minute each, and it contains lines 232 through 306.

In lines 232 through 239, each new job arrives and is inserted into the FIFO arrivals queue. The time of arrival provides a unique identification for the job. Lines 243 through 277 embody the memory management strategy. If the first element in the ascending memory queue is sufficiently large to handle the first job in the arrivals queue, then that memory hole is allocated to the job and the hole's size is adjusted accordingly. The loaded job is then removed from the arrivals queue and inserted into the execution queue.

Lines 281 through 305 simulate the execution of the jobs in the execution queue by parallel processing. One minute is subtracted from the time remaining for each job to account for their execution during the period since the last update. (Note that execution of the jobs in parallel may not be physically possible on many systems, but it is a useful simplification for our purposes.) Any job completions are counted, and the memory occupied is once again made available by insertion into the memory queue.

When 30 minutes have elapsed, control passes to line 310, and the final result is printed.

Several points should be noted about the given program. First, the simulation is run for only 30 minutes, so one would expect a maximum queue size of 30. However, the queues are all declared to be size 100. This is due to the nature of the memory queue. The execution and arrivals queues will have a maximum of 30 entries, because a job is entered only once into each of those queues. However, memory holes are constantly deleted, split up and re-inserted, which forces the memory queue pointers farther down the queue. Thus, with 30 jobs being considered, at least 30 *different* memory holes will be inserted into the memory queue. The size of the memory queue is somewhat dependent upon the data used, so a queue large enough to handle all kinds of data is used (i.e., size 100).

Second, procedures Q_OVERF and Q_UNDER are purely application-dependent. That is, one may wish to perform many different actions upon queue overflow or underflow, depending on the course of action specified in the application. We are required only to print out an error message and set the error flag.

In this section, we have attempted to convey the flavor of computer simulation. It is a very broad subject, one that can be studied in considerable depth, and we have clearly only scratched the surface. Armed with this brief introduction, though, you should be prepared for a more complete treatment of the subject should the need arise. We have also introduced in this section the important concept of priority queues, along with procedures for manipulating them. Priority queues are very common in simulation applications, but they have many important applications beyond the realm of simulation as well.

Exercise for Sec. 10-7

1. A grocery store firm is considering the addition of a new service counter in one of its stores. Currently, the store has three checkouts, but the customer volume has increased to the point where a new counter is warranted. To determine whether the new counter should be a regular counter or an express counter (i.e., eight items or less), a simulation of customer flow through the checkout area is required.

    Our initial simulation is of a checkout area consisting of one express counter and three regular checkouts. All customers with eight or fewer items are assumed to proceed to the express counter. Customers with more than eight items go to the standard checkout with the shortest waiting line.

    Customers enter the checkout area randomly, with the time of next-arrival determined by adding to the present time a random number chosen from the range [0, 360] seconds. (0 is interpreted as the simultaneous arrival of

```
0  0000   00001   PROGRAM MEM_SIM (INPUT, OUTPUT);
0  0000   00002
0  0000   00003   (* THIS PROGRAM IS A SIMULATION MODEL OF MEMORY MANAGEMENT IN A    *)
0  0000   00004   (* HYPOTHETICAL COMPUTER SYSTEM.  QUEUES ARE USED TO CONTROL       *)
0  0000   00005   (* AVAILABILITY OF MEMORY, JOB EXECUTION AND JOB ARRIVALS.         *)
0  0000   00006   (* PROCEDURES QINSERT, QDELETE, QFILE AND QPLACE ARE USED FOR      *)
0  0000   00007   (* QUEUE MANIPULATION.  ASSUME A MEMORY OF 10,000 WORDS, SO THAT   *)
0  0000   00008   (* THE MEMORY QUEUE HAS ONE ENTRY WITH ADDRESS 0000 ( FOUR DIGIT   *)
0  0000   00009   (* ADDRESSES) AND SIZE 10,000.  THE OTHER TWO QUEUES ARE EMPTY     *)
0  0000   00010   (* INITIALLY.  ASSUME THE SIMULATION IS TO BE FOR 30 MINUTES,      *)
0  0000   00011   (* WITH A NEW JOB ARRIVING EVERY MINUTE.  TIME OF ARRIVAL IS USED  *)
0  0000   00012   (* AS THE JOB IDENTIFICATION NUMBER.  EACH JOB'S CHARACTERISTICS   *)
0  0000   00013   (* ARE READ FROM THE INPUT STREAM AT THE TIME OF ARRIVAL.          *)
0  0000   00014
0  0000   00015   TYPE VECTOR = ARRAY(1..100) OF INTEGER;
0  0038   00016
0  0038   00017   VAR MEM_Q_ADDR,            (* ADDRESS OF HOLE QUEUE  *)
0  0038   00018       MEM_Q_SIZE,            (* SIZE OF MEMORY HOLE Q  *)
0  0038   00019       EXEC_Q_ID,             (* EXEC. JOB I.D. NUMBER Q*)
0  0038   00020       EXEC_Q_ADDR,           (* LOADED JOB'S ADDRESS Q *)
0  0038   00021       EXEC_Q_TIME,           (* REMAINING EXEC. TIME Q *)
0  0038   00022       EXEC_Q_SIZE,           (* JOB'S MEMORY SIZE Q    *)
0  0038   00023       ARR_Q_ID,              (* ARRIVAL JOB I.D. # Q   *)
0  0038   00024       ARR_Q_MEM,             (* ARRIVAL MEM. REQUEST Q *)
0  0038   00025       ARR_Q_TIME: VECTOR;    (* ARRIVAL EXEC. TIME Q   *)
0  0038   00026       MEM_REQUEST,           (* INPUT MEMORY SIZE AND  *)
0  0038   00027       TIME_REQUEST,          (* EXEC. TIME REQUESTS    *)
0  0038   00028       COMPLETIONS,           (* NUMBER JOBS COMPLETED  *)
0  0038   00029       MINUTE,                (* TIMING LOOP CONTROLLER *)
0  0038   00030       HOLE_SIZE,             (* LARGEST MEM. HOLE SIZE *)
0  0038   00031       MF1, MR1, MF2, MR2,    (* MEMORY QUEUE POINTERS  *)
0  0038   00032       EF1, ER1, EF2, ER2,    (* FRONT AND REAR POINTERS*)
0  0038   00033       EF3, ER3, EF4, ER4,    (* FOR EXECUTION QUEUE    *)
0  0038   00034       AF1, AR1, AF2, AR2,    (* FRONT AND REAR POINTERS*)
0  0038   00035       AF3, AR3,              (* FOR ARRIVALS QUEUE     *)
0  0038   00036       ADDR,                  (* ADDRESS OF MEMORY HOLE *)
0  0038   00037       ID,                    (* ARRIVALS Q FIRST JOB ID*)
0  0038   00038       MEM,                   (* ARRIVALS Q FIRST JOB   *)
0  0038   00039                              (* MEMORY SIZE REQUEST    *)
0  0038   00040       TIME,                  (* ARRIVALS Q FIRST JOB   *)
0  0038   00041                              (* EXECUTION TIME REQUEST *)
0  0038   00042       P, J : INTEGER;        (* POSITION IN QUEUE AND  *)
0  0038   00043                              (* TEMPORARY VARIABLES    *)
0  0038   00044       ERROR: BOOLEAN;        (* ERROR FLAG             *)
0  0038   00045
0  0038   00046       PROCEDURE Q_OVERF;
1  0000   00047       (* Q_OVERF IS INVOKED IF THE QUEUE IN QUESTION DURING AN
1  0000   00048          INSERTION IS FULL *)
1  0000   00049
1  0000   00050       BEGIN
1  003C   00051           ERROR := TRUE;
1  0044   00052           WRITELN ('0','*** AN ERROR OCCURS DURING INSERTION INTO ',
1  0068   00053               'THE QUEUE.');
1  007A   00054           WRITELN (' ','THE VECTOR IS FULL PRIOR TO INSERTION.' : 45);
1  009E   00055       END;
0  0038   00056
0  0038   00057       PROCEDURE Q_UNDER;
1  0000   00058       (* Q_UNDER IS INVOKED IF THE QUEUE IN QUESTION DURING A DELETION
1  0000   00059          IS EMPTY. *)
1  0000   00060
1  0000   00061       BEGIN
1  003C   00062           ERROR := TRUE;
1  0044   00063           WRITELN ('0', '*** AN ERROR OCCURS DURING DELETION FROM ',
1  0068   00064               'THE QUEUE.');
1  007A   00065           WRITELN (' ', 'THE VECTOR IS EMPTY PRIOR TO DELETION.' : 45);
1  009E   00066       END;
0  0038   00067
0  0038   00068       PROCEDURE QINSERT (VAR Q: VECTOR; VAR F, R: INTEGER; X: INTEGER);
1  0000   00069       (* GIVEN VECTOR Q AND FRONT AND REAR POINTERS F AND R, THIS
1  0000   00070          PROCEDURE INSERTS X AT THE REAR OF THE QUEUE.  AN EMPTY QUEUE
1  0000   00071          IS SIGNALLED BY F AND R BOTH HAVING A VALUE OF ZERO. *)
1  0000   00072
1  0000   00073       BEGIN
1  006E   00074
1  006E   00075           (* OVERFLOW CONDITION? *)
1  006E   00076           IF R >= 100
1  006E   00077           THEN Q_OVERF
1  007A   00078           ELSE BEGIN
1  008A   00079
1  008A   00080               (* INCREMENT REAR POINTER *)
```

Fig. 10-9   Program MEM_SIM: Simulation of memory allocation

```
1  008A  00081                        R := R + 1;
1  0096  00082
1  0096  00083                        (* INSERT NEW ELEMENT *)
1  0096  00084                        Q(R) := X;
1  00C0  00085
1  00C0  00086                        (* IS THE FRONT POINTER PROPERLY SET? *)
1  00C0  00087                        IF F = 0
1  00C0  00088                        THEN F := 1
1  00CC  00089                        END
1  00D4  00090       END;
0  0038  00091
0  0038  00092   PROCEDURE QDELETE (Q: VECTOR; VAR F, R, X: INTEGER);
1  0000  00093   (* GIVEN VECTOR Q AND FRONT AND REAR POINTERS F AND R, THIS
1  0000  00094        PROCEDURE DELETES THE FRONT ELEMENT FROM THE QUEUE AND PLACES
1  0000  00095        THAT ELEMENT INTO X.  AN EMPTY QUEUE IS SIGNALLED BY F AND R
1  0000  00096        BOTH HAVING A VALUE OF ZERO. *)
1  0000  00097
1  0000  00098   BEGIN
1  0086  00099
1  0086  00100       (* UNDERFLOW CONDITION? *)
1  0086  00101       IF F = 0
1  0086  00102       THEN Q_UNDER
1  0092  00103       ELSE BEGIN
1  00A2  00104
1  00A2  00105          (* DELETE FRONT ELEMENT *)
1  00A2  00106          X := Q(F);
1  00CC  00107
1  00CC  00108          (* IS QUEUE NOW EMPTY? *)
1  00CC  00109          IF F = R
1  00CC  00110          THEN BEGIN
1  00D8  00111             F := 0;
1  00DE  00112             R := 0
1  00DE  00113          END
1  00E4  00114          ELSE (* INCREMENT FRONT POINTER *)
1  00E4  00115             F := F + 1
1  00E8  00116       END
1  00F4  00117       END;
0  0038  00118
```

Fig. 10-9   Program MEM_SIM: Simulation of memory allocation (cont'd.)

two customers.) The number of items bought by each customer can also be approximated by selecting a random number in the range [1, 40]. The time taken for a customer to proceed through a checkout once the cashier begins "ringing up" his or her groceries can be calculated by assuming an average rate of 30 seconds per item (ringing plus wrapping time).

A random number can be generated by using the SIN function. For example, we choose an initial value for X. Finding an integer of three significant figures can be done by calling

SIN (X) * 1000.0

and truncating this result using the PASCAL built-in function TRUNC. The truncated value is assigned to an integer variable, say RANDOM. In other words, RANDOM is the value of the sine of X with the decimal place shifted to the right three places and no digits to the left of the decimal. Finally, finding a random number in the range (0, 360) can be done using the PASCAL MOD operator as follows

RANDOM MOD 361

For the next random number, we use the following assignment statement:

X := RANDOM – SIN (X) * 1000.0

```
0  0038  00119        PROCEDURE QFILE (VAR Q: VECTOR; VAR F, R: INTEGER; X: INTEGER;
1  0000  00120            VAR P: INTEGER; D: INTEGER);
1  0000  00121        (* GIVEN A VECTOR Q AND FRONT AND REAR POINTERS F AND R, THIS
1  0000  00122           PROCEDURE INSERTS X IN THE APPROPRIATE PLACE IN THE PRIORITY
1  0000  00123           QUEUE REPRESENTED BY Q.  P POINTS TO THE PLACE AT WHICH X IS
1  0000  00124           INSERTED.  D IS AN INTEGER PARAMETER SPECIFYING THE ORDERING
1  0000  00125           DIRECTION FOR THE QUEUE.  IF D > 0, THE QUEUE IS ASSUMED TO BE
1  0000  00126           IN ASCENDING ORDER FROM FRONT TO REAR; IF D < 0, THE QUEUE IS
1  0000  00127           ASSUMED TO BE IN DECREASING ORDER.
1  0000  00128           AN EMPTY QUEUE IS SIGNALLED BY F AND R BOTH HAVING A VALUE OF
1  0000  00129           ZERO. *)
1  0000  00130
1  0000  00131        VAR L: INTEGER;          (* TEMPORARY COUNTER      *)
1  0086  00132
1  0086  00133        BEGIN
1  0086  00134
1  0086  00135            (* OVERFLOW CONDITION? *)
1  0086  00136            IF R >= 100
1  0086  00137            THEN Q_OVERF
1  0092  00138            ELSE BEGIN
1  00A2  00139
1  00A2  00140                (* INCREMENT REAR POINTER TO ACCOMODATE INSERTION
1  00A2  00141                   OF NEW ELEMENT *)
1  00A2  00142                R := R + 1;
1  00AE  00143
1  00AE  00144                (* FIND APPROPRIATE POSITION FOR NEW ELEMENT *)
1  00AE  00145                IF F = 0
1  00AE  00146                THEN P := 1
1  00BA  00147                ELSE P := F;
1  00CE  00148
1  00CE  00149                (* IN WHICH DIRECTION IS THE QUEUE TO BE ORDERED? *)
1  00CE  00150                IF D > 0          (* ASCENDING ORDER *)
1  00CE  00151                THEN WHILE (X > Q(P)) AND (P < R) DO
1  0114  00152                        P := P + 1
1  0114  00153                ELSE WHILE (X < Q(P)) AND (P < R) DO
1  0162  00154                        P := P + 1;
1  0172  00155
1  0172  00156                (* SHIFT REMAINING ELEMENTS ONE POSITION *)
1  0172  00157                FOR L := R DOWNTO P + 1 DO
1  0198  00158                        Q(L) := Q(L - 1);
1  01EE  00159
1  01EE  00160                (* INSERT NEW ELEMENT *)
1  01EE  00161                Q(P) := X;
1  0218  00162
1  0218  00163                (* IS FRONT POINTER PROPERLY SET? *)
1  0218  00164                IF F = 0
1  0218  00165                THEN F := 1
1  0224  00166                END
1  022C  00167        END;
0  0038  00168
0  0038  00169        PROCEDURE QPLACE (VAR Q: VECTOR; VAR F, R: INTEGER;
1  0000  00170            X, P: INTEGER);
1  0000  00171        (* GIVEN A VECTOR Q AND FRONT AND REAR POINTERS F AND R, THIS
1  0000  00172           PROCEDURE INSERTS X AT POSITION P IN THE PRIORITY QUEUE
1  0000  00173           REPRESENTED BY Q.  THE QUEUE IS ASSUMED TO BE IN ASCENDING
1  0000  00174           ORDER FROM FRONT TO REAR.  AN EMPTY QUEUE IS SIGNALLED BY F
1  0000  00175           AND R BOTH HAVING A VALUE OF ZERO. *)
1  0000  00176
1  0000  00177        VAR L: INTEGER;          (* TEMPORARY COUNTER *)
1  007A  00178
1  007A  00179        BEGIN
1  007A  00180
1  007A  00181            (* OVERFLOW CONDITION? *)
1  007A  00182            IF R >= 100
1  007A  00183            THEN Q_OVERF
1  0086  00184            ELSE BEGIN
1  0096  00185
1  0096  00186                (* ADJUST ELEMENT POSITIONS ACCORDINGLY *)
1  0096  00187                R := R + 1;
1  00A2  00188                FOR L := R DOWNTO P + 1 DO
1  00C8  00189                        Q(L) := Q(L - 1);
1  011E  00190
1  011E  00191                (* INSERT NEW ELEMENT AT POSITION P *)
1  011E  00192                Q(P) := X;
1  0148  00193
1  0148  00194                (* IS FRONT POINTER PROPERLY SET? *)
1  0148  00195                IF F = 0
1  0148  00196                THEN F := 1
1  0154  00197                END
1  015C  00198        END;
```

Fig. 10-9 Program MEM_SIM: Simulation of memory allocation (cont'd.)

```
0  0038   00199
0  0038   00200   BEGIN     (* MAIN PROGRAM *)
0  0038   00201
0  0038   00202       (* INITIALIZE COUNTER, ALL QUEUE POINTERS, ALL QUEUES,
0  0038   00203          ERROR FLAG AND TIMING LOOP CONTROLLER *)
0  0038   00204       COMPLETIONS := 0;
0  003E   00205       MF1 := 0; MR1 := 0; EF1 := 0; ER1 := 0; AF1 := 0; AR1 := 0;
0  0062   00206       MF2 := 0; MR2 := 0; EF2 := 0; ER2 := 0; AF2 := 0; AR2 := 0;
0  0086   00207       EF3 := 0; ER3 := 0; AF3 := 0; AR3 := 0;
0  009E   00208       EF4 := 0; ER4 := 0;
0  00AA   00209       FOR J := 1 TO 100 DO
0  00CE   00210       BEGIN
0  00CE   00211           MEM_Q_ADDR(J) := 0; MEM_Q_SIZE(J) := 0;
0  011E   00212           EXEC_Q_ID(J) := 0; EXEC_Q_ADDR(J) := 0; EXEC_Q_TIME(J) := 0;
0  0196   00213           EXEC_Q_SIZE(J) := 0;
0  01BE   00214           ARR_Q_ID(J) := 0; ARR_Q_MEM(J) := 0; ARR_Q_TIME(J) := 0;
0  0236   00215       END;
0  023A   00216       ERROR := FALSE;
0  0242   00217       MINUTE := 1;
0  024A   00218
0  024A   00219       QFILE (MEM_Q_SIZE, MF2, MR2, 10000, P, -1);
0  0290   00220       QPLACE (MEM_Q_ADDR, MF1, MR1, 0000, P);
0  02CE   00221
0  02CE   00222       (* PRINT A HEADING FOR OUTPUT *)
0  02CE   00223       WRITELN (' ', 'MEMORY REQUEST', 'TIME REQUEST' : 22);
0  0304   00224       WRITELN;
0  0312   00225
0  0312   00226       (* ENGAGE TIMING LOOP *)
0  0312   00227       WHILE (MINUTE <= 30) AND NOT ERROR DO
0  032C   00228       BEGIN
0  032C   00229
0  032C   00230           (* READ INFORMATION FOR NEXT ARRIVAL AND FILE IN ARRIVALS
0  032C   00231              QUEUE *)
0  032C   00232           READ (MEM_REQUEST, TIME_REQUEST);
0  0350   00233
0  0350   00234           (* OUTPUT THE PRESENT REQUESTS *)
0  0350   00235           WRITELN (' ', MEM_REQUEST : 8, TIME_REQUEST : 23);
0  0386   00236
0  0386   00237           QINSERT (ARR_Q_ID, AF1, AR1, MINUTE);   (* FIFO QUEUE *)
0  03BC   00238           QINSERT (ARR_Q_MEM, AF2, AR2, MEM_REQUEST);
0  03F2   00239           QINSERT (ARR_Q_TIME, AF3, AR3, TIME_REQUEST);
0  0428   00240
0  0428   00241           (* IS ENOUGH MEMORY AVAILABLE TO SATISFY FIRST JOB IN
0  0428   00242              ARRIVALS QUEUE? *)
0  0428   00243           QDELETE (MEM_Q_SIZE, MF2, MR2, HOLE_SIZE);  (* LARGEST HOLE*)
0  045E   00244           QDELETE (MEM_Q_ADDR, MF1, MR1, ADDR);
0  0494   00245           MEM_REQUEST := ARR_Q_MEM(AF2);
0  04BE   00246
0  04BE   00247           (* QUEUE OVERFLOW OR UNDERFLOW? *)
0  04BE   00248           IF NOT ERROR
0  04BE   00249           THEN BEGIN
0  04CC   00250               IF HOLE_SIZE >= MEM_REQUEST
0  04CC   00251               THEN BEGIN
0  04D8   00252
0  04D8   00253                   (* REMOVE FIRST JOB FROM ARRIVALS QUEUE *)
0  04D8   00254                   QDELETE (ARR_Q_ID, AF1, AR1, ID);
0  050E   00255                   QDELETE (ARR_Q_MEM, AF2, AR2, MEM);
0  0544   00256                   QDELETE (ARR_Q_TIME, AF3, AR3, TIME);
0  057A   00257
0  057A   00258                   (* ADJUST HOLE ACCORDINGLY *)
0  057A   00259                   HOLE_SIZE := HOLE_SIZE - MEM;
0  0586   00260                   ADDR := ADDR + MEM;
0  0592   00261
0  0592   00262                   (* FILE NEW HOLE IN MEMORY QUEUE AND JOB IN
0  0592   00263                      EXECUTION QUEUE *)
0  0592   00264                   QFILE (MEM_Q_SIZE, MF2, MR2, HOLE_SIZE, P, -1);
0  05D8   00265                   QPLACE (MEM_Q_ADDR, MF1, MR1, ADDR, P);
0  0616   00266                   QFILE (EXEC_Q_TIME, EF3, ER3, TIME, P, +1);
0  0664   00267                   QPLACE (EXEC_Q_ID, EF1, ER1, ID, P);
0  06A2   00268                   QPLACE (EXEC_Q_ADDR, EF2, ER2, ADDR - MEM, P);
0  06EC   00269                   QPLACE (EXEC_Q_SIZE, EF4, ER4, MEM, P)
0  0714   00270                   END
0  072A   00271               ELSE BEGIN
0  072E   00272
0  072E   00273                   (* REINSERT FREE BLOCK *)
0  072E   00274                   QFILE (MEM_Q_SIZE, MF2, MR2, HOLE_SIZE, P, -1);
0  0774   00275                   QPLACE (MEM_Q_ADDR, MF1, MR1, ADDR, P)
0  079C   00276                   END
0  07B2   00277               END;
0  07B2   00278
```

Fig. 10-9   Program MEM_SIM: Simulation of memory allocation (cont'd.)

```
0  07B2  00279               (* TAKE 1 MINUTE OFF TIME REMAINING FOR EACH
0  07B2  00280                  EXECUTING JOB AND PROCESS ANY COMPLETIONS *)
0  07B2  00281               J := EF3;
0  07BA  00282               WHILE (J <= ER3) AND (EF3 <> 0) AND NOT ERROR DO
0  07E0  00283               BEGIN
0  07E0  00284                   EXEC_Q_TIME(J) := EXEC_Q_TIME(J) - 1;  (* ASSUME
0  07E0  00285                                                PARALLEL PROCESSING *)
0  0830  00286                   IF EXEC_Q_TIME(J) = 0
0  0856  00287                   THEN BEGIN
0  085E  00288                       COMPLETIONS := COMPLETIONS + 1;
0  086A  00289
0  086A  00290                       (* DELETE THIS JOB FROM EXEC QUEUE *)
0  086A  00291                       QDELETE (EXEC_Q_ID, EF1, ER1, ID);
0  08A0  00292                       QDELETE (EXEC_Q_ADDR, EF2, ER2, ADDR);
0  08D6  00293                       QDELETE (EXEC_Q_TIME, EF3, ER3, TIME);
0  090C  00294                       QDELETE (EXEC_Q_SIZE, EF4, ER4, MEM);
0  0942  00295                       WRITELN ('0', 'JOB ', ID : 2, ' IS COMPLETED ',
0  098A  00296                               'AT TIME ', MINUTE : 2);
0  09AE  00297                       WRITELN;
0  09BC  00298
0  09BC  00299                       (* RETURN NEWLY COMPLETED JOB'S
0  09BC  00300                          MEMORY TO MEMORY QUEUE *)
0  09BC  00301                       QFILE (MEM_Q_SIZE, MF2, MR2, MEM, P, -1);
0  0A02  00302                       QPLACE (MEM_Q_ADDR, MF1, MR1, ADDR, P)
0  0A2A  00303                       END;
0  0A40  00304                   J := J + 1
0  0A40  00305               END; (* OF PARALLEL PROCESSING *)
0  0A50  00306               MINUTE := MINUTE + 1
0  0A50  00307           END; (* OF TIMING LOOP *)
0  0A60  00308
0  0A60  00309           (* END OF SIMULATION *)
0  0A60  00310           WRITELN ('-', 'NUMBER OF JOBS PROCESSED: ' : 30, COMPLETIONS : 3)
0  0A96  00311
0  0A96  00312           (* FINISHED *)
0  0A96  00313 END.
```

```
-----------------------------------
| COMPILE TIME:    0.783 SECOND(S) |
|    NO WARNING(S) DETECTED        |
|    NO ERROR(S) DETECTED          |
-----------------------------------
```

Fig. 10-9   Program MEM_SIM: Simulation of memory allocation (cont'd.)

In setting up the simulation we should realize that prior to bringing a new customer into the checkout area, we must ensure that all customers who have had their groceries processed are removed from the waiting lines. Assume that no more than 10 customers are waiting in line at any one time for a regular checkout, and no more than 15 are waiting in line at any one time for an express checkout.

You are to formulate a program which simulates the checkout service just described. The desired output should contain the number of customers going through the checkout per hour, the total number of customers handled per hour, the average waiting time at each checkout, the overall average waiting time in minutes, the number of items processed at each checkout per hour, and the total number of items processed per hour. The waiting time is the time the customer spends in the checkout area.

Output having the following format is desirable:

	1	2	3	Express	Total
No. customers/hr	10	11	14	20	55
Avg. waiting time	2.80	3.01	2.96	0.22	1.94
Items processed/hr	192	261	210	65	728

```
--EXECUTION-->                        JOB 11 IS COMPLETED AT TIME 17
MEMORY REQUEST        TIME REQUEST
                                         800                    5
     500                 1
                                      JOB 16 IS COMPLETED AT TIME 18
JOB  1 IS COMPLETED AT TIME  1
                                      JOB 13 IS COMPLETED AT TIME 18
     300                 4
     9200                2                400                    6
     600                 4
                                      JOB 17 IS COMPLETED AT TIME 19
JOB  3 IS COMPLETED AT TIME  4
                                         253                    2
     400                10
                                      JOB 15 IS COMPLETED AT TIME 20
JOB  2 IS COMPLETED AT TIME  5
                                         632                    2
     500                 4               250                    5
     300                 5
     350                 6            JOB 20 IS COMPLETED AT TIME 22

JOB  4 IS COMPLETED AT TIME  8           321                    1

     400                 1            JOB 21 IS COMPLETED AT TIME 23
     1000                4
                                      JOB 18 IS COMPLETED AT TIME 23
JOB  9 IS COMPLETED AT TIME 10
                                         342                    2
JOB  6 IS COMPLETED AT TIME 10
                                      JOB 23 IS COMPLETED AT TIME 24
     200                 6
     600                 2               325                    2

JOB  7 IS COMPLETED AT TIME 12       JOB 19 IS COMPLETED AT TIME 25

     800                 5               123                    3
     300                 2
                                      JOB 24 IS COMPLETED AT TIME 26
JOB 12 IS COMPLETED AT TIME 14
                                         325                    8
JOB 10 IS COMPLETED AT TIME 14
                                      JOB 25 IS COMPLETED AT TIME 27
JOB  8 IS COMPLETED AT TIME 14
                                      JOB 22 IS COMPLETED AT TIME 27
     100                 5
                                         522                    3
JOB  5 IS COMPLETED AT TIME 15           3422                  10

     300                 2            JOB 26 IS COMPLETED AT TIME 29

JOB 14 IS COMPLETED AT TIME 16           322                    3

     400                 2              NUMBER OF JOBS PROCESSED:  26
```

Fig. 10-9 Program MEM_SIM: Simulation of memory allocation (cont'd.)

Simulate the situation in which there are four standard checkouts, using the same method of generating arrival times and number of items purchased. Your program should be designed so that the second simulation can be performed with very few changes to the original program.

10-8 LINKED LINEAR LISTS

Thus far, we have used the sequential allocation method to represent data structures in the computer's memory. Using this method of allocation, the address or location of an element in memory is obtained through direct computation.

An alternate storage-allocation approach is to use pointers or links (see Sec. 10-1) to refer to elements of a linear list. Recall from Sec. 10-8 of the main text that the approach is to store the address of the successor of a particular element in that element. This method of allocating storage is called linked allocation. In this section we examine the programming aspects of using linked lists in PASCAL. Such programming details cover the creation and manipulation of linked linear lists.

As an aid in introducing certain programming details related to linked allocation, let us consider a simple student registration application at a university. The information associated with each student can be represented by a record. Associated with each record is a set of properties such as student number, student name, and year of study. For a particular student, each property has a certain value. For example, a certain student might have a name of 'LYLE OPSETH', a student number of 75250 and a year of study of 1979. Conceptually, all the properties or fields in a record belong together, thus reflecting their relationship to one another. The structures discussed in Sec. 10-2 can be used to represent such a relationship.

In PASCAL, each programmer can create a template for a record structure by creating a programmer-defined data type as previously mentioned, and pointer variables that can point to instances of this structure. This facility permits the programmer to specify what fields are to be grouped together and in what order. This declaration also gives a name to the grouping or record.

For example, the statement

```
TYPE STUDENT_TEMPLATE = RECORD
        NAME: STRING(20);
        NUMBER,
        YEAR: INTEGER
        END;
VAR P: @STUDENT_TEMPLATE;
```

declares a record structure, which consists of the fields NUMBER, NAME, and YEAR. Such a declaration results in the definition of the node or record structure only. It does not allocate storage for the fields named. The declaration simply indicates the makeup of the record structure. The variable P is a pointer which can point to instances of STUDENT_TEMPLATE once an actual record in memory has been dynamically created.

The creation of actual records is controlled by using built-in procedure NEW elsewhere in the program. Specifically a record is created by the programmer in the following way:

```
NEW (P)
```

This procedure call allocates storage space for the three fields — NUMBER, NAME, and YEAR. Since many instances of the structure can be created in this way, a field name such as NAME is not enough for unambiguously specifying the name field. We must be able to reference, by the use of an address or pointer, a certain field within a particular record. This reference designator is a pointer variable which has as its value the address of the record in question. When the function NEW is called, a pointer variable is given as an argument and it receives the address of the newly created record. Note that the storage space created is for the data type to which the variable may point. For example, if we have the declarations for STUDENT_TEMPLATE and P as previously given, and Q is defined as a pointer to STUDENT_TEMPLATE, the procedure call

NEW (P)

creates storage for a new record with the given fields and sets P to the address of the newly created location. The procedure call

NEW (Q)

sets Q to the address of another record which is not the same one pointed to by P.

The reference of a particular record of a location in memory or of a field within this record is accomplished by using pointer qualification. For example, P@.STUDENT denotes the record generated by the last NEW statement for which P was the argument. The fields are referenced as P@.NAME, P@.NUMBER, and P@.YEAR. The PASCAL notation corresponds to the algorithmic notation STUDENT(P), NAME(P), NUMBER(P), and YEAR(P) of the main text.

At this point, a discussion on the difference between accessing dynamically created storage with the use of pointer variables and storage created at compile time is given. To access storage pointed to by Q, we use the PASCAL notation Q@. Note that we use Q@ as if it were a regular variable name. Memory for a record could be created statically at compile time as follows

VAR STUDENT: STUDENT_TEMPLATE;

in which case the accessing of any field in STUDENT is done via STUDENT. We could access the name of a student with either STUDENT.NAME or P@.NAME. Furthermore, memory may be allocated for non-structure data types. We can have a pointer pointing to a real value, which may be declared as

VAR P: @REAL;

In this case, we access the value pointed to by P after storage has been allocated with the procedure call NEW(P) by the reference P@. The @ signifies that P is a pointer to a location which is assigned at runtime. An assignment of the real value 2.2 to the location pointed to by P is simply P@ := 2.2. In the case of a structure, the sequence of assignment statements

P@.NAME := 'LYLE OPSETH';
P@.NUMBER := 75250;
P@.YEAR := 1979;

initializes NAME, NUMBER, and YEAR of the created record to values of 'LYLE OPSETH', 75250, and 1979, respectively.

Having created a record and placing its address in the pointer variable P by executing the procedure call NEW (P), the programmer is now in a position to use or change the values of the fields in the record. The following simple PASCAL program, which creates a record, assigns values to the three fields NAME, NUMBER, and YEAR, and outputs the results, illustrates this:

```
PROGRAM SAMPLE (INPUT, OUTPUT);
(* PROGRAM TO CREATE AND OUTPUT A RECORD *)
TYPE STUDENT_TEMPLATE = RECORD
            NAME: STRING(20);
            NUMBER,
            YEAR: INTEGER
     END;
VAR P: @STUDENT_TEMPLATE;
BEGIN
     NEW(P);
     P@.NAME := 'JUDY BLACK';
     P@.NUMBER := 79100;
     P@.YEAR := 1980;
     WRITELN (' NAME IS ', P@.NAME);
     WRITELN (' NUMBER IS ', P@.NUMBER: 5);
     WRITELN (' YEAR IS ', P@.YEAR: 4)
END.
NAME IS JUDY BLACK
NUMBER IS 79100
YEAR IS 1980
```

PASCAL allows not only the allocation of structures, but the freeing of such structures to available storage. This is accomplished by the procedure call

DISPOSE (P)

which causes the storage location indicated by pointer P to be restored to the availability area.

Pointer variables usually specify a memory address. An exception occurs when a pointer variable is assigned the special value NIL. This special value is not the address of some location in memory and, therefore, a record. NIL always has the same value and, consequently, it can be used as an end-of-list delimiter. The only comparisons which can be made between NIL and a pointer variable or between two pointer variables are those of "equal" and "not equal". NIL is similar to the NULL or empty address used in the algorithmic notation.

As another example involving pointers, consider the following problem. It is required to write a program which reads in N sets of data consisting of employee number, employee name, hourly wage, and hours worked. A record is created for each set of data consisting of an input set and an additional field denoting gross pay. The addresses of the created records are to be stored in a pointer array which is indexed by employee number. Assume that the employee numbers in the input are unique and that their values are between one and fifty. A program which performs the desired task for the following input is given in Fig. 10-10.

Employee Number	Employee Name	Rate	Hours
5	'LYLE OPSETH'	3.50	50
17	'JUDY RICHARDSON'	4.00	20
20	'HOWARD HAMILTON'	3.75	10

```
0  0000   00001   PROGRAM PAYROLL (INPUT, OUTPUT);
0  0000   00002   (* SAMPLE PAYROLL PROGRAM *)
0  0000   00003
0  0000   00004   TYPE POINTER = @EMPLOYEE;
0  0038   00005       EMPLOYEE = RECORD        (* REQUIRED DATA STRUCTURE CLASS *)
0  0038   00006           NAME: STRING(20);
0  0038   00007           RATE,
0  0038   00008           HOURS,
0  0038   00009           PAY: REAL;
0  0038   00010           END;
0  0038   00011   VAR MEMBER: ARRAY(1..50) OF POINTER;
0  0038   00012                               (* REFERENCE ARRAY FOR EMPOLYEES *)
0  0038   00013       NUMBER,                  (* EMPLOYEE NUMBER *)
0  0038   00014       N,                       (* NUMBER OF EMPOLYEES TO READ *)
0  0038   00015       I: INTEGER;              (* COUNTED LOOP VARIABLE *)
0  0038   00016       P: POINTER;              (* TEMPORARY POINTER VARIABLE *)
0  0038   00017
0  0038   00018   BEGIN
0  0038   00019
0  0038   00020       (* READ THE NUMBER OF EMPOLYEES TO INPUT *)
0  0038   00021       READ (N);
0  004A   00022       WRITELN (' ', 'NUMBER', 'EMPLOYEE NAME' : 16,
0  0080   00023           'WAGE RATE' : 21, 'HOURS' : 11, 'GROSS PAY' : 14);
0  00B6   00024       WRITELN;
0  00C4   00025
0  00C4   00026       (* PROCESS EMPLOYEES *)
0  00C4   00027       FOR I := 1 TO N DO
0  00E8   00028       BEGIN
0  00E8   00029
0  00E8   00030           (* CREATE A NODE *)
0  00E8   00031           NEW (P);
0  00FA   00032
0  00FA   00033           (* READ AN EMPLOYEE CARD *)
0  00FA   00034           READ (NUMBER, P@.NAME, P@.RATE, P@.HOURS);
0  0182   00035
0  0182   00036           (* PLACE ADDRESS OF CREATED NODE INTO ARRAY AND COMPUTE PAY *)
0  0182   00037           MEMBER(NUMBER) := P;
0  01AC   00038           P@.PAY := P@.HOURS * P@.RATE;
0  0200   00039           WRITELN (' ', NUMBER : 4, P@.NAME : 25, P@.RATE : 12 : 2,
0  0272   00040               P@.HOURS : 13 : 1, P@.PAY : 13 : 2)
0  02C2   00041       END
0  02C2   00042   END.
----------------------------------
| COMPILE TIME:   0.102 SECOND(S) |
|    NO WARNING(S) DETECTED       |
|    NO ERROR(S) DETECTED         |
----------------------------------
--EXECUTION-->
NUMBER   EMPLOYEE NAME          WAGE RATE    HOURS    GROSS PAY

   5     LYLE OPSETH              3.50        50.0      175.00
  17     JUDY RICHARDSON          4.00        20.0       80.00
  20     HOWARD HAMILTON          3.75        10.0       37.50
```

Fig. 10-10   Payroll Program using dynamic storage

First, the data type whose record structure consists of four fields having names of NAME, RATE, HOURS, and PAY is defined. Then a 50-element pointer vector named MEMBER whose associated subscript is any valid employee number is created and may point to instances of the EMPLOYEE structure.

The NEW (P) procedure call creates a record and stores its address in the pointer variable P. This address is then used to assign values to the four fields of the newly created record. The subscript of the vector element is given by the employee number read in. For the data of the three employees given earlier, three records whose addresses are stored into vector elements MEMBER(5), MEMBER(17), and MEMBER(20) are created. The program also outputs all related employee information.

Let us now discuss the representation of linked linear lists. This is accomplished by having a pointer field in a record contain the address of its successor. When pointers are used, all available space is allocated by the compiler. Similarly, the return of an unused record from a linked list to the availability area of memory is also handled by the compiler. We are, therefore, not concerned with available storage in the discussion to follow.

  In the example programs that follow we assume the record structure and pointer P are defined by the following

```
TYPE POINTER = @NODE
     NODE = RECORD
            INFO: STRING(5);
            LINK: POINTER
          END;
```

Notice that we define POINTER as a programmer-defined data type which points to instances of the NODE data structure. The following PASCAL function inserts a new record or node at the front of a linked list. The function has two parameters — FIRST and X. FIRST denotes the address of the first record in the list, while X contains the information contents of the new record.

```
FUNCTION L_FRONT (VAR FIRST: POINTER; X: STRING(5)): POINTER;
(* THIS FUNCTION INSERTS A NODE OR RECORD IN THE LINKED LIST
        WHICH WILL IMMEDIATELY PRECEDE THE RECORD WHOSE
        ADDRESS IS DESIGNATED BY FIRST. THE POINTER TO THE NEW
        RECORD IS RETURNED. *)
VAR P : POINTER;
BEGIN
      (* CREATE A NODE *)
      NEW (P);
      (* INITIALIZE INFORMATION AND LINK FIELDS *)
      P@.INFO := X;
      P@.LINK := FIRST;
      (* RETURN ADDRESS OF THE NEW NODE *)
      L_FRONT := P
END;
```

  This function can be invoked repeatedly, resulting in the construction of a linked linear list. Initially, we begin with an empty list. On each invocation of L_FRONT, a new node is inserted at the front of the existing linked list. The following sequence of five assignment statements in which LIST is a pointer variable creates a linked list of four records in a stack-like manner. That is, 'RICK' and 'BOB' become the information contents of the fourth record and first record, respectively.

```
LIST := NIL;
LIST := L_FRONT (LIST, 'RICK');
LIST := L_FRONT (LIST, 'PAUL');
LIST := L_FRONT (LIST, 'GRANT');
LIST := L_FRONT (LIST, 'BOB');
```

  We can also create a linked list by inserting a new record at the end of the existing list. To perform such an insertion first requires that the end of the existing list be found. That is, we must chain through that list until a LINK field with a value of NIL is found. At this point the new node can be inserted. The following PASCAL program segment in which SAVE and FIRST are pointer variables performs the required task:

```
SAVE := FIRST;
WHILE SAVE@.LINK < > NIL DO
        SAVE := SAVE@.LINK;
SAVE@.LINK := P
```

This program segment becomes part of the following function:

```
FUNCTION LEND (FIRST: POINTER; X: STRING(5)): POINTER;
(* THIS FUNCTION INSERTS A NODE OR RECORD AT THE END OF A
        LINKED LIST WHOSE FRONT NODE IS DENOTED BY FIRST, AND
        RETURNS THE ADDRESS OF THE FRONT NODE OF THE UPDATED
        LIST. *)
VAR P, SAVE: POINTER;
BEGIN
        (* CREATE A NEW NODE *)
        NEW (P);
        (* INITIALIZE CONTENTS OF NEW NODE *)
        P@.INFO := X;
        P@.LINK := NIL;
        (* IS THE ORIGINAL LIST EMPTY? *)
        IF FIRST = NIL
        THEN LEND := P
        ELSE BEGIN
                (* SEARCH FOR THE LAST NODE OF THE LINKED LIST
                        AND PERFORM INSERTION. *)
                SAVE := FIRST;
                WHILE SAVE@.LINK < > NIL DO
                        SAVE := SAVE@.LINK;
                SAVE@.LINK := P;
                (* RETURN FIRST NODE POINTER *)
                LEND := FIRST
                END
    END;
```

The following program segment creates the linked list of four records described earlier.

```
LIST := NIL;
LIST := LEND (LIST, 'BOB');
LIST := LEND (LIST, 'GRANT');
LIST := LEND (LIST, 'PAUL');
LIST := LEND (LIST, 'RICK');
```

Note that the performance of the function LEND degenerates progressively as the list gets larger. The traversal of such a long list to perform the next insertion can be avoided by keeping the address of the last inserted node. Using this approach, an insertion operation involves changing the link field of the last node (which has the value NIL) of the existing list to the address of the new node being inserted. The following function incorporates this modification to inserting a new record at the end of a list.

```
FUNCTION LLAST (VAR FIRST, LAST: POINTER; X: STRING(5)): POINTER;
(* THIS FUNCTION INSERTS A NODE OR RECORD AT THE END OF A
        LINKED LIST WHOSE FRONT NODE IS DENOTED BY FIRST. LAST
        IS A POINTER WHICH CONTAINS THE ADDRESS OF THE LAST
        NODE IN THE LIST BEFORE INSERTION. *)
VAR P: POINTER;
BEGIN
    (* CREATE A NEW NODE *)
    NEW (P);
    (* INITIALIZE CONTENTS OF NEW NODE *)
    P@.INFO := X;
    P@.LINK := NIL;
    (* IS LIST EMPTY? *)
    IF FIRST = NIL
    THEN BEGIN
        LAST := NEW;
        LLAST := P
        END
    ELSE BEGIN
        (* INSERT NODE AT END OF NONEMPTY LIST *)
        LAST@.LINK := P;
        LAST := P;
        LLAST := FIRST
        END
END;
```

Now that a number of insertion programs have been given, let us look at another equally important operation — that of deleting a record from a linked linear list. There are several ways of specifying which record is to be deleted. For example, we can denote the record to be deleted by giving its address. Another approach is to specify the INFO value of the record to be deleted. The procedure given in Fig. 10-11 is an implementation of the deletion operation for the latter approach.

Line 18 saves the value of the pointer which points to the front of the list. In line 19, a check is made for a deletion from an empty list. If the list is not empty, the procedure checks whether the first element in the list is the one to be deleted, and deletes it if it can. Otherwise, a search is made in the list for the desired element. The address of the current node being examined is stored in NEXT, while the address of the previous node that was examined is saved in the pointer variable PRED. Finally, the appropriate record is deleted from the list in line 46, if it is found; otherwise, an error message is printed.

The link field of the last record in a linked linear list can be changed from its NIL value to point to the first record in the list. The resulting circular structure is

```
0  0038   00011  PROCEDURE DELETE (VAR FIRST: POINTER; X: STRING(5));
1  0000   00012  (* FIND AND DELETE A RECORD WITH INFORMATION CONTENTS X FROM
1  0000   00013    A LINKED LIST POINTED TO BY THE VARIABLE FIRST. *)
1  0000   00014
1  0000   00015  VAR PRED, NEXT, SAVE: POINTER;
1  0058   00016
1  0058   00017  BEGIN
1  0058   00018      SAVE := FIRST;
1  0060   00019      IF FIRST = NIL
1  0060   00020      THEN (* INDICATE THAT LIST IS EMPTY *)
1  006C   00021          WRITELN (' ', 'LIST UNDERFLOW')
1  0090   00022      ELSE BEGIN
1  0094   00023          IF FIRST@.INFO = X
1  00AA   00024          THEN BEGIN (* DELETE FIRST RECORD *)
1  00B4   00025              FIRST := FIRST@.LINK;
1  00D6   00026
1  00D6   00027              (* RESTORE FRONT RECORD TO AVAILABILITY AREA *)
1  00D6   00028              DISPOSE (SAVE)
1  00D6   00029              END
1  0104   00030          ELSE BEGIN
1  0108   00031
1  0108   00032              (* INITIALIZE SEARCH FOR X *)
1  0108   00033              PRED := FIRST;
1  0110   00034              NEXT := PRED@.LINK;
1  0132   00035
1  0132   00036              (* PERFORM SEARCH FOR X *)
1  0132   00037              WHILE (NEXT <> NIL) AND (NEXT@.INFO <> X) DO
1  015E   00038              BEGIN
1  015E   00039                  PRED := NEXT;
1  0166   00040                  NEXT := NEXT@.LINK
1  017C   00041              END;
1  018C   00042
1  018C   00043              (* DELETE INDICATED RECORD, IF FOUND *)
1  018C   00044              IF NEXT <> NIL
1  018C   00045              THEN BEGIN
1  0198   00046                  PRED@.LINK := NEXT@.LINK;
1  01D4   00047
1  01D4   00048                  (* RESTORE RECORD WITH INFO X
1  01D4   00049                     TO AVAILABILITY AREA *)
1  01D4   00050                  DISPOSE (NEXT)
1  01D4   00051                  END
1  0202   00052              ELSE (* RECORD NOT FOUND *)
1  0202   00053                  WRITELN (' ', 'RECORD NOT FOUND')
1  022A   00054              END
1  022A   00055          END
1  022A   00056  END;
```

Fig. 10-11   PASCAL procedure for deleting a record from a linked list

called a circular list. Since the processing of such a circular structure can result in an infinite loop, it is desirable to add a list head record (with an address of HEAD) to a circular list. In so doing, a circular list can never be empty. An empty list is denoted by having HEAD@.LINK := HEAD. Usually, the INFO field of the list head is not used in processing a circular list. The following PASCAL procedure inserts a record in a circular list with a list head.

```
PROCEDURE CIFRONT (HEAD: POINTER; X: STRING(5));
(* THIS PROCEDURE INSERTS A RECORD WITH INFO X AT THE FRONT OF
      A CIRCULAR LINKED LIST WHOSE HEAD NODE IS DENOTED BY
      HEAD. *)
VAR P: POINTER;
BEGIN
      (* CREATE A NEW RECORD *)
      NEW (P);
      (* PERFORM INSERTION AND RETURN *)
      P@.INFO := X;
```

```
            P@.LINK := HEAD@.LINK;
            HEAD@.LINK := P
    END;
```

Certain applications require that the predecessor as well as the successor of a node or record in a linear list be known. Also, many of these applications require that the linear list be traversed not only from left to right but right to left as well. The node or record structure is expanded to accommodate these requirements easily. Such an expansion involves adding an additional pointer field to a record which gives the address of the predecessor of that record. The declarations now become

```
    TYPE POINTER = @NODE;
         NODE = RECORD
                LPTR: POINTER;
                INFO: STRING(5);
                RPTR: POINTER
                END;
```

where LPTR and RPTR are pointer fields which denote the predecessor and successor of a given node, respectively. Such a linear list structure is called a doubly-linked linear list. As was done for a circular linear list, it is very desirable to have the doubly-linked circular list with a list head record. Such a structure is called a circular doubly-linked linear list. An empty doubly-linked list has the following property for the pointers of its list head record:

```
    HEAD@.LPTR := HEAD and HEAD@.RPTR := HEAD
```

The following PASCAL procedure inserts a new record into a doubly-linked list to the immediate right of the specified record with address M. X contains the information contents of the new record.

```
    PROCEDURE DOUBLEI (HEAD: POINTER; VAR M: POINTER; X: STRING(5));
    (* THIS PROCEDURE INSERTS A NEW RECORD TO THE IMMEDIATE RIGHT
           OF RECORD M IN A DOUBLY-LINKED LINEAR LIST WHOSE HEAD
           NODE IS DENOTED BY HEAD. *)
    VAR P: POINTER;
    BEGIN
        (* CREATE A NEW RECORD *)
        NEW (P);
        (* INSERT NEW RECORD *)
        P@.INFO := X;
        P@.LPTR := M;
        P@.RPTR := M@.RPTR;
        M@.RPTR@.LPTR := P;
        M@.RPTR := P
    END;
```

Observe the use of a local pointer variable reference M@.RPTR@.LPTR in this program. This is equivalent to the algorithmic notation's use of nested pointers (i.e., LPTR(RPTR(M))).

The following procedure performs the deletion of the node specified by OLD in a doubly-linked linear list.

```
PROCEDURE DOUBLED (HEAD, OLD: POINTER);
(* THIS PROCEDURE DELETES THE RECORD SPECIFIED BY OLD FROM A
        A DOUBLY-LINKED CIRCULAR LIST WHOSE HEAD NODE IS
        DENOTED BY HEAD. *)
BEGIN
        (* DELETE INDICATED RECORD *)
        OLD@.LPTR@.RPTR := OLD@.LPTR;
        OLD@.RPTR@.LPTR := OLD@.RPTR;
        (* RETURN RECORD TO AVAILABILITY AREA *)
        DISPOSE (OLD)
END;
```

In this section we have presented the PASCAL basics of representing linear lists using dynamic storage. The next section gives PASCAL programs for several applications of linked linear lists.

Exercises for Sec. 10-8

1. Given a singly-linked list whose node structure and pointer types are declared as follows:

    ```
    TYPE POINTER = @NODE;
         NODE = RECORD
                INFO: STRING(20);
                LINK: POINTER
                END;
    ```

    write a function which counts the number of nodes in the list. The function is to contain one parameter (FIRST) which contains the address of the front node in the list.

2. Write a function which performs an insertion to the immediate left of the Kth node in a linked linear list. K = 0 specifies that a node is to be inserted into an empty list. The function is to have three parameters; namely,

    FIRST - address of the front node in the linear list.
    K - the Kth node in the existing list.
    X - information content of the new node.

    Assume the same node structure as in exercise 1.

3. Given two linked lists whose front nodes are denoted by the pointers FIRST and SECOND, respectively, obtain a function that concatenates two lists. The front node address of the new list is to be returned by the function. Assume the node structure declaration given in exercise 1.

4. Obtain a procedure which will deconcatenate (or split) a given linked list into

two separate linked lists. The first node of the original linked list is denoted by the pointer variable FIRST. SPLIT denotes the address of the node which is to become the first node of the second linked list. Assume the node declaration structure in exercise 1.

5. Write a procedure which inserts a node at the end of a circular list with a list head node, i.e., between the node which points to the list head and the list head node. The procedure is to have two parameters — HEAD, which denotes the head node, and X, which specifies the information content of the new node.

6. Formulate a procedure which deletes from a circular list with a list head (HEAD), a node whose information content is given by the string variable X.

7. An unknown number of cards are punched, each of which contains a student record with the following information: student number, name, college, sex, and year of study. Each field is separated by at least one blank, and the fields are in the order listed above. The sex is punched as M (male) or F (female). A trailer card with student number of 999999 and "dummy" information in the other four fields is placed at the end of the deck of cards.

    The college and year of study of a student may change. A series of update cards follows the initial deck. Update cards contain information on students who have made changes. The update deck is also followed by a trailer card having student number 999999 and dummy information in the other two fields. The update deck is then followed by a series of cards on which a college name is punched.

    Construct a program to create a linked list of the student records which is ordered by student numbers (smallest to largest). Then read the update cards and update this list. Once all update cards have been read, read the college names and output a well-organized report of all students in that college in alphabetical order. Do this for each college name read in. List the student number, name, sex and year of study for each of these students.

    Note that neither the original file cards nor the student cards are ordered, and it is possible that there may be an update card for a student who is not in the original file, in which case an appropriate error message is to be printed.

10-9 APPLICATIONS OF LINKED LINEAR LISTS

This section discusses three applications of linked linear lists and their associated PASCAL programs. The first application deals with the symbolic addition of polynomial expressions. The second topic describes the application of hashing functions to the operations of searching and sorting. The third and final application is an application of linked queues to radix sorting.

All of the applications are described in detail in Sec. 10-10 of the main text.

10-9.1 Polynomial Manipulation

In this section we concentrate on the symbolic addition of polynomials in three variables. For example, the addition of polynomial $x^2 + xy + x + y^2 + 2z^2$ to polynomial $2x^2 - 2xy + 3x - y^2 + yz$ yields the result $3x^2 - xy + 4x + yz + 2z^2$. A suitable representation of a polynomial in the three variables x, y, and z is given in the following PASCAL statement.

```
TYPE POINTER = @TERM
     TERM = RECORD
            POWER_X,
            POWER_Y,
            POWER_Z: INTEGER;
            COEFF: REAL;
            LINK: POINTER
            END;
```

We assume that the terms in the linked list that represent a polynomial are ordered. More specifically a term with address P precedes another term with address Q, if $P@.POWER\_X > Q@.POWER\_X$; or if these powers are equal, then $P@.POWER\_Y$ must be greater than $Q@.POWER\_Y$; or, if these y powers are equal, then $P@.POWER\_Z$ must be greater than $Q@.POWER\_Z$.

Two polynomials ordered in this way are added by scanning each of their terms only once. For example, a polynomial term $D_1 x^{A_1} y^{B_1} z^{C_1}$ in the first polynomial is added to its corresponding term $D_2 x^{A_2} y^{B_2} z^{C_2}$ in the second term if $A_1 = A_2$, $B_1 = B_2$, and $C_1 = C_2$. In this case the coefficient of the sum term is $D_1 + D_2$.

A general algorithm which uses the functions POLY_INSERT, for inserting a term into a polynomial such that its order is maintained, and POLY_LAST, which inserts a term at the end of a polynomial, and the procedures POLY_ADD, which adds two polynomials, and POLY_PRINT, which prints the resulting polynomial follows:

1. Repeat thru step 6 for all pairs of polynomials
2. Initialize the pointers to the polynomials to nil
3. Repeat for each term of the first polynomial
       Call POLY_INSERT to build linked list representing the polynomial
4. Repeat for each term of the second polynomial
       Call POLY_INSERT to build linked list representing the polynomial
5. Call POLY_ADD to add the two polynomials
6. Call PRINT_POLY to print the answer

Figure 10-12 is a PASCAL program that adds pairs of polynomials. The sample infix expressions used for this program are

$$7x^5y^4z^2 + 7x^5y^4z + 8x^2y^3 + 16xy^3z$$
$$19x^6y^4z + 23x^6y^4 + 3x^5y^4z^2 + 3x^2y^3 + 16xy^3z^2$$

and

$$x^2 + xy + x + y^2 + 2z^2$$
$$2x^2 - 2xy + 3x - y^2 + yz$$

For convenience, we assume that each term of the polynomials is given as four numbers, where the first number denotes the value of the coefficient, while the second, third, and fourth give the values of the exponents x, y, and z, respectively.

The end of the polynomials is denoted by a final term which has a coefficient value of zero.

The variables used in the main program are:

Variable	Type	Usage
POINTER	@NODE	Pointer type pointing to term structure for polynomial
NODE	RECORD	Structure used to store term of polynomial
POWER_X	INTEGER	Exponent of x in term of polynomial
POWER_Y	INTEGER	Exponent of y in term of polynomial
POWER_Z	INTEGER	Exponent of z in term of polynomial
COEFF	REAL	Value of coefficient of term
LINK	POINTER	Points to next term in polynomial
POLY1	POINTER	Points to the first node of the first polynomial
POLY2	POINTER	Points to the first node of the second polynomial
POLY3	POINTER	Points to the first node of sum polynomial
X	INTEGER	Exponent value of x
Y	INTEGER	Exponent value of y
Z	INTEGER	Exponent value of z
C	REAL	Coefficient of term
LAST	POINTER	Points to last node of polynomial

Variables used in the function POLY_INSERT are:

NX	INTEGER	Exponent of x of term to be inserted
NY	INTEGER	Exponent of y of term to be inserted
NZ	INTEGER	Exponent of z of term to be inserted
NCOEFF	INTEGER	Coefficient of term to be inserted
FIRST	POINTER	Points to the first term of the polynomial
NEWPTR	POINTER	Points to the term to be inserted
SAVE	POINTER	Temporary pointer variable
TEMP	POINTER	Temporary pointer variable
A	INTEGER	Value of the exponent of x of the term being examined
B	INTEGER	Value of exponent of y
C	INTEGER	Value of exponent of z
FLAG	BOOLEAN	Indicates if term inserted

Variables used in the procedure POLY_ADD are:

P	POINTER	Points to the first term of the first polynomial
Q	POINTER	Points to the first term of the second polynomial
R	POINTER	Points to the first term of the sum polynomial
PSAVE	POINTER	Points to the first term of the first polynomial
QSAVE	POINTER	Points to the first term of the second polynomial
A1	INTEGER	Exponent of x value from the first polynomial
A2	INTEGER	Exponent of x value from the second polynomial
B1	INTEGER	Exponent of y value from the first polynomial
B2	INTEGER	Exponent of y value from the second polynomial
C1	INTEGER	Exponent of z value from the first polynomial
C2	INTEGER	Exponent of z value from the second polynomial
D1	REAL	Coefficient value of the term from the first polynomial
D2	REAL	Coefficient value of the term from the second polynomial

Variables used in the function POLY_LAST are:

NX	INTEGER	Value of exponent of x
NY	INTEGER	Value of exponent of y
NZ	INTEGER	Value of exponent of z
NCOEFF	REAL	Coefficient value of term
FIRST	POINTER	Points to head of polynomial
NEWPTR	BOOLEAN	Temporary pointer variable

Variables used in the procedure POLY_PRINT are:

FIRST	POINTER	Points to the head of polynomial
SAVE	POINTER	Temporary pointer variable

Line 248 of the main program controls the processing of all the pairs of the polynomials to be added. Lines 245, 256 to 260, 265 to 270, and 280 read the terms of the two polynomials and call the function POLY_INSERT to build the two polynomials. Then, in line 275, POLY_ADD is invoked to add the two polynomials.

In the function POLY_INSERT, a new node is created first and the values of the coefficient and exponents are copied into its elementary items. Then a search is made to find where the new term goes in the polynomial. Line 44 determines whether the list is empty. If the list is not empty, a check is made to see if the new

```
0  0000   00001   PROGRAM POLY (INPUT, OUTPUT);
0  0000   00002   (* GIVEN THE PROCEDURES POLY_ADD, POLY_INSERT, POLY_LAST, AND
0  0000   00003      PRINT_POLY, THIS ALGORITHM INPUTS TWO POLYNOMIALS AND PRINTS
0  0000   00004      THEIR SUM. *)
0  0000   00005
0  0000   00006   TYPE POINTER = @NODE;
0  0038   00007        NODE = RECORD            (* TERM OF POLYNOMIAL *)
0  0038   00008          LINK : POINTER;        (* POINTER TO NEXT TERM *)
0  0038   00009          POWER_X,               (* EXPONENT OF X *)
0  0038   00010          POWER_Y,               (* EXPONENT OF Y *)
0  0038   00011          POWER_Z: INTEGER;      (* EXPONENT OF Z *)
0  0038   00012          COEFF: REAL            (* COEFFICIENT OF TERM *)
0  0038   00013          END;
0  0038   00014   VAR POLY1, POLY2, POLY3,      (* FRONT TERMS OF THE POLYNOMIALS *)
0  0038   00015       LAST: POINTER;            (* LAST TERM IN POLYNOMIAL *)
0  0038   00016       X, Y, Z: INTEGER;         (* POWERS OF X, Y, AND Z *)
0  0038   00017       C: REAL;                  (* COEFFICIENT VALUE OF INPUT TERM *)
0  0038   00018
0  0038   00019       FUNCTION POLY_INSERT (NX, NY, NZ: INTEGER; NCOEFF: REAL;
1  0000   00020          FIRST: POINTER): POINTER;
1  0000   00021       (* GIVEN AN ORDERED SINGLY LINKED LINEAR LIST WHERE FIRST
1  0000   00022          DENOTES THE ADDRESS OF THE FIRST TERM OF THE POLYNOMIAL,
1  0000   00023          THIS FUNCTIONAL PROCEDURE INSERTS A NEW TERM INTO THE
1  0000   00024          LINKED LIST AND PRESERVES ITS ORDER.  NX, NY, NZ, AND
1  0000   00025          NCOEFF CORRESPOND TO THE EXPONENTS FOR X, Y, AND Z AND
1  0000   00026          THE COEFFICIENT VALUE OF THE TERM. *)
1  0000   00027
1  0000   00028       VAR NEWPTR, SAVE, TEMP: POINTER;  (* TEMP POINTER VARIABLES *)
1  007E   00029           A, B, C: INTEGER;            (* TEMP INTEGER VARIABLES *)
1  007E   00030           FLAG: BOOLEAN;               (* INDICATES TERM INSERTED *)
1  007E   00031
1  007E   00032       BEGIN
1  007E   00033
1  007E   00034          (* CREATE A NEW NODE *)
1  007E   00035          NEW (NEWPTR);
1  0090   00036
1  0090   00037          (* COPY INFO INTO NEW NODE *)
1  0090   00038          NEWPTR@.POWER_X := NX;
1  00B2   00039          NEWPTR@.POWER_Y := NY;
1  00D4   00040          NEWPTR@.POWER_Z := NZ;
1  00F6   00041          NEWPTR@.COEFF := NCOEFF;
1  0118   00042
1  0118   00043          (* IS THE LIST EMPTY? *)
1  0118   00044          IF FIRST = NIL
1  0118   00045          THEN BEGIN
1  0124   00046             NEWPTR@.LINK := NIL;
1  0140   00047             POLY_INSERT := NEWPTR
1  0140   00048             END
1  0148   00049          ELSE BEGIN
1  014C   00050
1  014C   00051             (* DOES NEW NODE PRECEDE FIRST NODE OF LIST? *)
1  014C   00052             A := FIRST@.POWER_X;
1  016A   00053             B := FIRST@.POWER_Y;
1  0188   00054             C := FIRST@.POWER_Z;
1  01A6   00055             IF (A < NX) OR ((A = NX) AND (B < NY)) OR
1  01CA   00056                ((A = NX) AND (B = NY) AND (C < NZ))
1  01EE   00057             THEN BEGIN
1  01EE   00058                NEWPTR@.LINK := FIRST;
1  020C   00059                POLY_INSERT := NEWPTR
1  020C   00060                END
1  0214   00061             ELSE BEGIN
1  0218   00062
1  0218   00063                (* INITIALIZE TEMPORARY POINTER *)
1  0218   00064                SAVE := FIRST;
1  0220   00065                FLAG := FALSE;
1  0228   00066
1  0228   00067                (* SEARCH FOR PREDECCESSOR AND
1  0228   00068                   SUCCESSOR OF NEW NODE *)
1  0228   00069                WHILE (SAVE@.LINK <> NIL) AND NOT FLAG DO
1  0258   00070                BEGIN
1  0258   00071                   TEMP := SAVE@.LINK;
1  0276   00072                   A := TEMP@.POWER_X;
1  0294   00073                   B := TEMP@.POWER_Y;
1  02B2   00074                   C := TEMP@.POWER_Z;
1  02D0   00075                   IF (A > NX) OR ((A = NX) AND (B > NY)) OR
1  02F4   00076                      ((A = NX) AND (B = NY) AND (C > NZ))
1  0318   00077                   THEN SAVE := SAVE@.LINK
1  032E   00078                   ELSE BEGIN
1  033A   00079
```

Fig. 10-12 Program to sum two polynomials

```
1   033A   00080                                        (* INSERT NEW NODE *)
1   033A   00081                                        NEWPTR@.LINK := SAVE@.LINK;
1   036E   00082                                        SAVE@.LINK := NEWPTR;
1   038C   00083                                        POLY_INSERT := FIRST;
1   0394   00084                                        FLAG := TRUE
1   0394   00085                                        END
1   039C   00086                                    END;
1   03A0   00087                                    IF NOT FLAG
1   03A0   00088                                    THEN BEGIN
1   03AE   00089
1   03AE   00090                                        (* INSERT NEW NODE AT END OF LIST *)
1   03AE   00091                                        NEWPTR@.LINK := NIL;
1   03CA   00092                                        SAVE@.LINK := NEWPTR;
1   03E8   00093                                        POLY_INSERT := FIRST
1   03E8   00094                                        END
1   03F0   00095                                    END
1   03F0   00096                                END
1   03F0   00097    END;
0   0038   00098
0   0038   00099    FUNCTION POLY_LAST (NX, NY, NZ: INTEGER; NCOEFF: REAL;
1   0000   00100          FIRST: POINTER): POINTER;
1   0000   00101    (* GIVEN AN ORDERED SINGLY LINKED LINEAR LIST, WHERE FIRST
1   0000   00102       DENOTES THE ADDRESS OF THE FIRST TERM OF THE POLYNOMIAL
1   0000   00103       THIS FUNCTIONAL PROCEDURE PERFORM AN INSERTION AT THE
1   0000   00104       END OF THE LIST.  NX, NY, NZ, AND NCOEFF CORRESPOND TO
1   0000   00105       THE EXPONENTS FOR X, Y, AND Z AND THE COEFFICIENT VALUE
1   0000   00106       OF THE TERM. *)
1   0000   00107
1   0000   00108    VAR NEWPTR: POINTER;     (* TEMPORARY POINTER VARIABLE *)
1   007E   00109
1   007E   00110    BEGIN
1   007E   00111
1   007E   00112        (* CREATE NEW NODE *)
1   007E   00113        NEW (NEWPTR);
1   0090   00114
1   0090   00115        (* INITIALIZE FIELDS OF NEW NODE *)
1   0090   00116        NEWPTR@.POWER_X := NX:
1   00B2   00117        NEWPTR@.POWER_Y := NY;
1   00D4   00118        NEWPTR@.POWER_Z := NZ;
1   00F6   00119        NEWPTR@.COEFF := NCOEFF;
1   0118   00120        NEWPTR@.LINK := NIL;
1   0134   00121
1   0134   00122        (* IS THIS LIST EMPTY? *)
1   0134   00123        IF FIRST = NIL
1   0134   00124        THEN BEGIN
1   0140   00125            LAST := NEWPTR;
1   0148   00126            POLY_LAST := NEWPTR
1   0148   00127            END
1   0150   00128        ELSE BEGIN
1   0154   00129
1   0154   00130            (* INSERT NEW NODE AT END OF NONEMPTY LIST *)
1   0154   00131            LAST@.LINK := NEWPTR;
1   0172   00132            LAST := NEWPTR;
1   017A   00133            POLY_LAST := FIRST
1   017A   00134            END
1   0182   00135    END;
0   0038   00136
```

Fig. 10-12   Program to sum two polynomials (cont'd.)

term precedes the first term of the linked list. If not, a search is made in lines 69 to 85, and the new term is placed in its correct position.

Procedure POLY_ADD first stores the addresses of the two polynomials in temporary pointer variables. Then a loop is entered which is used to add the terms of the polynomials until the end of either polynomial is reached. Inside the loop, the current terms of the polynomials are compared. If the terms correspond, the coefficients are added and if the resulting value is not zero, this term is added to the end of the sum polynomial. This is done by calling the function POLY_LAST. Otherwise, the term that precedes the other term of the two polynomials is added to the end of the new polynomial. After exiting the loop, the unprocessed terms of the remaining polynomial are appended to the end of the new polynomial in lines 201 to 204.

```
0  0038  00137    PROCEDURE POLY_ADD (VAR P, Q, R: POINTER);
1  0000  00138    (* GIVEN TWO POLYNOMIALS STORED IN LINKED LISTS AND WHOSE
1  0000  00139        FIRST TERMS ARE DENOTED BY THE POINTER VARIABLES P AND Q,
1  0000  00140        THIS PROCEDURE SYMBOLLICALLY ADDS THESE POLYNOMIALS AND
1  0000  00141        STORES THE ORDERED SUM AS A LINKED LIST WHOSE FIRST NODE
1  0000  00142        IS DENOTED BY THE POINTER VARIABLE R. *)
1  0000  00143
1  0000  00144    VAR PSAVE, QSAVE: POINTER;  (* TEMP POINTER VARIABLES *)
1  0066  00145        A1, A2, B1, B2, C1, C2: (* TEMPORARY EXPONENT VARIABLES *)
1  0066  00146          INTEGER;
1  0066  00147        D1, D2: REAL;          (* TEMPORARY COEFFICIENT VARIABLES *)
1  0066  00148
1  0066  00149    BEGIN
1  0066  00150
1  0066  00151        (* INITIALIZE *)
1  0066  00152        R := NIL;
1  006C  00153        PSAVE := P;
1  0074  00154        QSAVE := Q;
1  007C  00155
1  007C  00156        (* END OF ANY POLYNOMIAL? *)
1  007C  00157        WHILE (P <> NIL) AND (Q <> NIL) DO
1  0094  00158        BEGIN
1  0094  00159
1  0094  00160            (* OBTAIN FIELD VALUES FOR EACH TERM *)
1  0094  00161            A1 := P@.POWER_X;
1  00B2  00162            A2 := Q@.POWER_X;
1  00D0  00163            B1 := P@.POWER_Y;
1  00EE  00164            B2 := Q@.POWER_Y;
1  010C  00165            C1 := P@.POWER_Z;
1  012A  00166            C2 := Q@.POWER_Z;
1  0148  00167            D1 := P@.COEFF;
1  0166  00168            D2 := Q@.COEFF;
1  0184  00169
1  0184  00170            (* COMPARE TERMS *)
1  0184  00171            IF (A1 = A2) AND (B1 = B2) AND (C1 = C2)
1  01A8  00172            THEN (* CORRESPONDING TERMS *)
1  01A8  00173                IF P@.COEFF + Q@.COEFF <> 0
1  01DE  00174                THEN BEGIN
1  01E6  00175                    R := POLY_LAST (A1, B1, C1, D1 + D2, R);
1  0234  00176                    P := P@.LINK;
1  0252  00177                    Q := Q@.LINK
1  0268  00178                    END
1  0270  00179                ELSE BEGIN
1  0274  00180                    P := P@.LINK;
1  0292  00181                    Q := Q@.LINK
1  02A8  00182                    END
1  02B0  00183            ELSE (* TERMS DO NOT MATCH *)
1  02B0  00184                IF (A1 > A2) OR ((A1 = A2) AND (B1 > B2))
1  02D8  00185                    OR ((A1 = A2) AND (B1 = B2) AND (C1 > C2))
1  02FC  00186                THEN BEGIN
1  02FC  00187
1  02FC  00188                    (* OUTPUT TERM FROM POLYNOMIAL P *)
1  02FC  00189                    R := POLY_LAST (A1, B1, C1, D1, R);
1  033E  00190                    P := P@.LINK
1  0354  00191                    END
1  035C  00192                ELSE BEGIN
1  0360  00193
1  0360  00194                    (* OUTPUT TERM FROM POLYNOMIAL Q *)
1  0360  00195                    R := POLY_LAST (A2, B2, C2, D2, R);
1  03A2  00196                    Q := Q@.LINK
1  03B8  00197                    END
1  03C0  00198        END;
1  03C4  00199
1  03C4  00200        (* IS POLYNOMIAL P PROCESSED? *)
1  03C4  00201        IF P <> NIL
1  03C4  00202        THEN LAST@.LINK := P
1  03E6  00203        ELSE IF Q <> NIL
1  03F2  00204            THEN LAST@.LINK := Q;
1  041C  00205
1  041C  00206        (* RESTORE INITIAL POINTER VALUES FOR P AND Q *)
1  041C  00207        P := PSAVE;
1  0424  00208        Q := QSAVE
1  0424  00209
1  0424  00210    (* FINISHED *)
1  0424  00211    END;
0  0038  00212
```

Fig. 10-12   Program to sum two polynomials (cont'd.)

```
0  0038   00213      PROCEDURE PRINT_POLY (FIRST: POINTER);
1  0000   00214      (* THIS PROCEDURE PRINTS OUT A POLYNOMIAL WHICH IS STORED AS
1  0000   00215         A LINKED LINEAR LIST WHOSE FIRST TERM IS POINTED TO BY
1  0000   00216         FIRST. *)
1  0000   00217
1  0000   00218      VAR SAVE: POINTER;        (* TEMPORARY POINTER VARIABLE *)
1  004E   00219
1  004E   00220      BEGIN
1  004E   00221
1  004E   00222          (* INITIALIZE *)
1  004E   00223          SAVE := FIRST@.LINK;
1  006C   00224
1  006C   00225          (* PRINT FIRST TERM *)
1  006C   00226          WRITE(' ', FIRST@.COEFF : 5 : 1, ' * (X**',
1  00B8   00227               FIRST@.POWER_X : 2, ') * (Y**', FIRST@.POWER_Y : 2,
1  011A   00228               ') * (Z**', FIRST@.POWER_Z : 2, ')');
1  0166   00229
1  0166   00230          (* PRINT REMAINING TERMS *)
1  0166   00231          WHILE SAVE <> NIL DO
1  0172   00232          BEGIN
1  0172   00233              WRITELN(' + ');
1  0184   00234              WRITE(' ', SAVE@.COEFF : 5 : 1, ' * (X**',
1  01D0   00235                   SAVE@.POWER_X : 2, ') * (Y**', SAVE@.POWER_Y : 2,
1  0232   00236                   ') * (Z**', SAVE@.POWER_Z : 2, ')');
1  027E   00237              SAVE := SAVE@.LINK
1  0294   00238          END;
1  02A0   00239          WRITELN
1  02A0   00240      END;
0  0038   00241
0  0038   00242  BEGIN  (* MAIN PROGRAM *)
0  0038   00243
0  0038   00244      (* INPUT FIRST TERM IN FIRST POLYNOMIAL *)
0  0038   00245      READ(X, Y, Z, C);
0  0080   00246
0  0080   00247      (* PROCESS ALL POLYNOMIALS *)
0  0080   00248      WHILE NOT EOF DO
0  0088   00249      BEGIN
0  0088   00250
0  0088   00251          (* INITIALIZE *)
0  0088   00252          POLY1 := NIL;
0  008E   00253          POLY2 := NIL;
0  0094   00254
0  0094   00255          (* INPUT AND CONSTRUCT FIRST POLYNOMIAL *)
0  0094   00256          WHILE C <> 0 DO
0  00A0   00257          BEGIN
0  00A0   00258              POLY1 := POLY_INSERT (X, Y, Z, C, POLY1);
0  00E4   00259              READ(X, Y, Z, C)
0  012C   00260          END;
0  0130   00261          WRITELN('-', 'FIRST POLYNOMIAL IS');
0  0154   00262          PRINT_POLY (POLY1);
0  0172   00263
0  0172   00264          (* INPUT AND CONSTRUCT SECOND POLYNOMIAL *)
0  0172   00265          READ(X, Y, Z, C);
0  01BA   00266          WHILE C <> 0 DO
0  01C6   00267          BEGIN
0  01C6   00268              POLY2 := POLY_INSERT (X, Y, Z, C, POLY2);
0  020A   00269              READ(X, Y, Z, C)
0  0252   00270          END;
0  0256   00271          WRITELN('0', 'SECOND POLYNOMIAL IS');
0  027A   00272          PRINT_POLY (POLY2);
0  0298   00273
0  0298   00274          (* ADD POLYNOMIALS *)
0  0298   00275          POLY_ADD (POLY1, POLY2, POLY3);
0  02C6   00276          WRITELN('0', 'SUM OF POLYNOMIALS IS');
0  02EA   00277          PRINT_POLY (POLY3);
0  0308   00278
0  0308   00279          (* INPUT FIRST TERM IN FIRST POLYNOMIAL *)
0  0308   00280          READ(X, Y, Z, C)
0  0350   00281
0  0350   00282      (* FINISHED *)
0  0350   00283      END
0  0350   00284  END.
```

```
------------------------------------
| COMPILE TIME:    0.692 SECOND(S) |
|     NO WARNING(S) DETECTED        |
|     NO ERROR(S) DETECTED          |
------------------------------------
```

Fig. 10-12 Program to sum two polynomials (cont'd.)

```
--EXECUTION-->

FIRST POLYNOMIAL IS


    7.0 * (X** 5) * (Y** 4) * (Z** 2) +
    7.0 * (X** 5) * (Y** 4) * (Z** 1) +
    8.0 * (X** 2) * (Y** 3) * (Z** 0) +
   16.0 * (X** 1) * (Y** 3) * (Z** 1)

SECOND POLYNOMIAL IS
   19.0 * (X** 6) * (Y** 4) * (Z** 1) +
   23.0 * (X** 6) * (Y** 4) * (Z** 0) +
    3.0 * (X** 5) * (Y** 4) * (Z** 2) +
    3.0 * (X** 2) * (Y** 3) * (Z** 0) +
   16.0 * (X** 1) * (Y** 3) * (Z** 2)

SUM OF POLYNOMIALS IS
   19.0 * (X** 6) * (Y** 4) * (Z** 1) +
   23.0 * (X** 6) * (Y** 4) * (Z** 0) +
   10.0 * (X** 5) * (Y** 4) * (Z** 2) +
    7.0 * (X** 5) * (Y** 4) * (Z** 1) +
   11.0 * (X** 2) * (Y** 3) * (Z** 0) +
   16.0 * (X** 1) * (Y** 3) * (Z** 2) +
   16.0 * (X** 1) * (Y** 3) * (Z** 1)


FIRST POLYNOMIAL IS
    1.0 * (X** 2) * (Y** 0) * (Z** 0) +
    1.0 * (X** 1) * (Y** 1) * (Z** 0) +
    1.0 * (X** 1) * (Y** 0) * (Z** 0) +
    1.0 * (X** 0) * (Y** 2) * (Z** 0) +
    2.0 * (X** 0) * (Y** 0) * (Z** 2)

SECOND POLYNOMIAL IS
    2.0 * (X** 2) * (Y** 0) * (Z** 0) +
   -2.0 * (X** 1) * (Y** 1) * (Z** 0) +
    3.0 * (X** 1) * (Y** 0) * (Z** 0) +
   -1.0 * (X** 0) * (Y** 2) * (Z** 0) +
    1.0 * (X** 0) * (Y** 1) * (Z** 1)

SUM OF POLYNOMIALS IS
    3.0 * (X** 2) * (Y** 0) * (Z** 0) +
   -1.0 * (X** 1) * (Y** 1) * (Z** 0) +
    4.0 * (X** 1) * (Y** 0) * (Z** 0) +
    1.0 * (X** 0) * (Y** 1) * (Z** 1) +
    2.0 * (X** 0) * (Y** 0) * (Z** 2)
```

Fig. 10-12   Program to sum two polynomials (cont'd.)

The function POLY_LAST creates and initializes a new term. Then, in lines 123 to 127, the list to which the polynomial is to be added is checked for being NIL. If it is, the address of the new node is returned; otherwise, the node is inserted at the end of the list and the address of the first node of the list is returned. Procedure PRINT_POLY prints the terms of the polynomial. Lines 226 to 228 print the first term, while lines 231 to 238 print the remaining terms of the polynomial.

10-9.2   Hash-Table Techniques

This subsection examines the programming aspects of a class of search techniques based on computing the position of a record in a table through the use of a hashing function. Such a function associates the key of a record with a particular position in the table. Since more than one key can be mapped into the same table position; collisions occur. These collisions can be resolved using two classes of collision-resolution techniques; namely, open addressing and chaining.

We examine the programming aspects of both methods in this subsection. The notions of hashing are also applicable to the operation of sorting. A program for sorting by address calculation is given.

Recall that a *key-to-address transformation* problem is a mapping or *hashing function* (HASH), that maps the key space (KEY) into an address space. This address space is usually an address to an element in a table. *Preconditioning* is often necessary to convert a key consisting of alphanumeric characters into a form that allows arithmetic or logical manipulation. Usually, the key space is larger than the address space, which often results in collisions between records.

Preconditioning is most efficiently performed by using the numerically coded representations of the characters in the key. To convert characters into their numerically coded representations we must first consider PASCAL's notion of sets which was introduced in Chap. 2. Recall that a set can be defined as

TYPE WEEKDAYS = (MON, TUES, WED, THURS, FRI);

The ordinal number of any element (or its position less one) can be obtained by using the built-in function ORD. ORD (MON) returns the value 0 as MON is the first element in the set. ORD (TUES) returns 1 and ORD (FRI) returns 4.

The function ORD can have characters in its argument. Characters comprise a set and a character precedes another character in the set if the first lexically precedes the second. That is, because 'X' < 'Y' then ORD ('X') < ORD ('Y'). The first character in the set is the one which is numerically coded as 0. Note that many characters exist in the character set of a computer but are unprintable and not found on a keypunch or computer terminal. Because of this, the ordinal value of a character is the same as its numerically-coded value and any call to ORD will return this value. For example, if characters are stored in EBCDIC representation, ORD ('A') returns the value 193, which is the base 10 value of A's storage representation 11000001 in base 2. Once we have the numeric representation of the alphanumeric characters, arithmetic or logical manipulation can easily be done on the characters.

Two hashing functions are required to generate an address. First, the preconditioned value of the key must be computed, and second, the mapping of the key into a table location is performed. These two hashing functions are often combined into one hashing function.

The *division method* of hashing, which is defined as

$$H(x) = x \bmod m + 1$$

can easily be given in PASCAL. Before the division method can be used, preconditioning of the key may be required. One method that can be used is a length-dependent hashing function.

Figure 10-13 gives a hashing function using the *length-dependent method*. With this method, the length of the key is used along with some portion of the key to produce a table address directly, or an intermediate key which is used with, say, the division method to produce the final table address. It is often difficult to convert alphanumeric characters directly to a table address; thus, in Fig. 10-13, the length-dependent method is only used for preconditioning. The hashing function obtains the internal binary representation of the first and last characters of the key and sums them along with the length of the key shifted left four binary places. Since the

```
0  0038   00025  FUNCTION HASH (SYMBOL: STRING(10); SIZE: INTEGER): INTEGER;
1  0000   00026  (* THIS FUNCTION COMPUTES THE HASH VALUE OF THE STRING
1  0000   00027      SYMBOL BY USING THE LENGTH-DEPENDENT METHOD *)
1  0000   00028
1  0000   00029  VAR LETTER: ARRAY (1..10) OF CHAR;      (* USED TO STORE SYMBOL AS
1  0000   00030                                                   CHARACTER STRING *)
1  0068   00031      LENGTH,                         (* LENGTH OF SYMBOL *)
1  0068   00032      VALUE: INTEGER;                 (* PRECONDITIONED VALUE *)
1  0068   00033
1  0068   00034  BEGIN
1  0068   00035
1  0068   00036      (* COMPUTE THE LENGTH OF THE SYMBOL *)
1  0068   00037      LETTER := SYMBOL;
1  0082   00038      LENGTH := 10;
1  008A   00039      WHILE LETTER(LENGTH) = ' ' DO
1  00B2   00040          LENGTH := LENGTH - 1;
1  00C2   00041
1  00C2   00042      (* COMPUTE THE PRECONDITIONED RESULT *)
1  00C2   00043      VALUE := ORD (LETTER(1)) + ORD (LETTER(LENGTH)) + 16 * LENGTH;
1  0104   00044
1  0104   00045      (* RETURN THE HASHED VALUE *)
1  0104   00046      HASH := VALUE MOD SIZE + 1
1  0110   00047  END;
```

Fig. 10-13   Example of a length-dependent hashing function

length of SYMBOL is not 256, we cannot use the LENGTH function as described in Chap. 5 to compute the length of the string. A search is made for the last nonblank character in the string instead. It is assumed that the symbol does not end with blank characters. The length of the key shifted over four places is obtained by multiplying the key's length by 16. Finally, the division method is used to compute the final table address. In this hashing function, SIZE stores the size of the address space, and should be a prime number.

Recall that hashing functions often map several keys into the same address. Collision-resolution techniques are required so that the colliding records can be stored and accessed. Open addressing and chaining are two classes of collision resolution used to resolve these conflicts. Open addressing searches for a free location in a table if the location that the key was hashed into is occupied.

Because of difficulties in deleting records with open addressing, a special value (DELETE) is used to denote that a record has been deleted. Recall that for look-ups, difficulty occurs when records have been deleted between the position where the record was hashed and where it is finally stored in the table.

One method of open addressing, called *linear probing*, uses the following sequence of locations for a table of m entries:

$$d, d + 1, ..., m - 1, m, 1, 2, ..., d - 1$$

where d denotes the initial hash position of the input key. Insertions fail if no unoccupied location is found and look-ups fail if either an empty position is reached without finding the record in question, or if the entire table has been searched.

Figure 10-14 gives a program that performs look-ups and insertions using the function OPENLP. The variables used in the main program are:

Variable	Type	Usage
HASH_TABLE	ARRAY(1..100) OF HASH_STRUCTURE	Array of structures storing records

HASH_STRUCTURE	RECORD	Hash-table structure template
K	STRING(10)	Key field of record
DATA	STRING(20)	Information field of record
FLAG	CHAR	Denotes whether record location is empty, occupied, or deleted
KEY	STRING(10)	Key of record to be inserted or looked-up
INFO	STRING(20)	Information field of record to be inserted or looked-up
M	INTEGER	Size of the hash table
NUM	INTEGER	Number of records to be inserted
INSERT	BOOLEAN	Logical flag for insertion or look-up
POS	INTEGER	Position of record looked-up
I	INTEGER	Counted loop variable

Variables used in function OPENLP are:

X	STRING(10)	Key value to be hashed for look-up or insertion
INFO	STRING(20)	Information field
INSERT	BOOLEAN	Specifies look-up or insertion
D	INTEGER	Hashed value of key
I	INTEGER	Counted loop variable
FINISH	INTEGER	Position of last record in table to look at during search
STOP	BOOLEAN	Used to terminate loop

The main program first initializes the hash table locations to empty. Then a loop is entered which calls the function OPENLP to insert the records into the table. Finally, look-ups are performed in lines 134 to 142.

In OPENLP, the initial position of the record in the table is calculated. The hash function used for this purpose is the one given in Fig. 10-13. Next, a scan of the table is made starting at the initial position. If the key value matches the key in the table, the position is returned if a look-up is required. For insertions, a negated index is returned if the record is already present. Then if the table location either is empty or contains a deleted record, the record is inserted if required. An empty location for a look-up indicates that the search key is not found and a negated index is, therefore, returned. Finally, if STOP has the value FALSE in line 105, either the table is full, or the search key was not found.

This program was tested on the following data. The keys 'FROG', 'WHALE', 'LYNX', 'SNAKE', 'BLUEJAY', 'BEETLE', and 'SALMON' were inserted. Look-ups were performed on 'LYNX', 'BLUEJAY', 'SALMON', JACKFISH', 'LADYBUG', and 'SNAKE'. Note that 'JACKFISH' and 'LADYBUG' were not previously inserted into the table.

Because of primary clustering, the efficiency of look-ups and insertions in the table decreases as the table becomes full. For a table, the probability of an insertion into any location increases as the number of locations immediately preceding that location that are contiguously occupied increases. This problem

```
0  0000   00001   PROGRAM PROBE (INPUT, OUTPUT);
0  0000   00002   (* THIS PROGRAM INPUTS RECORDS AND PERFORMS THE REQUIRED LOOK-UPS AND
0  0000   00003      INSERTIONS.  THE PROCEDURE OPENLP IS USED TO PERFORM OPEN ADDRESSING
0  0000   00004      USING LINEAR PROBING. *)
0  0000   00005
0  0000   00006   CONST M = 17;                    (* SIZE OF HASH TABLE *)
0  0038   00007
0  0038   00008   TYPE HASH_STRUCTURE = RECORD (* STRUCTURE OF HASH TABLE *)
0  0038   00009          K: STRING(10);     (* KEY FIELD *)
0  0038   00010          DATA: STRING(20);  (* INFORMATION FIELD *)
0  0038   00011          FLAG: CHAR         (* DENOTES IF RECORD LOCATION IS EMPTY (E),
0  0038   00012                                OCCUPIED (I), OR DELETED (D) *)
0  0038   00013          END;
0  0038   00014
0  0038   00015   VAR HASH_TABLE: ARRAY (1..M) OF HASH_STRUCTURE;
0  0038   00016                               (* HASH TABLE *)
0  0038   00017       KEY: STRING(10);        (* KEY FIELD OF RECORD *)
0  0038   00018       INFO: STRING(20);       (* INFORMATION FIELD *)
0  0038   00019       POS,                    (* POSITION OF RECORD *)
0  0038   00020       NUM,                    (* NO OF RECORDS TO INSERT *)
0  0038   00021       I: INTEGER;             (* COUNTED LOOP VARIABLE *)
0  0038   00022       INSERT: BOOLEAN;        (* LOGICAL FLAG FOR INSERTION
0  0038   00023                                  OR LOOK-UP *)
0  0038   00024
0  0038   00025   FUNCTION HASH (SYMBOL: STRING(10); SIZE: INTEGER): INTEGER;
1  0000   00026   (* THIS FUNCTION COMPUTES THE HASH VALUE OF THE STRING
1  0000   00027      SYMBOL BY USING THE LENGTH-DEPENDENT METHOD *)
1  0000   00028
1  0000   00029   VAR LETTER: ARRAY (1..10) OF CHAR;      (* USED TO STORE SYMBOL AS
1  0000   00030                                             CHARACTER STRING *)
1  0068   00031       LENGTH,                            (* LENGTH OF SYMBOL *)
1  0068   00032       VALUE: INTEGER;                    (* PRECONDITIONED VALUE *)
1  0068   00033
1  0068   00034   BEGIN
1  0068   00035
1  0068   00036       (* COMPUTE THE LENGTH OF THE SYMBOL *)
1  0068   00037       LETTER := SYMBOL;
1  0082   00038       LENGTH := 10;
1  008A   00039       WHILE LETTER(LENGTH) = ' ' DO
1  00B2   00040           LENGTH := LENGTH - 1;
1  00C2   00041
1  00C2   00042       (* COMPUTE THE PRECONDITIONED RESULT *)
1  00C2   00043       VALUE := ORD (LETTER(1)) + ORD (LETTER(LENGTH)) + 16 * LENGTH;
1  0104   00044
1  0104   00045       (* RETURN THE HASHED VALUE *)
1  0104   00046       HASH := VALUE MOD SIZE + 1
1  0110   00047   END;
0  0038   00048
0  0038   00049       FUNCTION OPENLP (X: STRING(10); INFO: STRING(20); INSERT: BOOLEAN):
1  0000   00050           INTEGER;
1  0000   00051       (* THIS FUNCTION PERFORMS THE TABLE LOOK-UP AND INSERTION
1  0000   00052          OPERATIONS AND RETURNS THE POSITION OF THE RECORD GIVEN BY X,
1  0000   00053          IF SUCCESSFUL.  OTHERWISE, A NEGATED POSITION IS RETURNED,
1  0000   00054          INDICATION AN ERROR.  THE HASHING FUNCTION HASH IS USED TO
1  0000   00055          CALCULATE AN INITIAL POSITION. *)
1  0000   00056
1  0000   00057       VAR D,                 (* HASHED VALUE *)
1  0062   00058           I,                 (* COUNTED LOOP VARIABLE *)
1  0062   00059           FINISHED: INTEGER; (* TERMINATES LOOP *)
1  0062   00060           STOP: BOOLEAN;     (* LOGICAL FLAG FOR FUNCTION RETURN *)
1  0062   00061
1  0062   00062       BEGIN
1  0062   00063           STOP := FALSE;
1  006A   00064
1  006A   00065           (* CALCULATE INITIAL POSITION *)
1  006A   00066           D := HASH (X, M);
1  0094   00067
```

Fig. 10-14   Program to enter records into a table using linear probing

can be solved by using *random probing*. A random sequence of positions is generated rather than an ordered sequence. Such a random sequence can be generated by the PASCAL statement

$$Y := (Y + C) \text{ MOD } M$$

```
1  0094   00068             (* PERFORM INDICATED OPERATION IF LOCATION IS FOUND *)
1  0094   00069                 I := D;
1  009C   00070                 FINISHED := D - 1;
1  00A8   00071                 IF FINISHED < 1
1  00A8   00072                 THEN FINISHED := M;
1  00BC   00073                 REPEAT
1  00BC   00074                     IF X = HASH_TABLE(I).K
1  00DE   00075                         THEN IF (NOT INSERT) AND (HASH_TABLE(I).FLAG = 'I')
1  0126   00076                             THEN BEGIN  (* POSITION OF RETRIEVED RECORD *)
1  0126   00077                                 OPENLP := I;
1  012E   00078                                 STOP := TRUE
1  012E   00079                                 END
1  0136   00080                             ELSE BEGIN  (* ERROR IN INSERTION *)
1  013A   00081                                 OPENLP := -I;
1  0144   00082                                 STOP := TRUE
1  0144   00083                                 END;
1  014C   00084                     IF ((HASH_TABLE(I).FLAG = 'E') OR (HASH_TABLE(I).FLAG =
1  01A2   00085                         'D')) AND NOT STOP
1  01AC   00086                     THEN IF INSERT
1  01BA   00087                         THEN BEGIN  (* PERFORM INDICATED INSERTION *)
1  01C4   00088                             HASH_TABLE(I).K := X;
1  01EC   00089                             HASH_TABLE(I).DATA := INFO;
1  0218   00090                             HASH_TABLE(I).FLAG := 'I';
1  0244   00091                             STOP := TRUE;
1  024C   00092                             OPENLP := I
1  024C   00093                             END
1  0254   00094                         ELSE IF HASH_TABLE(I).FLAG = 'E'
1  027E   00095                             THEN BEGIN
1  0288   00096                                 OPENLP := -I;  (* ERROR IN LOOK-UP *)
1  0292   00097                                 STOP := TRUE
1  0292   00098                                 END;
1  029A   00099                     IF I = M
1  029A   00100                     THEN I := 1
1  02A6   00101                     ELSE I := I + 1
1  02B2   00102                 UNTIL ((I = FINISHED) OR STOP);
1  02D4   00103
1  02D4   00104             (* TABLE OVERFLOW *)
1  02D4   00105             IF NOT STOP
1  02D4   00106             THEN BEGIN
1  02E2   00107                 WRITELN (' ', 'OVERFLOW OR LOOK-UP ERROR');
1  0306   00108                 OPENLP := 0
1  0306   00109                 END
1  030C   00110         END;
0  0038   00111
0  0038   00112 BEGIN
0  0038   00113
0  0038   00114     (* INITIALIZE HASH TABLE AND VARIABLES *)
0  0038   00115     FOR I := 1 TO M DO
0  005C   00116         HASH_TABLE(I).FLAG := 'E';
0  008C   00117     INSERT := TRUE;
0  0094   00118
0  0094   00119     (* INSERT REQUIRED RECORDS *)
0  0094   00120     READ (NUM);
0  00A6   00121     WRITELN (' ', 'INSERTED RECORDS ARE ');
0  00CA   00122     WRITELN ('0', 'KEY', ' ' : 7, 'INFORMATION FIELD', ' ' : 7,
0  0124   00123         'POSITION');
0  0136   00124     FOR I := 1 TO NUM DO
0  015A   00125     BEGIN
0  015A   00126         READ (KEY, INFO);
0  017E   00127         WRITELN (' ', KEY, INFO, ' ' : 6, OPENLP (KEY, INFO, INSERT)
0  01DE   00128             : 2)
0  0204   00129     END;
0  0208   00130
0  0208   00131     (* PERFORM REQUIRED LOOK-UPS *)
0  0208   00132     WRITELN ('-', 'POSITION OF LOOK-UP RECORDS ARE');
0  022C   00133     WRITELN ('0', 'KEY', ' ' : 7, 'POSITION');
0  0274   00134     READ (KEY);
0  0286   00135     WHILE NOT EOF DO
0  028E   00136     BEGIN
0  028E   00137         POS := OPENLP (KEY, INFO, NOT INSERT);
0  02CE   00138         IF POS > 0
0  02CE   00139         THEN WRITELN (' ', HASH_TABLE(POS).K, ' ' : 3, POS : 2)
0  0342   00140         ELSE WRITELN (' ', 'INVALID KEY IS ', KEY);
0  037C   00141         READ (KEY)
0  038E   00142     END
0  038E   00143 END.
```

```
-----------------------------------
¦ COMPILE TIME:    0.386 SECOND(S) ¦
¦    NO WARNING(S) DETECTED        ¦
¦    NO ERROR(S) DETECTED          ¦
-----------------------------------
```

Fig. 10-14   Program to enter records into a table using linear probing (cont'd.)

```
--EXECUTION-->
INSERTED RECORDS ARE

KEY        INFORMATION FIELD      POSITION
FROG       AMPHIBIAN                 3
WHALE      MAMMAL                   15
LYNX       MAMMAL                   14
SNAKE      REPTILE                  11
BLUEJAY    BIRD                     12
BEETLE     INSECT                   13
SALMON     FISH                      9


POSITION OF LOOK-UP RECORDS ARE

KEY        POSITION
LYNX          14
BLUEJAY       12
SALMON         9
INVALID KEY IS JACKFISH
INVALID KEY IS LADYBUG
SNAKE         11
```

Fig. 10-14   Program to enter records into a table using linear probing (cont'd.)

where Y is the previous position of the random sequence, C is a constant, and M is the size of the address space. C and M should be relatively prime to each other.

The program of Fig. 10-14 was rerun using the same data except that function OPENRP was used in place of procedure OPENLP. Figure 10-15 gives the function OPENRP and shows results obtained when the program was run. The variables used in OPENRP are:

Variable	Type	Usage
X	STRING(10)	Key field to be hashed for insertion or look-up
INFO	STRING(20)	Information field
INSERT	BOOLEAN	Determines if look-up or insertion required
D	INTEGER	Hashed value of key
J	INTEGER	Index for random probing
Y	INTEGER	Index for random probing
C	INTEGER	Constant used to generate next random position

First the initial position is calculated in the function OPENRP. It uses the hashing function described earlier. Then an initial probe is made into the table. If an insertion is required, and the position is empty or a deleted record is in this location, the new record is inserted. For a look-up, if the search key and the key in the table match, the position is found. If this position is empty, a negated position is returned. Otherwise, a loop is entered in line 98 to perform a search through the table. Each location in the table is scanned by computing the next location to be examined in lines 102 and 103. If the new position to be examined is the original position, an overflow or look-up error occurs, and the negated position is returned. In lines 118 to 121 an insertion, if required, is performed into an empty location or in a location that contains a deleted record. For look-ups, if the record position is empty, a negated position is returned since the search key was not found in the table. If it is found, the location of the record is returned.

While random probing solves the problem of *primary clustering*, it creates the problem of *secondary clustering*. All keys hashed into the same location generate the same random sequence. Another approach to solving this problem, called *double hashing*, requires two independent hashing functions. For example, if $H_1(x_1) = H_1(x_2)$ for $x_1 \neq x_2$, we can have a second hashing function H_2 such that $H_2(x_1) \neq H_2(x_2)$. An example of a double hashing procedure is given in Fig. 10-16. Only the functions OPENDH, HASH1, and HASH2 are given, and the output. The main program and data used are the same as in Fig. 10-14. Function OPENDH is the same as procedure OPENRP given in Fig. 10-15 except that line 66 has been replaced by two statements that call two independent hashing functions. The function HASH1 is the same as HASH which was used in previous programs. HASH2, on the other hand is used to generate a random constant value for C. In HASH2, the statement VALUE := X MOD + 1; is replaced by VALUE := X MOD (M – 2) + 1, thus giving an independent hashing function.

Recall that there are three main difficulties with open addressing. Colliding records tend to cluster. Also, table overflows are difficult to resolve, which requires a total reorganization of the table. Finally, record deletions are difficult. *Separate chaining* is one method that may be used to handle overflow records. Colliding records are chained in an *overflow area* which is distinct from the *prime area*. Thus, all records that are hashed into the same location are maintained in a linked list. Figure 10-17 gives a program using this approach. Note that the hash table merely becomes a vector of pointers to the linked lists. A value of NIL in any position of the hash table means that the corresponding linked list is empty.

The variables used in the main program are:

Variable	Type	Usage
POINTER	@RECORD_STRUCTURE	Pointer type to record structure
RECORD_STRUCTURE	RECORD	Structure for storing records
KEY	STRING(20)	Key field of record
DATA	STRING(20)	Information field of record
LINK	POINTER	Pointer to next record in linked list
HASH_TABLE	ARRAY(1..M) OF POINTER	Pointer vector representing hash table
POS	POINTER	Pointer for printing linked lists
X	STRING(20)	Key field of record to be inserted or looked-up
INFO	STRING(20)	Information field of record
M	CONST	Size of hash table
I	INTEGER	Counted loop variable

The variables used in procedure ENTER are:

X	STRING(20)	Key field of record to be inserted or looked-up

```
0   0038   00049   FUNCTION OPENRP (X: STRING(10); INFO: STRING(20); INSERT: BOOLEAN):
1   0000   00050        INTEGER;
1   0000   00051   (* THIS FUNCTION PERFORMS THE TABLE LOOK-UP AND INSERTION
1   0000   00052      OPERATIONS AND RETURNS THE POSITION OF THE RECORD IN
1   0000   00053      QUESTION, IF SUCCESSFUL.  OTHERWISE, A NEGATED POSITION
1   0000   00054      IS RETURNED. *)
1   0000   00055
1   0000   00056   CONST C = 7;                     (* RANDOM PROBE CONSTANT *)
1   0062   00057
1   0062   00058   VAR D,                           (* HASHED VALUE *)
1   0062   00059       J, Y: INTEGER;               (* INDICES FOR RANDOM PROBE *)
1   0062   00060       STOP: BOOLEAN;               (* LOGICAL FLAG FOR FUNCTION RETURN *)
1   0062   00061
1   0062   00062   BEGIN
1   0062   00063       STOP := FALSE;
1   006A   00064
1   006A   00065       (* CALCULATE INITIAL POSITION *)
1   006A   00066       D := HASH (X, M);
1   0094   00067
1   0094   00068       (* FIRST PROBE? *)
1   0094   00069       IF INSERT
1   0094   00070       THEN IF (HASH_TABLE(D).FLAG = 'D') OR (HASH_TABLE(D).FLAG = 'E')
1   00FE   00071            THEN BEGIN
1   00FE   00072                HASH_TABLE(D).K := X;
1   0126   00073                HASH_TABLE(D).DATA := INFO;
1   0152   00074                HASH_TABLE(D).FLAG := 'I';
1   017E   00075                OPENRP := D;
1   0186   00076                STOP := TRUE
1   0186   00077                END
1   018E   00078            ELSE IF X = HASH_TABLE(D).K
1   01B4   00079                THEN BEGIN
1   01BE   00080                    OPENRP := -D;
1   01C8   00081                    STOP := TRUE
1   01C8   00082                    END
1   01D0   00083                ELSE
1   01D0   00084       ELSE IF (HASH_TABLE(D).K = X) AND (HASH_TABLE(D).FLAG = 'I')
1   0234   00085            THEN BEGIN
1   0234   00086                OPENRP := D;
1   023C   00087                STOP := TRUE
1   023C   00088                END
1   0244   00089            ELSE IF (HASH_TABLE(D).FLAG = 'D') OR (HASH_TABLE(D).FLAG =
1   029E   00090                'E')
1   02A8   00091                THEN BEGIN
1   02A8   00092                    OPENRP := -D;
1   02B2   00093                    STOP := TRUE
1   02B2   00094                    END;
1   02BA   00095
1   02BA   00096       (* PERFORM SEARCH *)
1   02BA   00097       Y := D - 1;
1   02C6   00098       WHILE NOT STOP DO
1   02D4   00099       BEGIN
1   02D4   00100
1   02D4   00101           (* SCAN NEXT ENTRY *)
1   02D4   00102           Y := (Y + C) MOD M;
1   02EA   00103           J := Y + 1;
1   02F6   00104
1   02F6   00105           (* OVERFLOW? *)
1   02F6   00106           IF J = D
1   02F6   00107           THEN BEGIN
1   0302   00108               WRITELN (' ', 'OVERFLOW OR LOOK-UP ERROR');
1   0326   00109               OPENRP := 0;
1   032C   00110               STOP := TRUE
1   032C   00111               END;
1   0334   00112
1   0334   00113           (* PERFORM LOOK-UP OR INSERTION *)
1   0334   00114           IF INSERT
1   0334   00115           THEN IF (HASH_TABLE(J).FLAG = 'D') OR (HASH_TABLE(J).FLAG =
1   0394   00116                'E')
1   039E   00117                THEN BEGIN
1   039E   00118                    HASH_TABLE(J).K := X;
1   03C6   00119                    HASH_TABLE(J).DATA := INFO;
1   03F2   00120                    HASH_TABLE(J).FLAG := 'I';
1   041E   00121                    OPENRP := J;
1   0426   00122                    STOP := TRUE
1   0426   00123                    END
1   042E   00124                ELSE IF HASH_TABLE(J).K = X
1   0454   00125                    THEN BEGIN
1   045E   00126                        OPENRP := -J;
1   0468   00127                        STOP := TRUE
1   0468   00128                        END
1   0470   00129                    ELSE
```

Fig. 10-15   Program to solve record collisions using random probing

```
1  0470   00130              ELSE IF HASH_TABLE(J).FLAG = 'E'
1  049E   00131                   THEN BEGIN
1  04A8   00132                           OPENRP := -J;
1  04B2   00133                           STOP := TRUE
1  04B2   00134                        END
1  04BA   00135              ELSE IF HASH_TABLE(J).K = X
1  04E0   00136                   THEN BEGIN
1  04EA   00137                           OPENRP := J;
1  04F2   00138                           STOP := TRUE
1  04F2   00139                        END
1  04FA   00140      END
1  04FA   00141  END;
```

```
--EXECUTION-->
INSERTED RECORDS ARE

KEY         INFORMATION FIELD       POSITION
FROG        AMPHIBIAN                  3
WHALE       MAMMAL                    15
LYNX        MAMMAL                    14
SNAKE       REPTILE                   11
BLUEJAY     BIRD                      12
BEETLE      INSECT                     2
SALMON      FISH                       9


POSITION OF LOOK-UP RECORDS ARE

KEY         POSITION
LYNX          14
BLUEJAY       12
SALMON         9
INVALID KEY IS JACKFISH
INVALID KEY IS LADYBUG
SNAKE         11
```

Fig. 10-15   Program to solve record collisions using random probing (cont'd.)

INFO	STRING(20)	Information field of record
RANDOM	INTEGER	Hashed value of key
P	POINTER	Temporary pointer variable
STOP	BOOLEAN	Indicates procedure return

The main program first initializes the hash table to NIL. Then lines 103 to 108 read the records and call procedure ENTER to insert them into the appropriate linked list. Finally, the program outputs the linked lists formed by procedure ENTER.

In procedure ENTER, the hash value of the key X is first computed. Then line 68 checks whether or not the linked list where the record is to be inserted is empty. The hash table position will have a NIL value if it is empty. If the linked list is not empty a search is made to determine if the new record is already present. If not, in lines 86 to 90 the new record is inserted at the front of the linked list.

So far we have been concerned with searching using hashing functions. Next, we look at a method of sorting that uses an order-preserving hashing function.

Address-Calculation Sorting

An *order-preserving hashing function* has the property

$x_1 < x_2$ implies that $HASH(x_1) \leq HASH'(x_2)$

Such a hashing function can be used to sort records. Colliding records are stored in linked lists that preserve the order of the keys. The separate-chaining method of

```
0  0038  00025  FUNCTION HASH1 (SYMBOL: STRING(10); SIZE: INTEGER): INTEGER;
1  0000  00026  (* THIS FUNCTION COMPUTES THE HASH VALUE OF THE STRING
1  0000  00027      SYMBOL BY USING THE LENGTH-DEPENDENT METHOD *)
1  0000  00028
1  0000  00029  VAR LETTER: ARRAY (1..10) OF CHAR;      (* USED TO STORE SYMBOL AS
1  0000  00030                                            CHARACTER STRING *)
1  0068  00031      LENGTH,                             (* LENGTH OF SYMBOL *)
1  0068  00032      VALUE: INTEGER;                     (* PRECONDITIONED VALUE *)
1  0068  00033
1  0068  00034  BEGIN
1  0068  00035
1  0068  00036      (* COMPUTE THE LENGTH OF THE SYMBOL *)
1  0068  00037      LETTER := SYMBOL;
1  0082  00038      LENGTH := 10;
1  008A  00039      WHILE LETTER(LENGTH) = ' ' DO
1  00B2  00040          LENGTH := LENGTH - 1;
1  00C2  00041
1  00C2  00042      (* COMPUTE THE PRECONDITIONED RESULT *)
1  00C2  00043      VALUE := ORD (LETTER(1)) + ORD (LETTER(LENGTH)) + 16 * LENGTH;
1  0104  00044
1  0104  00045      (* RETURN THE HASHED VALUE *)
1  0104  00046      HASH1 := VALUE MOD SIZE + 1
1  0110  00047  END;
0  0038  00048
0  0038  00049  FUNCTION HASH2 (SYMBOL: STRING(10); SIZE: INTEGER): INTEGER;
1  0000  00050  (* THIS FUNCTION IS AN INDEPENDENT HASHING FUNCTION THAT
1  0000  00051      RETURNS THE HASHED VALUE OF X WHICH IS TO BE USED AS THE
1  0000  00052      CONSTANT FOR RANDOM PROBING. *)
1  0000  00053
1  0000  00054  VAR LETTER: ARRAY (1..10) OF CHAR;      (* USED TO STORE SYMBOL AS
1  0000  00055                                            CHARACTER STRING *)
1  0068  00056      LENGTH,                             (* LENGTH OF SYMBOL *)
1  0068  00057      VALUE: INTEGER;                     (* PRECONDITIONED VALUE *)
1  0068  00058
1  0068  00059  BEGIN
1  0068  00060
1  0068  00061      (* COMPUTE THE LENGTH OF THE SYMBOL *)
1  0068  00062      LETTER := SYMBOL;
1  0082  00063      LENGTH := 10;
1  008A  00064      WHILE LETTER(LENGTH) = ' ' DO
1  00B2  00065          LENGTH := LENGTH - 1;
1  00C2  00066
1  00C2  00067      (* COMPUTE THE PRECONDITIONED RESULT *)
1  00C2  00068      VALUE := ORD (LETTER(1)) + ORD (LETTER(LENGTH)) + 16 * LENGTH;
1  0104  00069
1  0104  00070      (* RETURN THE HASHED VALUE *)
1  0104  00071      HASH2 := VALUE MOD (SIZE - 2) + 1
1  0116  00072  END;
0  0038  00073
0  0038  00074  FUNCTION OPENDH (X: STRING(10); INFO: STRING(20); INSERT: BOOLEAN):
1  0000  00075          INTEGER;
1  0000  00076  (* THIS FUNCTION PERFORMS THE TABLE LOOK-UP AND INSERTION
1  0000  00077      OPERATIONS USING DOUBLE HASHING, AND RETURNS THE POSITION
1  0000  00078      OF THE KEY X, IF SUCCESSFUL. OTHERWISE, A NEGATED OR
1  0000  00079      ZERO POSITION IS RETURNED. HASH1 GIVES THE FIRST HASH
1  0000  00080      VALUE WHILE HASH2 IS AN INDEPENDENT HASHING FUNCTION FOR
1  0000  00081      THE SECOND HASHED VALUE. *)
1  0000  00082  VAR D,                      (* HASH1 VALUE OF X *)
1  0062  00083      J, Y,                   (* INDICES FOR RANDOM PROBE *)
1  0062  00084      C: INTEGER;             (* SECOND HASHED VALUE *)
1  0062  00085      STOP: BOOLEAN;          (* LOGICAL FLAG FOR FUNCTION RETURN *)
1  0062  00086
1  0062  00087  BEGIN
1  0062  00088      STOP := FALSE;
1  006A  00089
1  006A  00090      (* CALCULATE INITIAL POSITION *)
1  006A  00091      D := HASH1 (X, M);
1  0094  00092      C := HASH2 (X, M);
1  00BE  00093
1  00BE  00094      (* FIRST PROBE? *)
1  00BE  00095      IF INSERT
1  00BE  00096      THEN IF (HASH_TABLE(D).FLAG = 'D') OR (HASH_TABLE(D).FLAG = 'E')
1  0128  00097          THEN BEGIN
1  0128  00098              HASH_TABLE(D).K := X;
1  0150  00099              HASH_TABLE(D).DATA := INFO;
1  017C  00100              HASH_TABLE(D).FLAG := 'I';
1  01A8  00101              OPENDH := D;
1  01B0  00102              STOP := TRUE
1  01B0  00103              END
```

Fig. 10-16 Program to perform double hashing

```
1  01B8    00104                      ELSE IF X = HASH_TABLE(D).K
1  01DE    00105                          THEN BEGIN
1  01E8    00106                              OPENDH := -D;
1  01F2    00107                              STOP := TRUE
1  01F2    00108                          END
1  01FA    00109                      ELSE
1  01FA    00110              ELSE IF (HASH_TABLE(D).K = X) AND (HASH_TABLE(D).FLAG = ^I^)
1  025E    00111                  THEN BEGIN
1  025E    00112                      OPENDH := D;
1  0266    00113                      STOP := TRUE
1  0266    00114                  END
1  026E    00115              ELSE IF (HASH_TABLE(D).FLAG = ^D^) OR (HASH_TABLE(D).FLAG =
1  02C8    00116                      ^E^)
1  02D2    00117                  THEN BEGIN
1  02D2    00118                      OPENDH := -D;
1  02DC    00119                      STOP := TRUE
1  02DC    00120                  END;
1  02E4    00121
1  02E4    00122      (* PERFORM SEARCH *)
1  02E4    00123      Y := D - 1;
1  02F0    00124      WHILE NOT STOP DO
1  02FE    00125      BEGIN
1  02FE    00126
1  02FE    00127          (* SCAN NEXT ENTRY *)
1  02FE    00128          Y := (Y + C) MOD M;
1  0314    00129          J := Y + 1;
1  0320    00130
1  0320    00131          (* OVERFLOW? *)
1  0320    00132          IF J = D
1  0320    00133          THEN BEGIN
1  032C    00134              WRITELN (^ ^, ^OVERFLOW OR LOOK-UP ERROR^);
1  0350    00135              OPENDH := 0;
1  0356    00136              STOP := TRUE
1  0356    00137          END;
1  035E    00138
1  035E    00139          (* PERFORM LOOK-UP OR INSERTION *)
1  035E    00140          IF INSERT
1  035E    00141          THEN IF (HASH_TABLE(J).FLAG = ^D^) OR (HASH_TABLE(J).FLAG =
1  03BE    00142              ^E^)
1  03C8    00143              THEN BEGIN
1  03C8    00144                  HASH_TABLE(J).K := X;
1  03F0    00145                  HASH_TABLE(J).DATA := INFO;
1  041C    00146                  HASH_TABLE(J).FLAG := ^I^;
1  0448    00147                  OPENDH := J;
1  0450    00148                  STOP := TRUE
1  0450    00149              END
1  0458    00150              ELSE IF HASH_TABLE(J).K = X
1  047E    00151                  THEN BEGIN
1  0488    00152                      OPENDH := -J;
1  0492    00153                      STOP := TRUE
1  0492    00154                  END
1  049A    00155                  ELSE
1  049A    00156          ELSE IF HASH_TABLE(J).FLAG = ^E^
1  04C8    00157              THEN BEGIN
1  04D2    00158                  OPENDH := -J;
1  04DC    00159                  STOP := TRUE
1  04DC    00160              END
1  04E4    00161              ELSE IF HASH_TABLE(J).K = X
1  050A    00162                  THEN BEGIN
1  0514    00163                      OPENDH := J;
1  051C    00164                      STOP := TRUE
1  051C    00165                  END
1  0524    00166      END
1  0524    00167  END;
```

Fig. 10-16   Program to perform double hashing (cont'd.)

collision resolution with a separate hash-table can be used to represent this sorting process. The linked-lists are maintained in alphabetical order and after all records have been inserted into the table, the linked lists just need to be concatenated.

A general algorithm to perform the address-calculation sort follows:

1. Initialize hash table entries to NIL
2. Repeat thru step 4 while there are still input records

```
--EXECUTION-->
INSERTED RECORDS ARE

KEY          INFORMATION FIELD       POSITION
FROG         AMPHIBIAN                  3
WHALE        MAMMAL                    15
LYNX         MAMMAL                    14
SNAKE        REPTILE                   11
BLUEJAY      BIRD                      12
BEETLE       INSECT                     2
SALMON       FISH                       9


POSITION OF LOOK-UP RECORDS ARE

KEY          POSITION
INVALID KEY IS DUCK
INVALID KEY IS BIRD
INVALID KEY IS MONKEY
INVALID KEY IS MAMMAL
LYNX           14
BLUEJAY        12
SALMON          9
INVALID KEY IS JACKFISH
INVALID KEY IS LADYBUG
SNAKE          11
```

Fig. 10-16   Program to perform double hashing (cont'd.)

3. Input and hash a record
4. Insert record into appropriate linked list and preserve the order of the keys
5. Find the first nonempty linked list
6. Repeat for all remaining linked lists
       Concatenate the end of the previous nonempty linked list with the front of the next nonempty linked list
7. Print the sorted linked list

A program is given in Fig. 10-18 which performs an address-calculation sort. The key values used are:

CAT, DOG, PIKE, CANADA GOOSE, DOLPHIN, MAN, MALLARD DUCK, HORSE, and CANARY.

The variables used in the program are:

Variable	Type	Usage
POINTER	@RECORD_STRUCTURE	Pointer type to record structure
RECORD_STRUCTURE	RECORD	Structure representing records
K	STRING(20)	Key field of record
DATA	STRING(20)	Information field of record
LINK	POINTER	Points to next record in list
KEY	STRING(20)	Key field of record read
INFO	STRING(20)	Information field of record read
HASH_TABLE	ARRAY(1..M) OF POINTER	Vector of pointers representing hash table
M	CONST	Size of record table
RANDOM	INTEGER	Hashed value of key

I, J	INTEGER	Counted loop variables
P	POINTER	Pointer to insert record into hash table
S	POINTER	Pointer to insert record into hash table
HEAD	POINTER	Points to head of sorted linked list
NEWPTR	POINTER	Points to new record
BLANKS	STRING(256)	String of blanks

Variables used in the function HASH are:

KEY	STRING(20)	Key which is to be hashed
CHAR	STRING(1)	Stores first character of key
VALUE	INTEGER	Hashed value of key

The program initializes all elements in the hash table to NIL. The first record is read in line 53. Then a loop is entered to sort the records. First a new record is allocated and initialized. Then the key is hashed and the record is inserted into the appropriate linked list. Line 67 determines whether the record is to be inserted into a null linked list. If not, a search is made through the list and the record is inserted such that the order of the keys are preserved in increasing order. Then in line 93, the next record is read. After all the records have been processed, the nonempty linked lists are concatenated. Finally, the sorted table is printed in lines 121 to 128.

The function HASH returns a value that is order preserving by computing the position in the alphabet that the first character of the key is found. Then this preconditioned value is mapped into the address space.

10-9.3 Radix Sorting

The notion of radix sorting was introduced in the exercises at the end of Chap. 4 in the main text, and discussed further in Sec. 10-10.3 of the main text. In radix sorting, there are 10 pockets, one for each digit value. Each digit position is sorted, where all records having the same digit in the same position in the key field are placed into the same pocket. All digits are processed in turn, starting with the lowest-order digit.

For example, the table

73, 65, 52, 77, 24, 83, 17, 35, 96, 62, 41, 87, 09, 11

is first sorted by the low-order digits, giving

```
                                    87
          11  62  83       35       17
          41  52  73  24  65  96  77      09
Pocket:  0   1   2   3   4   5   6   7  8   9
```

This results, after joining the pockets together, in the table:

41, 11, 52, 62, 73, 83, 24, 65, 35, 96, 77, 17, 87, 09

```
0  0000   00001   PROGRAM CHAIN (INPUT, OUTPUT);
0  0000   00002   (* THIS PROGRAM INPUTS A SERIES OF RECORDS AND ENTERS THEM INTO A
0  0000   00003      HASH TABLE USING SEPARATE CHAINING.  PROCEDURE INTER IS USED
0  0000   00004      TO PERFORM THE INSERTION. *)
0  0000   00005
0  0000   00006   CONST M = 11;                (* SIZE OF HASH TABLE *)
0  0038   00007
0  0038   00008   TYPE POINTER = @RECORD_STRUCTURE;
0  0038   00009      RECORD_STRUCTURE = RECORD    (* RECORD STRUCTURE *)
0  0038   00010         KEY,               (* KEY FIELD *)
0  0038   00011         DATA: STRING(20);   (* INFORMATION FIELD *)
0  0038   00012         LINK: POINTER      (* POINTER TO NEXT RECORD *)
0  0038   00013         END;
0  0038   00014
0  0038   00015   VAR HASH_TABLE: ARRAY (1..M) OF POINTER;
0  0038   00016                          (* POINTER VECTOR REPRESENTING THE HASH
0  0038   00017                             TABLE *)
0  0038   00018       POS: POINTER;        (* USED TO PRINT LINKED LISTS *)
0  0038   00019       X,                   (* KEY FIELD OF NEW RECORD *)
0  0038   00020       INFO: STRING(20);    (* INFORMATION FIELD *)
0  0038   00021       I: INTEGER;          (* COUNTED LOOP VARIABLE *)
0  0038   00022
0  0038   00023       FUNCTION HASH (SYMBOL: STRING(20); SIZE: INTEGER): INTEGER;
1  0000   00024       (* THIS FUNCTION COMPUTES THE HASH VALUE OF THE STRING
1  0000   00025          SYMBOL BY USING THE LENGTH-DEPENDENT METHOD. *)
1  0000   00026
1  0000   00027       VAR LETTER: ARRAY (1..20) OF CHAR;
1  0068   00028                          (* USED TO STORE SYMBOL AS CHARACTER
1  0068   00029                             STRING *)
1  0068   00030          LENGTH,          (* LENGTH OF SYMBOL *)
1  0068   00031          VALUE: INTEGER;  (* PRECONDITIONED VALUE *)
1  0068   00032
1  0068   00033       BEGIN
1  0068   00034
1  0068   00035          (* COMPUTE THE LENGTH OF THE SYMBOL *)
1  0068   00036          LETTER := SYMBOL;
1  0082   00037          LENGTH := 20;
1  008A   00038          WHILE LETTER(LENGTH) = ' ' DO
1  00B2   00039              LENGTH := LENGTH - 1;
1  00C2   00040
1  00C2   00041          (* COMPUTE THE PRECONDITIONED RESULT *)
1  00C2   00042          VALUE := ORD (LETTER(1)) + ORD (LETTER(LENGTH)) + 16 * LENGTH;
1  0104   00043
1  0104   00044          (* RETURN THE HASHED VALUE *)
1  0104   00045          HASH := VALUE MOD SIZE + 1
1  0110   00046       END;
0  0038   00047
0  0038   00048       PROCEDURE ENTER (X, INFO: STRING(20));
1  0000   00049       (* GIVEN A POINTER VECTOR HASH_TABLE REPRESENTING A HASH
1  0000   00050          TABLE, EACH ELEMENT OF WHICH CONTAINS A POINTER TO A
1  0000   00051          LINKED LIST OF COLLIDING RECORDS, AND A HASHING FUNCTION
1  0000   00052          HASH, THIS PROCEDURE APPENDS THE GIVEN KEY (X) AND THE
1  0000   00053          INFORMATION FIELD (INFO) TO THE FRONT OF THE APPROPRIATE
1  0000   00054          LINKED LIST IF IT IS NOT ALREADY THERE. *)
1  0000   00055
1  0000   00056       VAR RANDOM: INTEGER;   (* HASHED VALUE OF KEY *)
1  0056   00057          P: POINTER;         (* TEMPORARY POINTER VARIABLE *)
1  0056   00058          STOP: BOOLEAN;      (* LOGICAL FLAG FOR PROCEDURE RETURN *)
1  0056   00059
1  0056   00060       BEGIN
1  0056   00061          STOP := FALSE;
1  005E   00062
1  005E   00063          (* COMPUTE THE HASH NUMBER *)
1  005E   00064          RANDOM := HASH (X, M);
1  0088   00065
1  0088   00066          (* IS THE LINKED LIST TO WHICH X BELONGS EMPTY? *)
1  0088   00067          WRITELN (' ', X, ' HASHED INTO ', RANDOM : 2);
1  00D0   00068          IF HASH_TABLE(RANDOM) = NIL
1  00F2   00069          THEN BEGIN
1  00FE   00070              NEW (P);
1  0110   00071              HASH_TABLE(RANDOM) := P;
1  013A   00072              P@.KEY := X;
1  0156   00073              P@.DATA := INFO;
1  0176   00074              P@.LINK := NIL;
1  0196   00075              STOP := TRUE
1  0196   00076              END;
1  019E   00077
1  019E   00078          (* PERFORM SEARCH FOR X *)
1  019E   00079          P := HASH_TABLE(RANDOM);
```

Fig. 10-17   Program to resolve collisions using separate chaining

```
1  01C8  00080              WHILE (P <> NIL) AND NOT STOP DO
1  01E2  00081                  IF X = P@.KEY
1  01F8  00082                  THEN STOP := TRUE  (* X IS ALREADY PRESENT *)
1  0202  00083                  ELSE P := P@.LINK;
1  0234  00084              IF NOT STOP
1  0234  00085              THEN BEGIN  (* X IS NOT IN THE TABLE *)
1  0242  00086                  NEW (P);
1  0254  00087                  P@.KEY := X;
1  0270  00088                  P@.DATA := INFO;
1  0290  00089                  P@.LINK := HASH_TABLE(RANDOM);
1  02D4  00090                  HASH_TABLE(RANDOM) := P
1  02F6  00091                  END
1  02FE  00092          END;
0  0038  00093
0  0038  00094  BEGIN  (* MAIN PROGRAM *)
0  0038  00095
0  0038  00096          (* INITIALIZE HASH TABLE *)
0  0038  00097          FOR I := 1 TO M DO
0  005C  00098              HASH_TABLE(I) := NIL;
0  0088  00099
0  0088  00100          (* INPUT VARIABLES TO ENTER INTO TABLE *)
0  0088  00101          WRITELN (' ', 'RECORDS HASHED TO');
0  00AC  00102          WRITELN;
0  00BA  00103          READ (X, INFO);
0  00DE  00104          WHILE NOT EOF DO
0  00E6  00105          BEGIN
0  00E6  00106              ENTER (X, INFO);
0  010C  00107              READ (X, INFO)
0  0130  00108          END;
0  0134  00109
0  0134  00110          (* PRINT OUT LINKED LISTS *)
0  0134  00111          WRITELN ('-', 'LINKED LISTS FORMED BY PROCEDURE ENTER');
0  0158  00112          WRITELN;
0  0166  00113          FOR I := 1 TO M DO
0  018A  00114          BEGIN
0  018A  00115              POS := HASH_TABLE(I);
0  01B4  00116              WRITE (' ', 'ROW ', I : 2);
0  01EA  00117              WHILE POS <> NIL DO
0  01F6  00118              BEGIN
0  01F6  00119                  WRITE (' ' : 2, POS@.KEY);
0  022E  00120                  POS := POS@.LINK
0  0244  00121              END;
0  0254  00122              WRITELN
0  0254  00123          END
0  0262  00124  END.
```

```
-----------------------------------
| COMPILE TIME:   0.312 SECOND(S) |
|     NO WARNING(S) DETECTED       |
|     NO ERROR(S) DETECTED         |
-----------------------------------
--EXECUTION-->
RECORDS HASHED TO

FROG              HASHED INTO 11
LION              HASHED INTO  5
PELICAN           HASHED INTO  2
WHALE             HASHED INTO  2
LYNX              HASHED INTO  1
SNAKE             HASHED INTO  9
BLUEJAY           HASHED INTO 11
BEETLE            HASHED INTO  4
SALMON            HASHED INTO  8
DUCK              HASHED INTO  9
MONKEY            HASHED INTO  2
WOLF              HASHED INTO  9


LINKED LISTS FORMED BY PROCEDURE ENTER

ROW  1  LYNX
ROW  2  MONKEY            WHALE            PELICAN
ROW  3
ROW  4  BEETLE
ROW  5  LION
ROW  6
ROW  7
ROW  8  SALMON
ROW  9  WOLF              DUCK             SNAKE
ROW 10
ROW 11  BLUEJAY           FROG
```

Fig. 10-17   Program to resolve collisions using separate chaining (cont'd.)

After sorting on the high-order digit, we obtain:

	17						65	77	87	
	09	11	24	35	41	52	62	73	83	96
Pocket:	0	1	2	3	4	5	6	7	8	9

giving the sorted table

    09, 11, 17, 24, 35, 41, 52, 62, 65, 73, 77, 83, 87, 96

The pockets can be maintained using linked lists with pointers to the first and last nodes.

A general algorithm to sort the keys containing m digits follows. Note that m successive passes are required.

1. Repeat thru step 4 for each digit
2. Initialize the pointers to the front and rear of the linked lists for each pocket to NIL
3. Repeat for each node in the linked list
   Obtain the jth digit of the key
   If the list for the appropriate pocket is empty, set the front and rear pointers to the address of the new node in the linked list,
   else add it to the end of the list
4. Find the first nonempty pocket and concatenate the nonempty pockets together

A main program and the procedure RADIX_SORT are given in Fig. 10-19. The program sorted the tables

    73, 65, 52, 77, 24, 83, 17, 35, 96, 62, 41, 87, 09, 22

and

    38, 52, 59, 53, 11, 76

This program assumes that the key field is read as a character string so that single digits can easily be removed from the keys. The variables used in the main program are:

Variable	Type	Usage
POINTER	@RECORD_STRUCTURE	Pointer type to table of records
RECORD_STRUCTURE	RECORD	Table of records
K	STRING(10)	Key field
LINK	POINTER	Pointer to next node in list
N	INTEGER	Number of records in table
KEY	STRING(10)	Key of record read
M	INTEGER	Size of key field
I	INTEGER	Counted loop variable
J	INTEGER	Counted loop variable

FIRST	POINTER	Pointer to first node in table
PREV	POINTER	Pointer used to build sorted table
P	POINTER	Address of new node
BLANKS	STRING(256)	String of blanks

Variables used in procedure RADIX_SORT are:

N	INTEGER	Number of records in table
M	INTEGER	Size of key field
FIRST	POINTER	Head of list to be sorted
T	ARRAY(0..9) OF POINTER	Pointers to first nodes in the linked lists of the pockets
B	ARRAY(0..9) OF POINTER	Pointers to last nodes in the linked lists of the pockets
I	INTEGER	Counted loop variable
J	INTEGER	Counted loop variable
TEMP	INTEGER	Index variable
R	POINTER	Pointer to current node in list
NEXT	POINTER	Pointer to next node in list
PREV	POINTER	Used to combine the pockets at the end of a pass
POINT	POINTER	Temporary pointer variable
D	STRING(256)	Current digit used to sort record
D_INT	INTEGER	Integer value of digit D
DIGITS	STRING(256)	String of digits

In the main program, line 101 controls a loop that sorts the tables. The next line reads the number of records in the table and the key size. Next, the table is read and built as a linked list. Procedure RADIX_SORT is called in line 128 to sort the table. Finally, lines 131 to 141 print the sorted table.

In procedure RADIX_SORT, line 49 controls the passes for each digit in the key. First the pointers for the pockets are initialized to NIL. Then line 61 controls a loop to distribute each record into the appropriate pocket. The jth digit is obtained and converted into its integer value. Then, the record is appended to the end of the appropriate pocket. Once all records have been placed into the appropriate pockets, the resulting linked lists are concatenated. Lines 83 to 85 search for the first nonempty pocket. Then the pointer to the last node of each nonempty pocket is set to the address of the first node of the next nonempty pocket. The pointer variable FIRST is set to the address of the first record of the sorted linked list.

EXERCISES FOR CHAPTER 10

1. Construct a program to subtract two polynomials in three variables.

2. Construct a program to multiply two polynomials in three variables.

3. Formulate a program for evaluating a polynomial of three variables which is represented by a linked list. The values for x, y, z are given as a, b, and c, respectively.

4. Using the division method of hashing with m = 101 and the ORD function in PASCAL obtain the hash values for the following set of keys:

```
0   0000   00001   PROGRAM ADD_CAL (INPUT, OUTPUT);
0   0000   00002   (* THIS PROGRAM INPUTS RECORDS AND SORTS THEM BASED ON AN ADDRESS
0   0000   00003      CALCULATION WITH A SEPARATE OVERFLOW AREA USING AN ORDER
0   0000   00004      PRESERVING HASHING FUNCTION. *)
0   0000   00005
0   0000   00006   CONST M = 13;              (* SIZE OF TABLE *)
0   0038   00007
0   0038   00008   TYPE POINTER = @RECORD_STRUCTURE;
0   0038   00009        RECORD_STRUCTURE = RECORD (* USED TO SORT RECORDS *)
0   0038   00010          K: STRING (256);        (* KEY *)
0   0038   00011          DATA: STRING(20);    (* INFORMATION FIELD *)
0   0038   00012          LINK: POINTER
0   0038   00013          END;
0   0038   00014
0   0038   00015   VAR KEY: STRING(256);        (* KEY OF RECORD *)
0   0038   00016       INFO: STRING(20);        (* INFORMATION FEILD OF RECORD *)
0   0038   00017       RANDOM,                  (* HASHED VALUE OF KEY *)
0   0038   00018       I,J: INTEGER;            (* LOOP COUNTER VARIABLE *)
0   0038   00019       NEWPTR,                  (* POINTS TO NEW RECORD *)
0   0038   00020       P, S,                    (* USED TO INSERT ELEMENTS *)
0   0038   00021       HEAD: POINTER;           (* HEAD OF SORTED LINKED LIST *)
0   0038   00022       HASH_TABLE: ARRAY (1..M) OF POINTER; (* POINTS TO OVERFLOW AREA *)
0   0038   00023       BLANKS: STRING(256);      (* STRING OF BLANK CHARACTERS *)
0   0038   00024       PROCEDURE CONCAT (VAR S1, S2, RESULT: STRING(256)); EXTERNAL;
0   0038   00025       FUNCTION HASH (KEY: STRING(256)): INTEGER;
1   0000   00026       (* THIS ORDER PRESERVING HASHING FUNCTION RETURNS TO HASH
1   0000   00027          VALUE OF KEY. *)
1   0000   00028
1   0000   00029       VAR CHARACTER: STRING(256);  (* FIRST CHARACTER OF KEY *)
1   004C   00030           VALUE: INTEGER;       (* HASHED VALUE OF KEY *)
1   004C   00031           ALPHAB: STRING(256); (* STRING OF ALPHABETIC CHARACTERS *)
1   004C   00032             FUNCTION INDEX (VAR S, PATTERN: STRING(256)): INTEGER;
2   0000   00033                EXTERNAL;
1   004C   00034             PROCEDURE SUB (VAR S: STRING(256); POS, NUM: INTEGER;
2   0000   00035                VAR RESULT: STRING(256)); EXTERNAL;
1   004C   00036
1   004C   00037       BEGIN
1   004C   00038           ALPHAB := 'ABCDEFGHIJKLMNOPQRSTUVWXYZ*/';
1   0052   00039           (* COMPUTE HASHED VALUE OF KEY *)
1   0052   00040           SUB (KEY, 1, 1, CHARACTER);
1   0086   00041           VALUE := INDEX (ALPHAB, CHARACTER);
1   00B0   00042           HASH := (VALUE + 1) DIV 2;
1   00C6   00043       END;
0   0038   00044
0   0038   00045   BEGIN
0   0038   00046       BLANKS := '                       */';
0   003E   00047
0   003E   00048       (* INITIALIZE HASH TABLE *)
0   003E   00049       FOR I := 1 TO M DO
0   0062   00050           HASH_TABLE(I) := NIL;
0   008E   00051
0   008E   00052       (* INPUT AND INSERT RECORDS INTO APPROPRIATE LINKED LISTS *)
0   008E   00053       READ (KEY, INFO);
0   00B2   00054       WRITELN (' ', 'UNSORTED TABLE IS');
0   00D6   00055       WRITELN;
0   00E4   00056       WHILE NOT EOF DO
0   00EC   00057       BEGIN
0   00EC   00058           CONCAT (KEY, BLANKS, KEY);
0   011A   00059           WRITELN (' ', KEY : 20, ' ' : 2, INFO);
0   0162   00060           NEW (NEWPTR);
0   0174   00061           NEWPTR@.K := KEY;
0   0190   00062           NEWPTR@.DATA := INFO;
0   01B0   00063           NEWPTR@.LINK := NIL;
0   01D0   00064           RANDOM := HASH (KEY);
0   01F4   00065
0   01F4   00066           (* INSERT RECORD INTO APPROPRIATE LINKED LIST *)
0   01F4   00067           IF HASH_TABLE(RANDOM) = NIL
0   0216   00068           THEN BEGIN  (* INSERT RECORD INTO EMPTY LINKED LIST *)
0   0222   00069               NEWPTR@.LINK := NIL;
0   0242   00070               HASH_TABLE(RANDOM) := NEWPTR
0   0264   00071               END
0   026C   00072           ELSE BEGIN (* INSERT RECORD IN MIDDLE OR AT END OF LIST *)
0   0270   00073               P := HASH_TABLE(RANDOM);
0   029A   00074               S := P;
0   02A2   00075               WHILE (S@.LINK <> NIL) AND (S@.K < KEY) DO
0   02E8   00076               BEGIN
0   02E8   00077                   P := S;
0   02F0   00078                   S := S@.LINK
0   0306   00079               END;
```

Fig. 10-18   Program to perform address-calculation sort

```
0  0316   00080                    IF (S = HASH_TABLE(RANDOM)) AND (KEY <= S@.K)
0  0366   00081                    THEN BEGIN (* INSERT AT FRONT *)
0  0366   00082                        HASH_TABLE(RANDOM) := NEWPTR;
0  0390   00083                        NEWPTR@.LINK := S
0  03AA   00084                    END
0  03B2   00085                    ELSE IF (S@.LINK = NIL) AND (KEY > S@.K)
0  03FC   00086                        THEN (* INSERT AT END *)
0  03FC   00087                            S@.LINK := NEWPTR
0  0416   00088                        ELSE BEGIN (* INSERT IN MIDDLE *)
0  0422   00089                            P@.LINK := NEWPTR;
0  0444   00090                            NEWPTR@.LINK := S
0  045E   00091                            END
0  0466   00092                END;
0  0466   00093            READ (KEY, INFO)
0  048A   00094        END;
0  048E   00095
0  048E   00096    (* FIND FIRST NON-EMPTY LINKED LIST *)
0  048E   00097    I := 1;
0  0496   00098    WHILE (HASH_TABLE(I) = NIL) AND (I < M) DO
0  04D0   00099        I := I + 1;
0  04E0   00100    HEAD := HASH_TABLE(I);
0  050A   00101    J := I + 1;
0  0516   00102
0  0516   00103    (* CONCATENATE THE NON-EMPTY LINKED LISTS *)
0  0516   00104    WHILE J <= M DO
0  0522   00105    BEGIN
0  0522   00106        IF HASH_TABLE(J) <> NIL
0  0544   00107        THEN BEGIN  (* FIND TAIL OF LINKED LIST *)
0  0550   00108            P := HASH_TABLE(I);
0  057A   00109            WHILE P@.LINK <> NIL DO
0  05A0   00110                P := P@.LINK;
0  05C6   00111
0  05C6   00112            (* LINK END OF THIS LINKED LIST
0  05C6   00113               TO THE HEAD OF THE NEXT *)
0  05C6   00114            P@.LINK := HASH_TABLE(J);
0  060A   00115            I := J
0  060A   00116            END;
0  0612   00117        J := J + 1
0  0612   00118    END;
0  0622   00119
0  0622   00120    (* PRINT LINKED LIST *)
0  0622   00121    WRITELN ('-', 'SORTED LIST IS');
0  0646   00122    WRITELN;
0  0654   00123    P := HEAD;
0  065C   00124    WHILE P <> NIL DO
0  0668   00125    BEGIN
0  0668   00126        WRITELN (' ', P@.K : 20, ' ' : 2, P@.DATA);
0  06DA   00127        P := P@.LINK
0  06F0   00128    END
0  06FC   00129 END.
```

```
-------------------------------------
| COMPILE TIME:    0.325 SECOND(S) |
|      NO WARNING(S) DETECTED       |
|      NO ERROR(S) DETECTED         |
-------------------------------------
--EXECUTION-->
UNSORTED TABLE IS

CAT                  FELIS CATUS
DOG                  CANIS FAMILIARIS
PIKE                 ESOX LUCIUS
CANADA GOOSE         BRANTA CANADENSIS
DOLPHIN              DELPHINUS DELPHIS
MAN                  HOMO SAPIEN
MALLARD DUCK         ANAS BOSCAS
HORSE                EQUUS CABALLUS
CANARY               SERINUS CANARIUS


SORTED LIST IS

CANADA GOOSE         BRANTA CANADENSIS
CANARY               SERINUS CANARIUS
CAT                  FELIS CATUS
DOG                  CANIS FAMILIARIS
DOLPHIN              DELPHINUS DELPHIS
HORSE                EQUUS CABALLUS
MALLARD DUCK         ANAS BOSCAS
MAN                  HOMO SAPIEN
PIKE                 ESOX LUCIUS
```

Fig. 10-18   Program to perform address-calculation sort (cont'd.)

```
0  0000   00001   PROGRAM SORT (INPUT, OUTPUT);
0  0000   00002   (* THIS PROGRAM INPUTS TABLES OF VALUES CONSISTING OF 2 DIGIT
0  0000   00003        NUMBERS (WHICH ARE READ AS STRINGS) AND SORTS THEM BY USING
0  0000   00004        PROCEDURE RADIX_SORT. *)
0  0000   00005
0  0000   00006   TYPE POINTER = @NODE;
0  0038   00007        NODE = RECORD              (* TABLE OF RECORDS *)
0  0038   00008           K: STRING(256);         (* KEY FIELD *)
0  0038   00009           LINK: POINTER           (* POINTER FIELD *)
0  0038   00010           END;
0  0038   00011
0  0038   00012   VAR KEY,                         (* RECORD KEY WHICH IS READ IN *)
0  0038   00013        BLANKS: STRING(256);        (* STRING OF BLANK CHARACTERS *)
0  0038   00014        N,                          (* NUMBER OF RECORDS IN TABLE *)
0  0038   00015        M,                          (* SIZE OF KEY FIELD *)
0  0038   00016        I, J: INTEGER;              (* COUNTED LOOP VARIABLES *)
0  0038   00017        P,                          (* ADDRESS OF NEW NODE *)
0  0038   00018        FIRST,                      (* ADDRESS OF FIRST NODE IN TABLE *)
0  0038   00019        PREV: POINTER;              (* USED TO BUILD TABLE *)
0  0038   00020         PROCEDURE CONCAT (VAR S1, S2, RESULT: STRING(256)); EXTERNAL;
0  0038   00021
0  0038   00022         PROCEDURE RADIX_SORT (N, M: INTEGER; VAR FIRST: POINTER);
1  0000   00023         (* GIVEN A TABLE OF N RECORDS ARRANGED AS A LINKED LIST
1  0000   00024              WHERE EACH NODE CONSISTS OF A KEY FIELD (K) OF M DIGITS
1  0000   00025              AND A POINTER FIELD (LINKK), THIS PROCEDURE PERFORMS A
1  0000   00026              RADIX SORT. *)
1  0000   00027
1  0000   00028         VAR T, B: ARRAY (0..9) OF POINTER;
1  0076   00029                                   (* ADDRESSES OF REAR AND FRONT
1  0076   00030                                        RECORDS IN QUEUES *)
1  0076   00031              I, J, TEMP: INTEGER; (* INDEX VARIABLES *)
1  0076   00032              R,                    (* ADDRESS OF CURRENT WORD *)
1  0076   00033              NEXT,                 (* ADDRESS OF NEXT WORD *)
1  0076   00034              PREV,                 (* USED TO COMBINE POCKETS
1  0076   00035                                        AT END OF PASS *)
1  0076   00036              POINT: POINTER;       (* TEMP POINTER VARIABLE *)
1  0076   00037              DIGITS,               (* STRING OF DIGITS *)
1  0076   00038              D: STRING(256);       (* DIGIT BEING EXAMINED *)
1  0076   00039              D_INT: INTEGER;       (* INTEGER VALUE OF D *)
1  0076   00040              FUNCTION INDEX (VAR S, PATTERN: STRING(256)): INTEGER;
2  0000   00041                   EXTERNAL;
1  008E   00042              PROCEDURE SUB (VAR S: STRING(256); POS, NUM: INTEGER;
2  0000   00043                   VAR RESULT: STRING(256)); EXTERNAL;
1  008E   00044
1  008E   00045         BEGIN
1  008E   00046              DIGITS := '0123456789*/';
1  0094   00047
1  0094   00048              (* PERFORM SORT *)
1  0094   00049              FOR J := M DOWNTO 1 DO
1  00B6   00050              BEGIN
1  00B6   00051
1  00B6   00052                   (* INITIALIZE PASS *)
1  00B6   00053                   FOR I := 0 TO 9 DO
1  00DA   00054                   BEGIN
1  00DA   00055                        T(I) := NIL;
1  0102   00056                        B(I) := NIL
1  0124   00057                   END;
1  012E   00058                   R := FIRST;
1  0136   00059
1  0136   00060                   (* DISTRIBUTE EACH RECORD INTO THE APPROPRIATE POCKET *)
1  0136   00061                   WHILE R <> NIL DO
1  0142   00062                   BEGIN
1  0142   00063
1  0142   00064                        (* OBTAIN JTH DIGIT OF KEY K(R) *)
1  0142   00065                        SUB (R@.K, J, 1, D);
1  0188   00066                        D_INT := INDEX (DIGITS, D) - 1;
1  01B6   00067                        NEXT := R@.LINK;
1  01D8   00068                        IF T(D_INT) = NIL
1  01FA   00069                        THEN BEGIN
1  0206   00070                             T(D_INT) := R;
1  0230   00071                             B(D_INT) := R
1  0252   00072                             END
1  025A   00073                        ELSE BEGIN
1  025E   00074                             POINT := T(D_INT);
1  0288   00075                             POINT@.LINK := R;
1  02AA   00076                             T(D_INT) := R
1  02CC   00077                             END;
1  02D4   00078                        R@.LINK := NIL;
```

Fig. 10-19   Program to sort records using the radix sort

```
1   02F4   00079                              R := NEXT
1   02F4   00080                          END;
1   0300   00081
1   0300   00082                          (* COMBINE POCKETS *)
1   0300   00083                          TEMP := 0;
1   0306   00084                          WHILE B(TEMP) = NIL DO
1   0334   00085                              TEMP := TEMP + 1;
1   0344   00086                          FIRST := B(TEMP);
1   036E   00087                          FOR I := TEMP + 1 TO 9 DO
1   0398   00088                          BEGIN
1   0398   00089                              PREV := T(I - 1);
1   03C8   00090                              IF T(I) <> NIL
1   03EA   00091                              THEN PREV@.LINK := B(I)
1   0432   00092                              ELSE T(I) := PREV
1   0460   00093                          END
1   0468   00094                      END
1   046C   00095              END;
0   0038   00096
0   0038   00097   BEGIN
0   0038   00098          BLANKS := '          */';
0   003E   00099
0   003E   00100          (* PROCESS EACH TABLE *)
0   003E   00101          FOR I := 1 TO 2 DO
0   0062   00102          BEGIN
0   0062   00103
0   0062   00104              (* INPUT NUMBER OF RECORDS IN TABLE AND SIZE OF KEY *)
0   0062   00105              READ (N, M);
0   0086   00106
0   0086   00107              (* INPUT TABLE *)
0   0086   00108              WRITELN ('-', 'UNSORTED TABLE IS');
0   00AA   00109              WRITE (' ');
0   00BC   00110              FIRST := NIL;
0   00C2   00111              PREV := NIL;
0   00C8   00112              FOR J := 1 TO N DO
0   00EC   00113              BEGIN
0   00EC   00114                  READ (KEY);
0   00FE   00115                  NEW (P);
0   0110   00116                  P@.K := KEY;
0   012C   00117                  P@.LINK := NIL;
0   014C   00118                  IF PREV = NIL
0   014C   00119                  THEN FIRST := P
0   0158   00120                  ELSE PREV@.LINK := P;
0   0186   00121                  PREV := P;
0   018E   00122                  CONCAT (KEY, BLANKS, KEY);
0   01BC   00123                  WRITE (KEY : 6)
0   01CE   00124              END;
0   01D2   00125              WRITELN;
0   01E0   00126
0   01E0   00127              (* SORT THE TABLE *)
0   01E0   00128              RADIX_SORT (N, M, FIRST);
0   020E   00129
0   020E   00130              (* PRINT THE TABLE AND FREE THE NODES FOR THE NEXT TABLE *)
0   020E   00131              WRITELN ('0', 'SORTED TABLE IS');
0   0232   00132              WRITE (' ');
0   0244   00133              PREV := FIRST;
0   024C   00134              WHILE PREV <> NIL DO
0   0258   00135              BEGIN
0   0258   00136                  CONCAT (PREV@.K, BLANKS, PREV@.K);
0   02AA   00137                  WRITE (PREV@.K : 6);
0   02D0   00138                  FIRST := PREV@.LINK;
0   02F2   00139                  DISPOSE (PREV);
0   0320   00140                  PREV := FIRST
0   0320   00141              END;
0   032C   00142              WRITELN
0   032C   00143          END
0   033A   00144   END.
--EXECUTION-->


UNSORTED TABLE IS
73   65   52   77   24   83   17   35   96   62   41   87   09   22

SORTED TABLE IS
09   17   22   24   35   41   52   62   65   73   77   83   87   96


UNSORTED TABLE IS
38   52   59   53   11   76

SORTED TABLE IS
11   38   52   53   59   76
```

Fig. 10-19 Program to sort records using the radix sort (cont'd.)

'ALBERTA'
'SASKATCHEWAN'
'MANITOBA'
'ONTARIO'

5. Write a PASCAL function procedure for the mid-square hashing method which extracts the middle N bits of the square of a five-digit key. The function is to have two parameters:

KEY - numerical key
N - number of bits to be extracted

The function is to return the hash value obtained in the computation.

6. Write a PASCAL function for the folding method of hashing. Assume that a three digit address (000 – 999) is required. The function, which has one parameter, is to return the desired hash value.

7. Compare the results of applying the division, midsquare, and folding hashing functions to a fixed set of keys. Make sure the ranges of these three functions are the same or almost the same for the keyset used. Which method distributes the keys most uniformly over the elements of the range?

8. Write a program, based on the linear probe method, for deleting a record from a hash table. This program is not to use a special value of DELETE. That is, each record position is to be either occupied or empty.

One approach that can be used is first to mark the deleted record as empty. An ordered search is then made for the next empty position. If a record, say, y, is found whose hash value is not between the position of the record just marked for deletion and that of the present empty position, then record y can be moved to replace the deleted record. Then the position for record y is marked as empty and the entire process is repeated, starting at the position occupied by y.

CHAPTER

11

TREES

So far, we have been concerned with the programming aspects of linear data structures. In this chapter we examine the programming details associated with tree structures. In particular, the dynamic method of storage allocation in PASCAL is used to give linked representations of tree structures. Also, programs for the application of trees to the area of symbolic manipulation of expressions, searching, and sorting are given.

11-1   INTRODUCTION

The notation and concepts of tree structures are given in the main text. In this section we summarize these notions.

A tree consists of a set of nodes and a set of lines or branches. A node from which there are no branches emanating is called a *terminal node* or *leaf node*. A nonleaf node is called a *branch node*. The following is a recursive definition of a tree:

A *tree* is a finite set of one or more nodes such that:

1. There is a specially designated node called a *root*.
2. The remaining nodes are partitioned into disjoint subsets T_0, T_1, T_2, ..., and T_n $(n \geqslant 0)$, each of which is a tree. Each T_i $(0 \leqslant i \leqslant n)$ is called a *subtree* of the root.

Another important notational convenience in dealing with trees is that of the *level* of a node. The level of the root node of a tree is 1. Otherwise, the level of any other node is 1 plus its distance from the root node. It is also convenient to define the degree of a node. The *degree* of a node is simply its number of subtrees.

If we order, say, from left to right, the children of a node at each level in the tree, the resulting tree is said to be *ordered*. A set of disjoint ordered trees is called a *forest*.

Finally, it is useful to restrict trees so that the degree of each node is at most 2. Also, it is convenient to distinguish between the left and right subtrees of each node. The following recursive definition specifies a binary tree:

A *binary tree* is a finite set (possible empty) of nodes consisting of a root node which has two disjoint binary subtrees called the left subtree and the right subtree.
An *empty binary tree* is a binary tree of zero nodes.

With this brief summary of tree notation, we proceed to examine how trees might be represented in the computer's memory. This is the topic of the next section.

11-2   STORAGE REPRESENTATION AND MANIPULATION OF BINARY TREES

The previous chapter was concerned with the storage representation of linear lists within the computer's memory. We will now extend these concepts to the representation of binary tree structures.

Although both linked and sequential storage allocation techniques can be used to represent binary trees, in this section we will emphasize the programming of linked storage structures in PASCAL. In Sec 11-3.3, however, a sequential storage structure will be used to represent a tree for the purpose of sorting.

First, PASCAL structures are used to implement a linked representation of binary trees in memory. Based on this approach, several programs, such as those for traversing and creating trees are presented. Second, the programming aspects of threaded binary trees are introduced. Finally, a program for the conversion of a general tree to a binary tree is presented.

11-2.1 Linked Storage Representation

As mentioned in the main text, an obvious representation of a binary tree involves storage nodes whose components are given by the following definition:

```
TYPE POINTER = @NODE;
     NODE = RECORD
            LPTR: POINTER;
            INFO: STRING(1);
            RPTR: POINTER
            END;
```

where LPTR and RPTR are pointer variables which denote the addresses of the root nodes of the left and right subtrees, respectively, of a particular node. An empty subtree has an address of NIL.

Recall that the *preorder traversal* of a binary tree consists of the following steps:

1. Process the root node.
2. Traverse the left subtree in preorder.
3. Traverse the right subtree in preorder.

The following PASCAL recursive procedure traverses in preorder a given binary tree with the node structure just given:

```
PROCEDURE RPREORDER (T: POINTER);
(*GIVEN A BINARY TREE WHOSE ROOT NODE
     ADDRESS IS GIVEN BY A POINTER VARIABLE T,
     THIS PROCEDURE RECURSIVELY TRAVERSES THE TREE
     IN PREORDER. )
BEGIN
     IF T < > NIL
     THEN BEGIN
          (* PROCESS THE ROOT NODE *)
          WRITE (' ': 5, T@.INFO);
          (* PROCESS THE LEFT SUBTREE *)
          RPREORDER (T@.LPTR);
          (* PROCESS THE RIGHT SUBTREE *)
          RPREORDER (T@.RPTR)
          END
END;
```

Observe that the preceding program also works for an empty binary tree (i.e., a tree that contains no nodes).

Similarly, the *inorder traversal* of a binary tree involves executing the following steps:

1. Traverse the left subtree in inorder.
2. Process the root node.
3. Traverse the right subtree in inorder.

A PASCAL recursive procedure for this traversal order is the following:

```
PROCEDURE RINORDER (T: POINTER);
(* GIVEN A BINARY TREE WHOSE ROOT NODE
      ADDRESS IS GIVEN BY A POINTER VARIABLE T,
      THIS PROCEDURE TRAVERSES RECURSIVELY THE TREE IN
      INORDER. *)
BEGIN
      IF T < > NIL
      THEN BEGIN
            (* PROCESS THE LEFT SUBTREE *)
            RINORDER (T@.LPTR);
            (* PROCESS THE ROOT NODE *)
            WRITE (' ':5, T@.INFO);
            (* PROCESS THE RIGHT SUBTREE *)
            RINORDER (T@.RPTR)
            END
END;
```

Of course, it is also possible to program the traversals of a binary tree in an iterative manner. In such an approach we require a stack to save upward-pointing information which will permit the ascent of the certain parts of the tree. Figure 11-1 illustrates this approach for preorder traversal. In this program a vector is used to simulate a stack.

Frequently, a binary tree may be destroyed during its processing. Consequently, a duplicate copy of the given binary tree, prior to such processing, may be required. Figure 11-2 exemplifies a PASCAL recursive function for the copying of a binary tree.

We terminate this section with a program for deleting an arbitrary node from a lexically-ordered tree. Recall that the general algorithm for deleting a node is the following:

1. Determine the parent of the node marked for deletion, if it exists; note that it will not exist if we are deleting the root node
2. If the node being deleted has either an empty left or right subtree,
   then append the nonempty subtree to its grandparent node (that is, the node found in step 1) and exit
3. Obtain the inorder successor of the node to be deleted.
   Append the right subtree of this successor node to its grandparent.
   Replace the node to be deleted by its inorder successor.
      This is accomplished by appending the left and right subtrees (with the aforementioned successor node) of the node marked for deletion to the successor node. Also the successor node is appended to the parent of the node just deleted (that is, the node obtained in step 1).

A PASCAL procedure which follows this general algorithm appears in Fig. 11-3. This procedure has one parameter that denotes the information contents of the node marked for deletion.

The procedure first initializes the pointer P to the root node of the tree. If the tree is empty, a message that the node to be deleted is not found is printed and the

```
0  0038   00012  PROCEDURE IPREORDER (T: POINTER);
1  0000   00013  (* GIVEN A BINARY TREE WHOSE ROOT NODE ADDRESS IS GIVEN BY A
1  0000   00014      POINTER VARIABLE T, THIS PROCEDURE ITERATIVELY TRAVERSES
1  0000   00015      THE TREE IN PREORDER *)
1  0000   00016
1  0000   00017  VAR P: POINTER;                    (* CURRENT NODE IN THE TREE *)
1  004E   00018      S: ARRAY (1..50) OF POINTER;  (* STACK *)
1  005E   00019      TOP: INTEGER;                 (* TOP INDEX OF STACK *)
1  005E   00020
1  005E   00021  BEGIN
1  005E   00022
1  005E   00023      (* INITIALIZE *)
1  005E   00024      IF T = NIL
1  006E   00025      THEN WRITE ('EMPTY TREE')
1  008C   00026      ELSE BEGIN  (* INITIALIZE STACK *)
1  0090   00027          TOP := 1;
1  0098   00028          S(TOP) := T;
1  00C2   00029
1  00C2   00030          (* PROCESS EACH STACKED BRANCH ADDRESS *)
1  00C2   00031          WHILE TOP > 0 DO
1  00CE   00032          BEGIN
1  00CE   00033
1  00CE   00034              (* GET STORED ADDRESS AND BRANCH LEFT *)
1  00CE   00035              P := S(TOP);
1  00F8   00036              TOP := TOP - 1;
1  0104   00037              WHILE P <> NIL DO
1  0110   00038              BEGIN
1  0110   00039                  WRITE (P@.INFO);
1  0138   00040                  IF P@.RPTR <> NIL
1  0152   00041                  THEN BEGIN
1  015E   00042
1  015E   00043                      (* STORE ADDRESS OF NONEMPTY RIGHT SUBTREE *)
1  015E   00044                      TOP := TOP + 1;
1  016A   00045                      S(TOP) := P@.RPTR
1  01A2   00046                      END;
1  01AE   00047                  P := P@.LPTR  (* BRANCH LEFT *)
1  01C4   00048              END
1  01CC   00049          END
1  01D0   00050          END
1  01D4   00051
1  01D4   00052      (* FINISHED *)
1  01D4   00053  END;
```

Fig. 11-1   Iterative preorder traversal of a binary tree (vector representation)

```
0  0038   00055  FUNCTION COPY (T: POINTER): POINTER;
1  0000   00056  (* GIVEN A BINARY TREE WHOSE ROOT NODE ADDRESS IS GIVEN BY
1  0000   00057      THE POINTER VARIABLE T, AND A NODE STRUCTURE (NODE), THIS
1  0000   00058      RECURSIVE FUNCTION GENERATES A COPY OF THE TREE AND
1  0000   00059      RETURNS THE ADDRESS OF ITS ROOT NODE. *)
1  0000   00060
1  0000   00061  VAR P: POINTER;              (* TEMPORARY POINTER VARIABLE *)
1  004E   00062
1  004E   00063  BEGIN
1  004E   00064
1  004E   00065      (* NULL POINTER? *)
1  004E   00066      IF T = NIL
1  004E   00067      THEN COPY := NIL
1  005A   00068      ELSE BEGIN
1  0064   00069
1  0064   00070          (* CREATE A NEW NODE *)
1  0064   00071          NEW (P);
1  0076   00072
1  0076   00073          (* COPY INFORMATION FIELD *)
1  0076   00074          P@.INFO := T@.INFO;
1  00B0   00075
1  00B0   00076          (* SET THE STRUCTURAL LINKS *)
1  00B0   00077          P@.LPTR := COPY (T@.LPTR);
1  00F2   00078          P@.RPTR := COPY (T@.RPTR);
1  013C   00079
1  013C   00080          (* RETURN ADDRESS OF NEW NODE *)
1  013C   00081          COPY := P
1  013C   00082          END
1  0144   00083  END;
```

Fig. 11-2   Recursive function to copy a binary tree

```
0  0038   00085   PROCEDURE TREE_DELETE (X: STRING(20); HEAD: POINTER);
1  0000   00086   (* GIVEN A LEXICALLY ORDERED BINARY TREE, THIS PROCEDURE
1  0000   00087      DELETES THE NODE WHOSE INFORMATION FIELD IS EQUAL TO X.
1  0000   00088      THE TREE IS ASSUMED TO HAVE A LIST HEAD WHOSE ADDRESS IS
1  0000   00089      GIVEN BY HEAD. *)
1  0000   00090
1  0000   00091   VAR P,                         (* NODE TO BE DELETED *)
1  0058   00092       PARENT,                    (* PARENT OF NODE TO BE DELETED *)
1  0058   00093       PRED, SUC,                 (* USED TO FIND INORDER SUCCESSOR
1  0058   00094                                     OF NODE P *)
1  0058   00095       Q: POINTER;                (* USED TO DELETE NODE P *)
1  0058   00096       D: CHAR;                   (* DIRECTION FROM PARENT NODE
1  0058   00097                                     TO NODE TO BE DELETED *)
1  0058   00098       STOP: BOOLEAN;             (* LOGICAL FLAG FOR PROCEDURE RETURN *)
1  0058   00099
1  0058   00100   BEGIN
1  0058   00101
1  0058   00102       (* INITIALIZE *)
1  0058   00103       STOP := FALSE;
1  0060   00104       IF HEAD@.LPTR <> NIL
1  0076   00105       THEN BEGIN
1  0082   00106           P := HEAD@.LPTR;
1  00A0   00107           PARENT := HEAD;
1  00A8   00108           D := 'L'
1  00A8   00109           END
1  00AE   00110       ELSE BEGIN
1  00B2   00111           WRITELN (' ', 'NODE NOT FOUND');
1  00D6   00112           STOP := TRUE
1  00D6   00113           END;
1  00DE   00114
```

Fig. 11-3 PASCAL procedure for deleting an arbitrary node from a binary tree

procedure returns to the calling program. In line 116, a loop is entered which searches for the desired node. The root of the current subtree is compared with the record to be deleted. If it is greater than the record to be deleted, a branch to the left subtree is made in lines 120 to 122; otherwise, a comparison is made to see if the root node is less than that of the given key. If this is the case, a branch to the right subtree occurs. If the node to be deleted has been found, the procedure first checks whether either subtree of this node is empty. If one subtree is empty, the pointer variable Q is set to the nonempty subtree of the marked node. Otherwise Q is set to the inorder successor of the node to be deleted. The two subtrees are then combined in lines 155 to 158. Finally, in lines 161 to 163, the pointer which points to the node to be deleted is set to the new subtree which has been formed. If line 170 is reached, the record to be deleted was not found in the tree.

11-2.2 Threaded Storage Representation

The storage representation of binary trees introduced in the last subsection suffers from two drawbacks:

1. It contains many NIL links.
2. The traversal of such a tree structure requires a stack. This requirement wastes both time and memory space.

The NIL links in this storage representation can be replaced by threads. A *thread* is a pointer which gives information about either the predecessor or successor of a given node in the tree. We "thread" a binary tree with a particular traversal order in mind. For the inorder traversal of a binary tree, threads are pointers that point to

```
1  00DE  00115  (* SEARCH FOR AND DELETE THE MARKED NODE *)
1  00DE  00116  WHILE (P <> NIL) AND NOT STOP DO
1  00F8  00117  BEGIN
1  00F8  00118      IF X < P@.INFO
1  010E  00119      THEN BEGIN  (* BRANCH LEFT *)
1  011C  00120          PARENT := P;
1  0124  00121          P := P@.LPTR;
1  0142  00122          D := 'L'
1  0142  00123          END
1  0148  00124      ELSE IF X > P@.INFO
1  0162  00125          THEN BEGIN  (* BRANCH RIGHT *)
1  0170  00126              PARENT := P;
1  0178  00127              P := P@.RPTR;
1  019A  00128              D := 'R'
1  019A  00129              END
1  01A0  00130          ELSE BEGIN  (* INDICATE NODE HAS BEEN FOUND *)
1  01A4  00131              IF P@.LPTR = NIL
1  01BA  00132              THEN (* EMPTY LEFT SUBTREE *)
1  01C6  00133                  Q := P@.RPTR
1  01DC  00134              ELSE IF P@.RPTR = NIL
1  0206  00135                  THEN  (* EMPTY RIGHT SUBTREE *)
1  0212  00136                      Q := P@.LPTR
1  0228  00137                  ELSE BEGIN  (* CHECK RIGHT SON *)
1  0234  00138                      PRED := P@.RPTR;
1  0256  00139                      IF PRED@.LPTR = NIL
1  026C  00140                      THEN BEGIN
1  0278  00141                          PRED@.LPTR := P@.LPTR;
1  02AC  00142                          Q := PRED
1  02AC  00143                          END
1  02B4  00144                      ELSE BEGIN
1  02B8  00145
1  02B8  00146                          (* SEARCH FOR SUCCESSOR OF P *)
1  02B8  00147                          SUC := PRED@.LPTR;
1  02D6  00148                          WHILE SUC@.LPTR <> NIL DO
1  02F8  00149                          BEGIN
1  02F8  00150                              PRED := SUC;
1  0300  00151                              SUC := PRED@.LPTR
1  0316  00152                          END;
1  0322  00153
1  0322  00154                          (* CONNECT SUCCESSOR *)
1  0322  00155                          PRED@.LPTR := SUC@.RPTR;
1  035A  00156                          SUC@.LPTR := P@.LPTR;
1  038E  00157                          SUC@.RPTR := P@.RPTR;
1  03CA  00158                          Q := SUC
1  03CA  00159                          END
1  03D2  00160                      END;
1  03D2  00161              IF D = 'L'
1  03D2  00162              THEN PARENT@.LPTR := Q
1  03F2  00163              ELSE PARENT@.RPTR := Q;
1  0420  00164              DISPOSE (P);
1  044E  00165              STOP := TRUE
1  044E  00166              END
1  0456  00167      END;
1  045A  00168      IF (P = NIL) AND NOT STOP
1  0466  00169      THEN (* SEARCH FOR INDICATED NODE HAS FAILED *)
1  0474  00170          WRITELN (' ', 'NODE NOT FOUND')
1  0498  00171  END;
```

Fig. 11-3   PASCAL procedure for deleting an arbitrary node from a binary tree (cont'd.)

higher nodes in the tree. These threads permit us to ascend the tree directly without having to store the addresses of nodes in a stack.

Since the left and right links of a node can be either a structural link or a thread, we must be able to distinguish between them. One way of doing this is to use a separate Boolean flag for each of the left and right pointers. The node or record structure using this approach is defined as:

```
TYPE POINTER = @NODE;
     NODE = RECORD
         LPTR: POINTER;
         LFLAG: BOOLEAN;
```

```
        INFO: STRING(20);
        RFLAG: BOOLEAN;
        RPTR: POINTER
        END;
```

where LFLAG and RFLAG are Boolean indicators associated with the left and right pointers, respectively. In particular, the following coding scheme distinguishes between a structural link and a thread:

    LFLAG = TRUE   denotes a left structural link
    LFLAG = FALSE denotes a left thread link
    RFLAG = TRUE   denotes a right structural link
    RFLAG = FALSE denotes a right thread link

Given the inorder threaded representation of a binary tree, the PASCAL function INS given in Fig. 11-4 returns the address of the successor of a designated node X. The first assignment statement in this program initializes P to the right link of X. If the RFLAG of node X has the value FALSE (i.e., if it denotes a thread link), then the inorder successor of X has been obtained and the contents of P are returned. If the test fails, however, we enter a loop which repeatedly branches left until a left thread is obtained. The function terminates with the return of this pointer value.

A similar PASCAL function for obtaining the inorder predecessor of a given node is given in Fig. 11-5 This program is similar to the program just given except that the roles of LPTR and RPTR are interchanged.

By repeatedly using function INS of Fig. 11-4, a threaded binary tree is easily traversed in inorder. A program which accomplishes this task is given in Fig 11-6. Note that the REPEAT loop will terminate when the inorder successor of a node becomes the list head node. At this point the traversal of the given tree is complete. Observe that the program first obtains the inorder successor of the list head node. In order for the right node to be found, the right link of the list head node must be a structural link which points to itself.

Up to this point, we have conveniently assumed that a threaded binary tree exists. We next examine programming modules which can be used to construct a threaded tree. The first programming module inserts a node between a given node, say X, and the node X@.LPTR. The required program appears in Fig. 11-7. Observe that two cases can arise. The first case involves the insertion of a new node as the left subtree of the designated node. The second case inserts the new node between the given node X and the node X@.LPTR. In this case the right link of the inorder predecessor of X before insertion is set to a thread link which points to a new node.

An analogous programming module is easily obtained for performing an insertion to the right of a designated node (say, between X and X@.RPTR). Such a program appears in Fig. 11-8. Note that the roles of LPTR and RPTR have been interchanged. Furthermore, the successor of the designated node (X) is required instead of its predecessor.

These two programming modules are used in the next program which inserts a given node into a lexically-ordered threaded binary tree. The insertion is to be performed at the leaf level, if no duplicate of that node already exists in the tree. The program which performs such an insertion appears in Fig. 11-9.

The program first initializes T to contain the address of the list head node of the tree. The program then, through a WHILE ... DO construct, controls the

```
0   0038    00017   FUNCTION INS (X: POINTER): POINTER;
1   0000    00018   (* GIVEN X, THE ADDRESS OF A PARTICULAR NODE IN A THREADED
1   0000    00019       BINARY TREE, THIS FUNCTION RETURNS THE ADDRESS OF THE
1   0000    00020       INORDER SUCCESSOR OF THIS NODE. *)
1   0000    00021
1   0000    00022   VAR P: POINTER;                        (* TEMPORARY POINTER VARIABLE *)
1   004E    00023
1   004E    00024   BEGIN
1   004E    00025
1   004E    00026       (* A THREAD? *)
1   004E    00027       P := X@.RPTR;
1   0070    00028       IF X@.RFLAG  (* FALSE DENOTES A RIGHT THREAD LINK *)
1   0086    00029       THEN (* BRANCH LEFT? *)
1   0090    00030           WHILE P@.LFLAG DO
1   00B0    00031               P := P@.LPTR;
1   00D2    00032
1   00D2    00033       (* RETURN ADDRESS OF SUCCESSOR *)
1   00D2    00034       INS := P
1   00D2    00035   END;
```

Fig. 11-4   PASCAL function for obtaining the inorder successor of a given node

```
0   0038    00037   FUNCTION INP (X: POINTER): POINTER;
1   0000    00038   (* GIVEN X, THE ADDRESS OF A PARTICULAR NODE IN A THREADED
1   0000    00039       BINARY TREE, THIS FUNCTION RETURNS THE ADDRESS OF THE
1   0000    00040       INORDER PREDECESSOR OF THIS NODE. *)
1   0000    00041
1   0000    00042   VAR P: POINTER;                        (* TEMPORARY POINTER VARIABLE *)
1   004E    00043
1   004E    00044   BEGIN
1   004E    00045
1   004E    00046       (* A THREAD? *)
1   004E    00047       P := X@.LPTR;
1   006C    00048       IF X@.LFLAG
1   0082    00049       THEN (* BRANCH RIGHT? *)
1   008C    00050           WHILE P@.RFLAG DO
1   00AC    00051               P := P@.RPTR;
1   00D2    00052
1   00D2    00053       (* RETURN ADDRESS OF PREDECESSOR *)
1   00D2    00054       INP := P
1   00D2    00055   END;
```

Fig. 11-5   PASCAL function for obtaining the inorder predecessor of a given
node

descent through the tree. A branch left is attempted if X is lexically smaller than the INFO field of the current node. If the left pointer of this node is a flag, procedure LEFT is called to insert a new node with information contents given by X as the left son of the current node; otherwise, the branch left is performed. If X is lexically greater than the information contents of the current node and the right pointer is not a flag the branch is made; otherwise procedure RIGHT is invoked to insert the new node as a right son of the current node. If the information contents of the node equals that of X, then a message indicating that a node already exists in the tree is printed and STOP is set to true to force the procedure to return to the calling program. The loop is repeated until either a new node is inserted into the tree or a node with the same information contents as X is found.

The previous subprograms (INP, INS, LEFT, RIGHT, INSERT_NODE and TINORDER) are all brought together in the main program given in Fig. 11-10. This program creates and traverses a lexically-ordered threaded binary tree. The following input data were used:

'DEER', 'DOG', 'RAT', 'DODO', and 'MOUSE'.

```
0  0038   00169  PROCEDURE TINORDER (HEAD: POINTER);
1  0000   00170  (* GIVEN THE ADDRESS OF THE LIST HEAD OF A BINARY TREE (HEAD)
1  0000   00171     WHICH HAS BEEN THREADED FOR INORDER TRAVERSAL, THIS
1  0000   00172     PROCEDURE TRAVERSES THE TREE IN INORDER. *)
1  0000   00173
1  0000   00174  VAR P: POINTER;                  (* TEMPORARY POINTER VARIABLE *)
1  004E   00175      STOP: BOOLEAN;               (* LOGICAL FLAG FOR PROCEDURE RETURN *)
1  004E   00176
1  004E   00177  BEGIN
1  004E   00178
1  004E   00179      (* INITIALIZE *)
1  004E   00180      STOP := FALSE;
1  0056   00181      P := HEAD;
1  005E   00182
1  005E   00183      (* TRAVERSE THE THREADED TREE IN INORDER *)
1  005E   00184      REPEAT
1  005E   00185          P := INS (P);
1  0080   00186          IF P = HEAD
1  0080   00187          THEN STOP := TRUE
1  008E   00188          ELSE WRITELN (' ', P@.INFO)
1  00D4   00189      UNTIL STOP
1  00D4   00190  END;
```

Fig. 11-6   PASCAL procedure for the inorder traversal of a threaded tree

```
0  0038   00057  PROCEDURE LEFT (HEAD, X: POINTER; DATA: STRING(20));
1  0000   00058  (* GIVEN THE ADDRESS OF THE HEAD NODE OF AN INORDER THREADED
1  0000   00059     BINARY TREE (HEAD), THE ADDRESS OF A DESIGNATED NODE X,
1  0000   00060     AND THE INFORMATION ASSOCIATED WITH A NEW NODE (DATA),
1  0000   00061     THIS PROCEDURE INSERTS A NEW NODE TO THE LEFT OF THE
1  0000   00062     DESIGNATED NODE. *)
1  0000   00063
1  0000   00064  VAR P,                           (* DENOTES ADDRESS OF NODE
1  0000   00065                                       TO BE INSERTED *)
1  0064   00066      TEMP: POINTER;               (* TEMPORARY POINTER VARIABLE *)
1  0064   00067
1  0064   00068  BEGIN
1  0064   00069
1  0064   00070      (* CREATE NEW NODE *)
1  0064   00071      NEW (P);
1  0076   00072      P@.INFO := DATA;
1  0096   00073
1  0096   00074      (* ADJUST POINTER FIELDS *)
1  0096   00075      P@.LPTR := X@.LPTR;
1  00CA   00076      P@.RPTR := X;
1  00EC   00077      X@.LPTR := P;
1  010A   00078      P@.LFLAG := X@.LFLAG;
1  0142   00079      P@.RFLAG := FALSE;
1  0164   00080      X@.LFLAG := TRUE;
1  0186   00081
1  0186   00082      (* RESET PREDECESSOR THREAD, IF NECESSARY *)
1  0186   00083      IF P@.LFLAG
1  019C   00084      THEN BEGIN
1  01A6   00085          TEMP := INP (P);
1  01C8   00086          TEMP@.RPTR := P;
1  01EA   00087          TEMP@.RFLAG := FALSE
1  0204   00088          END
1  020C   00089
1  020C   00090      (* FINISHED *)
1  020C   00091  END;
```

Fig. 11-7   Procedure to make a left insertion into a threaded tree

Figure 11-10 also gives the inorder traversal output.

Thus far, we have been concerned exclusively with binary trees. In the next subsection, the conversion of a general tree to an equivalent binary tree is examined.

```
0   0038    00093   PROCEDURE RIGHT (HEAD, X: POINTER; DATA: STRING(20));
1   0000    00094   (* GIVEN THE ADDRESS OF THE HEAD NODE OF AN INORDER THREADED
1   0000    00095      BINARY TREE (HEAD), THE ADDRESS OF A DESIGNATED NODE X,
1   0000    00096      AND THE INFORMATION ASSOCIATED WITH A NEW NODE (DATA),
1   0000    00097      THIS PROCEDURE INSERTS A NEW NODE TO THE RIGHT OF THE
1   0000    00098      DESIGNATED NODE. *)
1   0000    00099
1   0000    00100   VAR P,                        (* ADDRESS OF NODE TO BE INSERTED *)
1   0064    00101       TEMP: POINTER;            (* TEMPORARY POINTER VARIABLE *)
1   0064    00102
1   0064    00103   BEGIN
1   0064    00104
1   0064    00105       (* CREATE NEW NODE *)
1   0064    00106       NEW (P);
1   0076    00107       P@.INFO := DATA;
1   0096    00108
1   0096    00109       (* ADJUST POINTER FIELDS *)
1   0096    00110       P@.RPTR := X@.RPTR;
1   00D2    00111       P@.LPTR := X;
1   00F0    00112       X@.RPTR := P;
1   0112    00113       P@.RFLAG := X@.RFLAG;
1   014A    00114       P@.LFLAG := FALSE;
1   016C    00115       X@.RFLAG := TRUE;
1   018E    00116
1   018E    00117       (* RESET SUCCESSOR THREAD, IF NECESSARY *)
1   018E    00118       IF P@.RFLAG
1   01A4    00119       THEN BEGIN
1   01AE    00120           TEMP := INS (P);
1   01D0    00121           TEMP@.LPTR := P;
1   01EE    00122           TEMP@.LFLAG := FALSE
1   0208    00123           END
1   0210    00124
1   0210    00125       (* FINISHED *)
1   0210    00126   END;
```

Fig. 11-8   Procedure to make a right insertion into a threaded tree

11-2.3 Conversion of General Trees to Binary Trees

Recall that the natural correspondence conversion process converts a general tree (or, more generally, a forest) to a unique equivalent binary tree. The conversion process requires that a parent node be connected to its left offspring. Furthermore, all siblings at the same level within the same tree must be connected from left to right. This subsection presents a program which performs the required conversion.

As was done in the main text, we choose the level-number method to specify a general tree (or forest). The input of each tree is given in preorder.

A general algorithm for the required conversion consists of the following steps:

1. Create a list head node and stack its address and level number.
2. Repeat through step 6 while there still remains an input node.
3. Input a node description.
4. Create a tree node and initialize its contents.
5. If the level number of the input node is greater than the level number of the stack-top node
   then connect the parent to its left offspring
   else repeat while the level number of the stack-top node is greater than the level number of the input node
      pop the stack
      connect the siblings together
6. Push input node onto the stack.
7. Exit.

```
0  0038  00128  PROCEDURE INSERT_NODE (HEAD: POINTER; X: STRING(20));
1  0000  00129  (* THIS PROCEDURE INSERTS A NODE WITH INFORMATION CONTENTS X
1  0000  00130      AS A LEAF NODE IF IT IS NOT ALREADY THERE. *)
1  0000  00131
1  0000  00132  VAR P,                          (* ADDRESS OF NEW NODE *)
1  0058  00133      T: POINTER;                 (* ADDRESS OF CURRENT NODE *)
1  0058  00134      STOP: BOOLEAN;              (* LOGICAL FLAG FOR PROCEDURE RETURN *)
1  0058  00135
1  0058  00136  BEGIN
1  0058  00137
1  0058  00138      (* INITIALIZE *)
1  0058  00139      STOP := FALSE;
1  0060  00140      T := HEAD;
1  0068  00141
1  0068  00142      (* PERFORM INDICATED INSERTION IF REQUIRED *)
1  0068  00143      WHILE (T <> NIL) AND NOT STOP DO
1  0082  00144
1  0082  00145          (* FIND THE LOCATION AND APPEND NEW NODE *)
1  0082  00146          IF X < T@.INFO
1  0098  00147          THEN (* BRANCH LEFT *)
1  00A6  00148              IF T@.LFLAG
1  00BC  00149              THEN T := T@.LPTR
1  00DC  00150              ELSE BEGIN (* APPEND NEW NODE AS A LEFT SUBTREE *)
1  00E8  00151                  LEFT (HEAD, T, X);
1  0114  00152                  STOP := TRUE
1  0114  00153                  END
1  011C  00154          ELSE IF X > T@.INFO
1  0136  00155              THEN IF T@.RFLAG
1  015A  00156                  THEN (* BRANCH RIGHT *)
1  0164  00157                      T := T@.RPTR
1  017A  00158                  ELSE BEGIN
1  018A  00159                      (* APPEND NEW NODE AS A RIGHT SUBTREE *)
1  018A  00160                      RIGHT (HEAD, T, X);
1  01B6  00161                      STOP := TRUE
1  01B6  00162                      END
1  01BE  00163          ELSE BEGIN (* NODE ALREADY THERE *)
1  01C2  00164              WRITELN (' ', 'DUPLICATE NODE   ', X);
1  01F8  00165              STOP := TRUE
1  01F8  00166              END
1  0200  00167  END;
```

Fig. 11-9   Procedure for inserting a node into a lexically-ordered threaded tree

Figure 11-11 contains a program for the required conversion process. The variables used in the main program are:

Variable	Type	Usage
POINTER	@NODE	Pointer type to node structure
NODE	RECORD	Nodes of the tree
LPTR	POINTER	Pointer to the left subtree of the node
INFO	STRING(10)	Information field of the node
RPTR	POINTER	Pointer to the right subtree of the node
T	POINTER	Pointer to the head of the tree
HEAD	POINTER	Head node of the tree

Variables used in the procedure CONVERT are:

STACK	ARRAY(1..50) OF RECORD	Stack structure
NUMBER	INTEGER	Level number of nodes
LOC	POINTER	Address of node in the tree

```
0  0000   00001   PROGRAM THREAD (INPUT, OUTPUT);
0  0000   00002   (* THIS PROGRAM USES PROCEDURES INSERT_NODE AND TINORDER TO
0  0000   00003       CONSTRUCT AND TRAVERSE A THREADED BINARY TREE. *)
0  0000   00004
0  0000   00005   TYPE POINTER = @NODE;
0  0038   00006        NODE = RECORD             (* TREE NODE *)
0  0038   00007           LPTR: POINTER;         (* LEFT POINTER *)
0  0038   00008           LFLAG: BOOLEAN;        (* THREAD FLAG FOR LPTR *)
0  0038   00009           INFO: STRING(20);      (* INFORMATION FIELD *)
0  0038   00010           RFLAG: BOOLEAN;        (* THREAD FLAG FOR RPTR *)
0  0038   00011           RPTR: POINTER          (* RIGHT POINTER *)
0  0038   00012           END;
0  0038   00013
0  0038   00014   VAR DATA: STRING(20);          (* INFORMATION TO ADD TO TREE*)
0  0038   00015       HEAD: POINTER;             (* HEAD OF TREE *)
0  0038   00191
0  0038   00192   BEGIN
0  0038   00193
0  0038   00194       (* BUILD HEAD OF TREE *)
0  0038   00195       NEW (HEAD);
0  004A   00196       HEAD@.LPTR := HEAD;
0  0068   00197       HEAD@.RPTR := HEAD;
0  008A   00198
0  008A   00199       (* INITIALIZE *)
0  008A   00200       HEAD@.INFO := 'ZZZZ';
0  00AA   00201       HEAD@.LFLAG := FALSE;
0  00CC   00202       HEAD@.RFLAG := TRUE;
0  00EE   00203
0  00EE   00204       (* BUILD TREE *)
0  00EE   00205       READ (DATA);
0  0100   00206       WHILE NOT EOF DO
0  0108   00207       BEGIN
0  0108   00208           INSERT_NODE (HEAD, DATA);
0  012E   00209           READ (DATA)
0  0140   00210       END;
0  0144   00211
0  0144   00212       (* TRAVERSE TREE *)
0  0144   00213       WRITELN (' ', 'TREE IN INORDER IS');
0  0168   00214       TINORDER (HEAD);
0  0186   00215       WRITELN
0  0186   00216   END.
---------------------------------------
¦ COMPILE TIME:    0.400 SECOND(S) ¦
¦     NO WARNING(S) DETECTED       ¦
¦     NO ERROR(S) DETECTED         ¦
---------------------------------------
--EXECUTION-->
TREE IN INORDER IS
CAT
DEER
DODO
DOG
MOOSE
MOUSE
RAT
```

Fig. 11-10   Main program for constructing and traversing a threaded tree

TOP	INTEGER	Points to top of stack
LEVEL	INTEGER	Level number of input node
NAME	STRING(10)	Name of input node
PRED_LEVEL	INTEGER	Level number of the previous node
PRED_LOC	POINTER	Address of the previous node
P	POINTER	Temporary pointer variable
STOP	BOOLEAN	Indicates procedure reutrn

Procedures RPREORDER and RINORDER which are used to print the binary tree are similar to the ones given in Sec. 11-2.1. The stack used in the program is simulated by using an array of structures.

```
0  0000  00001  PROGRAM TEST (INPUT, OUTPUT);
0  0000  00002  (* THIS PROGRAM USES SUBPROCEDURE CONVERT TO BUILD A BINARY TREE
0  0000  00003       FROM A FOREST OF TREES.  SUBPROCEDURE IINORDER AND RPREORDER
0  0000  00004       PRINT THE RESULTING TREE. *)
0  0000  00005
0  0000  00006  TYPE POINTER = @NODE;
0  0038  00007       NODE = RECORD            (* TREE NODE *)
0  0038  00008          LPTR: POINTER;        (* LEFT POINTER *)
0  0038  00009          INFO: STRING(10);     (* INFORMATION FIELD *)
0  0038  00010          RPTR: POINTER         (* RIGHT POINTER *)
0  0038  00011          END;
0  0038  00012  VAR T, HEAD: POINTER;
0  0038  00013
0  0038  00014       PROCEDURE CONVERT (VAR HEAD: POINTER);
1  0000  00015       (* GIVEN A FOREST OF TREES WHOSE INPUT FORMAT IS OF THE FORM
1  0000  00016           DESCRIBED, THIS PROCEDURE CONVERTS THE FOREST INTO AN
1  0000  00017           EQUIVALENT BINARY TREE WITH LIST HEAD (HEAD). *)
1  0000  00018
1  0000  00019       VAR STACK: ARRAY (1..50) OF RECORD
1  005E  00020              NUMBER: INTEGER; (* LEVEL NUMBER OF NODES *)
1  005E  00021              LOC: POINTER     (* ADDRESS OF NODE *)
1  005E  00022              END;
1  005E  00023          TOP,                 (* TOP INDEX OF STACK *)
1  005E  00024          LEVEL: INTEGER;      (* LEVEL NUMBER OF INPUT NODE *)
1  005E  00025          NAME: STRING(10);    (* NAME OF INPUT NODE *)
1  005E  00026          PRED_LEVEL: INTEGER; (* LEVEL NUMBER OF PREVIOUS NODE *)
1  005E  00027          PRED_LOC,            (* ADDRESS OF PREVIOUS NODE *)
1  005E  00028          P: POINTER;          (* TEMPORARY POINTER VARIABLE *)
1  005E  00029          STOP: BOOLEAN;       (* LOGICAL FLAG FOR PROCEDURE RETURN *)
1  005E  00030
1  005E  00031       BEGIN
1  005E  00032
1  005E  00033          (* INITIALIZE *)
1  005E  00034          STOP := FALSE;
1  0076  00035          NEW (HEAD);
1  0088  00036          HEAD@.LPTR := NIL;
1  00A4  00037          HEAD@.RPTR := NIL;
1  00C4  00038          TOP := 1;
1  00CC  00039          STACK(TOP).NUMBER := 0;
1  00F4  00040          STACK(TOP).LOC := HEAD;
1  0122  00041
1  0122  00042          (* PROCESS THE INPUT *)
1  0122  00043          READ (LEVEL, NAME);
1  0146  00044          WHILE NOT (EOF OR STOP) DO
1  0158  00045          BEGIN
1  0158  00046
1  0158  00047             (* CREATE A TREE NODE *)
1  0158  00048             NEW (P);
1  016A  00049             P@.LPTR := NIL;
1  0186  00050             P@.RPTR := NIL;
1  01A6  00051             P@.INFO := NAME;
1  01C6  00052
1  01C6  00053             (* COMPARE LEVELS *)
1  01C6  00054             PRED_LEVEL := STACK(TOP).NUMBER;
1  01F0  00055             PRED_LOC := STACK(TOP).LOC;
1  021E  00056             IF LEVEL > PRED_LEVEL
1  021E  00057
1  021E  00058             (* THEN CONNECT PARENT TO ITS LEFT OFFSPRING *)
1  021E  00059             THEN PRED_LOC@.LPTR := P
1  0240  00060             ELSE BEGIN  (* REMOVE NODES FROM STACK *)
1  024C  00061                WHILE PRED_LEVEL > LEVEL DO
1  0258  00062                BEGIN
1  0258  00063                   TOP := TOP -1;
1  0264  00064                   PRED_LEVEL := STACK(TOP).NUMBER;
1  028E  00065                   PRED_LOC := STACK(TOP).LOC
1  02B0  00066                END;
1  02C0  00067                IF PRED_LEVEL < LEVEL
1  02C0  00068                THEN BEGIN
1  02CC  00069                   WRITELN (' ', 'MIXED LEVEL NUMBERS');
1  02F0  00070                   STOP := TRUE
1  02F0  00071                END
1  02F8  00072                ELSE BEGIN
1  02FC  00073
1  02FC  00074                   (* CONNECT SIBLINGS TOGETHER *)
1  02FC  00075                   PRED_LOC@.RPTR := P;
1  031E  00076                   TOP := TOP - 1
1  031E  00077                END
1  032A  00078             END;
```

Fig. 11-11   Procedure for the conversion of any tree to a binary tree

```
1  032A  00079                    IF NOT STOP
1  032A  00080                    THEN BEGIN
1  0338  00081
1  0338  00082                        (* PUSH A NEW NODE ON THE STACK *)
1  0338  00083                        TOP := TOP + 1;
1  0344  00084                        STACK(TOP).NUMBER := LEVEL;
1  036E  00085                        STACK(TOP).LOC := P;
1  039C  00086
1  039C  00087                        (* INPUT A NODE *)
1  039C  00088                        READ (LEVEL, NAME)
1  03C0  00089                        END
1  03C0  00090                    END
1  03C0  00091                END;
0  0038  00092            PROCEDURE IINORDER (T: POINTER);
1  0000  00093            (* GIVEN A BINARY TREE WHOSE ROOT NODE ADDRESS IS GIVEN BY A
1  0000  00094                POINTER VARIABLE T, THIS PROCEDURE TRAVERSES THE TREE IN
1  0000  00095                INORDER, IN AN ITERATIVE MANNER. *)
1  0000  00096
1  0000  00097            VAR P: POINTER;             (* CURRENT NODE IN THE TREE *)
1  004E  00098                S: ARRAY (1..50) OF POINTER; (* STACK *)
1  005E  00099                TOP: INTEGER;           (* TOP INDEX OF STACK *)
1  005E  00100                STOP: BOOLEAN;          (* LOGICAL FLAG FOR PROCEDURE RETURN *)
1  005E  00101
1  005E  00102            BEGIN
1  005E  00103
1  005E  00104                (* INITIALIZE *)
1  005E  00105                STOP := FALSE;
1  0076  00106                IF T = NIL
1  0076  00107                THEN BEGIN
1  0082  00108                    WRITE ('EMPTY TREE');
1  0094  00109                    STOP := TRUE
1  0094  00110                    END
1  009C  00111                ELSE BEGIN
1  00A0  00112                    TOP := 0;
1  00A6  00113                    P := T
1  00A6  00114                    END;
1  00AE  00115
1  00AE  00116                (* TRAVERSE THE TREE IN INORDER *)
1  00AE  00117                WHILE NOT STOP DO
1  00BC  00118                BEGIN
1  00BC  00119
1  00BC  00120                    (* STACK ADDRESS ALONG A LEFT CHAIN *)
1  00BC  00121                    WHILE P <> NIL DO
1  00C8  00122                    BEGIN
1  00C8  00123                        TOP := TOP + 1;
1  00D4  00124                        S(TOP) := P;
1  00FE  00125                        P := P@.LPTR
1  0114  00126                    END;
1  0120  00127
1  0120  00128                    (* PROCESS NODE AND RIGHT BRANCH *)
1  0120  00129                    IF TOP > 0
1  0120  00130                    THEN BEGIN
1  012C  00131                        P := S(TOP);
1  0156  00132                        TOP := TOP - 1;
1  0162  00133                        WRITE (P@.INFO);
1  018A  00134                        P := P@.RPTR
1  01A0  00135                        END
1  01AC  00136                    ELSE STOP := TRUE
1  01B0  00137                END
1  01B8  00138            END:
0  0038  00139
```

Fig. 11-11   Procedure for the conversion of any tree to a binary tree (cont'd.)

The main program calls procedure CONVERT to build the trees. Then it calls procedures RINORDER and RPREORDER to print the tree that has been built. In procedure CONVERT, the head node to the tree and the stack are first initialized and the first node's name and level are read. A loop is then entered which processes all nodes from the forest of trees. A tree node for this node is created and initialized. The level of this node is compared with the level of the top node on the stack. If its level is greater than that of the node on the top of the stack, this node is connected to the previous node's left offspring; otherwise, the top node on the stack is deleted

```
0  0038   00140          PROCEDURE RPREORDER (T: POINTER);
1  0000   00141          (* GIVEN A BINARY TREE WHOSE ROOT NODE ADDRESS IS GIVEN BY A
1  0000   00142             POINTER VARIABLE T, THIS PROCEDURE TRAVERSES THE TREE IN
1  0000   00143             PREORDER. *)
1  0000   00144
1  0000   00145          BEGIN
1  004E   00146
1  004E   00147              (* PROCESS THE ROOT NODE *)
1  004E   00148              IF T <> NIL
1  004E   00149              THEN WRITE (T@.INFO);
1  0082   00150
1  0082   00151              (* PROCESS THE LEFT SUBTREE *)
1  0082   00152              IF T@.LPTR <> NIL
1  0098   00153              THEN RPREORDER (T@.LPTR);
1  00CA   00154
1  00CA   00155              (* PROCESS THE RIGHT SUBTREE *)
1  00CA   00156              IF T@.RPTR <> NIL
1  00E4   00157              THEN RPREORDER (T@.RPTR)
1  010E   00158
1  010E   00159              (* FINISHED *)
1  010E   00160          END;
0  0038   00161
0  0038   00162          BEGIN  (* MAIN PROGRAM *)
0  0038   00163
0  0038   00164              (* BUILD TREE *)
0  0038   00165              CONVERT (HEAD);
0  0056   00166              T := HEAD@.LPTR;
0  0074   00167
0  0074   00168              (* PRINT OUT TREE *)
0  0074   00169              WRITELN (' ', 'TREE IN INORDER IS');
0  0098   00170              WRITE (' ');
0  00AA   00171              IINORDER (T);
0  00C8   00172              WRITELN;
0  00D6   00173              WRITELN ('0', 'TREE IN PREORDER IS');
0  00FA   00174              WRITE (' ');
0  010C   00175              RPREORDER (T);
0  012A   00176              WRITELN
0  012A   00177          END.
```

```
-----------------------------------
| COMPILE TIME:    0.355 SECOND(S) |
|     NO WARNING(S) DETECTED        |
|     NO ERROR(S) DETECTED          |
-----------------------------------
--EXECUTION-->
TREE IN INORDER IS
BRIAN     CLARENCE EMILE   DONALD   ANDY     IRIS    JANICE   GAIL     HEATHER  FLORENCE

TREE IN PREORDER IS
ANDY      BRIAN    CLARENCE DONALD  EMILE   FLORENCE GAIL     IRIS     JANICE   HEATHER
```

Fig. 11-11   Procedure for the conversion of any tree to a binary tree (cont'd.)

from the stack and has the right pointer of the new node on the stack set to the new tree node location. If the level of this node is actually less than the level of the node on the stack, the input has not been read in its proper order and STOP is set to true so that the procedure terminates. The level of the node just read and its location are pushed onto the stack. Finally, the next node's name and level are read.

The input data used for the program are:

First tree		Second tree	
Name	*Level*	*Name*	*Level*
'ANDY'	1	'FLORENCE'	1
'BRIAN'	2	'GAIL'	2
'CLARENCE'	2	'IRIS'	3
'DONALD'	2	'JANICE'	3
'EMILE'	3	'HEATHER'	2

The first tree is read in the order shown before the second tree is read.

Now that we have introduced the basics of programming tree structures, we are ready to apply these programming techniques to a variety of applications.

Exercises for Sec. 11-2

1. Given a pointer variable T which denotes the address of the root node of a binary tree, obtain a recursive PASCAL procedure for its postorder traversal.

2. Using a stack, formulate a recursive PASCAL procedure for the iterative inorder traversal of a given binary tree with root node location given by T.

3. Given a threaded binary tree for inorder traversal, write a PASCAL function which computes the number of leaf nodes in that tree. Assume that the address of the tree's root node is given by the pointer variable T.

4. Given a binary tree T which has been threaded for preorder traversal, construct PASCAL functions for obtaining the preorder predecessor and successor of a designated node.

5. Write a recursive procedure for converting a forest into an equivalent binary tree.

6. This problem concerns the operations of subtree insertion and deletion, as applied to general trees. Recall that a general tree can be converted to a binary tree using the natural correspondence algorithm discussed in the main text.

    It is most natural to discuss insertion or deletion of a subtree in terms of its relation to a parent node. Thus we define our two operations as follows:

    DELETE (N, I) and
    INSERT (N, I, T)

    DELETE deletes the Ith subtree of the node given by N. INSERT inserts the tree, with root T, as the new Ith subtree of the node given by N. For illustration consider the general tree

    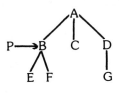

    If we execute

    INSERT (P, 2, Q)

where Q identifies the tree

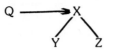

then we obtain the tree

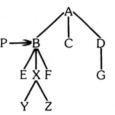

The complementary operation for restoring our original tree is then

DELETE (P, 2)

It is required to formulate PASCAL procedures for the operations of INSERT and DELETE assuming that we are given the binary tree equivalent to the general tree. It would be helpful if you examined what happens to the binary-tree equivalent of the general tree when these operations are performed.

11-3 APPLICATIONS OF TREES

In this section, we will look at four applications of trees. The first application considers the evaluation of an algebraic expression which is stored symbolically. Next, searching a binary tree is examined. In the third application, we study complete binary trees used for sorting. Finally, we examine the applicability of general trees to searching.

11-3.1 The Symbolic Manipulation of Expressions

In the previous chapter, we discussed the manipulation of polynomial expressions which were represented by linked lists. Binary trees, on the other hand, will allow us to add, subtract, multiply, etc., algebraic expressions symbolically.

Recall that nonleaf nodes in a binary tree are used for representing operators and that the left and right subtrees are the left and right operands of that operator. Unary operators, which have only one operand, have only a right subtree. Each node in the tree has three fields, a left pointer, an information field, and a right pointer. The values of the information fields are

0, 1, 2, 3, 4, 5, 6, and 7

which correspond to constants, variables, and the operations +, −, *, /, θ, and ↑, respectively. θ represents the unary minus operator. A leaf node of a tree is either a

```
0  0038   00086  FUNCTION EVAL (E: TREE_PTR): REAL;
1  0000   00087  (* GIVEN AN EXPRESSION WHICH IS REPRESENTED BY A BINARY TREE WITH A
1  0000   00088     ROOT-NODE ADDRESS OF E, THIS FUNCTION RETURNS THE VALUE OF THE
1  0000   00089     GIVEN EXPRESSION. *)
1  0000   00090
1  0000   00091  VAR F: TAB_PTR;              (* SYMBOL TABLE POINTER VARIABLE *)
1  004E   00092
1  004E   00093  BEGIN
1  004E   00094      E@.TAG := OPERATOR;
1  0070   00095
1  0070   00096      (* INVALID EXPRESSION? *)
1  0070   00097      IF (E@.NTYPE < 0) OR (E@.NTYPE > 7)
1  00B4   00098      THEN BEGIN
1  00B4   00099          WRITELN (' ', 'INVALID EXPRESSION');
1  00D8   00100          EVAL := 0
1  00D8   00101          END
1  00E0   00102      ELSE
1  00E0   00103
1  00E0   00104          (* EVALUATE EXPRESSION RECURSIVELY *)
1  00E0   00105          CASE E@.NTYPE OF
1  00FE   00106          0 : BEGIN
1  011A   00107              E@.TAG := OPERAND;
1  013C   00108              F := E@.VALUE_PTR;
1  015E   00109              EVAL := F@.
1  0174   00110              END;
1  0180   00111          1 : BEGIN
1  0180   00112              E@.TAG := OPERAND;
1  01A2   00113              F := E@.VALUE_PTR;
1  01C4   00114              EVAL := F@.
1  01DA   00115              END·
1  01E6   00116          2 : EVAL := EVAL (E@.LPTR) + EVAL (E@.RPTR);
1  0246   00117          3 : EVAL := EVAL (E@.LPTR) - EVAL (E@.RPTR);
1  02A8   00118          4 : EVAL := EVAL (E@.LPTR) * EVAL (E@.RPTR);
1  0308   00119          5 : EVAL := EVAL (E@.LPTR) / EVAL (E@.RPTR);
1  036A   00120          6 : EVAL := - EVAL (E@.RPTR);
1  039E   00121          7 : EVAL := EXP (EVAL (E@.RPTR) * LN (EVAL (E@.LPTR)))
1  03FE   00122          END
1  040E   00123  END;
```

Fig. 11-12   Function to evaluate algebraic expressions

variable or a constant, and its right pointer points to the position in the symbol table which gives the value of the variable or constant.

With this representation for an algebraic expression, we can evaluate this expression. A recursive algorithm for this problem is easy to formulate and is given as follows:

1. If the current node being examined is a constant or variable,
   then return the value of the node which comes from the symbol table
2. Return the values of the two subtrees of the node which are applied to the operator given by the information field

A PASCAL program to accomplish this task is given in Fig. 11-12. The variables used by this program are:

Variable	Type	Usage
NODE_POINTER	@NODE	Pointer type to tree nodes
TABLE_POINTER	@REAL	Pointer type to symbol table
NODE	RECORD	Tree node
LPTR	TREE_PTR	Pointer to the left subtree
NTYPE	INTEGER	Information field
RPTR	TREE_PTR	Pointer to the right subtree

VALUE_PTR	TAB_PTR	Pointer to symbol table
E	TREE_PTR	Address of the current node in the tree
F	TAB_PTR	Symbol table pointer

Note that the declarations for the structure NODE do not appear in the function EVAL since they are used as global variables. Also the symbol table exists only as pointers to dynamically allocated memory for storing REAL values. Since only one value is to be stored, a structure does not need to be created. Note that a separate pointer type is used for pointers into the symbol table rather than using one of the tree links because PASCAL allows pointer variables to point only to a particular data type.

The function EVAL is basically a CASE statement for the values 0 through 7. Each label tests the value of E@.NTYPE to determine what operation is required, or if the node represents a constant or variable. If E@.NTYPE has the value 0 or 1, then EVAL is set to the value stored at the location indicated by the pointer SYM_TABLE. Otherwise, EVAL is called recursively with the operation represented in E@.NTYPE applied to the subtrees of this node. Invalid values for NTYPE are determined by using an IF statement. If this occurs, an error message is printed and the value 0 is returned.

11-3.2 Binary Search Trees

Recall that binary trees are lexicographically (or lexically) ordered if for any given record in the tree, all records in its left subtree have values less than that of the root of the given tree or subtree, and all records in its right subtree have values greater than that of the root node. Insertions and searching can easily be performed on such a tree if it is stored using linked allocation. A new entry is inserted as a leaf node in the tree such that the tree's order is preserved. Note that to find a record in a tree, or the position where one is to be inserted, is merely a matter of comparing the value of the record with that of the root of the tree or subtree we are examining and branching right or left.

Since a search is required for insertions, the two algorithms of searching and inserting into a binary tree can easily be combined. Such an example is the following algorithm:

1. Repeat thru step 2.
2. If the value of the given record is less than that of the root of the subtree
   then branch left
         if the subtree is empty
         then if we are performing a search
               then the desired record was not found
               else create a new leaf and append it as the new left subtree
   else if the value of the given record is greater than that of the root of
         the subtree
         then branch right
               if the subtree is empty
               then if we are doing a search
                     then the record being searched for was not found
                     else create a new leaf and append it as the new right subtree
         else return the position of the record found

A program to perform this operation appears in Fig. 11-13. Note that for failures of insertions or look-ups, the pointer value NIL is returned. The variables used in the function are:

Variable	Type	Usage
POINTER	@NODE	Pointer type for the node structure
NODE	RECORD	Node structure of tree
LPTR	POINTER	Pointer to left subtree of node
INFO	STRING(20)	Information field of the record
RPTR	POINTER	Pointer to the right subtree of the node
HEAD	POINTER	Head node of the tree
INSERT	BOOLEAN	Denotes whether an insertion or look-up is required
ITEM	STRING(20)	Record to be searched for or inserted
PARENT	POINTER	Address of the parent node of the record to be inserted
T	POINTER	Temporary pointer variable
STOP	BOOLEAN	Indicates function return

In the program the pointer T is set to the head of the tree. Then a loop is entered to perform the search. The given record is compared with the root of the current subtree. If its value is less than that of the root node, a branch is made to the left subtree; otherwise, in line 59, a branch is made to the right subtree. After the branch is made, a check is made to see if the new subtree is empty. If it is and a look-up is required, the record is not in the table and the NIL value is returned. Otherwise, for an insertion, a new node is allocated and inserted as the appropriate left or right subtree. If the keys are equal, line 83 is executed. For look-ups, the position of the record is returned. For insertions, the record was already present in the tree, thus the NIL pointer value is returned.

11-3.3 Tree Sorts

In the previous section, we introduced a method of sorting using binary trees. A more efficient method, called a heap sort, uses a special form of a full binary tree called a heap. The root of the tree is the largest key in the tree. The next two largest keys are the left and right offspring of the root. Similar relationships exist for the remaining keys of the table. In general, a heap which represents a table of n records satisfies the following property:

$$K_j \leqslant K_i \text{ for } 2 \leqslant j \leqslant n \text{ and } i = j \text{ DIV } 2$$

Note that a heap can easily be represented by using a vector. The left and right sons of record in position i are 2i and 2i + 1. The parent of record i is i DIV 2 if i is not the root node. Thus, any path in the tree can easily be traversed.

To sort a table, we require two algorithms. The first algorithm must create a heap from the table. To do this, we can use the following high-level algorithm:

```
0  0038   00015   FUNCTION BINTREE (HEAD: POINTER; INSERT: BOOLEAN; ITEM: STRING(20)):
1  0000   00016         POINTER;
1  0000   00017   (* THIS RECURSIVE FUNCTION PERFORMS THE REQUESTED OPERATIONS
1  0000   00018      ON THE TREE STRUCTURE *)
1  0000   00019
1  0000   00020   VAR T,                            (* TEMPORARY POINTER VARIABLES *)
1  0064   00021       PARENT: POINTER;              (* ADDRESS OF PARENT NODE OF NEW ITEM
1  0064   00022                                        TO BE INSERTED *)
1  0064   00023       STOP: BOOLEAN;                (* LOGICAL FLAG FOR FUNCTION RETURN *)
1  0064   00024
1  0064   00025   BEGIN
1  0064   00026       STOP := FALSE;
1  006C   00027
1  006C   00028       (* INITIALIZE SEARCH VARIABLE *)
1  006C   00029       T := HEAD;
1  0074   00030
1  0074   00031       (* PERFORM INDICATED OPERATION *)
1  0074   00032       WHILE (T <> NIL) AND NOT STOP DO
1  008E   00033
1  008E   00034           (* COMPARE GIVEN ITEM WITH ROOT ENTRY OF THE SUBTREE *)
1  008E   00035           IF ITEM < T@.INFO
1  00A4   00036           THEN BEGIN  (* BRANCH LEFT *)
1  00B2   00037               PARENT := T;
1  00BA   00038               T := T@.LPTR;
1  00D8   00039               IF T = NIL
1  00D8   00040               THEN IF NOT INSERT
1  00E4   00041                    THEN BEGIN  (* SEARCH UNSUCCESSFUL *)
1  00F2   00042                        BINTREE := NIL;
1  00F8   00043                        STOP := TRUE
1  00F8   00044                    END
1  0100   00045                    ELSE BEGIN
1  0104   00046
1  0104   00047                        (* CREATE A NEW LEAF AND INSERT AS A
1  0104   00048                           LEFT SUBTREE *)
1  0104   00049                        NEW (P);
1  0116   00050                        P@.INFO := ITEM;
1  0136   00051                        P@.LPTR := NIL;
1  0152   00052                        P@.RPTR := NIL;
1  0172   00053                        PARENT@.LPTR := P;
1  0190   00054                        BINTREE := P;
1  0198   00055                        STOP := TRUE
1  0198   00056                    END
1  01A0   00057               ELSE
1  01A0   00058           END
1  01A4   00059           ELSE IF ITEM > T@.INFO
1  01BE   00060           THEN BEGIN  (* BRANCH RIGHT *)
1  01CC   00061               PARENT := T;
1  01D4   00062               T := T@.RPTR;
1  01F6   00063               IF T = NIL
1  01F6   00064               THEN IF NOT INSERT
1  0202   00065                    THEN BEGIN  (* SEARCH UNSUCCESSFUL *)
1  0210   00066                        BINTREE := NIL;
1  0216   00067                        STOP := TRUE
1  0216   00068                    END
1  021E   00069                    ELSE BEGIN
1  0222   00070
1  0222   00071                        (* CREATE A NEW LEAF AND INSERT AS A
1  0222   00072                           RIGHT SUBTREE *)
1  0222   00073                        NEW (P);
1  0234   00074                        P@.INFO := ITEM;
1  0254   00075                        P@.LPTR := NIL;
1  0270   00076                        P@.RPTR := NIL;
1  0290   00077                        PARENT@.RPTR := P;
1  02B2   00078                        BINTREE := P;
1  02BA   00079                        STOP := TRUE
1  02BA   00080                    END
1  02C2   00081               ELSE
1  02C2   00082           END
1  02C6   00083           ELSE BEGIN  (* A MATCH HAS OCCURRED *)
1  02CA   00084               IF INSERT
1  02CA   00085               THEN BINTREE := NIL
1  02D4   00086               ELSE BINTREE := T;
1  02E6   00087               STOP := TRUE
1  02E6   00088           END
1  02EE   00089   END;
```

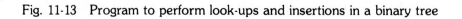

Fig. 11-13 Program to perform look-ups and insertions in a binary tree

1. Repeat thru step 3 for q = 2, 3, ..., n
2. Obtain the parent of the qth record
3. Repeat while the key of the qth record is greater than that of its parent
   exchange the records
   obtain the next parent of this record

Once we have created a heap, it is easy to obtain the largest key in the table. We can exchange this record, which is always the root of the heap, with the last record in the heap and re-sort the new heap which now has one less record in it. This is done in the following algorithm:

1. Repeat thru step 4 for q = n, n–1, ..., 2
2. Exchange the first record in the heap with the qth record
3. Compute the index of the largest son of the first record
4. Repeat while the son having the largest key is greater than that of the record
   exchange the records
   compute the index of the next largest son

These two algorithms can easily be combined into one program, which is given in Fig. 11-14. Note that the procedure CREATE is called by the main program to build a heap. After this, the main program performs a sort on the heap. The variables used in the main program are:

Variable	Type	Usage
K	ARRAY(1..50) OF INTEGER	The table to be sorted
N	INTEGER	Number of elements in the table
KEY	INTEGER	Key of record to be swapped
Q	INTEGER	Pass index variable
I	INTEGER	Index variable
J	INTEGER	Index variable of the largest son of the record
TEMP	INTEGER	Used to exchange the records

Variables used in the procedure CREATE are:

K	ARRAY(1..50) OF INTEGER	Table of keys for which to create a heap
N	INTEGER	Number of elements in the table
KEY	INTEGER	Key of the record to be inserted
Q	INTEGER	Number of insertions into the heap
I	INTEGER	Index variable
J	INTEGER	Index of the parent key

The following table was sorted by the program in Fig. 11-14:

52, 14, 89, 56, 42, 3, 25, 78, 42, 11, 56, 23, and 58.

```
0  0000   00001   PROGRAM HEAP (INPUT, OUTPUT);
0  0000   00002   (* THIS PROGRAM READS A TABLE INTO THE VECTOR K AND
0  0000   00003       SORTS IT INTO ASCENDING ORDER. *)
0  0000   00004
0  0000   00005   TYPE VECTOR = ARRAY (1..50) OF INTEGER;
0  0038   00006   VAR K: VECTOR;                (* CONTAINS THE KEYS OF THE RECORDS *)
0  0038   00007       N,                        (* NUMBER OF ELEMENTS OF VECTOR K *)
0  0038   00008       Q,                        (* PASS INDEX *)
0  0038   00009       I, J,                     (* INDEX VARIABLES *)
0  0038   00010       KEY,                      (* CONTAINS VARIABLE CONTAINING KEY
0  0038   00011                                    OF THE RECORD BEING SWAPPED *)
0  0038   00012       TEMP: INTEGER;            (* TEMPORARY VARIABLE *)
0  0038   00013
0  0038   00014     PROCEDURE CREATE (VAR K: VECTOR; N: INTEGER);
1  0000   00015     (* GIVEN A VECTOR K OF N ELEMENTS, THIS PROCEDURE CREATES AN
1  0000   00016         INITIAL HEAP. *)
1  0000   00017
1  0000   00018     VAR Q,                      (* NUMBER OF INSERTIONS *)
1  0056   00019         J,                      (* INDEX OF PARENT KEY *)
1  0056   00020         I,                      (* INDEX VARIABLE *)
1  0056   00021         KEY: INTEGER;           (* KEY OF RECORD BEING INSERTED *)
1  0056   00022
1  0056   00023     BEGIN
1  0056   00024
1  0056   00025         (* BUILD HEAP *)
1  0056   00026         FOR Q := 2 TO N DO
1  007A   00027         BEGIN
1  007A   00028
1  007A   00029             (* INITIALIZE CONSTRUCTION PHASE *)
1  007A   00030             I := Q;
1  0082   00031             KEY := K(Q);
1  00AC   00032
1  00AC   00033             (* OBTAIN PARENT OF NEW RECORD *)
1  00AC   00034             J := I DIV 2;
1  00BC   00035
1  00BC   00036             (* PLACE NEW RECORD IN EXISTING HEAP *)
1  00BC   00037             WHILE (I > 1) AND (KEY > K(J)) DO
1  00F6   00038             BEGIN
1  00F6   00039
1  00F6   00040                 (* INTERCHANGE RECORD *)
1  00F6   00041                 K(I) := K(J);
1  0142   00042
1  0142   00043                 (* OBTAIN NEXT PARENT *)
1  0142   00044                 I := J;
1  014A   00045                 J := I DIV 2;
1  015A   00046
1  015A   00047                 (* CHECK IF J SUBSCRIPT OUT OF BOUNDS *)
1  015A   00048                 IF J < 1
1  015A   00049                 THEN J := 1
1  0166   00050             END;
1  0172   00051
1  0172   00052             (* COPY NEW RECORD INTO ITS PROPER PLACE *)
1  0172   00053             K(I) := KEY
1  0194   00054         END
1  019C   00055
1  019C   00056         (* FINISHED *)
1  019C   00057     END;
0  0038   00058
0  0038   00059   BEGIN
0  0038   00060
0  0038   00061     (* READ THE KEYS *)
0  0038   00062     READ (N);
0  004A   00063     FOR I := 1 TO N DO
0  006E   00064         READ (K(I));
0  00A4   00065
0  00A4   00066     (* CREATE INITIAL HEAP *)
0  00A4   00067     CREATE (K,N);
0  00CA   00068
0  00CA   00069     (* PERFORM SORT *)
0  00CA   00070     FOR Q := N DOWNTO 2 DO
0  00EC   00071     BEGIN
0  00EC   00072
0  00EC   00073         (* OUTPUT AND EXCHANGE RECORD *)
0  00EC   00074         WRITELN (' ', K(1));
0  0114   00075         TEMP := K(1);
0  0120   00076         K(1) := K(Q);
0  014E   00077         K(Q) := TEMP;
0  0178   00078
0  0178   00079         (* INITIALIZE PASS *)
```

Fig. 11-14   Program to sort a table by using a heap sort

```
0  0178  00080              I := 1;
0  0180  00081              KEY := K(1);
0  018C  00082              J := 2;
0  0194  00083
0  0194  00084              (* OBTAIN INDEX OF LARGEST SON OF NEW RECORD *)
0  0194  00085              IF J + 1 < Q
0  019C  00086              THEN IF K(J + 1) > K(J)
0  01F6  00087                   THEN J := J + 1;
0  0208  00088
0  0208  00089              (* RECONSTRUCT THE NEW HEAP *)
0  0208  00090              WHILE (J <= Q - 1) AND (K(J) > KEY) DO
0  0246  00091              BEGIN
0  0246  00092
0  0246  00093                  (* INTERCHANGE RECORD *)
0  0246  00094                  K(I) := K(J);
0  0292  00095
0  0292  00096                  (* OBTAIN NEXT LEFT SON *)
0  0292  00097                  I := J;
0  029A  00098                  J := 2 * I;
0  02AA  00099
0  02AA  00100                  (* OBTAIN INDEX OF NEXT LARGEST SON *)
0  02AA  00101                  IF J + 1 < Q
0  02B2  00102                  THEN IF K(J + 1) > K(J)
0  030C  00103                       THEN J := J + 1
0  0312  00104                       ELSE
0  031E  00105
0  031E  00106                  (* CHECK IF J SUBSCRIPT OUT OF BOUNDS *)
0  031E  00107                  ELSE IF J > N
0  0326  00108                       THEN J := N;
0  033A  00109
0  033A  00110                  (* COPY RECORD INTO ITS PROPER PLACE *)
0  033A  00111                  K(I) := KEY
0  035C  00112              END
0  0364  00113          END;
0  036C  00114
0  036C  00115          (* FINISHED *)
0  036C  00116          WRITELN ('  ', K(1))
0  0394  00117  END.
-----------------------------------
| COMPILE TIME:     0.231 SECOND(S) |
|     NO WARNING(S) DETECTED        |
|     NO ERROR(S) DETECTED          |
-----------------------------------

--EXECUTION-->
          89
          78
          58
          56
          56
          52
          42
          42
          25
          23
          14
          11
           3
```

Fig. 11-14   Program to sort a table by using a heap sort (cont'd.)

The main program first reads the table and calls procedure CREATE to create the initial heap. Then a loop is entered in line 70 to perform the sort. The first and last records are exchanged for the current size of the heap, which is given by the value of Q. This places the largest key in the heap at the back of the heap. Then the heap is rebuilt. Line 90 controls a loop which exchanges the record that was swapped previously with its son having the greatest key value if possible. This is done by exchanging the record if possible, and obtaining the index of the son having the largest key.

In the procedure CREATE, line 26 controls a loop that builds the heap. This is done by considering heaps of size 2, then 3, and so on up to a size of n. For each heap, a new element is added at the back of the heap. This record ascends the heap if its key is greater than that of its parent. The loop in line 37 is used to control this process. Within the loop, the record is exchanged with its parent and the new parent of the record is computed.

In the next section, we examine the use of m-ary trees for searching. This involves using a trie structure.

11-3.4 Trie Structures

This section examines the application of m-ary trees ($m \geq 2$) for searching. A trie structure is a complete m-ary tree in which each node consists of m components, where each component may contain either a character string or the address to another node in the structure. The method of searching tries is analogous to digital searching which was described in Chap. 10.

A trie structure can be represented by a 27 x n array of character strings. The keys of the records are stored in the elements of this array. The 27 rows represent the blank character and the letters A through Z, respectively. The n columns represent the nodes in the trie structure. Note that node 1 is the root of the tree.

To access a node given a search key, we examine the first letter of the key. This gives the position (i.e., 1 through 27) of the component in the node that we should examine. If this component contains the key being searched for, the search is finished; otherwise, if the entry is a number, we go to the node that corresponds to that number. This process is repeated for the next letter in the key. Note that the blank symbol is used to denote the end of a word during the scan of a key.

Figure 11-15 gives an example of a main program that calls procedure TRIE_SH to perform searching in a trie structure. The variables used in the main procedure are:

Variable	Type	Usage
MATRIX	ARRAY(1..27, 1..12) OF STRING(20)	Type definition for trie structure
TRIE	MATRIX	Trie structure
NAME	STRING(256)	Key to search for in the trie structure
N	INTEGER	Number of nodes in the trie structure
ROW	INTEGER	Row NAME is found in TRIE
COL	INTEGER	Column NAME is found in TRIE
I	INTEGER	Counted loop variable
J	INTEGER	Counted loop variable
TEMP	STRING(256)	Temporary variable
BLANKS	STRING(256)	String of blanks

Variables used in the procedure TRIE_SH are:

NAME	STRING(256)	Key to search for in trie structure
TRIE	MATRIX	Trie structure
ROW	INTEGER	Component being examined
COL	INTEGER	Node being examined
K	INTEGER	Index variable

LENNAME	INTEGER	Length of name
CHAR	STRING(256)	Used to convert string numbers to fixed
NUMBER	STRING(256)	Used to convert string numbers to fixed
DIGITS	STRING(256)	String of digits
LETTERS	STRING(256)	String of letters
DASH	STRING(256)	Dash(-) character
STOP	BOOLEAN	Indicates procedure return

In the main program, line 109 reads the number of nodes in the trie structure. The elements of the trie structure are then read. Next, a loop is entered which inputs a series of keys and calls procedure TRIE_SH to find the position of the key in the table.

In the procedure TRIE_SH, COL is initialized to 1 because the first node is the root node. A loop is then entered which examines every character of the key (NAME). ROW is set to the value which corresponds to the letter being examined. The loop in line 48 allows the search to continue until an empty position in the trie structure is found or the search key is found. If the name is not found the position is not empty, a check is made to see if the element contains a number. If not, another name has been found and the search terminates. The number is converted to its integer form and COL is set to the new trie node that is to be examined. In lines 95 to 100, if the key is not found, ROW and COL are, therefore, set to zero before the procedure returns to the calling program.

EXERCISES FOR CHAPTER 11

1. A familiar example of symbol manipulation is finding the derivative of a formula with respect to a variable, say, x. The following rules define the derivative of a formula with respect to x where u and v denote functions of x:

   1. $D(x) = 1$
   2. $D(a) = 0$, if a is a constant or a variable other than x
   3. $D(\# u) = D(u) / u$, where # denotes the natural logarithm
   4. $D(-u) = -D(u)$
   5. $D(u + v) = D(u) + D(v)$
   6. $D(u - v) = D(u) - D(v)$
   7. $D(u * v) = D(u) * v + u * D(v)$
   8. $D(u / v) = D(u) / v - (u * D(v)) / v^2$
   9. $D(v ** u) = (v ** u) * (u * D(v) / v + D(u) * \# v)$

   These rules permit evaluation of the derivative D(y) for any formula y composed of the preceding operators. Based on the binary tree representation of an expression given in the text, formulate a program which differentiates a given expression according to the differentiation rules 1 through 9.

2. If we apply the differentiation rules of the previous exercise to a formula, certain simplifications can be made to the resulting derivative. In particular, certain redundant operations such as multiplications by 0 or 1 and

```
0  0000   00001   PROGRAM TRIETST (INPUT, OUTPUT);
0  0000   00002   (* THIS PROGRAM READS IN A TRIE STRUCTURE AND CALLS PROCEDURE
0  0000   00003      TRIE_SH TO PERFORM SEARCHES ON THE TRIE STRUCTURE. *)
0  0000   00004
0  0000   00005   TYPE MATRIX = ARRAY (1..27, 1..12) OF STRING(20);
0  0038   00006   VAR TRIE: MATRIX;           (* TRIE STRUCTURE *)
0  0038   00007       NAME: STRING(256);      (* KEY TO SEARCH FOR *)
0  0038   00008       ROW, COL,               (* POSITION OF KEY IN STRUCTURE *)
0  0038   00009       N,                      (* NUMBER OF NODES IN STRUCTURE *)
0  0038   00010       I, J: INTEGER;          (* COUNTED LOOP VARIABLES *)
0  0038   00011       TEMP,                   (* TEMPORARY CHARACTER STRING *)
0  0038   00012       BLANKS: STRING(256);    (* STRING OF BLANK CHARACTERS *)
0  0038   00013
0  0038   00014       PROCEDURE CONCAT (VAR S1, S2, RESULT: STRING(256)); EXTERNAL;
0  0038   00015
0  0038   00016       PROCEDURE TRIE_SH (NAME: STRING(256); TRIE: MATRIX; VAR ROW,
1  0000   00017          COL: INTEGER);
1  0000   00018       (* THIS PROCEDURE SEARCHES FOR NAME IN TRIE, THE TRIE STRUCTURE,
1  0000   00019          RETURNING ITS POSITION THROUGH ROW AND COL. *)
1  0000   00020
1  0000   00021       VAR K,                  (* INDEX VARIABLE *)
1  0084   00022           LENNAME: INTEGER;   (* LENGTH OF NAME *)
1  0084   00023           CHAR, NUMBER,       (* USED TO CONVERT NUMBER IN TRIE *)
1  0084   00024           DIGITS,             (* ARRAY TO AN INTEGER *)
1  0084   00025           LETTERS,            (* USED TO DETERMINE ROW POSITION
1  0084   00026                                  OF KEY IN STRUCTURE *)
1  0084   00027           DASH: STRING(256);  (* DASH TRIE STRUCTURE ENTRY *)
1  0084   00028           STOP: BOOLEAN;      (* LOGICAL FLAG FOR PROCEDURE RETURN *)
1  0084   00029
1  0084   00030           FUNCTION INDEX (VAR S, PATTERN: STRING(256)): INTEGER;
2  0000   00031              EXTERNAL;
1  0084   00032           FUNCTION LENGTH (VAR STR: STRING(256)): INTEGER; EXTERNAL;
1  0084   00033           PROCEDURE SUB (VAR S: STRING(256); POS, NUM: INTEGER;
2  0000   00034              VAR RESULT: STRING(256)); EXTERNAL;
1  0084   00035
1  0084   00036       BEGIN
1  0084   00037
1  0084   00038           (* INITIALIZE *)
1  0084   00039           DIGITS := '0123456789*/';
1  008A   00040           LETTERS := ' ABCDEFGHIJKLMNOPQRSTUVWXYZ*/';
1  0090   00041           DASH := '-*/';
1  0096   00042           COL := 1;
1  009E   00043           STOP := FALSE;
1  00A6   00044
1  00A6   00045           (* PERFORM SEARCH *)
1  00A6   00046           LENNAME := LENGTH (NAME);
1  00C8   00047           K := 1;
1  00D0   00048           WHILE (K <= LENNAME) AND NOT STOP DO
1  00EA   00049           BEGIN
1  00EA   00050               SUB (NAME, K, 1, TEMP);
1  011E   00051               ROW := INDEX (LETTERS, TEMP);
1  0148   00052               IF TRIE(ROW, COL) = DASH
1  0188   00053               THEN BEGIN
1  0192   00054
1  0192   00055                   (* MISSING NAME *)
1  0192   00056                   WRITELN (' ', 'NAME NOT FOUND');
1  01B6   00057                   ROW := 0;
1  01BC   00058                   COL := 0;
1  01C2   00059                   STOP := TRUE
1  01C2   00060               END
1  01CA   00061               ELSE IF TRIE(ROW, COL) = NAME
1  020E   00062                    THEN STOP := TRUE
1  0218   00063                    ELSE BEGIN
1  0224   00064                        TEMP := TRIE(ROW, COL);
1  0274   00065                        SUB (TEMP, 1, 1, TEMP);
1  02A8   00066                        IF INDEX (DIGITS, TEMP) = 0
1  02CE   00067                        THEN BEGIN
1  02D6   00068                            TEMP := TRIE(ROW, COL);
1  0326   00069                            CONCAT (TEMP, BLANKS, TEMP);
1  0352   00070                            WRITELN (' ', 'UNEXPECTED ', TEMP : 20,
1  0388   00071                               ' FOUND');
1  039A   00072                            ROW := 0;
1  03A0   00073                            COL := 0;
1  03A6   00074                            STOP := TRUE
1  03A6   00075                        END
1  03AE   00076                        ELSE BEGIN
1  03B2   00077
1  03B2   00078                            (* CONVERT COLUMN TO AN INTEGER *)
1  03B2   00079                            NUMBER := TRIE(ROW, COL);
1  0402   00080                            COL := 0;
```

Fig. 11-15   Program to perform a trie search

```
1  0408   00081                                    IF LENGTH (NUMBER) = 2
1  0426   00082                                    THEN BEGIN
1  042E   00083                                        SUB (NUMBER, 1, 1, CHAR);
1  0462   00084                                        COL := (INDEX (DIGITS, CHAR) - 1) *
1  048C   00085                                            10;
1  049C   00086                                        SUB (NUMBER, 2, 255, NUMBER)
1  04BC   00087                                        END;
1  04D0   00088                                    COL := COL + INDEX (DIGITS, NUMBER) - 1
1  04FA   00089                                    END
1  0502   00090                               END;
1  0502   00091                        K := K + 1
1  0502   00092                    END;
1  0512   00093
1  0512   00094            (* MISSING NAME? *)
1  0512   00095            IF NOT STOP
1  0512   00096            THEN BEGIN
1  0520   00097                WRITELN (' ', 'NAME NOT FOUND');
1  0544   00098                ROW := 0;
1  054A   00099                COL := 0
1  054A   00100                END
1  0550   00101        END;
0  0038   00102
0  0038   00103  BEGIN  (* MAIN PROGRAM *)
0  0038   00104        BLANKS := '                    */';
0  003E   00105
0  003E   00106        (* READ IN THE TRIE *)
0  003E   00107        ROW := 0;
0  0044   00108        COL := 0;
0  004A   00109        READ (N);
0  005C   00110        FOR I := 1 TO 27 DO
0  0080   00111            FOR J := 1 TO N DO
0  00A4   00112                READ (TRIE(I, J));
0  00FC   00113
0  00FC   00114        (* PERFORM SEARCH *)
0  00FC   00115        READ (NAME);
0  010E   00116        WHILE NOT EOF DO
0  0116   00117        BEGIN
0  0116   00118            CONCAT (NAME, BLANKS, TEMP);
0  0144   00119            WRITELN ('-');
0  0156   00120            WRITELN (' ', 'NAME SEARCHED FOR IS ', TEMP : 20);
0  018C   00121            TRIE_SH (NAME, TRIE, ROW, COL);
0  01C2   00122            WRITELN (' ', 'NAME IS IN ROW', ROW : 3, ' AND COLUMN', COL
0  020A   00123                : 3);
0  021C   00124            READ (NAME)
0  022E   00125        END
0  022E   00126  END.
```

```
--------------------------------------
| COMPILE TIME:    0.339 SECOND(S) |
|     NO WARNING(S) DETECTED        |
|     NO ERROR(S) DETECTED          |
--------------------------------------
--EXECUTION-->


NAME SEARCHED FOR IS CANARY
NAME IS IN ROW  2 AND COLUMN  2


NAME SEARCHED FOR IS EAGLE
NAME IS IN ROW  2 AND COLUMN  3


NAME SEARCHED FOR IS HELLO
UNEXPECTED HAWK              FOUND
NAME IS IN ROW  0 AND COLUMN  0


NAME SEARCHED FOR IS ZERO
NAME NOT FOUND
NAME IS IN ROW  0 AND COLUMN  0


NAME SEARCHED FOR IS SNOB
NAME NOT FOUND
NAME IS IN ROW  0 AND COLUMN  0
```

Fig. 11-15   Program to perform a trie search (cont'd.)

exponentiation to the first power can be avoided. Modify the program obtained in the previous exercise so that these simplifications are realized.

3. Construct a program which uses the function BINARY_TREE repeatedly to perform a sequence of insertions and/or searches. Use the following sequence of inputs:

TRUE	'THEN'
TRUE	'INTEGER'
TRUE	'ELSE'
TRUE	'READ'
FALSE	'ELSE'
TRUE	'WRITE'
TRUE	'TYPE'
FALSE	'VAR'

4. Construct a program for the deletion of an element from a trie structure whose organization is that given in the text.

APPENDIX

A

**REFERENCE
SUMMARY
FOR
PASCAL**

This appendix is an attempt to collect, in a form convenient for quick reference, many details of the PASCAL language as presented in this book. The information in this appendix is drawn primarily from the PASCAL User Manual and Report [Jensen and Wirth 1978].

Section A — Notation

To permit a simple and precise description of language features and constructs we employ what is known as a "metalanguage." In the metalanguage certain symbols, not part of the language itself, are used to describe how one forms valid elements of the language.

1.   Angle brackets, "<" and ">", are used to denote instances of something. For example,

<identifier>

denotes an instance of identifier. For example, ROOT, SUM and FILLER would all be instances of identifier.

2.   Square brackets, "[" and "]", are used to denote optional entities. For example,

IF <condition> THEN <statement>
[ELSE <statement>]

means that the ELSE clause is optional in an IF construct.

3.   Curly brackets (or braces), "{" and "}", are used to denote an item that can be repeated any number of times (including 0 times, unless information to the contrary is given). For example,

VAR <identifier> {, <identifier>}:<type> ;
    {<identifier> {, <identifier> }: <type> ;}

says the following is legal in PASCAL

VAR   SUM, A, B: REAL;
       FILLER, NAME: CHAR;
       FLAG: BOOLEAN;

Note that although <identifier> can in theory be replicated any number of times (according to the specification given), a limit may be imposed in practice.

4.   Upper-case words will be used to denote keywords in the PASCAL language.

Section B — Basic Concepts

1. Variable Names

A variable name (or identifier) in PASCAL consists of a string of alphanumeric characters beginning with a letter and followed by any combination of letters or digits. Some compilers permit the use of the special character underscore (_). In many compilers, the variable name must be unique in the first eight characters. In Manitoba PASCAL this is extended to 31 characters. No blanks are allowed within a variable name.

There are 35 reserved words of the PASCAL language that must not be used as variable names. These are

AND	DOWNTO	IF	OR	THEN
ARRAY	ELSE	IN	PACKED	TO
BEGIN	END	LABEL	PROCEDURE	TYPE
CASE	FILE	MOD	PROGRAM	UNTIL
CONST	FOR	NIL	RECORD	VAR
DIV	FUNCTION	NOT	REPEAT	WHILE
DO	GOTO	OF	SET	WITH

2. A Program

A PASCAL program is a collection of definitions, declarations, and statements. The first statement is a PROGRAM statement of the form

PROGRAM <program name> (INPUT, OUTPUT);

where INPUT and OUTPUT are examples of program parameters. The last statement of a program is

END.

Programs are entirely free-form.

3. Scope of Names

That part of a program in which an entity may be referenced by its name is known as the *scope* of the entity. The scope of an entity has nothing to do with when storage for the entity is allocated or released, or when the entity gets valid values; instead it indicates only where one is permitted to refer to the entity by its name. The scope of an entity depends on where it is declared or defined relative to the block structure of the program.

The rules of scope are basically quite simple. The scope of an entity is the block in which its declaration or definition appears, including any contained blocks, except those blocks (and blocks internal to them) in which the name is redefined. As a general principle, scopes are inherited inward; that is, within any block one can refer to all names accessible to the containing block that are not redefined in the present block. Examples of scope are given in Sec. 6-4.

4. Comments

A comment in PASCAL is delimited by the characters pairs "(*" and "*)". In some compilers, "{" and "}" may be used instead. Comments are intended to make the program more understandable and have no effect whatsoever on either the compilation or the execution of the program.

5. Constants

The following are available in PASCAL:

Integer constant - examples: 435, –13785, 0. Maximum magnitude: 2147483647 (i.e., $2^{31} - 1$)

Real constant (may or may not use "E" notation) - examples: –0.00087, 76.98E–5, 12E20. Magnitude: approximately 10^{-78} through 10^{76}.

String constant (or literal) - a sequence of characters enclosed in delimiting quotes ('). Examples: 'THE FINAL SUM IS' 'NAME   ADDRESS   PHONE NO.' '1221 AVE OF THE AMERICAS'

Logical (or Boolean) constant - there are only two possible logical constants: TRUE and FALSE.

Section C — Definitions and Declarations

PASCAL offers considerable data-structuring capability through the provision of a new standard data types along with a mechanism for extending these.

Any program or procedure (including functions) begins with a series of definition and declaration sections. Not all of these need be present, but those that are must be in the following order, and must be introduced by the indicated keywords.

1. Label Definitions (keyword LABEL)

All labels to be used in the program or procedure must be defined in this section. The basic format is

LABEL <label list>;

where <label list> is a series of labels separated by commas. For example.

LABEL HERE, THERE;

defines labels HERE and THERE.

2. Constant Definitions (keyword CONST)

Any numeric or string constants to be used in the program or procedure can be associated with identifiers in the constant definition section. The format of this section is

CONST {<identifier> = <constant>;}

At least one definition must be given if there is to be a constant definition section. For example

```
CONST PI = 3.14159;
      BREAK_CHAR = '#';
      ZERO = 0;
```

defines three constants as indicated. There are several system-supplied constants. For example, MAXINT is the largest possible integer that can be stored on the computer involved (on an IBM S/370, MAXINT is 2147483647), and NIL is a special pointer value that refers to no location at all.

3. Extended Data Type Definitions (keyword TYPE)

This section is used for programmer-defined data types. These can be of two flavors: sets, or types built upon previously-defined or system-supplied data types. The format of this section is

TYPE {<identifier> = <definition>;}

Once again, at least one definition is expected if this section is to be included. An example of a type definition is

```
TYPE DWARFS = (HAPPY, GRUMPY, SNEEZY, SLEEPY,
        DOC, BASHFUL, DOPEY);
     POINTER = @INTEGER;
     STUDENT = RECORD
        NAME: STRING(20);
        GRADES: ARRAY(1..5) OF INTEGER
        END
```

This defines a set DWARFS with seven elements, a pointer POINTER that points at integer values, and a record structure STUDENT with two components — NAME, a character string, and GRADES, an integer vector with five elements.

4. Variable Declarations (keyword VAR)

This section is used for the declaration of all "regular" variables to be used in the program or procedure. Four basic data types are allowed: BOOLEAN, CHAR, INTEGER, and REAL, as well as programmer-defined data types. The basic format of this section is

VAR {<identifier list> = <data type>;}

where as before at least one declaration is expected. The <identifier list> is a list of identifiers separated by commas. For example

```
VAR COUNT, TALLY: INTEGER;
    AVERAGE: REAL;
    FLAG: BOOLEAN;
```

defines COUNT and TALLY to be of type INTEGER, AVERAGE to be of type REAL, and FLAG to be of type BOOLEAN.

Section D — Executable Statements

In this section the executable statements of PASCAL are described in alphabetical order. While we attempt to be reasonably complete, we make no attempt to be exhaustive. A number of statements that are beyond the scope of this book have been omitted. In PASCAL, any executable statement can be given a label. To avoid repeating this in our specifications of the individual statements we will assume a general form as follows:

[label:] <statement>

Assignment statement

The assignment statement is used to assign values to variables. Its basic form is the following:

<variable name> := <expression>

The assignment statement is used to assign values to variables. Its basic form is the following:

<variable name> := <expression>

In general, the value of the expression on the right-hand side of the assignment operator ":=" is assigned to the variable named on the left-hand side.

BEGIN

This is *not* an executable statement. Rather, it marks the beginning of a *compound statement*.

```
BEGIN
        {<statement>}
END
```

A compound statement is permitted in a program anywhere that a single statement can be used.

CASE

The CASE statement allows selection of one of several courses of action, depending on the value of a *case selector*. Its basic form is

```
CASE <case selector> OF
        {labelled case}
END
```

Compound Statement

(See BEGIN).

CONST

This is *not* an executable statement. Rather, it introduces the constant definition section of a program or procedure. (See Sec. C).

DO

This is *not* an executable statement. Rather, it is part of the WHILE construct which is described elsewhere.

END

This is *not* an executable statement. Rather, it acts as a delimiter for several program constructs which are described elsewhere.

FOR

The FOR statement is used to control iteration. It is used specifically for counter-controlled loops. Its basic format is:

        FOR <loop control variable> = <start value> TO <end value> DO
            <statement>

The statement in the loop (which can be a compound statement) is executed for a sequence of values of the loop control variable, beginning with the start value and proceeding in unit increments until the value exceeds that given by the end value. TO can be replaced by DOWNTO, in which case the increment is –1, and iteration continues until the value of the loop control variable is less than that given by the end value.

FUNCTION

This is *not* an executable statement. Rather, it marks the beginning of a function definition. (see Sec. E).

GOTO

This statement is used to alter the normal flow of control in a program. The execution of the statement

        GOTO <label>

causes an immediate (unconditional) branch to the statement whose label is specified. This statement must be used with caution. Excessive use can have unfortunate consequences on the readability and understandability of a program. For this reason, we prefer that it be avoided.

IF

The IF statement normally causes execution of one of a specified pair of alternatives based on the evaluation of a given condition. It has the following basic form:

        IF <condition> THEN <statement 1>
        [ELSE <statement 2>]

<Statement 1> is executed if the <condition> (a Boolean expression) evaluates to true; otherwise <statement 2> is executed. Either of these (or both) can, of course, be compound statements. The ELSE portion is optional. If it is not present and the <condition> evaluates to false, execution proceeds with the next sequential statement. In the event that IF statements are nested, an ELSE relates back to the nearest unended preceeding IF.

LABEL

This is *not* an executable statement. Rather, it introduces the label definition section of a program or procedure. (See Sec. C).

PROCEDURE

This is *not* an executable statement. Rather, it introduces a procedure definition. (See Sec. E).

PROGRAM

This is *not* an executable statement. Rather, it introduces a program. (See Sec. B).

READ, READLN

These statements control the input of data. Their format is

```
READ (<input list>)
READLN [(<input list>)]
```

<Input list> is a series of variables into which values are to be read. READ always looks for the next item in the input stream. READLN begins a new line of input after the input list, if any, has been read, thus possibly ignoring parts of current lines.

REPEAT

This is a special form of iteration control that guarantees at least one execution of the loop (i.e., it is *bottom tested*). Its format is

```
REPEAT
  {<statement>}
UNTIL <condition>
```

Execution of {<statement>} continues as long as <condition> remains false. The loop terminates when <condition> becomes true.

TYPE

This is *not* an executable statement. Rather, if introduces the type definition section of a program or procedure. (See Sec. C).

UNTIL

This is *not* an executable statement. Rather, it is part of the REPEAT construct which is described elsewhere.

VAR

This is *not* an executable statement. Rather, it introduces the variable declaration section of a program or procedure. (See Sec. C).

WHILE

The WHILE statement provides a *top-tested* conditional loop. Its format is

        WHILE <condition> DO
            <statement>

<Statement> (which may be simple or compound) is executed repeatedly as long as <condition> remains true. The loop may execute zero times.

WRITE, WRITELN

These statements control the output of data. Their format is

        WRITE (<output list>)
        WRITELN [(<output list>)]

<Output list> is a series of values to be written. WRITE continues each write operation at the point where the previous one terminated; WRITELN begins a new output line after the output list, if any, has been written.

Section E — Functions and Procedures

1. Definition

Format:
        FUNCTION <name> {<parameter declarations>}: <type attribute>;
            [FORWARD;]

    or

        PROCEDURE <name> {<parameter declarations>};
            [FORWARD;]

        <declaration of local variables>
        BEGIN
            {<statement>}
        END

The <name> is used to invoke the function or procedure. At the time of the invocation, arguments are supplied to correspond to the parameters of the definition. The precise nature of this correspondence is described in the next subsection.

The declaration of a parameter indicates what type it expects the corresponding argument to be. Parameter declarations are similar in appearance to normal variable declarations except that only type information is permitted. The type declarations cannot be set or array definitions, for example. The following is an example of a set of parameter declarations in a procedure TALLY:

```
PROCEDURE TALLY (VAR INDEX, COUNT: INTEGER;
        VAR AVERAGE: REAL;
        SWITCH: BOOLEAN);
```

There is no RETURN statement in PASCAL. Return of control always takes place at the end of a function or procedure. The value of a function is assigned to the function name. A function can only return scalar values.

Finally, functions and procedures are meant to be defined before they are called. Where this is not possible, the attribute FORWARD is necessary to permit forward reference.

2. Argument-Parameter Correspondence

The basic concepts of correspondence are considered in Sec. 6-3. PASCAL permits parameter passing both by reference and by value. Call (or pass) by reference is applied when the parameter is preceded by VAR in the parameter declaration; otherwise call (or pass) by value is assumed. For example, in the procedure SUB, defined as follows:

```
PROCEDURE SUB (VAR S: STRING(256);
        POS, NUM: INTEGER;
        VAR RESULT: STRING(256));
```

call by reference is applied to parameters S and RESULT, and call by value is applied to parameters POS and NUM. It must be noted that call by reference can be used *only* when the argument is a variable. If a constant or expression is to be passed, then call by value *must* be used.

Section F - Built-in Functions

PASCAL provides a number of built-in functions to supplement the standard operators. In this book we are not interested in all of them. Those of interest are summarized in this section. A more complete list is found in the PASCAL report.

ABS (x)

The result is the absolute value of the numeric expression x, and is of the same numeric type as x.

CHR (i)

The result is the character whose ordinal number is i (i must be INTEGER), if such a character exists.

COS (x)

COS returns the real value that represents the cosine of x (expressed in radians). The argument x may be INTEGER or REAL and the result is REAL.

DISPOSE (p)

The argument p is a pointer variable. This function frees the storage pointed to by p, and returns it to the availability area.

EOF

EOF is a logical (or BOOLEAN) function that returns TRUE if and only if end-of-file occurs on input.

EXP (x)

EXP returns a real value that is given by e^x where e is the base of the natural logarithm system. The argument x may be INTEGER or REAL and the result is REAL.

LN (x)

LN returns a real value that is the natural (base e) logarithm of x. The value of x must be greater than 0. The argument x may be INTEGER or REAL and the result is REAL.

NEW (p)

The argument p is a pointer variable. This function allocates new storage (from the availability area) and sets p to point to it.

ODD (i)

This is a logical (or BOOLEAN) function that returns TRUE if and only if i is odd. The argument i is of type INTEGER.

ORD (s)

The argument s can be any ordinal type. The result is an integer, which is the ordinal number of s.

PRED (s)

The argument s can be any ordinal type. The result is the same ordinal type, and is the predecessor value of s, if such a value exists.

ROUND (x)

The result is the value of x rounded to the nearest integer. The argument x is of type REAL.

SIN (x)

SIN returns a real value that represents the sine of x, where x is expressed in radians. The argument x may be INTEGER or REAL and the result is REAL.

SQR (x)

The result is x^2. The type of the result (which is numeric) matches that of the argument.

SUCC (s)

The argument s can be any ordinal type. The result is the same ordinal type, and is the successor value of s, if such a value exists.

SQRT (x)

SQRT returns a real value that is the square root of x. The value of x must not be less than 0. The argument x may be INTEGER or REAL and the result is REAL.

TRUNC (x)

The result is the integer portion of the real argument x and is of type INTEGER.

INDEX